MEGALOPOLIS

The Urbanized Northeastern Seaboard of the United States

MILES

0   100

1950 metropolitan areas

Counties added by 1960 for this study

Compare with Figures 2 and 3 in text

The Main Street of the Nation

The Northeastern seaboard of the United States is today the site of a remarkable development — an almost continuous stretch of urban and suburban areas from southern New Hampshire to northern Virginia and from the Atlantic shore to the Appalachian foothills. The processes of urbanization, rooted deep in the American past, have worked steadily here, endowing the region with unique ways of life and of land use. No other section of the United States has such a large concentration of population, with such a high average density, spread over such a large area. And no other section has a comparable role within the nation or a comparable importance in the world. Here has been developed a kind of supremacy, in politics, in economics, and possibly even in cultural activities, seldom before attained by an area of this size.

3

A Very Special Region: Megalopolis

This region has indeed a "personality" of its own, which for some three centuries past has been changing and evolving, constantly creating new problems for its inhabitants and exerting a deep influence on the general organization of society. The modern trends in its development and its present degree of crowding provide both examples and warnings for other less urbanized areas in America and abroad and call for a profound revision of many old concepts, such as the usually accepted distinctions between city and country. As a result new meanings must be given to some old terms, and some new terms must be created.

Great, then, is the importance and significance of this section of the United States and of the processes now at work within it. And yet it is difficult to single this area out from surrounding areas, for its limits cut across established historical divisions, such as New England and the Middle Atlantic states, and across political entities, since it includes some states entirely and others only partially. A special name is needed, therefore, to identify this special geographical area.

This particular type of region is new, but it is the result of age-old processes, such as the growth of cities, the division of labor within a civilized society, the development of world resources. The name applied to it should, therefore, be new as a place name but old as a symbol of the long tradition of human aspirations and endeavor underlying the situations and problems now found here. Hence the choice of the term *Megalopolis*, used in this study.

Some two thousand years before the first European settlers landed on the shores of the James River, Massachusetts Bay, and Manhattan Island, a group of ancient people, planning a new city-state in the Peloponnesus in Greece, called it *Megalopolis*, for they dreamed of a great future for it and hoped it would become the largest of the Greek cities. Their hopes did not materialize. Megalopolis still appears on modern maps of the Peloponnesus but it is just a small town nestling in a small river basin. Through the centuries the word *Megalopolis* has been used in many senses by various people, and it has even found its way into Webster's dictionary, which defines it as "a very large city." Its use, however, has not become so common that it could not be applied in a new sense, as a geographical place name for the unique cluster of metropolitan areas of the Northeastern seaboard of the United States. There, if anywhere in our times, the dream of those ancient Greeks has come true.

An Urbanized Area with a Nebulous Structure

As one follows the main highways or railroads between Boston and Washington, D. C., one hardly loses sight of built-up areas, tightly woven residential communities, or powerful concentrations of manufacturing plants. Flying this same route one discovers, on the other hand, that behind the ribbons of densely occupied land along the principal arteries of traffic, and in between the clusters of suburbs around the old urban centers, there still remain large areas covered with woods and brush alternating with some carefully cultivated patches of farmland. These green spaces, however, when inspected at closer range, appear stuffed with a loose but immense scattering of buildings, most of them residential but some of industrial character. That is, many of these sections that look rural actually function largely as suburbs in the orbit of some city's downtown. Even the farms, which occupy the larger tilled patches, are seldom worked by people whose only occupation and income are properly agricultural. And yet these farm areas produce large quantities of farm goods!

Thus the old distinctions between rural and urban do not apply here any more. Even a quick look at the vast area of Megalopolis reveals a revolution in land use. Most of the people living in the so-called rural areas, and still classified as "rural population" by recent censuses, have very little, if anything, to do with agriculture. In terms of their interests and work they are what used to be classified as "city folks," but their way of life and the landscapes around their residences do not fit the old meaning of urban.

In this area, then, we must abandon the idea of the city as a tightly settled and organized unit in which people, activities, and riches are crowded into a very small area clearly separated from its nonurban surroundings. Every city in this region spreads out far and wide around its original nucleus; it grows amidst an irregularly colloidal mixture of rural and suburban landscapes; it melts on broad fronts with other mixtures, of somewhat similar though different texture, belonging to the suburban neighborhoods of other cities. Such coalescence can be observed, for example, along the main lines of traffic that link New York City and Philadelphia. Here there are many communities that might be classified as belonging to more than one orbit. It is hard to say whether they are suburbs, or "satellites," of Philadelphia or New York, Newark, New Brunswick, or Trenton. The latter three cities themselves have been reduced to the role of suburbs of New York City in many respects, although

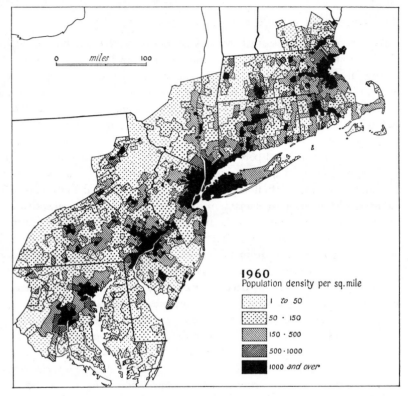

Fig. 1. The density of population according to the 1960 Census, by minor civil divisions. Compare with similar maps for 1940, p. 386, and 1950, p. 387, and with the maps of density by counties in 1960 on the end-papers at the front of this volume.

Trenton belongs also to the orbit of Philadelphia. (See Fig. 1, the distribution of population density.)

The "standard metropolitan areas," [1] first used by the U. S. Bureau of the Census in 1950, have clarified this confused situation somewhat but not entirely. For example, the New York–Northeastern New Jersey standard metropolitan area cuts across political boundaries to reveal the

[1] The U. S. Bureau of the Census defined a standard metropolitan area as "a county or group of contiguous counties which contains at least one city of 50,000 inhabitants or more. In addition to the county, or counties, containing such a city, or cities, contiguous counties are included in a standard metropolitan area if according to certain criteria they are essentially metropolitan in character and socially and economically integrated with the central city." In New England, "towns and cities, rather than counties, are the units used in defining standard metropolitan areas."

relationships of this vast region to the core city of New York. And yet the mechanical application of the term "standard metropolitan area" has resulted in the establishment of separate areas for Trenton, which is closely tied to both Philadelphia and New York, and for Bridgeport, which is for many practical purposes part of the New York area. Similar problems can be found in other parts of Megalopolis.[2]

Thus an almost continuous system of deeply interwoven urban and suburban areas, with a total population of about 37 million people in 1960, has been erected along the Northeastern Atlantic seaboard. It straddles state boundaries, stretches across wide estuaries and bays, and encompasses many regional differences. In fact, the landscapes of Megalopolis offer such variety that the average observer may well doubt the unity of the region. And it may seem to him that the main urban nuclei of the seaboard are little related to one another. Six of its great cities would be great individual metropolises in their own right if they were located elsewhere. This region indeed reminds one of Aristotle's saying that cities such as Babylon had "the compass of a nation rather than a city."

Megalopolis — Main Street and Crossroads of the Nation

There are many other large metropolitan areas and even clusters of them in various parts of the United States, but none of them is yet com-

---

[2] For the 1960 Census the term "standard metropolitan area" was changed to "standard metropolitan statistical area." The definition was modified and a somewhat different set of criteria used which resulted in breaking down several of the formerly recognized larger metropolitan areas into smaller such units. The results thus achieved may be more precise in some respects but in the case of Megalopolis they may cause some confusion. The New York–Northeastern New Jersey standard metropolitan area of 1950 has been replaced by four standard metropolitan statistical areas: one for New York in New York State and three in New Jersey, those of Paterson-Clifton-Passaic, Jersey City, and Newark. The stricter definition of metropolitan integration of adjoining counties now excludes Somerset and Middlesex counties, formerly classified as metropolitan. As a result the percentage of the population of New Jersey residing in metropolitan areas fell from 89.9 in 1950 to 78.9 in 1960 — a statistical trend surprising to those who know how much more metropolitan — or should we say Megalopolitan — the whole of New Jersey grew through the 1950's. To compensate for such an impression and for the separation between New York City and Northeastern New Jersey, a new term has been created and defined: "Standard Consolidated Areas," of which there were two (recognized for 1960) in the country: the New York–Northeastern New Jersey area (which included Somerset and Middlesex counties in New Jersey), and the Chicago–Northwestern Indiana area. The recognition of these broader areas was intended to stress "the special importance of even more inclusive metropolitan statistics" (see Executive Office of the President, Bureau of the Budget, *Standard Metropolitan Statistical Areas*, U. S. Government Printing Office, Washington, D. C., 1961). The metropolitan area of Philadelphia remained unchanged in both its Pennsylvania and New Jersey parts.

parable to Megalopolis in size of population, density of population, or density of activities, be these expressed in terms of transportation, communications, banking operations, or political conferences. Megalopolis provides the whole of America with so many essential services, of the sort a community used to obtain in its "downtown" section, that it may well deserve the nickname of "Main Street of the nation." And for three centuries it has performed this role, though the transcontinental march of settlement has developed along east-west axes perpendicular to this section of the Atlantic seaboard.

In recent times Megalopolis has had concentrated within it more of the Main Street type of functions than ever, and it does not yet seem prepared to relinquish any of them. Witness, for example, the impact of the Federal government in Washington, D. C., as it tightens up over many aspects of national life; the continued crowding of financial and managerial operations into Manhattan; New York's dominance of the national market for mass communication media, which resists all attempts at erosion; and the pre-eminent influence of the universities and cultural centers of Megalopolis on American thinking and policy-making. Megalopolis is also the country's chief façade toward the rest of the world. From it, as from the Main Street of a city, local people leave for distant travel, and to it arriving strangers come. For immigrants it has always served as the chief debarkation wharf. And just as passing visitors often see little of a city except a few blocks of its Main Street, so most foreign visitors see only a part of Megalopolis on their sojourns in the United States.

Just as a Main Street lives for and prospers because of the functions of the whole city, rather than because of any purely local advantages of its own, so is Megalopolis related to the whole United States and its rich resources. In general, Megalopolis itself was blessed only moderately by nature. It has no vast expanse of rich soils (there are some good soils but more poor ones), no special climatic advantages (its cyclonic climate is far from ideal), and no great mineral deposits (though there are some). In these respects it cannot compare with the generous natural potential of the Middle West or Texas or California. But it does excel in locational advantages — deep harbors of a drowned shoreline, on which its principal cities were early established, and a connecting-link relationship between the rich heart of the continent and the rest of the world. By hard work man has made the most of these locational resources, the most outstanding ones in an otherwise average natural endowment. As a result, early in its history Megalopolis became a dynamic hub of international relations, and it has maintained and constantly expanded that role to the present day. It is now the most active crossroads on earth, for people, ideas, and goods, extending its influence far beyond the national borders, and only as such a crossroads could it have achieved its present economic pre-eminence.

Megalopolis as a Laboratory of Urban Growth

Modern technology and social evolution provide increasing opportunity in urban pursuits on the one hand, and on the other steadily improving means of producing more agricultural goods with less manpower. The forces at work in our time, coupled with the growth in population, are, therefore, bound to channel a rising flow of people toward urban-type occupations and ways of life. As this tide reaches more and more cities they will burst out of old bounds to expand and scatter all over the landscape, taking new forms like those already observable throughout Megalopolis. This region serves thus as a laboratory in which we may study the new evolution reshaping both the meaning of our traditional vocabulary and the whole material structure of our way of life.

Tomorrow's society will be different from that in which we grew up, largely because it will be more urbanized. Nonagricultural ways of life will be followed by more and more people and will occupy much more space than they ever did, and such changes cannot develop without also deeply modifying agricultural life and production. So great are the consequences of the general evolution heralded by the present rise and complexity of Megalopolis that an analysis of this region's problems often gives one the feeling of looking at the dawn of a new stage in human civilization. The author has visited and studied various other regions of the world but has not experienced such a feeling anywhere else. Indeed, the area may be considered the cradle of a new order in the organization of inhabited space. This new order, however, is still far from orderly; here in its cradle it is all in flux and trouble, which does not facilitate the analyst's work. Nevertheless, a study of Megalopolis may shed some light on processes that are of great importance and interest.

A Study in Entangled Relationships

As the work of data-gathering and analysis progressed it became evident that the key to most of the questions involved in this study of Megalopolis lies in the interrelationships between the forces and processes at work within the area rather than in the trends of growth or the development of techniques. Thus the trend of population increase, easy to measure and perhaps to forecast approximately, provides less insight into the nature of the area than do the interrelations existing between the processes that caused the local population to grow, those that attracted certain kinds of people to Megalopolis, and those that supplied the swelling crowds with the means to live and work together there. Many of these processes are statistically measurable and some of them can be mapped, but the degree to which each of them stems from the others or determines them is a much more subtle matter, and is more basic to an understanding of what is going on and what can be done about it.

Most regional studies stay on the safer and more superficial grounds of statistical description and functional classifications. Had this report followed that pattern it would have been devoted mainly to summing up the abundant data available from the Censuses and other sources of general information about the various characteristics of Megalopolis. A description of natural conditions, such as topography, climate, hydrography, and vegetation, would have introduced a historical sketch to be followed by chapters on population, industries, trade, transportation and communications, the real estate market, other occupations, and descriptions of the main cities and of the general features of "rural areas." Such a report would have concluded with a description of present problems and forecasts of the future presented by means of graphs, based on the assumption that the trends of the past twenty to fifty years will continue for the next twenty years.

A mere compilation of such data would probably be of service to some people but it could hardly help those who need further insight into and understanding of the basic problems of the area. By attempting to find out more about the deeper processes and their entanglements, one may hope to achieve a more fundamental kind of knowledge, which can be applied to another area or projected into the future more safely, though not always more easily. This is why the present report is organized along a somewhat less classical outline, its goal being a more reasoned discussion and an objective analysis. For such complicated phenomena as the social and economic processes at work in Megalopolis there are, of course, numerous and interlocking determining factors. The author has endeavored to search for *all* these factors, keeping in mind their multiplicity and entanglements and avoiding any arbitrary choices among them.

Outline of This Report

Part One presents a sketch of the *dynamics of urbanization* and attempts to show, in terms of the region's history, why things have come to be as they are and where they are. Although this section is largely descriptive it cannot avoid raising some new questions.

Part Two takes up what may be called the *"modern revolution in land use."* The new mixture of urban and rural must be dissected and each part related to the others in the newly developing system. Separation between place of work and place of residence creates within the area the system of daily "tidal" movements involved in commuting. Over these are superimposed other currents, some seasonal and some irregularly recurrent. These reflect relations between different parts of Megalopolis that stem from more complicated needs than the simple journey from home to work. These other needs grow more complicated and more general as average family income rises and both goods and activities that were once considered dispensable come to be regarded as necessary by large numbers of Megalopolitans. As Montesquieu observed two centuries ago, on the eve of the Industrial Revolution, "It is the nature of commerce to make the superfluous useful and the useful necessary." Perhaps it is not commerce but just human nature that produces this sequence. At any rate it has certainly been proven true of the consumption of goods, and now it seems to apply to the consumption of activities and space. The modern urban revolution, so apparent already in the affluent society of Megalopolis, devours time and space as well as food and industrial goods, and the fulfilling of these needs requires many types of movements.

These various tidal movements involve a reshaping of land use. Much agricultural land has been taken over by residential and industrial development. On the remaining farms a new specialized type of agriculture is developing, which requires less space than did the old system of farming. Woods have spread over much of the land abandoned by the farms, and this expansion of forests calls for new methods and concepts of forestry management, to provide for recreational and other suburban needs and for a better conservation of the landscape and of wildlife. Simultaneously the old city cores or "downtowns" are evolving toward decline or renewal, while uptowns, suburbs, and outer suburbia are becoming interlocked in a new and still constantly changing web of relationships. Regional integration is taking on forms unknown a generation or two ago, and the old system of local, state, and national authorities and jurisdictions, which has changed little, is poorly suited to present needs.

New *patterns of intense living* that have become normal in Megalopolis affect not only land use. They also exert a strong influence on the economic and social foundations of society, and Part Three endeavors to describe the problems thus created. The density of activities and of movement of all kinds is certainly the most extraordinary feature of Megalopolis, more characteristic even than the density of population and of skyscrapers. It has become a means of maintaining economic growth and stabilizing society; but how far can it go without destroying itself? For example, the growth of Megalopolis owes much to the automobile, but highway traffic jams are beginning to strangle city activities and to take the pleasure and efficiency out of driving a car. At the same time cars contribute to the ruination of other means of transportation, made more necessary than ever by the massive tidal currents of people and goods. The self-defeating effect of dense concentrations may be observed also in other fields than transportation. Many industries, for example, are now aiming at decentralization. The intense living of Megalopolis makes a great deal of waste inescapable, waste of space and time as well as of materials. For a long time such waste may have seemed justifiable, for, paradoxically, the crowding that caused it brought higher economic yields. Now this crowding seems at times to defeat its own aims. Why and how does such intense living grow and threaten itself? Answers to these queries build up a general picture of a dynamic and prosperous society, obviously responsible for maintaining the growth of large-scale urbanization but responsible also for the problems the process creates and for finding the badly needed solutions.

It is easier to accept responsibility for solutions than to provide them. The many millions of people who find themselves *neighbors in Megalopolis*, even though they live in different states and hundreds of miles from one another, are barely becoming aware of the imperatives of such a "neighborhood." Part Four attempts to point them out. Responsible public opinion is becoming conscious of the problems involved, and the struggle to find solutions has started. It is especially difficult because no one problem can be tackled without affecting the others. Transportation, land use, water supply, cultural activities, use and development of resources, government and politics — all are interrelated.

Today it is essential that solutions be found to save this area from decay and to reassure the nation and the world about the kind of life modern urbanization trends presage for the future. Megalopolis has been built and often reshaped by its people. These people are now wealthier, better educated, and better endowed with technological means than ever. They ought to be able to find ways of avoiding decline of the area.

For the Better or for the Worse?

The preceding paragraph may seem to imply an unwarranted optimism about society's ability to control itself. True, history records a long list of brilliant civilizations that have sunk under the pressure of internal decay and external jealousy. We remember their names: Babylon, Corinth, Sparta, Athens, Rome, and many others. In the shadowy vistas of ancient times they vanished into the distance like shipwrecked ships loaded with ambition and precious cargo. Can such a fate be looming in the offing for Megalopolis? Modern urban sprawl is viewed by many as a threat to progress and general welfare. What is happening in Megalopolis today has been described as a pathological phenomenon, a sickness, a cancer. Such views are held by distinguished and respectable citizens of the area. One may well be alarmed by their invectives, all the more so as one does not have to go far away from Megalopolis to hear expressions of distrust and jealousy inspired by the amazing concentration of wealth and power in the great seaboard cities. Are people both in and out of this extraordinary region united in condemning it?

Urban growth in general has been discussed and condemned on moral grounds for a long time. Such debate is expectable and desirable, but on the whole history has shown the condemnation to be unjust, as can be seen by a brief review of some of the consequences of crowding.

Contrasts between rich and poor, for example, are especially striking in the crowded communities of cities. These may exist in rural areas too, but there they are diluted by scattering and veiled in greenery. The growth of urban pursuits (industries, trade, services) sharpens the contrasts by condensing them into a smaller area. Rich and poor live within short distances of one another and mix together in the streets in a way that often arouses righteous indignation. It seems brutally amoral to witness destitution neighboring on elegant sophistication, poverty mixing with prosperity. And yet, alas, a growing city's environment can hardly escape offering such sights. For many centuries there was an enormous difference between the advancement possible in trade and industry on the one hand and in farming on the other (though modern farm mechanization and subsidies to agriculture have substantially increased the profit possibilities of farming), and so to rise economically within the span of one lifetime has traditionally been easier in cities than in rural areas. The affluence of those who have so risen draws to the city large groups of humbler people, who come there to profit by the local abundance of money and the volume of spending and to serve the wealthier. In contrast to the more conservative "open" country, the "closed-in" city offers a more dynamic environment, socially and economically.

In cities, too, other vicious aspects of economic growth and social life have always been more evident than in the country. As urban development was accelerated by the Industrial Revolution, some of these vicious aspects became increasingly obvious. Slums and mobs grew worse than ever, making the urban landscape ethically and aesthetically shocking to those who cared about the people. From his sojourns in an industrializing western Europe, and especially from Paris during the French Revolution, Thomas Jefferson brought back impressions that reinforced his normal Virginian opposition to great cities and the development of manufactures or large-scale commerce. As slums and mobs became more general in European cities in the first half of the nineteenth century there arose more awareness about the classes of society and social injustice. There was more discussion of these matters, and the early Socialist doctrines were largely inspired by them. Then came the teachings of such philosophers as Fourier and Proudhon in France and Engels and Karl Marx in Germany, opposing great urban concentration as much as great concentration of capital. Engels' writings on the slums and working conditions in the then fast-developing British cities, such as Manchester, are well known. Because urban conditions of living and working were largely at the root of nineteenth-century Socialist doctrines, Karl Marx stressed that his theories applied much more to the industrialized countries of western Europe, which had accumulated large amounts of capital, than to the rural, little-urbanized countries to the east. Twentieth-century events have proved him wrong on this score, however, for communism has conquered the mainly rural countries, and the forms of socialism that developed in the more urban and capitalistic countries of the West have turned away from Marxism.

Crowding of population within a small area creates shortages of various resources, and most of the crowded people are bound to suffer in some ways because of the shortages. To alleviate them, to make crowding more bearable and the population happier, ways and means of constantly better distribution must be found. Otherwise no lasting growth can develop, and the whole enterprise will soon be doomed. From the struggle against such shortages have come some of mankind's most important advances. In the arid areas of the Middle East, for example, early civilization arose when people first congregated around the main springs and permanent rivers. As the settlement grew, the supply of both water and irrigable land became scarce. To insure survival of the people a proper distribution system had to be achieved, and rules and regulations had to be set up and accepted. Thus organized society, ruled by law, was born. Because authorities were needed to enforce law, political power arose, and people organized themselves to avoid more oppression than was necessary. Everywhere, the more crowded people have become in cities the more they have craved both security and freedom. Modern political life and its concepts of liberty, self-government, and democracy are the products of urban growth, the inheritance of cities in process of growth and development — places such as Jerusalem, Athens, Rome, Bruges, Florence, Paris, London, to mention only those that have been most studied by historians. And the same places, or similar urban centers, have contributed most of our scientific and technological developments, either because people there were struggling to solve pressing problems or because urban societies make possible a leisurely enough elite, some of whose members can devote themselves to disinterested research and a search for a better understanding of the universe.

Thus urban crowding and the slums and mobs characteristic of it may be considered growing pains in the endless process of civilization.

In the same way, the picture of Megalopolis is not as dark as the outspoken pessimists and frequent protests would seem to paint it. Crowded within its limits is an extremely distinguished population. It is, *on the average*, the richest, best educated, best housed, and best serviced group of similar size (i.e., in the 25-to-40-million-people range) in the world. The area is still a focus of attraction for successful or adventurous people from all over America and beyond. It is true that many of its sections have seen pretty rural landscapes replaced by ugly industrial agglomerations or drab and monstrous residential developments; it is true that in many parts of Megalopolis the air is not clean any more, the noise is disturbing day and night, the water is not as pure as one would wish, and transportation at times becomes a nightmare. Many of these problems reflect the revolutionary change that has taken place as cities have burst out of their narrow bounds to scatter over the "open" countryside. In some ways this suburban sprawl may have alleviated a crowding that had threatened to become unbearable, for residential densities of population per square mile have decreased. But new problems have arisen because of the new densities of activities and of traffic in the central cities and because the formerly rural areas or small towns have been unprepared to cope with the new demands made upon their resources. New programs are needed to conserve the natural beauty of the landscape and to assure the health, prosperity, and freedom of the people. In spite of these problems, however, available statistics demonstrate that in Megalopolis the population is on the average healthier, the consumption of goods higher, and the opportunity for advancement greater than in any other region of comparable extent.

Thus the type of urban growth experienced here generates many contrasts, paradoxes, and apparently contradictory trends. It calls for debate and naturally excites passionate opinions for and against it. Are its results for the better or for the worse? It is not for our generation to moralize on the matter, but to strive to make the outcome be for the better, whatever obstacles may be in the way. Megalopolis stands indeed at the threshold of a new way of life, and upon solution of its problems will rest civilization's ability to survive. In the search for such solutions there will be found no easy keys to success, no "gimmicks" or "open-sesames." Solutions must be thought out, ironed out, and constantly revised in the light of all the knowledge that can be acquired by all concerned. It is the author's hope that this report, a systematic and sometimes critical analysis of the past and present of Megalopolis, will contribute to the gathering of such knowledge and to its distribution. At the same time, it will tell the story of an extraordinary region as its people have made it.

PART ONE

THE DYNAMICS OF
URBANIZATION

On the Northeastern Atlantic seaboard, from Massachusetts Bay to the valley of the Potomac, there is an almost continuous chain of impressive cities along the old highway known as U. S. I. Along this axis, over a distance of about 500 miles, are five of the larger metropolitan areas in America — Boston, New York, Philadelphia, Baltimore, and Washington — each of which had a population of well over a million people in 1950.[1] Between them and in the interior immediately west of this axis there were a good dozen other metropolitan areas each with populations ranging from 200,000 to 800,000.

Such a constellation of large cities is unique in the country, not only

[1] There were nine other metropolitan areas in this category elsewhere in the United States.

17

because of the number of large units within the area and the size of its total population, but also because of the size of the main nucleus, New York City. Moreover, this region, here called *Megalopolis*, has assumed world leadership in the urban growth and metropolitan sprawl characteristic of so many regions in the middle of the twentieth century.

The urban chain that constitutes the backbone of Megalopolis is no new development in American history. Very early the seaboard area along U. S. I was urbanized from Lawrence, Massachusetts, to Alexandria, Virginia. Although colonial settlers engaged primarily in agricultural pursuits, from the beginning legislation in New England ordered settlement in groups, which were expected to become "towns." Most of these towns remained mere villages, but during the eighteenth century successful maritime activities developed a good many larger centers in the coastal areas and on the estuaries of the Hudson and the Delaware. By 1700 three towns in the colonies — Boston, New York, and Philadelphia — had more than 4,000 inhabitants each, and these assumed an early leadership.

By 1750 each of these three cities counted more than 12,000 people, and four other ports in New England had more than 5,000, a truly urban size for the period. South of the Potomac there were then only two towns of about 5,000 inhabitants. The overseas trading interests of the major seaports in the colonies were already important enough to cause serious concern in England and to play a notable part in starting the struggle for American independence.

By 1800 the United States had four cities with populations of 25,000 or more, all in this region — Philadelphia, New York, Baltimore, and Boston — and a half dozen towns in the same area had more than 4,000 people. After 1820 urban growth picked up new impetus. By 1850 New York and Philadelphia each had more than 300,000 people, and of the four American cities with populations ranging between 100,000 and 200,000, two (Baltimore and Boston) were in Megalopolis, while the two others (Cincinnati and New Orleans) were far to the west. Of the fifty-five cities then having 10,000 to 100,000 people, twenty-five were in Megalopolis, which was already shaping up a century ago. New York City had already established its supremacy within the area. In 1850 it had not only the largest population but also the highest density of any American city, 135.6 inhabitants per acre in the parts of the city "actually and fully settled." In terms of such crowding Boston and Philadelphia followed New York, far outdistancing the Western cities.[2]

[2] The Census of 1850 reported that "in the portions of the cities actually and fully settled, the number to the acre was as follows: Mobile 13.8, New Orleans 45.4, Cin-

By the turn of the century America was already heavily urbanized. Historians recognize the "rise of the city" as a major characteristic of the 1880's and 1890's. Although Midwestern cities scored the most rapid advances during this period, the principal grouping of large cities remained along the Northeastern seaboard. Here were to be found four of the six cities of the United States with populations above the half million mark (these four were New York, Philadelphia, Boston, and Baltimore), and in addition the area had fifty other cities of more than 20,000 inhabitants, a record at the time for a ribbon of land 500 miles long. Suburban sprawl and coalescence between neighboring urban centers were already becoming obvious here, and even the smaller cities had begun to show a scattering of suburban residences and industrial plants outside their municipal boundaries.

By 1890 population statistics revealed a vast crowded region extending from Boston to Baltimore.[3] The axis of this crowded region, the most densely populated in America, was no longer entirely along the seaboard or U. S. I. Between Providence, Rhode Island, and New Haven, Connecticut, for example, there was rural territory, but Worcester and Springfield, in central Massachusetts, provided an urban link between the Boston-Providence complex and the Connecticut Valley. Southwest of Philadelphia the axis of crowding again avoided U. S. I and the Fall Line, following instead the Pennsylvania Railroad's main line toward Lancaster and York and then turning southward toward Baltimore, Maryland. In fact, by 1900 it was evident that the urbanized area that first developed along the Northeastern seaboard was expanding well inland, though it remained east of the Appalachian ridges. Incorporated in it were Worcester and Springfield in Massachusetts, a scattering of towns along the Hudson River in New York State, and the growing cities on the coalfields and rich limestone basins of eastern Pennsylvania, such as Lancaster, York, Bethlehem, Allentown, even Reading and Harrisburg. Coalescence of the suburbs of these interior centers with those of the greater seaboard cities was far from complete, but they were beginning to extend arms toward each other.

The Census of 1910 introduced the concept of the *metropolitan district,*

cinnati 45.0, St. Louis 47.5, Philadelphia 80.0, Boston 82.7, New York 135.6." (J. D. B. DeBow, *Statistical View of the United States . . . being a Compendium of the Seventh Census,* Senate Printer, Washington, D. C., 1854.)

[3] Walter F. Willcox, "Density and Distribution of Population in the United States at the Eleventh Census," *Economic Studies,* published by the American Economic Association, The Macmillan Company, New York. See Vol. II, No. 6, December 1897, pp. 377–477.

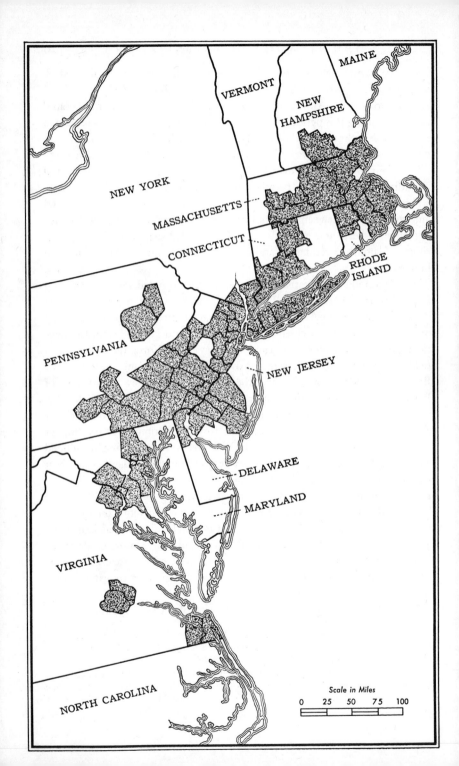

MAINE

VERMONT

NEW HAMPSHIRE

NEW YORK

MASSACHUSETTS

CONNECTICUT

RHODE ISLAND

PENNSYLVANIA

NEW JERSEY

DELAWARE

MARYLAND

VIRGINIA

NORTH CAROLINA

Scale in Miles

0   25   50   75   100

composed of one or more central cities and the contiguous suburban townships; by 1950 it was found necessary to replace this too-narrow and unique category with three definitions: *the urbanized areas, the standard metropolitan areas,* and *the metropolitan state economic areas.* The latter were established on a county basis for the whole country, and when these were mapped they showed an impressive and continuous stretch of counties classified as having a metropolitan-type economy from Hillsborough County in southern New Hampshire to Fairfax County in northern Virginia.[4] This continuous urbanized area (see Fig. 2) provided the writer with his first statistical demonstration of the coming of age of the region he has designated as *Megalopolis.* By 1960 this process of more or less loose urbanization had expanded over still more territory, filling up most of the lands between the Atlantic shores and the Appalachian foothills from Massachusetts Bay to northern Virginia.

The present limits and essential characteristics of this area will be defined more precisely in the first chapter. The characteristics are, of course, much more complex than can be revealed by a mere statement of density of population. Daily or periodic movements of population endow this whole area with its own system of tidal currents, similar to but much more complicated than the system of currents in a maritime basin. These currents within the moving human sea create in the various parts of Megalopolis at certain times of the day and of the year densities quite different from those recorded by the Census, which is concerned only with the number of residents (i.e., permanent nighttime occupants) of each place on the date when it is taken. This dynamic aspect of urbanization is a new development, and it is particularly striking in this region.

The area has other characteristics, too, that deeply affect the whole national economy. From 1900 to 1950 the *urban* population of the United

---

[4] See especially Donald J. Bogue, *State Economic Areas,* Bureau of the Census, U. S. Government Printing Office, Washington, D. C., 1951, and the folded map attached to this publication. It is based on 1940 Census data. Definitions of the various concepts adopted by the 1950 Census are given in the various volumes of the Census and summarized in the *County and City Data Book, 1952: A Statistical Abstract Supplement,* and *County and City Data Book, 1956,* Bureau of the Census, U. S. Government Printing Office, Washington, D. C., 1953 and 1957.

Opposite FIG. 2. Continuity of the counties with an economy of metropolitan type along the Northeastern seaboard, 1940–50 (as defined in his *State Economic Areas* by Donald J. Bogue, on the basis of 1940 Census data, and prepared for use by the U. S. Bureau of the Census in 1950). We took this outline as a starting point for the study of Megalopolis: see the end-papers at the front of this volume.

States increased by 66 million. This stupendous figure has made necessary one of the greatest programs of housing construction and equipment expansion known in human history, a program that has gone on at an accelerated rate. It was the equivalent of resettling in fifty years the total populations of the United Kingdom, the Netherlands, Norway, and Ireland put together. In practice it involved much more than such an operation, for a constant churning moved people around within urban territory during this half century. Megalopolis alone was responsible for at least a good fourth of this vast urban expansion.

Such dynamism is rather exceptional in terms of both the size of the regional phenomenon and the rate of growth. Three hundred years ago this region was just a small outpost of European colonization, without any "metropolitan" features at all. Today, and for some decades past, the region has surpassed all other areas in urban and metropolitan development. It has even undertaken to show to other nations the road to successful urbanization. To gain some understanding of the phenomenon and the processes involved we shall study what the situation has been in recent years, and under what conditions, geographical and historical, it has come to be what it is.

CHAPTER 1

Prometheus Unbound

Because of its concentration of people, wealth, and economic activities, Megalopolis stands out on the map of the present world as a stupendous monument erected by titanic efforts. It impresses deeply everyone who reaches it, whether by land, air, or sea. And yet Megalopolis, in spite of its unique qualities, is not an isolated urban development, for it is located in the very middle of that complex section of the globe's surface bordering on the North Atlantic, where urban concentrations of large masses of people on relatively small areas are often found. On the highly developed continent of North America, of which Megalopolis is the eastern façade, the industrialized Midwest, between the Great Lakes and the Ohio River, and the California seaboard form two other smaller but nonetheless impressive concentrations of riches, economic equipment, and educated people. Across the Atlantic, are the countries of western Europe, where on both sides of the North Sea and English Channel an intensity of urban dynamism comparable to that in Megalopolis may soon be attained. There and elsewhere in Europe urban concentrations have been developing for almost a thousand years, and individual cities are even older.[1] By such Old World standards the main cities of Megalopolis may seem brand new; but by American standards their 300 or so years of existence make them quite old. And they have an even older heritage, brought by the Old World immigrants who founded them and not forgotten by their descendants. This heritage played a great role in early American history, and it is to history we must appeal for explanations as to why and how this extraordinary urban concentration, this Megalopolis, arose here.

The Present Concentration as a Complex Regional Feature

Some of the major characteristics of Megalopolis, which set it apart as a special region within the United States, are the high degree of concentration of people, things, and functions crowded here, and also their variety. This kind of crowding and its significance cannot be described by simple measurements. Its various aspects will be shown on a number of maps, and if these could all be superimposed on one base map there would be demarcated an area in which so many kinds of crowding coincide in general (though not always in all the details of their geographical distribution) that the region is quite different from all neighboring regions and in fact from any other part of North America. The essential reason for its difference is the greater concentration here of a greater variety of kinds of crowding.

Crowding of population, which may first be expressed in terms of densities per square mile, will, of course, be a major characteristic to survey. As this study aims at understanding the meaning of population density, we shall have to know the foundation that supports such crowding over such a very vast area. What do these people do? What is their average income and their standard of living? What is the distribution pattern of wealth and of certain more highly paid occupations? For example, the outstanding concentration of population in the City of New York and its immediate suburbs (a mass of more than ten million people by any count) cannot be separated from the enormous concentration in the same city of banking, insurance, wholesale, entertainment, and transportation activities. These various kinds of concentration have attracted a whole series of other activities, such as management of large corporations, retail business, travel agencies, advertising, legal and technical counseling offices, colleges, re-

[1] Their "2000th anniverseries" were celebrated in 1951 by Paris and in 1958 by Lyon in France and Nyon in Switzerland. Rome, Athens, and Jerusalem are, of course, much more ancient.

search organizations, and so on. Coexistence of all these facilities on an un-equalled scale within the relatively small territory of New York City, and especially of its business district, i.e., Manhattan below 60th Street, has made the place even more attractive to additional banking, insurance, and mass media organizations. Thus have concentrations snowballed.

At the same time the concept of "standard metropolitan area" is based on the decentralization of certain urban functions. Residences, manufac-turing, and recreation facilities, for example, may be scattered around an old urban core in suburbs that may eventually cover an entire county or even a group of counties. However, the presence of a substantial urban core, with at least 50,000 inhabitants *residing in it when the Census is taken*, is an essential requirement of the metropolitan area. In Megalopolis today there are many such nuclei, and we have already noted their pro-liferation in recent times. At first most of the old "central cities" served only their own neighborhoods or separate hinterlands. As settlement ex-panded inland, competition arose between the major seaboard nuclei, and at the same time they developed some specialization of function. Special-ization made them more interdependent, while competition helped them all to grow. As suburbs and metropolitan areas expanded, they overlapped. Had one section of present Megalopolis been strangled by some other, it would have stopped growing and would have declined in terms of wealth and size of population. As long as *all sections grew*, it may be assumed that there was no duplication economically harmful to the whole region. Only recently have a few parts of the area begun to decline.

While much of the decentralization caused by overcrowding of the original sites developed within Megalopolis itself, some industrial, com-mercial, and managerial activities initiated in this area have spread beyond its limits, benefiting the whole country and sometimes other countries too.

Megalopolis is thus characterized by concentration of a great variety of phenomena — in short, by *manifold concentration* — and by a *polynuclear structure*.

Concentration of Population: Densities and Their Meaning

To determine population density we must assume at least broadly out-lined boundaries of the area. It must include the chain of contiguous coun-ties having a metropolitan economy in 1950, and their dense constellation of large central cities. Thus defined, Megalopolis stretches from southern New Hampshire to northern Virginia and from the Atlantic shores to the Appalachian foothills. How much of New Hampshire and of the foothills should be included will appear as the major characteristics are presented,

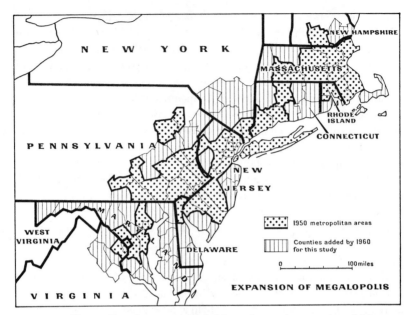

Fɪɢ. 3. For the purposes of this study, to the counties which were already considered metropolitan by 1950 (see Fig. 2) have been added those counties which belonged in the region of Megalopolis in 1960

one by one, on maps. Because of the size and dynamism of this phenomenon, details on the fringes matter little in our search for a better understanding of the development of this huge concentration. We shall, therefore, adopt some temporary limits (see Fig. 3). The main axis of the region is about 600 miles long and the width varies between 30 and 100 miles. The total area amounts to 53,575 square miles, or 1.8 per cent of the land area of the 48-state United States. On the other hand, the population of Megalopolis was close to 31.9 million in 1950, or 21 per cent of the total population of the continental United States. It was about 37 million in 1960. This region encompasses all of Massachusetts, Rhode Island, Connecticut, New Jersey, Delaware, and the District of Columbia, most of Maryland, large chunks of New York State and Pennsylvania, and slices of New Hampshire and Virginia.

This vast region remains extremely varied in many respects. Its urbanization [2] is old in some parts but quite recent in others. And its population keeps growing in numbers and expanding over more space.

[2] Our use of the terms "urban" and "urbanization" for the purposes of this exposition should not be confused with or construed in any way as critical of the terms

If, then, we estimate the total area of Megalopolis to be 53,575 square miles, the average density reached 596 inhabitants to the square mile by 1950 and close to 700 by 1960. No region of similar size in the United States can claim a density approaching 500. In fact, in 1950 no single state in the Union had a density of 200 per square mile other than those included wholly or partly in Megalopolis. The western half of California, where marked urbanization has developed recently, is a somewhat larger area, but it had not reached a density of even 150 in 1950. By 1960 it approached 200. In the whole world, too, densities like those of Megalopolis, occurring over comparable areas, are rare, being found only in northwestern Europe (mainly in the Benelux countries and, with slightly lower values, in West Germany and Britain), a few corners of the Mediterranean realm (northern Italy and the Nile Valley in Egypt), and some lowlands of eastern Asia (in parts of Japan, India, and China), where similar and even higher densities of population are relatively common.

Over an area as vast as Megalopolis the population is, of course, unequally distributed. In 1950 Rhode Island counted 749 inhabitants per square mile, New Jersey 643, Massachusetts 596 (exactly the average for Megalopolis), Connecticut 410, Maryland 237, Delaware 161, Long Island, New York, 371, and the District of Columbia 13,151! The smaller the size and the more urbanized the unit, the higher the density — a conclusion that could have been arrived at logically without much statistical analysis. And this is not necessarily a matter of individual large cities. In New Jersey, for example, no city had a population of even half a million in 1950. However, the state as a whole was suburbanized enough, either by its own central cities (14 of which had over 50,000 inhabitants each, enough to serve as the core of a standard metropolitan area) or by the great across-the-river cities of New York and Philadelphia, to average 643 inhabitants per square mile, a density quite close to that of Belgium-Luxembourg, with about twice New Jersey's area. In 1960 the population of

"urban territory," "urbanized districts," and "metropolitan areas" as used with specific definitions by the Bureau of the Census. When Census terms are used in this volume this is indicated, and the official meaning is respected. However, the Census Bureau has its own purposes and requirements, which often restrict the use of words and figures in order to achieve more accurate measurement and statistical description of extremely complex and varied phenomena. When it is necessary for such purposes, the Bureau does not hesitate to modify a definition of its own (that of "urban" was thus redefined for the 1950 Census) or to introduce new terms, such as "standard metropolitan area." While a regional study like the present one makes great use of Census data, its purposes are quite different. It seeks not only to describe phenomena but also to discover their "whys" and "hows," concerns that are beyond the official aim of the Census Bureau.

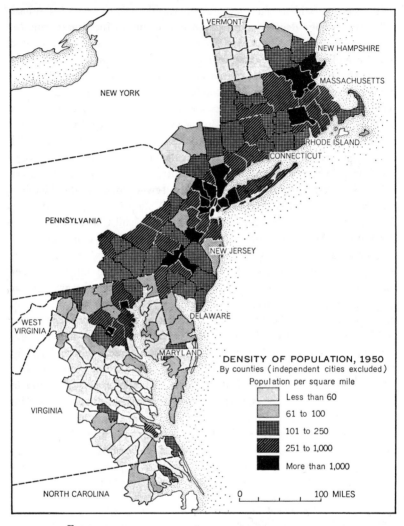

DENSITY OF POPULATION, 1950
By counties (independent cities excluded)
Population per square mile

- Less than 60
- 61 to 100
- 101 to 250
- 251 to 1,000
- More than 1,000

Fig. 4

New Jersey reached a density of 800 per square mile, the highest of the fifty states in the Union (see Fig. 1, p. 6).

A map of population density by counties rather than by states tells more about the internal structure of Megalopolis (Fig. 4). Over most of the area the 1950 density appears to have been much above 51 people per square mile, the national average, and for most of the counties (the few exceptions were located mainly on the fringes) it was above 100. No other area of similar size in the United States could boast of comparable densities on a county basis. On the national map (Fig. 5) another impressive though smaller group of counties south of the Great Lakes shows densities of more than 90 per square mile, but this industrial Midwestern belt shrinks to a scattering of disconnected nuclei when counties with densities greater than 150 are indicated (see Fig. 6). And yet counties with this density, or an even greater one, extend more or less continuously from Boston to Washington. These higher densities outline the old axis of crowding and urbanization that follows rather closely the Fall Line, the inland limit of seagoing ships. Megalopolis was indeed initiated as a seaboard phenomenon and it still bears the imprint of its origin.

The most striking feature of population distribution within and around Megalopolis is the thinning out of density on the mountain fringe to the northwest and in Virginia south of the Washington metropolitan area. On the whole, the densities are more continuously high from Pennsylvania to Massachusetts than south of the Mason and Dixon line. This contrast between north and south within Megalopolis seems to be fading gradually, however, as is illustrated by the higher rate of population increase in the counties south of Philadelphia in recent intercensal periods (see Fig. 9, p. 41). This trend will probably continue in the 1960's. Additional contrasts in density can be observed on maps plotted on the basis of minor civil divisions (see Figs. 45 and 46, pp. 163–164), but the county unit reveals enough for our purposes.

A simple map of population density delimits Megalopolis in a broad manner. However, to reveal its true character other criteria must be taken into account also. Greater densities, occurring over comparable areas and involving comparable masses of several dozen millions of people, can be found in northwestern Europe and in Far Eastern countries. In Europe, as in Megalopolis, urbanization and industrialization account for the high density, and this means higher incomes and standards of living (much higher in Megalopolis, of course, than in Europe). In the Far East and countries like Egypt, such densities exist not only in cities but even in purely agricultural regions, and the great crowding, rural or urban, in these areas means at the present time utter misery and deprivation, offering the greatest possible contrast with the way of life in Megalopolis. Asia's overcrowded areas are the poorest and least well equipped in the world, while the population of Megalopolis is undoubtedly the most affluent group of over 30 million people to be found anywhere in the mid-twentieth century.

These relationships can be seen by comparing maps of density of population in the United States and Megalopolis with those showing distribution of income (see Figs. 4, 5, 210, 220, pp. 28, 31 and 696, 717). Clearly, the higher population densities in Megalopolis usually coincide with higher income. The relation would be inverse in countries such as India or China, if adequate statistical data were available for the compilation of similar maps.

Thus the crowding in Megalopolis can hardly be called "overpopulation" in the sense of creating want. At least it does not create poverty for want of consumer goods. Any shortages it causes are of a new kind — for example, shortages of space for special uses such as gracious living for the average family, or for recreation. Population density alone, therefore, cannot define a way of life.

To understand the meaning of maps of population density it is necessary also to recognize the limitations of the Census data. The United States Census is taken on a given day, and people are counted at their places of residence. There is no information given as to where these people work, and of course in the huge complex of Megalopolis people do not always live near their place of work. They often commute not only to another township but even to another county or state. To some extent this is the result of the population density and of the resulting intensity of land use. The commercial and industrial civilization that produced Megalopolis has as one of its essential characteristics a very great, involved, and *constantly increasing division of labor among men.* And as such specialization increases and deepens, it results in a growing specialization of locations, a greater and more *complex division of labor for the land.* Thus, in New York and other "central cities" of Megalopolis to which most of these commuters go, there is a great numerical difference between the daytime and nighttime population. In Manhattan, for example, the 1950 Census population was given as 1,960,000 with 923,000 of these people employed locally. The total number of jobs on the island, however, was 2,571,000.[3] Thus the local population was joined on weekdays by some 1,600,000 people coming in to work, and by an additional number, indefinite but appreciable, of visitors, travellers, shoppers, and others. The total number of incoming persons may thus more or less equal the Census population, and

[3] See the data gathered by the Regional Plan Association in *People, Jobs and Land, 1955–1975, in the New Jersey-New York-Connecticut Metropolitan Region,* R. P. A. Bulletin 87, New York, June 1957.

Opposite Fig. 5. Population per square mile by counties in 1950 for the continental United States. *Courtesy of the U. S. Bureau of the Census*

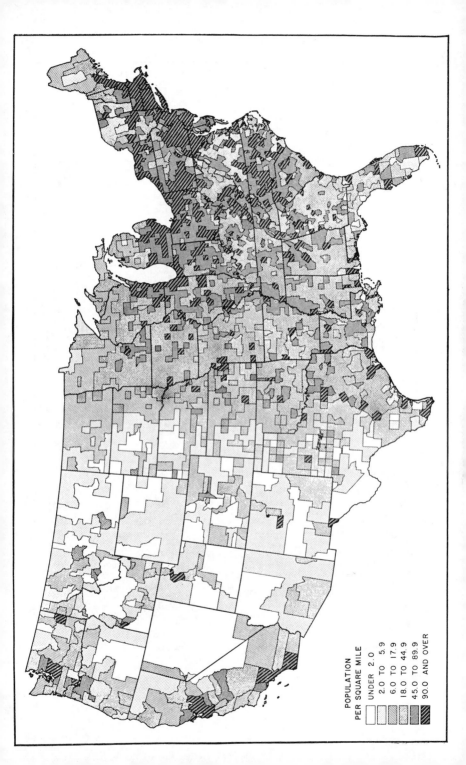

POPULATION
PER SQUARE MILE

UNDER 2.0
2.0 TO 5.9
6.0 TO 17.9
18.0 TO 44.9
45.0 TO 89.9
90.0 AND OVER

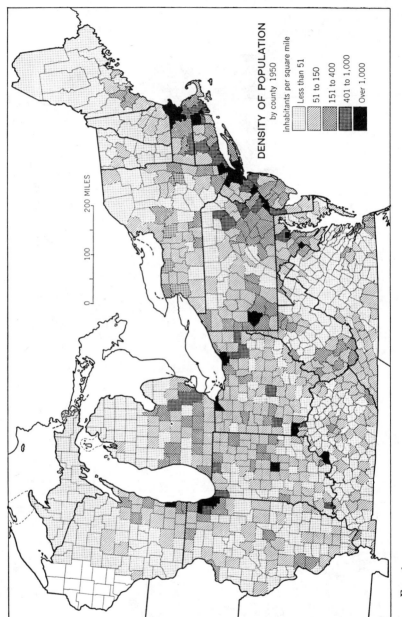

DENSITY OF POPULATION
by county 1950

inhabitants per square mile

Less than 51
51 to 150
151 to 400
401 to 1,000
Over 1,000

0   100   200 MILES

Fig. 6

for many hours of the day Manhattan's residential density of 89,096 per square mile may be approximately doubled, making it 180,000 per square mile. While Manhattan is an extreme case, it is not unique. Commuting to Newark in 1950 brought the daytime population of the city to 885,000, thus more than doubling the residential population of 439,000. In Washington, D. C., the 1950 daytime population included at least 200,000 more persons than were recorded in the Census. Philadelphia had 400,000 more people in the daytime, and Boston 270,000 more.[4] For all practical purposes the densities and masses of people to be serviced by local facilities are those of the peak hour, and this means much denser occupation of the land than could be inferred from the population density maps.

Such tides of higher population crowding do not occur only in central cities or business districts. They may also become a regular feature of areas in which manufacturing plants occupy most of the land, with their labor force partly housed in the neighborhood but partly commuting from more distant homes.

The most impressive tides are found in still other areas, and are of a seasonal rather than a daily nature. In summer many families in Megalopolis migrate to summer homes, from which the head of the family may commute, if not daily, at least weekly, to spend the week ends on the seashore, on a lake, or in the hills. At such seasons the population density of areas — sometimes they are entire groups of counties — serving as *summer pastures* for the city folks may be several times greater than the densities of the year-round population only. The *Vineyard Gazette*, weekly newspaper of Martha's Vineyard Island, carries on its front page the heading: "Martha's Vineyard Island — population: 6,000 in winter, 40,000 in summer." The former figure is that of the Census, taken on April 1, 1960. Obviously Cape Cod and Nantucket experience similar variations. The three Massachusetts counties (Barnstable, Dukes, and Nantucket) in which these resort areas are located were not included by the Census in any standard metropolitan area or designated as metropolitan state economic areas. It is hardly disputable, however, that in summertime all three are metropolitan suburbs of the Megalopolitan central cities and that most of the income and occupation of their year-round residents is derived from the activities of this season of dense population. We shall include these three counties in Megalopolis without hesitation, and we shall do likewise

---

[4] See Wilfred Owen, *The Metropolitan Transportation Problem*, The Brookings Institution, Washington, 1956, especially p. 271, Table 4. The 1960 Census gathered some data on commuting, which was not available to us as we went to press.

for various other seashore resort areas in Delaware and Maryland that are contiguous, at least on the county basis, to year-round Megalopolitan counties.

Summer pastures are not limited to the seashore. They are just as important in the upper Piedmont and the mountain ranges west of the seaboard cities. However, it does not seem as justifiable to extend the limits of Megalopolis into the Appalachian ridges and Adirondack valleys, for there local industries play a larger role in the economy, and also Midwesterners contribute to the summer tourists. We shall, therefore, limit Megalopolis to areas contiguous to districts densely occupied at Census time, and close enough to the places of work to make possible week end, if not daily, commuting in the summer. Thus, in New York State we shall include the Catskills but not the Adirondacks.

These daily and seasonal tidal currents in the population concentrations in Megalopolis raise questions about the usual distinctions between urban and rural.

Urban and Rural in Megalopolis

The U. S. Bureau of the Census revised for the 1950 Census the definition of territory classified as *urban places*. These include incorporated and unincorporated places of 2,500 inhabitants or more and densely settled urban-fringe areas. (Before 1950 unincorporated areas and urban fringes were not classed as urban.) This official definition still associates the concept of "urban" with a rather large group of people living together *in the same place;* it evokes a picture of dense grouping of a substantial population. All places not classified as urban are considered to be "rural," and the population resident (i.e., spending the nights) in rural territory is automatically called rural. The concept of "rural," whether applied to people or land, has long carried a meaning of close association with agriculture or forestry, or in any case of living off the land in a way that contrasts with the industrial and commercial pursuits of city folks. In the old order and through the centuries, *the distinction between urban and rural was basic in the division of labor,* serving to oppose two ways of life as well as to classify in two broad and clearly distinct categories all the various accepted economic activities. Urban population went to rural areas on vacation, for recreation purposes, but otherwise the two remained well separated, the urban way of life being characterized by dense concentration of population in small built-up areas, and the rural way by scattered settlement over vast and mainly green spaces. This distinction has long been true and useful; it still is true, in its ancient meaning, over large areas in

many countries; but in Megalopolis these terms need a good deal of revision to avoid the confusion that arises when the accepted meaning of
words is found to be too far divorced from the facts to be useful in describing them.

The human tidal currents within Megalopolis, which we hinted at
briefly when we discussed the actual meaning of population densities (and
which will be analyzed in greater detail later in this study), result mainly
from the scattering far beyond the "city walls," and beyond various limits
of local government, of people whose main work, interests, and income
are located in urban, built-up districts. These people, who are city folks
in daytime hours on weekdays, are residents of areas that often do not
qualify as "urban" according to the Census definition, even that of 1950.
As new areas are invaded by such people urban territory has to be extended and sometimes redefined. The number of places classified as urban
by the U. S. Census rose from 939 in 1880 to 2,262 in 1910, 3,165 in 1930,
and 3,464 in 1940. It would have reached 4,023 in 1950 if the definition
used in 1940 had not been revised; but with the revision, which included
unincorporated as well as incorporated places, the total number of urban
places rose in 1950 to 4,741. The urban element in the population of the
United States has, of course, increased greatly too. Between 1910 and 1950
it shot up from 42 million to 96 million people, or from 45.7 to 64.0 per
cent of the total.

This proliferation of urban places involves also a greater administrative
subdivision of the land. In rural territory this has been less marked, for the
number of places in such territory has risen much more slowly, remaining,
since 1930, between 13,000 and 14,000.[5]

Eventually the Bureau of the Census found that the two basic categories, rural and urban population, no longer met the needs for descriptive
purposes. A new category had to be introduced within the rural population — the *rural nonfarm* population. This established a definite distinction
between rural and agricultural. It might have been argued that with the
development of highly mechanized and larger farms and the disappearance of small farms the number of people needed to service the reduced
strictly agricultural population would increase, enough even to account
for about half of the population in some agricultural regions. Often those
servicing the farms live in some town and are thus classified as urban. But
even if we assume that their residences are scattered enough so that the
people are still counted as rural, it is difficult to classify as mainly agricul-

---

[5] The above figures on rural and urban places are from the *Statistical Abstract of
the United States: 1959*, Washington, 1959, p. 17.

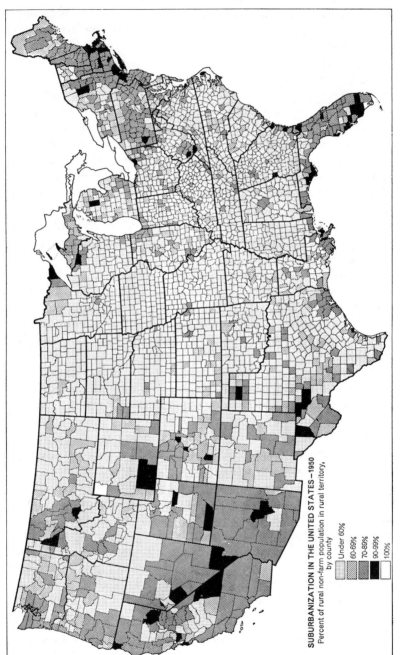

SUBURBANIZATION IN THE UNITED STATES—1950
Percent of rural non-farm population in rural territory,
by county

Under 60%
60-69%
70-89%
90-99%
100%

Fɪɢ. 7

tural an area in which the farm population may make up as little as one third or less of the rural population (from which any urban element is excluded).

The relative importance of the rural nonfarm population in rural territory may thus serve as a measure of the degree to which the territory considered is indeed rural in the old sense of the term.[6] Wherever a very large majority of the total rural population is nonfarm, the meaning of rural must be definitively divorced from an agricultural connotation; it must be assumed that the majority of the people resident in that area live from and by nonagricultural pursuits, that is, pursuits of an industrial, commercial, or other "urbanlike" nature. The map of the percentage of the nonfarm component in rural population in all counties of the United States according to the 1950 Census reveals various distribution patterns (see Fig. 7). It clearly shows east of the Rocky Mountains vast areas — most of the Great Plains and of the Southeast — where the farm element is marked (40 per cent or more of the total rural population). In some counties, though this is not shown on the map, it is dominant (50 per cent or more). Counties where the farm element constitutes about one third of the rural population and the nonfarm between 60 and 69 per cent may be considered transitional, where suburban influences must be at work, and there are not too many of them. East of the Front Ranges of the Rockies they seem to border on middle-sized developing cities; they are also found on the fringes of Megalopolis and even inside it (Lancaster and York counties in Pennsylvania, for example, or the Eastern Shore counties of Maryland) around developing but not yet large communities. Of the counties with more than 70 per cent nonfarm population in rural territory, the largest group on the map is found on the Northeastern seaboard. (This leaves out of consideration the Southwestern states, where the much larger size of counties and the special rural life of the desert establish conditions precluding valid comparison with the East.)

This Northeastern deruralized area almost straddles the Appalachian ranges in Pennsylvania and extends deep into northern New England, in both regions an obvious result of farm abandonment in the hills. But the general outline of Megalopolis, on a scale even larger than the frame already adopted, appears very clearly on the map. The evolution of nonfarm population in rural territory has been different here from that in

[6] Webster's Dictionary defines *rural* as follows: "Of or pertaining to the country, as distinguished from a city or town; designating or pertaining to country people, or country occupations, especially agriculture; rustic." Discussing synonyms, the Dictionary adds: "*Rural* especially suggests agricultural pursuits or simple community life."

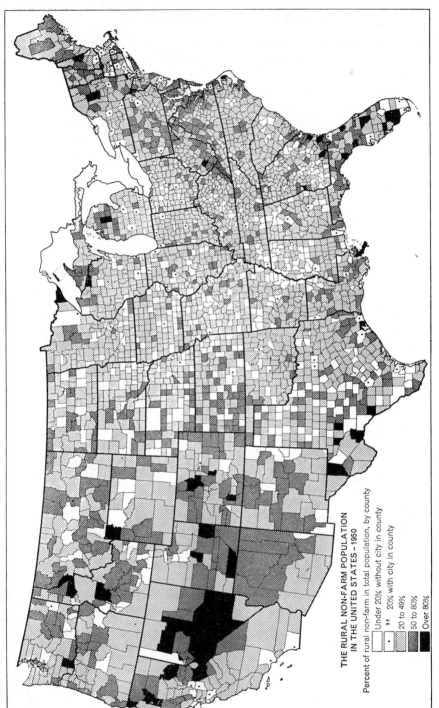

THE RURAL NON-FARM POPULATION
IN THE UNITED STATES - 1950

Percent of rural non-farm in total population, by county

Under 20% without city in county
" 20% with city in county
20 to 49%
50 to 80%
Over 80%

FIG. 8

other parts of the nation. Here distinction between urban and rural has taken novel and special forms.

There is little doubt, as one reflects upon the size of the invasion of rural territory by nonfarmers, that in and around Megalopolis a large degree of *de facto* suburbanization has been achieved in vast areas still considered nonurban. It was as a result of this emergence, outside the urbanized areas, of scattered nonagricultural population, depending on urban or suburban means of livelihood, that the need arose for the "metropolitan area" concept, which has already met with great success because of its usefulness. The Northeastern seaboard "patch" on the map of the nonfarm element in rural territory demonstrates, however, the enormous scale, in this particular part of the country, of a super-metropolitan sprawl welding together many contiguous or neighboring metropolitan areas. Around the counties that are metropolitan at the season of the Census (i.e., outside the summer season) there is thus a zone of transitional counties, on their way to fuller metropolitanization, or perhaps we ought to say "Megalopolitanization." This results from the needs of concentrated masses of population, which have developed a wide and complex network of "human tides."

Barring an unforeseeable event cancelling out all the present trends, there is little doubt that such a process of growing suburbanization or "metropolitanization" will go on in the parts of Megalopolis still considered rural. The total population and its density are growing. The larger cities are often saturated, at least in terms of their present residential capacity, and show signs of a declining Census population. As a leading population expert has observed:

> Although gains in the population of cities have been the normal condition, there have been many exceptions. One out of every ten of the cities which had 100,000 persons or more in 1940 reported a decline in population by 1950. All but one of these were located in the northeastern States.[7]

Although Megalopolis covers only a section of the whole Northeast, most of the declining large cities are within it. It is not surprising that in some of the most crowded places, where congestion is the most felt, solutions are sought, partly by migration within the region. This trend has been greatly accelerated since 1950. Even New York City has had to resign itself to a slight (1.4 per cent) decline in the number of its residents from 1950 to 1960.[8]

[7] Conrad Taeuber and Irene B. Taeuber, *The Changing Population of the United States*, John Wiley and Sons, New York, 1958, pp. 113–114.

[8] According to *Newsletter*, Department of City Planning, New York, January 1961 and *1960 Census of Population: Advance Reports*, PC(A2)-34, March 15, 1961.

To make clearer these trends of migration within Megalopolis and the general evolution toward a more equal, though yet extremely variable, density of residents throughout its vast area, let us turn to a map of the changes in population from 1930 to 1950. Prepared on the basis of minor civil divisions, this map offers a detailed enough picture (although some generalization was necessary to make it clear enough at this scale) for this region and its immediate environs. For this twenty-year period, encompassing a major depression and a World War, the growth was quite unequal within Megalopolis' territory. On the whole, however, it was much greater within it than in the surrounding areas. The main nuclei from which Megalopolis developed, and which in 1950 still contained about half of its total population, did not show much growth. In the great cities of Boston, Providence, New York, Philadelphia, and Baltimore no dark patches appear. Washington alone among the major cities had, in the District of Columbia, an accretion of more than 50 per cent. Around New York City even some of the immediate suburbs did not have as much as 50 per cent increase in the period 1930–50 (Fig. 73, p. 248).

The greatest increases, shown by the darkest patches, occurred *around* the major nuclei. On the whole, these areas of growth were disposed along the main Fall Line axis between the Boston and Washington metropolitan areas, but they also showed a tendency to shift somewhat away from this main line, chiefly toward the seashore but also at times inland. Connecticut and New Jersey, the two more obviously "suburbanized" states, had the largest areas of substantial growth (i.e., of more than 50 per cent and sometimes even more than 100 per cent). It ought to be remembered that these are figures of growth between Censuses, which do not take into account the summer-season migration that causes denser occupation temporarily on both sides of the central ribbon of more permanent concentration. There were very few cases of notable decrease (of more than 10 per cent) within Megalopolis; but there was a scattering of such areas in western Massachusetts and on the Eastern Shore of Maryland, where they covered somewhat more territory. There were much larger areas of definite decrease outside the boundaries we have tentatively outlined for Megalopolis, i.e., in Vermont and northern New Hampshire, in upstate New York, in the central ranges of Pennsylvania, and in Virginia. During those twenty years Megalopolis was still sucking some population out of the more agricultural areas remaining on its fringes (in Massachusetts and Maryland, for instance) and in its neighborhood (in northern New England and in Virginia). We know that similar trends continued in the 1950's. The special 1957 population Census of New York City and its

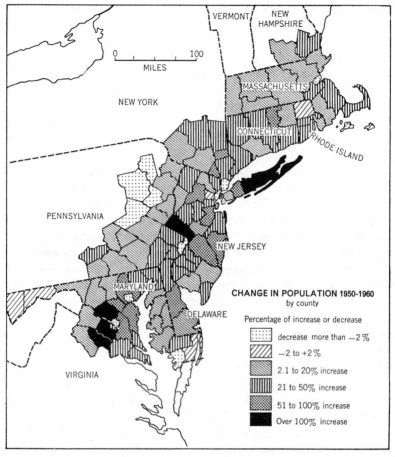

CHANGE IN POPULATION 1950-1960
by county

Percentage of increase or decrease

decrease more than −2%
−2 to +2%
2.1 to 20% increase
21 to 50% increase
51 to 100% increase
Over 100% increase

FIG. 9

New York suburbs first demonstrated that even this metropolis was losing population (in Manhattan, Brooklyn, and the Bronx) and that its distant suburbs were being populated at a faster rate than those closer to the city. This is well demonstrated by the changes in population during the intercensal period 1950–60 (see Fig. 9).

It is obvious, then, that residences and other forms of activity are being scattered so widely and rapidly throughout Megalopolis outside the old nuclei that a new and rapidly shifting map of land use is emerging all over the region. Communities originally dependent on one or another of the old main nuclei become part also of the orbits of other nuclei as these expand and overlap in constantly more complicated fashion. This is particularly true in such states as Connecticut and New Jersey, parts of which gravitate simultaneously into the orbits of large cities within the state (such as Trenton and Newark in New Jersey, or New Haven and Bridgeport in Connecticut) and into the vaster orbits of New York and Philadelphia, in the one state, and New York, Boston, and Providence in the other. The interconnections grow more and more entangled as more specialization develops in the labor force and in certain districts, and as the means of travel and communication between these various points are constantly being improved.

That a good deal of the land in the "twilight areas" between the cities remains green, either still farmed or wooded, matters little to the continuity of Megalopolis. The region as a whole is made up of many interdependent parts, and the increase in population and the tidal system of human movements through the area affect the sections that still keep a rural look just as well as the more built-up districts. The concentration most characteristic of Megalopolis is not merely continuous residential crowding. It is a different, perhaps more modern, kind, reflecting the sort of economic opportunity this area offers and also its extraordinary wealth, which seems both to result from and to cause concentrations of both people and opportunity.

The Concentrated Economic Opportunity

History has abundantly demonstrated that economic opportunity attracts people, a principle that seems so evident it hardly needs elaboration. For the last four hundred years no other part of the world has been as much associated as America with dreams of greater opportunity. These dreams made even Ellis Island into a legend. Megalopolis has been the principal entrance gate for immigrants coming into the United States, and New York has been the chief port of entry. It was thus not a random decision but a well-informed and considered one that set up in the midst of New York harbor the Statue of Liberty, that symbolic gift brought all the way across the ocean. To the immigrant, admission into this country was interpreted as a sort of liberation, and all modern political theory has recognized that the greater freedom offered by American laws and customs broadened the scope of economic opportunity available to those who came to the United States.

Many historians, economists, and geographers in America and in Europe have claimed repeatedly that the extraordinary economics of the Northeastern Atlantic seaboard of the United States, and the amount of liberation achieved here by immigrants from Europe, should be explained by the development of the natural resources abounding on the North America continent, by what was going on inland rather than by the evolution of the Northeastern seaboard itself. The resources supplied by nature were, first, the abundance of free land, at a time when agricultural production still formed the basis of wealth and international trade; then the abundance on the continent and within easy reach from the Northeastern seaboard of major sources of energy (i.e., waterfalls, coal, and oil) and of other major industrial raw materials (such as grains, cotton, timber, iron and copper ores), and even of gold and silver.

This theory is summed up by the popular reference to the "valuable piece of real estate" taken from the Indians, who were unable to develop it. As the settlement and development of the United States proceeded from the bases early established between the James River and Massachusetts Bay, the general control of the national economy remained in this section, and the concentration of economic opportunity also grew there. The really great opportunity was found, however, in the West — in the Great Plains, in California, in Oregon — where the actual liberation occurred, where the natural resources were located, where land long remained abundant and free. It would thus seem to be only because of the early start that population is now concentrated on the largest scale in Megalopolis; and the great recent rate of population increase on the Pacific coast, especially in southern California, would seem to demonstrate an already consummated relative decline of Megalopolis.

All these considerations have their factual and statistical foundations. The major natural resources of the United States are certainly located outside the region of Megalopolis and even, for most of them, at considerable distances. The only two major natural resources still present today within the area are the ocean, with its two assets of navigation and fisheries, and the coal basin of eastern Pennsylvania, situated at the very fringe of Megalopolis but included in our broadly outlined limits. Of the better agricultural land in the area little is still under cultivation, and the total acreage of high-quality soil originally available here seems rather negligible when compared to the vast expanse of richer soils in the Great Plains. Some ores (iron, copper, and others) were formerly mined within the area, especially in the early nineteenth century, but today these resources are only a memory. Of course all these various local natural riches played a role in earlier times. However, there is hardly any region of the world of similar size that could not boast of some equivalent natural endowment. There is nothing exceptional indeed in Megalopolis' natural

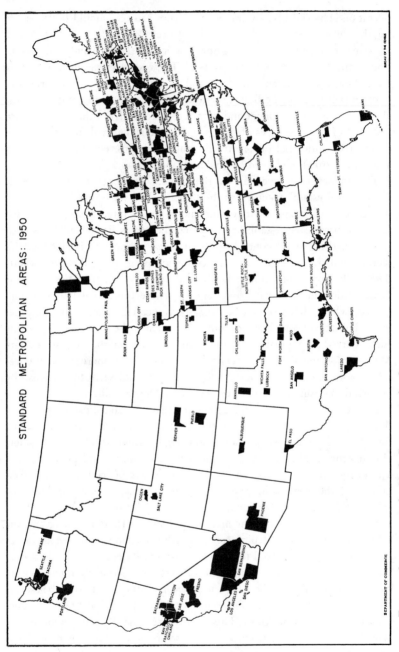

STANDARD METROPOLITAN AREAS: 1950

DEPARTMENT OF COMMERCE

BUREAU OF THE CENSUS

Fig. 10. *Courtesy of the U. S. Bureau of the Census*

potential, unless it is its geographical location, which enabled it to play its historical role as the landing wharf for European immigrants coming to a rich continent awaiting development. The question then arises: why did the population congregate here instead of gathering in better endowed, naturally richer areas farther inland? For at least a century there had been no serious obstacles in the way of internal migrations, but nowhere else did crowding reach such magnitude and intensity.

Great cities arose inland along the American nation's route of transcontinental march westward — Pittsburgh and Cleveland, St. Louis, Detroit, and Chicago, and many others, and finally the impressive and more recent great metropolises of Los Angeles and San Francisco on the West Coast. Each of these had its own period of spectacular growth when many reasons suggested projecting that moment's dynamics into the future and visualizing at that place the future center of population of the nation, the greatest urban and economic agglomeration. However, actual developments have not carried out the promise of such great hopes. Although it has moved westward, the mathematical center of population has remained a purely theoretical concept; it has recently been situated in southwestern Indiana (in 1940) and at Centralia, Illinois (1960), in areas of little density and tending to decline in population from 1940 to 1960. One ought, perhaps, to remember the fate of the original Megalopolis in the Greek Peloponnesus. In America the only area that has for the last 200 years retained the actual function of which the Greek Megalopolis, and at other times Pittsburgh, St. Louis, or Chicago, may have dreamed, is the one we have defined in this Northeastern seaboard, endowed by nature in a rather average way, certainly without any extraordinary natural resources on the spot to justify the harvest of skyscrapers and many multi-billion-dollar businesses now blooming there.

If people arriving in the United States did not all proceed inland toward the free open spaces full of natural wealth, it surely was because they found enough economic opportunity right on the seaboard, in the great cities and their suburbs. In fact, few parts of the country have had at any time as high a percentage of foreign-born population as the cities of what has become Megalopolis. Perhaps the newcomers were not adventurous enough, or not adjusted enough to the American scene, to take advantage of the opportunities offered in the more rapidly developing areas inland. Perhaps also they felt more assured by the rather satisfying perspectives in this crowded region. For although the crowded Eastern area did not provide the romantic freedom of the frontier or the immediate wealth of a small booming community (this did not occur as frequently as the popular "westerns" would seem to imply), it gave to individuals more privacy and more time to adapt themselves in their own manner to the New World to which they had been admitted. This was also an area with large groups of many different national origins, who could help and direct the first steps of a newcomer of their own nationality.

The seaboard cities were growing rapidly, even though their rate of growth, arithmetically computed, may have been less than that farther west. This slower rate of growth should not obscure the fact that from a very early time population numbers and densities have been greater here. An increase of 10 per cent is certainly less impressive than one of 25 per cent in the same period; but if, to begin with, the region that grew more slowly had five times, or even three times, as many people and jobs as the more rapidly growing region, the former's population and labor force will have increased much more in actual numbers than will those of the latter.

It thus appears that Megalopolis has had at least two distinctive characteristics in its growth: it has offered satisfying economic opportunities to massively increasing numbers of people; and it has provided for this expanding labor market without having any exceptional natural endowment in terms of local agricultural or mineral riches. As in the case of many another great city in the past, the cities of Megalopolis have had to rely on their wits to thrive. They seem to have succeeded well, for Megalopolis has grown not only by immigration from overseas and by the natural rate of increase but also by in-migration from other parts of the Union. In New York City and Washington this has been especially marked. Despite the relative lack of local natural riches, the seaboard has achieved a most remarkable concentration of labor force and of wealth. These two components of economic opportunity may be more easily measured if they are described.

Size and Nature of the Labor Market

The actual organization of resources that supports Megalopolis will be described and analyzed at greater length in future chapters. It may, however, be stressed at this point that the manifold and polynuclear concentration characteristic of Megalopolis has resulted from a complex and successful management of all the historical and geographical assets of the area, building up a very special and enormous labor market. The great cities of the region have all helped to make it become a vast hub servicing, in various ways, not only the national economy but also international relations. To find out how this "hub" is itself serviced today we shall have to roam the whole wide world. As early as the seventeenth century the seaside towns of New England and New York developed maritime activities to an extent causing worries in London. Cromwell's Navigation Acts were largely provoked by New England's threat to the profits English merchants expected from their overseas trade. Despite laws voted in Westminster, the maritime economy blossomed during the eighteenth century, increasingly so after independence. On the eve of the Civil War, competition by American clippers that sailed from Boston, New York, Philadelphia, and Baltimore again caused great worry to the British shipping interests. Greatly reduced in importance from 1860 to 1910, the merchant marine based on the seaports of Megalopolis resumed its expansion in the twentieth century, particularly after the two World Wars. Through all these periods, whether the ships crowding the harbors flew the American flag or the flags of other countries, the great seaports remained prosperous and expanded.

Whether they were directly maritime or serviced the commerce generated by the shipping, the activities derived from the seaport functions were a permanent and essential component in building up the labor market on the seaboard. Near the waterfront warehouses developed along with wholesale trade of imported goods, marine insurance, commercial banking, ship building and repairing, large-scale fisheries and processing of the catch, and many other trades and industries. The quasi-monopoly achieved by Manhattan as the capital of both finance and entertainment in America, and more recently in the world, owes a great deal to the extraordinary prosperity and expansion of the Port of New York, and in recent years to its coordination, once it became so crowded and so expensive, with the great maritime establishments of Massachusetts Bay and Delaware and Chesapeake bays.

The total tonnage of merchandise actually handled in the major ports of Megalopolis averaged close to 300 million short tons for the period 1953-56. If local traffic were excluded and only *foreign tonnage* (100 million tons) and *coastwise tonnage* were counted (in the United States coastwise traffic means such long-range navigation as shipments from the Gulf of Mexico, the West Coast, and even Alaska, distances equalling those involved in international navigation in Europe or South America), this figure would be reduced to 200 million short tons. Even this is equalled in volume only in the great system of seaports of northwestern Europe on both sides of the North Sea and English Channel (i.e., from Hamburg to Le Havre on the continent and from Southampton to Aberdeen in Britain). The total volume of goods loaded and unloaded in foreign trade for the whole of North America (from Alaska to Panama) amounted for the same period to 468 million short tons, of which 21.3 per cent went through Megalopolis. The whole foreign seaborne trade of the United Kingdom, populated by 50 million islanders, reached 148 million short tons in that period. These comparisons may help to make clear the enormous concentration of sea transport in the harbors of Megalopolis.

The maritime activity also brought to the same harbors a steady flow of immigrants from various parts of the world but essentially from Europe. Thus in this region the seaports generated an *abundantly supplied labor market* and also one *oriented toward trading and servicing* as well as, and perhaps more than, toward manufacturing. Labor in Megalopolis on the whole was geared toward the upper stages of economic activity – the more involved kinds of manufacturing and the "white-collar" professions – rather than toward the simple production of raw materials, and as the continent was developed, such specialization along the Northeastern seaboard increased. To be able to maintain this trend, the region needed a constantly improving level of education for its manpower, and it also remained an area of relatively high wages and salaries. At the time of the 1950 Census, Megalopolis, as defined for the purpose of this study, accounted for 21.2 per cent of the total population of the United States and for a slightly larger share, 22.8 per cent, of the total number of persons employed in the country. In actual numbers this concentration of employed persons was impressive: 12.8 million people were at work in Megalopolis in April 1950, and the figure has substantially increased since then. There are not many *nations* in the present world with much larger labor forces.

The concentration of *well-paid* personnel was most impressive too. For a good number of years the better average incomes in the country, as distributed by states, have been located in this seaboard area. In 1956 the average per capita income for the continental United States stood at $1,940; only eight states and the District of Columbia reported an average above $2,200. Delaware had the highest figure ($2,858), followed by Connecticut ($2,673), New Jersey ($2,443), California ($2,419), Nevada ($2,413), New York ($2,395), Illinois ($2,383), the District of Columbia ($2,371), and Massachusetts ($2,206). The somewhat lower average for Pennsylvania ($2,008) seems to indicate a figure in the $2200's for the part of the state included in Megalopolis, and Maryland ($2,102) and Rhode Island ($2,012) are not far below. Thus for all of Megalopolis the average personal income per capita in 1956 was well above $2,400. In the late 1950's this was undoubtedly the richest section in the country in terms

of *average personal income* and the richest group of nearly 40 million people in the world. That is, the people were better paid for their work. The population of Megalopolis is far from being one of leisurely wealth, for in 1960 the proportion of employed people in the total population was slightly higher than in the rest of the country.

This situation is not new. For quite some time Megalopolis has been the largest American market for well-paid labor. In 1929, when the national average personal income per capita stood at $703, among the forty-eight states only seven showed an average above $900. New York ($1,159), Delaware ($1,017), California ($995), Illinois ($957), Massachusetts ($913) — and the District of Columbia ($1,273) — all showed higher average incomes than any other states. In 1940, the national average was down to $595, and the District of Columbia was again at the top of the list with $1,170, almost double the national average, followed by eight states with figures above $750, the same states that showed more than $2,200 in 1956, but in a slightly different order: Delaware ($1,004), Connecticut ($917), Nevada ($876), New York ($870), California ($840), New Jersey ($822), Massachusetts ($784), and Illinois ($754). Rhode Island was just below the $750 level with $743.[9]

The shift of Connecticut and New Jersey toward the top of the list seems to be a result of the increasing suburbanization of these two states, particularly by out-migration from New York City and its immediate suburbs within New York State. The concentration of income within Megalopolis has changed little, it would seem, since 1929. However, from 1929 to 1956 the per capita personal income showed an increase in Megalopolis somewhat below the national rate of increase of 176 per cent (it was 162 per cent in New Jersey, 160 per cent in Connecticut, 171 per cent in Maryland, and 181 per cent in Delaware, but only 107 per cent in New York State). Throughout the country this rate was much higher in the farming areas than in the urbanized ones; and the successful development of the formerly depressed Southeastern states brought there such rates of increase as 320 per cent in South Carolina, 300 per cent in Georgia, and 291 per cent in North Carolina.[10] However, the nonfarm labor market of Megalopolis still remains without equal in terms of the opportunity resulting from both its size and its higher rate of compensation.

In 1956, in the total wage and salary disbursements in the continental

[9] The figures of average personal income by states in 1956, 1929, and 1940 are from the U. S. Bureau of the Census, *Statistical Abstract of the United States: 1958*, Table No. 393, p. 311.

[10] *Ibid.*, Table 395, p. 314.

United States (which amounted to $224,635 million), the share of the eight seaboard states from Massachusetts to Maryland, plus the District of Columbia, reached 33 per cent (or $72,373 million).[11] This figure is somewhat above the total for Megalopolis counted by county, for although it omits southern New Hampshire and northern Virginia it includes the much larger areas of upstate New York and western Pennsylvania. However, it remains obvious that Megalopolis' share of the national totals is greater for wages and salaries than it is for either people or industrial production.

The average pay is higher, despite the heavy concentration of rather poorly paid colored and Puerto Rican crowds in the central cities of Megalopolis, especially from Washington, D. C., to New York, because of the *kind* of labor predominant in the region. In such an urbanized area the labor market for farmhands is quite small, and the family-sized farm predominates here, which in some areas uses the help of migrant labor at harvest time. The nonagricultural employment has been steadily shifting from the "blue-collar" to the "white-collar" type of activity, from the industrial to the nonindustrial professions.

By 1950 the total value of agricultural products produced and sold in Megalopolis amounted to 5.1 per cent of the national total. This was far below the area's share of the nation's population (21.2 per cent) and still further below the share of the total national consumption of agricultural goods. But it was still above the percentage of the national land area included in Megalopolis (1.8 per cent), and since it was about one twentieth of the huge farm production of the United States it still formed a substantial volume and value of agricultural goods. However, its value, $1,257 million, seemed small compared to the 1950 value added by manufacture in the factories of Megalopolis. This value, $30,953 million, was 26.4 per cent of the national total, whereas the region had 21.2 per cent of the nation's population and 22.8 per cent of its total jobs. Manufacturing still plays a great part in the prosperity of Megalopolis, and even farming still makes a contribution, though a minor one. However, both have lost, before 1950 and since, in *relative importance*, both in terms of their proportion of the national total and in terms of their role within the region's economy.

Such trends develop in accordance with the logic of history. Formerly, when there were still few settlers west of the Appalachian ridges, the area of the present Megalopolis was the best developed in the United States in

[11] *Ibid.*, calculated from Table 394, pp. 312–315. The same area had 23 per cent of the population in 1960.

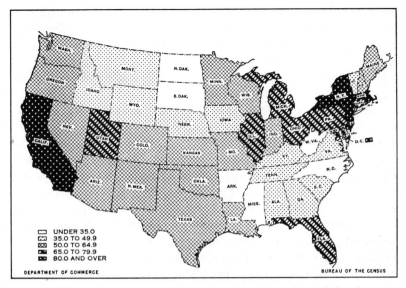

UNDER 35.0
35.0 TO 49.9
50.0 TO 64.9
65.0 TO 79.9
80.0 AND OVER

DEPARTMENT OF COMMERCE   BUREAU OF THE CENSUS

FIG. 11. Urban population as per cent of total population by state, 1950. *Courtesy of the U. S. Bureau of the Census*

terms of agriculture and contained most of the country's industries. Then settlement flowed into the Great Plains and developed there the richest farming region in the world. The Northeast could not and did not need to compete with the rural Middle West, and its farming shrank and evolved toward specialties depending on proximity to a large consuming market. In the latter part of the nineteenth century the great industrial belt developed from Pittsburgh to Cleveland and to Chicago, and other manufactures spread westward and southward, some of them having actually moved out of Megalopolis. As the whole country grew more industrialized, the share of Megalopolis in its total manufacturing was bound to decrease. That was still quite respectable in 1950 but it seems destined to decline slowly. This does not preclude a substantial and even growing volume, value, and perhaps employment in manufacturing industries — at least in some of them. Megalopolis cannot, of course, maintain the kind of economic leadership it has held for so long without constantly shifting its major industrial emphasis, according to the impulse of technology, toward the newer, more advanced kinds of manufactures, those usually requiring also greater numbers of workers.

A constantly shifting division of labor between the various sections of the country is steadily taking most of the textile plants out of New

England and New Jersey where these industries used to be so important.
But these areas are experiencing a spectacular growth in electronics, a
newcomer among major industries. Finishing industries requiring highly
specialized manpower are not the only ones to grow in Megalopolis. The
region has also seen steel mills rising or expanding near Baltimore and
Trenton, attracted by cheap ores from abroad and the size of the regional
market. But the labor force in Megalopolis is no longer basically concerned with manufacturing employment.

The fundamental change adding to the variety of the labor force has
been the steady growth of nonindustrial employment and of the white-
collar army in these great cities and around them. This has been a general feature in the nation and throughout the world in the twentieth
century, and the trend is still going on. In 1953 within the nonagricultural employment in the United States the nonindustrial sections equalled
and surpassed the figure of the industrial employment, each of these two
major sections of the labor force reaching about 25 million at the time.[12]
Since then industrial employment has been below this figure, while in
1959 nonindustrial employment exceeded 28 million jobs. Throughout
the nation the growth in job opportunities since World War II has been
mainly in nonindustrial activities, and in 1959 this category of employment was one third (or 7 million jobs) higher than in 1947.

Describing the major shifts in employment during the past fifty years
an expert listed first the shift from agricultural to nonfarm work.

In 1910, agricultural employment accounted for about 31 percent of total
employment in the United States. In 1956, it made up only 10 percent. In
1910, more than 11 million agricultural workers were required to produce the
food, fiber, and tobacco for the 92 million people in the United States. In 1956,
only about 6.5 million supplied similar needs for 168 million persons. . . . Employment in the trade and service industry divisions increased more rapidly
than total nonagricultural employment. . . . During the 1947–56 period, nonproduction workers have increased at a rate about 15 times as fast as production workers. Nonproduction workers, who represent less than one quarter
of total manufacturing employment, accounted for about three-quarters of the
total increase in employment in manufacturing during this period . . . Looking at the economy as a whole, the major changes appear to be (a) a long-term
rapid growth of the so-called " white collar " group of occupations; (b) a

---

[12] Data from "Recovery in the Labor Market," in *Federal Reserve Bulletin*, Washington, D. C., May 1959, pp. 471–476; based on figures from the Bureau of Labor
Statistics and following its definitions. *Industrial* employment includes manufacturing, mining, construction, transportation, and public utilities. *Nonindustrial* represents
trade, service, finance, and government. Domestic service and the self-employed are
not included.

slower growth in the "blue collar" occupations by a continuing rise in the skill level; (c) a sharp decline in employment among farmers and farm laborers; and (d) a faster than average growth among service workers.[13]

In the eighteenth and nineteenth centuries technological progress had been concentrating large masses of workers on the better sites for production. Urban growth was particularly spectacular then, in the midst of areas best fitted to produce large quantities of raw materials or finished goods needed for mass consumption. Cities grew in the middle of rich farming regions, on waterfalls, on coal basins, near iron-ore deposits, and at breaking points on transportation routes for the bulky essential cargoes. The twentieth century has modified these trends; its technology aims at producing and handling materials, light or bulky, with a minimum of human labor. The proletariat crowds that seemed the very essence of productivity a hundred years ago have gradually become less and less useful. Quantitatively, the labor force turns to the *nonproductive* functions in industrial as well as in nonindustrial occupations. In many manufacturing industries, for example, the clerical and laboratory staffs grow while the production workers scatter. Since nonindustrial occupations are more or less of a servicing and nonproductive nature, they increase their battalions of workers more rapidly than do the other divisions of the labor force.

If *servicing* in the widest sense of the term [14] becomes the main labor-demanding economic activity, *the major urban growth will shift from centers of large-scale production or redistribution to centers of massive consumption and decision-making*. Massive consumption of all kinds is, of course, found in and around the larger metropolises. The generation of new jobs by massive consumption centers will mean primarily a faster rate of growth for major metropolitan areas and for clusters of cities than for thinly populated districts, unless such districts, despite a thin density, contain some institution or group causing an especially heavy consumption of services. This would be the case in a fashionable resort area or in districts around certain military establishments. Especially snowballing will be white-collar occupations in and around what we call

[13] Ewan Clague, Commissioner of Labor Statistics, U. S. Department of Labor, *The Shifting Industrial and Occupational Composition of the Work Force during the Next Ten Years*, address to AFL–CIO Conference on Changing Character of American Industry, Washington, D. C., January 16, 1958. Quoted from a release of the U. S. Department of Labor.

[14] That is, including managerial and government occupations as well as retailing, domestic services, education, and entertaining. We do *not* follow here the classification of the Bureau of Labor Statistics (service workers, etc.).

"centers of decision-making." In such a category would be included centers where government agencies congregate and also places of considerable managerial, commercial, and financial activity.

Economic and political policies can never be entirely divorced for any length of time. Whether on the national or the local scale, both involve daily decisions dependent on laws and their administration as well as on the economic and financial processes at work in the country or in the locality. Although the nation's political capital is not in the same city as the main commercial and financial markets, all these major "decision-making" centers are located in Megalopolis except for five great cities situated in other parts of the United States.[15] No other place in North America has today a role in "decision-making" on both the economic and the political levels comparable either to Washington, D. C., or to New York City.

New York offers the largest concentration of financial power and industrial managerial authority in the Western world. Many corporations whose official headquarters are located elsewhere in the United States have found it necessary to put their main financial offices in Manhattan. In addition to those in Manhattan, the banks, trust and insurance companies, and corporation headquarters located in Boston and Philadelphia, in Connecticut and New Jersey, in Delaware and Maryland make Megalopolis' central axis the financial and managerial Main Street of the modern world, at least of those parts of it that do not gravitate in Moscow's orbit. On a national scale the essential managerial bureaus of the advertising industry, of publishing, mass media, and even of scientific research are found along this same axis.

No other section of the United States has a comparable "white-collar army," whether in size, variety, or authority. This concentration of white-collar occupations in Megalopolis does not prevent their growth in other sections of the country also, perhaps at even faster rates because much smaller numbers of workers are involved. But Megalopolis' specialization in these services and in decision-making functions favors the region's stability and growth despite the lack of massive natural resources locally and despite the gradual decentralization of industrial production and of the total volume of consumption.

[15] These five great cities are Chicago, Detroit, Pittsburgh, San Francisco, and Los Angeles. Each of them is indisputably an important policy-making center on the regional, and for certain specialized fields on the national, level. None of them, however, can claim to make decisions of the importance and at the rate of either New York City or Washington, D. C. They fall rather in the next category, in which we ought also to classify Boston and Philadelphia, which are in Megalopolis.

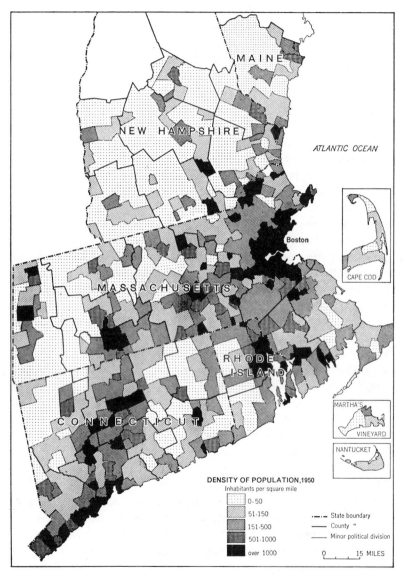

FIG. 12. Population density by minor civil divisions, 1950, in southern New England

This critical aspect of the economic crowding achieved in Megalopolis raises a host of questions. How the present situation came about, and by what involved processes this titanic concentration is still growing and spreading, despite symptoms of decentralization, are questions to be considered again on many of the following pages. At this stage it seems important to stress the growing dependence of employment *on human organization* rather than on resources extracted from nature's bounty. As involved technology and massive mechanization play a larger role in production and transportation, economic activities require more capital and credit to proceed. The money markets, either private or public, become a weightier factor in decision-making even at modest local levels.

Around the major concentration of capital and around the agencies managing large funds, vast bureaucracies develop. In the democracies public authorities share the responsibilities of financial management with private enterprise; instead of one central government bureaucracy there must develop, under the American system of government, many separate bureaucracies, some operating as agencies of the federal, state, and local governments while others, even more numerous, belong to the various corporate or other industrial organizations managing industry, commerce, capital, services, research, education, and so forth.

As years go by large organizational structures invade new fields previously reserved for the activities of individuals or small groups. Thus the white-collar battalions multiply. Thus the market expands for nonindustrial and nonagricultural employment around the centers of government and principal money markets. A new association takes shape in terms of geographical location between a mushrooming section of the labor force and the concentrations of capital and power. By this process Megalopolis has enormously benefited; indeed, its present greatness seems to rest upon it.

Wealth and Knowledge

Writing half a century ago, the historian Paul Mantoux [16] observed that the beginning of the Industrial Revolution in the eighteenth century was just one more step in the age-long evolution of the division of labor and of commercial exchange. These develop hand in hand, the progress of one opening new opportunities to the other. As Mantoux developed his analysis more deeply he came to link intimately the progress of both

[16] Paul Mantoux, *The Industrial Revolution in England in the Eighteenth Century*, Paris, 1906 (in French); second edition, revised (in English), Jonathan Cape, London, 1928.

commerce and the division of labor with the accumulation of capital, for development of the two former is impossible without growth of the latter, often at an even faster pace.

This evolution began with the appearance in prehistoric times of an urban life distinct from the rural. Urbanization can be described as the first major step in the early division of labor,[17] which proceeded more rapidly within urban populations mainly because they developed more specialization in the crafts and carried on more trading. The *market place* was, in the European Middle Ages, the distinctive mark and exclusive privilege of cities. In the past, urbanization could not be separated from the growth of commerce and of increasing specialization, and this relationship still holds. Capital may formerly have been accumulated largely as profits on the fruits of the land, but even then it was gathered and managed in towns, where it was put to work through the mechanisms of exchange and where crowding caused a greater density of consumption.

The concentration now observed in Megalopolis appears to conform to this general theory. This Northeastern seaboard region early developed trading activities and a more advanced division of labor. Its great market places were the first in America to gather substantial amounts of capital, which could be reinvested first in more trading and later in manufacturing. In this respect New England's seaboard and the main cities of the Middle Atlantic states led the nation from the start. This historical process explains their early and persistent progress in terms of both urbanization and capital accumulation, preparing the way for the present concentration of financial and managerial functions and the recent growth of the white-collar labor force.

Underlying the present phenomenon is the steady concentration of American wealth in Megalopolis. This came as a result of a long and complicated economic process, not separable, of course, from the concentration of managerial decision-making activities, for these activities depend on credit, banking operations, and competent legal and technical advice. The present concentration might not have been achieved if such a large share of American wealth had not been solidly anchored along this seaboard. With the multiple forms that wealth may assume nowadays, it may be difficult to arrive at any statistics demonstrating its geographical distribution. However, it is significant that so many of the higher

[17] According to the distinguished specialist on prehistoric economics, Gordon V. Childe, the "urban revolution" in the Middle East opened the dawn of history. See his *Man Makes Himself,* rev. ed., Mentor Books, New York, 1951.

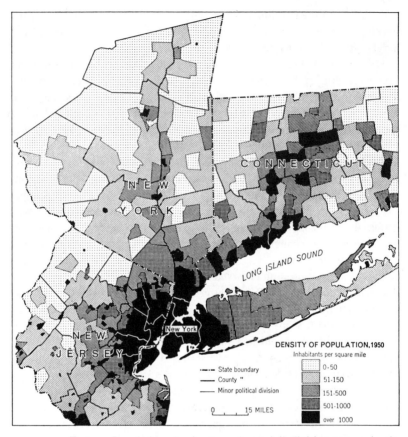

FIG. 13. Population density by minor civil divisions, 1950, in the Greater New York Metropolitan Region

individual incomes are found in the area of Megalopolis (see Figs. 210 and 220, pages 696, 717). This showed up as early as 1892, when a survey of the great American fortunes counted 4,047 millionaires (individuals or estates) throughout the United States. More than half of these were located in the area of Megalopolis, and more than one fourth were in New York City (1,103 in New York and 154 in Brooklyn; 269 in Boston; and 210 in Philadelphia).[18] A million dollars was great wealth indeed before 1900, and the affluent elite of the time in Megalopolis can well be

[18] According to "American Millionaires," in *The Tribune Monthly* (New York), Vol. IV, No. 6, June 1892, as reproduced and analyzed by Sidney Ratner in *New Light on the History of Great American Fortunes*, Augustus M. Kelley, New York, 1953.

estimated at more than 5,000 families, a figure representing a very substantial market. Many members of this stratum of metropolitan society had behind them several generations of wealth.

In Megalopolis there is also an unusual concentration of financial operations. At the present time, when securities holders are counted by the million, the New York exchanges handle close to 95 per cent of the national volume of operations in securities of all kinds. The region carries on more than its share of banking, too. On June 1, 1956, the total deposits in the banks of Megalopolis amounted to $81.3 billion, or 37.7 per cent of the national total (for 21.2 per cent of the nation's population), and the total assets held by these banks reached a little over $100 billion, or 40 per cent of the national figure. On the international level this concentration of credit may be better judged by comparing it with London, where in 1956 the eleven clearing banks had total assets amounting to about £15 billion, or close to $42 billion. To fully assess the volume of credit handled in Megalopolis it must be remembered that the Federal budget is administered in Washington, D. C., and that the velocity of the turnover of deposits in Megalopolitan banks is traditionally higher than in the rest of the country. (See Chapter 10 below for further details and references.)

In addition, control of wealth in other areas is concentrated in Megalopolis. There, particularly in Manhattan, are found the managerial and financial operations of many large corporations, foundations, and other organizations, the actual wealth of which may be spread over the whole country and beyond its borders. The accumulation of capital, at least in terms of commanding credit, has developed steadily in Megalopolis for at least two centuries. It has attracted to the area a very stratified and diversified labor force, which has kept subdividing itself with the increasing division of labor, under the impact of technological progress, and with the expansion (in terms of variety and of space) of Megalopolitan interests. This involved process of economic growth has somewhat divorced itself, in terms of geographical location, from the producing and processing industries it commands. Decisions made in Megalopolis may be carried out by farms, mines, factories, and warehouses scattered far away. The growth of the great seaboard cities may even be dissociated from the volume of goods handled in their harbors. They direct and profit by the flow of cargoes in distant places.

Because such accumulated and inherited wealth has long been established in the country's oldest commercial centers, Megalopolis has for some time had a tradition of wealth and easy spending not found for

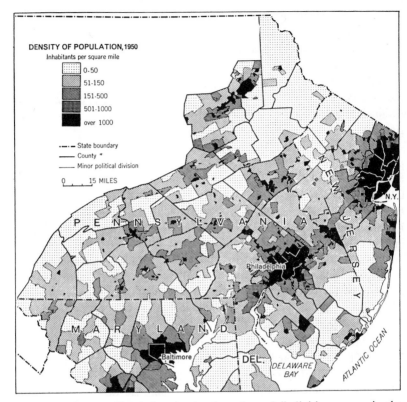

FIG. 14. Population density by minor civil divisions, 1950, in the New York-Philadelphia-Baltimore area

comparable numbers of people anywhere else in North America. The larger plantations of the South may have offered a more conspicuous image of gracious living, but they hardly represented any similar wealth, certainly not in terms of capital or credit. The wealthier families in the South were relatively few and scattered even around 1850, and there were few left after the Civil War. Megalopolis, however, has had an affluent elite for a long enough time and in large enough numbers to have created a special market for itself. Although the Puritan tradition may have kept a notable number of this elite from using their means ostentatiously, this group of higher-level consumers has nevertheless been responsible for the development of rows of luxury stores, trading in the best and most expensive goods the world can offer, the like of which, in terms of choice and quality, cannot be found in any other part of the country. This same elite seems also to explain the existence in Megalopolis (and especially in New York City) of a press aimed at an audience of higher level,[19] a press obviously different in style and interests from the more popular dailies and periodicals offered to the mass of the public. Such stratification in the press does not exist in other parts of the United States, although it is common in the larger European cities, where society is traditionally more stratified.

While the physical plant on which this wealth is founded may and must scatter, the brainwork of Megalopolis must maintain an intensity, rhythm, and efficiency that will retain in the area the actual command of the physical processes distributed so widely. It takes constant drive and unrelenting endeavor to keep growing and leading in the competitive world of men. Too often communities have rested on their laurels, or on their heaps of gold. The treasures of the Indies and Peru that were brought to Madrid and Lisbon did more harm than good, in the long run, to Spain and Portugal as centers of power and culture. They quenched the drive and the thirst for adventure that led the conquistadores overseas. They did not benefit the people's education in these countries. For a settled community it is easier to accumulate wealth than to keep it, for money and credit flow freely enough around the globe to cause financial centers and great markets to move. Venice, Florence, and Lisbon had their days of greatness as money markets and policy-making cities, and in time they lost to other cities. Megalopolis originally grew largely at the relative expense of the capitals of western Europe. Within Megalopolis itself, New York City at first gathered in a good deal of business formerly carried on by Philadelphia and Boston, while in recent years it has lost some of its financial supremacy to Washington. And the growth of Megalopolis did not prevent the largest single banking organization in the world from locating its present headquarters in San Francisco. Thus both past and present experiences show there is no guarantee that wealth and a large money market will remain concentrated where they are now. For their retention and growth a region needs other resources — *resources of the spirit*, which may, perhaps, be summarized briefly as *knowledge* and *the will to take risks and fight to win*. Knowledge, as full and up-to-date as possible, of the situation and of the risks involved is an obvious necessity for any sound policy- or decision-making activities.

The relationship between wealth and knowledge is, of course, a two-

---

[19] See, for example, such daily newspapers as *The New York Times, The New York Herald Tribune,* and *The Washington Post,* and weekly magazines such as *The New Yorker.*

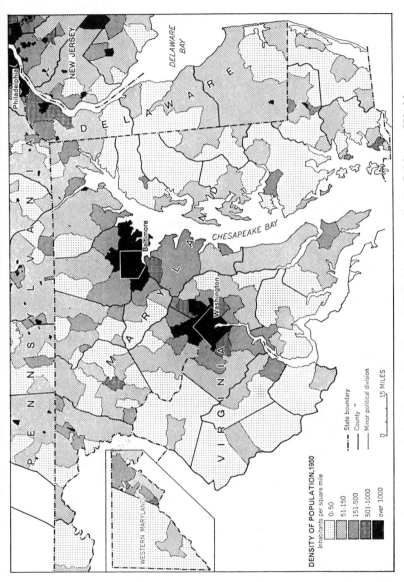

DENSITY OF POPULATION, 1950

Inhabitants per square mile

0- 50
51-150
151-500
501-1000
over 1000

State boundary
County "
Minor political division

0   15 MILES

Fig. 15. Population density by minor civil divisions, 1950, in the Baltimore-Washington area. Compare with the density in 1960 in the same area, p. 6.

way affair. Wealth needs education and knowledge and can afford to develop and improve them. Throughout history one can observe a broad geographical coincidence between centers of learning and centers of wealth. One certainly attracts and helps the other. Never has the location of wealth been completely dissociated from the location of learning. But over the centuries all these centers have moved from area to area, and often the migration of knowledge has preceded the migration of economic and political power. Which one ordinarily generates the growth of the other is a difficult question indeed and one that we need not try to answer.

It is important for this study, however, to record the thirst for education and knowledge that arose and expanded between New Hampshire and Maryland at a very early date, long before the area had accumulated much wealth. The historical role of this seaboard area in the upbuilding of the country and the higher densities of population and the greater size of the cities from the beginning favored the rise of centers of education and, in time, of learning. The gathering of wealth also created a market here for better education and for the study of various problems of trade, industry, health, and the arts. The "Ivy League" colleges are all in or near Megalopolis, where there is also a major concentration of rich museums. Affluent families, in larger number with each new generation, required more and better educational facilities for their children. Location on the Atlantic shore made it easier to draw on European scholarship, learned personnel, and other cultural resources.

The attitude toward education differed, however, from north to south. While most of the gentlemen of Virginia and more generally the Southern gentry accepted the rule then prevalent in Europe that education and knowledge were the privilege of the upper strata of society, settlers on the Northeastern seaboard reacted differently to the matter and emphasized the need for education of the masses. Massachusetts in the seventeenth century required that new settlements gather several families together under a parson and a teacher. In New England and the Middle Atlantic colonies the right to education was felt to be part, and an important part, of the freedom achieved by settlers in the New World. The eighteenth century's fight for enlightenment in Europe deepened the feeling of need, on both sides of the Atlantic, for a better and freer education of the people. The first stages of the Industrial Revolution made many responsible people understand the coming need for larger numbers of people educated well enough to take up the challenge of the new technology and make society benefit from it. Well known are the preachings along these lines of such leaders as Benjamin Franklin, Alexander Hamilton, and Thomas Jefferson, whose statement that "knowledge is power" has been widely quoted and whose writings are replete with concern for the education of the people.

The thirst for knowledge was indeed a practical one, related to the desire to achieve better living conditions, to develop more rapidly and more fully the resources at hand in this new land, and to keep abreast of progress in the rest of the world. These people, recently settled in small numbers on the edge of a vast, little known, and not too friendly continent, were in a precarious situation, and awareness of this gave them the incentive to educate themselves and be well informed. In their struggle toward such goals they were resourceful enough to discover and use many more riches in the region than a superficial survey would have suggested. The success they achieved was best measured in terms of their growing wealth, and in terms also of their leadership in the affairs of their nation and, in time, of the world.

As more wealth accumulated in Megalopolis, part of it was systematically used to acquire more cultural equipment. Until recently competent authorities in this region have felt that their cultural and artistic resources could not compare with those gathered for centuries by the richer cities and princes of Europe. They strove to emulate them, however, and managed to build up in Megalopolis what is becoming a leading concentration of such treasures in the world. This has been encouraged by tax laws that favor the establishment, by the great fortunes of the area, of foundations for the support of cultural and educational as well as charitable purposes. Megalopolis has many such foundations, some of which have become major institutions in the direction of science and art.

How much knowledge the people of the area have actually acquired as a result of all these efforts is difficult to measure, and yet a few numerical indices may help to evaluate it. Knowledge is essentially stored in the experience and learning mankind has accumulated in the past, and such stores are found in well-stocked and well-equipped libraries. As far back as we can go in history we find major libraries or clusters of them located at the centers of power and culture of each period.

Megalopolis may claim today the greatest concentration of large libraries in the world. In 1957 there were within the region eighteen libraries with more than one million volumes each, and twenty-six libraries holding half a million to a million volumes. This constitutes an amazing accumulation for an area or population of this size, as one can ascertain

Table 1

NUMBER OF LARGE LIBRARIES IN SELECTED AREAS

Number of Volumes in Library	Number of Libraries of These Sizes in:			
	Megalopolis	United States	Great Britain	France
500,000–1,000,000	26	83	16	13
More than 1,000,000	18	44	6	8

Source: *American Library Directory*, R. R. Bowker, New York, 1957.

from comparing Megalopolis in this respect with the whole of the United States, of Great Britain, and of France. This has been done in Table 1.

The figures in Table 1 are only a very general indication of the situation, but a significant one. Among the eighteen larger libraries in Megalopolis, five had more than three million volumes each in 1957, and they were the only five of such size in North America, while all of western Europe had only three. Besides the larger libraries, Megalopolis had some 155 substantial ones with 100,000 to 500,000 volumes each; and in this category several dozen were highly specialized collections offering particularly valuable opportunities for expert research.[20] Many specialized professional associations have national headquarters with such libraries located in Megalopolis. The research and reference opportunities in this area are indeed unequalled in any other part of the world (except for historical documents and publications antedating 1800, for which Europe's major libraries are often much richer).

The statistics of libraries and of the volumes on their shelves must be qualified by their degree of accessibility. The overwhelming majority of the great libraries in Megalopolis are readily available to the public at large, and the quality of their catalogues, indexing, and staff increases the accessibility of their material. In these respects the large American libraries surpass those of other countries. This accessibility means increased costs, but paying for these has proved to be a highly profitable investment, which has helped the American people as a whole to be better educated and informed.

To use and evaluate the materials thus stored, Megalopolis claims a high density of centers of learning, research, and higher education. Their quality is a more complex and debatable matter than is the case for libraries, and numerical indices are too often deceptive. It is interesting to note, however, that in 1940 and 1950 a relatively high proportion of

[20] The above figures are from the *American Library Directory*, R. R. Bowker, New York, 1957.

the adult population along the Northeastern seaboard had completed high school or gone on to more schooling. The maps showing the distribution of such educated people (see Figs. 190 and 191, pp. 619, 620) testify to the contrast still existing between schooling north and south of the Potomac, which a map of a more extensive area would demonstrate even more vividly. As has already been noted, the concern for education and knowledge never developed south of the Potomac to the same degree as it did from Massachusetts to the Delaware, despite the efforts of Jefferson and some other Southerners.

Certain aspects in the distribution of wealth and knowledge are peculiarly Megalopolitan. In great cities great wealth has always neighbored on slums and poverty, but the contrasts are particularly striking in Megalopolis. For many years a steady stream of immigrants, coming mainly from the poorer sections of Europe's population, entered America by way of the Northeastern seaboard, and many of the immigrants stayed there for at least some years. Today immigrants from overseas are few, and some of these are rather well off. But the labor market of the great cities still attracts large numbers of in-migrants from the poorer sections of the American population, especially Southern Negroes and Puerto Ricans, who congregate in the old urban areas and often live in slums. The contrasts between wealth and poverty are sharpened by differences in level of education, which make social mobility more difficult; and racial discrimination adds further handicaps.

At the same time Megalopolis as a whole is characterized by great economic and social mobility, provided by the region's rapidly growing economy and riches. This mobility attracts the more driving kinds of migrants, from other parts of the country and from abroad. To many of them money has come rapidly and in abundance; to a much greater number it comes slowly and with difficulty, rewarding long years of hard toil. Many have acquired wealth more rapidly than education, creating a lag between these two achievements of which a good balance makes for respectability. Such a lag reflects the size and accelerated rate of economic growth on the one hand and on the other the wide gamut of social strata involved in it. Along with the development of spectacular "*nouveaux riches*" fortunes, which have enriched the local folklore, the general level of standards of living and of education have steadily risen. In every generation parents, struggling upward and working hard, have striven to give their children a better education than they had themselves. Thus Megalopolis has grown and trained people who could give leadership to a growing nation, whether by going west or by staying on the

Northeastern seaboard in responsible jobs and supplying the personnel for the swelling ranks of the white-collar army.

In this New World, in a trading and manufacturing society, economic and social mobility has always been greater than in Europe because the framework inherited from the past was slight. True, similar conditions might have prevailed in other parts of America, but they did not. Even in the predominantly agrarian Southeast no mobility, no "easy" acquiring of wealth, no economic development could be observed on a similar scale. The Western frontier had greater mobility but on a local scale and for a short time. The rate and kind of development that went on for three centuries in Megalopolis was largely due to the urban activities of the area. It would have been impossible if the Northeast had had the same agrarian outlook as the Southeast, for instance. The difference of opinion as to what the American economy ought to be was clearly enough indicated by the theoretical debate in Revolutionary times between Thomas Jefferson and Alexander Hamilton. These men represented the choices already made at that time by Virginia and the South on the one hand and New England, New York, and Pennsylvania on the other. The emphasis on trade and manufacturing was characteristic of Megalopolis from its beginning and reflected the spirit in which it started.

Great concentration of wealth has been maintained in Megalopolis for little more than a century as yet. This is not long on history's scale. Many other such concentrations have lasted for a longer time. But this one arose out of an empty wilderness at an amazing speed, unmatched in any other of the various wildernesses settled or developed by Europeans after the fifteenth century's great discoveries. Two hundred fifty years after the first settlers began to arrive, the cities of the Northeastern seaboard had become some of the well-established major commercial centers of the world. Less than three hundred years after the founding of Boston in 1630, Megalopolis had achieved world leadership in economic matters and was close to supremacy. The development of Manhattan's famous skyline heralded in symbolic fashion a new era for this and many other parts of the world — an era of crowding, of both people and their accumulated works; an era of great affluence and building upward; an era of endeavor to reach higher and higher; truly an era of sky-scraping.

From at least the 1920's on, people who have seen this famous landscape have admired it and been awed by it, reacting in much the same way as did ancient travellers when they first saw Athens in the fifth century B.C., or as did Renaissance navigators when they first entered the port of Venice. In each case, despite the centuries that separate them, these sights have been offered by the metropolis of a great trading seaboard republic. What is happening in our time in Megalopolis recalls in many respects the blossoming of the great cities of the classical period and of the great Italian cities during the Renaissance. Like these predecessors Megalopolis was helped in its rise by its geographical location, its commercial vocation, its maritime trade, and the influx of people from afar, thirsty for adventure and material success. But in addition Megalopolis started far away from other centers of development, in a strange and difficult environment. That "valuable piece of real estate," the vast continent back of it, was at times as much a liability as an asset. Despite it all, Megalopolis became a huge success, so huge and so convincing that its ways of living and building are now imitated and discussed all around the globe.

This success grew out of an enormous amount of work put in unrelentlessly by large crowds through many generations. Most of the people who worked so hard and with great passion to build up this region were probably not conscious of the reasons for their drive. As Stephen Vincent Benét has put it, writing about New York City:

> It was high, but no one planned it to be so high.
> They did not think, when they built so. They did not say,
> "This will make life better, this is due to the god,
> This will be good to live in." They said "Build"
> And dug steel into the rocks . . .
> . . . So they built
> Not as men before but as demons under a whip,
> And the light was a whip and a sword and a spurning heel,
> And the light wore out their hearts and they died praising it.[21]

What was that "light"? Certainly not the sunshine itself, which is not so different over this area from what it is in some other parts of the world where nothing similar has happened. Perhaps the poet meant there was a light *these men had seen and had seen here, but which belonged inside them*, their deep beliefs, their education, their dreams. To say, as the poet does, "they did not think" and "they did not say" may be reporting too literally the results of a public opinion poll made among a haphazard sampling of people who were too busy. Through the years many answers could have been supplied by responsible people who participated in the upbuilding of Megalopolis, who thought things through

[21] Stephen Vincent Benét, "Notes to Be Left in a Cornerstone," first published in *The New Yorker*, copyright 1936, by Stephen Vincent Benét; also included in *Selected Works of Stephen Vincent Benét*, Holt, Rinehart and Winston, Inc.

and could say what they thought. Indeed, the whole tradition of this area, which largely became the American tradition, testifies to an education of the people that created and constantly rekindled the drive without which so much advanced labor, wealth, and power could not have been concentrated in the region.

The Tradition of Promethean Endeavor

Most of the settlements established in the seventeenth century along the coast on which Megalopolis was to rise were started by groups seeking a refuge from religious persecution at home.[22] This had not been the case in Virginia, and New Netherlands also was founded for purely business reasons. The Dutch sought to develop there a trading port and a base for privateering, but they showed religious tolerance and received at an early time a group of Portuguese Jews emigrating from Brazil. The Dutch colony was taken over by the English to become New York in 1664. However, for the colonies initially established by the English between Massachusetts Bay and the Potomac River religious considerations dominated. This was true of the Puritan settlement in Massachusetts, and it led to the political cleavage in New England, separating Rhode Island and Connecticut from the Puritan commonwealth. Maryland, started by the second Lord Baltimore in 1634, had been separated from Virginia because the first Lord Baltimore, a Roman Catholic convert, had been ordered out of Virginia on account of his beliefs. His son intended Maryland to become a refuge for English Roman Catholics, although it did not develop as such. Pennsylvania was started by the Quakers, under William Penn's leadership, as a "holy experiment," and the tolerance preached there soon attracted Mennonites, Hussite Moravians, and other sects.

The various companies that financed the first settlements in this area certainly had in mind materialistic considerations of profit as well as the charitable intent of helping persecuted people to a haven. But for the settlers, and especially for their leaders, *the idea of being on a mission* dominated their removal to the wilderness of America. It was not just a refuge these people were seeking. They were on a mission to conduct an "experiment" or an "errand" in the new environment. By creating in a new land a society ruled by the beliefs and laws of its faith, each

---

[22] The historical works on the early stages of American history are many. See, for instance, Samuel Eliot Morison and Henry Steele Commager, *The Growth of the American Republic*, rev. ed., Oxford University Press, New York, 1950. Chapters 3 and 4 of Volume 1 are especially pertinent.

sect felt it was accomplishing a pious act that should please the Creator and profit mankind, for the rest of the world could not fail to see how good and righteous the rules and beliefs were of a faith that succeeded on such an errand.

The Puritans in New England believed firmly in their "covenant" with God, and the sects that came to Pennsylvania in the divine mission on which they were engaged. To colonists with such beliefs the settlement of these lands was worth many sacrifices. To win with divine benediction the demonstration of the Faith's truthfulness in the eyes of the Old World was an enterprise that had to succeed. The effort would, of course, involve hard work for everybody, but it was aimed, as Perry Miller has put it, at the ultimate reward of a prosperity that "would be bestowed not as a consequence of labor but as a sign of approval upon the mission itself." [23]

Miller has shown, in the work from which we have just quoted, how the whole history of New England and the elaboration of the American national tradition are deeply rooted in the concepts of the early settlements about their "errand into the wilderness," their divine "covenant," and "commission," their holy experiments. It was indeed a rugged mission to undertake in a barely known new country, far away from the homeland and with little support at first. Success did not come early, and the first generations had to swallow much frustration.

The great hymn that Bradford, looking back in his old age, chanted about the landfall is one of the greatest passages, if not the very greatest, in all New England's literature; yet it does not resound with the sense of a mission accomplished — instead, it vibrates with the sorrow and exultation of suffering, the sheer endurance, the pain and anguish, with the somberness of death faced unflinchingly . . . We are bound, I think, to see in Bradford's account the prototype of the vast majority of subsequent immigrants . . . they came for better advantage and for less danger, and to give their posterity the opportunity of success. [24]

These later immigrants, who came in much greater numbers than the original groups, found the stage set for them, and they followed, whatever their faith, in the wake of the early tradition of the "errand." It was a beautiful one, and all the more appealing as those who held it were sure it could not fail.

[23] Perry Miller, *Errand into the Wilderness*, The Belknap Press of Harvard University Press, Cambridge, Mass., 1956; see p. 6.

[24] *Ibid.*, p. 4.

Thus developed in American society a tradition of Promethean endeavors. The ancient Greek legend of Prometheus would not have endured so long in the civilization inspired by the early Mediterranean cultures if it had not appealed to many people. Prometheus, says the legend, was an ancient hero, a Titan who endeavored to master some of the secrets of the gods and to achieve great improvements for mankind by bringing down to earth some of these secrets; he thus succeeded in bringing down fire for man to use. To punish him for his daring, Jupiter chained him to the top of a mountain while a vulture daily consumed his liver. There are varying versions of the myth of Prometheus, but its meaning is clear. Some individuals among men are possessed of such drive and aim at such heroic deeds that they benefit the whole of mankind, or at least their own community. But for such titanic endeavors they usually pay a penalty, in the form of constant dissatisfaction and perpetual worries as they seek for bigger and better results and for full and permanent security. There is hardly any progress not associated with frustration, as a prelude to spur it on and as a sequel.

One may perhaps interpret some episodes of the Bible, such as Jacob's wrestling with the Angel, which left him lame though blessed, as expressing a closely related concept. The Prometheus legend, however, conveys with special poignancy the human endeavor to penetrate the secrets of nature even in Heaven (fire was first known to men as the lightning in the sky) and to make it possible for men to use them for their earthly purposes. Thus it encompasses the notions of technological progress and of experimentation for practical purposes. Prometheus indeed undertook an errand into the wilderness, but with the obvious aim of bringing men closer to the gods, at least in terms of being able to use fire at will. The punishment that followed frustrated him but not future generations, although even today men do not yet feel satisfied with their present mastery of fire and energy.

Every nation has known periods of Promethean endeavors, though their intensity, quality, and duration have varied greatly. There can be little doubt of the high intensity and quality of the Promethean drive in such people as John Winthrop, William Bradford, and William Penn, and in their followers, whether or not they were conscious of the metaphysical implications of their "errand" and "experiment." This Promethean endeavor was long evident among the inhabitants of Megalopolis, and especially among their leaders. We may see it later in the "Great Awakening" of the 1740's in New England and the teaching of Jonathan

Edwards [25] of Connecticut. Still later Benjamin Franklin and most of the leaders of the Revolution improved and developed the tradition, especially as they insisted on the action necessary for Americans to make their country a better place to live in.

Early in the eighteenth century, near the beginning of the Industrial Revolution, a systematic and scientific classification was begun of information brought from all the known parts of the world. The most famous naturalists of Europe tried to evaluate the resources of the various continents, and especially those of America. Most of the scholarly opinions, based on spotty and vague reports, concurred in expressing great doubt that the resources of North America could be developed so as to support adequately a large population of European immigrants.[26] Faced with such opinions of reputed scholars Benjamin Franklin and Thomas Jefferson did their best, during their diplomatic missions in Paris, and John Adams did the same in London, to dispel this scholarly pessimism with data about American natural conditions and to lay the foundation for some optimism about their development. In his *Notes on Virginia*, originally written to give the French better information about his state, Jefferson dwelt at length on natural characteristics that would refute the assertions of European naturalists, especially Buffon.

American scholars, worried by the European debate, discussed at length the resources of their country and what ought to be done about them. Several influential members of the American Philosophical Society in Philadelphia repeatedly voiced their belief that the difficulties inherent in their natural environment could well be overcome and America be made into a good country to live in once this environment had been studied and became better known, and once knowledge had been applied, with whatever amount of work was needed.

On April 3, 1789, Dr. Nicholas Collin, then Rector of the Swedish Churches in Pennsylvania, read before the American Philosophical Society an address that was later printed as an introduction to the third volume of the Society's *Transactions*, under the title of "An Essay on Those Inquiries in Natural Philosophy, which at present are most beneficial to the United States of North America." Much of the program of

[25] To quote Perry Miller (*op. cit.*, p. 166): "What he [Edwards] marks . . . is the crisis of the wilderness' Awakening, in which the social problem was taken out of the arcana of abstract morality and put into the arena of skill, observation, and accommodation."

[26] See Gilbert Chinard, "Eighteenth Century Theories on America as a Human Habitat," *Proceedings of the American Philosophical Society*, Philadelphia, Vol. 91, No. 1, February 25, 1947, pp. 27-57.

research and reform it describes came to fruition in the nineteenth and twentieth centuries.[27]

Significantly, Collin began by listing the medical inquiries needed to improve the health of the people. He was not satisfied with the investigation of climate, marshes, and biological conditions of the land. He stressed the need for proper nutrition, clothing, housing, and so forth, to improve the general welfare.

Searching for general causes of the mentioned distempers in the popular diet, we should examine the following circumstances: excessive use of animal foods, especially pork; the common drink of inferior spirituous liquors both foreign and home made; not to mention a too frequent intemperance even in the best kinds . . . In the general modes of dress we plainly discern these defects: the tight bodied clothes, worn by both sexes, increase the heat of a sultry summer; the close lacing and cumbersome head-dresses of the ladies are especially injurious to health. The winter clothing is too thin for the climate of the northern and middle states, which is for several months at times equally cold with the North of Europe. Few persons preserve their feet from the baneful dampness of the slush occasioned by the frequent vicissitudes of hard frosts and heavy rains during the winter; . . . the American leather, though otherwise good, is very spongy: a defect owing to the precipitate process of tanning.

Collin was worried about the ravages caused by wars, both directly and indirectly (as, for instance, through the loss of property resulting from "disorders of paper money"). But, he adds, "such evils will under Providence be for ever prevented by the new confederation of the United States. The other cause is that gloomy superstition disseminated by ignorant illiberal preachers; the bane of social joy, of real virtue and of a manly spirit. This phantom of darkness will be dispelled by the rays of science and the bright charms of rising economy."[28]

Even more striking is Collin's program concerning the rural economy:

The United States possess a vast territory fertile in many valuable productions. They will therefore, if truly wise, make agriculture the principal source of prosperity and wealth . . . Agriculture has made a wonderful progress in several countries, since it became the business and favorite amusement of philosophers and men of taste. We may reap great advantage from the many excellent writings on this subject in the English, French, German and Swedish languages; but much more important is yet wanting in every part of this

---

[27] Nicholas Collin, "An Essay on Those Inquiries in Natural Philosophy, which at present are most beneficial to the United States of North America," *Transactions*, American Philosophical Society, Philadelphia, 1793, Vol. 3, pp. iii to xxvii.

[28] *Ibid.*, pp. vi–vii.

noble science. Besides, our local circumstances require in some cases peculiar methods . . .[29]

Machines for abridging human labour are especially desired in America, as there can be no competition between them and the arms of industrious labour, while these have full employ on her extensive lands; which must be the case for ages. Agriculture has the first claim to the exertions of mechanical genius, as the principal source of national prosperity. Extent of territory, improved by artificial industry, must yield a great quantity of products at so cheap a rate, as to bear exportation to very distant markets.[30]

Although Collin believed that the divine order of nature placed agriculture as the first and most indispensable of a country's economic activities, he did not neglect the other, more urban ones of industry and trade.[31] Maritime navigation and shipbuilding, inland canals with locks, city water supply and architecture, woodland management for timber and for pharmaceutical plants or chemical products — all these were surveyed by him as well as the fauna and the meteorological conditions. His conclusion is as follows:

In the works of Almighty power and infinite wisdom there can be *no chance;* the seasons revolve on the same fixed principles as the planets; and the apparent disorders lessen with our encreasing knowledge. The beautiful Creator discovers his marvels in proportion to our wants; if man has by a sublime sagacity traced the intricate path of the moon, why may he not explore the source of the tempest? Every country has native remedies against its natural defects . . . Let us therefore study nature, and nature's Ruler shall reward our labour.[32]

This is indeed as Promethean a statement as could be expected from the rector of some Protestant churches in a small nation, then counting less than four million people scattered along the shores of an immense and little-known continent. That the American Philosophical Society chose to publish this address as an *introduction* to an early volume of its *Transactions,* an unusual distinction, makes it a more significant expression of the Society's thinking and policy. Indeed, similar ideas and advice as to what Americans ought to do about their country are found in many other statements of that period. Another distinguished member of the American Philosophical Society, Dr. Benjamin Rush of Philadelphia, concluded a careful report on the climate of Pennsylvania and its physiological influence as follows:

[29] *Ibid.,* pp. vii–viii.
[30] *Ibid.,* p. xiii.
[31] It is interesting to find in Volume 4, 1793, of the Society's *Transactions* a detailed paper by the same Dr. Collin offering a design for the building of elevators.
[32] Collin, *op. cit.,* p. xxvii.

The sensations of heat and cold are influenced so much by natural circumstances, that we often mistake the degrees of them, by neglecting to use such conveniences as are calculated to obviate the effects of their excess. . . . In countries where heat and cold are intense and regular, the inhabitants guard themselves by accommodating their houses and dresses to each of them. The instability and short duration of excessive heat and cold in Pennsylvania, have unfortunately led its inhabitants, in many instances, to neglect adopting customs which are used in hot and cold countries to guard against them. . . . The number, height and vegetable productions of the mountains of Pennsylvania, afford a favorable prognosis of the future healthiness of the state . . . The variable nature of the climate of Pennsylvania does not render it necessarily unhealthy . . . *Perhaps no climate or country is unhealthy where men acquire from experience, or tradition, the arts of accommodating themselves to it.*[33]

The views expressed by Collin and Rush were not specifically Pennsylvanian but were widely held by the leaders of the Middle Atlantic states and New England. As the United States became independent, more thought was given to the future of the country, and it was decided from the start that "through the use of scientific knowledge, Americans would literally become the makers of their country." [34]

The emphasis on the use of serious and scholarly investigation for the making of policies, and on the application of science and technology to the daily needs and usage of the people, became and remained peculiarly American. The advancement of science and applied techniques in the years that followed was, of course, the work of many nations, though chiefly, through the nineteenth century, of those in western Europe. However, its results were put to work in the United States often more rapidly and on a larger scale than elsewhere. The gathering and redistribution of knowledge and useful information were quickly organized there, on a grand scale. The growing nation, expanding rapidly in population as well as in territory, was little concerned about the preservation of the status quo in any respect. This made for less of the kind of slowing down of progress that in many Old World countries had come to be accepted as a normal defense of the advantages inherited by the privileged classes. The more generous distribution of opportunity characteristic of the New World, which was the fruit of both the nation's age and its westward march, gave to American democracy the possibility of remain-

[33] Benjamin Rush, "Account of the Climate of Pennsylvania, and its Influence upon the Human Body. From medical enquiries and observations," *American Museum*, Vol. 6, 1789, pp. 250–254, and Vol. 7, 1790.

[34] Chinard, "Eighteenth Century Theories on America as a Human Habitat," *op. cit.*, p. 52.

ing a "Great Experiment" and of carrying on a liberation process that endeared it to those who, in other parts of the world, dreamed of greater freedom.

The historical and geographical conditions of the American experiment would not have sufficed to induce and maintain it in this way if the spirit of the mission, of the *errand into the wilderness,* had not permeated the national development and education. America had to become an exemplary commonwealth and to turn the natural conditions of the wilderness into comfort and civilization. That such endeavors had to succeed and to re-make nature and society was early agreed upon by the leaders of the Revolution. After long discussions of various designs for the great seal of the United States, Congress adopted, on June 20, 1782, the version favor-ably reported by its secretary, Charles Thomson, and on which John Adams, William Barton, and others had worked. While its crest bears the eagle with the escutcheon, seen in so many places and on every American military officer's cap, the reverse presents around an *unfinished* pyramid two mottos: *Annuit coeptis,* i.e., "God has favored the undertaking," and *Novus ordo seclorum,* i.e., "The new order of the ages." [35] Thus the idea of a holy experiment starting a new deal in history was inscribed on the great seal and, though little noticed, it appears today on every dollar bill! The Promethean tradition had lived on, on official documents as well as in practice, and it was and is especially apparent in the great urban areas of the Northeastern seaboard.

Prometheus Unbound

It may seem a curious paradox that more liberation was achieved by the Promethean impulses and progress in a thickly settled urban environ-ment than in the wilderness of the Western frontier. The wide open ex-panse of land freely distributed to the settlers or companies developing the area has been an extremely important factor in American history, but one that could last for only a limited period in every section of the country. The completion of the transcontinental march of the frontier did not ar-rest the growth of the American economy, and it was never the American idea that it would.

The substance of the "experiment" goes deeper than the land's surface. The American dream was of "unlimited resources," although it took a long time to be woven into the cloth of recognized economic theory.

---

[35] See Benjamin J. Lossing, "The Great Seal of the United States," in *Harper's New Monthly Magazine,* New York, 1856, Vol. 13, pp. 178–186.

Perry Miller has explained as follows the background of what he calls "the obsessive American drama, that of Nature versus civilization":

> Not only writers of such sophistication as Emerson and Melville raise the theme, *the* American theme, of Nature versus civilization. You can find it in the politics of Andrew Jackson, in the observations of foreign travelers, in the legend of Abraham Lincoln, in Stephen Douglas no less than in Francis Parkman. Once possessed of that view, you see that the United States became a nation in the late eighteenth century under the aegis of rationalism, but found itself obliged to conceive of itself in the nineteenth as still running the Puritans' errand into an apparently limitless wilderness. How then it can cope with New York, Detroit, Gary, becomes its problem; but the outlines of that problem were faintly perceptible from its beginning. John Winthrop had been worried about it even in the middle of the Atlantic: is any wilderness, in God's finite creation, really illimitable? [36]

The transcendentalists of the middle of the nineteenth century expressed the deep and growing worry of the American artist and intellectual concerning the onrushing success of utilitarian, progressive civilization. Thus the vultures were manifesting themselves around the Promethean success of an advancing frontier and expanding economy. Inseparable in the old Promethean legend were daring and successful endeavor toward progress and the deep, growing doubt this progress entails. In the 1840's these two aspects of the legend were manifested essentially in the more sophisticated elite of the Northeastern cities, and these aspects have been observed repeatedly in the development of Megalopolis since then.

Urbanization may indeed be one of the great *problems* of America; but urban growth, the piling of great quarries of stone into cities,[37] was a necessity for carrying on the *experiment for the improvement of society*. The Western frontier was, of course, a great force in the process of liberation and reorganization, as Frederick Jackson Turner and his school of historians have well demonstrated. But the possibility for the individual to move on and on, always farther away, to avoid being crowded was not necessarily making these individuals better. While the trend had long been characteristic of America, it came to an end by reason of geography at the beginning of the twentieth century. When the "Okies" moved from the Dust Bowl area westward in the 1930's, they did not go into a wilderness but rather to the West Coast cities and agricultural valleys. Although the frontier advancing against natural obstacles may still find more wasteland to improve in parts of the fifty states, such as southern Utah, Mon-

---

[36] Miller, *Errand into the Wilderness, op. cit.*, p. 205.

[37] This was forecast and hoped for as early as 1758 by Nathaniel Ames, the almanac maker from Massachusetts, as quoted by Miller, *op. cit.*, p. 207.

tana, and especially Alaska, the major endeavors have shifted toward the improvement of the thickly settled areas. *The frontier of the American economy is nowadays urban and suburban* ,rather than peripheral to the civilized areas. The Promethean endeavors may find here a tougher and more frustrating task, but one of greater magnitude in terms of opportunity for the improvement of society and in terms of impact on mankind's ways of life in the future.

Speaking at a conference on urban renewal in 1959, Adlai Stevenson remarked:

> We Americans have a penchant for believing that sufficient inputs of energy and dollars can solve any problem. We rush in where angels fear to tread and frequently we profit, but sometimes we learn why the angels, in their greater wisdom, have not joined us and preferred to stay aloft. Urban reconstruction is a case in point.[38]

The errand into the wilderness — the holy experiment — was not conceived just as a mission to settle people in an empty wilderness or to develop an underdeveloped territory. The "new order of the ages" was aimed at a new and better order of human living and working together. The target was a better society, a commonwealth so improved as to be accepted as an exemplary pattern by others elsewhere. The proximity of wild areas helped Americans to start a new system, liberated from the bonds of locally entrenched vested interests, but it did not always help a mission bent upon the improvement of the social neighborhood (in the widest sense of the latter term). The Massachusetts laws forbidding settlers to scatter individually and requiring new settlements to proceed by groups of four founders or more was often disobeyed as early as the late seventeenth century. Still New England was from early times settled in townships to a much greater degree than Virginia and other Southern regions. The lack of towns was often cited, from 1700 on, as the major reason for the poor educational facilities and the high cost of industrial products and trade services in Virginia as compared with Massachusetts.[39] The great cities or smaller towns did not necessarily provide more freedom at first than the plantation systems of settlement. The town proprietors and wealthy businessmen were much resented on the Northeastern seaboard in colonial times and even in the early nineteenth century. But the variety

---

[38] Adlai E. Stevenson, speaking at a conference of the American Council to Improve our Neighborhoods (ACTION), in Newark, New Jersey, on May 5, 1959, as quoted in *The New York Times*, May 6, 1959.

[39] See Jean Gottmann, *Virginia at Mid-Century*, Henry Holt and Company, New York, 1955, especially pp. 68–93.

and growth of economic activities in urban areas provided much new opportunity to newcomers; the educational facilities were better and opened the gates for social mobility; finally, the crowding in the cities caused an outcry for social justice that could not long be resisted by the proprietors. The freedom of movement forbade to the privileged individuals or groups any hope of keeping the poorer crowds down where they had gathered. If these had scattered the town might have dissolved, and its bosses would have been the main losers.

The Promethean endeavors that had long been confined to the dreams of European people, resigned to a status quo in their homelands, broke out of old bounds in this wilderness because it was a wilderness as well as because people here knew they were on an errand and part of an immense experiment. Scott Fitzgerald may have put it very clearly when he said that "France was a land, England a people but America was an idea." To pursue that idea the crowded city was probably as good an environment as an empty wilderness, and perhaps an even better one because it was closer to the ultimate problem.

So the Promethean impulses were unleashed on this Northeastern seaboard. There was almost limitless territory to tame in the background. The future bonds and vultures punishing success in the Greek legend seemed to be eliminated, because this errand was pursued by God-fearing people on a blessed undertaking. The obstacles put in their way by nature and men could be resolved by Americans through study, fact-finding, science, technology, and the improvement of society. While there was in time an end to the expanse of free land, the great cities of Megalopolis developed, through a finer division of labor, more exchange of services, more trade, and more accumulation of capital and people, a boundless vista of unlimited resources for an affluent society.

The expansion of Megalopolis could hardly have happened without such an extraordinary Promethean drive. As the frontier becomes more urban in its very nature,[40] as the wilderness to be tamed shifts in obvious fashion from the woods and the prairies to city streets and human crowds, the vultures that threatened Prometheus may be more difficult to keep away. How the unbound Promethean endeavors succeeded in building up the present Megalopolis and what their prospects are for tomorrow will be the concern of the following chapters.

[40] Even Frederick Jackson Turner, in his famous book *The Frontier in American History* (Henry Holt and Company, New York, 1920), recognized the role of the great cities of the Northeast in perpetuating the same basic ideals as the Western frontier. He foresaw the onrushing urbanization and industrialization as a potential new frontier. See pp. 299–334 in the 1958 reprinting.

CHAPTER 2

Earthly Bounds

The striking concentration of economic activities on which Megalopolis was founded arose through the stubborn endeavor of the inhabitants to make the "holy experiment" succeed as a result of their virtues and wits. It certainly required wits in large amount to succeed so well materially and to keep in this relatively small area the whole direction of so dynamic and vast an economy. It may be asked at this juncture whether local circumstances may have favored Megalopolitan growth and endeavors in some respects and perhaps restricted them in others.

How much was the experiment, as conducted on this Northeastern seaboard, influenced by what the early settlers termed their "earthly station"? Even though this region proved to be no Eldorado, no Garden of Eden, but a rather difficult wilderness, its inhabitants learned how to turn many of its environmental conditions into resources, shifting from one activity or technique to another as opportunity shifted with historical change and technological progress.

As one geographer has said: "A country is a reservoir where potential powers lie asleep, the development of which devolves on the inhabitants. They give them shape while molding them to their use and taste. Thus men establish new relationships between scattered features. For the random effects of local circumstances they substitute a new and coherent system of interlocking forces." [1] In the process the community cannot avoid receiving in some way the imprint of local circumstances. These bind together the elements of the newly established system. This has been true in Megalopolis, ever since its beginning in the seventeenth-century wilderness. Location, topography, geology, climate, and vegetation and wildlife have influenced the human endeavors that have at the same time molded and remolded these natural factors to the purposes of human communities. Even though the present foundation of the region's economy tends to be worldwide, local conditions continue to have some impact on what develops there.

The Seaboard's Location

The most basic asset of the region, and one of the more enduring ones, is its location on the Atlantic seaboard, facing Europe and in the middle latitudes. Started by seafaring people, Megalopolis has always depended on free access to maritime activities. As long as it was a small area of settlement stretched out along the coast, with a vast and little-known continent at its back, it needed contact with transatlantic navigation to secure supplies, market its products, maintain the freedom of opportunity offered by the sea lanes, develop cultural relations, and benefit by the knowledge and new experience of the rest of the civilized world. Without access to and from the high seas, the settlers of New England, New York, or Pennsylvania would have been confined economically and culturally to the narrow, astringent limits of a small settled section of the wilderness.

Accessibility by seagoing boats was therefore essential, and this need is well met along the submerged shoreline of the Northeast. In New England, where a landscape of fairly marked relief has been submerged, the shoreline is very irregular, with many embayments and estuaries, peninsulas and islands. Most of these irregularities reflect the bedrock topography, but in some places glacial deposition has contributed to them, for ridges of terminal moraine form the backbone of part of Cape Cod, and

[1] The author's translation of a famous passage by Paul Vidal de la Blache (see Chapter 1 of his *Tableau de la Géographie de la France*, Hachette, Paris, 1903).

of Long Island and other smaller islands; and in Boston Bay drumlins form islands. Southwest of New York City submergence of the flatter coastal plain has left fewer islands but the larger river valleys have been drowned to form the great estuaries of Delaware Bay and Chesapeake Bay, with its many tributary bays. These reach many miles into the interior. Longest of all, however, is the estuary of the Hudson River, a great arm of the sea extending inland 150 miles, as far as Albany. Part of this valley was overdeepened by glacial erosion.

The interpenetration of land and sea favored the multiplicity of settled sites from the early stages of colonization on. It did not stress the need for the kind of agglomeration that leads to urban growth, but it favored those settlers who wished to develop an economy based on trade, commercial exchange, and fishing. In the coastal plain the relatively open or gently rolling topography of the hinterland enabled tidewater to extend far inland along the major rivers, and these water routes were linked with overland routes carrying traders and explorers westward or northward (see Fig. 16). Climate as well as topography gave to the location in these middle latitudes, between 43° and 38° N., a favorably moderate character, so that accessibility is enhanced by the infrequency of frosts deep enough to freeze the navigable channels.

A still more important factor was the position on the Atlantic facing Europe, from which immigrants came and which contained the major markets for profitable commerce. It may also be worthwhile to mention the area's position close to the usual sea lanes linking western Europe to the West Indies. The ports of the area served at times as important bases for privateering attacks on the maritime communications of the Spanish colonial empire, and at other times as relay points in the trade between these regions. But Boston and New York traded also with more distant places, such as the African coasts, China, and Chile.

Thus the seaboard location was and still is essential mainly because it opened wide the horizons of oceanic navigation. However, it was also instrumental from early days in binding together the various towns of the tidewater, for coastwise navigation was an easy and inexpensive mode of transportation, particularly in an area of relatively scarce and expensive manpower. Until at least the 1840's a good deal of the passenger traffic between New York City and Washington or between Boston and Philadelphia, for example, went by water at least part of the way. For bulky shipments coastwise shipping remains important.

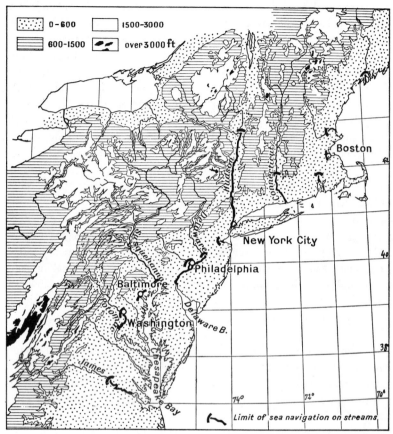

FIG. 16. Topography of Megalopolis and the surrounding areas. The extent of sea navigation on streams serves to indicate the accessibility inland for sea-going boats during the early period of settlement.

The Region's Topography

The region's structure and the processes of erosion active here have combined to endow Megalopolis with a diversified topography,[2] and its characteristics have contributed to the value of the region's location and to the pattern of development within it. They have also played a part in shaping its limits.

[2] For a scholarly analysis of the landforms in the region see Nevin M. Fenneman, *Physiography of Eastern United States*, McGraw-Hill Book Co., New York, 1938, especially Chapters 1-6.

The regional pattern is relatively simple. Megalopolis on the whole is squeezed between the sea and the higher mountain areas farther inland. In a very generalized way one may distinguish within it a flat coastal plain and a more dissected upland, separated from each other by the Fall Line, so named because it is marked by rapids and falls on the streams that cross it. From southern New England, where it starts, the coastal lowland widens southward, being made up first of scattered islands and then of broad peninsulas separated by estuaries. On the whole this lowland allowed an easy choice for early urban sites and space for farming around them. The more rugged upland reaches the coast in most of New England, but farther south it rises gently inland from the Fall Line, offering no insurmountable barrier to traffic or settlement. It is made up of groups of hills that are, in fact, dissected plateaus and advanced foothills of the Appalachian system of ranges. In the anthracite region of northeastern Pennsylvania Megalopolis actually includes part of the Appalachian Ridge and Valley province, but elsewhere it stops short of the mountains to the west. There the rise in altitude and the topographic features making traffic more difficult have limited the expansion inland of the denser settlement associated with and supported by urban types of economic activity. At the same time routes through these mountains to the rich interior are of great importance to the eastern cities.

Superimposed on this regional pattern are more complex local details. The vast area now covered by urban or suburban sprawl is a patchwork of small units offering a remarkable variety of physical characteristics and natural landscapes. For example, there are the glaciated hills of New England and New York State, where the surface is littered with bouldery moraine and where some of the valleys contain fertile deposits laid down in ice-marginal lakes or arms of the sea during the last retreat of the ice. In Long Island there are the low ridges of terminal and recessional moraine and the flat sandy outwash plains south of them. From New Jersey southward there are the broad expanses of the coastal plain, low and swampy near the shore, with lagoons and barrier beaches, but with a gently undulating landscape farther inland. Still farther inland is the rolling surface of the Piedmont upland, cut by deep river valleys. Despite man's impact, bringing into this original variety much uniformity and systematic coherence, a good deal of the diversity remains apparent. Though the differences in landscape between these small sections of Megalopolis may seem today far removed from the original differences of a century ago, there is still a differentiation based on the natural features. Nature's inheritance has been used constantly by the people in Megalopolis, though at each time and place the use has fitted into a system of relationships that have themselves been constantly varying (Fig. 17).

Thus the character of the coastline, the Fall Line terminating navigation on the rivers, the hills and valleys farther inland, and the routes through the adjacent mountains into the interior of the continent — all have played their part in fixing the sites of the major cities.

Such centers started, of course, in the coastal region. Not all parts of the coast were equally conducive to successful settlement, especially in dense urban nuclei. Northeast of the Hudson the shoreline is scalloped and rugged, with a multiplicity of creeks and a frequent alternation of rocky promontories and sandy beaches. Here are many convenient bays and straits, some of them large and well protected by islands and peninsulas, such as Boston and Narragansett bays and Long Island Sound; and there are numerous estuaries. Such a landscape was familiar to people from the shores of Britain or northwestern Europe and easy for them to manage for the development of maritime activities. South of the Hudson, however, many parts of the shore present a less neat line of contact of the land with tidal water because of the frequency of marshes, lagoons, sand pits, and sand bars. In such places the coastline is not always easily accessible to deep-sea boats. Because marshlands attract migratory birds they rank as excellent hunting grounds; but they also breed clouds of mosquitoes, which may infest a substantial area inland. Until the nineteenth century this impeded the population growth of seaboard cities. Parts of southern New Jersey and of the Delmarva Peninsula (between Delaware and Chesapeake bays) have therefore not been as hospitable for urban agglomeration and maritime activities as the regions farther north. Even here, however, the great estuaries of the larger rivers offer sheltered routes extending well inland. Despite a few sections of less convenient marine access there was thus a great deal of shoreline available for easy navigation, whether for fishing, trading, or, in the past, privateering. And today these waters are conducive to active boating for recreation. The few sections less accessible because of marshes and sand often provided good strategic shields for the areas of more intense maritime activity. On the whole, this was for well-trained seamen one of the more favorable seaboards. As urbanization crowded the area and mechanized equipment became available, much of the marshy ground was drained or filled and built upon, while other marshes and sandy areas were developed for recreation. Thus the natural features of the coastline, now greatly modified by man's works, can hardly be listed as obstacles to urbanization. They have merely restricted it locally and oriented its development, and this was more true in the past than

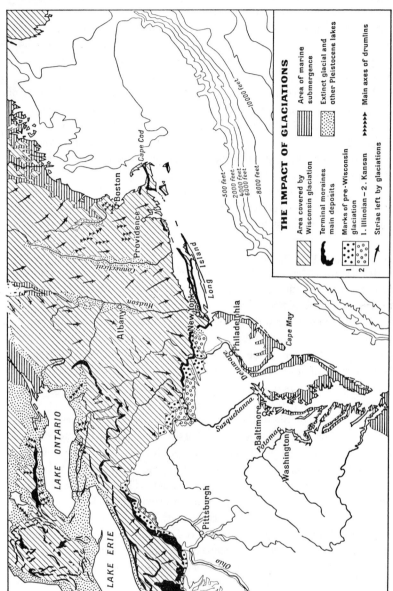

THE IMPACT OF GLACIATIONS

Area covered by Wisconsin glaciation

Area of marine submergence

Terminal moraines main deposits

Extinct glacial and other Pleistocene lakes

Marks of pre-Wisconsin glaciation
1. Illinoian — 2. Kansan

Main axes of drumlins

Striae left by glaciations

LAKE ONTARIO

LAKE ERIE

Pittsburgh

Ohio

Washington

Potomac

Baltimore

Susquehanna

Cape May

Delaware

Philadelphia

New York

Long Island

Albany

Hudson

Providence

Connecticut

Boston

Cape Cod

500 feet
2000 feet
4000 feet
6000 feet

10,000 feet

8000 feet

Fig. 17

it is now. The inheritance of their early impact is felt today mainly in the persistence of the major urban centers at some sites of early settlement.

In the localization of settlement sites the physical design of the shoreline was not the only important factor, for the topography inland was also significant. Neither coastal plain nor piedmont upland offered many barriers to movement and settlement. Barren rock areas are few and small, and most of the region has soils that are suitable for cultivation or pasture. In the glaciated area the scattering of boulders and stones impeded farming somewhat, but settlers from northwestern Europe knew how to clear the stones and build fences or houses with them.

Farther inland the topography rises into a complicated system of higher ranges and winding valleys, causing more trouble for through traffic and settlement. Only recently has there been penetration, by perennial suburban or interurban settlement, of some of these more hilly sections where they are fairly near the coast (such as the Berkshires in western Massachusetts, the Catskills in New York State, the Poconos in Pennsylvania, and Catoctin Mountain in Maryland). This trend reflects the immense demand for recreational activities arising with modern affluence in the crowded urban regions near by. The only part of Megalopolis with altitudes above 3,000 feet is found in such an area, in the southeastern Catskills (see Fig. 16). Such heights could not be considered suburban if they were not on the immediate fringe of as crowded a place as the New York metropolitan region. In that location they have acquired a recreational function that has brought to them dense crowds of urban people at certain seasons and on week ends. The Berkshires, Poconos, and Catoctin Mountain assume similar functions for other major urban agglomerations in Megalopolis, and for New York City also in the case of the first two.

Another more rugged part of Megalopolis is included for a different reason. This is the anthracite region of northeastern Pennsylvania, part of the Folded Appalachians. The early development of large-scale colleries and industries connected with them in the areas of Scranton, Wilkes-Barre, and Reading and their environs laid the foundations for a metropolitan growth there that is linked with eastern Pennsylvania and the basin of the Delaware River. By its historic past and present connections the urban development of the eastern Pennsylvania coalfield belongs to Megalopolis, even though it is situated on its fringe and is more dependent than any other section of the Megalopolitan economy on local natural resources. A metropolitan type of economy would not have developed there without the coal riches. But even they might not have had so much effect there had the area been less easily accessible from the main seaboard markets and had not the valley of the Susquehanna River made it accessible from various parts of both Pennsylvania and upstate New York.

Although in its early development it turned its back on the Appalachian Mountains, Megalopolis has from the very beginning had a keen interest in relations with the mountainous area and even more with the continental interior beyond it. Routes across the ranges to the west and north were considered an early and important asset. In the hinterland of the seaboard stretching from Boston to Baltimore, the mountain ranges are more broken up and easier to cross than farther south. The Hudson Valley provides an especially convenient corridor, accessible to oceanic navigation as far as Albany, and from there the Mohawk Valley leads westward, while the Lake Champlain depression offers an easy road northward. Thus the New York City area has convenient natural routes to both the Great Lakes and the St. Lawrence Valley. The valley of the Delaware River offers another but much longer and more difficult trans-Appalachian route northwestward from the Philadelphia-Trenton area. Other basins, valleys, and passes lead from the Lower Delaware and Susquehanna valleys toward Pittsburgh, whence the Ohio River provides a good waterway leading into the Mississippi Valley and the Great Plains. From Maryland and the Potomac River Valley the Cumberland Gap offers another route (today followed by U. S. Route 40) to the Ohio Valley and farther west. Not only did these valleys offer land routes, but the abundance of rivers and lakes, sections of which needed to be linked by short portage, favored penetration to the interior by men familiar with the techniques of water transportation. True, there was no such natural blessing as the great waterway of the Mississippi and its major tributaries seemed to offer for New Orleans' relations with the interior. But, on the whole, topography offered relatively slight obstacles to overland relations between the seaboard cities and the heart of the continent.

Thus the lay of the land has influenced Megalopolis both in its internal structure and in its relations with other regions. Megalopolis arose along the main axis of the seaboard, where there was easy penetration of the land by maritime transportation and trade. From the seventeenth century on, the Fall Line, followed now by U. S. Route I, attracted and localized the major urban centers and their early sprawl of suburban activities. And the general features of the region farther inland offered relatively easy routes to the trans-Appalachian realm. The localization of human activities was much more influenced by topography in the early days of settlement than it would be today, but this inheritance has remained a major factor in shaping present relationships.

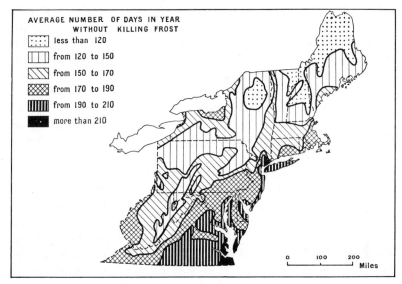

AVERAGE NUMBER OF DAYS IN YEAR
WITHOUT KILLING FROST
less than 120
from 120 to 150
from 150 to 170
from 170 to 190
from 190 to 210
more than 210

0   100   200
                    Miles

FIG. 18

Climate and Weather

To newcomers from western Europe the climate of the northeastern American seaboard seems remarkable for its extremes. The prolonged humid heat of the summer makes Europeans think of quasi-tropical weather, while the dry cold of winter takes on an almost arctic quality, especially in New England. The extreme variability of the weather, particularly the rapid rise or fall of temperature on certain days, has been a source of complaints among the inhabitants of this area as far back as records go.[3]

These climatic extremes are, however, somewhat more moderate in Megalopolis than in the areas to its north and west. Particularly important to an area so dependent on water transportation, both by sea and inland, is the duration of deep frosts in the winter. The frost-free period, being also the season of growth for vegetation, has had even more importance for agriculture than for transportation. It is noteworthy, therefore, that the average length of the growing season remains above 180 days along the seashore from Massachusetts Bay to the Hudson, then above 190 days in New Jersey, Delaware, and Maryland. With this long a period free from killing frosts, the probability of freezing of tidal estuaries and bays is reduced to rather brief periods in the year (see Fig. 18).

[3] See either the essay by Nicholas Collin, much quoted in Chapter 1, pp. 72–75 above, or Benjamin Rush, *American Museum*, Vol. 6, 1789, and Vol. 7, 1790.

The cold of winter grows more severe inland, especially with altitude, and also northward as soon as one enters Maine, even along its coast. Average temperatures for the month of January range between 24° to 32° F. in southern New England but decrease rapidly north of the northern boundary of Massachusetts (which almost seems to follow a climatological boundary), being 24° and 10° in Maine, New Hampshire, and Vermont, and decreasing still further in Canada. The contrast is just as striking within the State of New York, for the average January temperatures are about 30° F. near New York City (34.5° in recent years at New York's Central Park station) and range from 24° to 16° F. upstate. January is warmer, of course, as one goes south (32° to 36° F. in the vicinity of Washington, D. C., and in the state of Delaware) and cooler as one rises westward in the Appalachians (see Fig. 19). Such winter temperatures may seem severe by comparison with those experienced on the Atlantic coasts of Europe, but winter impedes traffic and transportation in Megalopolis only briefly and not too often, even though occasional sudden and deep snowfalls and deep freezing periods may occur in any part of the area.

As one proceeds from Megalopolis along the Atlantic seaboard the frost-free season lengthens, the winter grows milder, and the threat of prolonged ice and snow is more remote. But the length and tropical quality of the warm season increase, as does the frequency of hurricane disturbances from August to October. The July mean temperatures (see Fig. 19) vary between 72° and 68° F. in Massachusetts and between 78° and 68° in Maryland. The humidity is almost the same over the whole coastal area from Boston to Washington during the warm season, but there are longer uninterrupted humid and hot periods as one goes southwestward. On the whole, there is less differentiation in low-altitude areas throughout Megalopolis in summer than in winter. In certain years winter is indeed brief and mild around Washington, D. C., while it is always a marked season of some length around Boston.

The area of New York City appears on the maps of climatic averages as unique in several respects. It is remarkable for having a longer frost-free season than all surrounding areas, and also for somewhat more frequent breaks in the hot and humid weather in the summer than occur in the neighboring low-lying areas.[4] Although various explanations have been given for such climatic singularity in the vicinity of New York City, it may be suggested here that topography has something to do with it. The

[4] See the statistical data in the series, *Climates of the States,* U. S. Weather Bureau, 1959.

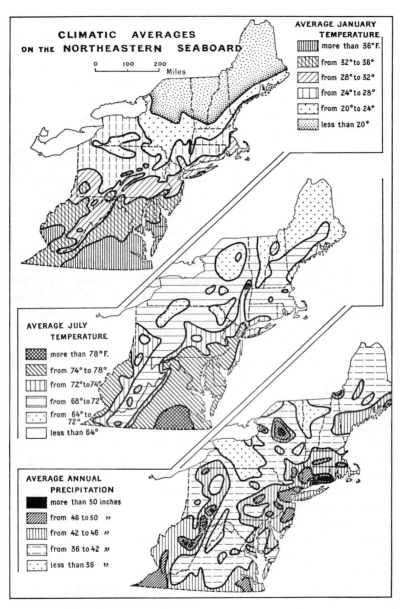

CLIMATIC AVERAGES ON THE NORTHEASTERN SEABOARD

AVERAGE JANUARY TEMPERATURE
- more than 36° F.
- from 32° to 36°
- from 28° to 32°
- from 24° to 28°
- from 20° to 24°
- less than 20°

AVERAGE JULY TEMPERATURE
- more than 78° F.
- from 74° to 78°
- from 72° to 74°
- from 68° to 72°
- from 64° to 72°
- less than 64°

AVERAGE ANNUAL PRECIPITATION
- more than 50 inches
- from 46 to 50 "
- from 42 to 46 "
- from 36 to 42 "
- less than 36 "

0   100   200
Miles

FIG. 19

corridors breaking through the uplands and highlands back to the estuary of the Hudson River favor currents of atmospheric circulation as well as transportation and trade.

The weather in Megalopolis as a whole is affected by the conflicting influences of the ocean and the continent. Situated in the middle latitudes, where winds from the west prevail, Megalopolis receives its weather most often from the continent, which furnishes cold air masses in the winter and in the summer warm tropical ones, which move from the Gulf up into the Great Plains. The corridors of upstate New York establish amid a rather hilly and complicated topography an invitation for air currents to move between such different climatic zones as the Atlantic Ocean off Long Island on the one hand and the Great Lakes and Quebec areas on the other. Thus the land relief may have helped New York City in terms of climate as well as trade. The greater variability of the weather thus obtained may be considered as an asset when it brings about welcome breaks in a long spell of summer heat, as cold winds blow from the north; but the same mechanism may be less pleasant as it causes icy winds and spells of low temperatures in the winter; icebreakers are at times needed to keep a channel open along the upper Hudson River, and on rare occasions they are even used in New York harbor. The meeting of arctic air masses with warm and humid maritime air may cause heavy snowfalls, such as the memorable 25.8 inches that fell on December 26, 1947, paralyzing the city for almost three days. In other seasons such meeting of air masses may cause fog or smog.

How much the weather in the great metropolitan areas, and the New York–Northeastern New Jersey one especially, may have been modified by the amount of heat generated by all the fuel consumed and machinery at work in the more crowded built-up districts remains a matter open to discussion. Air pollution and smog are certainly man-made. Some microclimatic influences are also certain within the fully built-up zones, but whether the whole circulation of air masses over the region has been affected remains in doubt. The slight and steady warming up of the climate in terms of decennial averages through the last fifty years seems certain, particularly in terms of less severe winters on long-range averages; but this trend has been observed in many other parts of the world and reflects a phenomenon of global magnitude. The reasons invoked to explain it remain hypothetical.

Except for this worldwide warming up, the climate of Megalopolis has stayed very much the same during the last 300 years, as can be seen from early accounts written by responsible local people. Since European climates had been the first to be studied carefully, they provided the "normal" standards, and in comparison with them Americans often stressed the greater variability of their weather and the greater heat of summer and cold of winter. An especially well-informed account of the climate of eastern Pennsylvania was published by Dr. Benjamin Rush in 1789–90 and it concluded with an almost lyrical description of the march of the seasons.

> It appears that the climate of Pennsylvania is a compound of most of the climates in the world. Here we have the moisture of Britain in the spring, the heat of Africa in summer, the temperature of Italy in June, the sky of Egypt in the autumn, the cold and snows of Norway and the ice of Holland in the winter, the tempests (in a certain degree) of the West Indies in every season, and the variable winds and weather of Great Britain in every month of the year.[5]

For comparison with other parts of the world lying at about the same latitude as Philadelphia, Rush cited the climates of Madrid and Peking, a choice that can be criticized because the more inland positions of both these capitals is bound to increase the contrast between cold and warm seasons and to decrease the moderating oceanic influences. Though he recognized that Peking's climate offered greater extremes, Rush was certainly right in observing: "The climate of China appears, in many particulars, to resemble that of Pennsylvania." [6] This remark reflects the dissymmetry of the continental masses, better known today. The Eastern seaboard of the United States has more similarities with the eastern section of Asia, while the West Coast is more like parts of western Europe and northwestern Africa.

Rush was certainly right in his conclusion [7] that if people make some adaptation "in dress, diet, and manners" the climate of his country was just as good for healthy life and development as any other. Despite its contrasts and variability, one can hardly find the Megalopolitan climate either debilitating or especially healthful. For men carrying on proper and reasonable activities it proves to be quite hospitable to dense settlement, rich farming, and the proliferation of industries. In recent times new devices have helped the inhabitants to condition their immediate environment to their taste by heating, cooling, and dehumidifying buildings, trains, and cars. Exposure to severe outside weather for any prolonged period of time is becoming almost an unusual accident in Megalopolis.

[5] Quoted from *American Museum*, Vol. 7, 1790, p. 337.
[6] *Ibid.*, p. 340.
[7] Quoted above in Chapter 1, p. 75.

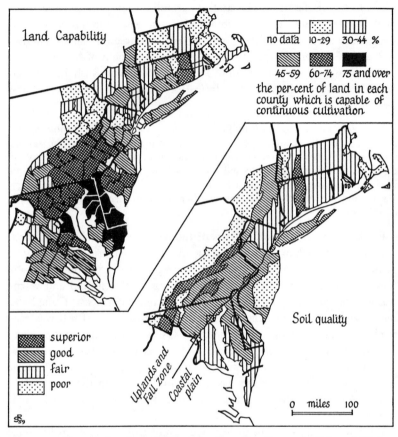

Fig. 20. Land capability and soil quality. Drawn by Edward Higbee on the basis of field research and data supplied by the U. S. Soil Conservation Service.

The abundant precipitation in the region, rather well distributed over the area (see Fig. 19) and through the year, insures an abundant enough supply of water for agriculture and forestry and, in the more recent stages of the region's development, for the great thirst of the cities and their industries and power plants. This abundance of fresh water, resulting largely from the climate as well as from the topography and geology of the region, may perhaps be rated as the greatest benefit locally bestowed by the climate. The variability of the weather occasionally brings about freak storms and the milder disturbance of fog or heavy snowfall, to disrupt sea and air navigation and land traffic. But it also favors the brevity of any such meteorological unpleasantness as heat or cold waves, and droughts or floods. The population of Megalopolis seldom has occasion for bitter complaints against the climate provided by nature. The worst conditions locally or occasionally deplored are often caused by the mismanagement of the natural endowment or by excessive crowding of people or machinery, or by both. Pollution or waste are man-made problems to be considered in the framework of later chapters.

Soils, Flora, and Fauna

Location, topography, and climate, considered for an area covering some 50,000 square miles, are still physical characteristics that men have been able to reshape in only small, localized details. For the biological environment, consisting of the soils, vegetation, and animal life, the story here is different. It is a long and involved story, some aspects of which remain obscure, but the end results have been substantial modification of the soils, flora, and fauna over the last three centuries.

Modern techniques allow for fertilizing soils that would in their natural condition be mediocre for farming. Continuous cultivation without proper fertilization may exhaust even the richest soils. Examples of both trends have occurred in the rural parts of Megalopolis, where a remarkable variety of kinds of soils has been observed. The main areas of major soil types and their productive capability at present are shown on two maps (see Fig. 20) prepared by Edward Higbee on the basis of field study and of data from the U. S. Soil Conservation Service. The very good soils (such as those in the Connecticut Valley or Lancaster and York counties in Pennsylvania) are not extensive enough in Megalopolis to be wastefully abandoned to nonagricultural uses. But the process of urbanizing and suburbanizing the whole extent of Megalopolis has developed an original system of economic forces from the play of which has arisen a new pattern of land use. In recent times the natural quality of the soil has had little impact on the actual elaboration of this pattern.[8]

The enormous supplies of agricultural goods needed by the huge markets of Megalopolis could not all have been produced within the area anyhow; and as the Middle West was settled and developed, the main bulk of farm production moved beyond the Appalachians. For about a century abandoned farmland in various parts of Megalopolis has been reverting to its natural vegetation, i.e., to wooded growth. This growth is, of course, quite different from what the first generation of European settlers must

[8] The present pattern of land use, how it came about, and its present trends are studied in Part II, Chapters 5, 6, and 7.

have seen in the region. From various available descriptions we know that in the early seventeenth century the Northeastern seaboard was heavily forested. The belief, accepted about fifty years ago, that the virgin American forest consisted mainly of softwood stands has been deeply shattered by recent experimentation and by careful study of historical testimonies. The northeastern forest was made up of mixed softwood and hardwood stands in Virginia as well as in New England.[9] There was some regional variety throughout the forests covering the area, reflecting variations in climate, physiography, and soils and following the involved rules of the succession of species. For even the primeval forest was not as changeless as the climate. The same species did not regenerate themselves indefinitely at every place. Even without any human influence, such natural factors as hurricanes, forest fires, prolonged droughts or frosts, insect pests, or changes in the animal population caused some evolution of the vegetation.

On its western fringe, in central New England, the pre-settlement forest was probably a mixture of tall white pines, hemlock, and some spruce with a good many broadleaf trees (such as beech, oak, hickory, birch, and sugar maple). These broadleaf hardwoods took on a more predominant role southward, in Connecticut, southern New York, and northern New Jersey. Farther south other more southern species became more prominent in the forest mixture. The original mixture found by early settlers had already been influenced by human action, for the Indians frequently used fire to clear the land and to hunt big game. The forested landscape is known to have had wide clearings maintained by the Indians either for cultivation or as grassy pastures attracting game.

After the development of European settlement human action became a predominating influence, reshaping the landscape several times in every part of Megalopolis. Woods were cut to provide land for farming as well as lumber for building, heating, and other purposes. Forest fires grew more frequent and devastating as the population increased in number. Most of the present forests bear little likeness to what the early settlers saw on this seaboard. Nevertheless as land is abandoned it generally returns to brush, which, once enough time is allowed, grows into forest. The management of these woodlands has become today a most important, though multifaceted, problem in land use, and it must be studied as such.[10]

[9] See especially Jean Gottmann, *Virginia at Mid-Century*, Henry Holt and Company, New York, 1955 (see Chapter 4, "The Forests: Their Use and Misuse," pp. 230–286); and R. T. Foster, "New England Forests: Biological Factor," in *New England's Prospect*, edited by John K. Wright, American Geographical Society, New York, 1933, pp. 213–223.

[10] See Chapter 7 below, pp. 341–383.

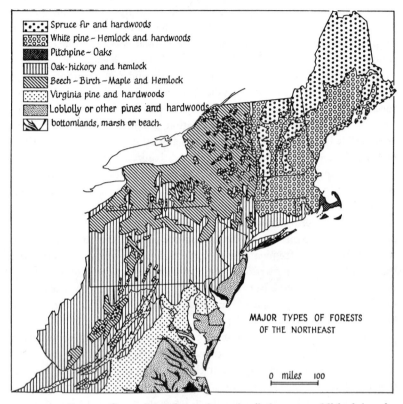

Spruce fir and hardwoods
White pine — Hemlock and hardwoods
Pitchpine — Oaks
Oak-hickory and hemlock
Beech – Birch – Maple and Hemlock
Virginia pine and hardwoods
Loblolly or other pines and hardwoods
bottomlands, marsh or beach.

MAJOR TYPES OF FORESTS
OF THE NORTHEAST

0   miles   100

FIG. 21. Generalized from three detailed maps published by the Society of American Foresters.

The forest cover is, of course, a perfect shelter for wildlife. The fauna of Megalopolis is much richer and more diversified than would be inferred from the usual interpretation of such concepts as urban, suburban, and metropolitan. Even in the heart of New York City practiced bird watchers can have a fine time identifying a great variety of birds that may come from the sea, from the coastal wetlands, or from the uplands, not to mention the migratory flights along the Atlantic flyway, which public authorities are striving to maintain across the whole length of Megalopolis. A whole book was recently written about the New York City's fauna.[11]

However, either through their uses of the land or through hunting and fishing, the inhabitants of Megalopolis have destroyed a great deal of the

[11] John Kieran, *A Natural History of New York City*, Houghton Mifflin Company, Boston, 1959.

wildlife that roamed the region on land, in the water, and in the air 300 years ago. This past destruction was all the more marked because the original abundance of wildlife was at first a great and manifold resource. Much of the first layer of the wealth upon which Megalopolis was built came from whaling and fishing in the Atlantic and from hunting beavers and other animals with valuable pelts, not to mention the hunting of wild turkey, geese, and other game for the local food supply. But as these resources were exhausted by overexploitation, the feeling for conservation arose and led to protective legislation and a good deal of restoration. Even in Virginia, most of which has been little urbanized as yet in comparison with Megalopolis, a study of the wildlife past and present led to the conclusion that "wildlife today is as much the result of systematic restoration as restored Williamsburg is." [12]

Melville's classical lament in *Moby Dick* about the approaching disappearance of the white whale did not suffice to save this species, and the whale is much less frequent a visitor, though now greatly respected and cared for, than it was two or three centuries ago on the shores of Long Island or Massachusetts. But deer are multiplying in the woods of Megalopolis, beavers have reappeared in various sections of it, wild turkeys may be observed in especially well protected spots, and in many places ring pheasants are becoming an almost common sight. Much of this restoration has been achieved through restocking, at least in selected sites.

The fight against some unpleasant elements in the wildlife, such as mosquitoes, is still going on and not always successfully. The rat, an animal commonly associated with human agglomeration, has been multiplying magnificently, occasionally causing serious worries in the major cities. Rats may outlive men and some day take over victoriously the urbanized areas where their densities have grown concurrently with human crowding. In a less dangerous and more picturesque way the seagulls benefit often by the pollution of coastal waters with human wastes.

Thus the fauna of Megalopolis has recently increased again in number and variety, largely as a consequence of the process of urbanization. For it was urban and suburban crowding that spurred on the conservation movement and measures such as the creation of parks in and outside the cities, of arboretums and wildlife refuges, of protective legislation regulating hunting and fishing.[13] Many are the needs of urban life, and one of them is for some preservation and partial restoration of nature within the

[12] Gottmann, *Virginia at Mid-Century, op. cit.,* see p. 298.
[13] Hans Huth, *Nature and the American: Three Centuries of Changing Attitudes,* University of California Press, Berkeley and Los Angeles, 1957.

limits and in the vicinity of cities. The flora and fauna of Megalopolis have thus been largely reshaped by man. Their present principal economic and social uses will be examined further in this study. It is significant, however, to observe at this point how much the natural resources of the region have been put to use by the inhabitants, how much these resources have been affected by local activities, and how organized public intervention has been needed to maintain some of the more desirable natural phenomena and to prevent their being washed away by the tide of urbanization.

The Area's Earthly Bounds

As one attempts to assess what the natural endowment of this region has meant to Megalopolis in the past, one comes to the conclusion that while no great natural obstacles were found in the path of settlement and economic development, the local conditions did not provide any extraordinary advantages either. One could find as many *local* reasons for economic growth in almost every other section of the American shores along the Atlantic or the Gulf of Mexico. The only physical characters that seemed to favor the development of Megalopolis here may be summed up by its *location*, meaning its position with relation to other areas on the continent and overseas, and perhaps the excellence of its *harbors* as seaports.

It was as a gate for deeper entrance into the North American continent, for people coming from the Atlantic and especially from northwestern Europe, that the location of Megalopolis could be considered advantageous in terms of distances, topography, and climate. Such potential advantages had to be implemented into a coherent system of regular relations between the two realms, one continental and the other oceanic. The cities of Megalopolis may rightly claim to have organized such a network of relations, rapidly and efficiently; and they have maintained it to this day, reaping from it enormous profits.

In this process of turning into huge assets the advantages of their position, the people of Megalopolis had to bring into being, sometimes by their own initiative and endeavor, dormant resources in many other areas in America and in other parts of the world. It was not, however, in those farflung enterprises that Megalopolitan endeavors encountered their worst problems; these arose right in the region itself, in the great cities and around them.

The life and prosperity of this region, which rest on a vast system of worldwide relations, remain closely bound also to its own locale. The story of Megalopolis emphasizes at its various stages these earthly but imperative bounds: the impact of local or regional conditions on the process of developing the assets of location and of its vested interests. In the earlier stages of settlement, for example, forests were a liability as well as an asset. They had to be cleared to establish farms and towns, and where dense forests surrounded the towns, they had to be policed to provide safe travel through them. Thus the forests, together with the marshes, the extremes of weather, the wildlife, and the occasional hostility of the Indians, were locally restricting factors.

A last physical characteristic of the region is its size. The proximity of the various towns in Megalopolis one to another created between them rivalries and competition leading to a historical process of selection of some rather than others for the localization of certain functions and for more rapid growth. Many a town that was an important center of economic activities in its own right until the end of the eighteenth century declined in the nineteenth. Sometimes from such a respectable status in the past it dropped down to the condition of a small town or suburb. The total area of Megalopolis, though covering more than 50,000 square miles, is not large enough to contain many cities the size of New York or Philadelphia. Despite the lively competition between the cities and the efforts at decentralization of various overcrowded activities, a specialization worked itself out, establishing *a new division of labor not only between groups of people but also between sections of the region, between places in Megalopolis.* As more major nuclei felt too crowded a finer division of labor in space shaped up, requiring more coordination and tighter links between more and more places. The era of the automobile helped the metropolis to explode over the countryside while still remaining coherent. But as these processes have gone on and on, despite the most beautiful highway system in the world, a dense network of railroads and airlines, an active navigation between huge and constantly improved seaports, traffic through Megalopolis is becoming a rapidly worsening problem. Thus the small size of the crowded region instead of restricting growth may have stimulated it; but a condition of saturation is a potential threat.

The crowding of people and their activities pollutes the waters and the air to a degree that in some sections, and especially in given atmospheric conditions, becomes a threat to general welfare and public health. Construction methods, equipment, and credit may have been improving and expanding, but slums and "grey zones," with their threat of more decay, are taking on proportions that could well run out of control.

The immense endeavor and skill that have brought such greatness and wealth to the region cannot proceed much further without applying more and more of their forces and means to the solution of problems thus accumulated within the area, the geographical value of which on the world map has been so splendidly developed.

The problems and their possible solutions belong in the field of land use as well as in the field of economic methods and structure, of social and governmental relations. The magnificent system of connections organized for Megalopolis with the outside world has brought about an acute need for another system of relations to be as skillfully organized or reorganized within the area itself. The prosperity of Megalopolis is today an essential foundation of the Western world, the whole of which would be shattered by the decay of this area. How deeply and intimately interwoven are the inside structure of Megalopolis and its network of outside relations may be better understood from the rapid sketch which follows of past and present trends.

CHAPTER 3

The Continent's Economic Hinge

The natural setting of Megalopolis provided a favorable location for the development of a great hub of relationships.

Historically, of course, this was the main gate through which came the great flow of immigrants that settled the continent and formed the American nation. Many people, especially in Europe, readily infer from this history that the abundance of cheap labor and skilled manpower supplied by the immigrants led to easy industrialization, and that on the resulting concentration of manufactures and on the large consuming market was then founded the greatest commercial and financial concentration of our time.

Although one could hardly overestimate the immense potentialities brought to this seaboard by the influx of immigrants, it must be recognized that the range of opportunity was broadened, for them and for those who had been there longer, by early and shrewd endeavors at large-scale commercial organization. These were first undertaken by the European sponsors of the first settlements, such as the Virginia Company, the Company of Massachusetts Bay, and the Dutch West Indies Company. The settlers quickly learned, however, how to organize for their own purposes instead of becoming merely outposts of European trade. Their endeavors to carry on an autonomous commerce started the American economy on the course that led first to independence and later to financial supremacy.

As the American economy grew, each of the main seaside cities developed a network of trade relationships on the continent and on the high seas. Standing at the contact of these two realms, the seaports assumed the role of *hinges* linking the development of these two foundations of the national economy. From period to period, the main weight of this seaboard's interest has oscillated from sea trade and overseas ventures to continental development and back again. Whether the general circumstances threw the door of the American economy open toward the outside or closed it to turn the main endeavors inland depended on decisions made in that *hinge*, the string of eastern cities. They alone in the country had enough capital, skill, and authority to elaborate such policies and profit by their application. How the hinge was formed and how it assumed this curious function become apparent as one reviews the stages of its growth.

On the Edge of the Wilderness

The early settlers came to these shores to find here a better life and greater freedom to organize their communities as they pleased. The success of their enterprises, they felt, would demonstrate the worth of their creed and testify to God's blessing upon them. In the eyes of the European governments that gave official sponsorship to the settlements, and of the merchants who financed and supported the migrations, the settlers were on a somewhat different errand. They were sent to stake out newly discovered and wild lands, to occupy them in the name of England, or the Netherlands, or Sweden, in a region believed to be strategically located and rich in goods that were lacking in northwestern Europe.

The location seemed, in the seventeenth century, to hold several promises. It was hoped that a Northwest Passage would be found near the area, leading to the spices of the East Indies. It was a base of operations on that new group of lands, still to be explored and developed, where it was hoped that there would be new markets for European manufactures and new sources of supplies for Europe. Last but not least, it was a base of operations close enough to the rich Spanish and Portuguese possessions farther south to permit participation in the Atlantic trade and in privateering developing in the Caribbean and on the sea lanes between the West Indies and Europe. The imperial value of this position increased as the English stake in the West Indies grew.

While the location seemed thus full of opportunities, the local abundance of resources needed in Europe was also significant. The pelts of many North American fur-bearing animals were highly valued in Europe. Dutch, English, and French hunted them and obtained them from Indians in exchange for a variety of European manufactures. The mineral wealth of the area quickly disappointed the settlers, who could not forget the glittering piles of gold and silver found in Peru and Mexico. But the forest stands of New England, New York, and Pennsylvania were a great asset, in terms of timber and naval stores, to the western European countries, whose own local forest supplies were already dwindling. Virginia early developed the cultivation and curing of tobacco, markets for which expanded rapidly. Pennsylvania and New York supplied grain and flour, particularly in demand in the West Indies. New England's proximity to the Grand Banks near Newfoundland led to the early development of fishing, and whaling was also carried on on a large scale, so that the seaports of these colonies produced exportable surpluses of salt fish (especially cod) and whale oil.

To encourage the settlement of the wilderness, impressive land grants were generously handed out in London to gentlemen considered worthy of the Crown's favor and able to direct the development of the newly acquired territory. These land grants left an obvious imprint on the region's map. The proprietors had their time of power and wealth, and their glory still lives in place names throughout Megalopolis. The grant made to William Penn is still commemorated in the name of the Commonwealth of Pennsylvania, while Lord Baltimore's grant shaped the state of Maryland and its great city of Baltimore. Among the large grants made in Amsterdam to Dutch patroons, the vast estate of the Van Rensselaer family is best remembered by historians as an economic success. In New England, town proprietorship developed on a smaller though often very profitable scale, often taking the forms of corporate organization.

Rural settlement on these grants was, of course, essential for the establishment of a solid link between the immigrants and their new country, between land and people. It was the foundation on which the American nation was built and it provided a large part of the basic resources for the people's sustenance. However, the profits it generated could not

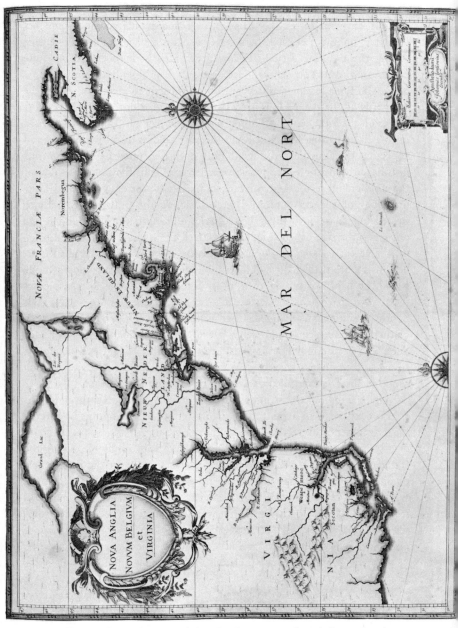

Fig. 22. An early map of the Northeastern seaboard drawn by the distinguished Dutch cartographer Johannes Jansson (middle seventeenth century). *Courtesy of the British Museum*

possibly have supported the urban growth and capital accumulation that occurred on the seaboard, between the Merrimac and Potomac rivers, during the colonial period. Towns grew rapidly here and were quite prosperous. Within a generation or two of their founding, Boston, New York, and Philadelphia had developed into substantial metropolises, by the standards of that time. This growth, and that of a dozen smaller seaport towns on the same coast, could not have taken place had the towns served only as regional markets supplying the surrounding rural population and exporting their surplus produce. This is well illustrated by developments in the southern English colonies, which were, from the point of view of the motherland, a much greater economic asset, for they supplied large quantities of tobacco and naval stores. There the only important city to develop in colonial times was Charleston, South Carolina, and it did not reach the size of 8,000 inhabitants until 1760, while Boston had 9,000 people as early as 1710. In that same year New York and Philadelphia both had more than 5,000, and Salem, Massachusetts, and Newport, Rhode Island, probably had more than 2,000 each. (The growth of these cities from 1650 to 1790 is shown on Figures 26a to 26e, pp. 114–115.) The Southern settlements avoided urban development by shipping out much of their produce from industrial wharves scattered along bays and rivers. Such a system could not fit the purposes of the Northeast's economy. Instead, it emphasized large-scale trade and maritime enterprises, which required the commercial organization of a large market place.

Empire building and overseas settlement in the seventeenth and eighteenth centuries had at its roots a strong mercantilist impulse. Whatever the idealism of the settlers who came into the wilderness, their errand could succeed only if their enterprise was materially profitable, laying the foundation for a better life for the new society. Many of the first settlers coming to Massachusetts and New Amsterdam, and later to Philadelphia, were skilled craftsmen. William Penn was proud in 1685 of the useful tradesmen in his city, among whom were carpenters, wheelwrights, shipwrights, boatwrights, shoemakers, and ropemakers. In 1677 a group of craftsmen in Boston could claim in a petition to the General Court to be "a very considerable part of the town," which supported 24 silversmiths by 1680, a sign of local wealth.[1]

The fur trade was one of the first sources of material available to merchants on the Northeastern seaboard. It drew off a good part of the pelts

---

[1] See p. 43 of Carl Bridenbaugh, *Cities in the Wilderness: The First Century of Urban Life in America, 1625–1742*, 2nd ed., Alfred A. Knopf, New York, 1955. Chapter 2 is especially pertinent.

The South part of Nevv-England, as it is Planted this yeare, 1635.

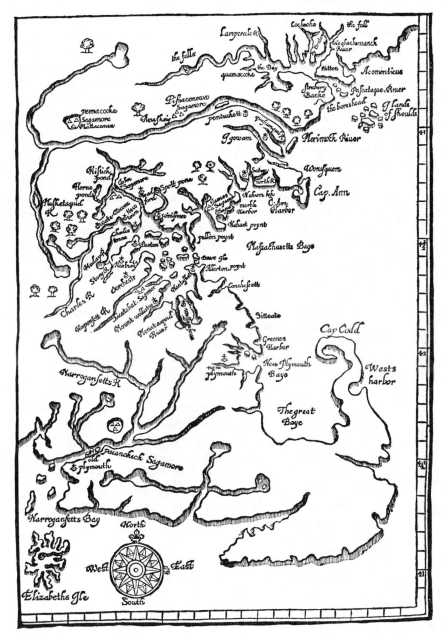

FIG. 23. *Courtesy of the British Museum*

that could be gathered to the west and north, and manufactures of quite a variety were imported or even made in the coastal towns to give to the Indians in exchange for the furs. This trade quickly pushed the commercial relations of the seaboard towns inland and brought them into brisk competition with the French trade network centered in New France.[2]

The New England forests produced some shipbuilding materials, especially the great masts that had become scarce in Europe and for which all European navies were hungry. From Boston and Portsmouth, New Hampshire, the mast ships "sailed with their precious cargo not only for England, as English law required, but also for many other destinations."[3]

Beginning with 1651 a series of *Navigation Acts*, adopted in Westminster, regulated maritime commerce in the British empire. They aimed at developing English sea trade to emancipate it from Dutch predominance in the seas around the British Isles. According to mercantilist practice, these acts gave to ships registered in English ports the monopoly of the trade between England and the colonies. All colonial produce and supplies had to be shipped in English ships, and trade with foreign countries had to go through the ports of England, with a few exceptions allowed. Ships from colonial ports were given, throughout the empire, virtually the same privileges as ships from London or Bristol. This was a valuable asset, and the middle and northern colonies rapidly took full advantage of it in the West Indies. It also led to substantial shipbuilding and ship ownership, especially in New England, where the main raw materials and skilled labor could be found in abundance.

As England had little use for what the northern colonies could export, besides furs and masts, merchants and seamen used their ingenuity to develop, instead of simple round trips to England, more intricate "triangular" routes of trade. There were several such triangles. The first and more lawful took flour from Philadelphia and New York, horses and cattle from Connecticut, and dried fish and lumber from Massachusetts to the West Indies. There these cargoes were exchanged for sugar, indigo, or coffee to be carried to England, wherefrom various manufactures were taken back to America. Ships from Newport shuttled between Rhode Island, the West African coast, and the West Indies, trading Negro slaves

---

[2] Edward C. Kirkland, *A History of American Economic Life*, Appleton-Century-Crofts, New York, 1951, pp. 38–42.

[3] Robert G. Albion, *Forests and Sea Power: The Timber Problem of the Royal Navy*, Harvard University Press, Cambridge, Mass., 1926. See also his "Colonial Commerce and Commercial Regulation," in *The Growth of the American Economy, An Introduction to the Economic History of the United States*, edited by H. F. Williamson, Prentice Hall, New York, 1944, pp. 66–81.

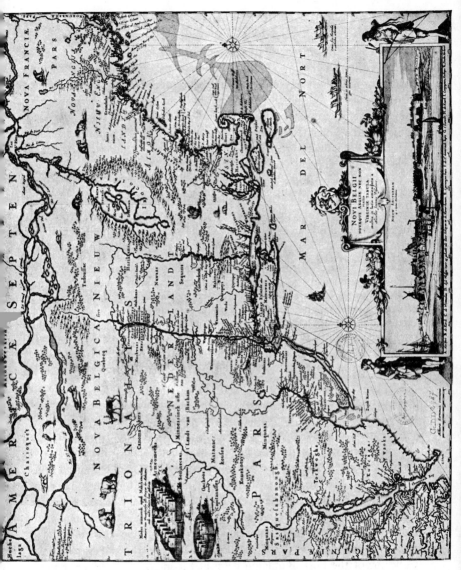

FIG. 24. The Northeastern seaboard in the 1650's: a detailed map
by the Dutch cartographer Nicolas Joannis Visscher, *circa* 1656.
The inset shows New Amsterdam as it appeared in the early 1650's
from a ship entering the East River. *Courtesy of the Bibliothèque
Nationale, Phot. SPBN*

for molasses, which, converted into rum, could be exchanged for more slaves. Other triangles went to foreign countries, for trade in commodities authorized by the Navigation Acts or even in spite of these, to make larger profits. Prices for many goods were more advantageous in the Spanish or French islands in the Caribbean, or on the continent of Europe, than in England. As the colonies were left free to import wine and salt from southern Europe, a brisk trade developed with that region. Besides regular trading on these commercial routes, a good deal of privateering went on throughout the North Atlantic and the Caribbean, based and financed in the ports of the middle and northern colonies.

These various maritime enterprises developed rapidly during the seventeenth century, especially in Boston and New York. In the first half of the eighteenth century they expanded to many other ports between the Merrimac and Potomac estuaries. As Carl Bridenbaugh has described it:

> The history of the colonial villages in the seventeenth century is primarily a tale of commercial expansion. In this period the five towns grew from wilderness settlements to fully developed little seaports challenging comparison with any European centers of the same size. The necessary corollary of this growth was the accumulation of capital, derived not only from the extension of wholesale trade by enterprising merchants but also from the small savings of prosperous tradesmen and artisans . . . "New England was originally a plantation of Religion, not a plantation of Trade" thundered John Higginson in his election sermon of 1663. "Let Merchants, and such as are increasing Cent per Cent remember this." [4]

And as trade grew the cities grew, and so did urban problems, especially in Boston and New Amsterdam.

From the pictures of New Amsterdam drawn on Dutch maps *circa* 1656 and 1673 (compare Figure 24 and the back end-papers) one may assess the rapid growth of the town and particularly of its port facilities in this brief period. Having become New York, it rapidly took over its share of the opportunities available to the English colonies, but it could not yet rival the rapid rise of Boston. Edward Randolph, sent from London to investigate Boston in 1675, reported a loss of about £100,000 annually to the Royal customs from the illegal operations of the port. Appointed Collector of the Port, Randolph described it in 1679 as "the mart town of the West Indies and a 'clearing house' for all the colonies in America." [5]

The founders of the great commercial hub of Megalopolis were the mer-

---

[4] Bridenbaugh, *Cities in the Wilderness, op. cit.,* p. 52.

[5] Writers' Program of the WPA in the State of Massachusetts, *Boston Looks Seaward. The Story of the Port, 1630–1940* (American Guide Series), Bruce Humphries Inc., Boston, 1941. See Chapter 1.

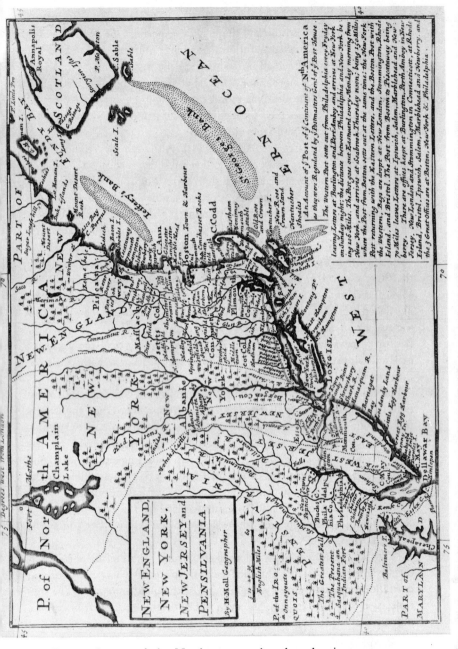

Fig. 25. A map of the Northeastern seaboard made *circa* 1730.
Courtesy of the British Museum

chants and seamen of Boston and the smaller seaports of the Northeast, for they refused to be satisfied with local trade and shuttling to England but were determined to "trye all ports," despite the regulations promulgated in London. To make more money and be able to expand their trade with greater autonomy, the Bostonians and their neighbors endeavored to exploit fully the resources their local environment could provide, both from local forest and farms and from the sea.

The sea offered the richer harvest at first. Although they found themselves competing there with many other nations, especially the French based in New France, and also with ships from England itself, the fishermen of eastern Massachusetts made a fortune on the Grand Banks off Newfoundland, which were found to be teeming with codfish. Just as Amsterdam was built on carcasses of herring, so the prosperity of Massachusetts was founded on the catching and drying of codfish. In 1636 the cod became the official symbol of Massachusetts, and the "sacred cod" hangs in the State Capitol in Boston. Dried cod found a thriving market in the West Indies, the southern colonies, and southern Europe. A little later daring fishermen in eastern Long Island added whaling to the harvesting of the sea. From Southampton, New York, and from Nantucket and New Bedford, Massachusetts, whalers set out to sea, hunting the large sea mammals and supplying the colonies and a good part of Europe with whale oil, then the main fuel for lighting.

For fishing, whaling, and trading the seaports needed ships, and these they built themselves. In Boston John Winthrop, who warned the settlers to "lookout to the West Indies," was also a shipbuilder. In 1710, twenty-one ships (totalling 1,520 tons) were launched in Massachusetts. The first schooner was built in Boston in 1716. In 1723 New England launched 700 ships. In 1721 the Lords of Trade in London rated shipbuilding as the most important and best managed among the various manufacturing industries in Boston, and London became worried by the costs of her own shipbuilding, which appeared to be almost twice as great per ton as the cost in Boston.[6]

New York was developing another emporium. Like Philadelphia, it had the advantage of the "bread trade," i.e., of exports of wheat and flour and corn meal supplied by the richer farming of the middle colonies. The specialization of New England, however, did not result entirely from a more difficult soil that had to be cleared of both woods and stones, and from a

---

[6] See *Boston Looks Seaward, op. cit.;* Albion, "Colonial Commerce and Commercial Regulation," *op. cit.;* and Samuel Eliot Morison, *The Maritime History of Massachusetts, 1783–1860,* Houghton Mifflin Company, Boston, 1921, pp. 12 ff.

colder climate. New Englanders deliberately preferred sea ventures and urban crafts to farming. William Bradford prophesized it early: "And let this spetially be borne in minde, y^t the greatest parte of ye Collonie is like to be imployed constantly, not upon dressing ther perticuler land and building houses, but upon fishing, trading, etc." [7] Processing codfish, whale blubber and bone was not enough for the industrious Yankees. They started making textiles, rivaling an old English specialty. And not only ships and masts were made and exported, but local timber resources were made into planks and boards, shingles and clapboards, staves, headings, and wine casks, most of which were exported to the Caribbean, Madeira, and more distant places. "Yankee ingenuity anticipated the modern prefabricated house by sending whole ready-to-assemble house frames to the West Indies." [8]

Although they started a little later, New York and Philadelphia followed fast in the wake of Boston, though with somewhat different specializations. New York was long the leader in flour milling, while Philadelphia developed cooperage and leather industries. Merchants played a very important part in the elite of every town, and in its prosperity, whether they engaged in retailing or in more impressive commerce on the seas with faraway customers. About 1700 New York became a capital of pirates and privateers, who went as far as the Red Sea and flooded the town's market with exotic silks and swords.[9] Steadily competition arose between the three major cities of the seaboard and between a dozen smaller towns in the area. By 1720 Boston fully dominated the commercial system of the American colonies. It was their "coin center," and New York, Connecticut, and Philadelphia were in various ways tributary to the Bay City,[10] which then counted about 11,000 inhabitants.

The population of the colonies north of Chesapeake Bay was still essentially distributed along the seacoast and in the valleys of the main navigable rivers (the Thames, the Connecticut, the Hudson, and the Delaware), as appears clearly on the map of settlement in 1700 (Fig. 26b). Around Chesapeake Bay and in Virginia it was also linked to navigable channels but was scattered somewhat farther inland. The concentration in towns

---

[7] William Bradford, *Bradford's History "Of Plimoth Plantation,"* Wright and Potter Printing Co., Boston, 1898, p. 57. See also Edward C. Higbee, "The Three Earths of New England," *Geographical Review*, Vol. XLII, No. 3, July 1952, pp. 425–438.

[8] Albion, "Colonial Commerce and Commercial Regulation," *op. cit.*, p. 77.

[9] New York City WPA Writers' Project, *A Maritime History of New York*, Doubleday, Doran and Company (American Guide Series), Garden City, N. Y., 1941. See Chapter 2.

[10] Bridenbaugh, *Cities in the Wilderness, op. cit.*, pp. 179 and 330.

FIG. 26. These maps (26a to 26e) give a general idea of the distribution of settlement and of urban growth on the Eastern seaboard from 1650 to 1790. See the legend on FIG. 26e. Maps reproduced by permission of their author, Dr. Herman Friis, and the American Geographical Society

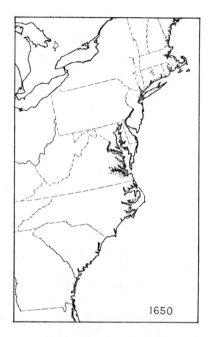

FIG. 26a

1650

FIG. 26b

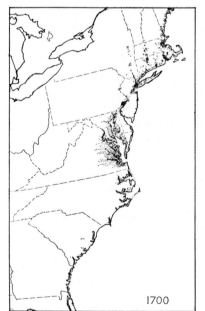

1700

FIG. 26c

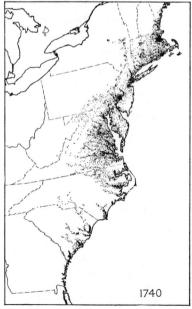

1740

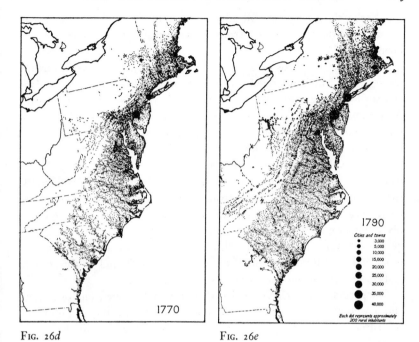

FIG. 26d   FIG. 26e

was already quite apparent in the northern region. Indeed, until about
1720 the middle and northern colonies developed essentially as seaboard
settlements more oriented toward the sea than looking inland. The occupance was restricted to the edge of the wilderness, and if it were true that
"the country makes the city," the "country" that made Boston and Salem,
Newport and New London, New York and Philadelphia extended as
much over the Atlantic Ocean and the Caribbean Sea as over the American
continent, and depended as much and perhaps more on England and the
sugar islands as on the land of the Algonquin Indians. By 1740, however,
things had begun to change.

More People, New Land, and More Trade

In 1713 the Treaty of Utrecht brought peace to Europe and to the
whole system in which the colonies lived; it opened "an era in which the
English colonies expanded westward, drew on new sources for their population, diversified their economic life, and began to enjoy the 'century of
enlightenment.' "[11]

[11] Samuel Eliot Morison and Henry Steele Commager, *The Growth of the American Republic*, 4th ed., Oxford University Press, New York, 1950, Vol. I, p. 91.

By 1740 the settlement had advanced inland substantially and had to some extent disengaged itself from the immediate proximity of the seaboard (Fig. 26c).

This greater emphasis on settlement inland was due to several factors: more people had immigrated and claimed more land; and peace on land and sea had made it easier both to settle and trade farther inland on the American continent, as well as to expand maritime commerce. The West Indies trade flourished from 1720 to 1740, as did the settlement of farmers in the hinterland of the seaboard in New York, Pennsylvania, and New England. As the sea trade expanded and the seaboard towns grew, the demand rose for more production of all sorts, including farm produce. At the same time the expansion of the rural settlement inland, while helping to increase agricultural and forest production, was also adding to the marketplace function of the towns. Thus maritime activities and continental development were intimately linked, the two growths reacting on one another and spurring each other on; and both contributed to the growth and enrichment of the seaboard cities.

The period from 1720 to the Revolution was, however, one of settling and developing the continent rather than of overseas enterprise, although the latter went on, flourishing and developing, at least until the 1760's. Most historians agree that immigration and population growth were the prime forces and problems of the time.

In respect to America the 18th century was preeminently the century of the foreigner; in 1760 the foreign born represented a third of the colonial population . . . Of all the factors at work in 18th century America none had greater influence than the immigration of the foreigners, for this made possible that vigorous expansion which is the dominant note of the age.[12]

This immigration of "foreigners" brought to the English colonies many nationalities besides the Englishmen who had predominated in the seventeenth century. Among them were Scots (who perhaps were not really foreigners after the Act of Union in 1707 had given them the run of the empire), Irish, French Huguenots, Swiss, and Germans. The latter two nationalities came largely to the middle colonies, lured by both greater religious freedom and the promise of abundant free land.[13] Because they were

---

[12] Curtis P. Nettels, *The Roots of American Civilization, A History of American Colonial Life*, Crofts, New York, 1938. See p. 383.

[13] See Eric F. Goldman, "Middle States Regionalism and American Historiography," in *Historiography and Urbanization; Essays in American History in Honor of W. Stull Holt*, edited by Eric F. Goldman, The Johns Hopkins Press, Baltimore, 1941, pp. 211–220; and also Herman R. Friis, *A Series of Population Maps of the Colonies and the United States, 1625–1790*, American Geographical Society, New York, 1940 (see especially the maps and pp. 10–33).

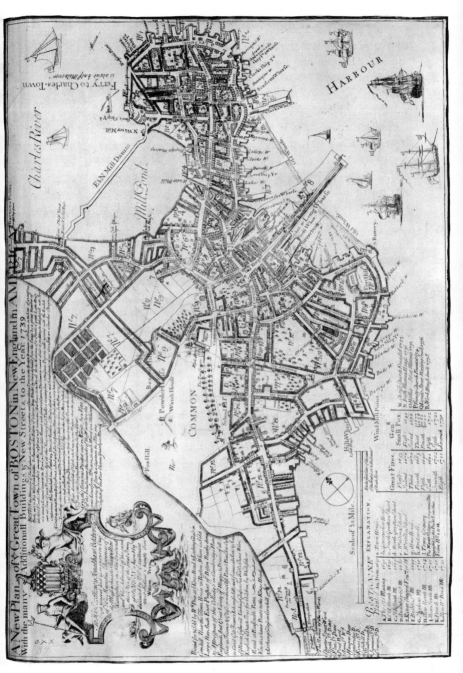

FIG. 27. *Courtesy of the British Museum*

farming people and because they often expected the wilderness to secure, through relative isolation, more freedom for their religious and social life, most of the Swiss and Germans arriving at that time proceeded inland. It was then that the "Pennsylvania Dutch" country was settled. The maps for 1740 and 1770 show a considerable progress of land occupation westward and southward. The rich limestone soils of southeastern Pennsylvania were well settled, largely by German immigrants, by 1750; these counties, especially Chester, Lancaster, and York, were densely populated indeed by 1770.[14] (See Figs. 28 and 29, and the maps by H. R. Friis, Fig. 26.)

This rural development of Pennsylvania, which went along with more settlement around the upper reaches of Chesapeake Bay, caused the structure of what was to become Megalopolis to extend south of the Delaware.

Baltimore was founded in 1729, largely because the local river bearing the humble name of Jones Falls afforded water power for mills which ground the wheat of German-settled Pennsylvania and up-country Maryland into flour, for which there was a brisk demand in the West Indies.[15]

Located farther inland and able easily to export both tobacco and flour, Baltimore quickly took over from Annapolis, the administrative capital and an older town, the role of principal seaport and market center of Maryland. It was also conveniently located on the overland route from Philadelphia southward.

For, although water transportation and coastwise navigation remained dominant, in the colonial economic system, traffic on the land was now rapidly rising in extent and intensity. The maps of population distribution show some moving away from the seaboard and the main valleys through all the colonies, from Maine to South Carolina. By 1770 (Fig. 26d) the population was already fairly dense all over the parts of New England we include in Megalopolis, as well as around the city of New York and in southeastern Pennsylvania. Another patch of higher density, though essentially rural, had developed on the modern location of the Washington metropolitan area. The distribution was still much affected by the major topographic features. South of the Potomac, however, there was greater scattering, reflecting the predominance there of the plantation economy.

[14] Most of the area was purchased by the Penn family in 1718. Lancaster, laid out in 1730, was a town of 2,000 in 1750. York was founded in 1741. The same year the Moravians established themselves at Bethlehem, far north of Philadelphia; and the Penns laid out Reading in 1748. See S. K. Stevens, R. W. Cordier, and F. O. Benjamin, *Exploring Pennsylvania: Its Geography, History and Government,* Harcourt, Brace & Company, New York, 1957, Chapter 4.

[15] Morison and Commager, *The Growth of the American Republic, op. cit.,* Vol. I, p. 100.

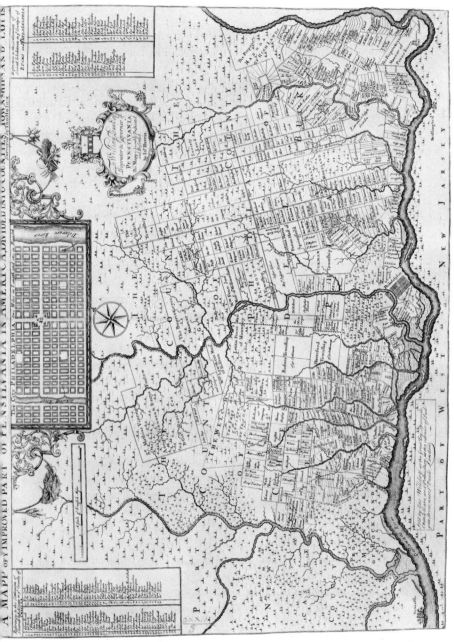

Fig. 28. An early map of Pennsylvania, with an inset reproducing the original plan of Philadelphia, drawn by the cartographer John Harris, London, early eighteenth century. *Courtesy of the British Museum*

Its dispersed and relatively self-sufficient economic cells left to the northern middle colonies the growth of almost all the manufactures, trades, and maritime enterprises.

The total population of the colonies, estimated at about 250,000 in 1700 (of which 170,000 were in the area from New Hampshire to Maryland), rose to 435,000 by 1715 and by 1750 it was close to 1,300,000 (of whom about one million lived in the present area of Megalopolis). By 1770 the total population had grown to about two and a half million, and the Congress estimate rated it above three million in 1774. On the eve of the Revolution the present region of Megalopolis must have held about three fifths of the total.[16]

Such a rapid increase in population was also accompanied by a substantial rise in the standard of living. True, of the total population figure in the 1770's about half a million were Negroes, most of them slaves, and about as many more were poor whites working as indentured servants on proprietors' estates and plantations, or as domestics and apprentices in the towns. Even so, around 1770 a country of some two million people, most of them white and many taxable, represented a very substantial market for a variety of consumer goods.

The expansion of settlement inland was, therefore, a natural and much needed move. It brought the settlers into closer contact and competition with the Indian tribes and with the French trading network, stretching inland from the estuary of the St. Lawrence to the delta of the Mississippi. The French, with their forts and their Indian allies, held with relative ease the barrier of the Appalachian ranges, restricting the inland advance of tradesmen and settlers. The fur trade suffered also from competition with the French, who drained many of the pelts collected in the interior of the continent toward Montreal. At the same time the clashes were becoming frequent on the sea to the north. New Englanders and settlers from New France disputed both the fishing grounds and the northerly routes of a profitable fur trade by sea, which had been opened in 1729 by Captain Atkins, sailing on the Boston ship *The Whale* to the "Eskimeaux Coast" beyond the Belle Isle Straits. Beaver pelts, seal skin, whalebone, and cod moved increasingly across these northerly seas, and by 1760 more ships departed from Boston toward Canada than toward the West Indies.[17]

Having enjoyed forty years of growth, prosperity, and agricultural and

[16] City population data in this chapter for the colonial period are based on Evarts B. Greene and Virginia D. Harrington, *American Population Before the Federal Census of 1790*, Columbia University Press, New York, 1932.

[17] *Boston Looks Seaward, op. cit.*, Chapter 2.

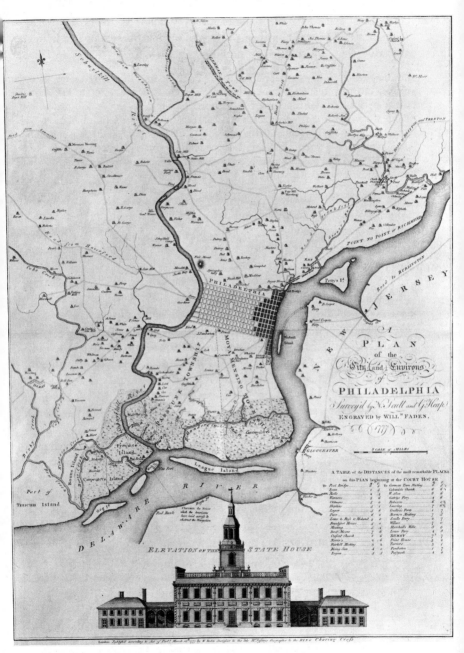

FIG. 29. *Courtesy of the British Museum*

commercial expansion, the colonies felt very annoyed, in the 1750's, by the limitations imposed on their progress in various directions by the few and sparsely populated French outposts. As one observer wrote in 1775:

> The French policy in hemming in our colonies to a narrow country along the sea coast by that well known chain of forts . . . was admirably calculated for the absolute destruction of all our settlements, as *colonies supplied by Britain with manufactures*, for they cut off the increase of plantations so effectually by their forts and the incursions of their Indians, that some hundred thousand people were, at the opening of the war, deprived of their agriculture, and would in a few years have all become manufacturers for sale, had not the evil been destroyed.[18]

This remarkable statement published in London in 1775, expresses the American settlers' viewpoint, though apparently it is concerned with a terrible threat to the interests of England. For want of lands all these people might turn to manufactures to compete with England instead of developing a larger market for her exports!

The Seven Years War between European powers (1756–63) became the French and Indian Wars in North America. In fact, since 1744 more or less continuous warfare had been going on along the borders of New England and New York. The British conquest of Canada (1759–60) and the defeat of the French in Europe and India brought an end to the immediate French pressure. The Peace of Paris in 1763 left France with only Louisiana on the continent of North America. In Canada, and again in the war with the Indians led by Pontiac in 1763, the British Redcoats gave good protection to the American traders and settlers. But the British crown then set forth with new plans to organize its much expanded colonial empire. From 1763 to 1774 a series of royal proclamations attempted to stop more settlers from occupying more land in the wilderness; and England especially disapproved of the commercial and industrial activities that prospered and grew in the seaboard cities.

For, while the major preoccupation and endeavors of the colonies had been of a continental nature from 1713 to 1763, the seaboard townsfolk had not, during that half century, neglected the fields in which they had made such a profitable start in the seventeenth century. After 1715, New York and Philadelphia grew at a much faster rate and began to challenge Boston's supremacy. A number of smaller coastal cities developed a market and maritime function of their own, some of them being still very close to one of the three leading ports but others being more autonomous be-

[18] *American Husbandry*, edited by Harry J. Carman, Columbia University Press, New York, 1939. See p. 22.

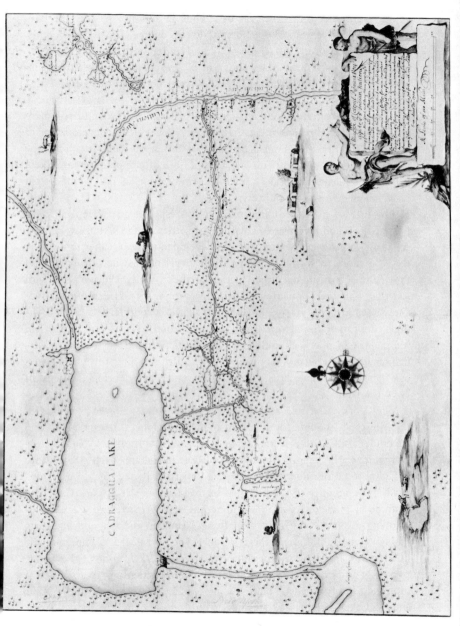

Fig. 30. An early map (*circa* 1700) of New York's hinterland as surveyed by Colonel Romer. Compare with the later map, Fig. 32. *Courtesy of the British Museum*

cause of distance and other factors. Thus in addition to such ports as Salem and Marblehead, Massachusetts, others such as Newport, Rhode Island, New Bedford, Massachusetts, New London and New Haven, Connecticut, and Baltimore, Maryland, had by 1775 become substantial centers of commerce in their own right. Most of these seaports were located between New York and Boston, and Boston remained the largest financial center, where active commerce since the 1630's had accumulated more capital available for investment. After 1740, however, the development of maritime enterprises did not proceed in Boston at the same pace as in the preceding hundred years. This was a result both of competition from New York and Philadelphia and of some decentralization of port activities toward smaller New England towns.

The rate of growth of Philadelphia was especially spectacular. It reflected the rapid westward expansion of settlement in Pennsylvania and western New Jersey (which was also developed under Quaker influence). By 1775 more roadways carrying traffic overland had been built around Philadelphia than in any other section of the colonies. Philadelphia, with less than half the population of Boston in 1700, surpassed the great Bay City by 1760, and by 1775 it claimed to be the second largest (after London) of all the cities of the British empire. Closer to the West Indies than Massachusetts, and well endowed with local products for export, Philadelphia also suffered less from the repeated British edicts forbidding various forms of sea trade or manufacturing, which had developed mainly in New England.

New York was rising rapidly, too. Its hinterland was more productive than Boston's, though not as much so as Philadelphia's. It carried out the triangular trades and privateering at least as well as Boston. It had a better and wider harbor, more difficult to police than the approaches to Boston. It had also a more liberal and mixed population. It developed busy shipyards. The number of ships owned by residents of New York City rose from 99 in 1747 to 447 in 1762 and 709 in 1772. Agriculture was also developing around New York — on Long Island, in the neighboring parts of New Jersey, and along the Hudson River northward.[19] The conquest of French Canada by the British opened up to New York in the 1760's two great and easy routes into the interior, and particularly to areas richly supplying the fur trade. The first route, straight north along the Hudson and the Lake Champlain depression, led to Montreal and the St. Lawrence

[19] *A Maritime History of New York, op. cit.; American Husbandry, op. cit.;* and U. S. Bureau of the Census, *A Century of Population Growth in the United States, 1790–1900,* Washington, D. C., 1909.

FIG. 31. The plan shows the City of New York in the late eighteenth century. *Courtesy of the Bibliothèque Nationale, Phot. SPBN*

Valley; the other, turning west from the Hudson along the Mohawk Valley, led in relatively easy fashion to the Great Lakes and the trans-Appalachian west. This topographic "Y" gave to New York a considerable strategic advantage; from the beginning it appeared on the early maps as highly valued by Dutch and English alike (see Figs. 24, 25, and 30) and even in the 1770's it was considered in London to be one of the major assets of the northern colonies (Fig. 32). The great "Y" proved to be of even greater significance to the trade of New York in the nineteenth century, but it played a role also during the eighteenth and indeed shaped the layout of the future State of New York.

A century of successful trade on the edge of the wilderness and all over the high seas brought to the main seaports substantial capital, most of which was invested locally, either in more trade and ships or in graceful living, real estate, and manufactures in the cities, as well as in land speculation farther inland. Boston money financed some of the activities of New York and Philadelphia, and many more in New England. Philadelphia capital went into land purchases and development of the surrounding country, as was well illustrated by the investments of the Penns and some other leading Quaker families. In New York a similar process went on; a famous privateer, Commodore Sir Peter Warren, acquired, with some of the profits reaped on the sea, a 300-acre estate north of the city on the present location of Greenwich Village. A whole class of rich merchants, ship owners, and land owners arose in the seaboard cities, forming by 1770 a wealthy elite, locally powerful and respected and displaying a conspicuous affluence, the signs of which were accepted even in the old Puritan commonwealth.

The colonies north of the Potomac were prosperous, and after 1763 their economy was to some extent in competition with the overseas interests of the United Kingdom. Such competition was mainly the result of the urban growth of the leading seaports, their overseas trade, their manufactures, and their obvious interest in directing the westward march of the frontier on the continent. The imperial reorganization undertaken by King George III brought one conflict after another in the relations between the central government and the American colonies. The Boston Tea Party symbolizes both the start of the American Revolution and the deep American interest in the freedom of trading on the high seas. However, this was certainly not the only cause of the Revolution. At least as important were the barriers that royal proclamations attempted to set to the free expansion of settlement westward, and the general policy of taxation and government without representation.

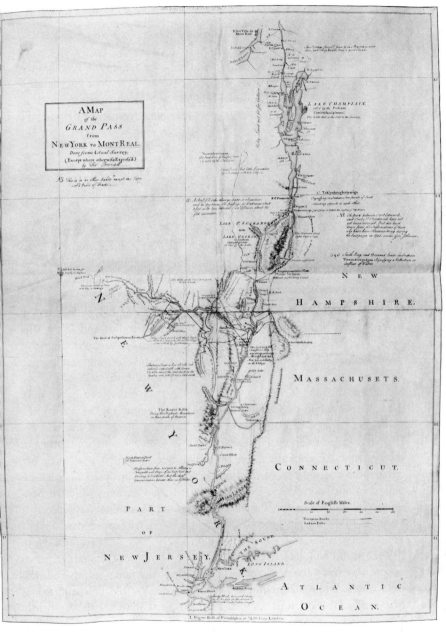

FIG. 32. The Great "Y" of New York's inland routes: Governor Thomas Pownall's map of the routes of New York's hinterland (*circa* 1756). *Courtesy of the British Museum*

The people inhabiting the Eastern seaboard had come of age enough to feel they could take their destiny in their own hands. This growth had been the result of a double economic process — the successful development of maritime enterprise and the settlement of the continent. Right after their victory, having achieved independence and begun reconstruction at home, Americans again switched the economic emphasis toward the oceans.

Continental Expansion and Maritime Profits

The Treaty of Paris, which terminated the Revolutionary War in 1783, brought freedom through independence and was followed by thirty years of expansion in both maritime commerce and inland settlement. This was a period of adolescence for the American nation, and the westward frontier then began its transcontinental march with great momentum. By 1790 settlers had already established themselves in respectable numbers in Kentucky and Tennessee, as well as around Pittsburgh in the Ohio Valley (see Fig. 26e). By 1810 the center of population of the United States was west of the Potomac, just south of Charlestown, Maryland. By 1820 it had moved just west of the present border between Virginia and West Virginia. The purchase of Louisiana, too, helped to make the development of the continental interior the major national endeavor during that period. But while the South was definitely looking westward, the seaboard of the Northeast, without forgetting its interests in continental expansion, built the most profitable and exciting sector of its economy on the sea.

It could perhaps be claimed that the remarkable success of overseas enterprises during these thirty years established the economic supremacy of this region in America for a long time. This development was all the more remarkable because the war and independence had disrupted the old system of colonial commerce, based on triangular navigation within the British empire and around it. But there was an old Massachusetts motto that a ship should "trye all ports." During the wars with Spain and France (1744–83) privateering had developed on a very large scale from Salem to Baltimore and had greatly contributed to the growth of the larger towns into prosperous entrepôts.[20] The privateering tradition was revived, this time against English ships, in the Revolutionary War. As independence at first restricted American access to British ports, trade with the British West Indies was carried on via the French or Spanish islands; American

[20] Carl Bridenbaugh, *Cities in Revolt: Urban Life in America, 1743–1776*, Alfred A. Knopf, New York, 1955, especially Chapter 2. Also Harold U. Faulkner, *American Economic History*, Harper and Brothers, New York, 1949.

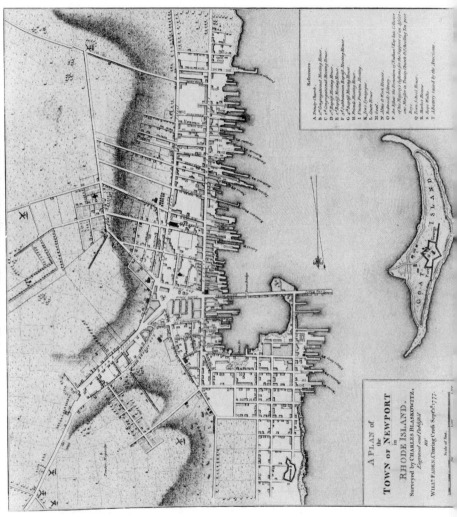

FIG. 33. *Courtesy of the British Museum*

Fɪɢ. 34. *Courtesy of the British Museum*

foodstuffs were necessary to feed the slave population of the sugar islands. By 1787 the main exchanges with the Caribbean area were restored, and a new and promising triangular route had been devised, this time to China.

In 1784 the *Empress of China*, a New York ship built in Baltimore, managed by a Bostonian, and financed by Philadelphians, sailed from Manhattan and around the horn to Whampoa, opening up the China trade for the Northeastern seaboard. The *Empress* took to Canton a cargo of ginseng (a stimulant obtained from a plant that grew abundantly in the Northeastern forests), woolens, and furs; she returned in 1785 with tea and silk, yielding good profits. That same year Elias Hasket Derby of Salem, a shipowner who had built a huge fortune on privateering, sent his *Grand Turk* to the Far East. In 1787 Captain Robert Gray of Boston sailed to the estuary of the Columbia River in the Pacific Northwest and found it teeming with seals and sea otters, the skins of which were highly valued in China. He proceeded with a cargo of pelts to Canton and returned to Boston with tea. Thus was "solved the riddle of the China trade," and a new triangle was inaugurated that led to the Pacific Northwest and China.[21] Trade was also carried on with Europe, and after 1794 it was resumed with English ports.

Legislation adopted in Congress in 1789 gave a boost to both American shipping and shipyards by establishing at the entrance of United States ports a duty of fifty cents per ton for foreign-built and -owned ships, while American-built ships paid thirty cents a ton if foreign-owned and only six cents if American-owned. The period from 1790 to 1807 was one of great maritime expansion and profits for Americans, and this was accomplished essentially by the ports of the Northeast.

During this period New York took a definite lead among American seaports and kept it, both because of the spaciousness and physical quality of its harbor and the drive and efficiency of its people. The tonnage of ships registered in the port of New York alone rose from 37,712 tons in 1790 to 71,693 in 1794 and 265,548 in 1812.[22] During the troubles preceding the Revolutionary War and until 1788 Boston's trade underwent a bad depression, but during the 1790's its activity became greater than ever. On one day in October, 1791, more than seventy vessels sailed out of Boston, and by 1797 its fleet was three times that of its neighbor, Salem, and second only to the tonnage of New York.[23]

During an average day in 1800, six trading vessels came to anchor or berthed at one of its [Boston's] many docks as others slipped out through the harbor's narrow entrance for other ports and seas. Throughout that year not less than 1600 vessels engaged in coastwise trade arrived at and cleared the port . . . Boston's advantages for trade are such that numbers of foreign vessels are attracted to the port, well assured of cargoes destined for many distant countries. In 1800, as in other normal times, Boston carried on much trade with the

---

[21] Morison, *The Maritime History of Massachusetts, op. cit.; A Maritime History of New York, op. cit.;* and Faulkner, *American Economic History, op. cit.,* Chapter 12.

[22] Statistical data cited here and in the previous paragraph are from *A Maritime History of New York, op. cit.*

[23] *Boston Looks Seaward, op. cit.*

West Indies and Canada and also with European countries and the Orient. In the year 1804 a total of 890 vessels from foreign ports entered the port of Boston.[24]

In this period Boston also developed an ice trade with the West Indies, shipping ice, cut on the frozen lakes and packed in pine sawdust, to Cuba and Jamaica and even to Brazil.

Philadelphia was both the largest city and busiest seaport immediately after the Revolution. Not until 1797 was it surpassed by New York in maritime commerce and not until around 1810 in population.

As in other large Atlantic ports, vessels and small craft from near-by places mingle with coasters from distant domestic ports and with the ships of foreign nations. Of the arrivals at Philadelphia in 1797, 800 were classed as coasters and 600 as foreign vessels. The products of all quarters of the world came to a temporary resting place on the many docks. Here are rum, muscovado sugar, coffee, and salt from the West Indies; strange packages from the Orient, marked in unrecognizable figures, containing tea, chinaware, silk, and spices; and direct imports from European countries of wines, fruits, drugs, and dry goods of many varieties. Ready for exportation are manufactured goods from the Philadelphia area, articles especially in demand in the southern states. Piled high are cases containing shoes, hats, gloves, books, saddlery, tinware and brassware, and ship chandlery. Among the exports, too, are wheat and flour, meats, cheese, mustard, loaf sugar, chocolate, soap, hair powder, starch, and vehicles.[25]

By the early 1800's Baltimore ranked fourth among American ports in terms of commerce with various ports of the world. Its rise on Chesapeake Bay was, however, explained more by its connections with the interior (southern Pennsylvania as well as Maryland) than by its harbor facilities and location. Still it acted as a small emporium for the upper Chesapeake country, concentrating on exports from plantations and small towns along the indented coast and in exchange redistributing imports from afar (such as sugar from the West Indies or hardware from Europe). Baltimore had even set up its own manufactures and in 1772 had claimed to have produced the first umbrella made in America.[26]

Its rapid growth at the time impressed a British visitor, who described it as follows:

[24] Ralph H. Brown, *Mirror for Americans: Likeness of the Eastern Seaboard, 1810,* American Geographical Society, New York, 1943, pp. 108–110.

[25] *Ibid.,* pp. 110–111.

[26] *Ibid.,* pp. 229–230; and Jean Gottmann, "Baltimore: un grand port industriel," in *Revue de la Porte Oceane, Le Havre,* V, Nos. 52–53, Aug.–Sept. 1949.

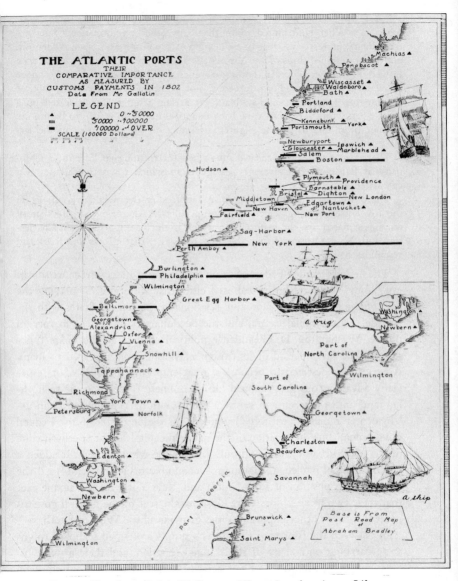

Fig. 35. Map from Ralph H. Brown, *Mirror for Americans: Likeness of the Eastern Seaboard, 1810*, American Geographical Society, New York, 1943. *Reproduced by permission of the American Geographical Society*

No town in the world, perhaps, has had a more rapid rise than Baltimore . . . What contributed more than any other circumstance to its extraordinary increase was that of its being a safe position as a place of deposit, out of the reach of ships of war during the War of Independence. Capital then flowed into it, commercial houses were established, and, the market once formed, such is the stability of credit and of habit, that even the foundation of Washington City, with all its advantages arising from its being seated on a great river, with every one of the back countries nearer to it than to Baltimore, has not been able to do the slightest prejudice to the prosperity of the latter . . .

There was a sum of $1,000,000 subscribed for forming an East India Company at Baltimore; the average passage from which town to Calcutta was calculated at 120 days.

There were several flourishing manufactures in the neighborhood, or in the town itself, among which was one peculiarly American, namely that of moss hair mattresses, the material for which is chiefly imported from Charleston and New Orleans, being the fine moss . . . that grows on trees and resembles hair.[27]

The newly founded Federal city on the Potomac added one more southern "joint" to the chain of seaboard cities that were already playing the part of the *hinge* in the economic relations of the United States with the outside. As a national capital and the headquarters of American foreign policy, Washington, D. C., added a political element to the hinge function. In the early period of its existence, Washington appeared to many Americans as destined to become a great emporium because of its especially advantageous geographical location. These forecasts came to nothing, and until the twentieth century the growth of Washington as an urban center remained entirely dependent on the activities of the Federal government. But the location of the national capital on the southern edge of the great urban chain could only benefit the whole system. It added a new residential nucleus to Baltimore's economic orbit and reinforced the metropolitan position of Philadelphia and New York, by the simple fact that these two metropolises were closer to the seat of the Federal government than were other important cities growing in the West or South.

In between the four major seaports a number of small seaboard towns were carrying on a share of the "hinge" function, and their growth increased rapidly after 1790. Their activities resulted either from an overflow from the major nuclei, as they became too busy and crowded, or from local initiative and endeavor. These smaller towns challenged the

[27] *Jeffersonian America: Notes on the United States of America Collected in the Years 1805–6–7 and 11–12 by Sir Augustus John Foster, Bart.*, edited with an Introduction by Richard Beale Davis, The Huntington Library, San Marino, California, 1954; see pp. 209–210.

"pull" of the larger centers but still tended to profit from their seaboard location and from the contribution made to the whole region by the leading and older seaports.

The great fishing industry of New England, for instance, had largely moved away from Boston. During the Revolution that great port was closed at times and when it recuperated it became busy with long-range trade rather than with fishing. The cod-fishing industry was gradually restored after 1783 and by 1800 it centered mainly in Massachusetts at Marblehead, Salem, Gloucester, Plymouth, Provincetown, and Yarmouth. It also moved northward to Portsmouth, New Hampshire, and York, Maine, and southward to New London, Connecticut, and Sag Harbor, New York. The fishing fleets in these towns were partly financed from Boston, but cod was becoming a specialty of these other, smaller ports. Whaling, which was rapidly developing, was concentrated in Nantucket, New Bedford, some of their smaller neighbors (Westport, Rochester, Wareham, Dartmouth), and the eastern end of Long Island. Whalers, looking for more whales, were ranging all over the Atlantic and were already going around the Horn into the Pacific Ocean.[28] Whalebone and oil were used in the United States or shipped to Europe and the West Indies.

More towns blossomed in the Connecticut Valley, Hartford and New Haven being the largest. The small town of Wethersfield specialized in the large-scale cultivation of onions for the near-by urban markets and for exports to the West Indies. Eastern Pennsylvania had an even more remarkable development of regional market towns at major inland crossroads on the Delaware River. Philadelphia, though dominant, did not monopolize the commercial port function, for Wilmington, Delaware, was also carrying on shipping and some manufacturing. In New Jersey, on the great road between Philadelphia and New York City, numerous small towns were growing steadily. Trenton, New Brunswick, Paterson, and Newark had already become noted in the early 1800's.

Thus the nuclei of Megalopolis were taking shape a century and a half ago, and the urban growth of that time received special stimulation from the remarkable maritime expansion of the period. The gross tonnage of the merchant marine rose from 487,477 in 1790 to 1,268,548 in 1807. In these same years the total value of foreign trade (in merchandise only) rose from $43.2 million to $146.8 million; in the latter figure almost $60 million

---

[28] Brown, *Mirror for Americans, op. cit.*, Chapter 5; Thomas Jefferson, *Report on Fisheries*, February 4, 1791 (*American State Papers, Commerce and Navigation*, I, pp. 8–22); and La Rochefoucauld-Liancourt, *Voyage dans les Etats Unis d'Amérique fait en 1795, 1796 et 1797*, Dupont, Paris, 1799, Vol. II.

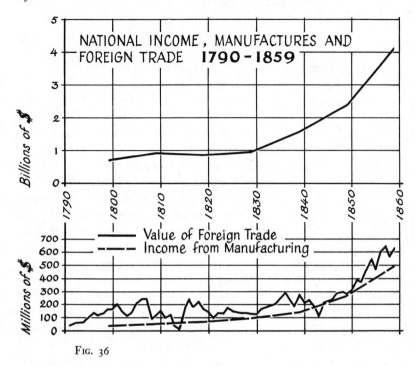

F<small>IG</small>. 36

were re-exports, an amount not to be equalled thereafter by United States re-exports until 1916, i.e., at the time of World War I.[29] The remarkable explosion of American maritime trade so soon after independence, and despite British predominance on the ocean, was fostered by the political circumstances resulting from the wars of the French Revolution and Empire. From 1792 to 1815, during most of which time France dominated the European continent, she and Britain remained almost constantly at war, trying to blockade one another. Through most of the period, and especially from 1793 to 1807, Americans had the opportunity offered by neutrality, in addition to their good position on the Atlantic and their long tradition of triangular trade with or without the official blessing of London or Paris.

After 1793 the great Northeastern seaports knew

a tremendous maritime boom. This boom was created chiefly by the opportunities in trade for neutral vessels where belligerents dared not sail. Such voyages risked seizures and other complications, but until the end of 1807 neutrality meant increased prosperity . . . Most important . . . was the recovery of

[29] U. S. Bureau of the Census, *Historical Statistics of the United States, 1789–1945,* Washington, D. C., 1949.

the profitable long haul of West Indian sugar across the Atlantic . . . England interfered and started to restrict the trade altogether, but finally winked at the subterfuge of breaking the voyage at some American port . . . Our trade statistics became suddenly inflated by the entry and quick withdrawal of hundreds of such cargoes, in which we had only a fleeting but very profitable interest . . . Good profits came from the freight money in "tramp" voyages between foreign ports where it was not safe for belligerents to enter . . . There was also steady business in the shuttle between America and England, while the number of vessels on the run to the Far East increased.[30]

The boom actually continued until 1807, as witnessed by shipping and customs statistics. It was then restricted to smaller proportions and became subject to irregular ups and downs, as the political picture evolved in Europe on the one hand and in British-American relations on the other. To avoid further trouble on the seas, President Jefferson imposed the Embargo of 1807 and asked for nonintercourse. Then the War of 1812 brought the British to the Northeastern seaboard and made it for a while unsafe for American vessels to trade even in Long Island Sound. When peace was restored, Napoleon had been defeated in Europe and all the European powers were returning to conditions of normal trade, which considerably limited American opportunities on the seas.

However, the exceptional period of 1793–1807 had brought notable profits and capital to the seaboard cities. National wealth grew from $1,150 million in 1790 to $2,518 million in 1807. This was a substantial rise but less rapid than the simultaneous growth of the merchant marine, which tripled, and of foreign trade, which expanded 3.5 times. Reduced to very little by the war with the British, foreign trade resumed its upward trend in 1815, reaching $229 million in 1816 (of which only $17 million were re-exports). The merchant marine, brought down to 1,159,000 gross tons in 1814, resumed a slower growth from 1815 on. The tonnage used in foreign trade had reached the period's peak of 981,000 in 1810, had lost one third by 1814 (674,000), and came back to about 800,000 gross tons by 1816–17, after which it fell again below 600,000.[31] The peak foreign-trade tonnage (981,000) was not reached again until 1847, when the Northeastern seaboard was engaged in another maritime boom.

Thus the United States went out to sea on a grand scale in the period that followed the Revolutionary War and that ended shortly after Waterloo. Some of the growth achieved during this boom in the volume of trade and shipping was retained afterward. That great adventure

[30] Robert G. Albion, "Foreign Trade in the Era of Wooden Ships," in *The Growth of the American Economy, op. cit.*, p. 159.
[31] *Historical Statistics of the United States, 1789–1945, op. cit.*

brought substantial gains for a generation, particularly to the Northeastern seaboard and its urban centers.

This same period was illustrated in American politics by the famous debate between Thomas Jefferson and Alexander Hamilton on general economic policy. Jefferson, representing an agrarian South, had had a close view of the Tory predominance in Norfolk, the only notable city in Virginia during the Revolution. He distrusted the mercantile interests of the large Northeastern cities and did not favor industrialization and urbanization for the United States, for in Paris, during the French Revolution, he had seen how city mobs can behave once they are excited by political demagogues. He disliked, and rightly so, the first social results of the Industrial Revolution in the larger European cities he had visited. His famous phrase, "Let our workshops remain in Europe," may remind one of Plato's *Laws*, in which the Athenian philosopher, mindful of the effect of mercantile interests and crowds of seamen on his city's politics, wanted his ideal republic isolated on an island and at a distance from the seashore; according to Plato's theory, matters of foreign relations and sea trade should be attended to by a small number of expert public servants. Jefferson's ideal for America was almost Platonic in this respect, and he opposed Hamilton's ideas stressing the need for the young Republic to develop trade and manufactures.

In the period of great maritime expansion from 1793 to 1807, the Northeastern cities were led by people who approved Hamilton's policy and ideas. Hamilton had been one of the founders and a director of the first bank established in New York City in 1784.[32]

But the population of the rural areas and the Southern planters distrusted and opposed these policies, from which they did not directly benefit. Jefferson was wary of the political entanglements into which the maritime ventures could lead. He tried to limit these effects but could not prevent the War of 1812. The re-establishment of peace on the continent of Europe and on the Atlantic Ocean by 1815 opened up a new historical period, and the pendulum of American economic activities and policies swung back inland.

From the Wharf to the Waterfall and the West

Although maritime activities and foreign trade showed progress for a few years after 1815, such trends resulted mainly from the reconstruction necessary after the disruption wrought by the War of 1812–14. While

[32] Allan Nevins, *History of the Bank of New York and Trust Company, 1784–1934*, privately printed, New York, 1934.

America was returning to "normalcy," so were the economies of the European powers and overseas relations. As a result, the era of quick and large profits for American ships on the Atlantic was closed for a time. Meanwhile the United States had grown in population (9.6 million people in 1820) and resources. Many more people had established themselves farther west and southwest on lands opened since 1783. However, the return to "normalcy" in foreign economic conditions brought about some shrinkage of transportation activity (especially on the sea) and of export markets for most agricultural commodities. In 1819 the realized private production income from agriculture was lower than it had been in 1809 ($294 million as opposed to $306 million), despite a population increase of 30 per cent in that decennial period. The proceeds from transportation showed a sharper decline ($176 million instead of $236 million), and so did the construction industry, which reflected slower expansion of urban centers (since rural construction at the time was largely a "do-it-yourself" proposition on farms and plantations). However, in 1819 manufacturing income scored an advance of about 17 per cent over 1809.[33]

The years 1815–30 are sometimes remembered in New England as the period when attention "shifted from the wharf to the waterfall," from maritime enterprise to inland development and from foreign trade to local manufacturing. The trend was not limited to New England. As the "right people" in the large Northeastern cities turned their main attention and interest toward the development of the rural areas of the continent, the old division between the Federalist and Republican (or Whig) parties faded away. In the "era of good feeling" a predominantly Republican Congress adopted economic policies embodying the main ideas of Hamilton's report on manufactures. A protective tariff was passed in 1816. The collapse of agricultural prices inland and the fear of the dumping of European manufactures on the American market united the country, and from 1816 to the 1830's both manufactures and the movement for their protection grew steadily. In a famous speech in March 1824, Henry Clay offered his "American System": to give the United States both prosperity and economic independence from Europe, the development of large industrial cities was necessary; they would supply the country with manufactures and the farmers with a consuming market for their produce.[34] By this time even Jefferson had abandoned his opposition to manufactures and urban growth and accepted them as an inevitable necessity in the

---

[33] Data in this paragraph are from *Historical Statistics of the United States, 1789–1945, op. cit.,* Part A.

[34] Faulkner, *American Economic History, op. cit.,* pp. 169–173.

growth of the nation. In 1785 he had written: "The mobs of great cities add just as much to the support of pure government as sores do to the strength of the human body." [35] In 1816, however, he admitted that "experience has taught me that manufactures are now as necessary to our independence as to our comfort." [36] The cities Jefferson thus accepted for his country seemed then destined to become more industrial than commercial, which to him seemed to limit the threat of the mercantile interests as an influence on foreign policy.

As manufactures were then favored, they naturally developed in or around the large Northeastern cities, where there was enough capital to finance them. The steady flow of abundant and cheap immigrant labor and the proximity to the consuming markets of the most densely settled and developed section of the country combined to foster the growth of the factories. Whether established on the waterfalls of the southern New England Piedmont or right in the older seaboard towns, manufacturing plants mushroomed in Massachusetts, Connecticut, and Rhode Island, financed largely by capital previously accumulated on the seas or wharves. In the 1810's and 1820's the Industrial Revolution was far enough advanced in Europe, and especially in England, to supply the Northeastern interests with the mechanized equipment necessary for a rapid start.

Thus during the first quarter of the nineteenth century Boston merchants organized manufacturing companies that built the factory towns of Waltham and Lowell where cotton cloth was made. Then Fall River, Providence, and Pawtucket joined the list of the textile towns. Textile mills multiplied also in Paterson, New Jersey, and in the suburbs of Philadelphia. New Haven, Berlin, and Middletown, Connecticut, made guns and pistols. In 1832 the Baldwin Locomotive plant was founded in Philadelphia. The Northeastern seaboard had much the largest concentration of manufacturing industries by 1840. Some diversified plants had scattered in the South (in Virginia and the Carolina Piedmont), in the Mohawk Valley, and beyond the Appalachians in western Pennsylvania and the Ohio Valley, but there was nowhere a concentration similar to what had already developed in Massachusetts and Connecticut or around Philadelphia.

These manufactures were still rather small factories and greatly dependent on the commercial organization that financed them locally, supplied them with raw materials, and marketed the goods produced. To function well, this commercial organization needed good transportation and efficient banking. Philadelphia, New York, and Boston, with their large groupings of experienced merchants, early became active money lenders to other towns and regions. After 1820 most of the American shipping was owned in New York and New England. Bankers of the large cities had enough capital and skill in money management to weather many storms. As they had successfully invested before 1815 in shipping, shipbuilding, and overseas trade, they saw in the 1820's the profits that could be obtained in financing better transportation between the newly developing Western areas and their cities.

In fact, an actual race was then started between New York, Philadelphia, and Baltimore for the trade with the trans-Appalachian regions. The seaboard South could communicate with the great Northeastern ports by coastwise navigation; but the regions along the Ohio River, the upper Mississippi, and the Great Lakes might well have looked downstream toward New Orleans if adequate waterway links had not been provided with the Northeastern seaboard. In Baltimore and Washington the idea of a canal linking Chesapeake Bay with the Ohio Valley via the Potomac Valley and the Cumberland Gap was advanced first by the Patowmack Company, presided over by George Washington himself. In the 1820's work on the canal was pushed, but it was already too late. In 1825 New York triumphantly inaugurated the Erie Canal, begun in 1817 and linking Buffalo, on Lake Erie, with the Hudson River at Albany by way of the Mohawk Valley. Another canal was constructed from Albany northward to Lake Champlain. Thus New York had completed a system of waterways putting to good use its strategic "Y" which, since the seventeenth century, had been expected to give it a favored position in the northwestern trade.

Most economic historians have recognized the Erie Canal as the major factor in New York's rise to supremacy in the Northeast. Reaching Lake Erie, it outflanked Niagara Falls and established a continuous water transportation route from as far as Lake Michigan to New York harbor, at a time when water transportation was much less expensive than wagon-borne traffic. But the vicinity of the Great Lakes was not then as well developed as was the Ohio Valley. In 1826 Philadelphia started building a canal system to Pittsburgh and the Ohio. The higher ranges of the Appalachians required a portage, however, for which a special rail link was devised. That canal opened in 1834, but its operation proved to be more cumbersome and expensive than that of the Erie Canal, and by 1844 the latter carried almost five times as much freight as the Pennsylvania Main

Line canal. As for Baltimore, its merchants preferred to push the Baltimore and Ohio Railroad in the 1830's and "in 1850 the Chesapeake and Ohio Canal staggered into Cumberland on the upper Potomac eight years behind the railroad." [37]

The canal race, first act of a century of competition in connection with the West, had thus been won by New York, which had established its primacy as a seaport and transportation hub. A similar race in railroad construction formed the second act. When the first steam trains began rolling in England around 1830, Americans were quickly convinced of the superiority of this means of transportation, which was so fast (more than 25 miles an hour!), would not freeze in winter, and could span hills and plains alike. The Atlantic Northeast once again went ahead rapidly with the new development. By 1840 there were 2,818 miles of railroad in the United States, 1,566 of which were in the Middle Atlantic States, 517 in New England, and 522 in the Southeast. From Boston trains began to roll to Worcester in 1835 and as far as to Albany in 1841. In contrast, the Baltimore and Ohio Railroad, chartered in 1827, did not reach Wheeling on the Ohio until 1852. The New York and Erie had reached Dunkirk on Lake Erie in 1851. The New York Central was organized in 1852 by merger of several small railroads operating between Albany and Buffalo. In the race to the West Philadelphia, despite its great past, had been falling behind New York.

In the 1830's the South had won the battle of the tariffs, forcing some reduction in the high tariffs that had favored the manufacturing Northeast. But at the same time the financial crises of the Jackson era enabled New York to strengthen its lead as a money market. The banks in Manhattan, having more capital and skill than any others in the country, united to deal with the crisis. As a result, New York recovered from the panic of 1837 more quickly than Philadelphia and the South, and thus it won the race for leadership in banking as well as in transportation. From that time on New York remained practically unchallenged as the country's leading seaport and money market, and when the "roaring forties" opened the whole Northeastern seaboard, led by New York, had established itself strongly as the dominant influence in the development of the West. So great was its dominance that it was able to take full advantage of the nation's growth as it turned once more toward foreign trade and maritime expansion.

---

[37] Kirkland, *A History of American Economic Life, op. cit.*, p. 237. See also Chester W. Wright, *Economic History of the United States,* McGraw-Hill Book Co., New York, 1941, Chapter 19.

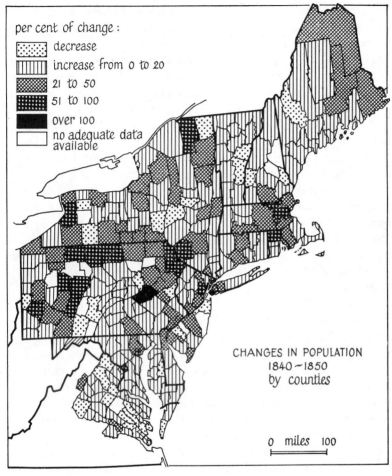

per cent of change :
    decrease
    increase from 0 to 20
    21 to 50
    51 to 100
    over 100
    no adequate data available

CHANGES IN POPULATION
1840–1850
by counties

0   miles   100

Fig. 37

The Worldwide Expansion at Mid-Century: 1840–60

The 1840's saw a new era of prosperity open both in Europe and America. The liberalization of foreign trade in England and in France coincided with a lowering of American tariffs. The United States increased the volume of its exports of grain, flour, tobacco, and cotton, and even of manufactured goods, sending these products both to rapidly industrializing European markets and to the developing Latin American countries. Exports of industrial raw materials amounted to $36 million in 1830, $75 million in 1840, $124 million in 1851, and $217 million in 1860; exports of foodstuffs, crude or processed, rose from $12 million in 1830 to $20 million in 1840, $25 million in 1851, and $51 million in 1860. The expanding United States, growing in population from 17 million in 1840 to 31 million in 1860, increased its imports as well. From 1843 to 1860 total foreign trade rose more rapidly than either the income from manufacturing or the total national income, though both these latter indices went up more steeply in that period than earlier in the century (see graphs, Fig. 36).

The urban centers on the Northeastern seaboard continued, of course, to finance a great deal of the inland development and of the upbuilding of the Western areas; and it was the swelling national market that bought most of the manufactures produced in ever growing quantities and variety in the seaboard area. But after the repeal of the Corn Laws in Britain in 1847 and the European revolutions of 1848, more attention was paid once again to maritime and overseas enterprises. In 1842 the American merchant marine engaged in foreign trade regained a tonnage comparable to that of 1815–17; in 1847, with 1,047,000 gross tons, it surpassed the previous record of 1810, and in the years 1855–60 it increased to 2.3–2.4 million gross tons.

At that time Boston, New York, Philadelphia, and Baltimore felt as if they were "ports of the world." The "golden age" of the extreme "clippers," the fastest sailing ships ever built, started around 1850, bringing a special glory to sailing vessels just before they surrendered the sea lanes to steamers. Baltimore had built the first clippers in the 1790's, streamlined, speedy schooners that were able to dodge foreign patrols at sea and easy to maneuver when approaching the land. The development of the China trade after 1845 and the gold rush to California in the 1850's called for larger, faster clippers. In 1847 Donald McKay built the famous *Ocean Queen*, of 1,300 tons, and many extreme clippers followed. In 1851 the specially built 100-foot schooner *America* won the yacht race around the Isle of Wight, starting the sailing classic known as the America's Cup races. Shipbuilding prospered as never before, with over 200,000 tons launched annually from 1848 to 1857 and up to 505,000 tons in 1855, and about 80 per cent of the national seagoing total was built in New England.

The waterborne foreign commerce that went through the port of New York was valued at $108 million in 1841, $197 million in 1851, and $393 million in 1860; in the latter year that port alone handled more than half the total foreign trade of the United States. The other ports trailed but with respectable amounts: Boston accounted for $31 million in 1841 and $58 million in 1860; Philadelphia handled $15 million in 1841 and $19 mil-

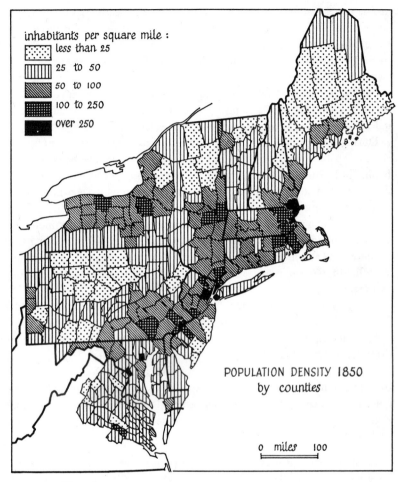

Fig. 38

lion in 1860; Baltimore $10 million and $18 million in the same years. The only other important seaports at that time were New Orleans and Mobile ($129 million and $40 million respectively in 1860). This trade went all over the world. The most important countries in these exchanges were, in order of importance, Britain, France, Cuba, Germany, Brazil, Canada, and China. In addition, both New York and Boston had very active sailing routes around South America and to the Mediterranean; and interests in the Far East were growing, for in 1854 an American naval squadron under Commodore M. C. Perry "opened Japan up" to foreign trade.

The American interests in the Pacific had been greatly expanded by the acquisition of California in 1846 and Oregon in 1848. A few years later the gold rush to California made the routes from New York and Boston to San Francisco among the most travelled of the sea lanes. Freight between the two cities went around the Horn, the long way, by fast clippers. Passengers and mail went by sea to the Isthmus of Panama, overland across it, and again by sea along the Pacific shores. In 1855 American capital built a railroad across the Isthmus to accelerate the trip.

During this period the Northeastern seaports received an unusually large influx of immigrants, swelling the harbor's traffic. The bad crops and famine in Ireland and the aftermath of revolutions in Central Europe and France helped the tide of immigration to rise. About 10,000 immigrants entered the United States in 1820, 25,000 in 1830, 92,000 in 1840, 315,000 in 1850, 180,000 in 1860. The decennial periods showed regular increases: the total immigration amounted to 599,125 in 1831–40, 1,713,251 in 1841–50, and 2,598,214 in 1851–60. The record year was 1854, when there was an influx of 460,000 immigrants, a figure not to be equalled afterward until 1873.[38]

The population of the larger cities of Megalopolis grew at a much faster pace after 1840 than before; this was especially clear for New York City, Philadelphia, Baltimore, and even Boston. After 1850 the rate of growth accelerated also for Newark and Jersey City, New Jersey, and for Worcester, Massachusetts, as well as for Chicago and Detroit. Not all of the immigrants stayed in the Northeast, and the general growth of the country was beginning to develop substantial urban centers out West (see Figs. 36 to 39), for the interior of the continent was gaining in importance within the national economy.

Down to 1850 American agricultural settlement had been limited to the forests and to the smaller prairies with scattered groves of trees by the pioneer's dependence on wood and running water. The large treeless prairies of Illinois and Iowa were devoid of shelter and remote from markets . . .

After 1850 the prairie farmer instead of the backwoodsman became the typical American pioneer.[39]

This was largely due to the mechanization of agricultural work and transportation. The McCormick family had come from northern Virginia to develop in Chicago a large-scale industry of agricultural machinery;

[38] *Historical Statistics of the United States, op. cit.*, Series B 331; and *Statistical Abstract of the United States: 1959*, U. S. Bureau of the Census, Washington, D. C., Table 109. See also Fig. 37.

[39] Morison and Commager, *The Growth of the American Republic, op. cit.*, Vol. I, p. 618.

and the railroads spread out of Chicago and the Ohio Valley to weave an expanding network through the Great Plains. In the Southern states tobacco and cotton had also moved somewhat westward, and the quantities harvested were greatly increased. Cotton production rose from 2,469,000 bales in 1849 to 5,387,000 in 1859; in the same decade tobacco went up from 200 to 434 million pounds, and wheat from 100 to 173 million bushels.[40]

The expansion of demand in the Eastern markets, swollen by population increase and the rising tide of immigration, was a major factor in this increase in production. Events in Europe helped too. Industrializing cities in western Europe imported more foodstuffs and raw materials; and in 1854–56 Britain and France found themselves at war with Russia, with the Crimean campaign cutting off European imports of grain from the Ukraine. Then prices of foodstuffs shot up — the price of wheat rose from $0.93 a bushel in 1851 to $2.50 in 1855 on the New York market, still the leading exporting port in the East — and trading in commodities futures started in Chicago at the Board of Trade.

This inland progress was to a large extent financed by Northeastern seaboard interests, especially by New York and Boston bankers; and the seaboard money markets were, of course, gathering more strength and profits as a result of the country's growth. The concentration of national credit and money management in the four large cities of Megalopolis was already obvious, and the hinge function was especially well illustrated by the flow of capital. As more banks were established all over the expanding United States, they all needed "correspondents" in the large Eastern cities, preferably New York and Boston. The concentration of funds in the principal commercial and industrial metropolises occurred for several reasons. Country banks, functioning according to the seasonal rhythm of local farming, had in certain periods surplus funds that they did not want to remain idle, while at other times they needed to borrow. A large bank with more all-year-round business, that could handle their needs most easily, was to be found only in the great seaports. Moreover, since many payments had to be made in the larger emporia for exports or imports, it was convenient to maintain balances in these places, which also gave good national standing to the notes of a small-town bank. In farming areas banks often had a lending capacity above local demand and wanted to take advantage of the better rates of larger markets, while banks in mill-towns could not keep the main balances of a local dominant firm, for the latter

[40] *Historical Statistics of the United States, op. cit.*, and Lewis Cecil Gray, *History of Agriculture in the Southern United States to 1860* (Carnegie Institution of Washington, Publication No. 430), Peter Smith, New York, 1941, Vol. II.

preferred to enjoy credit in a bank with many accounts of similar or larger size. They felt that local banks could be influenced too readily by local circumstances and by difficulties of the large local firm's treasury, while the large city banks would have enough resources to cope with such situations, unless they grew into national panics.

The commercial banks in the United States developed mainly as state-chartered institutions, under legislation often restricting a bank's activities and branches to the city or county of origin. In Louisiana banks could have branches all over the state (which greatly strengthened the five old New Orleans banks) but not beyond. These laws were aimed at preventing a single private bank from acquiring too great national influence and power. But, while limiting the concentration of funds in individual institutions to some extent, this fragmentation in fact favored concentration of money and credit in the larger commercial centers, in the great cities, and particularly in New York, which dominated foreign economic relations.

At the same time, the hubs of maritime commerce were best situated to transact banking business with overseas areas and obtain foreign funds to invest in the rapidly growing American economy. The second quarter of the nineteenth century saw much British capital invested in the United States. This flow of funds was organized, and then directed within the country, by banks in New York and Boston. At that time there arose the Anglo-American banking houses, which often took a leading part in the New York market. Almost all the American businessmen who started such business in London came from Boston, New York, Baltimore, or Philadelphia; and when the London Anglo-American houses opened branch offices on this side of the Atlantic, they were at first almost entirely in New York or Boston. As early as 1850 the main banking reserves of the United States were held in Megalopolis, especially in New York. This made the finances of the American economy more dependent on the ups and downs of foreign trade and European policies. The freezing of accounts in New York in 1857 gave to the financial panic that year a more general and more serious character than would have been the case otherwise. However, the banks in New York recovered from it most rapidly. For Pennsylvania the 1857 crisis was especially severe, and this increased the lead New York had already achieved over Philadelphia, and which it maintained for the rest of the century.[41]

[41] Harold F. Williamson, "Money and Commercial Banking, 1789–1861," and Muriel Hidy, "The Capital Markets, 1789–1869," in *The Growth of the American Economy, op. cit.*, pp. 250–302; also Chester W. Wright, *Economic History of the United States, op. cit.*, Chapters 24 and 25, pp. 416–480.

During this period not only commercial banking itself but also most of the other financial institutions important to money management grew chiefly in the four great Eastern ports, and the Federal government's financial and budgetary institutions developing in Washington. New York, Boston, and Philadelphia started the main bank clearing houses, the stock exchange boards, the savings banks, and the insurance companies. For all of these the volume of business, the size of the local population and market, and the scope of foreign relations were essential factors in locating the institutions and concentrating these types of business.

The role played by the maritime sector in the localization of Megalopolis was perhaps more decisive in 1840–60 than at any other period of American history. The legendary glitter acquired by the clipper's golden era is not merely a product of the historians' art. The growth and prosperity of the growing Megalopolis owed much to maritime activities, and in the 1850's these reached a peak not to be equalled for long afterwards. The American merchant marine, in peaceful and cordial competition, almost surpassed the British at a time when Britannia seemed to rule the waves more firmly than ever. Besides winning the America's Cup and establishing new records for circumnavigating the Americas (in 1851 the *Flying Cloud* sailed in eighty-nine days from New York's Narrows to San Francisco's Golden Gate) the clipper ships challenged the British on the run of the silk and tea trade and on the Australian routes. The *Oriental* of New York made it from Hong Kong to London in ninety-seven days, while the English-owned clipper *James Baines,* built by Donald McKay in Boston for the Australian Black Ball line, crossed from Boston to Liverpool in twelve and a quarter days and from Liverpool to Melbourne in sixty-three days. These passages long remained sailing records.

The American sea-going tonnage came close to that of the British in the early 1850's, though it was clearly outdistanced, especially in the tonnage of steamers, by 1860. This rivalry caused the British to worry lest "the Americans become the great carriers of the World," and the subject was debated in political meetings at election time. Even so, the American merchant marine was not keeping pace with the faster growth of foreign trade. Because of the emphasis on clippers and on large-scale whaling the American shipyards did not pay all the attention they deserved to the iron-built steamers increasingly used by the British and other European nations. The clipper illustrated the ardor with which the great seaboard cities looked at that time toward the sea and beyond it. Much of the money that the *hinge* area could then invest in the development of the continent was made on the sea or obtained overseas. The maritime venture still provided the best way for a newcomer to enter the restricted business-aristocracy circle then forming in Massachusetts and New York.

The Massachusetts mercantile group was apparently, during this period, pretty much of a closed corporation . . . It was not, nevertheless, impossible for a poor boy to work himself up to the position of an independent merchant, but his route would be by way of the fo'c'sle and quarter deck, and even here his chances would be considerably improved by being at least a distant and poor relative of the shipowner.[42]

These were the days of the merchant in American society. The cities of Megalopolis felt their leadership strongly established and they were preparing to make it last, despite the fast growth of the young national economy through the newly evolved network of "corporation." New York was dominating the rest of Megalopolis in many ways, and by 1860 had little rivalry to expect except perhaps for New Orleans, where another smaller hinge was taking shape between networks of strong relations expanding over the Mississippi basin on the one hand and to Mexico and the West Indies on the other. After 1860 the Civil War disrupted many of the trends that had characterized the 1850's. The internal struggle absorbed all the forces and the whole attention of the nation for a few years, after which too much had to be done in terms of reconstruction and reorganization to leave time and effort for looking toward the sea. For half a century the major attention of the whole country, including the Northeastern seaboard, turned inward.

Organizing a Vast Continent: 1861–1913

The Civil War naturally disrupted the operation of foreign maritime relations, especially for the South, blockaded by the Federal naval forces. The volume of foreign trade declined, owing to the blockade and devastation of the Confederacy (see Fig. 39). The tonnage of the merchant marine also dropped in the 1860's, and the greater part of the United States' imports and exports was carried under foreign flags. This was partly because a number of vessels were sold by American shipowners to aliens, who could then enjoy the advantages of neutrality in all American seaports. In 1862–65 these sales reached a total of 875,000 net tons,[43] plus probably some 300,000 to 400,000 more sold by Confederate shipowners,

---

[42] Kenneth W. Porter, *The Jacksons and the Lees*, Harvard University Press, Cambridge, Mass., 1937, Vol. I; quoted by Thomas C. Cochran, "Business Organization and the Development of an Industrial Discipline," pp. 303–318 in *The Growth of the American Economy, op. cit.* (see p. 304).

[43] *Historical Statistics of the United States, op. cit.,* Series K 115.

by far the highest four-year figure of American vessels transferred to other flags until the 1920's.

Manufacturing increased, especially in the Northeast, to supply the Union armies. But the principal effect of the Civil War on the growth of Megalopolis was to hand over to the large Northeastern cities the task of directing and financing the South's reconstruction after the North's victory. Without that victory the story of the continent's economy might have been different. As it was, the managerial function of Megalopolis was confirmed over the whole nation on the eve of a new westward expansion. For the years 1870–1900 were the great years of settlement and development of the West, between the Mississippi and the Pacific. As S. E. Morison has observed:

After Appomattox, national expansion and the protective tariff killed or atrophied many lines of commerce in which Massachusetts merchants had specialized; and the transatlantic cable made merchants, in the old sense, anachronisms. . . . The era of tramp steamers and four or five per cent profit had little attraction for merchants who could gain six to ten per cent by exploiting the great West. Many an old shipowner's ledger, that begins with tea and indigo and sixteenth shares of the ship *Canton Packet* and brig *Owhyhee*, ends up by recording large blocks of C. B. & Q., and Calumet & Hecla.[44]

During this period of expansion the railroads served as the major tool for the organization of the wide open spaces. They followed closely on the heels of the pioneers in covered wagons, at least along the main routes. In 1869 the first transcontinental railroad was completed, and the total mileage of railroads in operation rose from 35,085 in 1865 to 52,922 in 1870, 93,262 in 1880, and 166,700 in 1890. The movement of freight by rail went up from 39 billion ton-miles in 1882 to 79 billion in 1890, while the number of passenger-miles went from 7.6 to 12.2 billion. The railroads engaged also in various businesses connected with developing the lands they had been granted along the lines they built. The total capital and property investment of the railroads was valued at $1,172 million in 1867, some $5.4 billion in 1880, and $10.1 billion in 1890.[45] In this period the railroads were the most important sector of the national business. Their stocks and bonds continued until World War I to play a leading part on the stock exchanges, especially in New York, where most of this industry was financed. In the 1890's and early 1900's some of the most famous battles

---

[44] Morison, *The Maritime History of Massachusetts, op. cit.*, p. 370.
[45] *Historical Statistics of the United States, op. cit.*, Series K 19, K 1 to K 15.

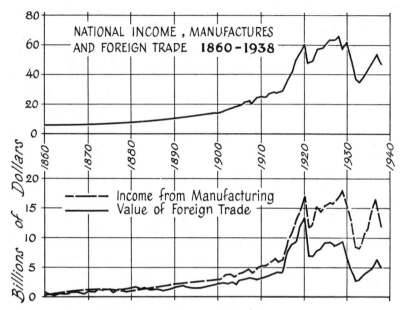

FIG. 39. The data apply to the United States as a whole.

between the Wall Street empire builders were fought over the control of major railroads of the West or even of the East. (See Fig. 205, p. 649.)

From the middle of the century, each of the leading Northeastern cities had its railroad leading west, and the competition between these roads to attract freight and passengers from inland areas reflected the rivalry that existed also between the seaports. Boston, New York, Philadelphia, and Baltimore vied for the freight to and from the West and the South, and for transporting it the railroads competed with waterways (i.e., canals and coastwise navigation). To New York, bulk shipments from the Lakes could come via the Erie Canal or by the New York Central or Erie Railroads. In 1865 the canal carried to the great city 844 million ton-miles, the New York Central 265 million, and the Erie Railroad 388 million. In 1872 about 85 per cent of the freight carried between New York and Philadelphia went by water. Then the major Northeastern railroads engaged in rate warfare to attract more customers. The Baltimore and Ohio, the Pennsylvania, and the New York Central fought bitterly in the 1870's and early 1880's, greatly lowering the cost of transportation from the cities of Megalopolis inland. Thus the rates from Chicago to New York per 100 pounds of grain went down from sixty cents in 1873 to forty cents in 1874 and thirty cents in 1875. Baltimore and Philadelphia tried to undersell New York, offering a rate as low as twenty cents in May 1876. In that year a carload of cattle could be moved from Chicago to New York for one dollar. The Baltimore and Ohio and the Erie lines were soon on the road to bankruptcy, but they continued to fight valiantly. In 1876 passenger fares from Cleveland to Boston were down to $6.50 and a little later immigrants were carried from New York to Chicago for a dollar a head.

These rate wars readjusted the shares of each of the major seaports in the total foreign trade and passenger traffic. The Northeastern seaports gained a good deal from the Southern ports. The post-Civil War attempt of New Orleans to resume an important role owing to its location near the mouth of the Mississippi was easily frustrated as rail transportation to the Northeast became so cheap. Traffic suffered on the Mississippi River and even on the Erie Canal. Philadelphia's quota in the nation's exports rose from 11 per cent in 1860 to twenty per cent in 1880.[46] There could be no doubt that the rail rate wars consolidated Megalopolis' function as the continent's commercial hinge and extended its great cities' influence westward. This would not have happened, of course, had there not been five great seaport cities on this seaboard to compete early in building each its own railroad and in encouraging rivalry between these; and it was all facilitated by capital locally accumulated through foreign trade and maritime ventures.

In the financing and control of the railroads the bankers in Megalopolis found their location convenient, for they could make up on the foreign-trade end of the haul some of the losses occasionally caused by the too rash competition between lines. They also succeeded in channelling a substantial amount of foreign capital into American railroad investment.

In 1907 over $6,000,000,000 of railroad stocks and bonds were held abroad, representing one-fourth of the entire value of the roads at that time. Of this amount Great Britain owned $4,000,000,000 and Germany one. In 1914 the *Wall Street Journal* estimated $3,400,000,000 worth of bonds, one-third of the outstanding railroad mortgage indebtedness, as held abroad.[47]

After several scandals and much corruption, the railroads were attacked by the "Granger movement," originating in the farming areas of the Middle West. From 1887 on, Federal regulation was increasingly applied to the railroads, and these regulations had to take into consideration the varia-

---

[46] William Z. Ripley, *Railroads; Rates and Regulation*, Longmans, Green, & Company, New York, 1912, Vol. II, "Finances and Organization." Also Faulkner, *American Economic History, op. cit.*, pp. 486–501.

[47] Faulkner, *op. cit.*, p. 492.

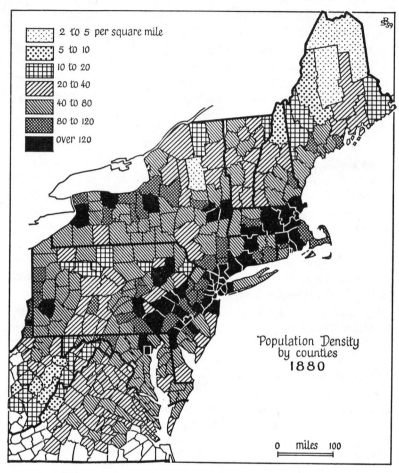

2 to 5 per square mile
5 to 10
10 to 20
20 to 40
40 to 80
80 to 120
over 120

Population Density
by counties
1880

0   miles   100

FIG. 40

tion in rates from section to section. Just as in the beginning of the century the Southeast complained of being harmed by the tariffs, so it claimed from the 1890's on that it was discriminated against by the railroad rates, which were lower in the Northeast. Federal regulation could not have been expected to reverse arbitrarily the situation it found, which resulted from a long inheritance, fierce fights, and the layout of the rail network.

The density of the rail network in the Northeast and its orientation toward the major seaboard hubs were not to be explained simply by historical roots. Besides its function for export and import the Northeastern seaboard was the major consuming market in the nation. It was the most

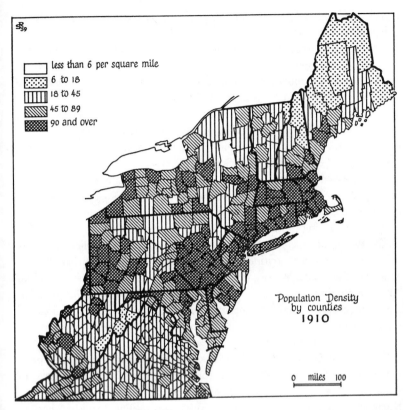

less than 6 per square mile
6 to 18
18 to 45
45 to 89
90 and over

Population Density
by counties
1910

0   miles   100

FIG. 41

densely populated sector (see Figs. 40 and 41), and the most heavily industrialized in 1880 as well as in 1910. However, by 1910 the westward march
of settlement and industrialization had substantially reduced the centralization of manufacturing in the region of Megalopolis. The bulk of the
heavy industries, developed on or near coal and iron deposits, were located
beyond the Appalachians, between the Ohio Valley and the Great Lakes.
Some southward migration of lighter industries had begun. But the Northeast still had the greatest concentration of people, of purchasing power,
and of diversified manufacturing among areas of similar size in the United
States. And when foreign trade was added to the needs of the regional
market, Megalopolis was logically the greatest hub of transportation and
communications in North America.

Still the rate of growth in this area from 1880 to 1910 was not comparable to that of the northern industrial Midwest. Many cities there,

especially Chicago, Pittsburgh, and Cleveland, seemed to be taking on some independence as sectional metropolises. As Frederick Jackson Turner began proclaiming that the age of the frontier was over, in the 1890's,[48] it looked as if the central position of Chicago and the steady growth of the Great Plains in population and wealth would take away the leadership from Megalopolis and transfer it to the heart of the continent. At that time it became popular to contend that New York was not really America, while Chicago certainly was. Canada, just across the Lakes and the Prairie boundary, was also growing rapidly in importance, both as a customer and as a supplier of the United States.

As the twentieth century opened, America was already pretty well urbanized. A. M. Schlesinger saw the growth of cities as the principal characteristic and driving force of the period 1878–98.[49] In an America that was becoming "a nation of cities" the present Megalopolis was certainly the greatest concentration of urban groupings. Earlier than any other region on the continent it had become essentially urban. It had achieved this status mainly by continuing to serve as "the gates" of America for immigrants and foreign trade, as America's major base for maritime ventures, and as America's principal commercial and financial hub, either for overseas relations or inland development — in short, by carrying on all the functions of the *hinge*.

This role of *hinge* was confirmed by the Northeastern seaboard's prosperity in the first years of this century, when the center of gravity of American economic activities was still turned inland, although some signs began to point again to increasing interests abroad. The Spanish-American War had given to the United States new responsibilities and interests in Puerto Rico and the Philippines, as well as in Cuba and the Caribbean area generally; Theodore Roosevelt's policies expanded the American stakes in Latin America; and the United States acted as mediator at international conferences dealing with distant disputes, such as the signing of the Portsmouth Treaty ending the Russian-Japanese conflict (1905) and the Algeciras Conference on Morocco (1906). Having become the leading world

[48] F. J. Turner in his famous essay on "The Significance of the Frontier in American History," in *Annual Report of the American Historical Association for 1893*, Washington, D. C., 1894 (see especially pp. 219–220), thought that the middle region of the Eastern seaboard before 1860, between the South and New England, was "typical of the modern United States." He saw "it was an open door to all Europe" and "it became the typically American region," bearing closer resemblance to the frontier than the other sections. But as the West developed after 1860 it became the real center of the nation.

[49] Arthur Meier Schlesinger, *The Rise of the City, 1878–1898* (*A History of American Life*, Vol. X), The Macmillan Company, New York, 1933.

producer and exporter of essential foodstuffs and many industrial raw materials, as well as a great importer of numerous other commodities, the United States could not remain disinterested in what happened in the major foreign markets for these various goods. The income realized in the country from manufacturing had become about equal to the income from agriculture in the period 1901–11; it surpassed it definitely from 1912 on. An equally important evidence of the predominance of urban pursuits was the fact that in every year after 1880 the income from trade, transportation, and service together was far above that from either manufacturing or agriculture.[50]

Although around 1910 the United States seemed close to economic self-sufficiency, it was a rapidly rising international power in terms of industry and commerce. The prosperity of its agriculture needed large exports, the markets for which were mainly in Europe. The half century of internal growth and development was brutally interrupted in 1914 by the start of World War I in Europe, and the Middle West then felt little interested in these transatlantic events; but Megalopolis, already responsible for the national economy, knew at once the powerful impact such events would have on American destiny. And the pendulum of the nation's economic activities swung outward again in decisive fashion.

To the Ends of the Earth

If some future historian, interested in the successive swings of the pendulum revolving on this *hinge*, ever scrutinizes its movements from 1914 to 1960, he may find it useful to distinguish three periods within these years. Each of the two World Wars drew the United States out to participate more actively than ever in the affairs of the outside world. And each time, for a few years after peace was restored, the United States was the only power able to fulfill the needs of the other former belligerents, who had to replenish their resources, temporarily exhausted or destroyed by warfare. In between these two periods of war and reconstruction, the years 1925–38 could be construed as a third period, in which internal economic preoccupations dominated the American scene.

The great prosperity of the late 1920's and the depression following it in the 1930's were not, however, exclusively or even specifically American phenomena, though the contrast they caused achieved its greatest amplitude in the United States. They belonged to an international cycle, which, despite a number of regional variations, brought about more economic nationalism and self-protecting measures in every important country on our

[50] *Historical Statistics of the United States, op. cit.,* Series A 154–163.

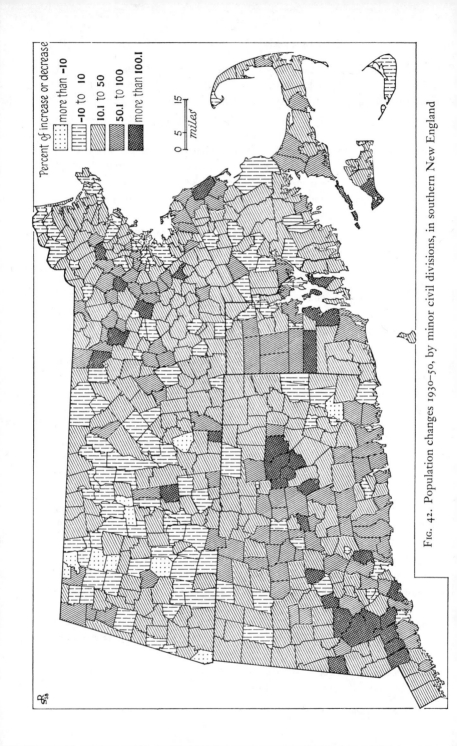

Percent of increase or decrease

more than -10
-10 to 10
10.1 to 50
50.1 to 100
more than 100.1

0   5   15
     miles

Fɪɢ. 42. Population changes 1930–50, by minor civil divisions, in southern New England

globe. In the very broad lines of this historical sketch it could thus be considered that the recent period, from 1914 until the 1950's, has been an epoch of outward accent in the American economy. After 1914 the economic system of the United States became in many ways more fully self-sufficient. Manufacturing industries proliferated on a huge scale, to supply the needs not only of the expanding national market but also of foreign customers; and the heavy foreign indebtedness was liquidated as a result of Europe's expenditures in America during World War I. The stupendous growth of American consumption, reflecting the rise of both population and standard of living, built up a production and financing machine so much bigger than any other national system that for a while it dominated the international economy as a whole. Such economic autonomy did not spell isolation, however. After 1920, New York became the world's banker, very much to the same extent that London and Paris had been in 1880–1910. There was some need of exporting to foreign markets, and interests abroad grew with international financing activities.

All these forces involved the United States as a senior partner in international economic and political affairs. The scope of the opportunity as well as the burden of the responsibilities incurred made it increasingly difficult for the American economy to turn essentially inward. The share of foreign trade in the national economy rose from 1915 to 1920, and the national income increased at the same time. Then the value of foreign trade stayed relatively low in the 1920's and 1930's, while the income from manufactures, though oscillating, remained quite high (see Fig. 39). But by that time the balance of foreign payments had become a more important source of profits than the export-import relationship could indicate. In 1938 the total value of foreign trade came up to about $5 billion, while the gross national product stood at $84.7 billion, and the balance of the international transactions of the United States showed a net outflow in the amount of $1.7 billion of funds on gold and short-term capital accounts. Still, the income received from investments abroad amounted to $383 million, while the payments made as income on foreign investments in the United States amounted to $200 million.[51]

The World War of 1914–18 liberated the United States from the bulk of its indebtedness to European capital and made it a great creditor nation. From a net indebtedness to foreign capital of about $3.9 billion in 1908 and

[51] This, despite the depression of the 1930's, was a striking contrast with the pre-World War I situation. For the years 1896–1914 the income from foreign investments received in the United States represented $760 million, as against $3,800 million paid to foreign investors in the country. See *Historical Statistics of the United States*, *op. cit.*

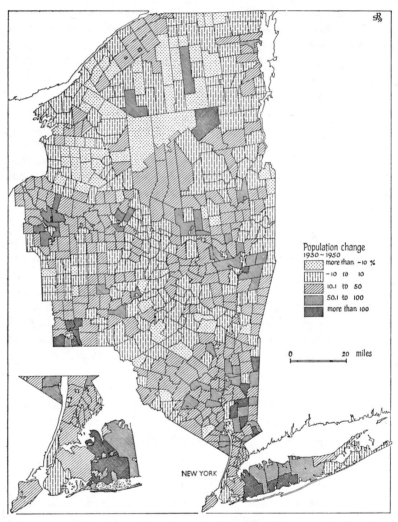

Population change
1930 – 1950

more than –10 %
–10 to 10
10.1 to 50
50.1 to 100
more than 100

0   20 miles

NEW YORK

FIG. 43. Population changes in New York State 1930–50, by minor
civil divisions

$3.7 billion in 1914, the investment balance swung to a net creditor's posi-
tion of $3.7 billion in 1919, $7 billion in 1924, and $12.1 billion in 1931.
During World War II large sums of foreign (especially western European) capital flowed to America, looking for secure and profitable investment at a time of great trouble abroad. The investment balance showed a
net indebtedness of $1.3 billion in 1940 and of $0.9 billion even in 1945, but

it had returned to a net creditor's position in 1946, rising to almost $15 billion in 1949 and more than $22 billion in 1957. In that year American investments abroad were estimated at $54 billion, and foreign investments in the United States at $31 billion.[52] The total deposits in all the member banks of the Federal Reserve System amounted then to $170 billion.

All these figures indicate a growing role in international banking. This function remains concentrated in Megalopolis, chiefly in New York City, with some decentralization toward Washington, seat of the Federal financial institutions and, since 1947, of the World Bank and International Monetary Fund. Some of these international financial activities were still located in Boston or Philadelphia in the 1950's, but to a decreasing extent. Outside Megalopolis the only place in the country with some significant international banking was San Francisco, oriented toward the Pacific area.

Megalopolis was able to rise so quickly to such eminence in the international economic system both because of its network of overseas relationships and because it kept the reins of direction of the national economy. This managerial role was not independent from the financial one and both had been built up, maintained, and reinforced through three centuries of stubborn and daring endeavor. Newcomers and well-established native people cooperated through the whole period to broaden the scope of opportunity in all directions, to "trye all ports," and to organize a system of entangled connections by sea, by land, and by air, reaching to every small town on the continent and to the ends of the earth abroad. These Megalopolitan endeavors were aided by competition between the old, early established seaboard cities, by the continent's development, and also by the course of history overseas. This same opportunity was open, however, except for the heritage of the past, to many other great cities or developing regions on other seaboards in America and elsewhere. The physical advantages locally available to Megalopolis in terms of climate, topography, and proximity to Europe were important in the early stages of American history, but they have not been of serious purport in the last hundred years, for the technology of transportation and manufacturing have reduced to very little indeed the practical influence of local physical circumstances.

By 1900 the growth of the American economy had brought about a good deal of decentralization from Megalopolis in terms of population numbers, value of manufactures produced, and volume of consumption.

[52] *Historical Statistics of the United States, op. cit.;* and *Continuation to 1952 of Historical Statistics of the United States, 1789–1945,* U. S. Bureau of the Census, Washington, 1954; and *Statistical Abstract of the United States: 1959, op. cit.*

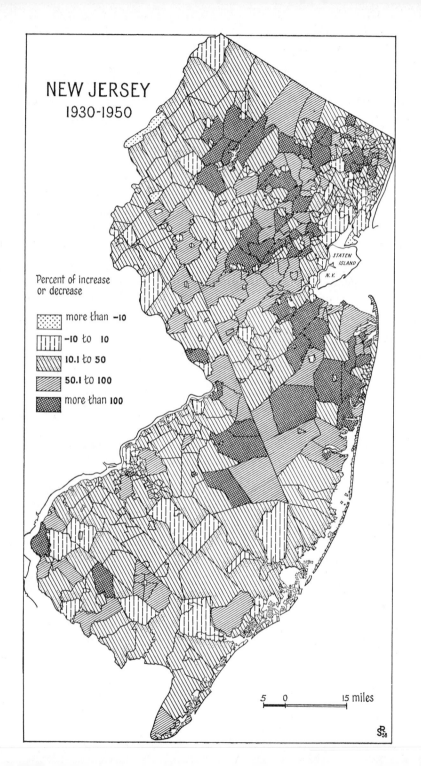

NEW JERSEY
1930-1950

Percent of increase
or decrease

more than −10
−10 to 10
10.1 to 50
50.1 to 100
more than 100

STATEN
ISLAND

N.Y.

5   0   15 miles

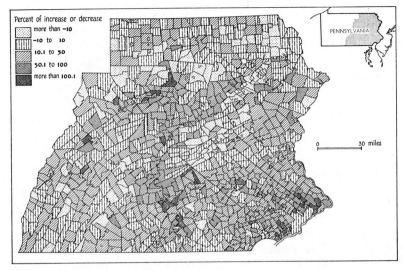

FIG. 45. Population changes in eastern Pennsylvania, 1930–50, by minor civil divisions

Just before 1914 Chicago appeared to be the rising metropolis that was destined soon to dominate the whole continent. The two World Wars, their aftermaths, and even the depression between them accelerated in various ways the trends toward a more equal distribution of employment, productive capacity, and consumption throughout the nation — that is, of economic development as a whole. But the *hinge* benefited in a certain number of new ways from the events that unfolded after 1914 and from the country's greater involvement in world affairs.

Megalopolis retained a good deal of manufacturing and services, especially those types that needed proximity to its enormous market, provided by one fifth of the nation's population and two fifths of its bank deposits. But much of the industry that had formerly been concentrated in the Northeastern seaboard area had been allowed to scatter through the country and even overseas. Megalopolitan interests even helped the scattering by financing and planning part of it. Still the area retained or developed specializations that have preserved its wealth and influence and that promote the growth of new branches of economic activity. These promise more profits, employment, and influence for the future.

International banking and credit management, with which we have al-

Opposite FIG. 44. Population changes in New Jersey, 1930–50, by minor civil divisions

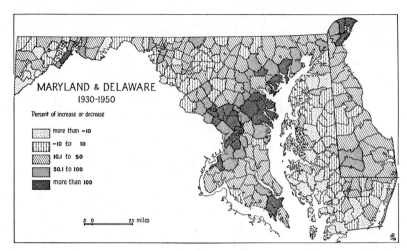

FIG. 46. Population changes in Maryland and Delaware, 1930–50, by minor civil divisions

ready dealt, furnish just one example. The main agencies of the Federal government, a source of employment that has grown rapidly since 1917 and may continue to grow for some time, are not all located in the District of Columbia, but are essentially in Megalopolis. While shipyards and aviation plants scatter, nuclear submarines are being built and based in southern New England, and the more advanced electronics industries are in good part located between New Hampshire and Virginia. Though the number and enrollment of colleges and universities are growing in every state, the cultural role of at least some of these educational institutions located in Megalopolis is still increasing its impact on the nation's life. The web of interconnections within Megalopolis, measured in terms of density of automobile and airplane traffic or of frequency of telephone calls, remains far more marked and more highly developed than in any other section of the country. (See maps in Chapters 11 and 12.) The automobile, the airplane, and the telephone may have seemed to be ideal tools for decentralizing activities away from a geographical location that had been favored by sea trade, canals, and railroads, but Megalopolis has overcome the threat to its growth.

The study of the mechanisms through which Megalopolis now functions, progresses, and protects its national and international role will take us into various problems, analyzed in the chapters to follow. In the post-1914 period the growth of the major cities has been less significant than in earlier times. More important are suburban sprawl and the redistribution of functions within Megalopolis itself. Describing the *hinge* function of the region should contribute to an understanding of the past. It may also help in assessing the foundations of the present system — its deep commercial roots and its dominant interest in coordinating the various economic processes, in America and through the world, in which Megalopolitan interests, initiative, capital, or personnel may participate. The United Nations headquarters on the East River in New York City is another symbol of the hinge's expanding function.

The present trends in the division of labor, in American involvement in international activities, in the growth of the interlacing of trades and services — all these should offer promise for Megalopolis if it remains true to its already long-standing tradition. A study of the mechanisms and oscillations of the hinge in the past naturally emphasized the system of relationships and the factors of growth linking Megalopolis with the rest of the country and the world. We shall now turn our attention from the outside relationships to conditions within the region itself, in order to comprehend better how, through successive stages, the consolidation of the whole region has been brought about.

CHAPTER 4

How the Cities Grew and the Suburbs Scattered

The story of the continent's economic hinge has revealed the successive stages of Megalopolis' efforts to become larger and wealthier, and this growth has involved the development of large *downtown* areas in the cities. They grew up from wharves, in the port cities, as well as from the market-place hubs of traffic and commercial transactions, from the centers of government and education, and from the sites of worship or recreation. Since time immemorial the city has supplied to the surrounding countryside properly serviced sites for the exchange of goods and ideas, for the administration of justice and politics, for the celebration of religious rites and other collective traditions, for education and relaxation. The crowding of people and the gathering of wealth in the cities of Megalopolis caused all these functions to be carried out on an impressive and rapidly widening scale.

So great was the pressure of all the people and all the activities seeking for a place in the cities along the seaboard or immediately back of it that the small areas first defined as "urban territory" had to be constantly expanded, and in this process of growth some of the functions originally carried on in the major cities had to be transferred elsewhere. Sometimes the shift was to new cities that would soon rival the older centers in size and prosperity (Washington grew thus as a center of government, and Baltimore as a port and industrial city). In other cases it was to suburbs, many of which were later absorbed by the legal extension of the central city's territory and some of which grew to become substantial cities in their own right, though they remained, at least in some respects, satellites of the larger metropolis from which they had sprung up. At a later stage certain categories of homes, plants, or stores that had been restricted to the well-defined bounds of urbanized districts became scattered farther away from the original nuclei, dispersed in such loose order that vast areas became *de facto* suburbs, with their population having no *raison d'être* for its existing distribution but its ties with a not-too-distant "downtown."

The process has taken on increasing complexity in the twentieth century. Urbanization in Megalopolis has covered an entire section of the country instead of being restricted to small areas within that section. "Downtown" businesses, such as department stores, warehouses, or fashionable restaurants, have scattered outside the cities, as have residences, characteristic of "uptown" city areas. Thus the urban region has acquired a nebulous, quasi-colloidal structure, with new patterns of land use. The result has been called "the exploding metropolis," a product of "the modern urban revolution." Before we analyze these new patterns, and the processes that have produced them, all of which are more advanced in Megalopolis than in any other part of the world, it is important to return once more to the history of the area. Having outlined the story of the external relations of the hinge, let us now focus on the evolution of its internal framework. The processes of city growth and suburban scattering began in Megalopolis two centuries ago, making it a *frontier* or pioneer area in these developments and an important element in American history. Reviewing its past development even briefly should help us understand the processes and complexities of this contemporary wilderness, so crowded as to make the seventeenth-century one seem empty.

Early Proliferation of Towns

Even in colonial times, along the seaboard between Portsmouth, New Hampshire, and Baltimore, Maryland, towns of some size multiplied in a fashion quite remarkable for the period. The planting of the colonial "villages" started in 1625–50. By 1690 four of them had grown to the status of respectable provincial centers, with many of the problems and conveniences then characteristic of urban life. Boston had 7,000 inhabitants, Newport 2,600, New York 3,000, and Philadelphia 4,000. In the Southern colonies, Charleston, South Carolina, counted some 1,100 people, but it was destined to remain isolated for some time as the only significant urban center south of Chesapeake Bay.

At that time, all the main urban activities in the English colonies in America were concentrated in these five towns, and, as Carl Bridenbaugh has well demonstrated,[1] they were already laying the foundations of American urban society. In the seventeenth century the four Northeastern seaports pioneered in developing commerce with both neighboring and far-away lands. They were successful market places, a function that had for ages been the privilege and the mainstay of cities in the Old World. However, even in 1700 they still did not have much countryside around them that was oriented toward them. Many of the commercial contacts of the scattered plantations and smaller villages were carried on by sea directly with England and other countries, without passing through any of the four larger ports. The eighteenth century saw both a rapid growth of the original "big four" and the scattered development along the coast of a good many other towns of respectable size.

By 1775 there were in the colonies eleven cities of more than 5,000 people each. Two of them were south of the Potomac — Charleston, South Carolina (about 14,000 inhabitants), and Norfolk, Virginia (about 6,000). The other nine were strung out from Massachusetts to Maryland — Boston (16,000) and Salem (5,300) in Massachusetts; Newport, Rhode Island (about 11,000; see Fig. 33, p. 129); New Haven (8,300), Norwich (7,300), and New London (6,000) in Connecticut; New York City (25,000); Philadelphia (40,000); Baltimore (6,000). In Connecticut and Massachusetts there were also eight townships with about 5,000 people. The area of these townships was large enough to hold several agglomerations of residences or one main town and a scattering of farmsteads, which would not qualify it for the category of "cities with more than 5,000 inhabitants." The number of such agglomerations testifies, however, to a density of population and of agglomerated nuclei suggesting the predominance of a rather generally well-grouped mode of settlement.[2]

---

[1] In his *Cities in the Wilderness: The First Century of Urban Life in America, 1625–1742*, 2nd edition, Alfred A. Knopf, New York, 1955.

[2] The figures above are mainly from Evarts B. Greene and Virginia D. Harring-

New England had some good reasons, stemming from its earliest social organization and evolution, to have many urban nuclei, most of them of rather small size. The founding fathers of Massachusetts did not authorize settlers to claim land and settle by themselves, in dispersal, as was done in Virginia. New settlement had to be authorized and to proceed by groups of four families or more, and each group had to secure the regular services of a parson and a teacher, a measure intended to provide for good religious behavior of the community and proper education of the children. These strict rules were, of course, not always followed. As early as 1700 the Puritan Commonwealth was bemoaning the license of individuals who took it upon themselves to break away from towns and rules and go alone into the wilderness to settle in isolation and greater freedom.[3]

There were many good reasons in colonial times for requiring such group settlements. First, Puritan society was based on the general concept of people living in communities, not as isolated and dispersed individuals. Religion could not be adequately practiced by isolated individuals or families; its regular observance required communities. Second, the strategy and economy of settlement fared better with larger numbers in towns. It was easier to police the place and defend it, and educational costs were less burdensome as more families shared them. Moreover, the common pasture was a help to the small farmer, and perpetuated a tradition brought over from England, to which the settlers were all the more attached since many of them had suffered because of the breaking up of the common lands in England during the "enclosures" trend of the seventeenth and eighteenth centuries. Last but not least, the system of town proprietors, generally applied throughout New England, gave higher profits and better expectations to those with vested interests, whether their holdings were as extensive as the grant of Sir James Hamilton, lord proprietary of the Narragansett country, or a smaller tract of land, usually a township, held

ton, *American Population before the Federal Census of 1790*, Columbia University Press, New York, 1932, and the older U. S. Bureau of the Census, *A Century of Population Growth in the United States, 1790–1900*, Washington, D. C., 1909. See also the maps by Herman R. Friis, Figs. 26a to 26e, pp. 114–115, and Carl Brindenbaugh, *Cities in Revolt: Urban Life in America, 1743–1776*, Alfred A. Knopf, New York, 1955, tables on pp. 216–217; the latter source estimates that twenty cities in the colonies had definitely more than 3,000 inhabitants and an urban way of life on the eve of the Revolution; only three of these twenty were south of the present area of Megalopolis: Norfolk, Charleston, and Savannah.

[3] Roy Hidemichi Akagi, *The Town Proprietors of the New England Colonies: A Study of Their Development, Organization, Activities and Controversies, 1620–1770*, Press of the University of Pennsylvania, Philadelphia, 1924.

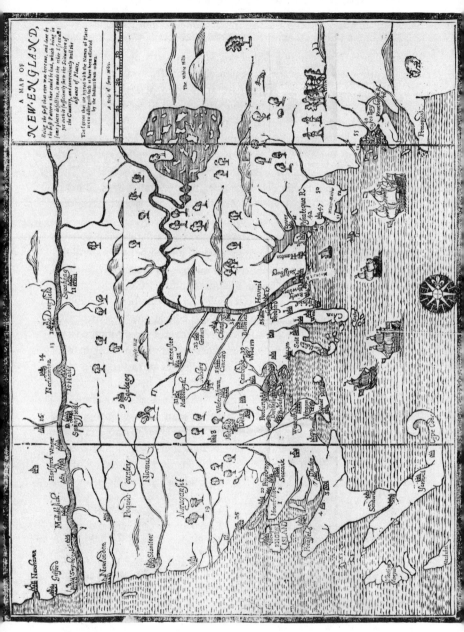

Fig. 47. One of the earliest maps made in Boston, and attributed to John Foster, *circa* 1677. Its technique is reminiscent of the sixteenth century. *Courtesy of the British Museum*

in common absolute ownership by a more modest group of original grantees or purchasers.

Breaking away from an existing township or removing to a new place of settlement by individuals was often caused by a desire for more independence and for social and economic freedom, but sometimes it was caused also by the lure of adventure in the wilderness. However, entire communities did also break and move away from old groups for either religious or economic reasons. It was because the rulers of Massachusetts banished them as heretics that Ann Hutchinson and Roger Williams founded on Narragansett Bay the settlements federated in 1644 as "the Rhode Island and Providence Plantations." Even earlier the foundations had been laid for another important split within New England. In 1635 groups from Watertown and Dorchester, Massachusetts, moved to Connecticut, and in 1636 Thomas Hooker led a community migration from Newtown, Massachusetts, to the Connecticut Valley. The reasons officially given for these moves were largely economic. For example, in June, 1634, the people of Newtown

told of the scarcity of their land, Hooker alleging "as a fundamental error, that towns were set so near to each other"; they instanced the fruitfulness of Connecticut and the danger of having it possessed by others; and finally they declared "the strong bent of their spirits to remove thither." To these arguments, Winthrop tells us "it was said" that such a removal outside the patent would be a breach of covenant . . . But during the winter the crowded feeling became contagious.[4]

Discussing what caused this "crowded feeling" and the removal of these various groups to the three "river towns" in Connecticut, Perry Miller shows that although early accounts insisted on economic motives, chiefly the desire for more and richer land, political and religious motives had actually been more instrumental and had probably been decisive. The three new Connecticut river towns adopted a fundamental law based on the same premises and philosophy as the Massachusetts theocracy, but instead of emphasizing "the principle that the wise, the able, and the good knew the purposes of the covenant better than most of those who entered it and should be allowed freedom to interpret it at their discretion" the Connecticut law, in more democratic fashion, insisted that the authorities "should be amenable to the fundamental laws of the society and the express will of the whole group."[5]

[4] Perry Miller, *Errand into the Wilderness*, The Belknap Press of Harvard University Press, Cambridge, Mass., 1956, pp. 23-24.
[5] *Ibid.*, p. 47; see pp. 16-47 for a full discussion of the situation.

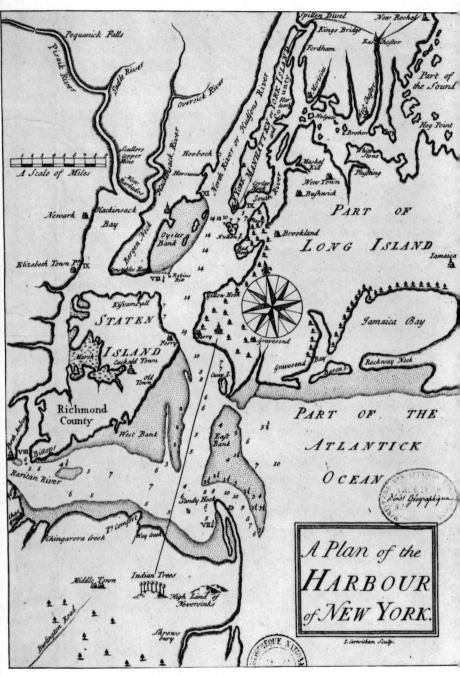

Fig. 48. *Courtesy of the Bibliothèque Nationale, Phot. SPBN*

The migration led by Hooker is interesting in many ways. While it confirms the fact that matters of legislation and government early influenced the multiplication of towns (and the rivalry between Hooker and John Cotton, the powerful Massachusetts leader, added another political element to it), it shows also that economic motives were put forward to cover up deeper feelings. The argument of *crowding* is easy to advance and difficult to refute. It leads us also to ponder the matter of crowding. It quickly grows unbearable if removal is in fact desired, and if people are not prepared to look for ways of alleviating such crowding locally (see Fig. 47 and Fig. 23, p. 107).

As Connecticut law shows the river towns' desire for the community's fuller participation in the administration of public affairs, we are not surprised to see the mushrooming of medium-sized but substantial towns along that river and the near-by seashore. By 1775 Connecticut had more towns (at least five of them) with 4,000–10,000 inhabitants than any of the other colonies. One might observe that it had more navigable rivers and a more indented coast, but it appears safe to assume that the spirit of the population was more decisive a cause than topographic features.

Towns did not multiply and prosper only in New England. By 1770 New York, and Philadelphia to an even greater degree, had far outdistanced Boston, and new towns were taking shape in New York State, New Jersey, and Pennsylvania. Some of them, such as Reading, were laid out by the Proprietors of Pennsylvania, but others sprang up from the desire of various religious sects to conduct their holy experiments in their own way. Thus the Moravians founded Bethlehem, and the Mennonites founded Lancaster. A few generations earlier Philadelphia and Annapolis had been started in a similar way. And several New Jersey towns were founded in the eighteenth century by groups of Quakers who settled there.

The two original impulses that brought English or Dutch settlers to this seaboard in the seventeenth century were the religious experiment to improve society and the commercial venture to develop another market place. A century later both impulses were still at work contributing to the rapid establishment of numerous and lively urban centers in the recently conquered wilderness. Urban communities provided better means of breaking free from the surrounding wilderness, from the impact of the natural environment, and of leading a more advanced way of life.

In 1750 there were only three cities in the colonies having more than 8,000 people, the three original nuclei of modern Megalopolis, and it is estimated that together they contained about 3.5 per cent of the country's

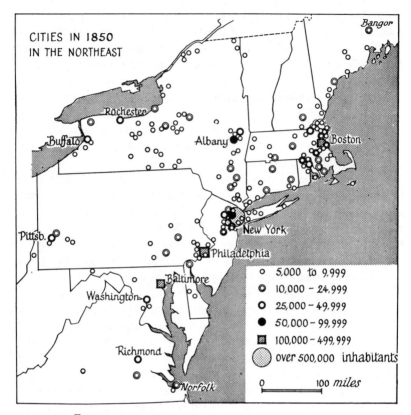

CITIES IN 1850
IN THE NORTHEAST

○	5,000 to 9,999
◉	10,000 – 24,999
◯	25,000 – 49,999
●	50,000 – 99,999
▨	100,000 – 499,999
⬤	over 500,000 inhabitants

0   100 miles

FIG. 49

population. In 1790 there were six such places (see Fig. 26e, p. 115); in 1810 eleven, containing 5 per cent of the population; in 1830 twenty-six, with 6.7 per cent; and in 1850 eighty-five, with 12.5 per cent of the total population. The urbanization of the United States was well on its way, and the early proliferation of towns in the area of Megalopolis had assumed such proportions as to set this section well apart in the still predominantly agrarian United States.[6]

A map showing the distribution of cities according to size in the Northeast in 1850 (see Fig. 49) testifies to both concentration and dispersal of urban centers. Only places with more than 5,000 people are shown, and their concentration appears in striking fashion first along the main seaboard axis from southeastern New Hampshire to Washington, D. C. (the

[6] U. S. Bureau of the Census, *A Century of Population Growth in the United States, 1790–1900, op. cit.*, figures from Table 4, p. 15.

axis of U. S. Route I), and second around the large cities, i.e., Boston, New York, and Philadelphia. There are four impressive "bunches" of cities: in eastern Massachusetts, in Rhode Island, around New York City, and on the Delaware. The impression of crowding is increased, of course, by the scale of the map, and some of the towns that seem adjacent to the New York "bunch" in New Jersey are situated thirty to forty miles from Manhattan, not a small distance in those days.

By mid-nineteenth century, however, roads were good enough to make traffic relatively easy between the various towns of southern New England, parts of New York, and the surroundings of Philadelphia. A great deal of transportation still went by water, but roads were playing a part, and railroads were already beginning to carry a good deal of the traffic. The scattering of towns of more than 5,000 inhabitants through New York State was closely linked with the better system of transportation through that area: the Hudson River and the Erie Canal, and the beginnings of what became, a few years after 1850, the New York Central and the Erie Railroads.

Transportation is the key to the development of the political, social, and economic history of New York in the years between 1825 and 1860. . . . Agitation for canals, railroads, or plank roads filled the newspapers and absorbed the attention of politicians. Every town — indeed every farmer — felt the impact of the changes brought about by the extension of canals, railroads, and highways. . . . The isolation of many rural communities was breaking down as citizens and goods flowed freely in and out. Merchants in both the upstate and metropolitan region, recognizing the crucial role of canals and railroads, looked with satisfaction upon the finest and most actively expanding transportation network in the country.[7]

Comparing the 1850 distribution of cities in New York State and in Pennsylvania demonstrates strikingly the close connection between urban growth on the one hand (in terms of both size of the metropolis and dispersal of the urban nuclei) and transportation network on the other. Pennsylvania was still limited in the east to the major lines of communication converging in Philadelphia and built mainly in the eighteenth century. It had been late in developing railroads and canals westward. By 1850 no substantial town had grown between the Harrisburg-York area (in the Susquehanna Valley) and the Pittsburgh area (in the Ohio Valley). Baltimore had been more active, and in western Maryland the town of Cum-

[7] David M. Ellis, James A. Frost, Harold C. Syrett, Harry J. Carman, *A Short History of New York State*, Cornell University Press, Ithaca, N. Y., 1957, pp. 244 and 255.

berland, at the famous gap, was already linked with tidewater by a good road, the B. & O. Railroad, and the Chesapeake and Ohio Canal. Cities grew and scattered, and from their market place at the crossroads commerce radiated quickly.

The expansion of trade in all directions, as outlined by our theory of the hinge (see Chapter 3, above), is thus finally responsible for the success of the urban growth in this region. The early proliferation was started by religious socio-political motives, but urban growth was maintained by the emphasis on commerce, material profit, and comfort. The richer Southern gentlemen had perhaps a more gracious mode of living on the large plantations, but they were rather few. In the Northeastern cities a quite comfortable way of life developed for many, with much more opportunity for recreation and education than in any other part of the world at the time, with the exception of western European cities.

It must also be stressed that this proliferation of cities was a deliberate process, often planned in advance; while this may not have been the case in colonial New England, it certainly was in Pennsylvania. William Penn carefully chose the site of Philadelphia; he instructed the commissioners of the Province in 1681 to:

Let the Rivers and Creeks be sounded on my side of Delaware River, especially Upland in order to settle a great towne, and be sure to make your choice where it is most navigable, high, dry and healthy. That is, where most ships may best ride, of deepest draught of water, if possible to Load or unload on ye Bank or Key side . . . Such a place being found out, for Navigation, healthy situation and good Soyle, for Provision, lay out ten Thousand Acres contiguous to it in the best manner you can as the bounds and extent of the Libertyes of said Towne.[8]

The rectangular territory thus assigned to the town was to be divided into equal rectangular blocks forming a regular orthogonal plan (see Figs. 29 and 50, pp. 121, 177) that was gradually settled. In 1822 Sidney E. Morse described it as follows:

The form of the ground plot of the proper city is an oblong, about one mile from north to south, and two from east to west, lying in the narrowest part of the isthmus between the Delaware and Schuylkill rivers, about 5 miles in a right line above their confluence. . . . All the houses built beyond the boundary line of the oblong city are said to be in the "liberties," as the jurisdiction of the corporation does not extend to that part of the town. Some of the streets in the liberties are irregular, but the city is regularly laid out in

---

[8] William Penn in a letter dated Sept. 30, 1681, published in the *Memoirs of the Historical Society of Pennsylvania*, E. Littell, Philadelphia, Vol. II, Pt. I, pp. 215–221 (see p. 216).

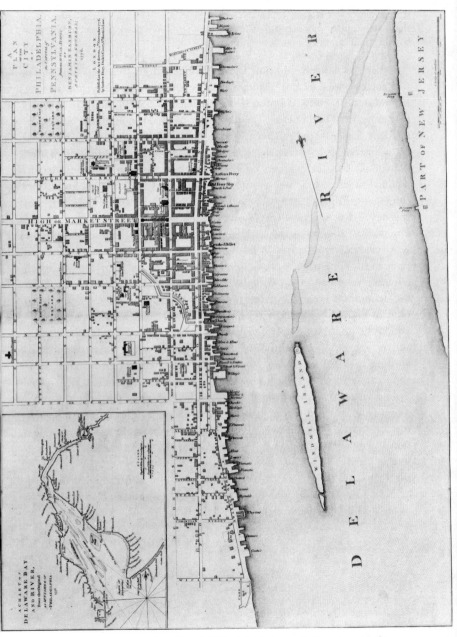

Fig. 50. A plan of the City of Philadelphia in 1776. *Courtesy of the British Museum*

streets which cross each other at right angles. . . . The number of squares in the original plan was 184, but as several of them have been intersected by new streets, their number now amounts to 304.[9]

Other towns were laid out by the Penns, such as Reading. Still others had been planned as local capitals, such as Annapolis in Maryland. In fact, a good deal of study had preceded the choice of the southern tip of Manhattan by the Dutch before the decision was made to establish New Amsterdam there. In the nineteenth century many a mill town was created by industrialists in Massachusetts, Connecticut, and New Jersey. Later, new small cities sprang up on the anthracite basin in Pennsylvania. In colonial times no city was as carefully planned as Philadelphia, and its orthogonal grid plan has been widely used throughout the United States to this day. After independence, however, it was decided (in 1791) to build a new city to serve as the Federal capital of the new nation, and its site was selected by George Washington on the Potomac, just below the river's falls. The plans were drawn by Pierre Charles L'Enfant (a French engineer who had come with Lafayette to fight in the Revolution) for the definite purpose of building a city for the Federal government "magnificent enough to grace a great nation." [10] Despite a long evolution in which the desire for better city development was far from being the only active factor, Washington, D. C., has on the whole been developed according to L'Enfant's plan, which the city did not outgrow until some 120 years after it became the seat of national government in 1800.

The vision that presided, at least on the highest level, over the planning of the national capital testifies to the fact that the creation of a new town, meant to become a great city, was already in the American tradition by 1790. The country's settlement had, in fact, proceeded as much by the growth of old and new urban centers as by the occupation of new rural space. This was a distinctive feature of the Northeastern seaboard, heralding the concentration of people, wealth, and power that has become so obvious in the twentieth century.

[9] Sidney E. Morse, *A New System of Modern Geography, or A View of the Present State of the World,* George Clark, Boston; Howe and Spalding, New Haven, 1822, p. 134.

[10] Federal Writers' Project of the Works Progress Administration, *Washington, City and Capital* (American Guide Series), U. S. Government Printing Office, Washington, D. C., 1937, especially pp. 35–67 and 91–129. See also Frederick Gutheim, *The Potomac* (Rivers of America Series), Rinehart and Company, New York, 1949, Chapters 1 and 11.

Growing Densities over a Vast Area

In later years Census after Census recorded a rapid growth of the Northeastern seaboard, in terms not only of the number and size of its cities but also of the total population of the area. After 1850, and even more noticeably after 1860, some of the farming districts within the region and on its fringes began to experience decreases of both population and tilled acreage. Nevertheless, densities of population, of towns, and of industrial and commercial establishments rose over the whole area and in most of its parts. The feeling of crowding began to be noted in the larger cities and their outer fringes and even farther away, but this crowding did not actually bring about a downturn of the curves showing major trends of economic activity. As witnessed by the case of the early Massachusetts settlers who in the 1630's migrated to Connecticut because they felt too crowded in Newtown, Dorchester, and Watertown, the notion of "crowding" and the "feelings" about it appear as an entirely subjective matter. Many past claims of overpopulation could be defined as a feeling prevailing in a community presently dissatisfied with its lot and local immediate prospect. One feels crowded when one wants change and believes he is entitled to another environment in which needed resources could be more easily developed.

The simple measure of the density of population does not, therefore, mean very much when given without some qualifications and comparisons with the past or with other regions elsewhere. The Bureau of the Census has published many maps showing the distribution of population densities throughout the United States since 1790. On the whole these densities have been calculated with more precision in recent times than formerly, but they are usually given by counties and with inadequate distinction between different degrees of density. For instance, most of the Census maps for United States as a whole show in one shade — that of the *highest* densities — all counties with more than 90 inhabitants per square mile.[11] The largest of these areas are situated in the northeastern quarter of the country (Fig. 5, p. 31). If a more detailed classification of densities is devised for that section, breaking up into several shades the densities greater than 100 per square mile, a quite different and much more correct picture is obtained (Fig. 6, p. 32).

[11] See the series of density maps for the successive Censuses in Charles O. Paullin's *Atlas of the Historical Geography of the United States*, American Geographical Society, New York, and Carnegie Institution, Washington, 1932; and Clifford L. Lord and Elizabeth H. Lord, *Historical Atlas of the United States*, Henry Holt and Company, New York, 1953.

However, the density of 90 per square mile is not often found outside the heavily industrialized and urbanized regions of North America. Compared to the average density of continental United States this 90-per-square-mile figure was about twice as great in 1940, almost three times as great in 1910, and eleven and a half times as great in 1850. In relative American terms 90 people per square mile formerly meant the beginning of crowding, at least outside large city limits (for within cities densities of more than 1,000 per square mile have been common for some time). By 1950 almost the whole of Megalopolis (with the exception of a few counties and most of Maryland's Eastern Shore) had county densities greater than 90 per square mile. In order to understand the past process of population distribution and growth, let us retrace the successive stages by which the various parts of the region achieved and surpassed this level of density.

The map showing the expansion, by 20-year periods (1790–1930), of the zone with county densities greater than 90 per square mile tells an interesting story (Fig. 51). Prior to 1810 only the main cities — Boston, New York, Philadelphia, and Washington — and their immediate suburbs showed high densities. The suburban patch was broader around Boston than around the other cities, for smaller towns, either seaports or mill towns on falls, mushroomed, after the Revolution, more quickly around the great Bay City than around the other regional capitals. Between 1810 and 1830 the Baltimore and Providence areas each added one county with the higher density, but the main area of increased crowding stretched from Philadelphia to New York City across New Jersey. This resulted chiefly from the rapid growth of small towns such as Newark, Elizabeth, New Brunswick, and Trenton along the much-travelled route, U. S. I, on that part of it joining the lower Hudson to the tidal Delaware. The highways and canals were rather good through this part of New Jersey, and as industrialization spread many towns found that this belt offered a combination of advantages — proximity to the markets of the two largest cities, location on the Fall Line, and easy access to the sea.

From 1830 to 1850, the accelerated rate of immigration and industrial development brought higher population density to wide areas. The Boston and Providence metropolitan areas coalesced. Higher density spread into the Connecticut Valley around New Haven, and in a broad suburban region around New York, including Westchester and Nassau counties. In Pennsylvania it spread widely from Philadelphia northward, to Berks, Lehigh, and Northampton counties. Suburban sprawl developed also around a good many notable Northeastern cities outside Megalopolis — Portland, Albany, Syracuse, Rochester, Buffalo, and Pittsburgh.

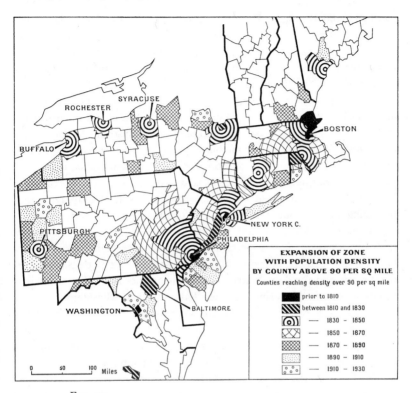

EXPANSION OF ZONE
WITH POPULATION DENSITY
BY COUNTY ABOVE 90 PER SQ MILE
Counties reaching density over 90 per sq mile

prior to 1810
between 1810 and 1830
— 1830 – 1850
— 1850 – 1870
— 1870 – 1890
— 1890 – 1910
— 1910 – 1930

FIG. 51

During the period 1850–1870 the high-density belt extending from greater Boston to Baltimore became practically consolidated except for the gap in York County, Pennsylvania. The patches around Boston and in Connecticut united via Worcester, Massachusetts, while Fairfield County filled in the gap between New Haven and New York. The sprawl progressed northward along the Hudson Valley and widened the high-density belt outlined prior to 1830 across New Jersey. In Pennsylvania the higher density area expanded both northward toward the coal deposits (Luzerne and Lackawanna counties) and westward toward the rich agricultural soils of Chester, Lancaster, and Dauphin counties. On the whole, with the exception of York County, the present limits of Megalopolis in Pennsylvania had been almost fully reached in the 1860's.

As the great development of the West unfolded after 1870, the expansion of the densely populated area on the Northeastern seaboard became slow and spotty. In the period 1870–90 York County, Pennsylvania, passed the 90-per-square-mile density, establishing the full continuity of the urban belt from Boston to Baltimore; Hillsboro County, New Hampshire, was added at the northern end; and the addition of a few more counties in Connecticut and New Jersey rounded up the shape of the central sector of the denser zone. In the history of American life this period is known as the era of "the rise of the city." One may notice relatively more sprawl developing in the western parts of Pennsylvania and New York State than on the seaboard proper. Cities grew on the coast and the Fall Line also, but in Megalopolis this rise was achieved mainly by industrial and commercial expansion within the large or medium-sized cities that had developed long before 1850. The densities grew along the main axes established in previous periods, without much expansion in space of the general area of crowding. Within the limits outlined by 1870, agriculture was already retracting, providing an easy source of more land for urban uses.

The periods 1890–1910 and 1910–30 continued in general fashion the trends of 1870–90. A few peripheral counties were added, bringing the limits of the densely occupied zone in closer contact with the seashore on one side and the Appalachian Mountains on the other. The main areal extension was in Maryland between Baltimore and Washington, D. C., bringing the District of Columbia into the continuously urban belt. During the years 1930–50, when the automobile and the highway took over the major role in the transportation system, helping relative dispersal, more territory was added on the fringes, and the internal gaps were filled in. By that time the criterion of 90-per-square-mile density on a county basis was no longer adequate for an understanding of the distribution of density.

In 1950 the average population density of the continental United States reached 50.7 inhabitants per square mile of land area. Over the 53,575 square miles of Megalopolis the density averaged 596.3, almost twelve times the national value. If the five biggest cities, containing more than half a million people each and having densities greater than 10,000 per square mile, were excluded from the totals of area and population for Megalopolis, the average density of the region would drop to 367, still seven times the national average (in which all cities are included), and greater than for any state except Rhode Island, Connecticut, and New Jersey, all three of which are parts of Megalopolis. The "crowding" in this region appears serious indeed, and much more intensive than in any other section of comparable size in North America.

The steady growth and sprawl of this "crowding" within the area must be analyzed in other ways, too, not just in terms of passing a 90-per-square-mile density. Its evolution through the eighteenth century was

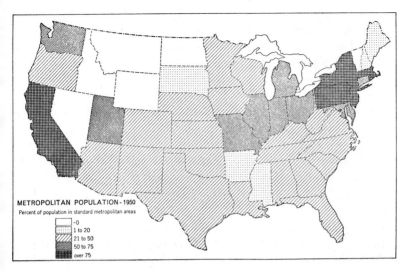

METROPOLITAN POPULATION · 1950
Percent of population in standard metropolitan areas
- 0
1 to 20
21 to 50
50 to 75
over 75

Fig. 52

demonstrated on the population maps by Herman R. Friis [12] (Figs. 26a to 26e, pp. 114–115). In those days little of the rest of the continent had been at all densely populated. By 1850, however, the situation was different. A density map by counties (Fig. 38, p. 145) shows a rather continuous stretch with density greater than 50 along the seaboard, with broad extensions inland and a wide area of such density south of Lake Ontario. This situation resulted largely from the distribution of cities of some size (Fig. 49), the populations of which are included in the calculation of county densities. And yet urban concentrations could not fully explain these densities, although they could explain the patches with densities greater than 100 per square mile scattered through the seaboard area and quite continuous through eastern Massachusetts. The changes in population that occurred in the intercensal period 1840–50, the "roaring forties" of the nineteenth century, show a good deal of growth in rural areas, including the Appalachian foothills on both sides of the range. But a few rural counties had begun to show a decline in population, owing chiefly to the lure of urban life on the one hand and of the Western frontier on the other (Fig. 37, p. 143).

Let us then consider the county density map of the 1880 Census (Fig. 40, p. 154), which shows most of modern Megalopolis with more than 80 people per square mile and a good deal of it with more than 120. The

[12] Herman R. Friis, *A Series of Population Maps of the Colonies and the United States, 1625–1790*, American Geographical Society, New York, 1940.

growth of population since 1850 had been greatest within the belt already densely occupied in 1850 (Fig. 38) and was chiefly in and around the nuclei of denser settlement as of that date. The most notable additions were two regions in Pennsylvania, one between Bethlehem, Lancaster, and Harrisburg and the other on the Scranton–Wilkes-Barre coal deposits.

The Lancaster limestone basin is one of the areas where the dense population reflects particularly rich soils rather than a maritime location. Indeed, until the 1870's Lancaster, founded by a hard-working group of settlers, could boast that it was the largest *inland* city — i.e., not situated on an easily navigable waterway. The Connecticut Valley is another area where rich soils have contributed to the density of population, but it enjoyed in early times the additional advantage of a navigable river (little used today).

By 1910 (Fig. 41, p. 155) the shape of the present Megalopolis seems pretty well outlined on the population density map. It is interesting to compare the 1910 map with the 1850 map (Fig. 38) and to note that the inland *rural* areas had generally either remained the same in density or had even lost people (particularly in northern New England). By 1940 the densities had become much higher in and around the urbanized districts, and a map of *densities by minor civil divisions* (Fig. 121, p. 386) shows much sharper contrasts in densities than the map by counties would suggest. However, this concentration of more people on less space was to be expected in this region as a result of the trends apparent in the successive Census counts of the nineteenth century. These contrasts sharpened through the 1940's, although the rate of growth was much more rapid in the less densely occupied southern parts of Megalopolis than in the more "saturated" northern sector.

In 1957 this writer published a map of Megalopolis based on the 1950 Census, and his attention was directed to its similarity to a map of "the main region of dense population in the United States" based on the 1890 Census and published in 1897.[13] The main difference between the two maps lies in the fact that in 1890 the zone of greatest density extended south only to Baltimore, while in 1950 it stretched farther, to Washington and the two adjacent suburban counties in Virginia. This difference results from two new factors, at work since 1915: the growth of the Federal government's activities and economic impact, and the steady rejuvenation

---

[13] Walter F. Willcox, "Density and Distribution of Population," in *Economic Studies*, published by the American Economic Association, The Macmillan Company, New York, Vol. II, No. 6, December 1897; the map referred to is in Chapter 2, facing p. 404.

and economic development of the Southeast. It is interesting to note that in 1950 as in 1890 the belt of high density connected Boston and the Connecticut Valley via Worcester, rather than via eastern Connecticut, and linked Philadelphia with Baltimore by way of Lancaster and York counties instead of the shores of the upper Chesapeake. This general axis of population crowding had already been established in the eighteenth century and it has shown remarkable stability.

The stability of the general outline, in terms of axis and of limits, especially in the years 1870–1940, did not mean stagnation or self-sufficiency. Megalopolis grew and was indeed consolidated during this period. Some of the growth represented a shift of farm population from rural regions within Megalopolis and on its fringes into the towns, but a much larger part of the population increase came from farther away, either from other parts of the continent or from overseas. The related emptying of various sectors of the Megalopolitan territory did not necessarily mean decline of these areas but rather, in most cases, a conversion from farming uses to "outer-suburbia" status. Similarly the size of the crowded areas and of the business activities attracting the crowds made it gradually less pleasant and more expensive to keep either residences or factories and warehouses inside the old city limits. Suburbs sprawled, and the intramural Census population of the cities — that is, that within the city boundaries — became more stabilized, or even, in some cases, declined, because Censuses count people at their places of residence, while cities, within their official boundaries, tended to contain fewer residences and more places of work and recreation. In some cases industrial plants and certain kinds of recreation also moved out to the suburbs and farther.

At the scale of the metropolitan areas bordering on one another in Megalopolis, the density according to the Census (i.e., according to usual nighttime residence) does not mean very much. At the county scale it may sometimes be significant, but in other cases it is deceptive. At the scale of minor civil divisions it is more significant, showing residential distribution (especially if some generalization is allowed, as in the case of Figures 1 and 122, on pp. 6, 387, where the scale required it). But the distribution at noontime on a working day may be quite different, for many of the people are at work, most of them in the cities of the neighborhood. Residential densities are the only kinds we have yet had systematically supplied for large areas by actual Censuses, and in a region like Megalopolis they are only *one* of the various indicators of the migrations of economic activities. Suburban sprawl, even if it is immense and disconcerting because of its *nebulous* structure, does not spell decline of the old urban centers; on the contrary, it may well mean that their power of attraction is greater than ever.

The Lure of the Cities

The proliferation of crowded urbanized districts did not occur throughout Megalopolis just because the opportunities of the hinge were well exploited by local merchants, bankers, and manufacturers. People were lured to the mushrooming cities by the promise of an urban way of life. Cities always grow by pulling people from the surrounding rural countryside, sometimes from far away, and also from other smaller towns, developing more slowly or declining. The question is often asked whether the *pull* of the urban center or the *push* off the countryside was the decisive factor in the process, but this has only a theoretical and, for our purposes, a very limited significance. *Pull and push* may work together to the same end for certain categories of people in a given area, or the pull of cities in one area may be fed by the push off the land in distant parts, as when Boston and New York "pulled" Irish immigrants pushed off the countryside of Ireland in 1840–60 by famine.

Megalopolitan cities received a constant influx of newcomers from Europe, because they stood at the Atlantic gates of the United States. From the latter part of the nineteenth century on they received immigrants also from Latin America (especially in New York) and from Canada (especially in New England). And all through their history people came from various parts of the then settled continental space to establish themselves in the cities. As Carl Bridenbaugh has eloquently shown,[14] even in colonial times the leading cities in the Northeast had built up an active intellectual life with a diversity of cultural activities, which was accompanied by the emergence of an urban gentry of substantial wealth and increasing numbers. The Revolution, however, was viewed by the mass of common citizens as giving the people a larger share in the opportunities and the government of American cities. The authority locally acquired by wealthier merchants and the town proprietors was almost as much at stake as that of governors and controllers appointed from London. As the development of large-scale commerce and manufactures began on the Northeastern seaboard shortly after the Revolution, the economic opportunities offered by urban life expanded at the same time that the social structure was being made more supple. Both these trends increased the social mobility in the cities and also their "pull" on not-too successful farmers farther inland and on immigrants, who could choose between

[14] Especially in his *Cities in Revolt, op. cit.,* Chapters 4, 5, 9, and 10.

staying in the seaboard cities and proceeding westward to the free lands of the frontier.

It was in the nineteenth century, and especially during its second half, that rural exodus toward cities developed on a large scale in both the United States and Europe, and the cities of Megalopolis thus received a flow of newcomers from both continents. A. M. Schlesinger has described how urban life and work attracted increasing numbers of people from the farms, especially in the latter part of the century.[15] As early as the 1880's and 1890's inland sections of the Northeast, from Maine to Pennsylvania, offered the spectacle of abandoned farms, fields returning to brush, and woods swallowing old crumbling stone walls and even buildings. The tilled area of New England reached its maximum around 1850 and has been shrinking ever since, for the cities offered a more attractive way of life, especially to young people and to women, while the agricultural development of the Great Plains made general farming less profitable on the smaller fields and poorer soils of the Northeast.

The rural exodus became a rather general trend in all advanced countries after 1850. Machines and fertilizers replaced farm hands in agricultural production. Meanwhile, city life offered a more sheltered existence, with fewer risks and responsibilities for the average worker and with easier access to recreation for adults, to education for youngsters, and to wealth for the greedy. Whether people were conservative or adventurous, the city could provide a better deal than the country, unless they yearned for isolation and for that feeling of independence and achievement many find in constant exposure to open space and in contact with Nature's physical processes.

The last quarter of the nineteenth century also witnessed the coming of age of a generation of refined philosophers reconciled to urban life and society. The condemnation of large urban growth had been much in vogue earlier among intellectuals who admired the philosophies of Jefferson, Thoreau, Emerson, and even Henry Adams. Although a more "pro-urban" tradition in America could have claimed Benjamin Franklin, Alexander Hamilton, Walt Whitman, and many other great patrons, the anti-urban attitude had remained more fashionable.[16] This attitude had

[15] Arthur Meier Schlesinger, *The Rise of the City, 1878–1898 (A History of American Life,* Vol. X), The Macmillan Company, New York, 1933, especially Chapters 3 and 4.

[16] We are indebted in these matters to a report on the history of the development of philosophical concepts concerning cities, prepared especially for this study by Professor Morton White of Harvard University and Mrs. Lucia Perry White. See their article, "The American Intellectual versus the American City," in *Daedalus,*

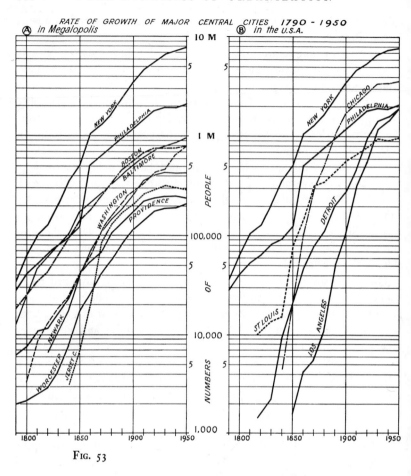

FIG. 53

very complex roots: aesthetic reactions against the drabness and ugliness of most urban landscapes, and against the slums and stench found in some parts of cities; ethical disapproval of so much mixing of obvious poverty with ostentatious wealth and of the strict discipline imposed on crowds of laborers; the knowledge of demagogic and corrupt practices in city halls; the old theory that life in "natural conditions" was more healthful and morally better than in an "artificial" urban environment; the new ideas calling for the conservation of "natural" landscapes and modes of life. All these factors, and many more, contributed to the fashionable

Journal of the American Academy of Arts and Sciences, Wesleyan University Press, Middletown, Conn., Winter 1961, pp. 166–179.

condemnation of the city, which in a certain society remains alive to this day.

The effects of this attitude were not all unfavorable to the city. One may regret that such people as Ralph Waldo Emerson, Henry Adams, or Henry James, expressing their disgust for State Street, kept themselves and many of their followers from endeavoring directly to improve Boston's politics and government. But a similar state of mind brought about many of the reforms in housing, water supply, public health, and labor legislation. Such progressive steps would not have been taken as early as they were in America without a great deal of stubborn and consistent criticism of certain features of city life and growth. Thoreau himself took the trouble to recommend large parks for every city, a measure implemented by later generations.

A study such as Oscar Handlin's on the life of the immigrants in Boston before 1880 [17] demonstrates eloquently that social reforms were greatly needed. They were achieved after 1880, by a generation that set its mind on improving the American city. The literature on urban growth and problems became extremely rich in the latter part of the nineteenth century. Among the people who taught or came of age then were William James, John Dewey, and Jane Addams, as well as many others. In badly governed Boston a wave of protest brought reforms that made great contributions to American life. As Arthur Mann has put it:

> The last twenty-five years of the nineteenth century were the seed bed of modern America. Boston's reformers met the challenge raised by the forces remaking their nation; . . . with an optimism and zeal reminiscent of the age of Ralph Waldo Emerson and Bronson Alcott, they rejuvenated the languishing spirit of reform to meet the problems of the modern, urban-industrial culture. Together with fellow liberals in other American cities they created a new climate of opinion that stimulated urban dwellers to rally behind the progressive creeds of Theodore Roosevelt and Woodrow Wilson.[18]

In this same period the movement for the conservation of natural beauty and resources scored its first practical successes. Through the efforts of George P. Marsh, Frederick L. Olmsted, Gifford Pinchot, and others, public parks were created in the cities and the conservation of forests and natural sites of special interest became a concern of national and state governments. Olmsted won the competition for the plan of Central Park in Manhattan in 1858, but resigned the position of architect-

[17] Oscar Handlin, *Boston's Immigrants, 1790–1880: A Study in Acculturation*, rev. ed., The Belknap Press of Harvard University Press, Cambridge, Mass., 1959.

[18] Arthur Mann, *Yankee Reformers in the Urban Age*, The Belknap Press of Harvard University Press, Cambridge, Mass., 1954, p. 240.

in-chief of the park in 1863, discouraged by the constant struggle this project involved. But in November 1882, Olmsted's diary mentions work he was conducting simultaneously on public projects in fifteen cities, among which were Washington, D. C., Boston, Providence, Bridgeport, Newport, Albany, Quincy, and Wellesley.[19]

It was shortly before the turn of the century that Frederick Jackson Turner heralded the passing of the frontier and enunciated his well-known theory of its role in American history. The lively debate aroused by Turner's ideas, which still goes on, has sometimes discussed the relative influence of the frontier and of the early urbanized Northeast on the development of the American nation and its character. Actually Turner's frontier theory does not exclude a very important role for the North-eastern cities. In his original paper of 1893, Turner proclaimed that "the true point of view in the history of this nation is not the Atlantic Coast, it is the Great West." [20] He said in the same paper, however, that "the Middle region" on the Atlantic seaboard (from New York to Pennsylvania) was "the typically American region" before the Great West was opened, and that it was from the "Middle region" that the frontier started on its westward march. In 1925, in a private letter to A. M. Schlesinger, Turner commented: "There seems likely to be an urban reinterpretation of our history." [21]

To some extent such an interpretation has developed on broad lines in the twentieth century, but it has been developed to a greater degree by European scholars, studying world history as a whole, than by Americans, among whom Lewis Mumford has probably been the most active and popular exponent of such ideas.[22] American historians, though often critical of the excesses of "the frontier interpretation," have been on the

[19] Hans Huth, *Nature and the American: Three Centuries of Changing Attitudes,* University of California Press, Berkeley and Los Angeles, 1957, especially Chapters 4 and 10.

[20] Frederick Jackson Turner, *The Frontier in American History,* Henry Holt & Company, New York, 1920. See p. 38 of the 1958 edition.

[21] Quoted by Arthur Meier Schlesinger in "The City in American History," *Mississippi Valley Historical Review,* 1940, XXVII, p. 43. In this paper Professor Schlesinger opened a broad debate on that reinterpretation, which was again discussed in cautious and stimulating fashion by William Diamond, in "On the Dangers of an Urban Interpretation of History," in Eric F. Goldman (ed.), *Historiography and Urbanization, Essays in American History in Honor of W. Stull Holt,* The Johns Hopkins Press, Baltimore, 1941, pp. 67–108. Turner himself seems to have begun such an urban reinterpretation when he called on urbanization and industrialization to provide new frontiers, in Chapters 11 and 12 of *The Frontier in American History, op. cit.*

[22] Especially in his *The Culture of Cities,* Harcourt, Brace & Company, New York, 1938.

whole wary of urban determinism in the first 300 years of their own past. As A. M. Schlesinger has wisely concluded, these attitudes reflect "the historian's central problem: the persistent interplay of town and country in the evolution of American civilization." [23]

In the special case of the cities in the *hinge* area the interplay was obvious, but there it was even more complicated than merely "town and country," for it involved also the sea and the resources reached by the network of overseas contacts. The seaports rarely used the sea for themselves alone; in most cases they used it to serve the needs and exploit the resources of their country. It was the products of American forests, farms, and towns that the seaboard merchants traded overseas; they needed West Indian molasses and rum to supply more Negro slaves to plantations in the South as well as in the Caribbean; they dried cod and imported or manufactured hardware for the domestic market as well as for export; and the New York money market founded its strength on its relations with the scattered banks in rural areas even more than on its credit in London. If it appears obvious that the rapid development of the Great West provided the opportunity for the Northeastern seaboard to erect as magnificent a commercial and industrial structure as it did, it is just as evident that the Great West would not have developed so rapidly and might not have grown so great in the nineteenth century had not the urban centers of the Atlantic seaboard provided it with the equipment, the capital, and even the people who built it up, and, in the twentieth century, with the overseas markets and supplies that helped it to go on and on.

Turner was probably much more conscious of this interplay of interests than some of his more enthusiastic followers or worst critics have acknowledged. He compared the effects of the advancing Western frontier in America to the spread of Hellenistic colonization in antiquity, from the metropolises in Greece over most of the Mediterranean world. Both great historical processes brought new lands and resources into the circuits of the civilized world, producing more wealth, new centers of culture, and new institutions; [24] in both cases the planting of new people on new lands started from great trading cities serving as home bases,[25]

[23] In "The City in American History," *Mississippi Valley Historical Review, op. cit.*, p. 43.

[24] Turner, *The Frontier in American History, op. cit.*, p. 38.

[25] The Greek term *metropolis*, i.e., "mother-city," meant a large and older city from which groups went to plant new city-states in new territory to be Hellenized and developed. As Phocaea founded Marseille, Lawrence, Kansas, was founded under the leadership of people from Lawrence, Massachusetts; the name was seldom repeated but the spawning of towns was frequent,

the existence and strength of which made the whole expansion possible. Indeed, one could take advantage of Turner's comparison of the frontier in the American West to the Mediterranean for the ancient Greeks and suggest that the Northeastern seaboard was blessed with both the continental frontier and the maritime one, as it used its location to play the part of the hinge.

The interplay of the hinge with the interior of the continent involved the exchange not only of goods and capital but also of people. Through-

FIG. 54 (*a, b, c*). Graphs of population migration by states, 1870–1950. Each graph shows for one state the migration in and out of it for the intercensal periods from 1870–80 to 1940–50. See legend and scale on Fig. 54a. The columns serving as background provide a scale, each column's height being equal to 5 per cent of the state's population at census time.

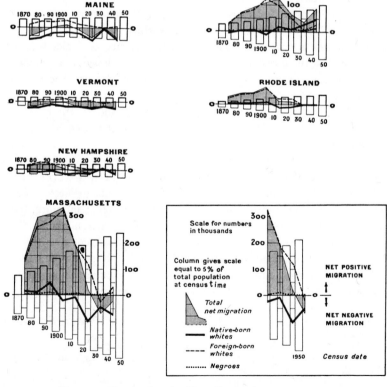

FIG. 54a. Graphs for the New England states

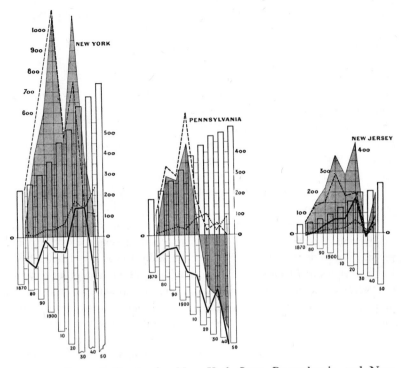

FIG. 54*b*. Graphs for New York State, Pennsylvania, and New Jersey

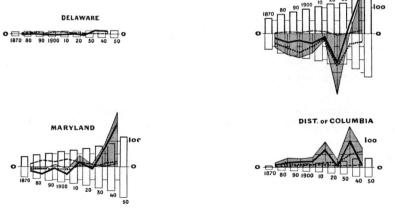

FIG. 54*c*. Graphs for Delaware, Maryland, Virginia, and the District of Columbia

out their history all the large cities of the Northeastern seaboard have had a varying but substantial fraction of their population made up of immigrants — people born in other states of the Union. At the same time the cities have sent people born within their bounds, or immigrants who had lived there for a good time, out west to the towns as well as to the open country. Even as early as 1850, Philadelphia County, Pennsylvania, counted 10.7 per cent of its residents born in the United States but out of the state; and such residents amounted to 18 per cent of the population in Providence County, Rhode Island, 20 per cent and 16 per cent respectively in Middlesex and Suffolk counties, Massachusetts, 8.2 per cent in New York County, New York, 10 per cent in Hartford and New Haven counties, Connecticut, and as might be expected, 36 per cent in the District of Columbia.[26]

The net migration trends after 1870 for the various states from Maine to Virginia (see Figs. 54a to 54c; note common explanatory legend, p. 192) show significant diversity on the seaboard. The northern New England states of Maine, New Hampshire, and Vermont register a negative net balance of migratory native whites for practically the whole period, 1870–1950, except for a temporary and slight improvement during the depression of the 1930's, when people looked for security by going home to the small farms and towns. For these states the total net migration was positive only in New Hampshire prior to 1910 and in Maine in the period 1890–1910; this was due to a net influx of foreign-born whites, which tapered off after 1920.[27]

Southern New England presents a somewhat different picture. The total population of this area rose rather regularly between 1870 and 1950, particularly in Massachusetts. However, for the Bay State as well as for Rhode Island the net migration balance was favorable only until 1930, and this favorable balance was due mainly to the inflow of foreign-born whites (i.e., to immigration). Connecticut shows a positive balance for total net migration and for foreign-born and Negroes for the whole period, 1870–1950, and the balance is positive even for the native-born with the exception of two intercensal periods, 1870–80 and 1900–1910. The lure of Connecticut for native-born Americans seems to have been

[26] According to J. D. B. DeBow, *Statistical View of the United States . . . , Being a Compendium of the Seventh Census,* The Senate Printer, Washington, D. C., 1854.

[27] The graphs in Fig. 54, *a* to *c,* and the comments that follow are based on data from Everett S. Lee, Ann Ratner Miller, Carol P. Brainerd and Richard A. Easterlin, *Population Redistribution and Economic Growth, United States 1870–1950,* Vol. I, American Philosophical Society, Philadelphia, 1957.

greatest in all of New England, and one wonders whether proximity to New York City has not been a decisive factor.

New Jersey, situated on the other side of New York, is also adjacent to Philadelphia and far enough south to have attracted substantial numbers of Negro in-migrants (see Fig. 54*b*). The curves are more accentuated for New Jersey than for Connecticut, and the total balance was slightly negative in the depression years. During the last ninety years New Jersey's attraction for migrants has been much greater than that of any state in New England.[28]

New York and Pennsylvania are more complicated. Each of these greater states has a western section beyond the bounds of Megalopolis and looking westward. However, urbanization in their seaboard areas was on a much greater scale, and these areas were responsible for most of the rise of population and the attraction of out-of-state migrants after 1870. The balance of total migration has remained consistently positive for New York State, but it has been negative for Pennsylvania since 1910, increasingly so in each decade. The growth of New York City and its metropolitan region has been much more rapid than that of Philadelphia, especially since 1890. Pennsylvania suffered also from the decline of its coal-mining areas (in and beyond Megalopolis) and from the fact that its mountainous western areas are more difficult for travel, particularly in the automobile era, than are the routes forming the famous "Y" in New York State. The migration of native-born whites *out* of Pennsylvania was especially strong throughout the period, accelerating after 1910; but the migration of foreign-born whites and Negroes remained positive. In New York State also there was some net out-migration of native-born whites, but it was not as sharp as in Pennsylvania and in 1920–40 there was a net in-migration. Throughout the period the influx of both foreign-born whites and Negroes into New York State remained very important, with a clear predominance of the former until 1930 and of the latter after 1940.

The statistics by states are all deceiving in some respects, for they are not independent one from another. Thus the suburban sprawl from both New York City and Philadelphia generously spilled over into New Jersey; some of the native-born white migration from both New York State and Pennsylvania certainly went into New Jersey, helping that state to maintain a positive balance for this category of migrants after 1880. Similar trends have probably worked in favor of Connecticut, Maryland,

[28] John E. Brush, *The Population of New Jersey*, Rutgers University Press, New Brunswick, N. J., 1956; especially in his Chapter 2 on population growth, pp. 15–38.

and Delaware. Washington, D. C., experienced, of course, a brisk growth, especially after 1915, for the national capital attracts newcomers from all over the Union, both white and Negro. Its metropolitan sprawl has spilled into both Maryland and Virginia, especially since 1930, contributing to the positive balances of these two states, although Baltimore, too, has contributed a large share to the Maryland growth, and in the same period several large urban areas have also arisen in Virginia at substantial distances from the Potomac.

The analysis of these graphs thus reveals the interconnections developed by Megalopolitan growth between neighboring states. Further, it shows that for a long time urbanization has been steadily proceeding southward from the shores of Massachusetts. Indeed, the maritime parts of Massachusetts and the small state of Rhode Island were the first to be affected by predominantly urban and suburban development. The urban proportion in the population exceeded 80 per cent in Rhode Island in 1880 and in Massachusetts in 1890. The seaboard was gradually conquered as such urbanization spread southward.

The trend south did not, however, proceed with entire regularity. The two cities of New York and Washington have expanded more rapidly than the other large nuclei in Megalopolis (see Figs. 53 and 54). They still lure more people of various origins to come and live within their walls or in their metropolitan orbits than do other centers of attraction. This has been true not only of native Americans in Washington, attracted by the rising role of Federal politics and government, or of immigrants in the case of New York, the main port of entry. The picture appears far more complex, and the attraction of these two centers is much more generalized.

Additional data and analyses concerning such trends within Megalopolis will be presented further on in this study. We may perhaps point out at this stage that both Washington, D. C., and New York City have, since the beginning of this century, assumed an increasing share of the managerial and policy-making functions that were more diffused throughout the nation in the nineteenth century. This is the result of historical trends and events that this study has already reviewed briefly. It is also the result of New York's choice location and of the constant endeavors of its people and their leaders. Even during the worst years of the great depression, while Washington attracted people because of the rapid rise in employment of government agencies during the New Deal, New York City also attracted people owing to the size and variety of its labor market even then, and because of the extraordinary development of its charities and assistance organizations. Speaking of the situation that developed through the 1930's in terms of rural exodus, Mayor Fiorello La Guardia of New York testified in 1940:

> Now, cities that are more humane are penalized for it, because where provision is made, and care given, it is always an attraction, and therefore you will find that certain cities in the country that are more attractive than others for this kind of people are penalized.[29]

New York was one of these; and it did not stop being so in the prosperous 1950's, or it would probably not have attracted such large numbers of underprivileged people, especially the Puerto Ricans.[30] Indeed, New York City, as the main port of entry of immigrants for over a century, has had a great deal of experience in handling newcomers who arrive poor and in need of help to adapt to a new way of life. The city has a social framework organized for this work, and once such an organization is well established and well known it attracts migrants.

This is not, of course, a type of attraction existing only in New York City (although it has been developed there to an exceptional degree). A city has always been a refuge for country people in case of trouble, when help was needed, especially the kind of help that is provided by public services. These have always been better organized where there is crowding, accompanied by sharper social differences, and where there is some concentration of agencies and resources for help; rich cities, crowded with not-so-well-to-do hard-working people, just could not function without providing some help regularly to the destitute and the less fortunate. It has been observed in recent years in India that in case of local famine not only people but also sacred cows from rural areas gather in the cities, expecting more help and care in these better organized communities.

Whether these characteristics of cities, a factor in their power to lure migrants, result from the specific features of urban economy, or whether they are simply produced by the mechanisms of crowding, is an interesting question, which could be debated at length. Certainly, on the one hand, "the crowding of people into small space bears with it a tremendous

[29] See *Interstate Migration*, Hearings before the Select Committee to Investigate the Interstate Migration of Destitute Citizens, House of Representatives, 76th Cong., 3rd sess., Part I, New York City Hearings, July 29–31, 1940, p. 3.

[30] See Elena Padilla, *Up from Puerto Rico*, Columbia University Press, New York, 1958; and Oscar Handlin, *The Newcomers: Negroes and Puerto Ricans in a Changing Metropolis*, New York Metropolitan Region Study, Harvard University Press, Cambridge, Mass., 1959. See also Gunnar Myrdal, *An American Dilemma*, Harper and Brothers, New York, 1944, Chapter 8.

increase in specialized demands. . . . A more complicated system of administration is necessary to handle the complex problems of engineering, law, finance and social welfare." [31] But still no city can succeed in developing such a system if it does not have an economic base sound enough to provide the employment and the revenue that will sustain population growth. The migrant, therefore, is not lured by the promise of charity alone; though this may be an element in time of crisis, the lure of the city, if it is to be enduring, must be rooted in the reasonable expectation of economic growth. In the city, however, because there is crowding and because of the economic activities pursued, one may be certain of finding a more *organized* society. The tighter social structure will provide more welfare through organization of the people, more shelter, more security, less individual responsibility.

Recently it has been observed that bigness in economic enterprise has caused many people to delight in being "organization men." These kinds of organization grow in urban centers and have in our time apparently contributed a good deal to suburban sprawl, at least of a certain kind.[32] Before the trend became suburban it was urban. Urban life and activities provide city dwellers with some of the advantages of "organization" in this same sense.

Whether these characters of urban society are in the long run desirable or not is a moral and ethical question. Whether individuals produced by a more organized or a less organized society are preferable has been debated for a long time and rather academically. Phenomena of crowding and the need for organization to adjust resources to needs caused the birth of civilization in the Middle East in ancient times.[33] Would it have been better to provide less well — to let some of the people die off, so that a few survivors could go on living a dispersed "frontier" way of life — and to avoid the evils of government and the emergence of civilized but tightly knit nations? The answer to these questions is a matter of personal judgment. It might be worthwhile for historians and economists to examine the relations that may exist between the trends toward a "welfare state" and the dense crowding on limited areas that have developed since the Industrial Revolution.

[31] Don Martindale, "The Theory of the City," prefatory remarks to a translation of Max Weber's *The City*, The Free Press, Glencoe, Ill., 1958, p. 13.

[32] William H. Whyte, Jr., *The Organization Man*, Simon and Schuster, New York, 1956.

[33] See particularly Henri Frankfort, *The Birth of Civilization in the Near East*, Indiana University Press, Bloomington, Ind., 1951, and Doubleday Anchor Books, Doubleday & Co., Garden City, N. Y., 1956.

The Widening Gamut of Urban Occupation

Urban centers have always been set aside from rural areas because of their specialization in manufacturing, trade, and services (the administration of government and religion being here considered a public service). The variety of occupations has always been greater in the city than in rural areas; and the evolution of urban activities has constantly increased and refined the variety. This process has kept the city from stagnation. It has brought about constant changes in the social structure and greater mobility of people and of the pattern of land use. This has often been emphasized by scholars of diverse specializations who have studied urban life.

An organization which is composed of competing individuals and of competing groups of individuals is in a state of unstable equilibrium, and this equilibrium can be maintained only by a process of continuous readjustment. . . . Concentration of populations in cities, the wider markets, the division of labor, the concentration of individuals and groups on special tasks, have continually changed the material conditions of life, and in doing this have made readjustments to novel conditions increasingly necessary. Out of this necessity there have grown up a number of special organizations which exist for the special purpose of facilitating these readjustments. The market which brought the modern city into existence is one of these devices.[34]

The main cities of modern Megalopolis started as seaports and markets. Our review of their past as an economic hinge has shown that they soon attracted craftsmen, and manufacturing developed in them in the eighteenth century, spurred on at the time of the Revolution by the political situation and later by the whole process of the growth of the American economy. The Northeastern seaboard began to industrialize on a large scale early in the nineteenth century, and by the end of that century the United States could claim to be the greatest industrial nation on earth (Europe was still little aware of American primacy). Megalopolis was then only one of the important industrial regions in the nation but it could still claim to be the most important one.

The growth of manufactures in Megalopolis through the nineteenth century and the first half of the twentieth was too enormous and complicated a process to be described here. It was steady and diversified during all this time. The earliest industries were linked to sea trade: shipbuilding and outfitting, flour-milling and rum-making for export, food preservation

[34] Robert Ezra Park, "The City: Suggestions for the Investigation of Human Behavior in the Urban Environment," in *American Journal of Sociology*, XX, March 1916, reprinted in *Human Communities* (Vol. II of the Collected Papers of R. E. Park), The Free Press, Glencoe, Ill., 1952, pp. 27–28.

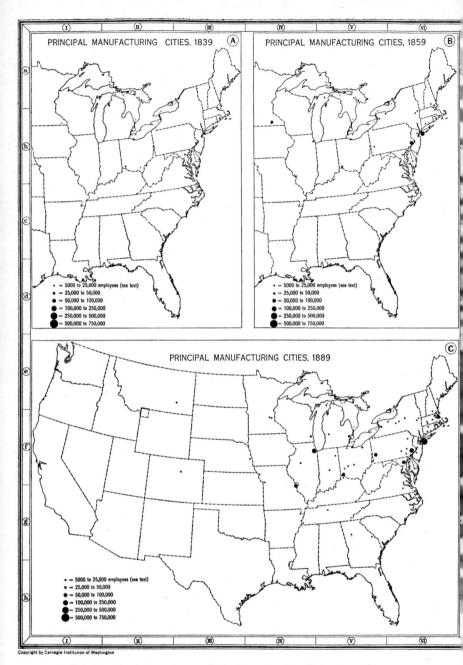

FIG. 55. Evolution of manufacturing, 1839–89. *Reproduced by permission of the Carnegie Institution of Washington, from C. O. Paullin,* Atlas of the Historical Geography of the United States, *plate 133*

for sea voyages. As settlement progressed diverse basic industries scattered through America. Iron works functioned in every colony before the Revolution, although most of them were in seaboard areas from eastern Massachusetts to Maryland; by 1860 they had spread to every state east of the Mississippi, but after 1840 and for a long time the greatest center of large-scale production was in the region of Pittsburgh. Eastern Pennsylvania also had an important iron industry, with many blast furnaces operating on anthracite coal between Philadelphia and Scranton. Philadelphia led as a center of locomotive building, but Paterson, New Jersey, was also active in that field after the 1850's.

Owing to the demands of their construction industries and shipyards, Boston, New York, and Baltimore developed large metal smelting and refining plants before 1860, while the Naugatuck Valley of Connecticut specialized in textiles. Rhode Island was the first to be successful with a large-scale cotton textile industry. In 1815 "there were within 30 miles of Providence 140 cotton manufacturers employing 26,000 hands and operating 130,000 spindles." [35] From there cotton and wool factories spread to Massachusetts and then southward to New Jersey and the region of Philadelphia. Arms manufacturing began in New England with Eli Whitney and Simeon North, and this led to the manufacture of other precision machinery, including clocks. Footwear and woodenware factories also developed. Pennsylvania led in making of glassware, paper, iron, and some types of heavy machinery. Wilmington became the headquarters of du Pont's chemical industry. Baltimore led the country in canning.

After 1870 the center of gravity of heavy industry in America moved across the Appalachians to the triangle formed by the great cities of Pittsburgh, Cleveland, and Chicago. Various specialties scattered all over the Middle West and even to the Pacific Coast. Textiles began to migrate to the Southeastern states, rich in cotton and cheap labor. One may follow this steady dispersal of manufacturing throughout the continent on maps in the *Atlas of the Historical Geography of the United States*,[36] noting the changing distribution of manpower, of value added by manufacture, and of the principal industries. Before 1859 Megalopolis was the only

[35] Harold F. Williamson (ed.), *The Growth of the American Economy*, Prentice Hall, New York, 1944; see also Victor S. Clark, *History of Manufactures in the United States*, McGraw-Hill Book Co., New York, 1929, 3 vols.

[36] Paullin, *op. cit.*, see plates 133–137, giving much greater detail than our Figures 55 and 56 for the years up to 1930. See also National Bureau of Economic Research, *Trends in the American Economy in the Nineteenth Century* (Studies in Income and Wealth, Vol. 24), Princeton University Press, Princeton, 1960, especially Part IA.

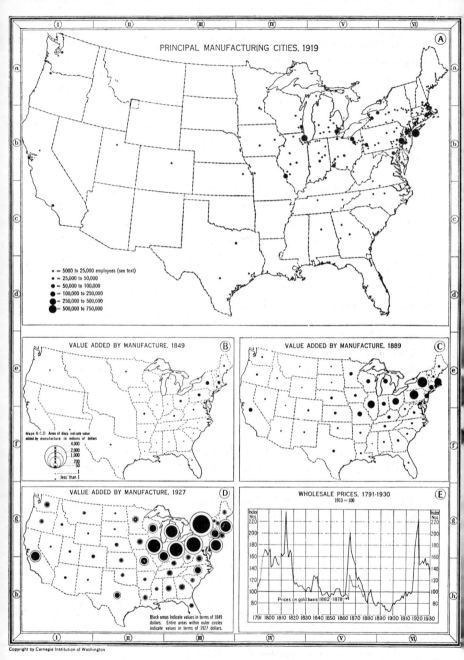

Fig. 56. Evolution of manufacturing, 1889–1927. *Reproduced by permission of the Carnegie Institution of Washington, from C. O. Paullin*, Atlas of the Historical Geography of the United States, *plate 134*

region in America to be intensively industrialized. In 1889 it still had by far the greatest industrial concentration, and even in 1919 this was true in numbers of employees; but the trans-Appalachian areas had risen more rapidly in terms of value added by manufacture and in this respect they had well outdistanced Megalopolis by the 1920's.

While certain industries continue to migrate out of Megalopolis, and others decline in their share of the national total, some new ones still prefer to locate in this area. The general trend is for the region to retain or attract industries requiring large numbers of skilled workers and proximity to consuming markets. In 1950 Megalopolis still had a higher share of the total value added by manufacture in the United States (26.4 per cent) than of the total population (21.2 per cent). *The size of the consuming market* in the area kept the clothing industry important there (in this field New York City used to be the towering capital, and it still remains a leading center, especially for women's and children's garments), increased the scale of the printing facilities,[37] and brought to the seaboard impressive new steel mills, both in Baltimore and on the Delaware.[38] And since 1940 there has grown up in Megalopolis the greatest concentration of electronics industries in the world, largely owing to the attraction of the New England and Greater New York and Philadelphia areas for these manufactures, as the result of a complicated set of factors concurring to make the location advantageous for this new and quickly expanding industry.[39]

How labor has had to adjust to a constantly changing industrial system has been well described, in the case of Philadelphia, by Gladys L. Palmer. There appears to be a basic stability due to advantages and specializations inherited from the past, and a varying degree of adaptation to new needs and demands.[40] It should also be noted that a good deal of industrial

[37] Max Hall (ed.), *Made in New York*, New York Metropolitan Region Study, Harvard University Press, Cambridge, Mass., 1959. See especially "Women's and Children's Apparel," by Roy B. Helfgott, pp. 135–239, and "Printing and Publishing" by Eric Gustafson, pp. 19–134.

[38] See Earl B. Shaw, *Anglo-America: A Regional Geography*, John Wiley and Sons, New York, 1959, especially pp. 102–105, and James C. O. Harris, "Steel," in *Mineral Facts and Problems*, U. S. Bureau of Mines, Washington, D. C., 1956, pp. 801–824.

[39] See the analysis for the New York region by James M. Hund, "Electronics," in *Made in New York*, op. cit., pp. 241–325; and our Chapter 9, below.

[40] Gladys L. Palmer, *Philadelphia Workers in a Changing Economy*, University of Pennsylvania Press, Philadelphia, 1956. Also the two volumes in the New York Metropolitan Region Study, *Anatomy of a Metropolis*, by Edgar M. Hoover and Raymond Vernon, Harvard University Press, 1959, and *Wages in the Metropolis* by Martin Segal, Harvard University Press, 1960.

migration has been taking place within the region of Megalopolis itself, increasingly in recent decades. Thus plants leave the too-crowded and too-expensive locations inside large cities to establish themselves in smaller towns with good transportation connections to the larger cities and beyond. They also move from highly industrialized areas such as southeastern New England, to less industrialized environments, which can still be found easily in Megalopolis south of the New York–Northeastern New Jersey metropolitan complex. Such moves may be motivated by a variety of reasons, ranging from labor relations to the desire for greater areas of inexpensive land for expansion. They have caused much churning within the region, have consolidated the areal pattern of industrialization and urbanization, and have pushed Megalopolis definitely southward (see Figs. 42 to 46, and 58, 59).

The most important trend of the twentieth century in the distribution of manpower does not, however, result from the migration of plants and factories. It stems from the remarkable fact that while modern technological progress has been effective in reducing the number of hands needed to produce given quantities in agriculture, mining, and manufacturing, it has also considerably increased the personnel needed to give full service in the nonproduction activities. As the *quantities* of goods to be manufactured keep on increasing, the total manpower occupied in the production of manufactures has still been rising but at a much slower rate than nonproduction industrial employment and employment in the white-collar or personal services categories. These trends are not new (see Figs. 136 and 170, pp. 456, 569). They have been changing the structure of the American labor force continuously for at least a century.[41] Since 1870 the trend has been definitely toward *less growth* in manufacturing employment and more in the complex of the white-collar occupations plus the service workers in maintenance, trade, and transportation. In 1919 in a total *nonagricultural* employment of 26,829,000 the manufacturing and construction industries accounted for 43 per cent, mining for 4 per cent, transportation and public utilities for 13 per cent, trade, finance, insurance, government, and the various services for 40 per cent. By 1957 nonagricultural employment had climbed to 52,162,000, almost double the 1919 figure; and the percentage accounted for by the manufacturing and construction industries had come down to 38, while the combined total of trade, finance,

[41] See Chapter 1 above, pp. 46–54, and the sources indicated in the footnotes on those pages. See also National Resources Committee, *The Structure of the American Economy*, U. S. Government Printing Office, Washington, D. C., Part I. *Basic Characteristics*, June 1939; *Part II. Toward Full Use of Resources*, June 1940.

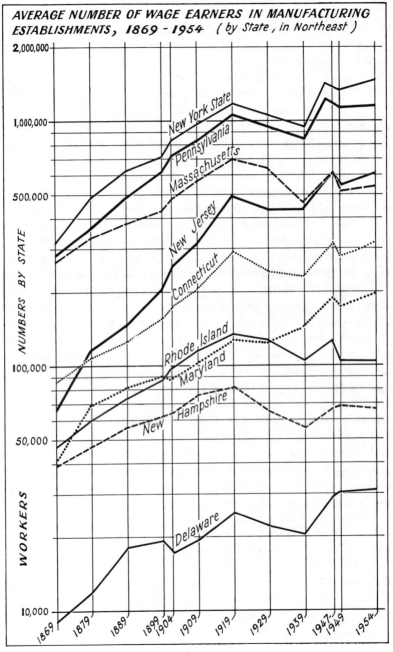

AVERAGE NUMBER OF WAGE EARNERS IN MANUFACTURING ESTABLISHMENTS, 1869 - 1954 (by State, in Northeast)

NUMBERS BY STATE

WORKERS

New York State
Pennsylvania
Massachusetts
New Jersey
Connecticut
Rhode Island
Maryland
New Hampshire
Delaware

2,000,000
1,000,000
500,000
100,000
50,000
10,000

1869 1879 1889 1899 1904 1909 1919 1929 1939 1947 1949 1954

FIG. 57

government, and other services had risen to 53 per cent.[42] In this latter group, which will soon account for *more than half of the total employment in the nation,* the variety of jobs and professions has constantly proliferated, owing to the affluence of society and to new problems arising from higher average incomes or from legal and technological developments. The latter have caused increased specializations among lawyers, physicians, dentists, and engineers, as well as among maintenance people. The greater average affluence has also caused new professions to appear, providing certain expert advice or special service now needed by many but formerly needed by only a few families and corporations.

In the manufacturing and construction industries many more people are employed in laboratory, secretarial, and managerial activities, creating new specialized professions and decreasing the numbers of workers in the trades and services. Thus the gamut of urban occupations has been quickly widening, and it promises to continue to create new specialties and new trades. How this professional evolution affects urban society and mode of life will appear in the forthcoming chapters of this volume analyzing its patterns of intense living. It must be pointed out at this stage that in the process *manufacturing becomes a less important component of the large city* and that the proximity of a large agglomeration of available labor becomes a less important factor in determining industrial plant location, although the consumer market keeps all its attraction. Since such trends have been operating in Megalopolis for some time they have contributed to the decentralization of its physical plants of production, pushing them out into suburban areas or satellite towns, thus increasing the average density of occupation on the fringes of metropolitan areas, consolidating Megalopolis in some regions, and somewhat expanding its limits.

At the same time the newly created or rapidly developing economic activities appear much more interconnected because they use more narrowly specialized personnel. Such establishments depend much more than do modern large-scale manufacturing plants on access to as large as possible a pool of competent and qualified labor. It is much easier to recruit and train the workers needed to operate an automobile plant or an oil refinery than it is to find personnel for the research, financial, and managerial divisions of the same corporation. Many companies find it advantageous to locate their financial headquarters close to institutions serving their various needs, such as stock exchange, large banks and investment firms, offices of specialized corporation lawyers, insurance brokers, accounting firms,

[42] Bureau of the Census, *Statistical Abstract of the United States: 1959,* U. S. Government Printing Office, Washington, D. C., 1959, Table 269, p. 210.

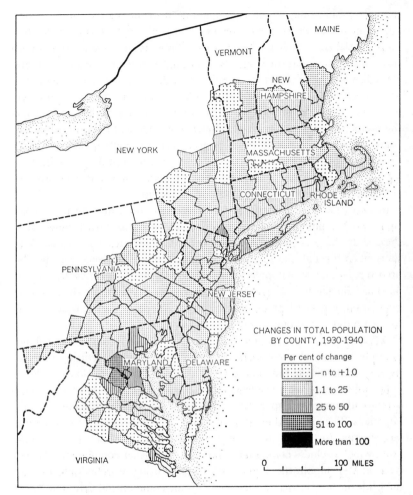

FIG. 58

advertising agencies, major news agencies, centers of economic research, good caterers, and so forth. This kind of concentration has been the reason for the growth of the business districts in central cities, particularly in Manhattan, Boston, and Philadelphia. Similar entanglements have concentrated the various activities of the mass-media market in Megalopolis and especially in the hub of Manhattan.

A city was a more stable unit when it had only a small minority of its population actually engaged in carrying on or servicing large-scale business, with most of the population engaged in factory work, local retail

trade, transportation, or construction. The widening of the gamut of occupations has displaced the center of gravity of employment toward the
more specialized, better-paid categories of jobs. Such workers are less tied
down to one location for living and working than if they had been tilling
the soil, working at a factory bench, or tending a small store. The rapid
growth of Megalopolitan cities, their industrialization, and the importance
of immigrants or in-migrants in their population have all helped to make
these cities more unstable, more subject to change and churning than has
been the case in less rapidly evolving urban centers. Nevertheless, although
the present occupational evolution is more advanced in Megalopolis, it is
a general characteristic of modern Western civilization, and it greatly increases with the whole density and rate of activities.

In 1950 the balance between manufacturing and white-collar occupations was beginning to shift in major cities on the seaboard. Since then
these shifts have accelerated, as has been demonstrated by various Censuses taken through the 1950's and in 1960. How this balance was distributed throughout Megalopolis in 1950 is shown to some extent by Figure
60. The "checkerboard" graphs indicate, for cities with more than 100,000
population, a general predominance of manufacturing over trade in the
total employment, though there are exceptions, among which Washington,
D. C., is naturally the leading one. Bridgeport, Connecticut, is a striking
example of a middle-sized seaboard city in which manufacturing remains
by far the dominant function. Graphs showing the proportion of white-
collar jobs among male residents complement the checkerboards to some
extent and stress the importance (still increasing) of this category of occupations. The picture thus attained is, of course, incomplete. Even for the
larger cities, for which there are graphs, the data given are for residents
only, which excludes commuters who reside in smaller communities. Moreover, in Megalopolis the dispersal of manufacturing, warehousing, and retail trade outside the major nuclei has become common and easy, and many
of these activities are therefore scattered in communities having fewer
than 100,000 people, for which no graphs are shown. In contrast, the "office industries" keep on concentrating in the major hubs or in a few new
suburban locations carefully selected for special purposes.

Suburban Sprawl and Metropolitan Integration

To alleviate the crowding of larger cities, divers solutions have been
tried, all of them resulting from the free interplay of temporary or permanent factors. Each of these solutions has increased the crowding of the
districts around and between the major nuclei. This is demonstrated by

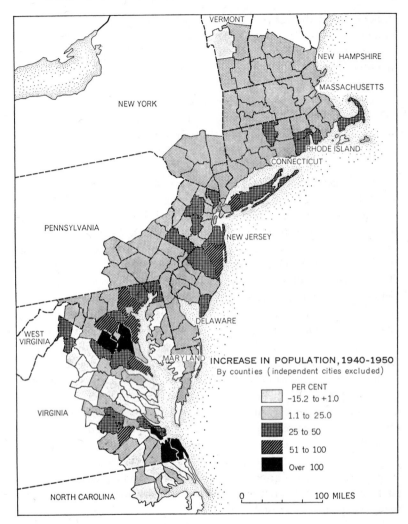

INCREASE IN POPULATION, 1940-1950
By counties (independent cities excluded)

PER CENT
-15.2 to +1.0
1.1 to 25.0
25 to 50
51 to 100
Over 100

0   100 MILES

FIG. 59

the maps showing the distribution of cities and densities of population in the region since 1850 (see Figs. 38, 40 to 46, 49, 58, 59, pp. 145, 154–155, 158–164), and by the changes occurring in the distribution of population.

The persistence of the early principal axis of settlement and traffic as a factor orienting recent crowding is obvious on the map showing (by counties) the spread of population densities greater than 90 per square mile (Fig. 51). It is apparent also in the more detailed maps showing population changes during the 1930–50 period (Figs. 42 to 46, pp. 158–164). Areas with decreasing or more or less stable population (i.e., having increases of less than 10 per cent in a period when the nation grew by 23 per cent) are found chiefly on the periphery of Megalopolis, in zones emptied by the attraction of the quickly growing sectors and not yet reached by the sprawl. But small patches of decline or stability are found also inside Megalopolis, and some of these correspond to the greater cities and some of their immediate suburbs, reflecting the slower pace of *residential* growth in the older, more crowded, more fully urbanized zones. These seem to have reached a sort of "saturation" in terms of residences.

For changes in distribution of place of work the picture is somewhat different. A map of the region showing changes in the distribution of manufacturing by minor civil divisions would probably be quite like the map of changes in population (i.e., residential change). Manufacturing shifts for the period 1939–54 have been mapped by counties in Figure 138 (p. 459), and this map has a good deal in common with the residential map. On a similar map of white-collar employment there would be more deviations from both residential and manufacturing trends as regards dispersal within the region; greater gains would be shown for major central cities. But the office industry apparently accepts more distant commuting.

It is apparent, then, that suburban sprawl was formerly and still is determined largely by the scattering of manufacturing establishments, away from the areas already too crowded by such plants and into districts with good transportation facilities and within easy reach of one or more major central cities. Because locations between several such large markets are often especially favored, there has been a more rapid growth of *interurbia* along the axial roads and railroads than in outlying districts on the fringe. Nevertheless, the size of the New York City market has induced a substantial manufacturing growth, especially in the 1900's in central Long Island; and certain industries prefer tidewater access and therefore accept a somewhat peripheral coastal location.

Thus manufacturing expansion and displacement have caused Megalopolis to grow and consolidate — as an urban area and as an entangled chain of metropolitan regions — both along the main axis of U. S. 1 and toward the tidewater edge. The automobile, better highways, and the relative emptying in previous decades of some adjacent areas have enabled workers in the old or new centers of employment to scatter their residences within reasonable distances of their place of work. Generally, to save time and money, people have preferred to keep this "reasonable distance" between home and job as low as possible.

But with the growing affluence of society, a rising level of education, and more leisure time on the whole, the suburban sprawl has been increasingly influenced by recreational considerations, which affect the choice of the main residence and in some cases of a secondary one. To have a major residence out of town while having one's principal source of income from an urban occupation came early to be recognized as a sign of distinction and of substantial wealth. Country houses, in rural surroundings but close enough to town for a round trip during the day, have been traditional symbols of a sort of aristocratic way of life: thus since the Renaissance the *villas* of rich merchants have dotted the landscape around Florence; and in the eighteenth and nineteenth centuries such suburban castles or manorial homes were scattered around Paris and other European metropolises.

The same trend had been early observed on the Northeastern seaboard of the United States. From the 1760's on, such suburban houses, either principal or secondary residences, proliferated around Boston, New York, and Philadelphia and in Rhode Island. Early examples of these elegant suburbs are the village of Cambridge near Boston, Greenwich Village on Manhattan, and the whole area of the Schuylkill Hills overlooking the Delaware near Philadelphia; farther away from the cities country houses on larger estates took on a manorial appearance in the 1780's and 1790's, rivalling the most famous mansions on the Virginia or South Carolina plantations.[43] This trend continued through the nineteenth century, as much larger numbers of middle-class citizens were able to afford elegant living, although perhaps on a more modest scale than the leading families. The latter, of course, always set the fashion and mode. S. E. Morison has well described the situation in Massachusetts:

Yachting in Massachusetts resulted from a new custom of the merchants, a summer residence by the sea. In Colonial and Federalist days, Boston and Salem were so salty themselves that the few who felt the need of a "change of air" took it inland, at a country seat. Horticulture was the gentlemanly hobby for a shipowner. But as Massachusetts turned inland for profit, she returned seaward for pleasure.[44]

The new fashion started in 1817 at Nahant and expanded gradually to many former fishing villages. One of these, Swampscott, developed after 1842, had by 1920 become "part summer resort, part bourgeois suburb of Lynn and Boston." [45] A similar destiny has come to most of the New England sea front in Connecticut, Rhode Island, and Massachusetts, and since

[43] Bridenbaugh, *Cities in Revolt, op. cit.*, pp. 248 and 336–342.

[44] Samuel Eliot Morison, *The Maritime History of Massachusetts, 1783–1860*, Houghton Mifflin Company, Boston, 1921, p. 244; see pp. 244–249.

[45] *Ibid.*, p. 245.

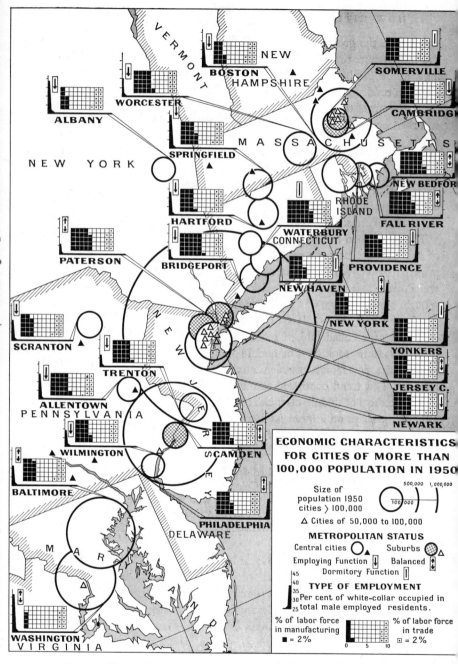

FIG. 60. Economic characteristics based on data and classification in *Municipal Yearbook: 1959*.

1910 many of the former summer residences have been occupied for most of the year.

There has been a similar evolution on Long Island, where many of the beautiful seaside estates of the period 1860–1910 have now been taken over by tax-exempt institutions or restricted clubs, or have become public parks, while others have been broken up into building lots and developed for all-year-round residences. The creeks and peninsulas of Maryland's shores on Chesapeake Bay may soon follow in a similar evolution.

Since the merchant princes of Boston and New York first took up yachting and seaside residences, this vogue has become so popular throughout the United States that Americans were estimated to have spent $2 billion on boating alone in 1958; [46] more than one fourth of this expenditure certainly took place in Megalopolis.

For recreational reasons, residences have pushed out toward the seashore on one hand and also toward wooded areas, scenic valleys in the inland hills, and lakes in New Jersey as well as in Massachusetts. The automobile era and the improvement of highway networks have added more incentives to dispersal "within reasonable distance," and by 1950 centers of employment had scattered so widely through the whole region between the tidewater and the steep inland ranges that very few districts of Megalopolis were beyond reasonable distance to some place of work. A vast tide of residential dispersal went beyond the axial belt where crowding was obvious and increasing.

Thus metropolitan regions have grown toward each other and have joined and even penetrated one another. And the adjacent space, perhaps not yet classified in 1950 as part of a standard metropolitan area, has acquired a type of rural economy entirely dependent on the adjoining urbanized zone. Megalopolis has thus grown to be the curious urban region that it is. To an observer who flies over its expanse at some altitude it may look largely wooded and thinly populated. The number of commuters who go daily from one of its metropolitan areas to another may seem too small, to persons who rely only on official statistical data for their judgments, to support the concept of an integrated super-metropolitan growth over all this section of the country. The integration, however, is an indisputable fact; it penetrates deeply the whole social and economic structure of the region and of its various and many parts. We shall better comprehend it as we proceed to analyze its modern patterns of land use and how its people live and work.

[46] Estimate in *Business Review*, Federal Reserve Bank of Philadelphia, July 1959, p. 11.

PART TWO

THE REVOLUTION
IN LAND USE

Exploding far beyond city limits, the seaboard metropolises have converted vast areas to urban and suburban modes of life and land occupation, and in several ways these new forms of land use and social reorganization have introduced revolutionary changes. Within the vast territory of the United States this large section specializes in urban pursuits while some other sections specialize in agricultural production. The long-accepted opposition between town and country has therefore evolved toward a new opposition between *urban regions*, of which Megalopolis is certainly the most obvious and advanced case, and *agricultural regions*, the largest and most typical of which is found in the grain-growing Great Plains.

The agricultural regions have always had towns and urban centers in their midst, for they were and are dotted with such groupings of dense population on tightly built-up small areas. Most of these urban dwellers live there in order to service the farms, but in a few cases cities within an agricultural region have developed industrial and trading activities, the horizons of which extend beyond the scope of the local region. Inversely, today an urban region such as Megalopolis encompasses farming areas, some of which may produce certain kinds of agricultural goods on a scale quite comparable to that of farms in agricultural regions. However, the occupation of the land for such farming purposes in an urban region appears entirely subordinated not only to the near-by urban market but also to a whole organization of society and to a system of land values quite different from those that can be found in the predominantly agricultural countryside.

The major "revolution" takes place in our understanding of how society is organized, how land is occupied, and how the various professions actually function. The picture we shall now sketch and analyze for Megalopolis results from a gradual evolution. The common man's knowledge about it, however, has lagged behind the actual changes. Apparently even most experts in social and economic fields have been so absorbed each in his own specialty that they have had little time to observe the interrelations between the trends, the entanglements linking the "facts" as defined by each expert. Thus the immense and complex process that has been steadily modifying the morphology of this whole region's lands and people was recognized only when its strangeness and its problems hit our eyes and our daily lives with overwhelming force.

Let us now try to shed the old ideas and images inherited from an education and a vocabulary that have not kept up with the changes going on around us, and let us start to explore with due curiosity and the many tools at our disposal this new "wilderness" that has grown up in Megalopolis. We may often be surprised: perhaps by the hint at the kind of farmers in the area suggested by the New Jersey Department of Agriculture report that a company has been established to furnish "cow-sitters" for dairymen who have to be absent from their farms; [1] or perhaps by the expansion of the forested area and the proliferation of deer in the immediate proximity of highly urbanized and densely occupied districts. In some aspects we may find this urban region much "wilder," and in others much more "civilized," than would be expected. At times it may be demonstrated that it was as people became more urban that the landscape came to look wilder. A new integration is thus being ironed out between concepts and trends we have been trained to separate and oppose. The analysis must start with the new symbiosis integrating what used to be "urban" and "rural," and then proceed with an examination of the component parts.

[1] *The New York Times*, January 17, 1960 (brief notes by W. E. Farbstein).

C H A P T E R   5

The Symbiosis of Urban and Rural

In Megalopolis in the 1950's the interpenetration of urban and rural had achieved a complexity and a size yet unknown anywhere else on the globe. In this gradual symbiosis two seemingly conflicting trends have worked together: urban people and activities have taken on more rural aspects and traditionally rural pursuits have acquired urban characteristics. Some sectors of an urbanized region have come to look the way rural countryside used to, while districts specializing in agricultural production have begun to resemble built-up suburbs. The whole pattern of land use has changed rapidly.

One may, of course, compare the process observed in Megalopolis to what has been happening since the beginning of the present century in the most urbanized and crowded parts of northwestern Europe: in England, around London and in the Midlands especially, in Holland and central Belgium, in the Greater Paris area of France, in the Ruhr industrial basin of Germany. Each of these regions is much smaller in area and more densely populated than Megalopolis. It is also more "fenced in" because of a narrower national economy whose boundaries impose many more barriers to movement than exist within the vast area of the United States. In fact, these European regions may be seriously in danger of running out of space. In Megalopolis the fully urbanized and built-up sectors are many and of impressive size, but there still remains a great deal of thinly occupied space devoted to woods, fields, and pasture. Seen from a plane the contrast between the built-up and the wooded districts is striking, and even now (1960) there is a general predominance of woods in terms of square miles.

On closer examination, however, we shall find that present and future use of these green spaces within Megalopolis is completely dependent on the march of urbanization. We shall also discover that, while the actual crowding is still localized and open land is available on a much larger scale than is usually recognized, present trends indicate an urgent need for new policies if Megalopolitan populations are not to find themselves even more fenced in than are the people in other highly urbanized regions of the world.

The Pull, the Push, and the Land

In the nineteenth century, migrations between rural and urban areas followed the typical pattern of "push off the land" and "pull of the cities." A profitable expansion of agricultural production required more machines and chemicals and fewer hands, and displaced farm workers were attracted to cities by new jobs in industry and by a life that was more glamorous and definitely easier, especially for the womenfolk. This pattern still applies today to migrations from the agricultural lands of the Great Plains to the metropolitan areas of the United States, and to the rural exodus so prominent now in many underdeveloped countries.

In Megalopolis, however, this pattern has been considerably modified and complicated by a new system of forces. Some of the old type of push and pull still goes on, but *within the same space* a new *pull of inner suburbia* attracts manufactures and certain types of residents, while *a pull of outer suburbia* attracts other categories of residents and some retail trade, and both of these pulls are balanced by the *push* out of the old city territory fostered by various economic and social factors. That is, Megalopolis experiences an exodus from the cities to neighboring zones that had been rural. At the same time other migrants from far-away towns and farms come to crowd the central cities. Thus urban growth goes on and on, both within the territory officially designated as urban and outside it.

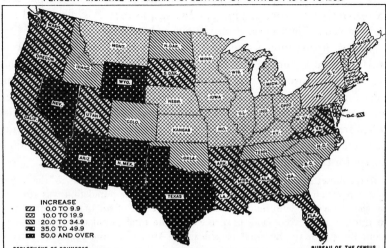

PERCENT INCREASE IN URBAN POPULATION BY STATES : 1940 TO 1950

INCREASE
0.0 TO 9.9
10.0 TO 19.9
20.0 TO 34.9
35.0 TO 49.9
50.0 AND OVER

DEPARTMENT OF COMMERCE   BUREAU OF THE CENSUS

Fig. 61. *Courtesy of the U. S. Bureau of the Census*

The first state in the Union to see its population become predominantly *urban* (according to official Census definition) was Rhode Island, which in 1850 had 55.6 per cent of its population so classified. In the same Census Massachusetts followed closely with 50.7 per cent. In New York State the urban element reached 50 per cent in 1870, while New Jersey recorded 54.4 per cent in 1880, Connecticut 50.9 per cent in 1890, Pennsylvania 54.7 per cent in 1900, Maryland 50.8 per cent and New Hampshire 51.8 per cent in 1910, and Delaware 54.2 per cent in 1920. The national average reached 51.2 per cent in 1920. Among the states outside Megalopolis none had an urban majority before 1900. In that year Illinois and California passed the half-way mark, and in 1910 Ohio, Oregon, and Washington State were added to the list, which Indiana, Michigan, and Wisconsin joined in 1920. Megalopolis showed, therefore, a clear precedence in this respect over other sections of the United States.

As early as 1930, however, the proportion of the population officially classed as urban began to decrease in several states, a trend that was general in Megalopolis in 1940 and 1950, especially if, for comparison's sake, the old definition of urban population, omitting unincorporated places and urban fringes (see p. 34 above), is applied to 1950 Census data. Using that definition the percentages of the population classed as urban in 1930, 1940, and 1950 for some representative states were: Massachusetts — 90.2, 89.4, 87.9; Rhode Island — 92.4, 91.6, 88.4; Connecticut — 70.4, 67.8, 64.1; New

Jersey — 82.6, 81.6, 79.6. In Maryland the change was from 60.0 per cent in 1920 to 59.8 in 1930, 59.3 in 1940, and 54.4 in 1950. A similar trend can be observed in New York, Pennsylvania, and Delaware.

That is, urbanization has spilled over the boundaries of the territory formerly defined as "urban" and has scattered rather widely. It was for this reason that in 1950 the Bureau of the Census redefined urban population, including for the first time the inhabitants of densely settled urban-fringe areas and of unincorporated places of 2,500 or more people outside the urban fringe. This new definition showed a substantial increase in the urban percentage over 1940, and over the 1950 count by the old definition, except for two states, Massachusetts and Rhode Island.

Massachusetts and Rhode Island stand in marked contrast to the other States in which the urban and rural distribution of the population was affected by the change in definition. In these States the net effect of this change was to transfer 3.5 percent and 4.2 percent of the total population, respectively, from the urban to the rural classification. Among all the remaining States, however, the change in urban definition resulted in net shifts of population in the opposite direction . . . The use of whole minor civil divisions as units required the inclusion of their sparsely settled areas. Under the greater refinement of the new definition, these sparsely settled areas reverted to rural territory with the result that in Rhode Island and Massachusetts the change in definition resulted in a net increase in population classified as rural.[1]

There can be no doubt, of course, that these states, like the others in Megalopolis, were in reality much more urbanized in 1950 than in earlier years. But some of the actually urban people, and apparently increasing numbers of them, reside *outside urban territory*. The statistics given above show that since 1920, and even more since 1930, urbanization has gone beyond old territorial bounds in Megalopolis and has scattered to such a degree that in certain districts it is a problem to know how to classify sparsely settled areas. They may look rural, but it may be more correct to recognize them as urban.

One understands better what has been happening as one looks at the distribution of the *rural nonfarm population* within the region. In 1950 the proportion of the rural nonfarm element in the *rural* population (all urban elements being excluded for the purposes of this query) varied from county to county but was for almost all of Megalopolis greater than 70 per cent, while the national average stood at 58 per cent (see Fig. 63). The 1950 figures represent considerable change since 1930 (when the nation

[1] U. S. Bureau of the Census, *U. S. Census of Population 1950, Vol. II: Characteristics of the Population, Part I: United States Summary*, U. S. Government Printing Office, Washington, D. C., 1953, pp. 14–15. All figures of urban percentages above from 1940 and 1950 Censuses.

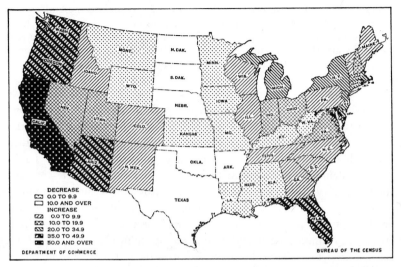

Fig. 62. Percentage decrease or increase in the rural population by states, 1940–50. *Courtesy of the U. S. Bureau of the Census*

averaged 44 per cent), and even more since 1940; for in Megalopolis the percentage of nonfarm population in rural territory had declined in many counties during the 1930's (see Fig. 64) as a result of the depression. The nonfarm population in rural territory depends either on jobs in urban areas within commuting range or on the servicing of farms and vacationers; and as industrial, farming, and touristic activities were all seriously reduced by the great depression, the rural nonfarm population obviously felt the brunt of the situation more than either farm or urban people. Many nonfarm rural residents then moved to other areas: to cities, to be close to eventual job openings; to farms, on which survival is easier in critical periods; and sometimes to areas far outside Megalopolis. During the 1940's, however, the nonfarm element spread again over rural territory within Megalopolis, and a comparison of 1950 figures with those of 1940 or 1930 is rather striking (see Figs. 63 and 64). This rise is all the more significant because in all states but Rhode Island and Massachusetts the redefinition of urban territory in 1950 transferred to that category the more densely settled and less agricultural areas that had still been classified as rural in the 1940 Census.

These various movements of people demonstrate what Donald J. Bogue, distinguished interpreter of American population statistics, has noted, that rural nonfarm population "has been residentially more mobile than either the urban or the rural-farm population." He goes on, however, to say that:

This differential seems to reflect the growth of suburbs and the building up of more dense settlements in the vicinity of metropolises, rather than a flow of population to open country, villages, or hamlets. As new subdivisions are created in suburban areas, they attract a flow of families from the central city. Such subdivisions tend to be classed as rural-nonfarm rather than urban.[2]

While this is certainly true for most of the country, one could take exception, insofar as a good deal of Megalopolis is concerned, to the conclusion that the nonfarm tide reflects "the growth of suburbs, and the building up of more dense settlements in the vicinity of metropolises rather than a flow of population to open country, villages, or hamlets." To be sure, the definition of "dense settlement" always was a variable concept; and the density of the population in the rural parts of Megalopolis is rather high by average American standards. On rural roads, along which the nonfarm occupance penetrates the rural lands, there are often groups of a dozen or so homes close enough to one another to produce what might be called a hamlet or village. But over large areas the distribution of buildings is quite sparse. As noted above, the sprawl of nonfarm population during the 1940's went deep into country that was still classified as rural even by the 1950 definition.

Woodland, which is often held to be the antithesis of urban land use, remains quite important throughout Megalopolis, making up nearly half of the total area. Outside the main cities in practically every county of the region, more than 12 per cent of the area was wooded in the middle 1950's (see Fig. 112, p. 342, based on U. S. Forest Service data); in most of the New England part of Megalopolis this proportion in woodland reached more than 60 per cent; in other counties, not situated along the main historical axis of crowding from New York City to Baltimore, it remained greater than 30 per cent. These are quite high percentages. The predominance of woods in the landscape outside the main metropolitan nuclei is obvious to anyone who has recently traveled through the area. This predominance does not prevent, and seems even in a way to favor, high density of population and especially of rural nonfarm population.

If we look at a few samples of land use and building distribution in areas of New England we may understand how such landscapes are brought about and are now functioning. The "dense dispersal" of houses through areas predominantly under woods and brush (see Figs. 67, 68, 69, 70, and 71) cannot be supported, indeed, by any source of income located in the immediate vicinity of these residences. Their occupants must work at

[2] Donald J. Bogue, *The Population of the United States*, The Free Press, Glencoe, Ill., 1959, p. 379.

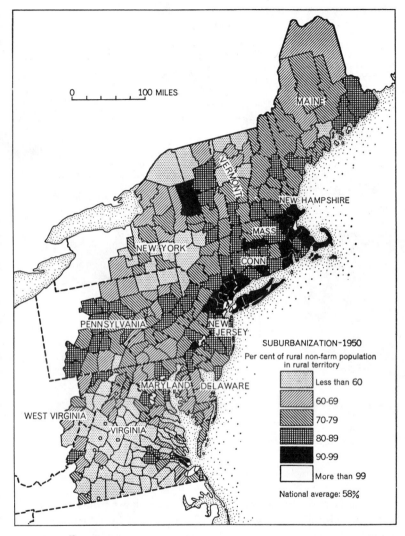

SUBURBANIZATION-1950
Per cent of rural non-farm population
in rural territory

Less than 60
60-69
70-79
80-89
90-99
More than 99

National average: 58%

Fig. 63

something other than forestry or farming. The few patches of land used for agricultural purposes are far too small and too scattered to enable the area to support so dense a residential dispersal.

While such is the case in New England and in some parts of New York, other areas farther south and southwest, in New Jersey, Pennsylvania, Delaware, Maryland, and northern Virginia, show a greater stability of

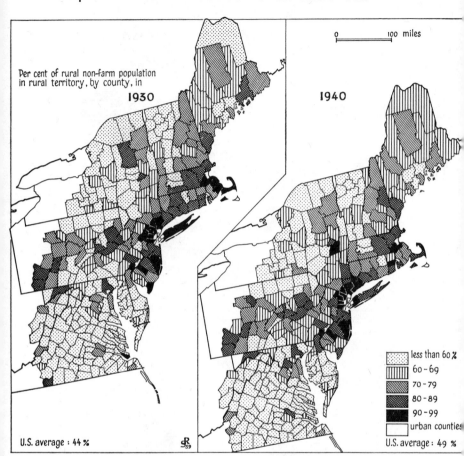

Per cent of rural non-farm population
in rural territory, by county, in
1930

1940

0   100 miles

less than 60 %
60 - 69
70 - 79
80 - 89
90 - 99
urban counties

U.S. average : 44 %

U.S. average : 49 %

FIG. 64. Suburbanization in the Northeast in 1930 and 1940, according to the same index as on Figs. 7 and 63

farms and of agricultural uses of the land. The higher proportion of the land in woods in New England seems to be caused by a complex set of factors, and paradoxically the earlier urbanization and higher densities of population in that area seem to have accelerated the trend pushing the farmland out and pulling the forest in. The poorer quality of the soils, the greater length of winters, and the somewhat marginal geographical location may have played a part too. However, through the 1950's one could easily observe obvious signs of the spreading of woodland in almost every large region of the United States east of the Mississippi. There were few localized sectors that stood out as exceptions to this rule. And this general trend went on in a large part of the country where the population density was rising, the suburbs were sprawling, and the output of many farm products was increasing.[3]

Push or pull? Within Megalopolis many forces are pulling and pushing at the same time, creating new patterns of land use. It may be surprising to recognize these new patterns as dependent upon the march of urbanization in the region. That such dependence exists in other parts of the world, too, has been shown by several recent surveys of land use in the vicinity of large European cities.

Agricultural Economics in a Suburban Setting

Both farming and sylvan land uses in Megalopolis will be systematically examined later in this study (see below, Chapters 6 and 7); but before we look at each in detail it is important to realize how entangled they are one with another and how deeply and daily they are both involved with the life of the cities. A few localized examples may illustrate these complex relationships and help us to appreciate the unique organization of the region.

Although occupying only 1.8 per cent of the land area of the continental United States, and having half of its territory covered with woods and brush, Megalopolis produced 5.1 per cent of the total value of farm products sold in the country in 1950. These figures suggest some districts of quite intensive farming within the region. The most remarkable of these is probably Lancaster County, Pennsylvania. It is the heart of the "Pennsylvania Dutch" area, reputed for its picturesqueness, the beautiful architecture of its farm buildings, and its skillful but often archaic agricultural methods. In size it is average by national standards, with 945 square miles, but Lancaster ranked thirteenth in the nation (among some 3,100 counties) in value of farm products sold, according to the *United States Census of Agriculture: 1954*, and it was *clearly first among all the counties east of the Mississippi*.[4] This value amounted to $80,151,000, almost equally divided between livestock and livestock products, poultry and poultry products,

[3] These processes have been studied in detail for the whole Commonwealth of Virginia in Jean Gottmann, *Virginia at Mid-Century*, Henry Holt and Company, New York, 1955; see Chapters 4 and 5. Similar trends have been observed by the writer in eastern France and by the German geographer Prof. Wolfgang Hartke in southern Germany.

[4] The twelve counties with higher values were all in the West: nine of them in California (where Fresno County was first in the nation) and one each in Arizona, Washington, and Colorado. The estimates for 1958 published by the magazine *Sales Management: The Magazine of Marketing* in its annual "Survey of Buying Power" (May 10, 1959, pp. 56–58) ranked Lancaster fourteenth and gave it second place in the East, behind Aroostook County, Maine, which had almost tripled the value of its crops from 1954 to 1958, possibly a statistical error.

and dairy products. These products came from some 7,951 farms, averaging 63 acres in size and covering 82.4 per cent of the county's land area. Only two farms had more than 1,000 acres each; and only 10 per cent of the farms were classified as part-time. Lancaster was therefore a region intensively cultivated by many small commercial farmers. However, 615 of the latter declared over $25,000 each in value of products sold in 1954. This made a remarkable density of rich farms, which accounts for the county's total farm wealth and its leadership in such a vast section. These figures could hardly be understood without knowing the local emphasis on animal products. It was the fattening of livestock and the production of large quantities of poultry and dairy products that explained the wealth of these farms.

The extent of this animal husbandry was impressive. In 1954 Lancaster counted 146,848 head of cattle and 41,195 hogs and pigs. With 3.8 per cent of Pennsylvania's land area in farms, this remarkable county fed 8 per cent of the state's cattle and 7 per cent of its hogs and generated 18 per cent of Pennsylvania's revenue from poultry raising. Despite the quality of the limestone soils and the skill and hard labor of the farmers, the county's earth could not feed adequately all the animals on its farms especially since the large buildings of so many farms take up part of the land, some farmland is wooded, and some is devoted to profitable industrial crops, especially tobacco leaf. Lancaster County therefore imported most of its animal feeds, largely from the Middle West. Increasingly the Lancaster farmers have specialized in raising, fattening, and milking animals to obtain high-priced products, the sale of which is profitable in the great urban markets within easy reach.

Dairy products, especially fluid milk, are regularly picked up by trucks of some company that specializes in distributing them in certain cities. Once the necessary contracts are signed with specialized organizations, providing for the feed and other supplies on the one hand and for the marketing of the produce on the other, a farmer with adequately equipped buildings and a little land can securely engage in producing large quantities of fluid milk for the urban consumer. Similar mechanisms work just as well for poultry and eggs. A good many Lancaster farmers have given up tobacco and other cash crops to turn to poultry.

As this writer visited a farm near the town of New Holland in Lancaster County in 1959, he began to understand the density of large farms standing on almost every hilltop as far as the eye could reach. One of these hilltops, however, was occupied by half a dozen brick houses, lower and less impressive structures that looked residential. The farmer explained that, not

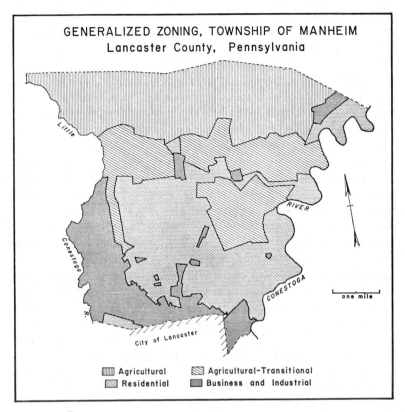

GENERALIZED ZONING, TOWNSHIP OF MANHEIM
Lancaster County, Pennsylvania

☐☐☐ Agricultural   ☒ Agricultural-Transitional
☐ Residential   ▤ Business and Industrial

FIG. 65

needing all his land for his intensive animal husbandry, he had started to develop a few acres for suburban residences. These houses are not too crowded together, and they are in a choice location, set in beautiful and healthful rural surroundings, and within some ten miles of an industrial town.

Thus urban and rural come to interpenetrate one another even in the heart of the rich agricultural Pennsylvania Dutch country. Such sights are no longer uncommon as one leaves the primary highways to wander along the rural roads in many parts of Megalopolis where farming goes on.

Farmers like those of Lancaster, Chester, or York counties in Pennsylvania, specializing in animal husbandry, supply good meats, milk, eggs, and poultry to the urbanized parts of the neighborhood and to more distant metropolises. Properly speaking, tillage and pasturage become secondary, almost complementary activities on their small farms, and the farmer's work consists mainly in "processing," by means of his animals, feeds procured from afar. For this he needs some skills, some equipment, some capital investment, and good contracts to assure that supplies will come in regularly and his produce will be sold regularly at a good profit. Gradually such a farmer evolves toward a contractor's status, with little need to care about the quality of his soil, the weather, or the extent of his land. But he must learn more about his animals' health and nutrition, the processing of the milk and eggs, the legal aspects of his contracts, his insurance, the needs and trends of the city markets.

Thus the farmer's profession evolves, not becoming less noble or more "artificial" but merely keeping up with the times and with the opportunities of his location. In a way it could be claimed to be *less* "artificial" than the vast classic grain- or cotton-growing farms in the Great Plains, for the Megalopolitan farms produce fewer surpluses and cost the taxpayer less in terms of subsidies. This kind of specialized agriculture either *processes agricultural raw materials* through the farm animals, to obtain finished consumer goods that bring a premium price on the market, or it *grows some special crops* that are in particular demand in the cities and that require proximity to the consumer because they spoil rapidly (fresh vegetables, flowers, certain berries, for example). Such farming is more directly adapted to the market's balance of demand and supply. It still benefits from all the devices for easy profit that legislation may afford, such as the soil bank or some tax deductions, but it contributes less to the huge stockpile of surpluses that cost the American taxpayer a few billion dollars each year.

This close relationship between farm production and urban consumption has been organized by large private firms distributing the goods and by public authorities. Among the latter the Federal agencies have been particularly concerned, since the 1930's, with protection of the farmers' interests, while local government agencies in urban areas have been more concerned with the protection of the consumer.

Fluid milk illustrates this well. It has become one of the major "cash crops" of the Megalopolitan farms and has made dairying quite popular and profitable in the rural sectors of the Northeast. This economic trend has resulted both from the huge milk consumption in the region and from the existence of legislation delimiting "milksheds" for the major cities in Megalopolis. The latter factor, rooted in public health regulations enacted by municipal authorities, appears indeed as the decisive one, governing the overall picture of production and distribution of fluid milk (and fresh cream) in Megalopolis.

A "milkshed" is established by a city or a state government for health reasons: they restrict the fluid milk and sometimes the cream supplies legally admitted for sale to the produce of farms in the area through which the responsible authority sends its inspectors to make sure that the methods of production, processing, and transportation meet the city's (and in some respects the state's) requirements. In this way, a city "licenses" a certain area to produce milk and cream for its consumption, and the area thus licensed becomes the city's milkshed. It is deemed a great opportunity and a privilege for a rural area to have a large city's market thus reserved for its dairy products. To be sure, its farmers must comply with the rules and requirements set — an example of local government concern for the consumer. But the prices fixed for milk consumed in the larger cities are, with the help of Federal support, high enough to pay the cooperating farmers well.[5]

Since the suburbs and satellites of a large central city normally follow its supply system they both benefit by the organized controls in the milkshed and swell the market it serves. Location inside the milkshed of a large metropolitan area is thus a substantial asset. For a producing district it is especially advantageous to be located in an area where two large milksheds overlap. This happens often in Megalopolis (see Fig. 66), where metropolitan areas each with more than a million inhabitants neighbor on one another. Lancaster County finds itself situated in the milksheds of New York City, Baltimore, and Philadelphia, a choice location indeed. Boston's milkshed overlaps only slightly with New York City's according to the map, but there is a transitional area in the so-called "Connecticut" milkshed, parts of which at times gravitate toward either New York or Boston. Since these are high-priced markets it is occasionally difficult for the Connecticut cities to obtain local milk, especially at a lower rate.

In southern New England, five major milk markets are located between the Boston and New York metropolitan markets . . . The situation demon-

[5] See A. C. Dahlberg and H. S. Adams, *Sanitary Milk and Ice Cream Legislation in the United States*, Bulletin of the National Research Council, No. 121, National Academy of Sciences–National Research Council, Washington, D. C., July 1950; by the same authors, *Sanitary Milk Control and Its Relation to the Sanitary, Nutritive and Other Qualities of Milk*, National Academy of Sciences–National Research Council, Publication No. 250, Washington, D. C., 1953; and William Bredo and Anthony S. Rojko, *Prices and Milksheds of Northeastern Markets* (Northeast Regional Publication No. 9), University of Massachusetts Agricultural Experiment Station, Bulletin No. 470, Amherst, Mass., August 1952; we are also indebted for a good deal of information to the U. S. Department of Agriculture, Washington, D. C., to Cornell University's Department of Agricultural Economics, and especially to the Department of Health of the City of New York.

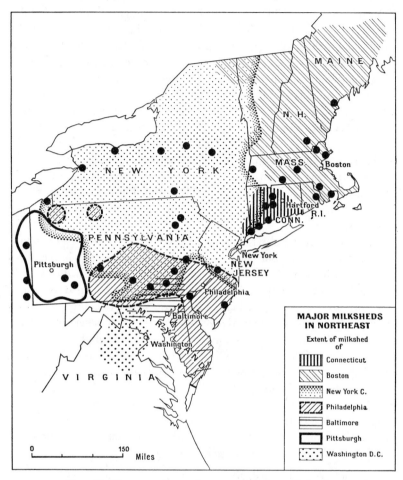

FIG. 66. The map shows the extent of the milksheds around 1950. The large black round dots indicate medium-sized cities (New Haven, Trenton, Wilmington, etc.) located within the milksheds of larger cities with which they may sometimes have to compete for supply. The clustering of such medium-sized cities in Connecticut, close to New York City, resulted in the establishment of a Connecticut milkshed.

strates uniquely the influence of two dominant markets on the relationships and adjustments of less important markets. The competition of New York City and Boston forces these five southern New England markets to reach for supplies in a northwesterly direction. The Connecticut markets are strongly influenced by New York City; but Providence, Hartford and Spring-field present an intermediate position, being subject to competition from both primary markets in western Vermont and eastern New York; Worcester, Lowell-Lawrence-Haverhill, and Portland are distinctly Boston satellites.[6]

A situation of tight supply in relation to the demand could cause not only a rise in prices but also difficulties for the supply of smaller intermediate markets. This is true in New Jersey and Pennsylvania as much as in New England. In recent years, however, the supply of fluid milk has been rather abundant in the Northeast and appears likely to be maintained at a level avoiding serious competition between consuming markets. This emphasis on dairy farming in Megalopolis is due to the large and stable size of the demand, and also to the abundance of capital ready for investment in large and well-equipped farm enterprises, providing suburban areas with the opportunity for *comfortable gentleman-farmer living*. For such farmers it is appropriate to be able to call on "cow-sitters" such as were announced recently in New Jersey (see p. 216 above). In some sectors of Megalopolis such gentleman-farmers may be able to afford to raise horses and fatten beef cattle, somewhat more expensive propositions than dairying.

For people having a large enough income from other sources than the farm, the cost of farm operation may seem worthwhile, for it still brings some benefits and provides for at least part of the year the setting of an elegant and healthful way of life. Analyzing Megalopolitan agriculture, Edward Higbee describes belts of estate farms (see pp. 314–318 below). With growing affluence and shorter working hours in the cities, more people can afford, if not rural estates, at least part-time farms on which they may establish their year-round residence. This modern category of gentlemen-farmers consists of people *who are farmers because they are indeed gentlemen*, with a large enough income from urban sources, rather than gentlemen because they own large farms, as used to be the tradition.

Of course, not all agriculture in Megalopolis is founded on milk, horses, and premium cattle, although a good deal of it is. Poultry farms have been an increasing and profitable industry, too, which often allows for a more genteel mode of life than the old type of farm on which grain and hay had to be produced in large quantities. Edward Higbee insists also on the important role specialized crops are playing on Megalopolitan farms, and on the role these hold in the national output of such products (see pp. 269–275). It is remarkable that in two opposite corners of the country, in Megalopolis and in California, are found the major dense concentrations of specialty crops. In California these concentrations can be explained in terms

[6] Bredo and Rojko, *op. cit.*, p. 52.

of climate and the development of irrigation at least as much as in terms of nearness to large urbanized regions; but in Megalopolis the proximity to the market and its size are the only significant factors.

How much and how long the economic circumstances in Megalopolis will favor such farming in practically suburban conditions is a question hard to answer for the future. As in any other industry in a complex and vast world of interconnected but different regions, the success of one enterprise depends on its competitiveness with many others that are constantly evolving within the area and far away from it. Feeding cows and poultry on farms in Megalopolis with feeds produced in the Middle West may not always be as profitable as it has been recently. Maintaining such farms may become too onerous if the present rules of taxation change, if the distribution of income is modified, or if New York City decides to extend its milkshed to Wisconsin and Minnesota! A continuing and uncontrolled sprawl of urban uses of the land could go on devouring land at a pace that would run many farms out of business. Or farms could be run out of the landscape if they were reduced to buildings in which feed was processed into dairy, poultry, and meat products by animals given only brief outings at set hours in a small green yard. Such poultry or dairy farms can already be observed in rather urban, built-up surroundings in some spots in Megalopolis.

To try to project far into the future would be of little use, because of the great variety of new factors likely to come into play among the forces determining suburban land uses. A study of the present circumstances of Megalopolitan agriculture still seems worthwhile, however, for it helps one to understand the play of factors now at work in this area, and the similar processes that are now developing in or are likely to come to other urbanizing areas.

Green Belts, Suburbs, and Social Aims

Agricultural production used to be the great consumer of land space. This cannot be expected any more in Megalopolis. In the whole United States the land area in farms has recently been increasing only slowly (it went from 956 million acres in 1920 to 1,159 million in 1950), despite a rapid increase in population; and in 1954 it seemed to have shrunk slightly (by one million acres) in relation to 1950. The 203 million acres of increase in the period 1920–50 included a rise of 157 million acres in the area of grassland and pastures in farms, and of 52 million acres in the area of woodlands in farms; the area of cropland remained remarkably stable. Mechanization and other devices to increase yields of crops have made expansion

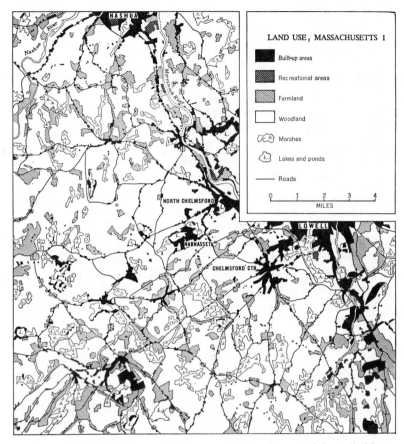

Fig. 67. Land use of the area south and west of Lowell, Massachusetts. Generalized from a detailed map drawn as a result of a field survey by the Graduate School of Geography of Clark University (about 1950).

of the farm area dependent on livestock needs. While the numbers of horses and mules (which were important feed consumers prior to 1920) decreased rapidly, the number of cattle rose from 66.6 million head in 1920 to 95 million in 1954 and was expected to approximate 100 million by 1960;[7] American production and consumption of beef and veal had been increasing and were expected to go higher.

Although some fattening of cattle may still take place in the southern

[7] U. S. Bureau of the Census, *Statistical Abstract of the United States: 1959*, U. S. Government Printing Office, Washington, D. C., 1959.

half of Megalopolis, it seems likely that the types of farming that may be expected to survive in an urbanized region are not those asking for more land. In fact, the area in farms in the entire Northeastern section (i.e., from Maine to Maryland) has been shrinking and still follows a downward trend. In 1950 cropland in this section accounted for 18.1 per cent of the land area, pasture and grazing land for 9.9 per cent, forest land (exclusive of parks and other special uses) for 55.9 per cent, and special uses (such as urbanized districts, highways, farmsteads, parks, wildlife refuges, military camps, airports, etc.) for 5.7 per cent.[8] The Northeastern region as defined above is, of course, much larger than Megalopolis and includes to the north and west of it areas more forested and less urbanized. It would be safe, nevertheless, to assess land uses in Megalopolis in the 1950's as follows: about one half wooded (including this time parks outside cities), one third actually used in farming (either tilled or grazed), and about 15 per cent devoted to special uses (chiefly buildings and roads).

In recent times the tilled area in Megalopolis, as in surrounding areas, has been shrinking in favor of the spread of both woods and urban uses. These trends have progressed at different rates in the various parts of the region. For instance, the pace of urban and woodland sprawl has been faster, and their proportionate extent greater, east of the Hudson River than west of it. Whatever the local variation, it must be recognized that the major competition for land is between urban uses and woodlands, and that *about half of the whole area of Megalopolis is green* in a relatively unproductive way.

Over many sections of Megalopolis woods have been gaining for some time. Connecticut had woods on probably one third of its land area in 1850 but on two thirds in 1950. Although since 1941 suburban sprawl has been biting quite frequently into wooded area on the periphery of the larger metropolitan areas, the abandonment of tilled land has been proceeding more rapidly than "special uses" have expanded. The proportion of land in woods (including rather recent brush) has been on the rise in most of the United States east of the Mississippi, and this seems destined to continue for some time.

The forest cover, however, can be made to serve multiple purposes. The technical opportunities offered by the extent and expansion of woodlands are examined in Chapter 7; but the social meaning of such abundant green spaces close to the great metropolises and around the smaller cities of an

[8] H. H. Wooten, *Major Uses of Land in the United States,* U. S. Department of Agriculture, Technical Bulletin No. 1082, Washington, D. C., October 1953 (see Tables 14-15).

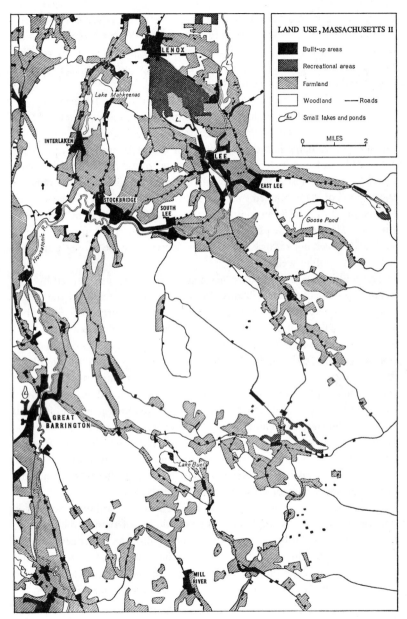

LAND USE, MASSACHUSETTS II

Built-up areas

Recreational areas

Farmland

Woodland ——— Roads

L. Small lakes and ponds

0 MILES 2

LENOX

Lake Mahkeenac

L.

INTERLAKEN

LEE

STOCKBRIDGE

SOUTH LEE

EAST LEE

Goose Pond L.

L.

Housatonic R.

GREAT BARRINGTON

L.

Lake Buel

MILL RIVER

Fig. 68. Land use generalized from a map by the Graduate School of Geography of Clark University (as on Fig. 67).

urbanized region must be dealt with first. The forest cover is a good protection for the soil, to preserve its fertility and to defend it against erosion; it contributes to conservation of water supplies; it provides an environment favorable to the proliferation of wildlife (unless too much hunting takes place) and to various recreational activities.

A policy of forest management concerned mainly with fostering wooded areas because of these basic values to suburban communities would not prevent these woodlands, once wisely preserved, from producing slowly but surely a valuable harvest of timber for industrial uses. Such programs are already in force in some national or state forests and in woods owned by various other institutions. How the average individual forest owner in the region could be induced to adopt such sound principles of management for his piece of land is an important though difficult question. Before we turn to it, it may be helpful to ask ourselves whether the preservation of such wide green belts is or is not of actual interest for the people and a contribution to public welfare.

The multiplicity of purposes that can be simultaneously served by adequate forest management already enumerated above provides the beginning of a general answer. Conservation of such resources as soil, timber, water, and wildlife has for some time been widely recognized in America as desirable. The recreational needs of the growing and crowded population of near-by cities and suburbs can be partly satisfied by woodlands which can provide for excursions, hiking, some hunting and fishing, and that "change of air" that was talked about in the seaboard cities as early as two centuries ago, at which time it was considered a privilege available only to those wealthy enough to own country estates. In a society that grows constantly more industrial and commercial, more divorced from an entirely rural environment (in the old meaning of "rural"), easy access to woods becomes also an educational asset for youngsters, who should not lose all physical contact with free natural processes.

At least since the time of Thoreau and Emerson, a stubborn current in American thought has emphasized the "goodness" of nature, the necessity for men to keep in touch with "natural" environment and processes. Perry Miller has singled out as the "American drama" and "*the* American theme" that "of Nature versus civilization." [9] In no other country, perhaps, has the elite of the nation insisted as much on "the evil of urbanization" as in the

[9] Perry Miller, *Errand into the Wilderness*, The Belknap Press of Harvard University Press, Cambridge, Mass., 1956, especially pp. 204–205; see also Hans Huth, *Nature and the American: Three Centuries of Changing Attitudes*, University of California Press, Berkeley and Los Angeles, 1957, a more popular and matter-of-fact approach.

United States, where in the twentieth century urbanization has taken on its most impressive form and where its spread is devouring space in the most notable way.

The Megalopolitan types of forestry and agriculture are certainly not the purest forms of virgin Nature. With the relatively high density of population that has existed in this region for a century or two, they could not be. But on the whole they are still "natural enough" to provide city folks, who spend most of their time in an environment of bricks, cement, glass, and steel, with an environment where flora and fauna develop according to the basic laws of Nature, even though they are under the influence and supervision of civilization. In fact, the green parts of Megalopolis have been repopulated with some of the original natural wildlife, owing to police enforcement of rules protecting these animals.[10] Deer and even beavers would not be appearing as they do in the forests of Megalopolis had the local people not been civilized enough to apply conservation policies.

The farms and woods that still subsist in Megalopolis help introduce within a densely urbanized region *vast sectors* where greenery predominates, mainly in the form of woods. The metropolitan regions of the seaboard have their green belts, much more green and wide than those envisioned by Ebenezer Howard, the British apostle of the "garden city" idea in the 1890's.[11] Perhaps one could claim that in 1960 Megalopolis, except for the densely built-up districts, is predominantly a "garden-and-park suburban region"; however, one should not insist on such a formulation, for it suggests the idea of a "beautiful paradise" for a region in which the great majority of the population still live in crowded and decaying neighborhoods with little benefit, if any, from the woods spreading in not-too-distant areas. But it must be stressed that many Megalopolitan residents, actually a sizable minority, have set their homes in semi-dispersed order amid woods and fields and along rural roads, in such a way that they cannot be seen by a traveller crossing the area along the major thoroughfares. This dispersal is difficult to realize unless one takes the trouble to follow smaller, winding roads and find out the occupations or sources of income of the residents whose homes stud, in variable but increasing densities, those rural, predominantly wooded zones that give the general landscape an "abandoned," almost wild look.

In most cases the inhabitants of these more scattered residences belong

[10] It may be appropriate here to remind the reader that our modern word *police*, as well as the word *politics*, came from the old Greek *polis*, the ancient city-state.

[11] Ebenezer Howard, *Garden Cities of Tomorrow*, Faber and Faber, London, 1945, with a preface by F. J. Osborn and an introductory essay by Lewis Mumford; first published under the same title in 1902.

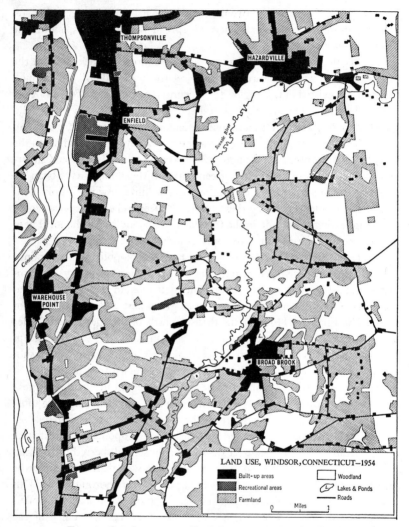

FIG. 69. Land use generalized from a map by the Graduate School of Geography of Clark University (as on Fig. 67).

to income brackets above the average. Such homes are usually more expensive to acquire and to maintain; they call for two-car families and for a heavier use of these cars than do town homes; they are better enjoyed by residents with shorter hours of work in town, so that more leisure time can be spent in the rural setting (that is, if commuting does not bear too heavily on the daily schedule). However, it ought to be recognized that this trend is an old and deep-seated one in Megalopolis, and perhaps in a large part of the nation. It explains the rise and spread of the rural non-farm population. It makes it evident that a great part of the woodland so apparent in the landscape is not "abandoned" but has in fact been converted directly or indirectly to suburban use. Such dispersed homes must offer substantial advantages, in terms of pleasant living, since so many American families have acquired them, despite their occasional inconvenience and somewhat higher cost.

A few examples of this scattering are shown here on maps based on detailed local surveys, most of which were completed around 1950 (see Figs. 67, 68, 69, 70, 71, and 72). Since a great deal of additional scattering took place during the 1950's, a full appraisal of it would require detailed counts from the 1960 Census and perhaps more recent maps of land use than are available. But this writer has reached his conviction on the matter through studying documents as well as through field research in various parts of Megalopolis: in Connecticut, Massachusetts, New Jersey, Maryland, and Virginia. He believes this trend is marked in many parts of the United States outside of Megalopolis, but that it is especially important here, where densities are higher and the pressure of suburban expansion is greater.

Following the attraction of many people from rural areas to crowded urban centers, the modern evolution of American life has involved the recent resettling of a good deal of the previously emptied rural countryside with sparsely distributed residences. Because these have held much attraction for families who can afford them, many rural roads have been transformed into loosely and irregularly built-up avenues. The homes have their backs to large blocks of green land stretching between roads.

If this trend were to continue without planning or regulation, more and more roads would cut across the now green blocks of territory, subdividing them and eventually producing an irregular but relatively dense pattern of homes with gardens around them. The rural advantages that attracted people to such areas may be lost in a few years in sections close enough to the major axis of Megalopolitan growth. By 1960 this had happened in a few sectors, but many more homes are still being scattered in sections that are as yet sparsely occupied.

The affluence of society, the excellence of the highway network, the widespread ownership and use of automobiles, the rapid expansion of retail trade services in rural areas, the growing disadvantages of city middle-class residences — all these are contributing factors that have concurred to make this wide dispersal easy throughout a region where woods were increasing in area. Obviously it could not go on and on indefinitely without

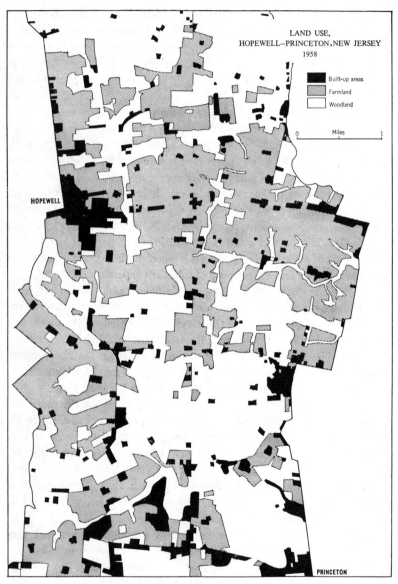

FIG. 70. Land use generalized from a map by the Graduate School of Geography of Clark University (as on Fig. 67), 1958.

ruining the present fragile balance of rural and urban in such "outer suburbia," clogging up roads with too much traffic, ruining woods and landscape, making commuting increasingly lengthy and unpleasant, and reversing the trends of migration within the region.

However, from what has happened in recent years a few conclusions can be formulated. In 1961 there is still a good deal of land space available in Megalopolis for residential, recreational, or other use, although it is irregularly distributed throughout the region. People who lead an urban kind of life seem to prefer rural surroundings for their homes and leisure. Land use may be planned so as to extend these advantages, which are recognized by philosophic theory as well as by common practice, to a greater number of people. Some planning is needed, lest overdevelopment of outer suburbia defeat its very aims and suburbanize the lands in deplorable fashion. The present abundance and expansion of woodlands should not mislead responsible people into a false sense of security and cause them to throw away the great opportunity that is now within their reach, to preserve some green areas for the future.

The Fear of Running Out of Space

While Megalopolis is not yet running out of space, there is in many quarters a deep-seated fear that such a situation may arise soon and that once this has happened it will be too late to do anything about it. We must realize, of course, that these feelings are based partly on reasoning, partly on emotions, and partly on particular local situations in certain districts. In addition the term "running out of space" is very vague and has been used in discussing a number of quite different problems.

First, of course, came *the old human fear of running short of agricultural space and therefore short of food.* Many times in history, agriculture has won legislative support because people were afraid of bringing famine about if they did not protect the farmers supplying them. The present production and distribution of the food supply does not call for any such anxiety, but various projections can be drawn to forecast a situation in which either America or the whole of mankind would be faced with starvation; Malthus had already so threatened the human race almost two centuries ago.

At present Megalopolis has probably the best-fed population in the world; of all groups of people of similar size (i.e., between 30 and 40 million) it enjoys the most abundant and varied supply ever obtained; and it wastes more food than any other group. Its sources of supply are scattered all around the earth, but the main ones are located in the Middle West and on the Great Plains. A situation could be imagined in some distant future in which these parts of America would become highly industrialized and urbanized, to the point of having little or no surplus of grain and meat to ship out to Megalopolis. Then, we are told by conservation experts, Megalopolis would badly need the good soils of the Connecticut Valley, of the limestone basins of Pennsylvania, and of some other areas that have been and are increasingly being invaded by urban and suburban uses of the land.

It is the professional duty of soil specialists and agricultural experts to worry about such prospects. However, anyone who attempts to follow and understand the modern evolution of land use must recognize that in the advanced countries of Western civilization, despite a recent acceleration of population growth, means of food production have expanded more rapidly than consumption needs. If the technology of agricultural production keeps on improving, Megalopolis should not be too seriously concerned with saving the better-quality soils, which at best represent a relatively small fraction of its total area. To cause the food supplies to fail one has to visualize a breakdown of the commercial, cultural, and political system on which the whole structure of Megalopolis is founded, and in the event of such a catastrophe much more than the supplies of food would be at stake. A concentration of activities as complex and dense as those that have developed in this urban region could not subsist without the vast network of outside relationships that has been built up. It may be safe to assume that as long as people will find it beneficial to congregate here, they will also find sources of food supply.

Assuming that most of the agricultural products consumed within the region will come from the outside, as is already the case, a more immediate threat is that Megalopolis might run out of space for living — that the whole area might become so crowded that people would not be able to move freely about it, and that there would be no choice left as to where to live, how to live, what to do for recreation, where to work. To have "enough space" has often meant to individuals *the free choice of "a place in the sun,"* and such individual freedom to choose one's mode of life and to change it has long been associated with free land, especially in American history. This association of man's freedom and the abundance of free open land has underlined the whole epic of the frontier and the legend of the West. As a person brought up with such concepts looks at what is developing in Megalopolis, fear may arise concerning the crowding of people and the scarcity of space (because it is so expensive) in the sections where the instruments of growth and prosperity are located. For what good is ample land, being increasingly wooded, in northwestern Massachusetts or

Fig. 71. Dispersal of buildings in the southern part of Bucks County. Reduced from county maps of the State of Pennsylvania.

in the Appalachian foothills of Pennsylvania to a New Yorker or a Washingtonian? He cannot consider commuting 100–200 miles to his place of work, and he cannot find any equivalent job in those parts of Megalopolis where space is plentiful.

The map of population change by minor civil divisions in 1930–50 (Fig. 73) shows that the most rapid growth has occurred in suburban and interurban zones along the main historical axis of Megalopolis, the economic hinge, where are concentrated the great opportunities that cause the people of this area to congregate here. That Megalopolis has attracted so many people shows there is no threat to put them in homes out of range of easy access to their places of work, for such a threat would have kept these people from coming to the area. The concentration developed because the economic and social lure of this area was strong enough to make people accept either the physical discomforts of crowding, commuting, and poorer housing, or the greater expense of comfortable living in a more desirable area. The population of Megalopolis did not, therefore, prefer this location because there was enough land here to provide for the free choice of open spaces. It came prepared to be "fenced in" in this respect, with the exception of the more privileged few who could afford to pay for open space even here. Megalopolis was expected to provide other satisfactions, other opportunities.

Nevertheless, many of the families resident in the region live in relatively rural surroundings, and even in built-up suburbs many more live in individual detached houses with adjoining lawns or gardens. This provides for a bit of greenery at the door and for a little more privacy, more freedom of movement about the home, often less polluted air than in more crowded sections. Such an arrangement also usually involves longer commuting to work; it devours more land and more of other commodities; but the occupant may feel less "fenced in" and have a greater sense of "freedom of movement" than if he occupied the same floor space in an apartment house.

It thus becomes obvious that people come to Megalopolis in order to be *within reach* of a certain kind of work, and that their endeavor is to find within a radius of *easy access* to that work conditions of living as pleasant as possible in terms of space, greenery, society, and access to recreation. Lack of space is synonymous with lack of accessibility to *the* work and *the* home desired.

Many places of work have been migrating themselves, largely to get out of too-crowded environs. In the case of manufacturing, migration of a plant to a new location is often planned in terms of advantages of transporting goods, and little thought is given to the problem of housing personnel.

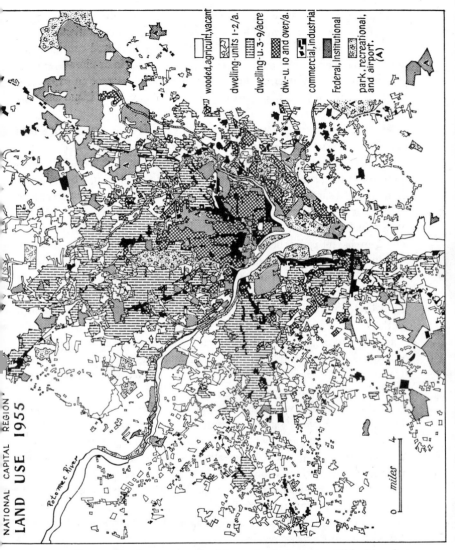

FIG. 72. Land use generalized from detailed maps published by the
National Capital Planning Commission, Washington, D. C.

When the employees follow the plant, meeting their residential needs causes
some discomfort for older residents and new problems for local government, some defacing of the landscape and perhaps traffic jams. However,
Megalopolis still has enough absorbing capacity in most of its sections to
accommodate a good deal of such migration of industry and its personnel,

The situation is somewhat different and calls for more concern in the case of office industry and of the services requiring concentration. Despite many attempts at decentralization from the more congested central cities, most of the white-collar employment remains located in or close to central business districts. Manhattan especially continues to attract an expanding "white-collar army," a large part of which lives outside the island and outside New York City.

However, sometimes a large agency moves a few thousand office jobs outside such a location toward the periphery of the urbanized or metropolitan area, and it usually displaces also the residences of some of its employees. In fact, such moves are intended to help them scatter their homes in more rural surroundings, to make their driving to work easier, to relieve somewhat the congestion of the old downtown, and to make cheaper and easier the expansion of offices and related services. Thus a major insurance company has moved its headquarters from Hartford, Connecticut, to a new sylvan-looking location a dozen miles from town. Decentralization on a larger scale has been tried around Washington. Federal agencies or bureaus moved out of the District of Columbia during World War II and have continued to do so. Thus the Pentagon was built in Arlington, Virginia, south of the Potomac, and a good many other office buildings of military bureaus followed it to that area. The U. S. Bureau of the Census has most of its central offices in rather rural surroundings at Suitland, Maryland. In 1958 the U. S. Atomic Energy Commission moved out to Germantown, Maryland, 27 miles from Washington.

The whole area in which the office industry is concentrated is extended by such moves. New "satellite downtowns" are created in the outer ring of the metropolitan area, where they function with some autonomy, but the very existence of such decentralized groups of offices depends on remaining in the working orbit of the central district of which they are offshoots. The headquarters of the U. S. Atomic Energy Commission obviously could not function if it did not have quick access to conferences at the White House, the Capitol, the Pentagon, the Department of State, and a dozen or more other agencies.[12]

One major insurance company, or two, may move to the periphery of

[12] The civilian employees of the executive branch of the Federal government working in Washington, D. C., still numbered 209,000 in 1959 despite many endeavors at decentralization; this number was lower than during World War II (269,000 in 1942, 244,000 in 1944) and the Korean War (237,000 in 1951) but higher than in either 1940 (137,000) or 1947 (182,000). (Data from the U. S. Civil Service Commission's *Monthly Report of Federal Employment,* issues of February 1955, March 1955, and October 1959.)

Hartford County or even to an adjacent county, but the offices of lawyers or of advertising firms that have regular business with several insurance companies would find it more efficient to be located at a central point more easily and equally accessible to all the clients. The sites chosen for the transferred offices must still be determined largely by their accessibility to and from the city of Hartford.

"Running out of space" appears to mean almost exactly "running out of easy access to desired places." With a very good transportation system, *access* is not as much a matter of distance measured in miles as a matter of organization of traffic in terms of time, comfort, and cost involved in the necessary transportation. Some scattering of residences around centers where business congregates has almost always existed, and it has always been a proof of wealth, for those having the more scattered homes could afford the time and money needed to provide themselves with comfortable access to wherever they needed to go. The advent and generalization of the automobile, of good hard-surfaced highways, of higher average standards of living, all foster more dispersal for more people. The "exploding" suburban sprawl, the rapid changes in the distribution of population within Megalopolis, especially since 1920, are all consequences of the *greater freedom of access* obtained as a result of these economic and technical achievements. Because so many people have taken advantage of these trends there is a constant threat that means of transportation (highways, railroads, etc.) will become inadequate; and a constantly greater part of what ought to be leisure time is spent travelling in more or less comfortable conditions from home to work, from work to home, to places of recreation, and so forth.

There is still a third meaning to "running out of space" in the mushrooming metropolitan areas of our day, and that is the fear of becoming *short of access to open space*, especially to what the average citizen wants for recreation. Open spaces still exist over substantial areas in the Northeast, and there are many more of them in other parts of the country. When an inhabitant of Megalopolis in mid-twentieth century complains of their disappearance he means those he can easily reach, that are "near by." He may know of the vast expanse of virgin or wild forests in the Amazon basin, in central Quebec, or in the Yukon, but access to those areas from Worcester, Massachusetts, or Reading, Pennsylvania, takes too much time and money to be easy. In fact, the two cities just mentioned, both of medium size and located on the fringe of the more densely occupied axial belt of Megalopolis, are relatively well situated in terms of access to open terrain. A resident of Brooklyn, New York, or Newark, New Jersey, is less fortunate in this respect.

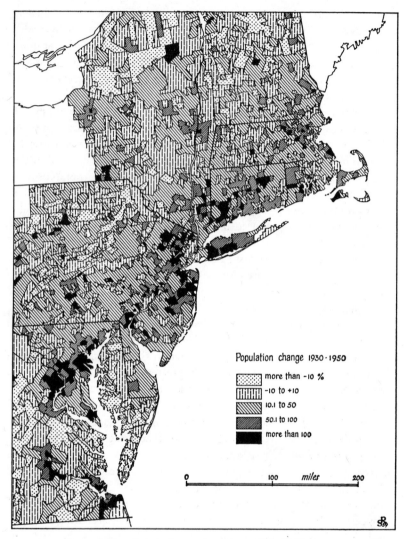

Population change 1930-1950

- more than -10 %
- -10 to +10
- 10.1 to 50
- 50.1 to 100
- more than 100

0   100   *miles*   200

FIG. 73. Population change by minor civil divisions, 1930–50. Generalized from detailed maps reproduced above in Figs. 42 to 46.

To provide urban centers with access to open space is mainly to satisfy recreation needs: hunting, fishing, boating, skiing, hiking, and the general desire to play and to get out to the country "for an outing." The more crowded an area, the greater is the psychological need for some open space — and the more difficult it is to provide. During the past century, as cities

have grown bigger and suburban sprawl has become more general, parks
have been established in cities and towns. As these have grown increasingly
crowded, more parks (state or even national) have been set aside for recreation in not-too-distant locations, some of them at lake or seashore sites
with fishing, boating, and bathing facilities.

The main axis of Megalopolis, along U. S. I and the Fall Line, *stretches
rather conveniently between a scalloped seaside and the steep Appalachian
foothills*. Recreational facilities have been set up on both sides, attracting
the city crowds according to their tastes and moods in the two different
directions. Originally this helped curtail crowding, but now that nearly
everybody has acquired a car, and a great many have a boat and a small
country place also, the ways of access to open space, either on land or at
sea, have grown increasingly congested. On the days when people usually
have the most leisure and the most desire to go out — on summer week ends
or certain holidays — the accessibility declines to its lowest level, for so
many people are on the move. "Open space" thus seems to be retreating
farther away from those who long for it. As more people have gone toward the sea, for example, the ocean shores have become more and more
crowded, more difficult of access.

The matter of "space needs" becomes first of all a matter of accessibility,
that is, of ease of movement, through the whole region. The concentration
of numerous central cities with their high-density districts in a lengthy
axial belt from Boston to Washington has left some space available on both
sides of this belt. Until 1950 the evolution of both population growth (see
Fig. 73) and farmland (see Figs. 67 to 72) helped to maintain or expand
"open space" within striking distances of the cities. However, during the
1950's new trends of increased dispersal seem to have made the situation
somewhat more complicated. The scattering of residences along smaller
rural roads should make the access of the woods back of these homes more
difficult for the outside public; and to find large blocks of actually open
space one may have to go farther from the major central cities.

On the map showing changes in the proportion of wooded land by counties from 1946 to 1956 (see Fig. 113, p. 345) some increase can be seen in
the vicinity of the northern and southern nuclei, but in the central part of
Megalopolis, especially in New Jersey, expansion of woodland seemed to
have been overtaken by suburban sprawl. Thus conditions vary from one
part of the region to another; but it is not yet too late to arrange for access
to more and better "open space" and to plan the scattering of industrial
plants so as to provide reasonable accessibility from these to places of residence and of recreation.

A growing symbiosis of urban and rural activities and landscapes has been in progress recently through most of the area of Megalopolis, resulting from private initiative as well as legislation. What the situation is and how it can be handled may be more fully realized once the local people abandon the old, outdated concepts distinctly separating urban and rural land use. A synthesis of the two could lead to better urban life, closer to the "park and garden city" dream, and could bring about a more efficient use of space.

A Multiple-Purpose Concept of Land Use

Studies of land use stress quite different features of an area depending on the scale at which it is examined. Most surveys of land use are detailed analyses of small areas, such as a township or a county, stressing interesting details that must, to be meaningful, fit into a scheme of well-defined and separate categories of land uses. Studies of much larger regions, such as the whole United States, are intended for different purposes and must adopt a scheme of land-use categories that may have little in common with those used in surveys of small areas. In either case, the various uses of the land are generally represented separately, each one being a distinct use not to be mixed with any other on the map, in order that the map may give a picture of distribution of land use in space.

In some situations, however, the overlapping of certain uses must be shown and brought into the scheme adopted. Such mixtures in the uses of the land are sometimes shown on maps, but they are seldom systematically used, with the exception of some "miscellaneous" categories such as "mixed farming" or "suburban development," the latter always evoking a mixture of urban and semi-rural conditions. These mixed uses are usually assumed to occupy small sectors and are represented on a map only when they seem to be indispensable in describing a transition between separate categories. We have been used to thinking according to these classified, clear-cut categories in many fields of study. How much more difficult would analysis and even description be if we could not use the terms of well-established classifications! In daily practice, however, especially in the use of resources as they are offered to us, matters seldom fit into easy classifications; they fit less and less when changing economic phenomena, endowed with great fluidity, are classified in terms of old, somewhat outdated categories.

Consider, for example, a waterfall. Formerly it was thought of merely as an obstacle to navigation and a source of energy. Today it is significant in other ways too. Falling water still serves to generate power, and dams may be built to control it for this purpose. However, such dams may also

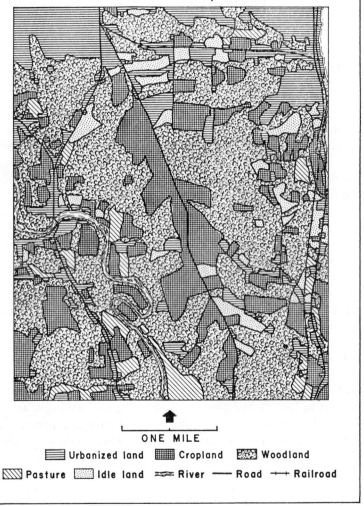

COMPETITION FOR LAND
HARTFORD COUNTY, CONN.

ONE MILE

Urbanized land   Cropland   Woodland

Pasture   Idle land   River   Road   Railroad

Fig. 74. Generalized from maps and field study by Edward Higbee.

serve to regulate the flow of the stream for navigation or to provide water for irrigation or for the needs of a city. Often the same reservoir can be put to recreational uses. The stream, the dam, and the reservoir can be made to serve all these purposes at the same time, and such multiple-purpose dams have become common. This does not mean, of course, that *all* the water whose flow is regulated by such a dam will be made to serve all these purposes. Although some water may serve first to produce electricity and then to irrigate a field or to sustain navigation, most of it is used, once it leaves the reservoir, for one final purpose — either urban water supply, or irrigation, or navigation, or some other use.

In similar fashion a certain unit of land, when it is large enough, whether it covers a few dozen acres or hundreds of square miles, can easily be put to several uses. Sometimes these uses can be made of one area at the same time; or the various uses may be adjacent in space but contemporaneous; while others may succeed one another on the same space at different times. Thus on a farm some of the land is used for buildings, some for roads, while still other sections are in cultivated fields, woods, or pasture. However, either cropland or woodland can also serve under certain conditions as pasture. In fact, the more efficient types of modern farming have a rotation of crops on fields that are also grazed at given times provided for in the rotation cycle. In urban land uses a more formal approach has predominated. A multiplicity of uses of the same piece of land can, of course, be achieved by building in height over it. The surface built upon is multiplied as many times as there are stories, and sometimes the stories are used for different purposes — for example, the ground floor for residential occupance or offices or manufacturing.

Such a variety of uses of the same building has not been in vogue, however, over most of Megalopolis. In fact, zoning has tended to emphasize specialization of districts within urban and suburban areas. To create a new "downtown" in zones previously considered to be "rural" it is often necessary to create a new town or division. Business districts strive, while occasionally expanding in one or the other direction, to continue to concentrate all the offices or business establishments they can in as compact an area as possible. Good residential districts defend themselves against invasion or infiltration of industrial plants, small stores, or cheaper kinds of housing. All such attitudes, defending a status quo and protecting the existing local interests, favor in the long run a strict legal separation of land uses in space. Such separation may lead through a slow process to full liquidation of certain uses.

Despite regulations and local resistances, the infiltration of commercial and industrial land uses into what were residential or agricultural zones proceeds slowly, either by outflanking zoned areas and invading neighboring districts that are less strictly protected, or by obtaining the official blessing of the local authorities. Towns seldom resist a change that ought to increase their revenue by lifting land-value assessments and therefore tax receipts. Thus industrial uses of the land are often permitted close enough to good residential districts to upset an existing balance. We have seen how a scattering of more or less grouped residences amidst woods and fields adds to the mixing of land uses. The planners too often deal with small areas only, or with units defined by the limits of a municipality, and have little or nothing to do with what develops in between the more congested units of land space, for which alone their professional advice is usually sought.

The congested areas are already quite congested. For any activities that can be decentralized from them, including centers of mass employment that do not necessarily require immediate proximity to other such centers, there are still worthwhile sites within Megalopolis. Enough dispersal could take place, close to the axial belt that serves as the actual Main Street of the nation, to help greatly to relieve pressures in the most congested areas. If the dispersal followed accepted policies of preserving local multiple-purpose use of land units, it could develop without defacing the landscape or suppressing too much of the open spaces that still cover about three fourths of the total area of Megalopolis.

To what degree the interpenetration of the various rural and urban uses had progressed by 1950 may be assessed by examining and comparing a few maps, worked out for the whole area of Megalopolis on the county-unit basis (see Figs. 126, 134, and 150, pp. 402, 441, 485). These maps show how often, and over how much of the region, manufacturing and residences mix together; and how and where manufacturing mixes with agriculture. Percentages in the labor force have been combined with percentages of land area occupied and other data to arrive at a few simple indices (see p. 402). The general lesson demonstrated by these maps is that a great deal of interpenetration has already taken place between industrial and agricultural activities and between both these uses of the land and residential and recreational uses. The highly urbanized areas (those counting over 85 per cent of their resident population as urban) have been singled out. It is in vast sections where more than 15 per cent of the population is rural that the mixtures of land uses can best be observed, especially in eastern Pennsylvania (where farming is still very important), in parts of New Jersey, and in most of Connecticut. There is little doubt that similar maps based on 1960 data would show even more mixing.

This interpenetration still leaves most industrial and commercial activ-

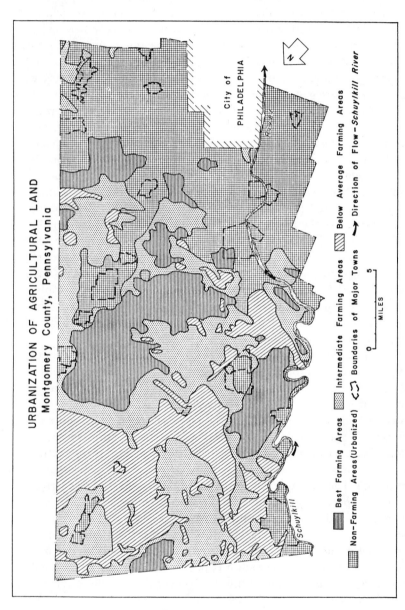

Fig. 75. Generalized from field study by Edward Higbee.

ities at a certain number of sites clearly distinct from the rest of the land if one looks at a very detailed map (Figs. 67 to 72, 74, and 75) or examines the terrain itself. But if these sites are distant enough from one another and from massive concentrations of residences, green open spaces can extend between them, having their own uses, but also serving as green belts from which all, urban and rural people alike, benefit in the long run. Lancaster County, Pennsylvania, which we cited as an outstanding example of successful and rich Megalopolitan farming, can also boast a high density of nonfarm population and a substantial industrial development. Of the total employment in the county in 1950, only 11.7 per cent was in agriculture, while 40.3 per cent was in manufacturing. In 1954 the total value of farm products sold amounted to $80.1 million, while the value added by manufacture in the county was $288 million, the manufacturing payroll was $150 million, the payroll of wholesale trade establishments was $14.2 million, and the receipts of selected service trades were $21 million. In 1950 and 1960 the county formed a separate metropolitan area, adjoining those of Philadelphia (to which Chester County belonged), York, Harrisburg, and Reading. Despite such location it had achieved a good balance of multiple activities.

The remarkable vitality of agriculture in Lancaster County may be explained by its geographical position, by the special quality of the local people, deeply attached to traditions and to the farming way of life, and by the good quality of the soil that has attracted this kind of settler since the eighteenth century.[13] Perhaps the stern character of the social and religious tradition of some of the sects that settled there, the Mennonites and the Amish especially, has helped to keep the farms as active as they are. Their prosperity today has not prevented rapid industrialization of the towns in the county (including the small ones), growth of suburbs, and a great deal of interpenetration of urban and rural life. By 1959 this process had led to a rather pleasant and well-balanced combination of agriculture, industry, and commerce. Many notable Lancastrians still believed that most of their county's income came from the farms, while manufacturing was in fact by far the major component of the local economy; but it had been kept from overrunning the landscape.

A somewhat similar evolution may be observed in some counties of Connecticut and western Massachusetts, but the financial proceeds of agriculture and the role of farms in the landscape is much more restricted there than in Lancaster, York, or Chester counties, Pennsylvania. In southern

---

[13] See Frederic Shriver Klein, *Lancaster County Since 1841*, revised edition, Lancaster County National Bank, Lancaster, Pa., 1955.

New England woodland areas predominate, and many of these have little productive function. Similar interpenetration of urban and rural exists, but with different combinations of the various categories of land use.

Accepting this process of interpenetration of urban and rural in Megalopolis could lead to a fruitful concept of a way of life. Some of the qualities of both the city and the country might be preserved, integrated, and even, with adequate local policies, balanced. The present situation results chiefly from a free expansion of formerly urban land uses infiltrating into rural territory where land is now less needed than previously for the "rural" aspects of the economy. Such infiltration developed to provide pleasant residences, but it can easily develop into a tide of blight. Whether programming and planning to preserve a multiple-purpose land use may save this region with its "synthetic" way of life and land use for the future is a question to which the answer remains doubtful but which is worth asking. Any way of life is, of course, "artificial" for it is man-made. In Megalopolis, however, a large number of inhabitants reside on rural-looking premises while otherwise leading an urban way of life. The scattering of residences thus achieved amidst greenery which often is actual woodland is quite different from the regular rows of houses of the English "garden cities."

In his Princeton lectures of 1930, Frank Lloyd Wright spoke of the modern city, which he saw on the way to "dissolution":

The dividing lines between town and country are even now gradually disappearing as conditions are reversing themselves. The country absorbs the life of the city as the city shrinks to the utilitarian purpose that now alone justifies its existence. Even that concentration for utilitarian purposes we have just admitted may be first to go, as the result of impending decentralization of industry . . .

Natural parks in our country are becoming everywhere available. And millions of individual building sites, large and small, good for little else, are everywhere neglected. Why, where there is so much land, should it be parceled out by realtors to families, in strips 25', 50' or even 100' wide? This imposition is a survival of feudal thinking, of the social economies practiced by and upon the serf. An acre to the family should be the democratic minimum if this machine of ours *is a success!* [14]

Whether the "Broad Acres City," as Wright called it elsewhere, is indispensable to a democratic society will long remain a moot question. History has demonstrated that rural societies breed tyranny as well as other forms of government. Density of residence often has produced more free-

[14] Frank Lloyd Wright, *The Future of Architecture*, Horizon Press, New York, 1953, pp. 175–176.

dom than the open countryside. But on the whole Wright foresaw the quasi-colloidal dissolution of certain urban functions in rural territory. In 1961, Fairfax County, Virginia, vividly illustrated this trend as it asked to become a separate city.[15]

The symbiosis of urban and rural in Megalopolis, creating new and interesting patterns of multiple-purpose land use over large areas, gives to this region a rather unique character. Like the downtown business districts with powerful skylines, this aspect of Megalopolis will probably be repeated in slightly different but not too dissimilar versions in many other regions of a rapidly urbanizing world. It must be studied both for itself and as an experiment offering lessons of more general portent. Having broadly outlined its entanglements and promise, we must now look more closely at the main components of the regional mixture: the agriculture in Megalopolis, the forests with their uses and problems, and the urban or "special" types of occupation of the land.

[15] On the authority of a heretofore unused law of the state of Virginia, the county of Fairfax (414 square miles, with a 1960 population of 275,000) signed an agreement with the small town of Clifton (population 230) to consolidate in order to form a new and single city. The 1960 Census recognized 78 per cent of the county's population as urban. The county was threatened with annexation of parts of its territory by the neighboring cities of Falls Church and Alexandria. To preserve its integrity it felt a sufficient sense of community to form what under Virginia's constitution is called an independent city; if its petition were approved, Fairfax would become by far the largest city in area in Virginia, and the second largest in the country. Its population increased by 140 per cent in 1940–50 and almost tripled in 1950–60. Its population density of 664 to the square mile would be somewhat low for an American city, yet higher than that of such cities as Rome, New York, or Concord, New Hampshire, and not much lower than that of Middletown, Connecticut, or Taunton, Massachusetts. There could hardly be a better illustration of the symbiosis of urban and rural than the consolidation that was being discussed in Fairfax in 1960–61.

CHAPTER 6

Megalopolitan Agriculture

Agriculture, by occupying more acres than do cities and suburbs, still dominates the landscape in large sectors of Megalopolis, but it is in constant retreat. On the fringe of advancing urbanization the farm has little survival power and ultimately gives way to more intensive uses of land. It is the main source of open space available for new housing, industry, highways, woods, and recreational areas. Compensating for the threat to its existence are the economic advantages of being close to a vigorous and expanding market. It is an odd yet logical coincidence that some of America's most efficient and prosperous farms are those about to be liquidated by the city. This threat of extinction has been cited as an agricultural problem, but actually the individual farmer is enriched by the increased market price of his real estate. It is to the urbanized area that the threat is serious, be-

This chapter is by Edward Higbee; abridged and edited by Jean Gottmann.

cause when existing open space between metropolitan complexes has once disappeared the present problems of congestion and communication will be compounded.

Agriculture and animal husbandry in Megalopolis have a sophistication that sets them apart from the more common types observed in the nation's rural heartland. There are some resemblances between farming on the fringes of Eastern cities and that conducted in better Western irrigation districts. Land values are high, costs of production are elevated, and competition is severe, so management must be superior to survive. The efficient producer is well compensated in the market place. As some farms are eliminated by urban growth, others benefit by the improved market that results where more people are supplied by fewer producers. To the consumer the economics of Megalopolitan agriculture may be a foretaste of that day when there will be few if any agricultural surpluses in the United States.

Distinctive Features

In the broad picture of American agriculture the small area occupied by Megalopolis attracts little attention. The total quantity of its output is a minor part of the national whole. Almost everything grown could be produced elsewhere in the country, often on better soil at less cost. Megalopolitan agriculture is significant because it has the best market in the country, the most customers with the highest incomes. Logically, the farms of Megalopolis specialize in perishables for direct human consumption.

The dairyman, for instance, provides milk for home delivery rather than for makers of butter and cheese. He markets a valuable finished product rather than a raw material for a factory. Every dairyman knows that there are wide variations in milk values at the farm. These differences depend not so much upon the milk itself but upon where the farm is located and how the milk is ultimately consumed. A Minnesota dairyman may raise twin heifers from his best registered Guernsey. If he keeps one and sells the other to a farmer in Connecticut, some day a quart of milk from the Connecticut cow will be worth twice as much as a quart from the cow that stays home. Similarly, a market gardener on the fringe of Boston, who irrigates his land with city water, may raise the same kind of sweet corn as a grower in southern Wisconsin, yet the market values of the crops are different. There are not enough people in Wisconsin to eat all of its native corn, which is therefore sold by the ton to canners rather than by the dozen to housewives. The direct consumer's market is the Megalopolitan farmer's particular advantage.

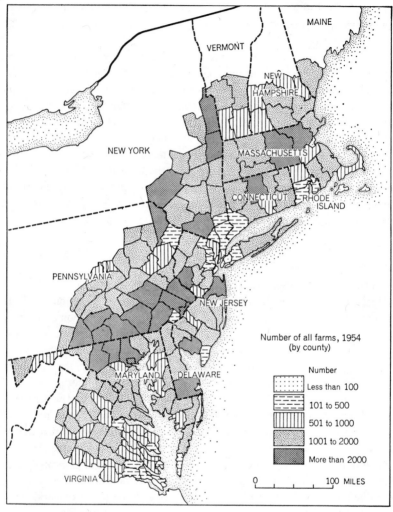

Fig. 76

Commercial farmers in Megalopolis therefore usually specialize in live-stock or in crops of high value such as market vegetables, fruits, and nurs-ery materials. The animal husbandmen, for the most part, buy feed grains from outside Megalopolis rather than produce all they need on their high-priced land with high-priced labor. Their time is too valuable to be spent raising grain. It is far more profitable for them to work inside their "factories" taking care of their birds or cows than it would be to labor in the fields like a Corn Belt farmer. Naturally such Northeastern business-men have little sympathy with Federal price supports designed to help the Middle West by keeping the market price of corn high. And for the same reasons the Northeastern dairymen favor any action that may restrict the entry of cheap Middle Western milk into the Megalopolitan area. They know it is clearly to their advantage to bring in cheap grain from across the Appalachians, but they do not want cheap milk to reach their custom-ers by the same route.

One might say that these specialists, whether dairymen or poultrymen, are essentially manufacturers who buy a low-cost raw material in the form of feed grains and sell a high-priced product such as meat or milk. The cultivation of ordinary crops is less profitable than cultivation of the mar-ket. The same is true of market gardening. Garden produce requires much hand labor. Thus the value of the product reflects the high cost of man-power more than any other expense. This, too, is therefore a system of converting cheap raw materials, such as seeds and fertilizer, and often ir-rigation water, into valuable consumer goods by the use of high-priced equipment and labor. It is not an enterprise for anyone who is pinched for credit but is rather an entrepreneurial activity with frequent turnover of inventory. It calls for business judgment and skill of the highest order.

From the standpoint of acres, Megalopolitan agriculture has long been in decline. However, in terms of production per acre and per farm it is still a vigorous, expanding industry. Commercial farms on the urban fringe are particularly productive. *In average value of farm products sold per acre New Jersey, Rhode Island, and Connecticut lead all other states in the Union* (see Fig. 77). Eight counties in Megalopolis are among the first hundred in the United States in the value of all farm products sold. On the basis of productivity per acre, the entire Megalopolitan area is one of the foremost agricultural districts in the United States. It is matched only by the best irrigated valleys of the Pacific states and by the leading fruit and vegetable counties of Florida. This condition is even more surprising when it is realized that commercial farms, except on Long Island, account for a smaller percentage of all farms than is the case in the nation's agricultural heartland. In other words, despite the large number of part-time and resi-dential farms, which market very little produce, the commercial farms are able to keep the average productivity of all farms well above the national level, second only to the Central Valley of California.

The farms of Megalopolis have also a high value per acre. In 1954 New Jersey surpassed all other states in the Union in this respect, with an aver-age per-acre value of farms of $403. Rhode Island, where agriculture rep-

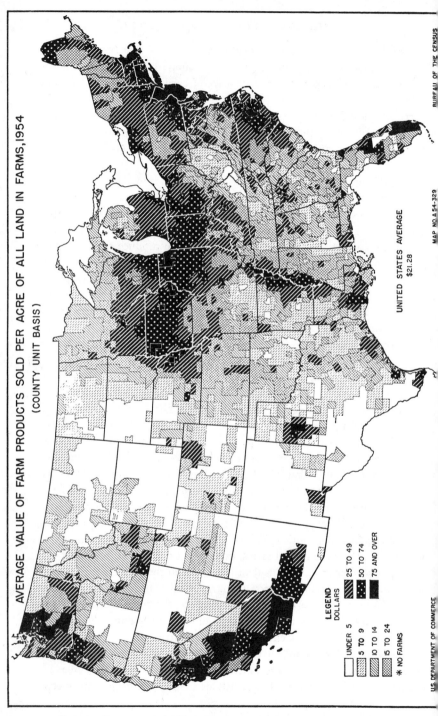

AVERAGE VALUE OF FARM PRODUCTS SOLD PER ACRE OF ALL LAND IN FARMS, 1954
(COUNTY UNIT BASIS)

UNITED STATES AVERAGE
$21.28

LEGEND
DOLLARS

☐ UNDER 5
5 TO 9
10 TO 14
15 TO 24
25 TO 49
50 TO 74
■ 75 AND OVER
* NO FARMS

U. S. DEPARTMENT OF COMMERCE   BUREAU OF THE CENSUS

MAP NO. A 54-329

Fig. 77. *Courtesy of the U. S. Bureau of the Census*

resents less than 2 per cent of the state's economy, was second ($343), Connecticut was third ($301), and Massachusetts was sixth ($223). These four states are typically Megalopolitan and, in the case of New Jersey and Connecticut, typically suburban within Megalopolis. Of the twelve states that lead the nation in the per-acre value of farms, seven lie entirely or partially within Megalopolis (see Fig. 78).

There are several reasons for the high value of farms in Megalopolis. Among the less important is soil quality, and the most significant is location. Some of the poorest soils and most valuable acres are in New England and New Jersey (see Fig. 20, p. 94). A farm with good soil usually commands a better price than one of the same size with poor soil, but only if their locations are equal. The rockiest pasture ten miles from Boston is more valuable than the finest black loam in central Illinois. For commercial farms the role of location in raising the per-acre value has already been discussed. Here is a large and high-priced market, and to meet some of its needs Megalopolitan commercial farmers have developed specializations that give a high per-acre productivity. However, as has already been noted, a large percentage of the farms of Megalopolis are part-time and residential. All farms within Megalopolis have real estate potentials that enhance their worth.

Suburbia in the Northeast does not always advance *en masse* upon farm lands. Often it grows by mycelial extensions that parallel the country roads. It enmeshes but does not entirely obliterate the back country that lies between. Frequently the ribboned extensions of one city merge with the threaded advances of others, while much open space remains thus enveloped, some of it in agriculture and some idle. Farms that are caught in such a network of suburban tentacles gain a residential value that often exceeds their agricultural worth. They may become more valuable to the commuter than to the commercial farmer. Or, as sometimes happens, the farmer becomes a commuter and only incidentally a tiller of the soil. Approximately half of the farmers of Rhode Island hold city jobs. They live on the land and engage in part-time husbandry but ride off in the morning to work in town.

Along the seacoast, too, rural properties take on high value for non-agricultural reasons. They are sought after not for the harvests they might yield but for the agriculturally worthless beaches they possess. Martha's Vineyard Island is a case in point. Not quite a century ago its most desirable lands were those with heavier textured soils that are found occasionally in the interior. On them good pasturage could be established, and sheep herding was then a good business. Sandy coastal lands, particularly

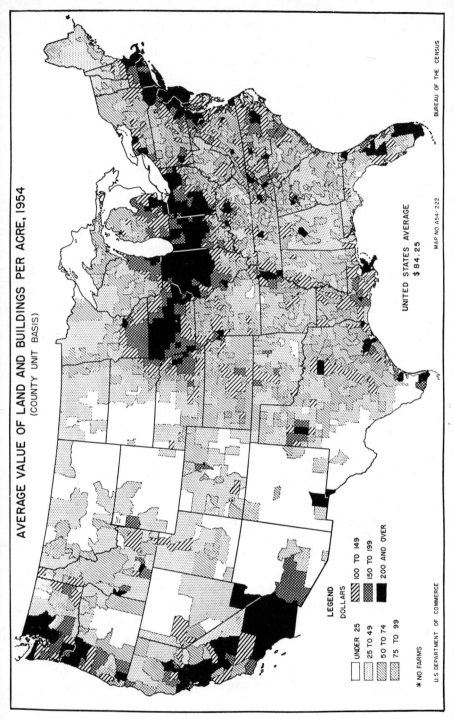

AVERAGE VALUE OF LAND AND BUILDINGS PER ACRE, 1954
(COUNTY UNIT BASIS)

LEGEND
DOLLARS

UNDER 25
25 TO 49
50 TO 74
75 TO 99
100 TO 149
150 TO 199
200 AND OVER

* NO FARMS

UNITED STATES AVERAGE
$ 84.25

U.S. DEPARTMENT OF COMMERCE
BUREAU OF THE CENSUS

MAP NO A54-222

FIG. 78. *Courtesy of the U. S. Bureau of the Census*

those on the southern shore facing the Atlantic, were despised and allowed to vegetate into tangles of thornbush and vines. Today agriculture as a business is almost extinct on Martha's Vineyard. Fewer than six per cent of the Island's resident population are farmers. And yet farms fronting on the sea are in great demand at fabulous prices. Most of them lie fallow — overgrown with the loveliest profusion of beach peas, bayberry, greenbriar, wild rose, beach plum, honeysuckle, goldenrod, and poison ivy. The crop they raise is serenity, an article hard to come by in Megalopolis and for which those who are able will pay a handsome premium.

Because these high land values introduce a strong element of speculation into the ownership of land in Megalopolis, tenancy is sometimes high. The working farmer may be unable to finance ownership of land that is priced beyond its agricultural worth. Rentals, however, are usually low, often amounting to no more than the taxes. By renting, dairymen can add temporarily to pasture or hay land with no outlay of capital. Vegetable gardeners also find rental attractive, especially if they desire fields on the edge of town where they can more easily market what they grow. From time to time these farmers must find new places to rent as former fields are sold, but they prefer to put up with this inconvenience rather than invest in land, unless they wish to be as much speculators as farmers.

In the Census statistics the full extent of such tenancy does not always show up, and this is especially true in New England. There much farmland is rented, but the tenancy rate appears deceptively low on the map of farm tenancy (see Fig. 79), for the Census considers a man a tenant only if he rents a whole farm from another, not if he rents pieces of farms from others to increase the size of his operations. In New England it is common for persons to own and live on farms but to work in town and do no farming at all. Often the larger part of such a farm remains in woods, with only a small part cleared, and the owner may rent these cleared patches to commercial farmers while retaining occupancy of the house and control of the woodlands.

The rate of tenancy may reflect other influences, too. In the old tobacco district of southern Maryland, for example, it is high because the production of tobacco requires much cheap labor. A study published in 1950 [1] showed that an average of 459 man-hours were required to grow and process one acre of tobacco with 24 man-hours needed to grow and harvest an acre of corn. In terms of the amount of labor needed to raise it,

[1] Reuben W. Hecht and Glen T. Barton, *Gains in Productivity of Farm Labor*, U. S. Department of Agriculture, U. S. Government Printing Office, Washington, D. C., 1950.

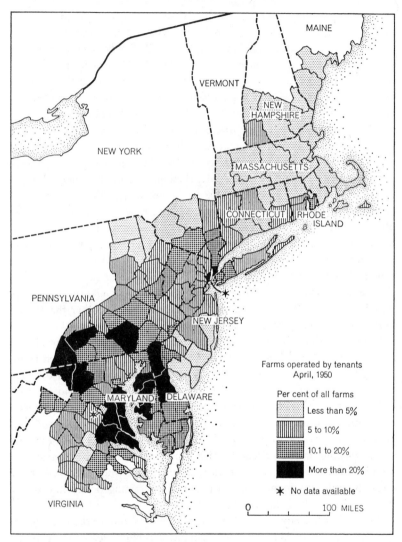

Fig. 79

tobacco is a costly commodity with a market value that is comparatively low. Thus the people who cultivate this crop cannot expect to earn high wages. Many persons who can afford to own a good farm do not spend their time on tobacco, for that would bring them wages of less than a dollar an hour; so they rent the farm to a tenant, usually on a share-crop basis.

As a general rule the farms of Megalopolis are much smaller than the national average of 242 acres, most of them being 50 to 100 acres in size (see Figs. 80 and 81). On the Delmarva Peninsula and in several Appalachian counties they are larger, approaching the national average in some instances. But in the most highly urbanized counties the average size of farm is lower. This is true regardless of soil capability and is as pronounced in New England as it is in southeastern Pennsylvania. In rural areas exceptionally small farms are to be found in Barnstable County, Massachusetts (Cape Cod), and in Ocean and Atlantic counties, New Jersey (the Atlantic City area). These are all summer resort counties and are thus, in a sense, seasonally urbanized. Small farms are popular just as vacation retreats. Moreover, the types of commercial farming characteristic of these areas — cranberry production in Massachusetts and poultry raising in New Jersey — do not require large areas of land (see Fig. 82).

One of the striking features of farms in southern New England and in southeastern New Jersey, Delaware, and Maryland is the high proportion of wooded land (Fig. 116, p. 359). A common explanation for this anomalous situation in an area of high land values is that the soil is too rocky, sandy, or poorly drained. There are other more subtle reasons. Frequently the farmer just does not need the wooded land. If he is a dairyman or poultryman it is often more profitable, as has been noted, for him to buy cheap Midwestern feed grains rather than to raise them. If he is a market gardener he usually needs only a few acres to keep himself fully occupied.

For example, a commercial vegetable grower near Vineland, New Jersey, has 10 acres, yet he has never cleared more than 5.8 acres. The remainder is still in woods, although the soil is as good as that on the land now cleared. The 5.8 acres are all that can be profitably cultivated. That area, however, is completely serviced by overhead sprinkler irrigation. It has been so intensively double-cropped and triple-cropped and interplanted that in recent years the farmer has actually grown the equivalent of the yield of more than 25 acres on the 5.8 acres of land. To raise multiple harvests on a few fields is more profitable than to spread his efforts and his capital over a larger area. To operate only a few acres in this intensive way requires a good deal of expensive equipment.

Thus agriculture in Megalopolis is decked with surprises, inconsistencies, and even contradictions. Perhaps this is because its very existence is something of a contradiction in what is essentially an urban and suburban region. And it is location in such a region that accounts for the distinctive features of Megalopolitan agriculture.

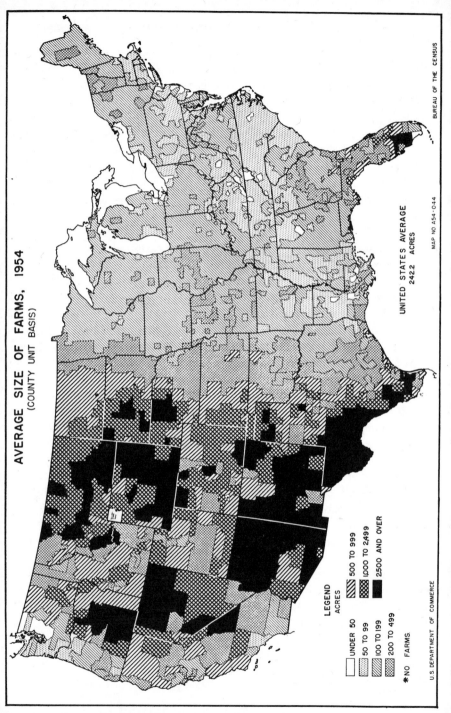

Fig. 80. *Courtesy of the U. S. Bureau of the Census*

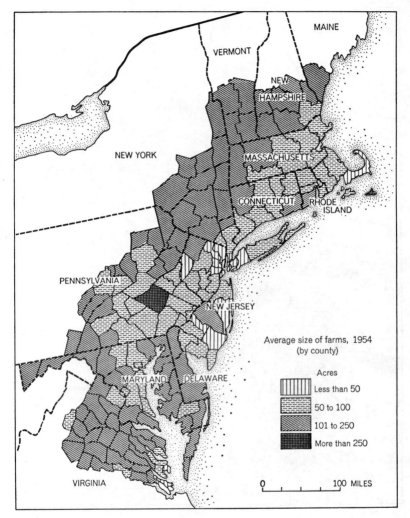

FIG. 81

Where Megalopolis Excels

A wide variety of types of farm activity is characteristic of Megalopolis. A few counties lead all others in the United States in their particular specialties, while many are prominent in the national picture. (See Table 2.) In the production of horticultural specialties Megalopolis is the most important area in the United States, outranking regions of similar size in California and Florida. These specialties are particularly tailored to the refined

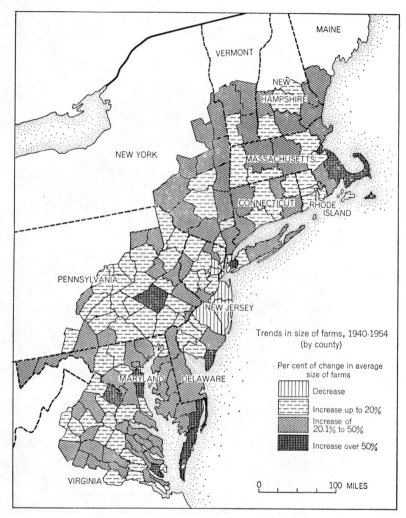

Trends in size of farms, 1940-1954
(by county)

Per cent of change in average
size of farms

Decrease

Increase up to 20%

Increase of
20.1% to 50%

Increase over 50%

0   100 MILES

FIG. 82

taste and ample purse of the big cities. They include all items grown under glass, landscape nursery stock, cut flowers, mushrooms, bulbs, and flower seeds. It is also of interest to note that Megalopolis is second only to a comparable area in California in the value of vegetables harvested for sale. The leading position of Megalopolis in the national poultry supply picture is its most remarkable agricultural achievement.

Study of the distribution of farm activity in Megalopolis shows that

Table 2

NATIONAL RANK OF MEGALOPOLITAN COUNTIES IN SPECIALTY PRODUCTION, 1954

County	State	Specialty	Rank Among All U. S. Counties
Barnstable	Massachusetts	Cranberries	1
Chester	Pennsylvania	Mushrooms	1
		Nursery stock	3
		Whole milk	4
Hartford	Connecticut	Cigar-wrapper tobacco	1
Suffolk	New York	Ducks	1
		Potatoes	2
Sussex	Delaware	Broilers	1
		Value of all poultry products	1[a]
Lancaster	Pennsylvania	Value of all poultry products	3
		Value of all farm products	13[b]
Monmouth	New Jersey	Chicken eggs	2
Orange	New York	Dry onions	4
Nassau	New York	Nursery stock	6
Gloucester	New Jersey	Tomatoes	7
Adams	Pennsylvania	Cherries	9
Atlantic	New Jersey	Sweet potatoes	9

Source: Bureau of the Census, *U. S. Census of Agriculture: 1954,* U. S. Government Printing Office, Washington, D. C., 1956.

[a] Twenty-three counties in Megalopolis were among the first fifty counties in the United States in the value of all poultry products sold.

[b] Out of the first twenty-two counties in the United States in the value of all farm products, nineteen were in western irrigation districts, one was in Florida, and two were in Megalopolis (Lancaster, Pennsylvania, and Sussex, Delaware).

dairying, market gardening, and poultry husbandry, the three leading types of agriculture, are characteristic of distinct types of regions.

Dairying predominates on cheaper lands on the western fringe of Megalopolis. Its greatest concentration is in the Pennsylvania Piedmont and in the first series of Appalachian limestone valleys beginning in Frederick County, Maryland, and extending into the Hudson Valley by way of Lancaster County, Pennsylvania, Sussex County, New Jersey, and Orange County, New York (Fig. 88, p. 287). The soils of the Piedmont and of the limestone valleys are among the best in Megalopolis, but the land is some of the cheapest because it lies west of the main areas of urban expansion. This is important because of all the farmers in Megalopolis the dairyman usually requires the most land.

Horticultural specialties are grown on the most expensive farm real estate. They are commonly produced on the very edge of the largest cities, sometimes within the cities themselves. Cut flowers and nursery stock bring a better price to the grower in localities close to the consumer. Labor and greenhouse costs are the major items of expense to the average horticulturalist. The cost of land, even though it would be considered high by most farmers, is proportionately less important than being near the customer and close to a supply of labor. The specialized horticulturalist is wise to buy a choice location if it will enhance the market value of his product.

To some extent this same principle applies to that kind of market gardening that is not easily mechanized or otherwise subject to cheap mass production. Many growers of melons, bush fruits, squash, peas, beans, lettuce, and tomatoes rent land within city limits, land that is waiting development. They may have their own sales stands or direct contact with wholesale and retail outlets. The Borough of Richmond (Staten Island), which is part of New York City, still has 60 commercial farms that together produced specialty crops worth nearly $1 million in 1956. Some of the more popular Chinese and Italian restaurants in New York City operate their own vegetable farms on near-by Long Island. In contrast, however, vegetable crops that are cultivated by mechanical methods or are produced in great quantity for canning or freezing are not commonly grown in expensive locations. Long Island potatoes are a conspicuous exception, but that industry is receding before the advance of urbanization.

A long growing season that begins early in the spring and ends late in the fall is essential to the grower of vegetables and horticultural specialties. Frosts do not bother the dairyman since perennial hay and pasture grasses are resistant, but they are a major hazard to the horticulturalist. He finds it profitable, therefore, to farm near the sea where the climate is more moderate, and the Atlantic Coast margin of Megalopolis, with its several peninsular formations and Long Island, is the most desirable location in the United States for the cultivation of many summer fruits and vegetables. The soils are not as fertile as those of the limestone valleys where dairying predominates, yet they respond very well to heavy fertilization and irrigation. There is more irrigation where vegetable crops and horticultural specialties are grown in Megalopolis than in any other comparable area in the humid Eastern United States (see Fig. 83). For its size, Megalopolis is also one of the most important consumers of commercial fertilizers. The natural deficiencies in soil productivity are more than compensated for by the techniques of heavy fertilization and supplementary irrigation.

Poultry husbandry, as it has developed in Megalopolis, is more of a factory enterprise than an agricultural art. Because he buys all his feed, the

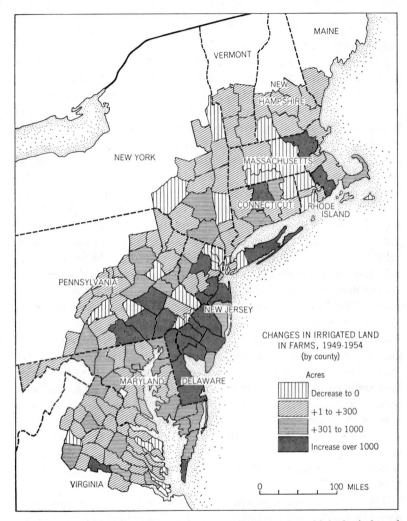

FIG. 83. The map shows the actual acreage by which the irrigated area in each county increased or decreased between 1949 and 1954.

poultryman needs no land for crops. Because his birds spend all or most of their lives indoors, very little if any range is necessary. This being the usual case, the cost of land is relatively unimportant to the grower because he needs so little. He invests his capital in buildings and equipment. Nearness to market and relatively mild climate throughout the year are characteristics of site that the poultryman prefers.

The Survival of Agriculture in Megalopolis

The fact that agricultural production is increasing in Megalopolis while the land devoted to farming is declining indicates that the farmer makes special adjustments to survive. As is illustrated by the wooded areas of New England and southern Maryland, land is not as important as the way it is used. The trend of agriculture in Megalopolis is away from common field crops that are fed to livestock. Emphasis is on the commodities that man consumes directly. To raise the latter successfully requires a greater investment in labor and equipment than in land. The contrary is true of the Corn Belt and Wheat Belt. There land is cheaper, yet it is the major resource with which the farmer works.

Another pertinent fact is the prospect of capital gain that every farmer hopes to enjoy. Although he may not need the land himself, and it would not be profitable for him to clear it of woods and use it, the real estate value of those unproductive acres is steadily increasing. The farmer, therefore, holds them for the biggest harvest of all — sale to the advancing city. As one dairyman remarked who lives in the Connecticut Valley on the fringe of the Hartford metropolitan area, "We farmers raise three crops. We go onto a place in our youth and raise a family. We spend our working years producing milk. When we are ready to retire we harvest enough capital gain from the land to keep us in our old age." This man and thousands of other farm owners look upon agriculture as a means of holding land for speculative gain, which is certain to occur owing to increased population pressure and urban expansion. They know that farmland so close to the great cities and satellite towns has residential or recreational value in addition to, and often more important than, its farm assets. That is why an acre of unproductive woodlot in Essex County, Massachusetts, is worth more than an acre of the best limestone hayland in southwest Virginia.

There is more than a superficial resemblance between the specialized agriculture of Megalopolis and the specialized agriculture of California and Florida. In the latter places the primary asset is a mild climate during the winter when most other parts of the country experience killing frosts. Having a national market to satisfy, and with competition reduced or eliminated, it pays the farmers of California and Florida to extract the greatest yields from a limited number of tillable acres. By irrigation and heavy fertilization it is possible to get maximum yield for each hour of labor invested. A comparable situation prevails in Megalopolis in summer. The climate of its maritime portion is cooler in summer than most other parts of the densely populated East and it is warmer in spring than the continental interior. Since the largest consumer's market in the country is at their doorstep and since labor is costly here, it pays the farmers of Megalopolis to strive for the highest yields per acre and per hours of labor by using irrigation and heavy fertilization for specialty-crop cultivation.

Land Capability and Regional Aspects

To be suitable for intensive cultivation a soil should be productive and it should resist erosion. These two characteristics are implied in the term "land capability." Some land is capable of tillage year after year, while some should be kept in permanent hay or pasture. Other soils are so poor that they should not be used for agriculture at all but should be left as woods, as marsh, or as recreation grounds. If vegetative cover is removed in such areas, the soil will erode or drift. In Megalopolis land of such low quality is generally found on steep slopes in the interior uplands of glaciated New England and in sandy places along the seacoast.

Since the late 1930's, the U. S. Soil Conservation Service has surveyed the soil over much of Megalopolis. When the data from these surveys are translated into cartographic form, they reveal significant differences from place to place (see Fig. 20, p. 94). The land capability data for the various sections are not always entirely comparable, but the deviations are not great except in the case of Connecticut. There stoniness was disregarded in making capability classifications because it is possible to remove stones from the soil with bulldozers and stone pickers. In contrast, in Massachusetts and Rhode Island, as well as elsewhere in glaciated terrain, stoniness was rated as a handicap to intensive tillage wherever the stones actually had not been removed. For an insight into the strong effect of stones upon soil capability in New England it is fortunate that these two different standards were used in adjoining states where the same soil types are common. Figure 20 shows land capability expressed as the percentage of total area in each county that is suitable for continuous intensive cultivation either with or without special erosion control measures. Technically such areas, which are the finest kinds of agricultural land, are rated as land-capability classes I and II. Included in Figure 20 there is also a map showing the variations in soil quality in rather general categories. The patterns of the two maps are somewhat similar.

The agricultural history of Megalopolis has been a varied one. While the soils have not, in themselves, determined the course of that history, nor even dictated the present patterns of rural land use, they have exerted much influence.

It is rather remarkable that William Penn, who came somewhat late as colonizer to the Eastern seaboard, should have secured the best agricultural lands. Perhaps for the evolution of American agriculture that was a fortunate circumstance, for of all the major colonizers Penn was the most diligent in bringing truly skillful farmers to this continent. He intended to operate his holdings in the best tradition of the English manor by locating tenants on his land in order to collect rents from them and their descendants in perpetuity. It is beside the point that Penn's financial ambitions went unrealized. What is significant is that he successfully encouraged able farmers from the Swiss and German Rhineland to settle on the finest soils of eastern America. They practiced such measures as adding lime to the soil to improve clover culture. They built fine barns for their cattle at a time when many settlers from Britain allowed theirs to run without shelter. They took care to conserve manure and were reputed to improve the land they cultivated at a time when it was the common custom to deplete the soil. Surpluses of wheat and pickled meats shipped from the port of Philadelphia helped feed fledgling industrial cities in New England, which could not secure sufficient supplies from their own hinterlands. Virginia, the Carolinas, and the West Indian sugar colonies also drew upon America's first corn belt, which developed at Philadelphia's back door.

In the early days of American settlement, when the principal merchant cities and seats of government were comparatively small, a city did not require extensive hinterlands. A fine port and a reasonable quantity of good agricultural land near by were sufficient if conditions and materials for industry were good. In those days even Boston and New York had their gardens, although it is apparent from the maps of soils and land capability that there are few spots on the Atlantic Coast more inhospitable to the farmer than the regions of eastern Massachusetts where Bradford's Pilgrims and Winthrop's Puritans chose to settle. It is no wonder that the early years of Plymouth County were blighted by death from malnutrition, or that the first dissident groups to leave the parent colonies settled on the Connecticut River and Narragansett Bay, the garden spots of southern New England.

With good care land may improve in productivity beyond its best natural condition. This has been true of the shale and limestone valleys of Megalopolis. The richest farmland of the area, now or in colonial times, lies in the limestone and shale sections of Pennsylvania, Maryland, Virginia, and New York. Only the limited area of these rich soils on the fringe of Megalopolis has minimized their importance in accounting for the nation's agricultural wealth. Nowhere else, except in some of the irrigated valleys of the West, does one find the general agricultural community as productive as in Lancaster County, Pennsylvania, where the first American corn belt was born. The limestone valley of Lancaster has a gently undulating surface that is almost entirely tillable. Not all limestone terrain is so completely suited to intensive cultivation, but where plowing is inadvisable the land is usually good for pasture and meadow. The shale landscape of neighboring York County is one of smooth-sloped rolling hills, ideally suited to contour cultivation in alternating strips of perennial grasses and annual crops of corn, wheat, and oats. Aesthetically, there is no more beautiful rural landscape in Megalopolis than the verdant, carefully tended hills of York along the course of the Susquehanna River. It is the prototype of idyllic farm country.

Loudoun County, Virginia, lies just beyond Washington's expanding suburbs, which have so deeply invaded adjoining Fairfax County. The Piedmont of Loudoun County is a landscape of green woodland and green meadows. It is one of the foremost areas of grassland agriculture in Megalopolis. To a somewhat lesser degree this is true also of all the Piedmont north of Virginia. For many decades the livery stables of Washington, Baltimore, and Philadelphia were supplied with hay from Piedmont farms. Good grass has been their specialty for generations, and nowhere else within Megalopolis are the productivity and beauty of good meadows rated more highly. From the standpoint of soil productivity there is no better conservation practice than maintenance of these perennial meadows of legumes and grasses, which are grazed by beef and dairy cattle. Sod on the rolling hillsides protects them from erosion that otherwise might cause damage, as it did to the southern Piedmont of the Carolinas and Georgia under cotton and tobacco.

The Coastal Plain is an area of highly variable soils that range from excellent loams to nonagricultural sands and clays. Because of flatness of terrain and slight elevation above sea level, many areas of the Coastal Plain are artificially drained to make them usable for agriculture. The watercourses are typically meandering streams, and efforts at artificial drainage by the construction of open ditches are relatively frequent.

Types of Farms: Commercial, Part-Time, and Residential

The distinction the U. S. Bureau of the Census makes between commercial, part-time, and residential farms is significant. A commercial farm is one that markets at least $1,200 worth of products or is the principal source of income of its operator. A part-time farm is one that markets between $250 and $1,199 worth of products annually and is not the principal source of family income.[2] A residential farm is one that markets less than $250 worth of products annually.

It is quite apparent, in view of today's prices, that part-time and residential farms are not important as productive units. They make only a slight contribution to the total farm yield of Megalopolis (carrying from 0.5 per cent in Delaware to 2 per cent in Rhode Island and 5 per cent in Virginia, a state chiefly outside Megalopolis), although they make up a relatively large proportion of all farms, varying from a low of 20 per cent in Delaware to highs of 44 per cent in Rhode Island and 48 per cent in Virginia (see Table 3). However, they do have an impact upon the region's rural culture and its real estate values, and this will be discussed in a later section (see pp. 310–319).

Few counties in Megalopolis still have more than 20 per cent of their labor force engaged in agriculture (see Fig. 84). They are somewhat tangent to the main axis of Megalopolis, and the most important of them are on the Delmarva Peninsula, where commercial husbandry, supplying important amounts of poultry products, fresh vegetables, and crops for canning, remains a major economic activity. Other counties with a high percentage of the labor force employed in agriculture are to be found in the commercial farming area of southern Maryland, an old tobacco district. In contrast to these two areas, where a high percentage of the labor force employed in agriculture is associated with a high percentage of commercial farming, northern Virginia is an example of its association with a high percentage of part-time and residential farming. This section is just beyond the rim of Megalopolis, an area of low population density where many of those engaged in agriculture must supplement their farm earnings by other work. Here the agricultural economy for a large number of small land holders is depressed and would benefit by urban and industrial growth. In those counties within commuting distance of Washington, the high rate of part-time and residential farming means that the farm there is often a place on which to enjoy living rather than a place on which to earn a livelihood.

[2] More specifically, the Bureau of the Census defines the commercial farm as one from which products worth at least $1,200 are sold annually, or from which products worth from $250 to $1,199 are sold annually and: a) the operator works less than 100 days per year at nonfarm employment; or b) the combined income of the operator and his family from nonfarm sources is less than the value of all farm products sold. The part-time farm is one from which products worth $250 to $1,199 are sold annually and: a) the operator works off the farm 100 days or more each year; or b) the income of operator and family from nonfarm sources is greater than the value of all farm products sold.

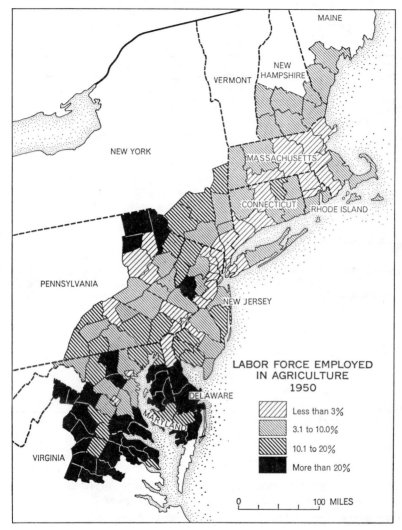

LABOR FORCE EMPLOYED
IN AGRICULTURE
1950

Less than 3%

3.1 to 10.0%

10.1 to 20%

More than 20%

0   100 MILES

FIG. 84

Part-time and residential farms are definitely smaller than commercial farms (see Table 3) and tend to be relatively close to cities, where all types of farms are of relatively small size. Away from the immediate fringe of the cities, where the farms are larger and more dominantly commercial, there has been a tendency in Megalopolis, as in the rest of the country, for farms to increase in size in recent years. Improvements in

Table 3

COMMERCIAL, PART-TIME, AND RESIDENTIAL FARMS AND THEIR
PRODUCTS IN MEGALOPOLITAN STATES, 1954[a]

States	Class of Farm	% of All Farms	% of All Dairy Prods.[b]	% of All Poultry Prods.[b]	% of All Veg. Prods.[b]	% of All Marketed Farm Prods.[b]
Entirely or chiefly within Megalopolis						
Massachusetts	Commercial	64	98	97.5	96	98
	P.-T. and Res.	36	—	1.5	2	1
Connecticut	Commercial	61	99	98	97.5	98
	P.-T. and Res.	39	—	1	2	1
Rhode Island	Commercial	56	99.5	97	96	98
	P.-T. and Res.	44	0.5	3	4	2
New Jersey	Commercial	75	99.5	99	99	98
	P.-T. and Res.	25	—	0.5	1	1
Delaware	Commercial	80	99.5	100	99.5	99.5
	P.-T. and Res.	20	—	—	0.5	0.5
Maryland	Commercial	68	98.5	98.5	97.5	98.5
	P.-T. and Res.	32	—	1.5	2	1.5
Partly within but chiefly outside Megalopolis						
New York	Commercial	73	99	97	97	98
	P.-T. and Res.	27	—	2.5	1	1
Pennsylvania	Commercial	64	98	96	93.5	97
	P.-T. and Res.	36	0.5	3	3	2
Virginia	Commercial	52	96	96	95	94
	P.-T. and Res.	48	3	4	3.5	5

Source: Computed from the *U. S. Census of Agriculture: 1954.*

[a] Calculations were made to the nearest half of one per cent.

[b] When totals do not equal 100 per cent it is because allowance is made for the production of what are called abnormal farms: agricultural experiment stations, public and private institutions.

farm technology have made it possible for one man to take care of more land and more animals than was formerly the case. In Megalopolis another explanation for the increase in average size of farms is that the smaller farms nearest to the centers of population are the ones most likely to be eliminated by urban sprawl, leaving the larger farms in the outlying rural areas to exert a greater impact upon the statistics (see Fig. 82). This situation is not likely to prevail in counties that have been slow in suburban growth or relatively stable in recent years.

In southeastern Pennsylvania, particularly in Lancaster County and to a lesser degree in Chester and York counties, there are many general-purpose commercial farms, each engaging in many enterprises on a substantial scale. It is not unusual to find a farm in Lancaster County with a fine

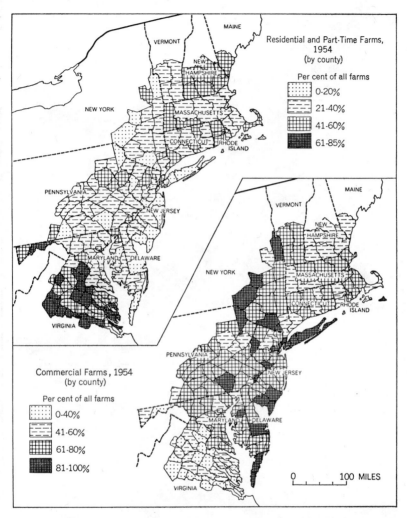

dairy herd, a feed lot stocked with beef cattle, a pen of hogs, a large flock of poultry, and, in addition, plots of tobacco, hay, and grain. Farms of this kind require a good deal of family labor or cheap hired help. When families are large and women and children can be depended upon to perform hard and responsible jobs, then the type of diversified farming reminiscent of "Old MacDonald" is not only profitable but surprisingly productive.

The majority of Megalopolitan commercial farms, however, are stream-

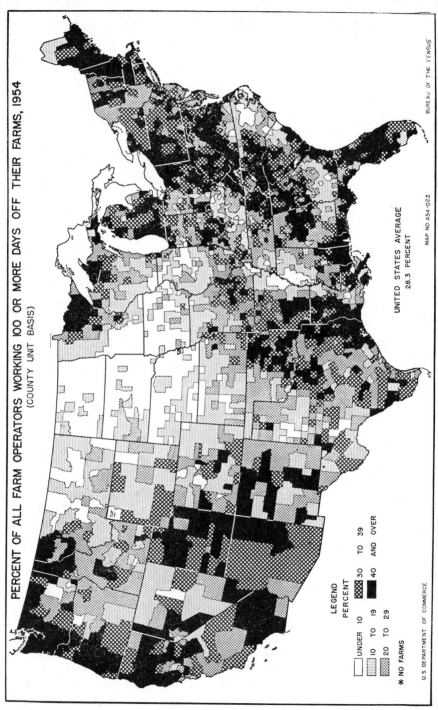

Fig. 86. *Courtesy of the U. S. Bureau of the Census*

lined modern specialty enterprises. Diversified operations, while they may be profitable, do not generally reach the peak of efficiency attained on specialty farms, where a single product is the dominant or exclusive interest of the operator. Many farmers in the vicinity of large Eastern cities are ingenious individualists who study market possibilities and develop a specialty to satisfy a particular need. Thus there are gardeners who raise a strange assortment of exotic vegetables exclusively for Chinese restaurants and food shops. There are those who produce sod for landscape contractors, flowers for wholesale florists, and game birds for the gourmet and delicatessens. The center of mushroom production in the United States is in southeastern Pennsylvania within overnight shipping distance of Washington, Philadelphia, New York, and Boston. The geographic location of these specialty enterprises is commonly a matter of calculation rather than accident. These farmers are in a better position to negotiate with wholesale outlets if they deliver their products personally than if they were to ship by consignment from more distant areas where land might be cheaper. Thus close contact with the market is a major asset, but one that is paid for dearly.

In terms of value, dairy and poultry products are the leading specialties, followed by fruits, vegetables, and horticultural products. Even in New Jersey, the Garden State, poultry products lead all others in value (see Table 4). These most important types of commercial farming in Megalopolis will be considered separately in the following sections.

Dairy Farming

The advantage of dairying in Megalopolis rather than in Wisconsin or Minnesota, which are at the heart of America's dairyland, is apparent in the data of Table 5: the Rhode Island dairyman receives more than twice as much money for his milk, pound for pound. In fact, only in Florida does the average dairyman receive more for his product (an average of $6.89 per hundred pounds in 1957) than in Rhode Island. Dairymen in Connecticut and Massachusetts rank fourth and fifth in the nation in the prices they receive per hundred pounds of milk. Moreover, New Jersey and Rhode Island rank second and third among the states in production of milk per cow (California leads with an average of 8,590 pounds). In 1957 owners of the 3.3 million cows in the Megalopolitan states received more money for 23,144 million pounds of milk than the owners of 4.6 million cows in the three leading Midwestern states received for 32,596 million pounds of milk. The advantage enjoyed by the Megalopolitan dairyman is a good market protected by milkshed regulations (see

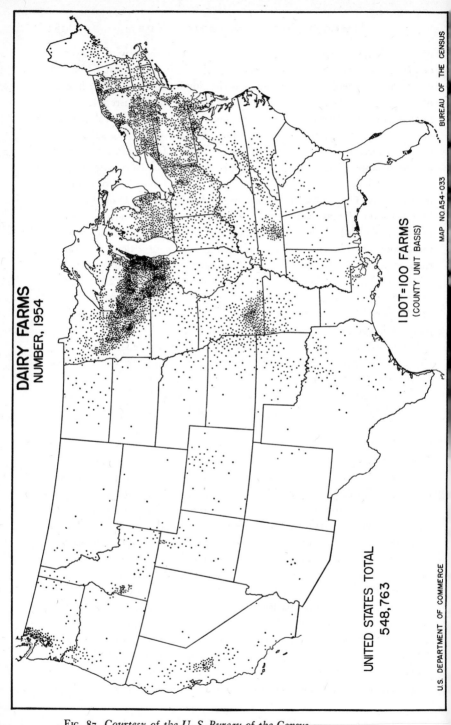

FIG. 87. *Courtesy of the U. S. Bureau of the Census*

Table 4

RELATIVE VALUE OF ALL FARM PRODUCTS SOLD
IN MEGALOPOLITAN STATES, 1954

(*Percentages*)

States	Cash Grains: Wheat, Corn, Oats, Soybeans	Veg., Fruits, Nuts, Hort. Spec.	Tobacco	Dairy Prods.	Poultry Prods.	Cattle, Calves, Hogs	Other
Entirely or chiefly within Megalopolis							
Massachusetts	—	26.5	6.1	29.6[a]	29.3	5.8	2.7
Rhode Island	—	22.0	—	40.8[a]	23.5	4.2	9.5
Connecticut	—	12.7	17.8	29.2	29.3[a]	3.5	7.5
New Jersey	4.1	27.8	—	21.6	32.9	6.1	7.5
Delaware	13.2	10.8	—	8.5	58.5[a]	3.6	5.4
Maryland	13.9	11.3	7.9	28.6[a]	22.0	12.7	3.6
Partially within but chiefly outside Megalopolis							
New York	4.1	18.2	—	50.0[a]	11.7	7.0	9.0
Pennsylvania	9.6	11.6	1.8	35.9[a]	19.1	14.6	7.4
Virginia[b]	7.4	10.4	19.5[a]	14.5	15.9	18.6	13.7

Source: U. S. Census of Agriculture: 1954, Vol. II, pp. 922–925.

[a] Leading commodity.

[b] Peanuts accounted for 5.5 per cent of Virginia's marketed farm products in 1954.

pp. 228–231). Most of his production goes into bottles to be consumed as fresh milk or cream. The bulk of Midwestern production goes into butter and cheese.

It will be noted that the average value of milk in New York and Pennsylvania is lower than that in the states that are entirely within Megalopolis. This is because a large proportion of the milk produced in New York and Pennsylvania enters the market as manufactured products such as butter and cheese, rather than as fresh bottled milk and cream. As might be expected, there is great pressure on the part of dairymen in the cheap milk states to sell their products in Megalopolis. There is equally strong effort on the part of dairymen in the favored market areas to produce all the milk that is needed so that milk shipments from the outside will not be necessary. The result of this competition is a streamlined refinement of the dairy industry in New Jersey and New England.

Except in years of drought the majority of dairymen in New York and a very large number in Pennsylvania try to grow on their own farms all the hay necessary to feed their cows and at least a substantial share of the grain. Thus they compensate for the somewhat lower market value of their

Table 5

DAIRY PRODUCTION, AMOUNT AND VALUE, 1957

States	Thousands of Milk Cows	Av. Annual Milk Yield per Cow (Lbs.)	Total Milk Yield (Million Lbs.)	Av. Price to Farmer per 100 Lbs.	Total Value of All Milk (Millions)
Entirely or chiefly within Megalopolis					
Massachusetts	113	7,250	819	$6.16	$50.4
Rhode Island	17	7,750	132	6.64	8.7
Connecticut	107	7,020	751	6.33	47.5
New Jersey	146	7,910	1,155	5.56	64.2
Delaware	33	6,000	198	4.67	9.2
Maryland	236	6,500	1,534	4.84	74.2
Partially within but chiefly outside Megalopolis					
New York	1,365	7,350	10,033	4.29	430.4
Pennsylvania	943	6,860	6,469	4.64	300.1
Virginia	388	5,290	2,052	4.91	100.8
9-State Totals	3,348				$1,085.5
Leaders in Mid-western Dairyland					
Wisconsin	2,293	7,380	16,922	3.37	$570.2
Minnesota	1,386	6,760	9,369	2.99	280.1
Iowa	1,004	6,280	6,305	2.86	180.3
3-State Totals	4,683				$1,030.6

Source: *Milk: Farm Production, Disposition, and Income, 1956–57*, U. S. Department of Agriculture, Washington, April 1958.

milk. Moreover, many dairymen in the central sections of these states sell surplus hay for shipment to southern New England and New Jersey. Southern New England also imports hay from northern New England, and from Canada.

In states where the market for fresh milk is excellent there is strong emphasis upon good pasture for cows and upon the production of grass-legume silage. Hay is the major field crop, except near the sea, where conditions for drying it are poor because in the summer humidity is high and rains are frequent. Relatively few feed grains are raised because it is more profitable to buy them and to use the time saved to care for more animals in the barns.

In fact, the general trend among dairymen in Megalopolis is to reduce field labor time and to increase the time spent in livestock husbandry. As farmland becomes increasingly valuable and less extensive around the big cities, it is likely that milk production will actually increase. Some day a situation similar to that in Los Angeles may occur. There the majority of

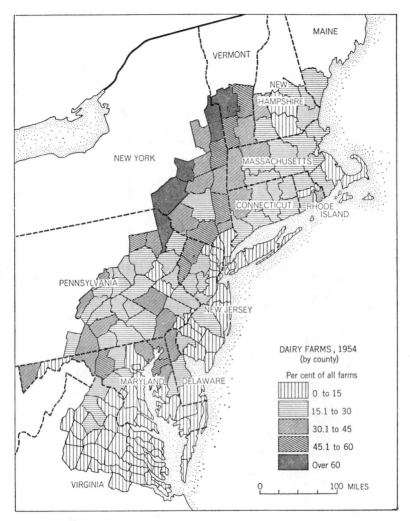

DAIRY FARMS, 1954
(by county)

Per cent of all farms

0 to 15
15.1 to 30
30.1 to 45
45.1 to 60
Over 60

0   100 MILES

FIG. 88

dairymen buy all grain and hay, and some have no pastures for cows during their lactation. On the outskirts of Los Angeles it is not uncommon to
keep as many as 250 milking cows on ten acres of land. The Megalopolitan
dairy farms have not reached this extreme, but they are 42 per cent more
mechanized than are dairy farms in the Midwest, and keep 39 per cent
more cows, on just about the same amount of land. The Wisconsin-Minnesota farms raise 28 per cent more acres of small grain, whereas the Meg-

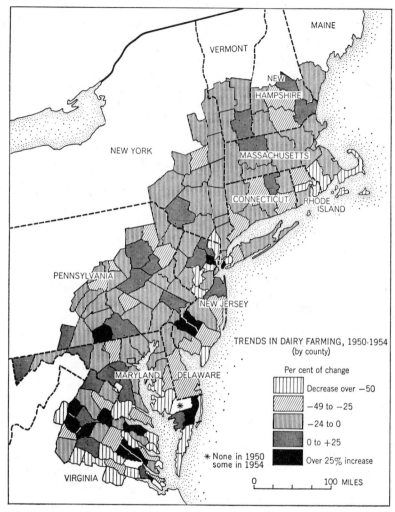

FIG. 89

alopolitan farms raise 29 per cent more acres of hay. It is more expensive per unit of feed value to ship hay than it is to ship grain. The Megalopolitan farmer, therefore, raises hay and about as much corn as the Middle Western dairyman, because corn can be used either as ensilage or as grain and stover.

There is a larger proportion of dairy farms in the counties of Appalachia and the Piedmont than in the counties of the Coastal Plain (see Fig. 88).

Table 6

QUANTITATIVE CHARACTERISTICS OF TWO DAIRY AREAS, 1954

Characteristics	Atlantic Coast Area (Megalopolis)	Northern Lake Area (Wisc.-Minn.)	% (+ or −) of Megalopolis' Deviation from Wisc.-Minn. (Per Farm)
Number of dairy farms	26,073	124,501	
Average per farm:			
Cows	25	18	+39
Acres	152	157	−3
Total investment in land and buildings	$27,274	$15,212	+79
Total investment in machinery	$6,823	$4,797	+42
Acres of cropland harvested	73	74	−1
Acres of cropland pastured	18	15	+20
% of cropland in:			
Small grains	23	32	−28
Corn for all uses	26	27	−4
Hay	49	39	+29
Milk sales per cow	$351	$201	+78
Pounds of milk per cow sold annually	7,200	6,594	+9
Price received per 100 lbs. of milk	$4.87	$3.05	+60

Source: U. S. Census of Agriculture: 1954, Vol. III, Pt. 9, Chapter 5.

This is due partly to inferior soils that are found on much of the Coastal Plain and partly to the competition of cities for the land. Since pasture and hay represent low-intensity land utilization, the dairy industry retreats to the western edge of Megalopolis rather than trying to remain at its center. That should be true as long as dairymen attempt to raise most of their hay and continue to pasture cattle. Eventually a substantial number of dairymen may shift to the "milk factory" system. Already fewer farms are producing more milk, as is brought out in Figures 89 and 90. That the number of dairy farms is declining is obvious in most counties, although there are some increases on the fringe of Megalopolis and in a few counties very close to New York City, Washington, and Philadelphia.

An outstanding example of Megalopolitan dairy farms is the Walker-Gordon enterprise of Middlesex County, New Jersey, one of the most remarkable dairy farms in the United States. Walker-Gordon and its associates have a herd of 2,800 milking cows and young stock together with

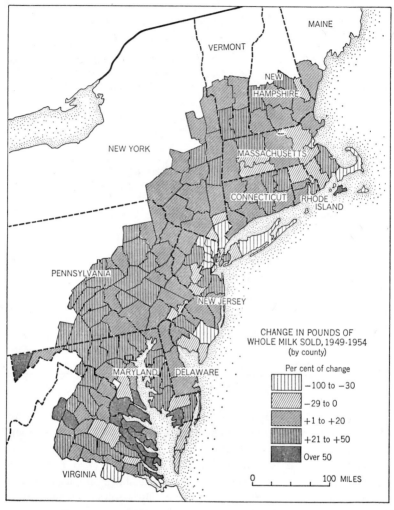

FIG. 90

2,400 acres of land at Plainsboro, New Jersey. Every day of the year the company milks 1,650 cows to obtain an average of 26,000 quarts. All this milk is produced under such conditions as to qualify for the premium certified milk market.

With an uncommonly good sense of geography, the Walker-Gordon farm was established in the New Jersey countryside half way between

New York City and Philadelphia. These were and still are the two best milk markets in the East and both are served by the main-line Pennsylvania Railroad, which has a spur running into the Walker-Gordon farm. Today this location, which is only forty-three miles from New York's Holland Tunnel and forty-four miles from Philadelphia's City Hall, is directly in the path of growing suburbanization. While the purpose of Walker-Gordon remains what it was over half a century ago, it has been forced to make a number of adjustments in the face of urban competition for its land and labor.

Formerly all the land and cattle at Walker-Gordon were owned and managed by the company. In the days of low-cost labor and low taxes economic survival was possible, but as the land, taxes, and skilled manpower all became more expensive, new solutions had to be devised. The best field and animal husbandry requires the utmost talents of skilled and interested men. Walker-Gordon has found that managers of this type must have a personal stake in their enterprise. Today the company's 2,400 acres near Plainsboro are divided into individual farm units of approximately 300 acres each. Each unit is leased to an able and trustworthy man who has proven his ability during previous employment with the company. All these farms are utilized solely to raise feed for the 1,650 milking cows. The cattle are housed not on the scattered farms but in a community of thirty-five barns clustered about a central milking plant, which is called the rotolactor. There is an incentive in the farm leasing system that encourages the best management. Rents paid by the lessees conform to terms that are common to that part of New Jersey. The company, however, guarantees to buy all the feed which is produced at fixed contract prices. All grain and other concentrate feeds are bought and shipped in from outside the area. It is not feasible or profitable to raise grain on such expensive land. The farmers who raise corn and alfalfa on the company's farms have nothing to do with the care or ownership of the dairy cows. These cattle are the special interest of contract herdsmen.

The management of the cattle is somewhat more complicated. In contrast to the days of company ownership the animals are now the property of individual herdsmen, each one of whom may be under contract with the company to provide fifty to a hundred and fifty milking cows at all times. While they are in milking condition, which is usually ten months during the year, the cattle are housed in the thirty-five company barns adjacent to the rotolactor. The company supplies all feed at wholesale cost and delivers it to the barns. The owners of the herds feed and bed their

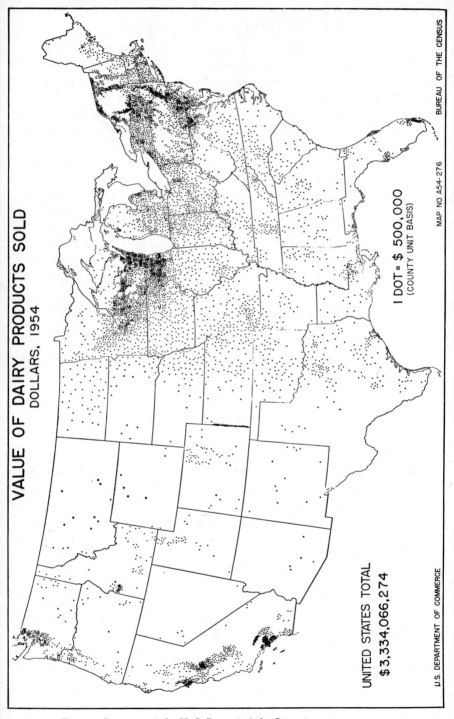

VALUE OF DAIRY PRODUCTS SOLD
DOLLARS, 1954

1 DOT = $ 500,000
(COUNTY UNIT BASIS)

MAP NO A54-276

BUREAU OF THE CENSUS

UNITED STATES TOTAL
$3,334,066,274

U.S. DEPARTMENT OF COMMERCE

FIG. 91. *Courtesy of the U. S. Bureau of the Census*

own cattle but they do not milk them. This is done at company expense in the sanitary milking parlor, which the cows visit in shifts twice daily on a fixed schedule.

Because a dairy cow requires about two months of rest between lactations, the dairy herdsmen must provide replacements for each cow temporarily retired. Many of these dairymen have their own lands in more distant rural communities where land is less costly. They must be within a day's trucking distance of Plainsboro, so eastern Pennsylvania's mountain valleys are used to pasture the dry cows until they calve and freshen. The cost of keeping them in the hill country is low compared with the price of buying a new cow, and the productive value is much higher because all of these cows have been bred by artificial insemination from one of the twelve proved sires kept by Walker-Gordon for its herdsmen. By such selective breeding the quality of all the herds is constantly improving.

It is by ingenious methods such as these that more dairy cows of Megalopolis may be housed near the market and yet be fed from the produce of cheaper lands some distance away. Even Walker-Gordon, despite its ingenious pioneering, is obliged to give way to growing suburbia. With land taxes mounting as new schools and highways are built, the company has sold some of its more valuable road front properties to research laboratories and other commercial organizations in order to help the local units of government increase their tax base. The shrinkage will very likely continue, but the central unit of barns and rotolactor should be able to function indefinitely.

The tendency of the Megalopolitan dairy industry to produce more milk on fewer farms and on less land is good business. Feed grains are, at the moment, one of the major surplus commodities of American agriculture. They are for sale at bargain prices, and their cost of transportation is low. As long as the Corn Belt continues to produce more grain than it can profitably feed to its own animals there will be cheap surpluses available to the dairymen and poultrymen of Megalopolis. If the livestock industry of Megalopolis is vulnerable in any sense, it is to the Corn Belt's control of the nation's feed grain supply.

Poultry Farming

Since 1930 there has been a revolution in the methods of poultry husbandry. Before that time most farms had a flock of laying hens as a side line, and almost all commercial supplies of eggs and poultry meat came from those flocks. Today the industry is becoming more highly specialized, with breeds of birds being raised for specific purposes. The all-

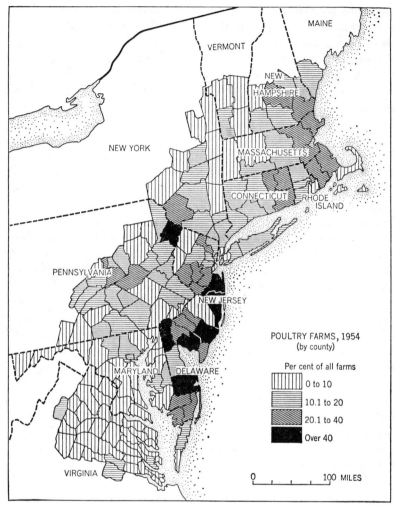

purpose chicken is now as obsolete as are dual-purpose cattle. With scientific improvements in breeding and feeding have come marked reductions in the costs of poultry production. This has attracted capital and encouraged specialization, so that today, particularly in Megalopolis, poultry husbandry is a highly refined enterprise.

Only twenty years ago it required more than four pounds of feed to produce a pound of broiler. Today not quite three pounds are needed. The time needed to raise a bird for market has also been reduced, which means a saving in labor and overhead costs. In recent years comparable improvements have been made in the breeding and feeding of egg-laying chickens. The kind of specialization that came early to the dairy industry developed later with poultry. Owing to the fact that poultry are fed entirely on concentrated feeds and not on roughage such as hay or pasture grasses, the specialized poultryman needs very little land. His kind of animal husbandry is therefore better suited than dairying to the costly real estate of the urban fringe.

The principal poultry region of the Northeastern United States coincides with the densely populated parts of Megalopolis. The importance of poultry husbandry in the commercial agriculture of this area is illustrated by the fact that 15.2 to 35.2 per cent of all commercial farms specialize in poultry. Among the commercial farms with less than 30 acres of land, poultry husbandry is the specialty of more than 53 per cent, while for the United States as a whole that percentage stands at 13.8. It is apparent that a highly specialized form of husbandry has found a particularly favorable environment on the fringe of the great cities.

Poultry farms are concentrated along the seaboard and in some Appalachian counties (Fig. 92), and the locational pattern shows almost no correlation with soils. For example, among the counties with marked emphasis on poultry farms New Castle and Sussex counties in Delaware lie in a region of better-than-average soils, whereas Atlantic County, New Jersey, and Pike County, Pennsylvania, lie in areas of poorer-than-average soils. In eastern Massachusetts, too, poultry husbandry is prominent on poor soils, underdeveloped and stony soils. The map (Fig. 92) indicates that location near large cities may be desirable but not necessary. New Jersey and northern Delaware are very close to the markets of New York and Philadelphia. In contrast, southern Delaware and Appalachian Pennsylvania are at some distance, but because of rapid truck transportation facilities this is no handicap.

The production of broilers is more highly regionalized than the production of chicken eggs, which are supplied in large numbers by more counties in Megalopolis (see Fig. 94). The Delmarva Peninsula stands out conspicuously as the center of the broiler industry. In 1954, for example, there were 1,299 farms producing broilers in Sussex County, Delaware, and the average farm sold a little more than 40,000 birds. Mild winters there are an advantage in reducing the overhead costs of shelters and heating. Perhaps more important is the fact that this type of highly refined husbandry has been practiced in this area for many years, and some of the foremost technical advances have been developed there and widely adopted.

Recent trends in egg production (see Fig. 95) indicate that most of the

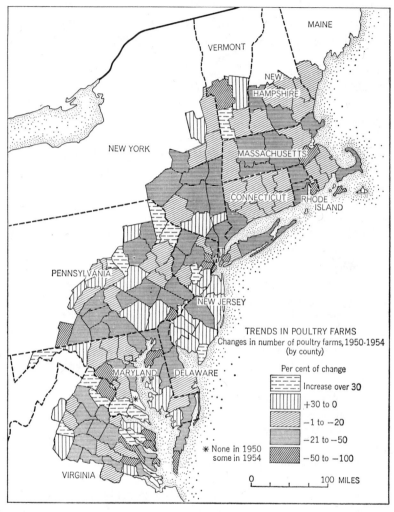

FIG. 93

counties making the fastest growth are on the Coastal Plain. However, what is a large percentage gain on Cape Cod and on the Eastern Shore of Maryland is not a really large increase in actual production (see Figs. 94 and 95). By 1954 New Jersey not only was the most important supplier of eggs but also was making the most substantial growth of all the states in Megalopolis.

It is a favorite hobby of people with city jobs and farm homes to keep

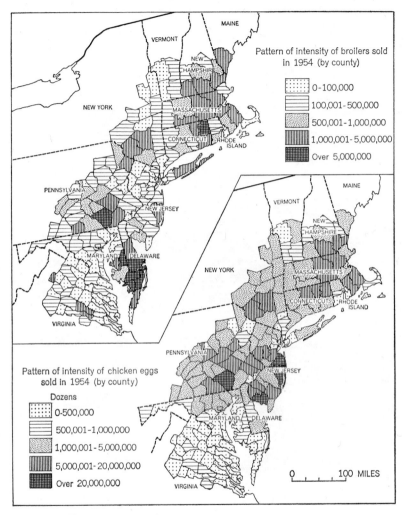

Pattern of intensity of broilers sold in 1954 (by county)

- 0-100,000
- 100,001-500,000
- 500,001-1,000,000
- 1,000,001-5,000,000
- Over 5,000,000

Pattern of intensity of chicken eggs sold in 1954 (by county)

Dozens
- 0-500,000
- 500,001-1,000,000
- 1,000,001-5,000,000
- 5,000,001-20,000,000
- Over 20,000,000

0 ____ 100 MILES

FIG. 94

a flock of chickens, but if time and overhead are accounted for, this rural side line is seldom profitable. Competition in the poultry industry is now so severe that only the most efficient large-scale operations return a reasonable profit. Bigness is necessary to pay for the best labor-saving devices — high capital investment per employee is the rule in the *commercial* poultry industry — and only such devices make it possible for manpower to be employed efficiently. With an abundance of such automatic machinery

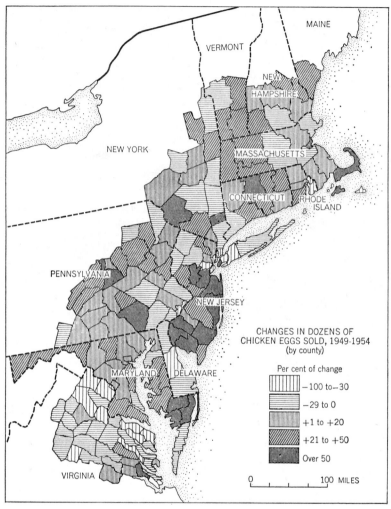

CHANGES IN DOZENS OF
CHICKEN EGGS SOLD, 1949-1954
(by county)

Per cent of change

	−100 to −30
	−29 to 0
	+1 to +20
	+21 to +50
	Over 50

0   100 MILES

F ɪɢ. 95

and with prepared feeds delivered in bulk, one man can handle an operation of large size. At times, however, even such large and efficient enterprises lose money. Feed costs are the most important item in current
expenses, and the spread between these costs and the market value of poultry products is generally very narrow. A close squeeze between these two
factors may mean a loss even for commercial poultry farms whose yearly
sales are $25,000 or greater. Presumably, such large-scale poultrymen with

the best labor-saving equipment find it profitable to hire help. On the other hand, it is significant that about one quarter of the operators of commercial poultry farms work off the farm for more than 100 days a year. Apparently they are not well enough equipped to keep themselves profitably employed full time. Moreover, the data on small-scale poultry farms show that on the average they have a loss or make very low profits. Clearly, then, the advantage of modern poultry husbandry seems to lie with large-scale, full-time enterprises having the most efficient equipment. Raising chickens is no longer a good side line for the part-time hobbyist unless he discounts the value of his labor and is able to take an occasional setback.

In Megalopolis, however, such amateur and semi-professional poultrymen are numerous enough to contribute significantly to the strong competitive pressures the poultrymen must face, pressures stronger than those to which the dairymen are subject. This internal aspect of the competition will probably diminish in coming years, as their inefficient methods subject hobby producers to more frequent losses. But the external pressures from outside Megalopolis are a more serious threat. Eggs are not as perishable as milk, and broilers can be kept by freezing. Since both eggs and broilers are worth much more per pound than milk, they can be transported for a lower percentage of their market value. Moreover, they are not protected by any "milkshed" type of legislation. Production can therefore be concentrated outside Megalopolis, wherever there is some definite local advantage. Georgia, for example, favored by comparatively low labor costs, is the leading state for broiler production. During recent decades many Georgia farms have given up cotton, which requires much cheap hand labor. It was necessary to find substitute employment, and broilers have proved profitable. For eggs, California, Iowa, and Minnesota are the top suppliers. Feed grains are cheap in Iowa and Minnesota, and in the Middle Western area it has always been a practice to convert surplus feed grains into more valuable livestock products. Egg production there is thus not new. However, it may increase still more, developing along the "factory" lines found in Megalopolis and California, as a result of the U. S. Department of Agriculture's Soil Bank Conservation Reserve program.

This program, designed to retire land from surplus crop cultivation, appeals to marginal grain farmers in the Corn Belt and to cotton producers on poor soil. It permits producers of surplus field crops to withdraw their entire cultivated acreage from production for periods up to ten years, and they receive attractive payments for each acre not planted. The *fields* may be devoted to forestry or wildlife, but there is no reason why the farmers cannot convert their *sheds and barns* into poultry houses. If this occurs on a larger scale than it has already, the poultry farmers of Megalopolis may pay heavily for having opposed high parity payments to grain and cotton farmers, which might have kept them in those businesses. Now with parity payments dropping to lower levels, the Conservation Reserve program acquires greater appeal. Should many marginal cash-grain growers convert to poultry while drawing government subsidies for not working in the fields, they would be in a favorable position to undersell the Eastern producer who buys high-cost feed, employs expensive labor, and operates on more valuable real estate.

An unusual poultry specialty is the raising of ducks on Long Island. The Long Island duck is a name to conjure with in New York restaurants and food shops. The story of where it is raised and where it is sold is a neat tale of geography, economics, and persistent culture habits. Fat duck is not a common American staple. Rather it is more to the taste of the Chinese and central Europeans. There is a greater demand for fat duck in New York City than anywhere else in the United States precisely because there are more people there who have clung to Old World dietary customs. Ducks are comparatively easy to raise and they put on weight more rapidly and more economically than any other market bird or animal. However, ducks with the best market finish should be produced where there is plenty of fresh running water. For these several reasons the southern shore of eastern Long Island is a choice spot for duck farms — or was until summer vactioners and commuters began to bid up land values of the better waterfront properties, making it difficult for commercial duck raisers to compete or even hold their own. The immaculate cleanliness of Long Island ducks in the shop windows of Manhattan's Chinatown and East Side indicates that somehow they still find space to swim despite suburban sprawl (see Fig. 96).

Cash Crops and Specialized Farms

The states of Megalopolis depart widely from the normal pattern of cash-crop farming in the United States. There is a greater emphasis upon items for direct human consumption rather than upon those that are fed to livestock. Field crops grown for sale tend to be specialty types that require relatively little land but a high degree of skill and considerable hand labor. Much of the labor is seasonally employed and is recruited largely from the Southern states, the West Indies, and the student population of the United States during the summer recess.

New Jersey and Delaware rank first and second among all states in hav-

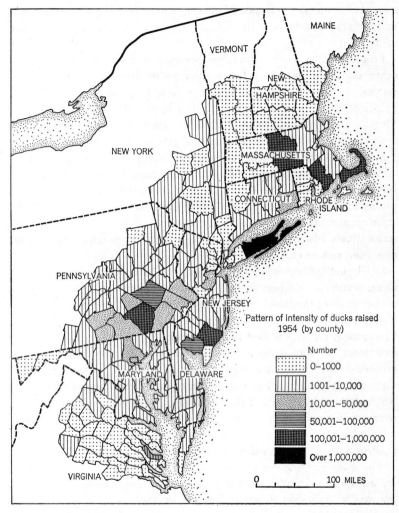

Pattern of intensity of ducks raised
1954 (by county)

Number

0–1000

1001–10,000

10,001–50,000

50,001–100,000

100,001–1,000,000

Over 1,000,000

0   100 MILES

FIG. 96

ing the highest proportions of their cash-crop acreage devoted to vegetables. New York and New Jersey rank first and second in space devoted
to floral plants and cut flowers grown under glass. Of the country's top
twenty counties in the production of nursery and greenhouse specialties,
ten are in Megalopolis. Seven states in Megalopolis are among the first
eight in the United States on the basis of the value of horticultural specialties in the total of all crops sold. For instance, slightly more than 44 per

cent of all crop sales in Rhode Island are of nursery and greenhouse products, whereas the average for the country as a whole is less than 4 per cent.

Fruits, tobacco, nursery stock, greenhouse products, white potatoes, and other vegetables are the primary interests of Megalopolitan cash-crop farmers. In the three states of southern New England these account for 97 per cent of all marketed crops. In this respect the field-crop farms of Megalopolis are more like those of Florida, where the average for the same is 93 per cent, or California, where it is 58.6 per cent. Table 7 indicates the great importance of tobacco in the cash-crop economy of Connecticut. It is not generally regarded as a tobacco state, however, for the total value and volume of the harvest are low compared with those of more prominent tobacco states, such as North Carolina and Virginia. A similar situation prevails in Rhode Island with respect to potatoes. On the national scene Rhode Island is not a prominent grower, but potatoes are its most important cash crop.

In Virginia tobacco is grown on small farms, under a share-crop arrangement, in rural areas where there is little or no opportunity for full-time or part-time work in urban centers. Tobacco in Connecticut is grown in the Connecticut River Valley, which is the industrial heartland of the state. Connecticut tobacco is used for cigar wrappers and binders. The recent emergence of homogenized leaf binders that are machine-made from crushed whole leaves has strongly reduced the planting of binder tobacco since the 1954 Census. For the moment shade-grown leaf wrappers are still in demand by makers of the best cigars, but growers are apprehensive over possibilities that these, too, may eventually be made by a modified homogenized-leaf process. This would eliminate an ingenious and specialized form of agriculture for which Connecticut is famous.

The shade techniques are designed to produce in the Connecticut Valley a product similar to what is grown in the humid tropical climate of Sumatra.[3] Cultivation is accomplished with the aid of irrigation under enormous field "tents" of cotton netting, which diffuse the sunlight, cut down wind movement, and promote somewhat higher relative humidity. The result is a fast-growing, thin, pliant leaf, practically without blemish or prominent veining, which satisfies a fastidious market. The tent-covered tobacco plots are more like enormous cotton greenhouses than ordinary farm fields. The mass-scale hothouse environment is almost as artificial as that created by man for himself in the near-by cities and suburbs.

[3] Edward Higbee, *The American Oasis,* Alfred A. Knopf, New York, 1957, pp. 198–201.

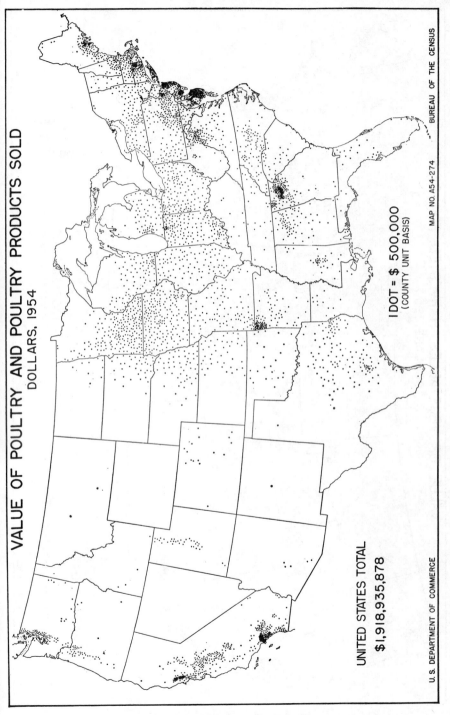

FIG. 97. *Courtesy of the U. S. Bureau of the Census*

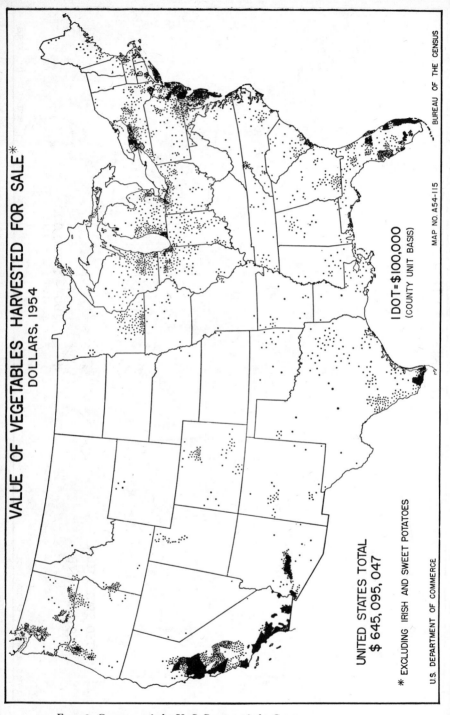

FIG. 98. *Courtesy of the U. S. Bureau of the Census*

Table 7

VALUE OF FRUITS, VEGETABLES, AND HORTICULTURAL SPECIALTIES
IN THE CASH-CROP ECONOMY OF MEGALOPOLIS

(*Percentages of All Crops Sold*)

States	Vege-tables	Fruits & Nuts	Horti-cultural Specialties	Tobacco	White Potatoes	Total of These 5 Groups
Entirely or chiefly within Megalopolis						
Massachusetts	13.2	26.5	34.7	17.1	5.3	96.8
Rhode Island	8.3	7.2	44.2	—	37.8	97.5
Connecticut	6.8	9.5	27.9	46.3	6.5	97.0
New Jersey	35.1	17.0	23.8	—	6.0	81.9
Delaware	24.0	4.4	12.3	—	8.6	49.3
Maryland	15.7	7.3	8.2	22.9	1.1	55.2
Partially within but chiefly outside Megalopolis						
New York	17.4	26.9	18.7	—	13.9	76.9
Pennsylvania	8.9	14.4	22.5	6.1	9.9	61.8
Virginia	5.8	13.7	3.8	40.9	2.5	66.7
Other leaders in these products						
California	13.3	35.2	4.2	—	3.9	58.6
Florida	22.0	53.2	7.8	6.5	3.8	93.3
United States Total	5.3	9.8	3.7	8.0	3.0	29.8

Source: Calculated from the *U. S. Census of Agriculture: 1954.*

The tendency in recent years has been toward specialization in cash-crop farming just as in animal husbandry. The amateurs are dropping out, while fewer professionals are raising more commodities on a larger scale. It is apparent in Table 8 that "large-scale" as applied to fruits, vegetables, and specialty crops does not necessarily mean big acreages. A characteristic of such farming is that labor is more important than land. For instance, only about 4,000 acres of muck soils in Orange County, New York, have enabled its growers of dry onions to rank fourth in the United States.

Sometimes it is by luck or accident that a farmer discovers some specialty that will enable him to keep his land in production in the face of rising property values and higher taxes. In Megalopolis, farming is more than a business; it is also a way of life, and to most farmers the land is home as well as a place to work. It is perhaps where one was raised, or where he came as a young man just married and where his children were born, and where he may hope to retire and enjoy seeing his children prosper in their turn.

Take, for example, the case of Philip Jones, Jr., the operator of White Hills, a 260-acre dairy and Christmas tree farm in the Town of Shelton, Fairfield County, Connecticut. The suburbs are closing in on White Hills. Land values and consequently taxes are reaching the point where even dairying for the bottled milk trade is becoming unprofitable. If Mr. Jones were to sell his 260 acres he could realize perhaps a quarter of a million dollars, but he would have to give up a way of life that he enjoys and that is something money alone cannot buy today, in increasingly congested southwestern Connecticut. Also one never knows what will happen to the value of money, but the value of a producing farm on the fringe of Megalopolis can only increase. The Christmas trees are the hope of the future at White Hills.

"It may sound strange, but without the trees the dairy couldn't pay its way." Mr. Jones was about to explain what every farmer on the edge of suburbia knows about taxes. "They would drive me out of business. They keep going up every year, while the price of milk drags. I get 9½ cents a quart for the milk you pay 29 cents to drink. But I've found that Guernseys and blue spruce are a good combination."

It all happened when luck was supported by some Yankee instinct for opportunity. Nineteen years ago the Christmas tree business began when Jones won a 4-H Club award for having done a particularly fine bit of woodlot thinning. He had taken a piece of choked-up, cut-over woodland on his father's farm and hacked out the "wolfs," the "sprouts," and the "cripples." That left more room and sunlight for the good trees that remained. With the $40 in prize money he bought pine and spruce transplants from the state forestry nursery to set out on a rocky place on the farm, "which wasn't much good for pasture. The trees grew well so we had to thin them. I found that folks would buy them for Christmas trees."

The advantage of growing such an exotic item as a Christmas tree on the fringe of the market was related by Mr. Jones. "We get 70 cents a foot for the trees. The average house tree is around 6 to 6½ feet. Some folks like to cut their own. They bring the kids out and make a big thing of cutting the tree. We have one plot for these woodchoppers. They swarm all over the place. We put price tags on every tree so they know the cost before they cut."

Fire is a problem of Mr. Jones and his 100,000 trees. He plants them in scattered patches, leaving open spaces of pasture in between. "That's where the cows are a big help. They keep the pasture down. If a fire gets started it will not travel across well-pastured ground. We let the cows in the plantings when the trees are small. They eat the grass and skip the trees."

Table 8

TRENDS IN FRUIT AND VEGETABLE FARMING IN MEGALOPOLIS

States	Thousands of Acres		Thousands of Farms		Average No. of Acres per Farm	
	1930	1954	1930	1954	1930	1954
A. Land in Fruit Orchards, Vineyards, and Planted Nut Trees						
Entirely or chiefly within Megalopolis						
Massachusetts	45.7	16.5	11.9	1.8	3.8	9.1
Rhode Island	5.5	1.8	1.5	0.25	3.7	7.2
Connecticut	22.2	12.7	8.4	1.8	2.6	7.0
New Jersey	54.8	28.5	8.5	2.5	5.7	11.4
Delaware	21.1	2.1	4.5	.2	4.7	10.5
Maryland	42.2	16.1	19.5	1.8	2.1	9.0
Partially within but chiefly outside Megalopolis						
New York	412.1	174.4	76.9	14.3	5.3	12.0
Pennsylvania	273.9	114.3	105.6	20.3	2.6	10.5
Virginia	220.3	85.4	89.5	11.7	2.5	7.2
B. Land in Vegetables Harvested for Sale (Except Potatoes)						
Entirely within Megalopolis or almost so						
Massachusetts	24.7	20.3	8.3	2.5	3.0	8.1
Rhode Island	2.2	1.8	0.9	0.24	2.4	7.5
Connecticut	9.1	12.7	3.7	1.2	2.5	10.6
New Jersey	94.9	145.9	12.0	5.1	8.0	28.6
Delaware	33.3	40.0	6.9	1.4	4.8	28.6
Maryland	119.9	94.0	19.2	5.3	6.2	17.7
Partially within but chiefly outside Megalopolis						
New York	131.6	184.9	35.8	10.9	3.4	17.0
Pennsylvania	54.2	96.1	32.9	11.8	1.6	8.1
Virginia	47.3	72.7	20.4	7.0	2.3	10.4

Source: U. S. Census of Agriculture: 1954, Vol. II.

Hired labor is always a problem for farmers on the Megalopolitan edge. Christmas trees call for seasonal work at planting time, pruning time, and cutting time. Mr. Jones says, "Its easier to hold my labor by keeping dairy cows. With trees alone I couldn't afford steady help. We are fortunate to have college boys at Christmas time when we need the most labor. They get their recess just when we need them and it seems they all have to make $50 for a gift for somebody special." Mr. Jones has to earn more than the Maine and Canadian growers. They raise their stock on cheap

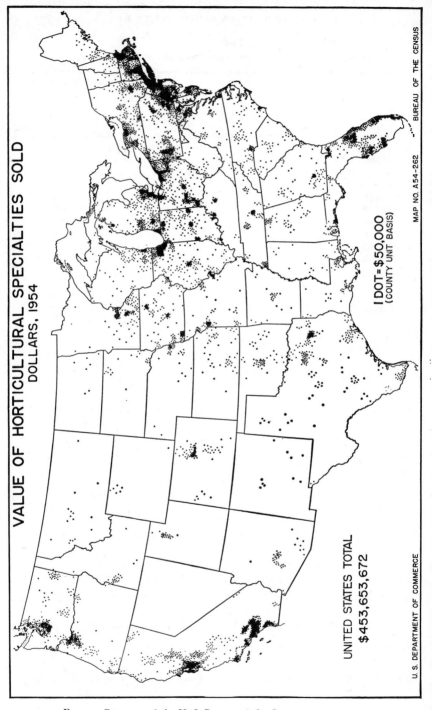

FIG. 99. *Courtesy of the U. S. Bureau of the Census*

land that might not be worth more than $15 an acre. White Hills farm is in the $1,000-an-acre area just out of Bridgeport, where some people commute daily to New York. One can stand on a high point in the middle of the farm and see at each point of the compass a farm being subdivided. "It's all going around here," Jones remarked. "I'd have to go too if it were not for the trees. I have sixty acres in trees and I'm planting more. Within thirty miles of me there are two million people. More and more of them are becoming my customers. As long as they keep coming I can keep the farm and I'll keep the cows too, to remind them of what Connecticut was before it grew into subdivisions and factories." [4]

Another specialized cash-crop enterprise is Seabrook Farms, with its central offices and processing plant in Cumberland County, New Jersey. Seabrook Farms is the nation's largest grower and packager of frozen vegetables. Because much of its output goes to market under various brand names, Seabrook is not as well known to the consumer as to the wholesaler. The organization is so large it employs a staff of professional guides. Its executives are as likely to be in New York, St. Louis, or Philadelphia as they are to be in their home offices — flown there in company planes by company pilots.

Each year the acreage of Seabrook Farms changes. Today it is 54,000 acres. In 1893 it was 78. Seabrook is something of an empire controlling its own lands as well as outlying colonies of contracted farms. It operates some 19,000 acres of its own. In addition it absorbs the produce of 35,000 acres owned by 1,169 "neighbors," who are scattered across several counties in southern New Jersey and in adjoining Delaware, Maryland, and Pennsylvania. During the summer packing season Seabrook Farms frequently harvests, packages, and freezes one million pounds of vegetables and fruits in a day. In a recent year it marketed more than 100 million pounds, almost one tenth of the national output.

Around the main farm new industries are already in operation, and suburbs are springing up. Local farm labor, once cheap and plentiful, has been drained off by the new factories and the new roads, which make it possible to commute to work in Wilmington, Camden, or Philadelphia. The growing populations of near-by cities improve the market for all types of food, but at the same time the progress of urbanization raises the cost of farm labor. To meet this challenge, Seabrook Farms is placing

---

[4] From Edward Higbee's notes on an interview with the farmer while making his field study of Connecticut. See also "New England's Christmas Tree Industry," in *New England Business Review*, Federal Reserve Bank of Boston, December 1956, pp. 1–3.

greater reliance on contracts with other farmers to raise the needed crops than on extending its own properties. This works to the mutual advantage of all parties, for land prices also are rising and now are generally thought to exceed their agricultural value. Seabrook cannot afford to tie up its capital in overpriced land. Small farmers feeling the pinch of higher taxes and generally mounting expenses are reluctant to gamble on an uncertain market and the possibility of being forced to sell their land prematurely just as it is rising greatly in value for subdivision development. An association between the processor and more than one thousand individual farmer-contractors has therefore become a kind of economic symbiosis whereby each sees a better way of surviving as the city closes in. A complex but profitable multi-contractual structure underpins the commercial farming of Megalopolis that works for the wholesale market.

Part-Time and Residential Farms

Part-time and residential farms are important for their impact upon the cultural landscape of Megalopolis, but their productivity is of slight significance. Their contribution to the market supply of agricultural commodities is as small as one per cent or less in several states. Most of their produce is for the tables of their owners, who generally earn their livelihood in the city. A few have other sources of income, such as pensions and investments, most of these being residential farmers who live on country properties but do not raise commodities for the market. If they do any farming at all it is chiefly as a hobby. They are as likely to bestow harvest-time gratuities upon their friends as they are to dispose of anything in the market place.

Several years ago two rural sociologists wrote:

There was a time when the interests of agriculture and the rural people of New England might have been considered with little reference to other types of land use than agriculture. Today this is not possible. The *part-time farmer, small-scale, and back-yard producers* have all become integral parts of the economy of Southern New England, as urban spheres of influence have widened. The invasion of rural areas by commuting urban workers, and by summer vacationers, has caused profound changes in the agricultural pattern, and may continue to do so. Rural areas, therefore, are no longer agricultural areas primarily, and the strictly farming residents may comprise but a small minority of the total of those who reside in a given open country section. The characteristics common to this part of the region are evidently to be found in other parts of the United States, if the increasing body of literature on this subject can be taken as an index.[5]

[5] William R. Gordon and Gilbert S. Meldrum, *Land, People and Farming in a Rurban Zone*, Rhode Island Agricultural Experiment Station, Kingston, 1942.

The proportion of part-time and residential farms is high in all Megalopolitan states. However, because they are smaller in average size than are
the commercial types they do not occupy as much of the total rural space
as their numbers would otherwise suggest. The crop and livestock interests
of part-time and residential farmers seem to be similar, while both are
somewhat contrary to those of specialized commercial farmers. In Delaware, where poultry products represent 58.5 per cent of all marketed farm
commodities and where commercial farms produce 99.5 per cent of everything that is sold, the part-time and residential farms definitely shy away
from the poultry business, which elsewhere is often a favorite interest.
Dairying is a comparatively minor activity of the part-time and residential
farms, as it requires more labor and attention than other forms of livestock
husbandry that are carried on in an avocational manner. In every area commercial farmers are the professional specialists, while part-time and residential farmers hold only amateur standing. However, despite this lower
occupational status, their farms usually have a higher value per acre of
land and buildings. They are often closer to the cities, where land values
are higher. Also the ratio of the value of buildings to the area of land is
often greater. Rhode Island is a conspicuous exception, as the average size
of all its farms is rather small; thus commercial farms also tend to be
highly developed in terms of buildings per acre.

Part-time and residential farms are frequently established on poorer soils
than are the commercial farms. However, when nearness to the city and to
the city job is important, the part-time or residential farmer who earns a
high income in town can easily afford to outbid the commercial farmer
for land. This is notable in the fashionable trend toward five-, ten-, and
twenty-acre "ranches" on the outskirts of Washington, Philadelphia,
and New York, where a country property is considered a social asset —
and sometimes a prerequisite. Among the most suitable products for the
part-time and residential farm are cane and vine fruits, poultry, garden
vegetables, and horticultural specialties wherever these are not the major
interest of neighboring commercial farms (see Tables 9 and 10).

The part-time and residential farms are much alike in that a half to four
fifths of their operators work at least 100 days a year off the farm. Approximately one quarter of the operators of residential farms do no off-
farm work at all. In as much as a farm is not classified as "residential" if
its annual sale of produce exceeds $249, it is apparent that many are owned
by persons of independent means who are retired, pensioned, or otherwise
favored with outside income, and thus are not obliged to work either at
farm labor or away from the farm.

These types of farm seem to increase in numbers with urbanization and

Table 9
Some Characteristics of Part-Time and Residential Farms, 1954[a]

States	Pt.-T. & Res. Farms as % of All Farms			% of All Farmland by Type of Farm			Per-Acre Value of Land and Buildings			% of Operators Working off Farm 100 Days or More		% of Operators Not Working off Farm	
	Pt.-T.	Res.	Both	Pt.-T.	Res.	Both	All Farms	Pt.-T.	Res.	Pt.-T.	Res.	Pt.-T.	Res.
Entirely or chiefly within Megalopolis													
Massachusetts	14	22	36	8	12	20	$218	$243	$246	81	69	12	24
Rhode Island	13	31	44	9	19	28	310	267	292	77	63	16	29
Connecticut	11	28	39	7	13	20	289	294	378	73	69	23	25
New Jersey	9	15	25	4	5	9	401	588	680	78	63	16	29
Delaware	9	11	20	4	2	6	153	177	326	80	56	14	27
Maryland	12	20	32	5	5	10	177	206	346	75	64	15	26
Partially within but chiefly outside Megalopolis													
New York	11	16	27	5	6	11	92	108	141	81	68	14	24
Pennsylvania	15	21	36	9	8	17	134	313	170	80	65	12	25
Virginia	16	32	48	10	22	32	106	115	132	68	58	22	31
Midwestern farm areas													
Wisconsin	6	6	12	3	2	5	101	102	127	82	64	10	26
Iowa	4	4	8	1	0.5	1.5	199	203	330	77	58	16	31
Illinois	7	9	16	2	1	3	230	162	193	76	53	14	33

Source: U. S. Census of Agriculture: 1954, Vol. II, Tables 3 and 4.
[a] Percentages are to the nearest whole number. When totals do not equal one hundred there is an allowance for institutional farms.

Table 10

Size and Products of Part-Time and Residential Farms in Megalopolis, 1954

States	Average Size (Acres)[a]			All Goods Sold by Pt.-T. Farms, %[a]					All Goods Sold by Res. Farms, %[a]				
	All Farms	Pt.-T.	Res.	Crops	Poult. & Poult. Prods.	Dairy Prods.	Other Livestock Prods.	Forest Prods.	Crops	Poult. & Poult. Prods.	Dairy Prods.	Other Livestock Prods.	Forest Prods.
Entirely or chiefly within Megalopolis													
Massachusetts	83	48	44	43	30	7	17	3	39	28	4	25	4
Rhode Island	77	50	44	36	48	3	13	—	32	39	3	26	—
Connecticut	89	57	41	33	34	5	26	2	47	23	1	29	—
New Jersey	73	29	22	53	35	1	11	—	54	29	—	16	—
Delaware	129	52	24	75	9	1	15	—	52	30	—	18	—
Maryland	120	52	31	53	19	3	24	1	31	35	3	30	1
Partially within but chiefly outside Megalopolis													
New York	143	68	54	40	23	13	21	3	33	25	5	31	5
Pennsylvania	102	63	48	38	23	8	29	2	30	24	5	38	3
Virginia	108	67	43	44	10	10	33	3	29	15	8	44	4

Source: U. S. Census of Agriculture: 1954, Vol. II, Table 10.
[a] Acres and percentages are given to the nearest whole number.

with better opportunity for rural people to commute to city jobs. The percentage of farm operators who work 100 or more days away from their farms is quite high in most of the nation except in the western Corn Belt, the Wisconsin-Minnesota Dairy Belt, and the Great Plains (see Fig. 86, p. 282). In 1954 about 30 per cent of all farms in the United States were either part-time or residential. The part-time or residential farm is an important solution to the low level of farm income wherever poor soils or the small size of the operating unit makes it desirable for the owner to find outside employment. Many farmers today do not have either the land or the capital to modernize and expand their facilities so as to become substantial commercial operators. The recent rate of technological change in agriculture has put them in the obsolete position that the pioneer subsistence farmer found himself in a hundred years ago. The best solution to an undersized or undercapitalized farm is for the owner to take a city job; he is thus more likely to attain a higher standard of living. The U. S. Department of Agriculture reports that 56 per cent of our farmers produce only 9 per cent of the nation's marketed agricultural products.[6] It is obvious that a great many more farmers would join the ranks of the part-time and residential fraternity if there were widely distributed opportunity for industrial employment. In Megalopolis this opportunity exists, and that is another reason for the comparative prosperity of its rural regions.

Isolated *estate farms* are found in every part of the nation and on the outskirts of every large city, but there are only a few rural communities where the estate either dominates the landscape or is sufficient in numbers to affect the character of local taste and society. The gentleman farmer in most agricultural areas is respected for his wealth but he is looked upon as a speculating interloper who, as a hobby, trims his property in ways that are beyond the means of ordinary working farmers. He is an outsider who has bought his way into the club but never quite belongs.

In Megalopolis the country squire is at home. It is his territory and has been since the first lands were granted by the kings of England to their favorites. While a stone-walled meadow stocked with Angus on the Island of Aquidneck is not a passport to Newport society's top drawer, it could be a help. The "Main Line" of Chester County is to the fox-hunting executives of Rittenhouse Square what Westchester County is to Madison Avenue. The larger the metropolis, the broader is its outlying belt of estate farms to which the men who make decisions can retire and relax in a formal sort of informality with their own kind. For the privilege of keep-

---

[6] Harold G. Halcrow, *Impact of Property Taxation on Connecticut Agriculture*, University of Connecticut, Storrs, Conn., 1956.

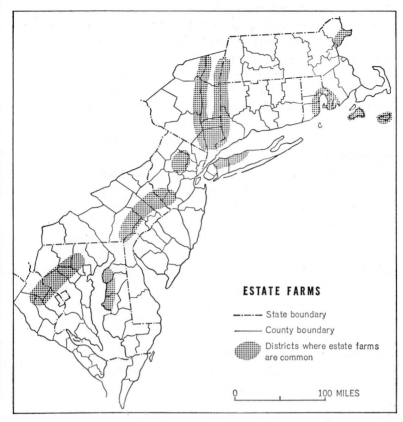

FIG. 100. A generalized sketch of the main areas in Megalopolis where estate farms are found in large numbers, according to field surveys in 1957

ing expensive land in farms near the city they pay a premium that the ordinary agriculturalist could not afford.

Precisely because the owner of an estate can do things that the working farmer cannot afford, he makes an important contribution to the beauty of landscape in Megalopolis, which is lacking in many other American communities where ownership of a country land is not a tradition in the upper circles of urban society. In the Middle West there are persons with a farm background who are now leaders in business and civic affairs, but to many of them a farm is a business rather than a cultural institution. One of the most charming features of New York is the facility with which one can leave the heart of Manhattan and arrive within a few minutes in the estate country of Westchester County. There, on the outskirts of the most congested real estate in America, exist delightful rural landscapes because it is a custom among the elite to keep these "too valuable" areas out of the hands of "developers." This same aesthetic respect for the countryside as a tradition rather than a commodity is common in parts of the Southern states and is growing in the Southwest. Of all sections of America none is so fortunate as Megalopolis in having so many rural communities of this character.

They are found north of Boston and south of Washington, as well as in many places in between. Figure 100 is a generalized sketch showing where estate farms are a common feature of the landscape. There is no sharp line delimiting the areas characterized by estates from those with a larger proportion of working farms, but the estates are more numerous on the outskirts of the largest cities. Estates may also be found in the professional farming areas, just as professional farmers may have properties in zones where estates predominate.

Doughoregan Manor, a few miles west of Baltimore, is an estate farm with a long history. It was the home of Charles Carroll of Carrolton, a signer of the Declaration of Independence. It had been granted by Lord Baltimore to his attorney general, an earlier Charles Carroll. The farm is now a modern dairy and beef enterprise of 2,500 acres. Originally the Manor was 13,000 acres. In the shrinking process it has contributed lands for settlement, roads, schools, and part of a Franciscan monastery. The way land has been used at Doughoregan Manor is the way land has been used on the Piedmont from the days of slavery and tobacco to the present time. This is not exactly a coincidence, for in times past the Carroll family helped to shape the agricultural history of Maryland.

In the records at Doughoregan Manor there is a report dating from the early days of the wheat era that at harvest time there were "forty slaves in a row swinging cradles across the fields." As Baltimore grew, so did the number of work horses in the stables of the manor. Hay became a profitable crop, just as it did for other Eastern farmers close to the big cities. This was the beginning of grassland farming, which is such a marked feature of the Piedmont. When the automobile and motor truck arrived, Doughoregan Manor turned to dairy cattle and a herd of Angus.

Today suburban Washington and Baltimore are growing toward a fusion with one another. The rural lands in between the cities are going into subdivisions, and large farms are being partitioned into small estates of from five to twenty acres. If it were not that Doughoregan Manor has long been regarded as a family trust to be passed from one generation to

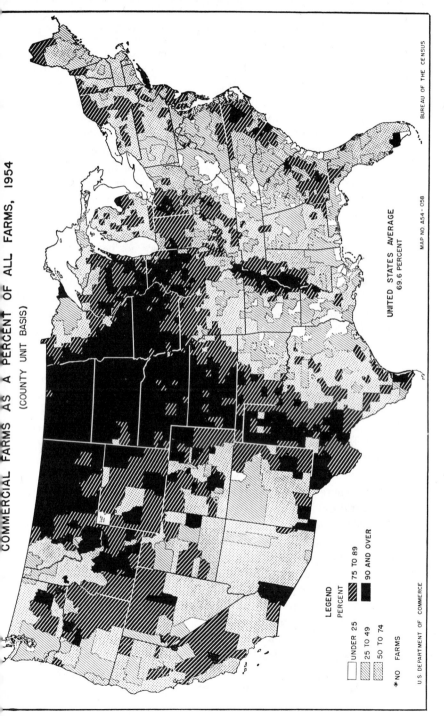

COMMERCIAL FARMS AS A PERCENT OF ALL FARMS, 1954
(COUNTY UNIT BASIS)

BUREAU OF THE CENSUS

MAP NO. A54 - 058

UNITED STATES AVERAGE
69.6 PERCENT

LEGEND
PERCENT

UNDER 25

25 TO 49

50 TO 74

75 TO 89

90 AND OVER

* NO FARMS

U S DEPARTMENT OF COMMERCE

FIG. 101. *Courtesy of the U. S. Bureau of the Census*

the next, it too might have been carved up into little pieces before now. Perhaps the fact that the buildings are very old and maintained with simplicity has also protected it.

The great estates are disappearing in Megalopolis. Their later twentieth-century counterparts are more viable models with smaller acreage and small houses, some without cultivated fields or livestock other than riding horses. The cause of the disappearance is not the initial cost of land, or today's more expensive buildings, which persuade the rich to restrict themselves to small properties. The inheritance tax, income tax, and local property taxes have now reached the point where even individuals with high salaries or lucrative investments cannot afford to hold land because it is beautiful. Even if one generation is so fortunate as to establish a country retreat, the succeeding generation may not be able to pay the inheritance tax if the estate is too elaborate. The result is a change in the style of estate farms. If they are large they must be as functional as possible to survive. While they cannot make a profit in most instances, they must endeavor to recoup as much of their operating costs as they can. Only if an estate is very small with a simple residence can it afford the luxury of a field of goldenrod and daisies.

Considering the lack of foresight many American communities have shown in failing to purchase parks or other recreation grounds before urbanization spread, it is fortunate that in some places there are individuals whose private properties preserve a green belt of natural countryside for all to see. To understand the aesthetic value of the estate farm to a community in Megalopolis, one must take a Sunday drive. In every state of Megalopolis there is a belt of rural loveliness preserved by private subsidy in the form of estates, which working farmers could not afford to keep from the encroaching cities. It seems that only with wealth earned in the cities is it possible to maintain green farmland.

As the population of Megalopolis grows and the amount of open countryside is reduced, the no-trespassing signs appear in greater number on fences, woodlots, and swamps. Only a few decades ago, before super-highways and mass travel by automobile, farmers seldom objected to an occasional city excursionist who hiked over their fields or asked permission to hunt at the proper season. Today a man who would welcome all comers would be mobbed. His fields would be trampled, and he would run the risk of being shot in his own woods if he let hunters in.

To most people in Megalopolis, the country is not just farmland. It is open space where a man can stretch and feel free. The more urban congestion increases, the greater becomes the urge in some people to get away to the country, at least on week ends, for a summer vacation, or for a hunting trip. But as their number increases so do the restrictions raised in their paths by harassed landowners who would also like to be left alone. In recent years thousands of persons have found a private solution for themselves. Many farms are now purchased just for their recreational value. Sometimes agricultural operations are suspended. In other instances the cropland is rented to a tenant while the owners reserve the woodlands, meadows, pond sites, and waterfront for their recreational pleasures. The farm house and barns are converted into club houses and dormitories. Neighbors, social clubs, scout troops, gun clubs, office clubs, professional associations, unions, churches, companies, and just groups of friends pool their resources to buy a farm so they will have a place to go for play and relaxation. From one end of Megalopolis to the other these properties are becoming increasingly conspicuous. They are found in every rural section from the submarginal sandstone ridges of Appalachia to the finest estate districts on Long Island. The type and amount of space purchased varies with the size of the purse the group possesses. It may be a cheap woodlot or an exhausted gravel pit. It may be a rolling Piedmont dairy farm with meadows that could be converted to a golf course for a quarter of a million dollars. For instance, Upper Heathworth is such a farm on the eastern shore of Chesapeake Bay in Queen Anne County, Maryland. It has been developed as a gun club. The farm is only 280 acres, of which twenty-five are marsh. This latter is its most important asset, for it is a resting and feeding area used by migratory waterfowl along the water's edge. Meadows of cattails and other aquatic plants have a primeval appearance attractive to thousands of geese and ducks.

The Farm as Space

Since Megalopolis is the consequence of spreading urbanization, it is inevitable that its growth should eliminate agricultural land. Some kinds of farms are more viable than others, but eventually the city overwhelms almost all of them because their land is less intensively developed than the land of the city. It costs too much to keep a farm in terms of what it yields. There comes a time when even the wealthy do not keep their estates. Portions of the Frederick W. Vanderbilt and Franklin D. Roosevelt farms at Hyde Park on the Hudson have become national shrines; on the balance of them are the usual kinds of subdivisions, roadside drive-ins, and shopping centers. One of the Vanderbilt stables is a summer theatre. Trees that President Roosevelt planted as a reforestation project have been removed for subdivision developments — yet they were eighty miles from New

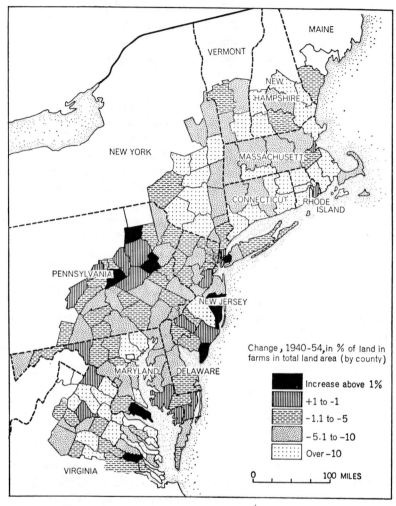

FIG. 102

York City. Hay and trees can never pay as well per acre as motels, split-levels, or apartment houses. Dairy cattle and poultry may be kept profitably in urban areas only if they are as compactly housed as people and maintained in the same way, with feed brought to them from cheaper land. Agriculture must become a factory culture if it is to survive in the heart of Megalopolis. The alternative is to step aside as the city moves forward.

As the modern city grows it absorbs rural land at an accelerating rate. The automobile and better highways enable the city to reach far out into

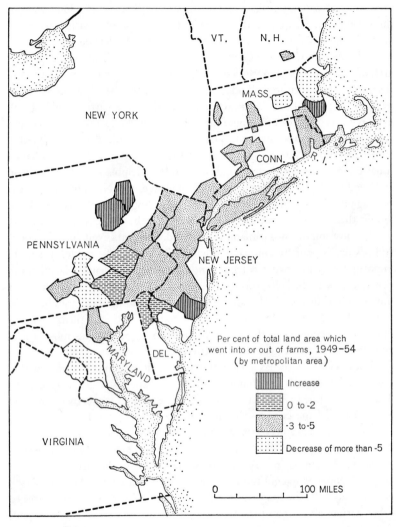

Fig. 103

the rural districts to create suburbs. In metropolitan areas the rate at which land went out of farming was about twice as great during the five-year period 1949–54 as it was during the twenty-year period 1929–49 (see Figs. 102 and 103). The areas in which land is coming into agriculture are marginal districts, such as northeastern Pennsylvania and southwestern New Jersey.

A number of agricultural conservationists and some farmers are alarmed at the rate at which farmlands are disappearing. They take a long view of the nation's food supply and recognize that our present surpluses are an anomaly in what is more generally a hungry, undernourished world. They know that when the Gadsden Purchase of 1853 filled out the present area of the American Southwest, we had twenty acres per capita of land that could be cultivated. Today we have a little less than three. With growth of population the per-capita area of arable earth would shrink even without the loss of a single farm. However the farms themselves are vanishing as the cities expand. The maps of generalized soil quality and land capabilities (Fig. 20, p. 94) show that the cities of Megalopolis are usually located on the better kinds of soil. Philadelphia is on Coastal Plain and Piedmont, not in the Poconos. Providence and Newport are in the Narragansett Basin, not in the granitic New England uplands. In Megalopolis the best places for farms seem to be the best places for cities also.

The most important farmland is cropland. Soil that is suitable for woods and pasture is poor by comparison with soil that is truly arable. It is more important to know what is happening to tillable soil than to farmland in general. The U. S. Soil Conservation Service has made some estimates of how much of this particular kind of land was lost to nonfarm uses between 1942 and 1956 (see Table 11). Most of the conversions of tillable land to public uses occurred in the years previous to 1947, whereas most of the conversions to private uses have occurred since that date.

Almost every state has a Committee on Soil and Water Conservation Needs. These boards are composed of farmers and agricultural specialists. They have studied recent changes in land use in their respective states and have estimated the changes that may occur by 1975. In Table 12 we see some of the conclusions of these committees. With the exception of Massachusetts, it is expected that the loss of cropland to other uses will continue at the same rate as in 1942–56. In some states, if the present pace of cropland conversion continues for another hundred years, all cropland will be eliminated. In the long run the farm cannot withstand the pressures of urbanization, and urban pressures are now weakest against the poor soils that are in woodlands.

A strong factor influencing the decline of cropland and pasture acreage is the growing opportunity for urban employment available to commuters living on relatively unproductive farms. While the farmhouse remains a suitable residence, field operations may be discontinued. In these instances woodland growth eventually covers former fields and pastures. The net influence of urbanization, therefore, may be a strong decline in open farmland but very little change in total woodland. For as some woodland is

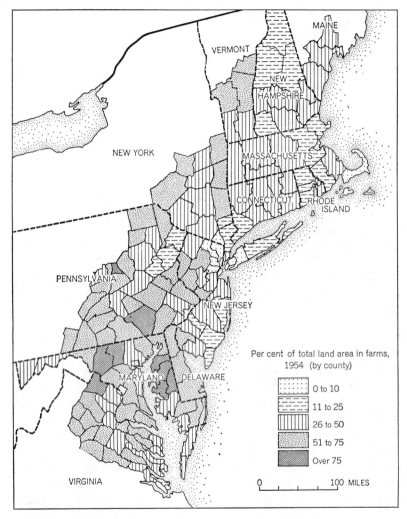

Per cent of total land area in farms,
1954 (by county)

0 to 10
11 to 25
26 to 50
51 to 75
Over 75

0   100 MILES

Fig. 104

urbanized or suburbanized, other woodland comes into existence by volunteer growth as active farming ceases in the commuter belts around cities.

The deviation of Massachusetts from the general trend is of more than passing interest. The committee for that state has estimated that its cropland will increase. If one considers the agricultural geography of Massachusetts it is apparent that in the western part of the state, with the exception of the Connecticut River Valley, there is considerable low-priced

Table 11

CONVERSION TO NONFARM USES OF LAND SUITABLE FOR CULTIVATION, 1942–56

States	Total Acres Converted to Nonfarm Uses	Acres Converted to Private Nonfarm Uses[a]
Entirely or chiefly within Megalopolis		
Massachusetts	110,000	70,000
Rhode Island	13,000	9,000
Connecticut	50,000	36,000
New Jersey	160,000	105,000
Delaware	38,000	22,000
Maryland	190,000	105,000
Partially within but chiefly outside Megalopolis		
New York	710,000	480,000
Pennsylvania	280,000	190,000
Virginia	460,000	250,000

Source: Unpublished estimates made by the U. S. Soil Conservation Service.

[a] Chiefly urban and suburban development. For each state the difference between the two columns represents the acreage converted to public nonfarm uses (roads, parks, military establishments, etc.).

stony land that could be brought into crop production if the stones were removed. In Massachusetts it is likely that there will be about as sharp a conversion of present cropland to nonfarm uses as in other states. But counter to that trend will be the conversion of much stony pasture to cropland through the removal of the stones. Several thousand acres in southern New England, chiefly in Massachusetts, have been renovated in this manner in recent years. The net loss of combined cropland and pasture to nonfarm use will follow the trends observed in other states.

The trend in Virginia and Maryland toward more pasture is contrary to the general picture. It is apparent that the new pastures will come largely from present cropland. This is consistent with the present marked shift to grassland farming in these two states. The growing seasons in Maryland and Virginia are longer than farther north, and well-managed pasture in a long growing season can be a very efficient use of land. According to estimates, the ratio of cropland decline in Maryland and Virginia will be much greater than the average increase of pasture; these states will also experience the normal conversion of an agricultural base to nonfarm uses. Much land of poor quality will revert to woodland as the farmers find employment in towns and cities.

If one were to project future trends solely on the basis of what is now

Table 12

EXPECTED CHANGES IN MEGALOPOLITAN LAND USE, 1955–75

(*Thousands of Acres*)

States	Cropland			Open Pasture			Woodland		
	1955	1975	% of Change	1955	1975	% of Change	1955	1975	% of Change
Entirely or chiefly within Megalopolis									
Massachusetts	551	583	+5.9	113	59	−47.8	3,251	3,122	−4.0
Rhode Island	69	55	−20.2	12	9	−25.0	434	398	−8.3
Connecticut	467	390	−16.4	128	70	−45.3	1,988	1,977	−0.5
New Jersey	1,086	950	−12.5	94	80	−14.9	2,229	2,071	−6.6
Delaware	515	465	−9.7	26	24	−7.7	392	371	−5.4
Maryland	2,124	1,677	−21.0	417	775	+47.5	2,920	2,820	−3.4
Partially within but chiefly outside Megalopolis									
New York	7,864	6,300	−19.6	3,222	2,700	−16.2	14,450	14,637	+1.3
Pennsylvania	7,250	6,400	−11.7	1,848	1,700	−8.0	14,688	14,637	—
Virginia	4,831	3,500	−27.5	2,771	3,500	−20.8	15,832	16,150	+2.0

Source: Unpublished estimates by state committees on soil and water conservation needs.

happening to farmlands, it would seem that agriculture should become extinct in Megalopolis. However, from earlier analyses of the types of husbandry that are prominent in Megalopolis, it might reasonably be assumed that this will not happen. As the better land is taken up by the city, the farmer will still have alternatives providing he wants to continue in business. For instance, he can do as some are doing now — buy grain from outside the region and keep more animals than ever. If he is a vegetable grower he can grow more on less land by irrigating and by applying more fertilizer and pesticides. A comparison of Figures 83, 98, 99, and 102 (pp. 273, 304, 308, 320) shows that irrigation is increasing significantly in counties where vegetable and specialty crops are prominent and where generally there is a decline of land in farms.

A basic consideration in the sale of farmland to city people is the fact that the farmer makes a substantial capital gain. Thus rewarded he can go on to poorer soil farther from the cities, spend some of his capital gain, and bring inferior acreage into production. This is happening throughout Megalopolis. Long Island and New Jersey potato growers have sold out and gone to Delaware where the land is cheaper. By spending more money for drainage and fertilizer they can raise as many potatoes as before. Rhode Island dairymen, who have sold expensive land, have managed to stay in business by buying hayfields and pastures for dry stock in central Massachusetts where land is cheaper. With investment in fertilizers and stone removal, the new land can be made to yield well.

Land that is not considered cropland today will become cropland tomorrow, but at the price of much investment. To stay in business the farmer will spend money to *make* good quality land, whereas formerly nature provided it without much assistance. This means a higher capitalization per acre in the future than has been necessary in the past. The city will get its food, but at a higher cost.

Public Demand for Land

The public demand for farmland is very strong. Private interests buy land for housing, industry, and commerce, but as cities grow they must be serviced by more water reservoirs, more roads, more airports, and more recreation grounds. Unless proper precautions are taken, these public demands can actually impair the public welfare by cutting deeply into the agricultural land base. Recently Professor David Rozman of the University of Massachusetts reported that, exclusive of roads, 11.1 per cent of the area of Massachusetts is in public ownership, and he concluded, ". . . it is found that many towns with good and medium agricultural land have extensive areas in public holdings." He suggests that if agricultural lands must be used by public agencies because of their location, then, "in order to counteract further loss of land to agriculture, due to constantly increasing new public and private uses of land in rural areas, a special effort should be made to rehabilitate an equal amount of land in suitable areas to become available for agricultural use." [7]

In the rural townships of Massachusetts,[8] public property represents 10.6 to 19.4 per cent of the total property evaluation. The community is affected in two ways by such public land acquisition: the agricultural base is reduced, which ultimately raises the local cost of food; and when highly taxed agricultural land is withdrawn for public use in preference to low-taxed stony woodland, then a heavier burden of taxation is shifted to surviving private properties, which must pick up the tab for those that become public and tax-free. Professor Rozman has shown that tax-exempt public property amounts to 25 per cent or more of the total valuation in 48 out of 312 Massachusetts townships. It is common for a public authority to buy agricultural land to create a water reservoir in a rural township

[7] David Rozman and Ruth E. Sherburne, *Public Landownership in Rural Areas of Massachusetts*, University of Massachusetts, Amherst, 1955.
[8] Those with less than 10,000 persons.

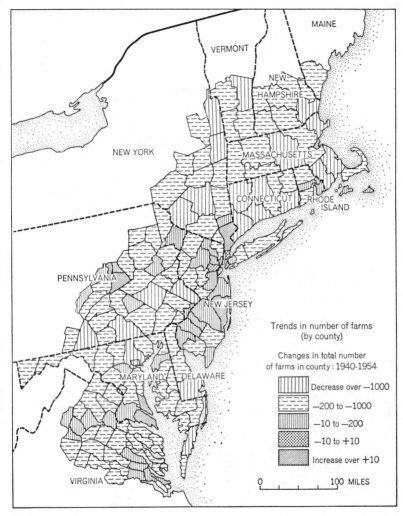

FIG. 105

or an airport for a city in an urbanized township. By reducing the tax base of the rural township an additional burden is placed upon the surviving farms in the area, which must make up the deficit.

The significant part that property taxes play in the economy of Megalopolitan farms is well demonstrated by Professor Harold G. Halcrow of the University of Connecticut, who studied 91 Connecticut farms that were "typical of commercial family-type agriculture." For twelve of these

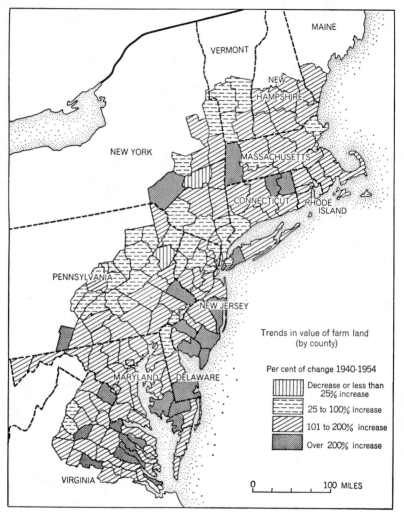

FIG. 106

farms there was a net loss even before property taxes were paid. The property taxes represented 19–44 per cent of net income *before* the property taxes were paid for thirty-seven other farms, and 8–14 per cent for the remaining forty-two.[9] It is easy to understand how such pressures force the operator of the commercial family-type farm to give up or

[9] Harold G. Halcrow, *Impact of Property Taxation on Connecticut Agriculture*, University of Connecticut, Storrs, Conn., 1956.

move into the back country. Only part-time, residential, and estate farmers with city incomes can pay such taxes.[10]

A More Rational Use of Land

Agricultural technicians possess a considerable body of knowledge about soils and land capability that urban planners might profitably use if they wish to save the unsuspecting home-buyer from flooded basements, septic tank failures, and other consequences of land misuse. Twenty years ago agricultural engineers working in rural areas on problems of flood control and soil conservation learned that it is cheaper in small watersheds to use properly vegetated floodways than to build concrete culverts, flumes, and spillways. Such areas are also more pleasing to view than concrete, of which the city ordinarily has enough without substituting it for grass and trees.

Because the competition for land between farm and city has reached an advanced state in Megalopolis, some agriculturalists believe positive action should be taken to regulate the use of land according to its physical capabilities. They fear that the present policy of allowing developers to pursue the cheapest course often conflicts with the long-range interest of the total community. Belford Seabrook of Seabrook Farms in New Jersey has made a study of land resources in his state and of the urbanization of agricultural lands. In a speech before the Soil Conservation Society of America at Trenton, Mr. Seabrook drew attention to the fact that only about 15 per cent of the land in New Jersey is suitable for agriculture and that 85 per cent is nonarable in its present condition. He suggested that "we consider some special zoning and planning for agriculture." Specifically, he proposed for New Jersey:

1. To reappraise the land and the agricultural potential in each municipality. Then make a land use study of the capability of the land. Follow this with a master plan on which the best land use will be evident. Some barren, rocky, and rough terrain, which would never be good for industry or agriculture, might be ideal for housing with parks and woodland in the rougher places.

2. For every present acre used by agriculture there are six other acres in New Jersey that are not used for anything. This is obvious proof that there

---

[10] Halcrow (op. cit.) has shown that in Connecticut, Rhode Island, Massachusetts, and New York the tax rates on farms, in dollars per acre, are much higher ($4.81, $3.15, $4.20, and $2.08 respectively in 1954) than the United States average ($.85 in 1954), and that the increases in the last half century have been greater in these states than in the country as a whole. In 1909–13, for example, the rates in these four states were $.48, $.46, $.81, and $.41, respectively, and the average for the United States was $.21.

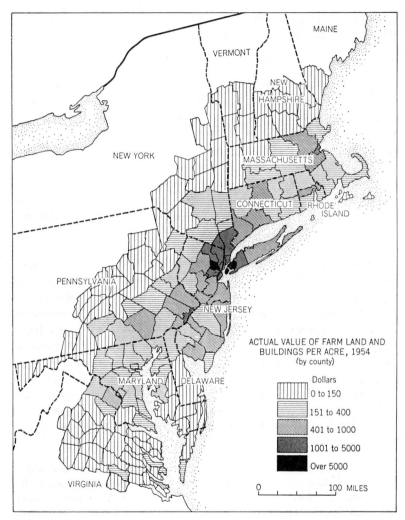

ACTUAL VALUE OF FARM LAND AND
BUILDINGS PER ACRE, 1954
(by county)

Dollars
	0 to 150
	151 to 400
	401 to 1000
	1001 to 5000
	Over 5000

0   100 MILES

Fig. 107

is enough land area for everyone if we use and distribute it wisely and properly.[11]

Mr. Seabrook explained the advantages of agricultural "A" zoning, which would prohibit urban development in designated rural areas where

[11] Belford L. Seabrook, "New Jersey's Vanishing Farmland," a paper delivered at the annual meeting of the New Jersey Chapter, Soil Conservation Society of America, January 23, 1957, quoted with permission from the text communicated to Edward Higbee by the author.

soils are of superior quality for farming and where the agricultural community is well established.

"A" zoning aims at protection of the farmer against rising taxation. Urban development penetrating farmlands can cause a farmer's tax bill to rise, even though he may have done nothing to promote this development. Competing urban development raises a farmer's taxes in two ways. First, when his land becomes surrounded by subdivisions, it increases in market value. When this rising market value produces a "trend," the assessor values his land in a higher bracket. But even if his assessed valuation remains the same, a farmer may still find his taxes rising. This is because the cost of services for the new subdivisions have added to the tax rates. Six hundred new families in an area call for a new elementary school. The cost of sewers, drainage facilities and other utilities add to the tax burden.

If industry and home builders could be encouraged to look at all the other available land first before they take over flat, fertile fields, it would be a real achievement.[12]

The people of Manheim Township in Lancaster County, Pennsylvania, have taken positive action along the lines proposed by Mr. Seabrook. Lancaster County is particularly conscious of the value of good soil, and the farmers are a strong political element even though the county is a part of Megalopolis. Figure 65, p. 227, shows the zoning now in effect in Manheim Township. The agricultural area is restricted to farming and services related to farming. In the words of the official zoning ordinance, the "Agricultural Zoning District is intended, primarily, to preserve farm or agricultural areas in Manheim Township in Lancaster County, Pennsylvania, one of the finest natural agricultural counties in the world . . ." The Agricultural Transitional Zoning District is designed as a protective buffer to prevent compact urbanization from threatening the Agricultural District. All new houses built in the Agricultural Transitional Zoning District must have two acres of ground. This is enough to discourage the usual kind of compact development. Manheim Township was the first political unit in the eastern United States to protect its best agricultural district by setting up a protective zone around it. The principle of agricultural zoning was first developed in California, where a number of counties followed the lead of Los Angeles, which protected its most important dairy areas by zoning them exclusively for agriculture.

Since the prospect of agricultural zoning does not appeal to most farmers, it is not likely to be extensively accepted at the present time. This fact may seem rather incongruous to the urbanite, who may have looked upon the retreating agricultural frontier as "the farmer's problem." Actually very few farmers are deeply disappointed when urban interests buy them

[12] *Ibid.*

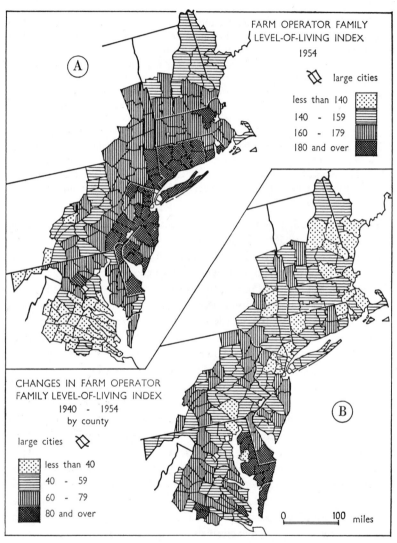

FIG. 108. The farm operator family level-of-living index, as defined by the U. S. Department of Agriculture, is based on four selected statistical items. The maps measure only variations: between counties in 1954, and between two Census years, 1950 and 1954.

out for a thousand dollars per acre or more. For agricultural purposes the soil itself is generally worth no more than a fraction of the selling price. The sale of the land may mean giving up a favorite spot, but even the old homestead loses its appeal when all the farms around it go into industry, residential developments, and shopping centers. The capital gain that comes when a farmer surrenders to the city is a handsome reward. He naturally feels much better about the deal than the suburbanite who follows him with a split-level on an eighty-foot lot and a thirty-year mortgage. The "poor farmer" can grieve at his leisure on Miami Beach while the "rich city slicker" works the rest of his able lifetime to pay for taking his land.

When Fairfax County, Virginia, sought to institute agricultural zoning by establishing a three-acre minimum for house lots in agricultural districts, the farmers went to court in protest. They claimed that they were discriminated against because developers could not afford to pay top prices for their properties if they had to cut them into miniature-sized farms instead of conventional house lots. A long legal battle ensued. The county's Board of Supervisors set up in 1959 a two-acre zoning ordinance hoping to protect the western part of the county. So, although there are exceptions, when the chips are down few agriculturalists regard the competition for land as "the farmer's problem." All of which makes many wonder just whose problem it is.

Judging by what has happened in the past, the farmer in Megalopolis will continue to produce more food on less land while the cities grow in size and population. It is not likely that the farmer will be eliminated. The chances are that he will continue to follow the same successful tactics that others have used in the past. The amount of farmland has declined since 1920 in the Megalopolitan states, in some cases drastically. The general trend for crop acreage has been downward. But counter to the shrinking land base of agriculture has been the truly remarkable increase in the production of poultry, milk, and eggs, products that have been the favorites of Megalopolitan farmers for many years (see Table 13) and for which comparatively little land is needed if coarse feed grains are shipped in from the Corn Belt. These products and market vegetables are the perishables for which the city pays a good price, and market vegetables, too, can be grown in great quantities on comparatively little acreage.

Two changes have occurred on the agricultural scene since 1920 that have helped the Megalopolitan farmer produce more on less land. One has been progress in plant and animal breeding. The increased production of milk per cow is significant, and there is every indication that this kind of progress will endure. The second change, which might easily be over-looked, is that horses have been replaced by mechanical power. Not only is power farming more efficient in getting higher yields per unit of land and per man, but by almost eliminating the draft horse it has reduced the need for pasture and hay.

There is no evidence to suggest that the agricultural systems of Mega-lopolis will not be able to make future adjustments just as efficiently as they have in the past. There is only one condition and that has already been discussed: coarse feed grains, and eventually more hay, will have to be shipped into Megalopolis from outside. The commercial farmer is un-likely to compete with the suburbanite for land on which to raise feed grains and hay, although he may rent hayland from investors as some New England dairymen are doing now. Also the Megalopolitan farmer is not going to give up one of the best markets for perishable commodities in America. As his land base shrinks, his production will increase. This is the husbandman's probable solution to the competition for land between farm and city. But what of the city itself?

The disappearance of farmland in Megalopolis is a matter to which few city people have given thought. Even professional urban land plan-ners seem more concerned about the niceties of street patterns and where to draw the colored lines that separate single-family districts from multi-family districts than about what the wisest use would be of the square miles of fresh farmland being lost when they are urbanized on the out-skirts. Not all farmland in Megalopolis will be urbanized, but within the next century it is probable that commercial agriculture will substantially disappear between the larger cities along their main routes of spread. When this open land is gone a sort of grey zone will set in if, meanwhile, that space has not been used to avert rather than to promote congestion and obsolescence.

By fanning out from cities in flanking attacks upon the country, suburbs spring up in the most unexpected places. Where two cities are close to-gether the intervening rural space becomes peppered with new develop-ments. This kind of leapfrogging sprawl outflanks some farms while it overruns others. The rural community is destroyed, yet the urban com-munity is not established. Investors who see the way things are going buy the remaining farms. They know the land will be used for building some-time and that it will increase in value faster than money loaned at interest to a bank. Also, the investor prefers to pay taxes on capital gains from land speculation rather than the steeper taxes on income earned as interest or dividends. This much land is taken out of farming that may not go into urban use for several years. Meanwhile the people in the suburban devel-

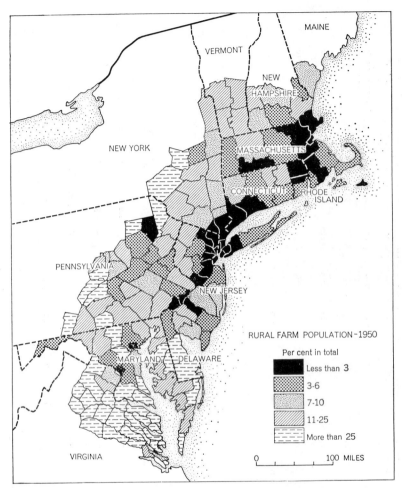

RURAL FARM POPULATION-1950

Per cent in total

Less than 3
3-6
7-10
11-25
More than 25

0   100 MILES

Fɪɢ. 109

opments have the comfortable but temporary sensation of being in the country. They even see woodlands replace cultivated fields, a sight that may enhance their sense of illusion.

In December 1957 soil conservationist Edwin F. Owens made a reconnaissance study of land use on 41,000 acres of the Wissahickon-Sandy Run Valley, which is on the outskirts of Philadelphia in Montgomery County. Among the suburban towns in the area are Roslyn, Willow Grove, Ambler, and Flourtown. The purpose of the study was to locate, if possible, open areas where several flood-water impoundments could be made without condemnation of houses or the relocation of power lines

Table 13
Agricultural Changes in States Entirely within Megalopolis, 1920–54

Census Table		Massachusetts		Rhode Island		Connecticut		New Jersey		Maryland		Delaware	
		1920	1954	1920	1954	1920	1954	1920	1954	1920	1954	1920	1954
1	Land in farms (1,000 acres)	2,494	1,439	331	154	1,898	1,137	2,282	1,665	4,757	3,896	944	814
1	Land in crops harvested (1,000 acres)	562	331	62.0	34.9	458	285	997	788	1,991	1,571	448	412
1	Land pastured[a] (1,000 acres)	876	422	110.9	44.7	784	389	335	318	892	974	101	112
16	Land in corn[a] (1,000 acres)	39.4	26.4	8.0	5.9	49.8	33.0	190	190	515	498	136	169
16	Oats threshed or combined (1,000 acres)	9.5	1.8	1.2	0.14	10.8	1.6	71	34	49	72	4.7	9.9
16	Wheat threshed or combined (1,000 acres)	—	—	—	—	—	—	85	55	664	186	126	33
16	Hay harvested (1,000 acres)	420	237	43.2	20.7	310	210	289	227	370	447	63	55
16	Vegetables exc. potatoes (1,000 acres)[b]	24.7	20.3	2.1	1.8	9.1	12.7	95	146	120	94	33.3	40.0
13	Milk cows (1,000 cows)	147	107	21.4	15.8	112	101	130	139	162	219	33.0	31.0
13	Whole milk sold (1,000,000 lbs.)	478	713	80	107	317	680	485	1,024	256	1,247	59	167
13	Chickens sold (1,000)	966	14,858	142	1,607	532	18,998	1,377	16,825	1,618	47,469	434	62,204
13	Chicken eggs sold (1,000,000 dozens)	6	42	1.0	3.9	4.0	36.4	8.7	172.4	10.6	17.7	2.8	5.8
13	Horses and/or mules (1,000)	50.9	6.0	6.6	0.6	38.9	4.0	78	8	174	23	37.1	4.0
13	Hogs and pigs (1,000)	104.1	105.9	12.8	6.9	61.0	17.9	139	185	306	230	38.6	41.1

Source: U. S. Census of Agriculture: 1954, Vol. II.
a For acreages in pasture and in corn the first figures given, in each state column, are for 1925. No data are available for 1920.   b Harvested for sale.

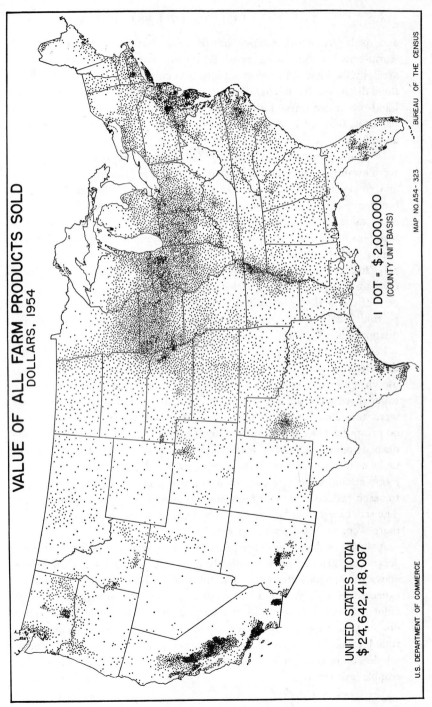

FIG. 110. *Courtesy of the U. S. Bureau of the Census*

and roads. As suburbanization has progressed in the valley, the rate of storm-water runoff has increased. Roofs and pavements of new suburban areas, by shedding water more rapidly than cultivated fields, have hastened flood discharge that has damaged urbanized areas farther down the valley. Land use at the time of the survey was found to be: agriculture 25–30 per cent, forested land 10 per cent, urban development 35–40 per cent, and idle land 25 per cent.

Idle land consisted chiefly of abandoned farms that had been sold and were awaiting urbanization. Most of this land is growing up into brush and young trees. Many years may pass before all this idle land is utilized, but because it is scattered among built-up zones it has already lost much of its value as far as economic regional planning is concerned. Of seventeen possible sites for the construction of impoundments, only three were "open." That is, these were the only properties with enough contiguous acres to make a catchment basin where there were no houses to condemn or roads and power lines to relocate. New construction on 35 to 40 per cent of the land was so sprinkled through the old farm country that opportunity to acquire undeveloped land for flood control had almost disappeared.

Fairfax County, Virginia, is part of suburban Washington and one of the fastest-growing counties in the United States. In the past decade land-use changes came so suddenly in Fairfax County that some unfortunate experiences were unheeded until recently. In several places subdivisions were started on land far removed from trunkline sewers where there was no prospect of being tied-in for many years because intervening space remained undeveloped. In some of these subdivisions it was found that septic tanks would not drain without costly excavation and crushed-rock fill. In a few instances the new communities were forced to resort to outhouses for each residence because there was no possible way to remove sewage. The soil, classified as belonging to the Orange series, was impervious, and there were no local sewer systems.

A similar problem has developed in a new seaside resort district in New Jersey, constructed on hydraulic land-fill and perched less than a foot above the groundwater table. The fill is all sand and normally would be expected to drain well, but the groundwater table is so high that sewage effluent does not flow readily from septic tanks. There was a time when one or two persons might have experimented with such a location and found it unsatisfactory. Seeing this, others would have shied away. Today whole subdivisions are erected and sold in a few months before possible trouble is suspected.

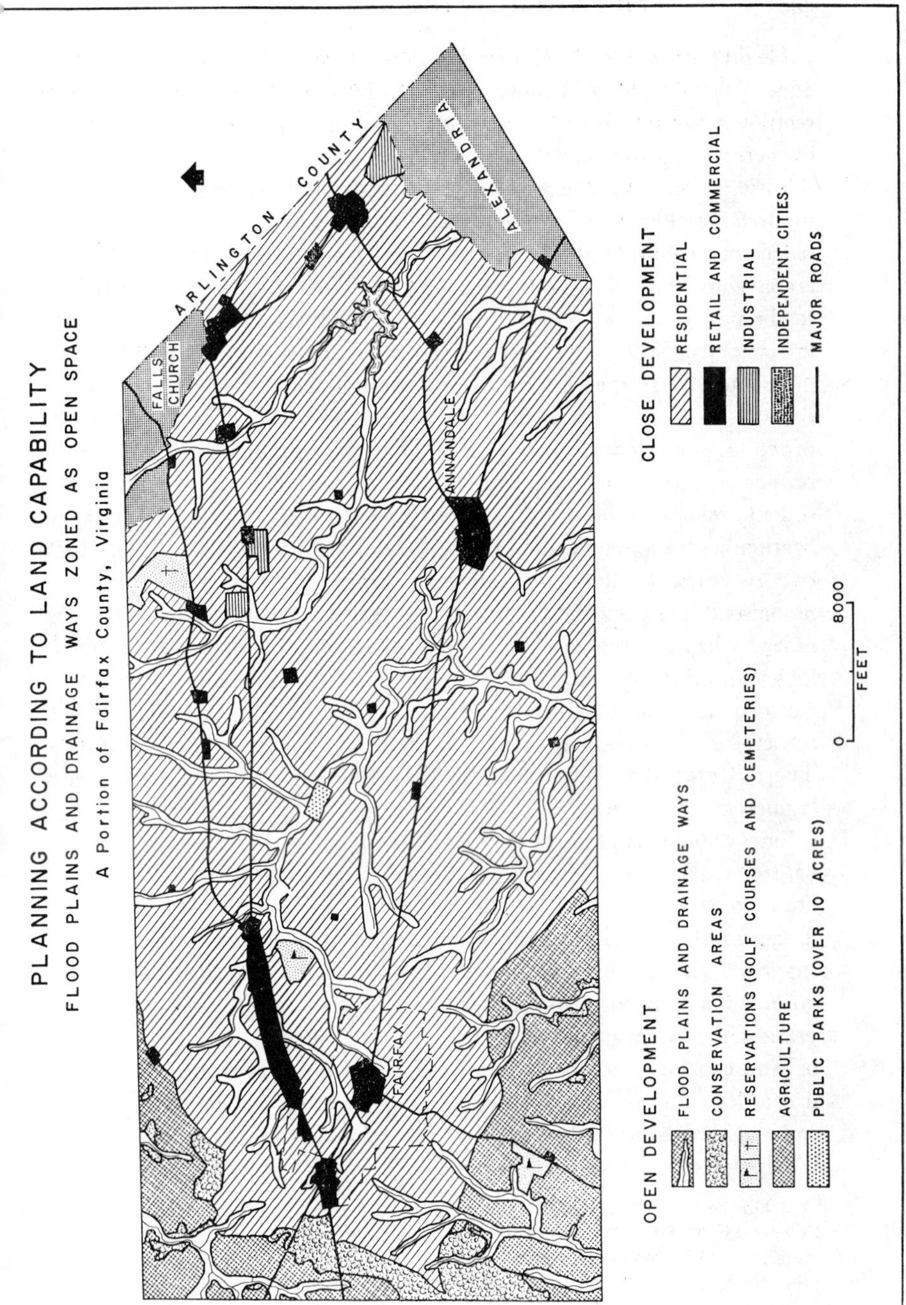

PLANNING ACCORDING TO LAND CAPABILITY
FLOOD PLAINS AND DRAINAGE WAYS ZONED AS OPEN SPACE
A Portion of Fairfax County, Virginia

OPEN DEVELOPMENT

FLOOD PLAINS AND DRAINAGE WAYS
CONSERVATION AREAS
RESERVATIONS (GOLF COURSES AND CEMETERIES)
AGRICULTURE
PUBLIC PARKS (OVER 10 ACRES)

CLOSE DEVELOPMENT

RESIDENTIAL
RETAIL AND COMMERCIAL
INDUSTRIAL
INDEPENDENT CITIES
MAJOR ROADS

0   8000
        FEET

ARLINGTON COUNTY
ALEXANDRIA
FALLS CHURCH
ANNANDALE
FAIRFAX

FIG. 111

Having learned the hard way, but determined to benefit by the experience, Fairfax County, Virginia, became the first in the United States to employ a soil scientist as a permanent advisor to its various departments concerning matters that involve soil capabilities (see Fig. 111). Planning the use of land according to soil types and terrain conditions is basic to modern agriculture. It is routine procedure for a surveyor of the U. S. Department of Agriculture to prepare a soil map of every farm that cooperates with local soil conservation districts. The farmer then uses the land to the best purposes consistent with its capabilities. He leaves waterways in sod or forest cover. He does not plow steep slopes. He practices the most intensive tillage on soils that are level, drain well, and resist erosion. By such measures the land does not deteriorate with use. It may even improve as time goes on through the application of fertilizers, the use of proper rotations, and the planting of trees on rough land to stabilize the soil and reduce runoff on too exposed land. This kind of rational land utilization has been practiced on the best farms of Megalopolis for more than twenty years. But it is still a novelty to employ the services of soil technologists in planning the urbanization of present farms. This is surprising indeed when it is realized that it is far more expensive to construct buildings than it is to plant alfalfa. Public investment in school sites, roads, recreational areas, flood-control projects, and water-supply reservoirs would be better safeguarded by technical appraisal of land capabilities in advance. There is critical variation in the behavior of different soils, which most laymen do not suspect.

Since thousands of acres of present farmland or woodland will be urbanized each year in Megalopolis, it would be wise if the city and its satellite municipalities were to adopt the concept of using land according to its capabilities, which has long been a scientifically directed practice in agriculture. Farms that operate according to their land capabilities could go on producing for centuries without danger of soil erosion and deterioration. If cities were designed and built according to the proper criteria of land capability and with vision for future needs as they expand, then urban development would last much longer without having to be torn up and renewed because the land was not used with proper forethought in the first place.[13]

[13] During the course of field observation that preceded preparation of this chapter, Edward Higbee was given invaluable assistance on the land by local staff members of the U. S. Soil Conservation Service. The maps of land capability and soil quality were prepared from unpublished manuscript data kindly furnished by state soil scientists. Major discrepancies at state lines are due to different standards of value. These two maps are not in this chapter but appear on Fig. 20, p. 94.

CHAPTER 7

The Woodlands, Their Uses and Wildlife

As has already been mentioned, the natural vegetation of Megalopolis was a rather dense forest cover. Today, in spite of all the great metropolises and the suburban sprawl it encompasses, Megalopolis still has vast forested areas within its bounds. A wooded appearance still predominates in this great urban region. True, the general aspect of the landscape may at times be misleading, for while from a distance the wealthier suburban towns in New Jersey, Connecticut, and Maryland may look like wooded districts the greenery is in fact densely stuffed with dwellings. Americans prefer a separate one-family house for a home, and this does not quite fulfill the "American dream" unless the house has some open space about

This chapter is by Henri Morel and Jean Gottmann.

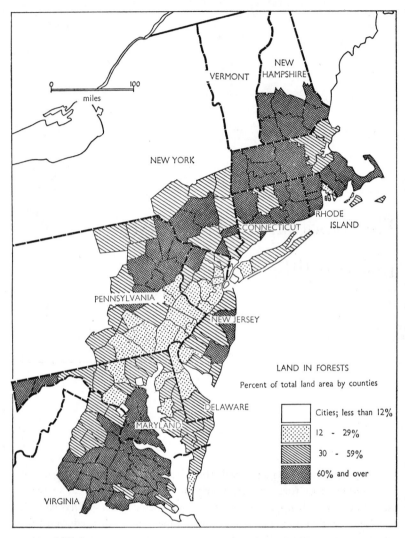

LAND IN FORESTS
Percent of total land area by counties

Cities; less than 12%

12 - 29%

30 - 59%

60% and over

FIG. 112

it, usually a lawn in front and a few trees around the building. However, even excluding such park-like suburbs, and the public parks located in cities or fully urbanized districts, there is plenty of *actually forested space* in Megalopolis, covering about half the region's land area.

This predominance of woodlands results from the imbalance between expanding urbanization and shrinking agricultural lands. More formerly tilled farm acreage is being abandoned and is reverting to wooded growth than is being consumed by urban and related special uses, and this has been true for some time.[1] The relationships vary from one part of the region to another, but the general result is that half of the area is forested, which creates enormous problems of forest and land management. These cannot be shelved under the pretext that it is natural growth and that "nature takes care of itself." The present land use and landscape of the region and its flora and fauna are a major public concern for the people who are crowded in the cities and suburbs, all the more so as the present woodlands are a product of urbanization and a major resource of suburban and urban living.

In the vast and far-reaching urban system of Megalopolis, even at considerable distances from city limits the flora and fauna are affected by various closely interwoven human activities pertaining to industry or trade, recreation or farming. Forestry is thus directly under the impact of the whole regional process of urbanization. A comprehensive picture of the use and management of the woods in Megalopolis must constantly be referred to this background, commanded by urban crowding and growth.

The Extent and Expansion of the Woodlands

Megalopolis is heavily wooded. Discounting parks and gardens in the fully urbanized sectors, the total area of woodlands in the middle 1950's made up about 48 per cent of the land area of the region as defined in this study.[2] With this substantial forest area, 16.2 million acres, Megalopolis has remained a typical part of the forested eastern United States, (i.e., east of the Great Plains).[3] However, this total woodland area is irregularly distributed, for it has been broken up into many parts and in some sections has been reduced to small patches.

Along almost all its inland periphery, Megalopolis is surrounded by

[1] See Edward Higbee's analysis of the competition for the land between farm and city in Chapter 6 above, pp. 319–340; see also pp. 222–239 in Chapter 5.

[2] These figures, like most of the other statistical data on forests in this chapter, are based on the Forest Survey conducted in 1953–56 by the Northeastern Forest Experiment Station of the U. S. Forest Service, Upper Darby, Pennsylvania. The advice, publications, and unpublished data generously contributed by this Station's staff have been of invaluable help to the authors of this report. Much help and data have also been supplied by the Forest Services of the various seaboard states, from New Hampshire to Virginia.

[3] Large sections of the United States that are more than 50 per cent forested are northern New England, most of the Appalachian Mountain ridges, the Southeastern states, and some of the high mountain ranges in the West.

predominantly forested regions, as can be seen on the map showing the proportions of the total land area that are wooded (see Fig. 112). Forests cover more than 60 per cent of the land at the two extremities of the region — in most of southern New England (except for a few counties around the main cities) and in southern Maryland and northern Virginia — and this high percentage of forested area continues both north and south of the region's boundaries. A third wide district as heavily wooded includes the Appalachian foothills and ridges, extending from the Catskills in New York toward the anthracite basin of northeastern Pennsylvania.

A much less wooded area (with woodlands occupying 12 to 29 per cent of the individual counties) stretches from the New York metropolitan region to the District of Columbia along the main axial belt of heavier crowding, pushing inland on the Pennsylvania and Maryland Piedmont and invading the Coastal Plain in Delaware. The central belt of heavy population crowding continues from the New York area toward Boston; but there is much more forest east of the Hudson Valley than southwest of it, where farming still occupies a larger part of the land.

Nowhere in a densely populated country can physiography alone explain the distribution of forests. In Megalopolis as elsewhere it has been determined by a variety of factors, most of them economic; but it is the land economics resulting from urbanization that have exerted the decisive influence here. The lowest proportions of woodland are found in the most densely built-up counties, for in a naturally wooded environment one has to clear land to build. Forested land is often relatively cheap and attractive to developers, and it has receded a good deal before the urban sprawl, a condition that was especially obvious in New Jersey during the 1950's. While receding in the newly developed sectors, the woods have been expanding on their periphery. Farmers often just let the trees grow on much of their land, waiting for the price of the land to come up and for a realtor to buy it for building. It is a good way to let the investment grow, while a minimum of expensive labor is used and some dividends may be obtained in the form of grazing, hunting, timber cutting, or benefits from the Soil Bank.[4] Such forest areas occupy lands that have not yet been pre-empted by the real estate market. Others, however, exist to meet specific needs of urban populations, especially recreation and water supply. Thus urban developments determine the supply of land for forests, and it is significant that even in recent years this supply has been increasing. During the years 1946–56, for example, the wooded area in the whole

[4] See Chapter 6 above, pp. 258–340.

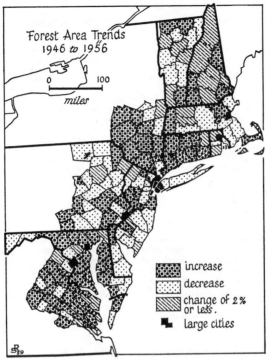

Forest Area Trends
1946 to 1956

0   100
miles

increase
decrease
change of 2% or less.
large cities

FIG. 113

of Megalopolis expanded somewhat, and this spread probably continued until 1960.

Knowing the agricultural evolution of the region helps to shed light on this increase in wooded area. It is a trend of rather long standing, having started (at least in southern New England) in the middle of the nineteenth century, and since World War II it has characterized most of the counties of Megalopolis (see Fig. 113). Land use has been shifting at a rapid pace under the pressure of urbanization, and relative stability of forest area (i.e., less than 2 per cent of change, one way or the other, in the proportion of forested area) was not common in Megalopolis during the years 1946–56. Rhode Island was the most stable of the Megalopolitan states in this respect, and New Hampshire (only two of its counties are included in the region) was fairly so. Other stable areas were scattered — in central Massachusetts, northeastern Connecticut, northern New Jersey, eastern Pennsylvania, central Maryland, and northern Virginia. In other counties the forested area has decreased, especially in Massachusetts, on

Table 14

FOREST LAND AS PART OF TOTAL LAND AREA IN MEGALOPOLIS, BY STATES

(*Thousands of Acres*)

States	Total Land Area	Forest Land				
		Total	Commercial	Noncommercial		
				Total	Productive	Nonproductive
Connecticut	3,135	1,990	1,973	17	11	6
Delaware	1,266	454	448	6	—	6
Maryland[a]	4,138	1,989	1,983	6	—	—
Massachusetts	5,035	3,288	3,259	29	18	11
New Hampshire[a]	2,908	2,325	2,306	19	—	—
New Jersey	4,814	1,958	1,910	48	17	31
New York[a]	7,458	3,785	3,456	330	—	—
Pennsylvania[a]	4,857	1,319	1,298	20	—	—
Rhode Island	677	434	430	4	4	—
Virginia[a]	4,897	2,729	2,671	58	—	—

Source: Compiled from the *Forest Statistics* series published during the 1950's as part of a nationwide forest survey for the individual states, except Virginia, by the Northeastern Forest Experiment Station (Upper Darby, Pennsylvania), Forest Service, U. S. Department of Agriculture. Statistics for Virginia were compiled from the *Forest Statistics* series by the Southeastern Forest Experiment Station (Asheville, North Carolina) in cooperation with the Virginia Department of Conservation and Development, 1957.

[a] For the states of Maryland, New Hampshire, New York, Pennsylvania, and Virginia only those parts included in Megalopolis are listed here.

Long Island, in New Jersey, on the Pennsylvania Piedmont and foothills, in Delaware, and in Washington's immediate suburbs. For the region as a whole, however, the increases have been greater than the decreases in acreage. Most of Connecticut, the counties in New York north of New York City, parts of eastern Pennsylvania and central New Jersey, and much of Maryland have recorded substantial additions to their wooded areas. Oddly enough, there seems to have been more wooded area added in the outer suburbs of the larger cities (except around Boston and Providence, where the land was already heavily wooded, and on Long Island) than in the more rural outlying sections of Megalopolis. One could almost say that afforestation in Megalopolis has progressed southward with urbanization and higher population densities. It would be more realistic to interpret these trends as representing the balance between the land supply needed by urban sprawl and that made available by decrease in cultivated area. Expansion of both cities and pastures cut into the woodlands in the eastern valleys and Piedmont of Pennsylvania, in southern New Jersey, and in Delaware; where some tilled farmland was given up, as in parts of Connecticut and Maryland, the woods advanced; where suburbs sprawled, as on Long Island, and there was no compensating abandonment of tilled land to forests, the woods retreated.

Thus the picture is a complex one, dominated by the interplay between urban developments and tilled farmland. For the whole region the forested area increased somewhat in the years 1946–56. From a good deal of field study it seemed safe to recognize a further advance in the total wooded area during the late 1950's. If woods occupy half of Megalopolis and are gaining, this fact alone would be important enough to call for an examination of the uses of these woodlands. We already know these uses are manifold and especially valuable to nonfarm crowded people. It would be unwise to conclude that because the forests are so broadly distributed and are expanding in the area there is no cause for worry. Having 16 million acres of forest for a population of almost 32 million (in 1950, and 37 million in 1960) means only half an acre per inhabitant in Megalopolis. This is not enough, for such a multiple-purpose resource, to relieve us from all concern and from the need for careful study.

The Forest Types in Megalopolis

Spread over the long and diversified region between the seashore and the steep Appalachian ranges, cut into many pieces, submitted to many human influences, the forests of Megalopolis could not be homogenous. They show, indeed, great variety.

The forests of eastern United States are well known for their diversity of tree species. For the sake of classification botanists and foresters have defined forest types, each of which consists of a given association of species and has a certain appearance. In practice, however, these types are not always easy to recognize, for biological phenomena and man's influence upon them are not easily reduced to simple formulas. The forest cover that remains on the same plot of ground changes as its very duration modifies the ecological conditions. Thus there are *pioneer stands* that grow after a major disturbance, such as a fire or a clearing for cultivation; and these are replaced, at the end of a long and undisturbed evolution, by *climax stands,* made of a mixture of species in which shade trees predominate. Intermediate between these two types are stands showing evidence of repeated cuttings, which may acquire various aspects and different species composition as man's actions modify them. Thus not only the geographical distribution of forests but also the types of trees comprising them have been and are constantly being modified by past and present uses and misuses man has made of them.

In Megalopolis the intermediate types are predominant. Climax forests are almost nonexistent nowadays in the Northeast, and pioneer formations are found only where they reclaim burned or abandoned land. Variations of these types frequently intermingle. The complexity of individual forest formation is therefore great, and it is further increased by physiographic contrasts. In a broad and rather generalized way, however, four main forest belts can be recognized: a pine belt along the seaboard from Massachusetts to southern Maryland; a mixed hardwood belt (with oaks predominating) in most of the Piedmont from Connecticut to Virginia; a northern hardwood belt (red oak and red maple mixed with white pine) in Massachusetts and farther north; and a mountain type (with some spruce, hemlock, and balsam fir) in the Catskills and Berkshires.[5]

Numerous other divisions and types can be distinguished, for a detailed examination of each of the four main belts shows much variety and complexity. A map of forest types, still very generalized but based on detailed surveys made by the Society of American Forests, provides a slightly more variegated picture of the Northeast (see Fig. 21, p. 97).

In the southern part of the *coastal pine belt* (Delmarva Peninsula) there is a great variety of species. The loblolly pine associates with hardwoods (sweet gum, yellow poplar, hickory, and white oak) in the woods and grows on abandoned fields, for it is a pioneer species. Given adequate fire protection its pure stands are colonized by hardwoods, and in due time a climax may be attained, with more oaks and hickories and fewer pines. In the Coastal Plain of New Jersey other yellow pines (pitch pine mostly, with some short leaf and Virginia) dominate. The "pine barrens" of that state are characterized by pitch pine with shrub oaks, interspersed with cranberry bogs and swamps where white cedar is found. Pitch pine is still dominant on the sandy coastal soils of Long Island, Connecticut, and Cape Cod. In eastern Massachusetts the pine stands contain a variety of oaks. Repeated cuttings of the valuable softwoods in the pine belt cause a rise in the proportion of hardwoods.

In the less maritime and colder climate inland from the Fall Line the mixed hardwood belt develops, the predominant species being red and white oak, yellow poplar, elm, hickory, and maple. Chestnut was eliminated by the blight, and white oak has retreated as a result of too much cutting. Other oak species appear on dry sites at elevations greater than 900 feet. On abandoned fields in the Piedmont of Maryland and Virginia, loblolly and Virginia or scrub pines are the pioneers, with the latter often being the chief one. Yellow poplar is the main pioneer in eastern Pennsyl-

[5] This description in general terms of the forest types in Megalopolis is based on data from Emma Lucy Brown, *Deciduous Forests of Eastern North America*, Blakiston, New York, 1950; *Forest Cover Types of North America (Exclusive of Mexico)*, published by the Society of American Foresters, Washington, D. C., 1954; and the Forest Survey publications of the Northeastern and Southeastern Forest Experiment Stations, *op. cit.*

vania, especially in Chester, Lancaster, and York counties, and it is succeeded northward in Bucks County by red cedar, which continues into New Jersey. On the glaciated soils from northern New Jersey eastward, the oak-hickory type is well established, introduced on new lands by a pioneering mixture of grey birch and red maple; and white pine appears more frequently as one progresses northward.

Everywhere in Megalopolis repeated cuttings have favored mixed hardwoods, which have sprouted back after each cut, producing a coppice-like new forest. As its composition changes, the more valuable species tend to scatter while the less desirable ones take over. This is true of the *northern hardwood* belt as well, where old stands of sugar maple, yellow birch, and beech are growing rare, and hemlock has been almost eliminated. In their places are widespread coppices of red oak, maple, basswood, and beech. White pine is abundant on abandoned fields, and grey birch on recently burned areas.

The *mountain-type forest* is more common on the ridges farther west, but within Megalopolis it occurs in the higher parts of the Catskills and the Massachusetts Berkshires. It consists of a mixture of red spruce, hemlock, and balsam fir. Probably it was once more extensive and has been restricted by human action.

The Past Story of the Forests

When the first European settlers arrived, the area that is now Megalopolis was clad with deep forests, in which Indians had made clearings by burning to facilitate travel and attract game. Although such burning had been carried out for many centuries, most of the forest consisted of stands old enough to be classified as climax types. Then the forests retreated as settlement progressed, and by 1800 no major forest within the region had been spared, for farmland was secured by clearings, and timber and firewood were in great demand. Small woodlots were left dispersed over the countryside to supply the rural needs of those days. By 1825 about half of the land in the Northeast had been cleared.[6]

As the westward march of settlement crossed the Appalachians and entered the rich agricultural lands of the Midwest, farmland acreage on the

[6] Historical data are from the following sources: Survey of the Northeastern Forest Experiment Station, *op. cit.;* U. S. Department of Agriculture, *Trees: Yearbook of Agriculture, 1949,* U. S. Government Printing Office, Washington, D. C.; Stanley W. Bromley, "The Original Forest Types of Southern New England," in *Ecological Monographs,* V, No. 1, January, 1935, pp. 63–89; and *Proceedings, Society of American Foresters Meeting: Forest Land Use in Transition* (Syracuse, N. Y., 1957), Society of American Foresters, Washington, 1958.

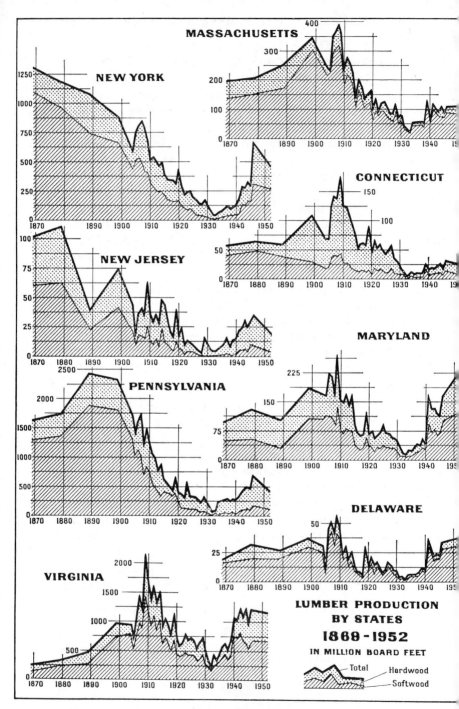

LUMBER PRODUCTION
BY STATES
1868-1952
IN MILLION BOARD FEET

Total — Hardwood
Softwood

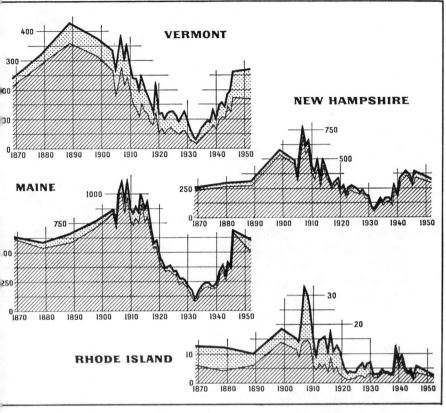

FIG. 114*b*. See legend on Fig. 114*a*.

Northeastern seaboard stopped expanding, and pioneer species began to reclaim abandoned fields and pastures. But from the 1830's on, industry needed more timber, and steam sawmills entered the forests, claiming the older stands for lumber and the second growth for charcoal and other uses. Thus there were more and more cuttings of both softwoods and hardwoods.

The more valuable trees were taken out in larger numbers as soon as they were merchantable, and *since industry preferred softwoods a hardwood invasion developed, changing the composition of the stands*. Gradually the commercial value of the forest declined as a result, and cutting therefore decreased. How the waves of this "mining of the forest" rolled southward from New England to Virginia, receded, and rose again may be followed on the graphs of lumber production by states from 1869 to

1952 (see Figs. 114a and 114b).[7] Most of the timber supply in Megalopolis had been exhausted by the time of the Civil War, and adjacent northern New England, upstate New York, and western Pennsylvania were heavily cut over from 1870 to 1890. Megalopolis saw a new surge of lumbering around 1910 when, fifty years after the Civil War, the stands had grown back again. The generalized low from 1925 to 1940 was due to the depletion of the stands even more than to reduced consumption during the depression. Every new wave of cutting in Megalopolis must take more hardwood, willy-nilly, for the softwoods, having been treated in expendable fashion, no longer expand much.

The more recent cuttings have often applied the "commercially selective" method, taking only the best trees and leaving the less valuable ones standing. Thus the desirable species tend to be eradicated, and a valueless coppice of hardwoods has spread over most of the Megalopolitan woodlands. A few forests, however, where conservation practices have been undertaken, have received better care.

In other ways, too, man's actions have affected forest growth and also the usefulness of the woods to the people. Among these other influences are the use of fire and hunting practices.

Formerly the Indians burned the forest to produce fresh and sweet pasture liked by deer, and they used fire also to clear the land and to make war. These practices are no longer carried on. However, the abundance of people in the area has caused many forest fires (see pp. 355–356), and these, by providing the environment for pioneer species, have been a potent factor in changing the composition of the woodland.

The European settlers, better equipped for hunting than the Indians were, went after the available game with such thoroughness that by 1900 they had almost wiped out deer, grouse, and wild turkey. The retreat of the woods helped, and game became so scarce in the Northeast that action had to be taken to reintroduce and protect it. Laws were passed forbidding deer hunting (in Connecticut) or doe shooting (in Pennsylvania in 1907 and in New York in 1912), new stock was brought in from the West, and refuge areas were set up.

Because of this protection and because the brush-stage woods that followed the heavy cuttings provided ideal conditions for deer, they came back in large numbers in the 1920's. As the forests grew older, however, their carrying capacity decreased. The deer began to feed upon the farms,

---

[7] Based on Henry B. Steer, *Lumber Production in the United States, 1799–1946*, U. S. Department of Agriculture Miscellaneous Publication No. 669, Washington, D. C., 1948; brought up to date from the Forest Survey data.

where they were shot at by the farmers. In addition, many died of malnutrition or were killed by feral dogs. But in spite of these losses many forested parts of Megalopolis became overpopulated with deer, which were too well protected by law.[8]

Since the "deer problem" is now one of overabundance, new legislation has encouraged regulating the hunting of deer. The rules vary from state to state. Some states protect the does and let the buck deer be hunted, while others have "buck laws" protecting the males too. The length of the hunting season varies, as does the maximum number of deer that can be shot. Massachusetts has never protected does, and since 1941 Connecticut has authorized farmers to kill at any time to protect their crops, although there is a two-month hunting season with permits. These states have no actual problem of overabundance. The situation is worse in the "buck law" states. New York State has two large "reservoirs" of deer in the Catskills and the Adirondacks, with a herd estimated at 400,000 head in 1955. The open season lasts two weeks for bucks but only one day for does, and the bag limit is set at one deer a season. This keeps the annual legal kill around 73,000 deer. Pennsylvania, with its mountains, has a similar overabundance of deer, with about a million head, mostly small animals with poor antlers. The official kill stands around 100,000 annually. New Jersey, Delaware, and Maryland seem also to have too many deer.[9]

For the woods, *overabundance of deer means overbrowsing*, and this results in elimination of young seedlings of species palatable to the deer, which happen to be also the more valuable commercially. Not only does this change the composition of the growth undesirably, but it also helps the spreading of the coppice and the coming in of grasses and shrubs.

There has been still another great change in hunting practice. Traditionally the hunter has been the farmer, who shot deer and grouse to provide his table with game and to protect his crops from these potential agents of damage. Today's hunter is from the city and is very different. He is not utilitarian but is after any animal that provides good sport. He believes in conservation and is more law-abiding. He is against and shoots at stray dogs, which menace all game and especially deer in winter, and

[8] Durward L. Allen, *Our Wildlife Legacy*, Funk and Wagnalls Company, New York, 1954, especially pp. 135–150; also Leslie A. Williamson, *Report on Deer in Connecticut*, Connecticut State Board of Fisheries and Game, Hartford, 1948 (mimeographed).

[9] Estimates from Allen, *op. cit.*; U. S. Department of the Interior, Fish and Wildlife Service, *Big Game Inventory for 1955* (Wildlife Leaflet 387), Washington, D. C., June 1957; Commonwealth of Pennsylvania, Fish and Game Division, *Annual Report for the Year 1957*, Harrisburg, Pennsylvania.

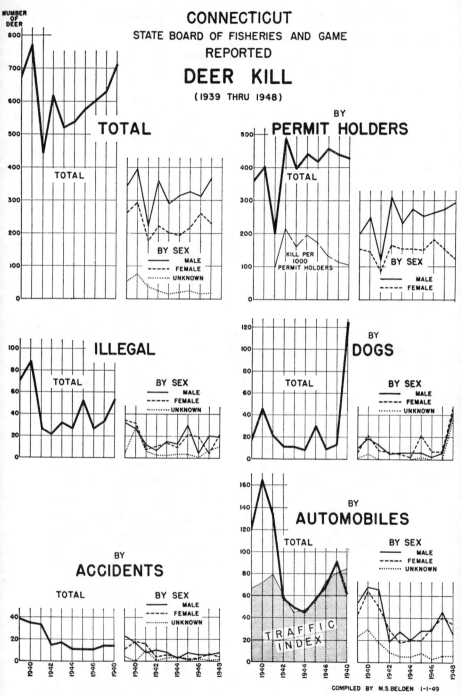

Fig. 115. *Courtesy of the Connecticut State Board of Fisheries and Game*

which thus, from the farmer's point of view, are protectors of his crops. Such attitudes result in protecting game close to the cities and suburbs, with resultant damage to the forests. Moreover, the urban hunter who drives into the forest seems seldom to walk much farther than one mile away from his car. A good part of the range thus remains unreached by the majority of hunters and there is undershooting of overabundant game! In various ways therefore, deer have profited much by the urbanization of the environment in Megalopolitan forests, and they continue to modify the forest types, generally for the worse (Fig. 120).

Forest Fires

Environmental conditions favoring forest fires are influenced by weather — a dry spell makes the underbrush and grass inflammable; by climate — the hazard is relatively low in the normally rainier regions, like New England; and by type of forest — the pine belt is an area of unusually great fire hazard. Obviously, then, forest fires are seasonal, and the hazard is unevenly distributed. However, few fires, usually less than 4 per cent of the known cases, are started by lightning or other natural causes. *Most fires are set by men, and large concentrations of people have always meant fire risk.* Forest fires therefore occur where man creates a fire risk in a forest environment favorable to the setting and spreading of fire.

All the available statistical data demonstrated these relationships quite clearly — that forest fires are essentially man-made, and that more people mean more fires.[10] However, rural and urban people do not cause fire in the same way. City people may act out of ignorance or carelessness, as when fires are set by smokers and campers. In contrast, the farmer uses fire as a tool, generally a dangerous device that gets out of control. It is chiefly rural people who are responsible for the debris- and brush-burning fires and sometimes for the incendiary fires. In the pine belt, for instance,

[10] This can be demonstrated statistically by the following data, supplied by the offices of the New Jersey State Forester and the Maryland State Forester (see the mimeographed "Forest Fire Report, Spring 1958" of the latter).

Causes of Forest Fires	New Jersey, 1958 No. of Fires	Maryland, Spring 1958	
		No. of Fires	% of Fires by Cause
Railroads	36	5	3
Campers	11	4	3
Smoking	550	48	34
Debris or brush burning	113	37	26
Incendiarism	138	28	16
Lumbering	—	1	1
Lightning	2	2	1
Miscellaneous	35	22	16

burning has long been practiced to encourage huckleberry growing, and in the Southeast burnings are still practiced to prepare the topsoil for the regeneration of pines, which are pioneer trees.

To recreation and tourist areas and to woods close to housing developments the urban crowds obviously bring a serious fire risk. That urbanization increases the threat to the true forests can also be illustrated statistically. In Massachusetts 1957 was a disastrous year in terms of forest fires, with 1,751 fires per million acres of forest in the state. However, the coastal tier of counties from Essex to Barnstable and Nantucket, more urbanized and touristic, had a greater density of fires — 2,820 per million acres of woodland — in spite of the fact that they are endowed with a damp climate. In Rhode Island in the same year 160 of the 244 forest fires occurred in Providence County alone. The whole of New York State had a density of 146 fires per million acres of forest, but its Megalopolitan section had 231. The figures for New Hampshire, Pennsylvania, New Jersey, and Maryland tell the same story. The risk of forest fire is highest in the areas around the large cities, as a result of week end driving, hiking, picnicking, camping, hunting, and other outdoor activities of the urbanites.[11] Attempts at educating the public have brought some results, but that they are not yet satisfactory is shown by the high incidence of smoking as a cause of forest fires.

As the frequency of forest fires in Megalopolis has increased, fire-fighting organizations have been set up. To stop a fire it is essential to get to the spot as soon as possible after the outbreak, and so a good alarm system, a favorable network of roads, and density of population are helpful factors. As a result, although many forest fires are started in Megalopolis, they are usually put out quickly, and the area burned per fire is small. This average area amounted in 1957 to 8.7 acres in New Hampshire, 4.7 in Massachusetts and Rhode Island (only 2.6 in Providence County), 4.2 in Connecticut, 17 for the whole of New York State (but 3.9 in Westchester County), 3.4 in Maryland (but only 2.4 in the heavily populated area near Baltimore or Washington). In the pine belt the type of forest increases the hazard and the average acreage burned. On the whole, however, over most of Megalopolis fires contributed to the degradation of the forests much more in the past than they do nowadays, despite the propensity of urbanites to scatter fire. It has proved difficult to teach people not to start fires but easy to train them to fight fire well.

[11] The above statistics are from "Forest Fire Statistics for the Calendar Year 1957," a report of the U. S. Forest Service, mimeographed, or were compiled from data supplied by the various State Forest Services.

Present Condition of the Forests

A long historical evolution, during which many factors have been at play, has produced the present condition of the forest stands in Megalopolis. Half of the land in the area grows trees, but how valuable a resource are these trees as producers of wood? The forest survey conducted by the U. S. Forest Service in the 1950's has gone into that problem in great detail. The data thus collected have been set forth in a series of publications,[12] which drive home the foregone conclusion, that *the woodlands are understocked, and that the proportion of saw-timber trees is below average.* In addition, the percentage of the more desirable softwood trees has dropped.

This situation is found commonly over most of the Northeast and in the Central Atlantic region, where forests have been depleted by excessive or overselective cuttings, but it is worse around the big cities than farther away from them. In New England, for example, stocking is better and the coniferous trees are more abundant as distance from the axial belt of Megalopolis increases.[13] This trend is obvious also in the detailed statistics for New York State, but less clear in Pennsylvania, where the forests in coal-mining regions have been especially depleted for pit props. In the pine belt the situation is somewhat better, for there are more pines and they grow more rapidly.

[12] See the publications of the Forest Survey by the Northeastern Forest Experiment Station, Upper Darby, Pa., and of the Virginia State Forest Service, *op. cit.* — especially the series of reports for each state entitled *The Timber Resources of . . .* We have particularly used these for Massachusetts (1956), Rhode Island (1957), Connecticut (1957), New Jersey (1958), Delaware (1959), Maryland (1955). These are supplemented by more detailed publications on *Forest Statistics* for each state. We have used also the valuable volume by the Forest Service, U. S. Department of Agriculture, *Timber Resources for America's Future,* Forest Resource Report No. 14, U. S. Government Printing Office, Washington, D. C., 1958.

[13] The following table was compiled from data in *Timber Resources for America's Future,* pp. 506–509. The average quantity of saw timber per acre is a good index of a forest's productive potential.

State	Saw Timber Stands (Millions of Board Feet)	Commercial Forest Area (1,000 Acres)	Average Quantity of Saw Timber per Acre (1,000 Board Feet)
Vermont	8,547	3,713	2.3
Maine	28,226	16,601	1.7
Massachusetts	2,659	3,259	0.8
Connecticut	1,859	1,975	0.9
Rhode Island	165	430	0.4
New Jersey	1,660	1,910	0.8
Maryland	6,771	2,897	2.3
Delaware	1,234	448	2.7

Broadly speaking, close to the metropolises there are fewer large and valuable trees per acre because of a very active demand for forest products and because owners care less about conservation programs. Megalopolitan forests are still peppered with small sawmills, an outgrowth of the local demand, which they cannot satisfy, and these mills apply cutting methods that further jeopardize the future supply. There is not much of a market at present for low-quality hardwoods, though some people hope that industries may adjust to the situation and use more hardwoods for pulping. Moreover, incentives could be provided to encourage the growth of more saw timber, of a better, more desirable quality, close to the markets. However, this has proved as yet to be no easy proposition, and this is especially regrettable because wood is generally costly to transport long distances.

Forest Ownership

Private ownership dominates Megalopolitan woodlands. There are no Federal forests in the region, and state and county forests have been established only recently under the impulse of the conservation movement. The policy of preserving forests by public ownership [14] has been active mainly in the West and South. The forest-industry type of ownership, well developed in other parts of the country, is not important in Megalopolis either, though 8 per cent of the commercial forest land in Massachusetts is so owned.

In the privately owned forests small holdings predominate, many of them being woodlots on active or abandoned farms (see Fig. 116). The proportion of woodland included in farms is higher where more of the land is wooded (compare Figs. 112 and 116). For example, in the heavily forested states of Rhode Island and Connecticut more than half of the commercial forest land is in holdings of less than 100 acres, and less than 10 per cent of it is in holdings of more than 500 acres. These proportions would be true also for Massachusetts if the 250,000 acres owned by the forest industry there were discounted. Similar conditions prevail in New Jersey, Delaware, and Maryland.

The forest owners belong to various social groups. Many of them are urbanites, for many people who have moved from the farms to the cities have kept or later inherited some woodlots, which looked like good investments requiring little care. This pattern of ownership indicates an increasing separation between forestry and agriculture, a trend not peculiar

[14] Luther Halsey Gulick, *American Forest Policy: A Study of Government Administration and Economic Control*, Duell, Sloan & Pearce (for the Institute of Public Administration), New York, 1951.

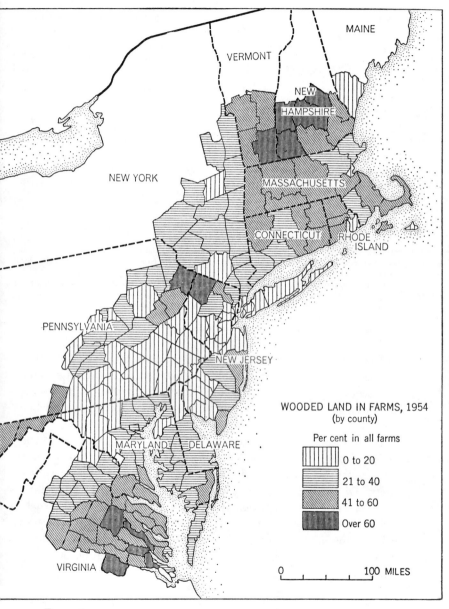

MAINE

VERMONT

NEW HAMPSHIRE

NEW YORK

MASSACHUSETTS

CONNECTICUT RHODE ISLAND

PENNSYLVANIA

NEW JERSEY

MARYLAND DELAWARE

VIRGINIA

WOODED LAND IN FARMS, 1954
(by county)

Per cent in all farms

0 to 20

21 to 40

41 to 60

Over 60

0   100 MILES

Fig. 116

Table 15

COMMERCIAL FORESTS IN MEGALOPOLIS BY OWNERSHIP AND BY SIZE CLASS

(*Thousands of Acres*)

States	Total Area	Public Ownership			Private Ownership	
		Federal	State	County & Municipal	Farm	Other
Connecticut	1,973	1	122	32	526	1,292
Delaware	448	1	10	2	217	218
Maryland[a]	1,983	53	26	15	822	1,066
Massachusetts	3,259	29	280	90	740	2,120
New Hampshire[a]	2,306	5	65[b]	—	792	1,444
New Jersey	1,910	1	130	50	320	1,409
New York[a]	3,456	26	97	18	898	2,418
Pennsylvania[a]	1,298	14	128	24	380	754
Rhode Island	430	—[c]	13	13	79	325
Virginia[a]	2,671	93	4	12	2,563[d]	—

Source: Compiled from the *Forest Statistics* series published during the 1950's for the individual states by the Northeastern Forest Experiment Station (Upper Darby, Pennsylvania), Forest Service, U. S. Department of Agriculture and the Southeastern Forest Experiment Station (Asheville, North Carolina).

[a] For the states of Maryland, New Hampshire, New York, Pennsylvania, and Virginia only those parts within the limits of Megalopolis are included here.

[b] State, county, and municipal figures are combined.

[c] Less than 0.5 thousand acres.

[d] Farm and other private ownership figures are combined.

to Megalopolis but one that is an important factor in the evolution of the landscape. As may be seen in Table 15, the woods included in farms now represent a fraction, often small, of all the commercial forest area. There are no available data on the number of nonresident forest owners, which is likely to be rather high.

The forest is still an important component of all large estates remaining in Megalopolis, but this kind of forest ownership was more common thirty years ago, for increased taxation has broken up many large private estates. Of those that have survived, some have been bought by clubs or have become public recreation areas. In this region forests are used less and less for grazing or timber growing and increasingly for recreation. Public ownership of woodland is being urged increasingly, especially on the periphery of the region, where such land is still available at not too high a price.[15]

[15] See Shirley A. Siegel, *The Law of Open Space*, Regional Plan Association, New York, 1960; and *The Place for Open Space: Final Report of the Park, Recreation and Open Space Project*, RPA Bulletin 96, Regional Plan Association, New York, 1960.

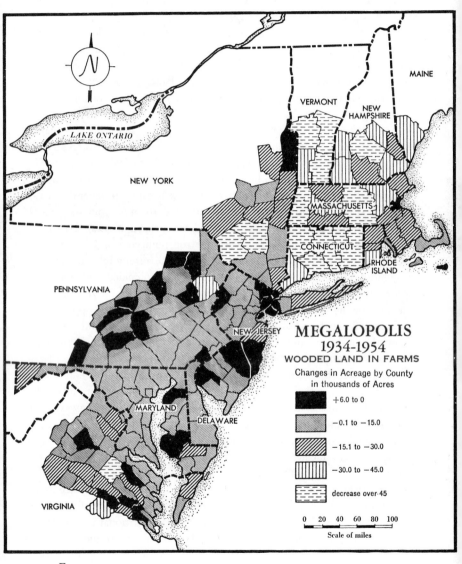

MEGALOPOLIS
1934-1954
WOODED LAND IN FARMS

Changes in Acreage by County
in thousands of Acres

+6.0 to 0

−0.1 to −15.0

−15.1 to −30.0

−30.0 to −45.0

decrease over 45

0   20   40   60   80   100
Scale of miles

Fig. 117

Parks and Recreation

The recreational needs of the crowded urban centers have caused suburban parks to multiply, and these are responsible for a good deal of the forest acreage in public ownership. Some parks are located in the suburbs proper, others at some distance in the midst of "rural" country. In Megalopolis the interpenetration of rural and suburban often makes it difficult to classify parks in these categories. Parks were created by communities wherever wooded land was available for the purpose and as close as possible to the city.

Any park has this in common with the city parks, that it is not managed for timber production but only for amenity and recreation. State and county parks are now numerous in Megalopolis, but of recent origin. The movement to establish them began around 1900 and has gathered impetus only since 1928. Before automobile ownership became so general tourism was not as widespread through the countryside, for most tourists went to one special spot by train. Those who did roam through rural territory — hikers, hunters, or fishermen — were not too numerous and could easily obtain access to most privately owned land. The automobile era caused a revolution in this situation, all the more so as it coincided with increased leisure time in many occupations. Large crowds of motorized urbanites took to the highways to "get out into the country" at every opportunity, to escape from their usual environment of concrete, steel, and stone and from the noise and polluted atmosphere of the city. Tidal waves of invaders descended upon the rural lands, and as a result the disturbed landowners posted their lands, turning them into fenced-in and legally closed properties. The strongest reaction came, logically enough, from city folks who had acquired rural residences or summer homes to get away from the crowds. Thus the urban resident's opportunities for outings shrank rapidly in Megalopolis. Responding to popular demand, county or state authorities set aside areas for the driving tourists' recreation, as well as for amenity. Often these areas were wooded.

State parks should not be confused with national parks, which are much larger and are located in areas of outstanding scenic or scientific interest. There are no national parks in Megalopolis, only "national monuments," which usually take very little space. State parks are more modest enterprises, which vary greatly in size and even in kind, some having a historical or educational significance while others are merely areas for play. Most of them are in a pleasant setting but are small, for land is expensive in Megalopolis. In this man-made and man-crowded region the patchwork of

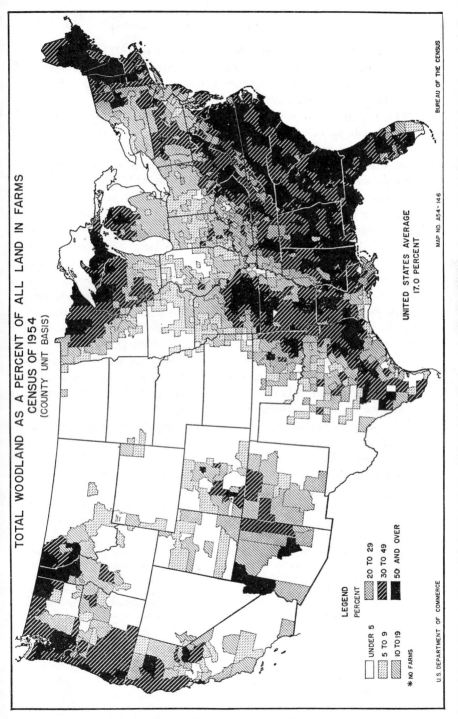

FIG. 118. *Courtesy of the U. S. Bureau of the Census*

scattered state parks is unique. Not only does it provide a much-desired contact with Nature, but it is also an expression of wealth and prosperity, for nowhere else in the world have as many areas been set aside for the sole purpose of public recreation.

By 1960 the metropolitan region of New York had a magnificent system of state parks, easily accessible via a radiating network of highways and parkways, many of which were designed to lead to these recreation areas. The achievements in New York State in terms of parks and parkways are especially impressive.[16] Long Island probably owes much of its attraction as a New York suburban area to its thirteen state parks. About one third of the Long Island shore is publicly owned. The famous Jones Beach State Park received ten million visitors in 1957 (more than 200,000 people a day on summer week ends). In the Heckscher State Park, farther away from the city, bathing and camping grounds are set amid a young but beautiful forest, already full of deer. Along the Hudson Valley north of the city there is a chain of parks starting with the Palisades Interstate Park, just across the river from upper Manhattan, and continuing by way of the popular Bear Mountain and Taconic State Parks to the Catskills, where a mountainous forest preserve extends over 234,610 acres and is protected by iron-clad regulations incorporated in the State Constitution. Farther north, beyond the rim of Megalopolis and the range of a one-day motor trip, lies the Adirondacks Forest Preserve.[17] Most of these parks and preserves are "functional," that is, they are organized for active recreation, permitting swimming, picnicking, camping, hiking, and skiing, and sometimes they are equipped with such facilities as hotels, cabins, boat basins, and golf courses.

Despite it all there is, in season, so much crowding in most parks that the present open space available around New York City is considered by many to be inadequate. In 1958 the New York Metropolitan Regional Council and the Regional Plan Association jointly undertook a "park,

[16] See the publications of the State Council of Parks, Division of Parks, New York State Conservation Department, Albany, New York, especially *New York State Parks: Thirtieth Anniversary, 1924–1954*, 1954, and *New York–New Jersey Metropolitan Region: Recreation for 19 Million in 1975* (Speeches at the New York–New Jersey Metropolitan Regional Recreation Conference), 1958. Also *Recreational Facilities in Westchester*, a report by the Westchester County Department of Planning, White Plains, N. Y., 1956. Much of the park and parkway development has been a result of the periodic efforts of Robert Moses.

[17] E. W. Littlefield, "Impact of Shifting Land-Use Patterns on Forest Policies and Programs," in *Proceedings, Society of American Foresters Meeting: Forest Land Use in Transition, op. cit.*, pp. 5–9; and W. D. Mulholland, "Forest Recreation in New York," *ibid.*, pp. 18–20.

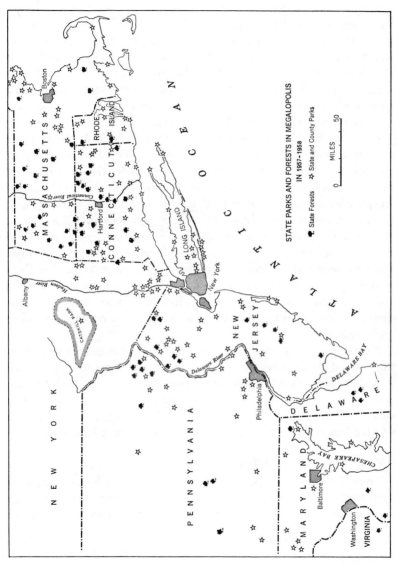

STATE PARKS AND FORESTS IN MEGALOPOLIS
IN 1957-1958

■ State Forests   ☆ State and County Parks

0   50
    MILES

F1G. 119

recreation, and open space project" to study the existing possibilities and needs, and to prepare a program for meeting the challenge of forthcoming urban growth.[18] As has been shown above, the New York region is relatively well endowed with parks, largely as a result of local wealth, for many state parks originated with an individual's gift and have been enlarged as more private funds have become available. The surroundings of Philadelphia and Baltimore, however, are much less well supplied with parks, and parts of New Jersey and Connecticut are quite deficient in park space (see Fig. 119). The need for it is recognized, however, and more state parks are now being laid out or planned.

The administrative action needed to create or maintain parks may come from other authorities than the state government. Often a county or municipality acts, and in New England parks are traditionally the responsibility of townships, many of them being very small as a result. In Connecticut, besides sixteen state parks totaling 20,000 acres, there were, in 1955, 509 county and township (mostly the latter) parks covering 14,875 acres. A similar situation exists in Rhode Island. In 1955 Massachusetts had twenty-six state parks averaging 1,000 acres each, all created since 1936, and 1,207 municipal and county parks averaging 14 acres each. New England has great touristic resources owing to its cooler summer climate, its rocks, lakes, and woods, and its history, and these attractions bring in millions of visitors from the outside each year. This requires more and more park facilities.[19]

Experience in Megalopolis has shown that new parks awaken an increasing demand by urbanites for the out-of-doors, for when new open space is made available it quickly becomes crowded and inadequate. This response probably demonstrates that, although crowds have lived and can survive without parks, these answer a deep human yearning. The people of Megalopolis are likely, therefore, to ask for more and more parks.

State Forests and Wildlife Sanctuaries

From the forester's standpoint parks are specialized forest areas, with their own type of management aimed at a pleasant environment and with no concern for timber production. State forests are different. They are

[18] The four reports resulting from this study were published in 1960. See the two volumes mentioned in footnote 15, p. 360 above; also Marion Clawson, *The Dynamics of Park Demand*, RPA Bulletin 94, New York, 1960.

[19] Marion Clawson, *Statistics on Outdoor Recreation*, Resources for the Future, Washington, D. C., 1958; also Sen. Doc. No. 610, The Commonwealth of Massachusetts, *Report of an Inventory and Plan for Development of the Natural Resources of Massachusetts*, Boston, January 1958.

Table 16
NATIONAL WILDLIFE REFUGES IN MEGALOPOLIS

State and Refuge	County	Date Established	Acreage	Purpose
Maryland				
Blackwater	Dorchester	1-23-33	11,216	Canada geese, ducks, muskrats, quail
Chincoteague (also in Va.)	Somerset	5-13-43	418	Greater snow geese, American brant, ducks, shorebirds, gulls, terns
Glenn Martin	Somerset	12-27-54	2,482	Ducks, geese
Patuxent Research Refuge	Anne Arundel, Prince Georges	12-16-36	2,679	Experiment station
Susquehanna	Harford, Cecil	8-24-39	16,410	Whistling swans, canvas-backs, red-heads, ruddy ducks, ring-necked ducks
Delaware				
Bombay Hook	Kent	6-22-37	13,810	Greater snow geese, black ducks, blue-winged teal, gadwell, shorebirds
Killochook (see also N. J.)	New Castle	2-3-34	580	Waterfowl
New Jersey				
Brigantine	Atlantic	10-5-39	12,807	American brant, ducks, shorebirds, gulls, terns, rails
Killochook (see also Del.)	Salem	2-3-34	907	Waterfowl, muskrats
New York				
Elizabeth Alexandra Norton	Suffolk	12-27-54	113	Waterfowl
Wertheim	Suffolk	6-7-47	1,799	Waterfowl
Massachusetts				
Great Meadows	Essex	5-3-44	210	Waterfowl
Monomoy	Barnstable	6-1-44	2,921	Black ducks, elders, scoters, shorebirds
Parker River	Essex	12-30-42	6,405	Black ducks, greater swans, Canada geese, shorebirds

Source: U. S. Department of the Interior, Fish and Wildlife Service, *List of National Wildlife Refuges — 1955,* Wildlife Leaflet *372,* Washington, D. C., December 1955.

usually located farther from the cities, and since their purpose is the conservation of a natural resource they are still available for the production of timber, and recreation is only secondary. They are an asset to the state's economy.

As a rule state forests in Megalopolis have been acquired since 1900, through gifts of land and purchases of low-value areas and also, in New York State, through reversion to the state for nonpayment of taxes. Most of these areas had been heavily cut over in the past, and they have seldom been planted or improved, but they receive good fire protection. They were set aside for their watershed significance and with the idea of reserving some timber growth for the future.

As the motorized crowds thronged the countryside, the state forests were made available for recreation also and were equipped with such facilities as camping grounds, picnic areas, and hiking trails, which take only a small fraction of the productive area. Fishing and hunting are permitted but are subject to regulations. State forests are important in Massachusetts (168,870 acres), Connecticut (122,641 acres), and New Jersey (158,682 acres). In other parts of Megalopolis they are more restricted, but their acreage is expanding as most of the states proceed with land acquisition programs. Combining recreation opportunities with a promise of timber production, the state forests are an interesting long-range investment.

There are other open areas, often wooded, set aside for various purposes, but which contribute also to recreation. Megalopolis has a great many wildlife sanctuaries (see Table 16), some of which are maintained by the U. S. Fish and Wildlife Service. Many more are under the care of state or local authorities, or are even privately established and managed. Some of these refuges attract visitors but they do not offer facilities for the general public, in order to preserve the "wild" character of their sites. Still other places are classified as "conservation areas," most of them being arboretums or bird sanctuaries. Long Island and New Jersey especially have a rich dowry of such preserves. Indirectly they have great value for recreation, for they help maintain a more abundant and diversified fauna in Megalopolis.

Hunting and Hunters

The study of the forests has brought us to consider wildlife and recreation. Megalopolitan people love to go hunting, and this kind of recreation has some bearing on land use. Hunting has long ceased to be a necessity, as it used to be for the early settlers who hunted to provide their table with meat and to protect their crops and flocks against destructive animals. To the modern urbanite hunting is just a sport, a leisurely pastime, with no actually useful purpose.[20] Nevertheless, the number of hunters drawn from urban areas has been on the increase.[21] If the game population has held its own in the region, it seems largely because of the inefficiency of urban hunters, their usual ignorance of wildlife habits and of the terrain, and the bag limit system.

Most of the urbanite hunters find plenty of game in Megalopolis, and within a short radius of their city homes. With the exception of the wealthier, who go to more distant grounds looking for more excitement, the hunters make it a one-day sport, as they go shooting for a few hours of spare time; and the records show that a very small proportion of the hunting licenses issued in the region are taken out by out-of-state residents. Beyond the bounds of Megalopolis this proportion increases rapidly, especially in northern New England.

Where do all these hunters go shooting? Legally the game belongs to the state and the land to its owner. Fifty years ago one could hunt on private open land, for this was considered part of the traditional American rights and freedom; but as the density of hunters has increased, posting against hunting has spread. The landowners' attitude is justified by the lack of caution and of outdoor education of most hunters, and by their great numbers. Gradually the habit developed for a group of hunters (often a "club") to obtain the privilege of shooting on a given property by agreement with the owner and usually for payment of rent. Thus posting became profitable. It is estimated that in New York 70 per cent of the

[20] The differences between urbanites and farmers in their ways of hunting deer have already been stressed. See pp. 353–355 above.

[21] The following table, based on Marion Clawson's *Statistics on Outdoor Recreation, op. cit.* (pp. 146–147), shows the number of hunting licenses issued in the various states around Megalopolis and their relation to the national total:

Number of Hunting Licenses (In Thousands)

State	1938	1945	1948	1952	1956
New Hampshire	50	65	101	95	87
Massachusetts	71	85	121	116	118
Rhode Island	8	9	12	13	13
Connecticut	27	34	48	52	55
New York	650	545	784	867	976
New Jersey	128	126	141	166	168
Pennsylvania	606	607	847	1,070	932
Delaware	16	15	21	18	19
Maryland	63	83	112	126	148
Virginia	136	152	259	414	382
U. S. Total	6,899	8,791	11,392	13,902	14,462

FIG. 120. *Reproduced (from a print in color) by permission of* The New Yorker. *Drawing by Mr. Garrett Price, Copyright* © *1958, The New Yorker Magazine, Inc.*

hunting is done on private land — 45 per cent on unposted property (mainly upstate) and 25 per cent on posted land by agreement with the owner. The remaining 30 per cent occurs on public lands.[22] In Connecticut and New Jersey, farmers register with the state to be guaranteed that nobody will hunt on their land without their written permission.

Sportsmen's clubs, which provide hunting for the happy few, are appearing all over Megalopolis. This, however, may be likened to the case of private versus public beaches. As the popular demand increases, more space for hunting must be provided. This becomes all the more difficult as dwellings scatter increasingly in the forests and, for obvious safety reasons, shooting must be restricted close to the buildings. The state agencies responsible for organizing and regulating hunting try to prevent posting and to widen the state-owned areas that can be opened to the general public. Various systems of cooperation with the farmers have been worked out. New Jersey and Pennsylvania have been buying public hunting grounds with funds derived from hunting-license fees. The public lands almost everywhere become so crowded in the hunting season that they are considered dangerous territory.

Finally, the hunter without land but willing to pay for hunting privileges finds in Megalopolis an increasing number of commercial shooting preserves, privately managed on a business basis and artificially but fully stocked with game. These are located in the vicinity of large cities, offering an expensive sport.

The Supply of Game: Farms and Wetlands

To keep the game abundant and within reach of so many hunters is no small problem. It is the task of the state game divisions, and they are faced with a difficult situation. Modern "clean" farming, making excessive use of herbicides, insecticides, and other chemicals, is not favorable to wildlife. For example, there are not enough insects left in the fields today to support many game birds. Because of poor cover and poor feeding conditions the popular bobwhite quail has been on the wane since 1930.[23] The decrease in grain cultivation on Megalopolitan farms, too, has worsened the food supply for game. Some valuable game birds, such as the wild turkey and the heath hen, have been practically eliminated. In contrast, new forest growth since 1910 has brought back deer in overabundance, and also the ruffed grouse, once almost gone. Skunks seem to be multiplying, too,

[22] Data kindly supplied by the New York State Division of Fish and Game.
[23] E. A. Moss in a paper quoted in "Bobwhite Quail," report of the Connecticut Board of Fisheries and Game, 1948, mimeographed.

feeding upon garbage as they do, and raccoons are reported to be increasing around the cities. Rabbits, too, are thriving, though they are not developing into a menace as they have in Europe. Nevertheless, in spite of these more favorable conditions for some species, the general trend for natural game, living in disturbed conditions, is to decrease.[24]

Since the types of farming characteristic of the area do not favor game, the greatest local opportunity for its increase lies in the woodlands. However, it is as difficult to "sell" good game management to private forest owners as it is to "sell" them good forestry methods. It is easier to obtain good results on publicly owned lands, and since the 1920's state and federal agencies have been working at the problem of improving hunting in the vicinity of the metropolises. Their goal is to provide more game, by protecting the "natural" game and by introducing new species. Wildlife refuges have been established, state game lands have been acquired, and habitat-improving practices, such as special cutting of trees and planting of shrubs, have been undertaken. Considerable effort has gone into these habitat improvement projects, but time is needed to produce results, and the responsible agencies cannot wait. Therefore, to maintain an adequate game population close to the cities another device must also be used — the artificial stocking of game. Farther from the cities, in New Hampshire, for example, natural reproduction can supply the bulk of the demand for game. But in Megalopolis the carrying capacity of the land cannot supply a crop of game great enough to meet the high demand.

Artificial stocking has been undertaken chiefly for pheasants, but also to a lesser degree for bobwhite and wild turkeys. A first attempt to stock cock and hen pheasants so that they could settle and populate the area proved impractical, for the environment was not favorable enough and there were too many predators. It became apparent that any bird in excess of the carrying capacity was eliminated, for recovery of banded birds that had been released was disappointing.[25] The earlier the artificially reared birds were released the greater was the percentage lost. Then came

[24] Gardiner Bump, Robert W. Darrow, Frank C. Edminster, and Walter F. Crissey, *The Ruffed Grouse: Life History, Propagation, Management,* New York State Conservation Department, Albany, 1947; Helenette Silver, *A History of New Hampshire Game and Furbearers,* New Hampshire Fish and Game Department, Concord, N. H., 1957.

[25] Durward L. Allen has reported these experiments in *Our Wildlife Legacy, op. cit.,* Chapter 12. In 1944 and 1945, of 15,520 cock pheasants released in Massachusetts after banding, only 9.1 per cent were shot or recovered. In the same years release of 19,050 banded pheasants in New Jersey led to only an 8 per cent recovery. In carefully controlled areas in New York, the kill percentages on stocked pheasants were 18.5 and 16.2.

the idea of *releasing the birds only a short time before shooting,* so that the hunters would have a chance at them before the unfavorable local environment caused their natural death. That is what is practiced in the state public hunting grounds in Megalopolis, and most of the states have pheasant farms for this purpose. These pheasants released just in time to be shot are very costly — about two dollars each in Connecticut, for example, where 7,952 were released in 1941 and 14,023 in 1957.[26] In Massachusetts 41,583 cock pheasants were thus produced in 1957; in Pennsylvania three farms supply about 75,000 pheasants a year; and in New Jersey the Rockport farm, one of the world's biggest, produces 40,000 adult cocks a year. State game farms also produce other birds, such as "wild" turkeys, bobwhites, and mallards, but grouse cannot be reared economically enough for large-scale distribution. Thus there is a whole industry maintained by state agencies to supply hunters with game ready to be shot.

The supply of game is still another story with respect to *waterfowl.* These birds are mostly migratory and cannot be raised on farms, for they require a special natural environment. *Abundance of waterfowl means plenty of wetlands.* Migrating birds follow a small number of routes from wintering to summering grounds across North America, and Megalopolis has one of them, the famous *Atlantic Flyway,* which stretches along the continent's rim from Labrador to the Antilles and South America.

The Atlantic coast is a regular avenue for travel, and along it are many famous points for observing both land and water birds. About 50 different kinds of land birds that breed in New England follow the coast southward to Florida . . . Resting places are afforded at convenient intervals . . . Many thousands of coots, widgeons, pintails, blue-winged teal, and other waterfowl and shorebirds regularly spend the winter season in the coastal marshes and the inland lakes and ponds of Cuba, Hispaniola and Puerto Rico.[27]

Typical users of the Atlantic Flyway are the Atlantic brants, which breed in the north of Canada and on the coast of Greenland but winter on the Atlantic seaboard, chiefly at Barnegat Bay, New Jersey. Parts of the Flyway in Megalopolis are regularly used by canvasbacks, redheads and scaups, the white-winged scoter, and Canada geese.

Wetlands are essential as feeding and resting places for migrating waterfowl (tidal marshes along seashore and rivers are highly favorable for

[26] Connecticut State Board of Fisheries and Game, *Pheasant Policy,* Hartford, 1957, mimeographed.

[27] Frederick C. Lincoln, *Migration of Birds,* U. S. Dept. of the Interior, Fish and Wildlife Service Circular 16, U. S. Government Printing Office, Washington, D. C., 1950, pp. 53–55.

them), and are also necessary to the survival of more sedentary birds. However, this waterfowl habitat is shrinking in Megalopolis despite the creation of new bird refuges. An extensive new survey of wetlands was completed in 1954,[28] and its findings, compared with those of earlier surveys made in 1906 and 1922, demonstrate *a drastic reduction of Megalopolitan wetlands in quality* (through pollution, management for cranberry production, etc.) *as well as in extent.* Vast stretches of wetlands have disappeared in recent years through drainage (especially in the form of ditching for mosquito control) or through filling for building, highway construction, rubbish dumps, and other purposes.

To combat the shrinkage of wetlands, the U. S. Fish and Wildlife Service has sponsored a policy of acquisitions. In addition, almost every seaboard state has purchased some wetland for wildlife management. Massachusetts, for example, has two important wildlife refuges, at Parker River and Monomoy; Connecticut has bought about 2,000 acres of coastal tidal marshes as reserves for hunting and other forms of recreation. Special techniques have been devised and applied with success, especially in New Jersey: salt marshes are improved for waterfowl by diking, insuring control of the water level; inland ponds are dried up, planted to game food, then inundated again, with the water level controlled. To make better use of such improved ponds in New Jersey, New York, and Pennsylvania, new species of birds have been introduced to supplement the native stock — thus far pintails, gadwalls, and redheads. This dual policy, of acquisition and improvement of existing wetlands on the one hand and creation of new small waterfowl areas on the other, gives excellent results. It has kept enough game along the Megalopolitan section of the Atlantic Flyway so that urbanites can still go duck hunting close to their cities.[29]

---

[28] Samuel P. Shaw and C. Gordon Fredine, *Wetlands of the United States, Their Extent and Their Value to Waterfowl and Other Wildlife*, U. S. Dept. of the Interior, Fish and Wildlife Circular 39, U. S. Government Printing Office, Washington, D. C., 1956. There is also a series of detailed publications covering each of the states. Specialists have pointed out that the U. S. Department of Agriculture, paying subsidies to encourage drainage with the view of increasing agricultural land, is working at cross-purposes with the Department of the Interior, which seeks to protect waterfowl. No drainage of a waterfowl area ought to be undertaken unless it is proved to produce good farmland needed in that region, at low enough cost to make farming economical.

[29] *The New York Times* reported on August 25, 1959, large numbers of herons of various species (the big common egret as well as the blackish, seldom-seen glossy ibis) nesting at the 31-acre sanctuary of State Harbor, New Jersey, adjacent to a growing development of summer residences, about thirty miles south of Atlantic City. Thus this policy also benefits non-game birds such as herons.

Migratory game, constantly crossing the lines between states, is a Federal responsibility. Managing resident game is the business of the states.

Fishing, Fishermen, and Fish

Whereas fishing in inland waters, like hunting, used to be primarily a sport for rural people, now increasing numbers of urbanites indulge in it. From 1941 to 1958 the numbers of fishing licenses issued rose in Massachusetts from 125,000 to 228,000; in Connecticut from 39,000 to 108,000; in New Jersey from 73,000 to 151,000; in Pennsylvania from 391,000 to 687,000. In the whole United States this rise was even steeper, advancing from 8,000,000 in 1941 to 20,000,000 in 1958.[30] In Megalopolis there is also the resource of salt-water fishing — both along the seashore and the so-called "deep-sea fishing" — which has grown very popular, especially with the development of boating. No license is required to fish in the sea, which probably accounts for the slower increase in number of fishing licenses in Megalopolis than in the rest of the United States, and also for the fact that in Megalopolis, from New York State to Virginia, more people buy hunting than fishing licenses. The latter situation is reversed in New England, however, perhaps because there is plenty of good lake fishing in the latter area.[31]

The average fisherman finds his range restricted by posting, just like the average hunter and for the same reasons. Many anglers from the city have no idea of the damage they cause in the field, and too many cases of vandalism have been reported. The state agencies in charge of fishing have tried to persuade landowners to reduce posting, but to little avail. Therefore, just as in the case of hunting they have had to embark on a program of land acquisition or leasing in order to provide anglers with places to fish. In Massachusetts and Connecticut a policy of leasing fishing rights is being abandoned in favor of the purchasing of permanent fishing rights on stream banks.[32]

[30] Data from Clawson, *Statistics on Outdoor Recreation, op. cit.* pp. 142–143, and U. S. Bureau of the Census, *Statistical Abstract of the United States: 1959*, U. S. Government Printing Office, Washington, D. C., 1959, p. 196.

[31] In 1958 the number of paid licenses issued for fishing and hunting respectively (excluding duck stamps) was 228,000 and 126,000 in Massachusetts; 108,000 and 55,000 in Connecticut; 819,000 and 975,000 in New York State; 151,000 and 188,000 in New Jersey; 687,000 and 972,000 in Pennsylvania; and 98,000 and 161,000 in Maryland. In the continental United States there were 20.18 million fishing licenses and 14.76 million hunting licenses. It may perhaps be noteworthy to remark that since hunting is on the whole a more expensive and dangerous sport than inland fishing, it is particularly suited to the more affluent and daring population of Megalopolis, especially outside of thrifty New England.

[32] A report for 1957 of the Massachusetts State Division of Fisheries and Game

Access to the water edge is another problem. Massachusetts law entitles the general public to fish in all ponds that are at least twenty acres in size, but the riparian landowner often posts his land against trespassers and closes the access.

Because the demand for fishing and other water sports has grown so pressing, the public has asked for the use of reservoirs, opening a lasting dispute. The huge needs of the cities for water supply have led to the establishment of impressive reservoirs, as close as possible to the urban centers, and at first glance they would seem to offer great recreational opportunities. But city water must be kept pure, and public health considerations conflict here with recreational activities. It is almost impossible to protect a whole watershed, but the water in the reservoir must be protected, and often it is necessary to acquire and isolate a strip of land (usually planted with evergreens) around the reservoir to prevent its pollution. When subsequent filtration is not practiced, only very limited public use of reservoirs is tolerable. When it is practiced, fishing and boating are sometimes considered possible, although the American Water Works Association opposes fishing in reservoirs altogether. The opening of recreational facilities on the edge of the Compensating Reservoir of Hartford, Connecticut, and on Penacock Lake, near Concord, New Hampshire, has had disappointing results. On the other hand, the Wachusett and Quabbin reservoirs in Massachusetts have been opened to fishing without any serious difficulties, although there has been a great deal of criticism of the policy of the state of Massachusetts on the matter.[33] In New York, state law requires New York City to allow boating and fishing on its reservoirs, subject to "reasonable regulations," and several thousand boating and fishing permits (free of charge) are issued each year.[34]

Once fishing grounds have been provided to satisfy the fisherman *they must be supplied with fish.* Here there must be a differentiation between cold-water and warm-water species, corresponding to two different kinds of fishing. Most anglers in warm waters go after bass, chain pickerel, or pike, for these provide more exciting sport than do panfish (suckers, gold-

(Boston, mimeographed) stated: "The Director was authorized to obtain permanent public fishing rights on streams by purchase or easement where possible, rather than by renewal of leases every five years as is presently done. This procedure will prove to be more economical in the long run, and will insure that such areas will forever be available to fishermen."

[33] See the *Journal of the American Water Works Association,* New York, Vol. 49, No. 9, September 1957. Concerning afforestation around reservoirs see Vol. 38, No. 10, October 1946.

[34] See Annual Reports of the Department of Water Supply, Gas and Electricity of the City of New York; also Theodore De Lo Coffin, "Sanitation of the Croton Watershed," *Water Works Engineering,* Vol. 95, 1942, pp. 1440–1442 and 1462.

shiners, and minnows), which are therefore usually neglected. Thus in warm water predator species are more sought after than are "forage fish," and in the long run this modifies the balance of fish population. In cold water, trout fishing is specially favored.

The seashore, particularly in the bays, also provides desirable fishing. Chesapeake Bay, for example, is rich in migratory species such as shad, and also in sedentary species such as black bass, king fish, flounder, hard head, channel bass, white and yellow perch, sunfish, and eels.

However, both along the seashore and in the rivers the waters and their fish population have been substantially affected by human action.

First, water temperature has warmed up in the rivers. This has been a worldwide trend resulting from deforestation, dam construction, and industrialization, and Megalopolis certainly has been no exception to this rule. In many cases cold-water species have declined or disappeared. There have been a few exceptions, however. For example, the operation of New York City's reservoirs on the upper courses of both branches of the Delaware River involves releasing water to the river, and since this water is drawn from the bottoms of the reservoirs the river has been made cooler downstream. As a result trout, which had disappeared around 1900, flourish again in the Delaware River. Trout are native to Megalopolis and were formerly widespread, but today they are found only where the water is still cold enough.

Second, in the industrial parts of the region water pollution has been and still is heavy, and this depletes fish food and reduces the oxygen content of the water. Many species suffer, especially cold-water fish, which need more oxygen.

Third, dams hamper the travel of migratory species. For instance, dams built on the Merrimack and Connecticut rivers put an end to the salmon and shad runs by 1857. Quite apart from dams, the Atlantic salmon is now entirely extinct in all the rivers in Megalopolis, for the waters are too warm for its taste. The shad, however, has been able to adjust to changing conditions, with man's help (such as the fish elevator built into the Holyoke dam on the Connecticut River), and it is now holding its own in the Connecticut and Hudson rivers and in some Maryland and Pennsylvania rivers.

Fourth, some waters are artificially stocked with fish. The brook trout, once widespread but now eliminated where the waters have become too warm, is very popular with fishermen, and a rising demand for it created a difficult problem for the state fisheries divisions. First they stocked rivers with trout fingerlings, but this method proved inefficient and was discontinued. Attempts at stream improvement proved to be costly and unsatisfactory. Finally the problem was solved, as was that of providing a supply of game, by using mature stock. Now in Megalopolis all possible streams, whether cold or warm, and many ponds are supplied at the beginning of the open season with artificially reared adult trout of legal size and ready to be caught. Because of the unfavorable conditions that prevail in many cases, these trout are given no choice but to be caught or die a natural death within a short time. About 80 per cent of them are caught. This intensive trout fishing has become a simple give-and-take proposition, independent of environmental conditions. State fisheries agencies in Megalopolis maintain large hatcheries, rearing millions of trout annually. New Jersey's state hatchery at Hackettstown is one of the largest in the world. To reduce their costs some of these agencies now stock many streams with brown trout (introduced from Europe and more adaptable) instead of the native brook trout.[35] And Maryland uses large numbers of rainbow trout introduced from the Pacific Coast.

Other species besides trout that have needed restocking are black bass, pickerel, and pike perch. Warm-water fish, too, have been depleted, and the relative abundance of the various species has changed because anglers catch their preferred species, producing the same effects as do "selective cuttings" in the forests.

Because of the large urban population there has come to be a tremendous pressure of hunters and fishermen, which at first resulted in depletion of fish and game. More recently, to keep these sportsmen happy, government agencies have undertaken artificial repopulation of the fishing and hunting grounds with newly introduced or artificially reared species of fish and game. Nowhere, except around a few other large cities, are hunting and fishing so much a product of man's own work.

A Multiple-Purpose Forest Management

Forests are the natural environment of Megalopolis. Study of them has led us to analyze what kind of contact urbanites achieve today with Nature. When they go hunting or fishing they find themselves dealing with a completely unreal world, built up through a great deal of effort and at high cost, to satisfy the yearnings for what have become socially desirable sports. Wildlife and woodlands of today are very different in aspect and are used very differently from what they were before this region became so crowded and wealthy.

A new balance between land uses is gradually being established, in

---

[35] See *Program for 1957 of the Connecticut State Board of Fisheries and Game*, Hartford, 1957. The Pennsylvania Fish Commission has made this change also.

which the forest is a sort of leftover in the landscape and its management stresses the recreational value of the woods. The urban population needs the recreation it can find in the woodlands, and such a concept in management seems necessary. For this reason alone expansion or at least preservation of the forested area is desirable, insofar as the needs of agriculture and urbanization allow. However, in addition to contributing to the decor of living and to the means of recreation, woods benefit the region in various other ways. They provide a good vegetation cover for the soil. Although more research is needed on the interrelations between forest and water, we do know enough about them to use afforestation as a regulator of the flow of water. Woods decrease runoff, even on steep slopes, encouraging the infiltration of water in depth, and they are probably instrumental in maintaining the stability of underground aquifers. In a heavily urbanized region such as Megalopolis water controls are *essential for both water supply and flood protection.* The cities and industries have a huge and growing thirst for water (see pp. 729–735 below). At the same time, since most of the urban settlement developed in early times along bays and navigable rivers, Megalopolis has a serious flood problem, especially on flood plains next to the Piedmont or foothill areas where the runoff from the higher lands is a threat.[36] Forested areas in the Catskills are advantageous for the water supply of New York City by reducing siltation in the reservoirs, and they reduce the threat of floods in the areas downstream from them. In New England, also, many forests protect the watersheds of city reservoirs. Good forest management thus serves the water needs of urban centers.

Without conflicting in any way with the interests of water policy, or in any serious way with those of recreation, better management of woodlands could also *help produce more and better timber than is now the case.* There is a considerable market for saw timber and wood products in Megalopolis, and in time of economic difficulties it may be important to have such a resource at hand locally.

During the recent world war this country did experience severe shortages of lumber, paper and pulp. . . . However, this shortage was not a timber shortage, as subsequent production shows, but solely a manpower and transportation shortage. . . . The transportation aspects of the problem stem from the bad distribution of forests with respect to the centers of use and shipment. This is due in part to the failure to grow trees in New England

[36] Gilbert F. White *et al., Changes in Urban Occupance of Flood Plains in the United States* (University of Chicago, Department of Geography Research Paper No. 57), University of Chicago Press, Chicago, November 1958; also E. A. Colman, *Vegetation and Watershed Management,* The Ronald Press, New York, 1953.

and Lake States where there were once extensive forests. To this extent the shortage was due to mistaken farm policies and to bad forestry practices in the period up to 1900, and to the failure to re-establish the forestry of these regions since that time.[37]

These remarks by Luther Gulick apply perfectly to Megalopolis in 1960. It is important to realize that lumber production for industrial uses is *compatible with both recreation and watershed management*. Some care must be taken to avoid undesirable interferences, but this should not cause trouble. Once they have been well planned, recreation uses do not require much land. Even if they were multiplied significantly, sites for camping, picnics, and sports activities would occupy only a small fraction of the total wooded area of Megalopolis.

To organize these forests for industrial production purposes is, how-ever, no simple question of "management" but, at the present stage of decay, involves reconstituting or restoring the woodlands. The stands are now understocked in commercially desirable species such as pine, black, white, and red oak, yellow poplar, sugar maple. They could be restored through various practices: weedings or release of selected trees, thinnings for saw timber, improvement cuttings (eliminating the *less* desirable trees), and plantings. All these techniques are expensive, require technical knowledge, and produce results only in the long run.

There is, however, no use trying to manage a forest, the stands of which are not properly stocked and of suitable age categories. The preliminary work of restoring must be done first, and as a rule the landowners are not prepared to do this expensive job. They have often a speculative turn of mind and look for immediate returns. They are afraid of taxation and want to get money out of the land, not to put any into it. Generally the system of land taxation, especially the assessment system (general prop-erty tax *ad valorem*), does not encourage sound forest management.[38]

Since privately owned forests predominate in Megalopolis, the problem seems to require improving the technical knowledge of the owners. In this respect the results achieved have been rather disappointing so far. Forestry techniques are difficult to assimilate, and results require persist-ence and time; and the landowners may not have enough time to achieve much results before they retire. Up to now two kinds of efforts have been attempted to improve private woodlands, one based on *regulation*, the other on the creation of *incentives*.

Regulations exist in only a few states. In Maryland, Massachusetts, New

[37] Gulick, *American Forest Policy*, op. cit., p. 133.
[38] U. S. Forest Service, *State Forest Tax Law Digest*, Washington, D. C., 1957.

Hampshire, and New York the law provides for specific regulations to be developed by local boards. These regulations, varying from place to place, are recent, for they have been established since 1945.[39] On the whole their influence has been only slight except in Massachusetts,[40] where "compulsory advice" is required. Most of the regulations set fixed rules, which cannot apply to every particular case, for forestry is a more involved art than most people think, and recipes are not enough. The success in Massachusetts is due largely to the fact that competent advice is adjusted to every particular case.

Most states provide free advice to private forest owners through extension services. Such cooperative forest management services are partially supported by Federal funds. Planting of abandoned land with desirable species, the seedlings being distributed by the state agencies, is very popular but gives poor results. Once planted, the trees are often neglected. In recent years, the *soil bank* program has given new impulse to the planting of trees on formerly farmed land (see above, p. 344). The new Agricultural Conservation Program (A.C.P.) provides Federal cost-sharing for pruning crop trees, release of seedlings from competing vegetation, site preparation for natural reseeding, fencing against livestock depredations, and so forth. This program, operating through the Agricultural Stabilization and Conservation Committees (A.S.C.), is too recent to be judged. It ought to be remembered that forestry needs long and continued efforts to produce results, and in these programs only the cost of the preliminary steps is shared by the government. Subsidy is an important incentive but does not eliminate the need for continued technical advice. Cooperative management programs must be complemented by free "compulsory advice" from well-trained foresters.

Once a cooperative management system is made attractive through free delivery of seedlings, tax exemptions, and the like, a landowner may well be induced to let his woods be supervised by a professional forester. Such arrangements assume that the forest services have a large enough personnel, adequately trained, and that a suitable market can be found for woodland products obtained during the restoration period. These products are largely wood of secondary species left predominating in the stands after

[39] See *Forest Practices Developments in the United States: 1940 to 1955,* Society of American Foresters, Washington, D. C., 1956.

[40] In Massachusetts regulations are based on a "compulsory advice" principle. Before cutting, every landowner *must* notify the State Forest Service, which examines the area and writes out a plan for cutting according to good practices. An inspector verifies compliance after the cut. Most violations occur because of ignorance of the law.

"commercially selective" cuttings. Good forest management should be co-ordinated also with hunting policies. At present the main crop of game obtained in the forests is deer, the overabundance of which hampers the improvement of the stands. It would be worthwhile to help develop species of game that could thrive in the woodlands and provide good shooting without damaging the trees or seedlings much. Some selective species of pheasants would probably do, as they are woodland creatures in other parts of the world.

Men have recently acquired powerful tools for shaping the environment they live in. But to avoid being deceived by their own deeds, they must be careful to keep a certain kind of balance with Nature.[41] The landscape can be managed as a whole to a multiple-use end, but this is not easy to achieve, for old uses and concepts are still projected into the present and the future. In Megalopolis the challenge has been partially met, at the cost of a great deal of money and effort. The average urbanite who goes hunting or fishing seldom realizes what kind of large and involved organization public authorities have had to set up and maintain to make these sports available for him. Large staffs of experts, a whole industry of big farms and hatcheries, constant land acquisition, and a good deal of research are all necessary to organize an artificial environment in which a fragile temporary balance with Nature provides for some of the major recreational needs of the people.

To provide enough for the future may be neither too difficult nor too costly if the general public and responsible government authorities can cooperate to achieve a better management of woodlands and other types of open space. The growing importance of *suburban forestry* is being recognized increasingly by specialists.[42] Public opinion is becoming better aware of the need for conservation and of the intricacy of managing the natural endowment as a lasting resource. However, many people, who find it "natural" to fish trout and shoot game carefully readied for them by government agencies on land acquired for that special purpose, would still resist the principle of government interference in privately owned woodland management. Education of the public is probably the indispensable prerequisite for making Megalopolis a pleasanter place to live in.

[41] See Raymond F. Dasmann, *Environmental Conservation*, John Wiley and Sons, New York, 1959.

[42] See George A. Garratt, "Effects of Land-Use Trends on Forestry Needs and Opportunities," in *Proceedings, Society of American Foresters Meeting: Forest Land Use in Transition, op. cit.*, pp. 9–14; and Henry W. Hicock, "The Suburban Forest," in *Frontiers of Plant Science*, Vol. 9, No. 2, Connecticut Agricultural Experiment Station, New Haven, Conn., 1957, p. 2.

The American forest problem, as Luther Gulick has remarked, "is not in the forests. It is in the character of our people." [43] The Promethean character of Megalopolitan development and of its people becomes quite obvious as one reflects upon what has been done in this region with forests and wildlife. A comprehensive land-use program is urgently needed in the woodlands submitted to the many pressures of Megalopolitan growth. As Gulick has said:

The forests are not just trees. They are timber, water, perhaps climate; they are wildlife habitat, grazing for stock, and recreation for man. They are windbreak, flood break, monotony break. And looking into the future, they will unquestionably become a major raw material and chemical of extraordinary versatility, because, after all, they are renewable, in the magic balance of sunshine and nature.[44]

One wonders how areas so full of worthy functions could ever have been labeled "open space" and treated, in terms of economics, as "abandoned land" or a "leftover" in the landscape. The forest could provide for some of the imperative needs of Megalopolis. The present woodlands still offer abundant green space which must be used with due skill and foresight. The present trends of woodland expansion in this region cannot be projected to the year 2000.

[43] *American Forest Policy, op. cit.,* p. 171.   [44] *Ibid.,* p. 171.

C H A P T E R   8

The Urban Uses of the Land

Most of the land area of Megalopolis is covered with farmland or woodland, the use of which is largely determined, as we have seen in the preceding chapters, by the presence within the region of a large population of urban or suburban character. The way of life of these people, their income, their professions, and the density of the population all play a role. Although the land actually occupied by urban or so-called "special" uses adds up to only a small part of the whole area (probably close to 20 per cent of it by 1960),[1] it holds the vast majority of the people, dwellings, and places of work — that is, all that makes Megalopolis into a huge urban region. The land use is also determined, of course, by the region's relations with the outside world and with other sections of the country.

How the densely occupied, more obviously urbanized parts of Megalopolis are used cannot be fully described in this chapter nor even in one

[1] See above, Chapter 5, p. 234.

volume. These pieces of land, though aggregating no more than 10,000 square miles, house more than thirty million people — one fifth of the American nation, about one tenth of the whole world's manufacturing capacity, and probably close to one fifth of the world's big-business management. For an area of such immense concentration of population and of industrial and commercial activities description of the various local uses of the land would require a great many pages of text and maps. In many respects the details of industrial or residential land use are similar to those of other large urban and industrial centers in America. It may not be very fruitful or indeed worthwhile to go into these land uses in great detail. It is more significant for the purposes of this study to find out what features of land use are characteristic of the region and what trends are developing.

The Nebulous Structure of Megalopolis

The unity of Megalopolis as an urban region was founded on the relative integration in one continuous system of contiguous standard metropolitan areas along the Northeastern seaboard. To these the author has added a few adjacent districts not always classified as "metropolitan," at least not in the 1950 Census. Between and around the urban nuclei is territory classified as metropolitan but rural, or even as altogether nonmetropolitan, and the uses of such territory have been dependent on the push or pull developed by the urban centers. Thus the rapid expansion of the area devoted to urban uses of the land has been a prime factor in imposing urbanization as the essential force that directs land use throughout the whole region. How it has progressed in the recent past may be ascertained by scrutinizing a few maps of population density. The generalized map of density by minor civil divisions for 1940 (Fig. 121) shows massive concentration in a few large noncontiguous blocks of land in which the density was everywhere more than 150 per square mile and often more than 500. Two of these blocks are especially impressive — one between Massachusetts and Narragansett bays (the Boston-Providence complex), the second around New York City. Three other blocks are significant, though more modest in size — the area along the tidal Delaware (from Trenton, New Jersey, to Wilmington, Delaware), the area around Baltimore, and the area around Washington, D. C. Much smaller areas of obviously urban concentration are found scattered through Massachusetts, Connecticut, and eastern Pennsylvania. Their dispersal outlines the actual frame of Megalopolis.

The density of population is measured on the basis of administrative

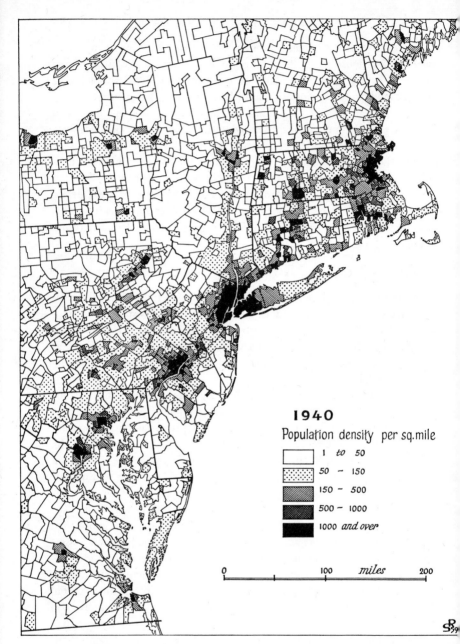

1940

Population density per sq. mile

	1 *to* 50
	50 – 150
	150 – 500
	500 – 1000
	1000 *and over*

0   100   *miles*   200

FIG. 121. Compare this distribution of the density of population by minor civil divisions in 1940 with the same for 1950 on Fig. 122 and for 1960 on Fig. 1 (p. 6).

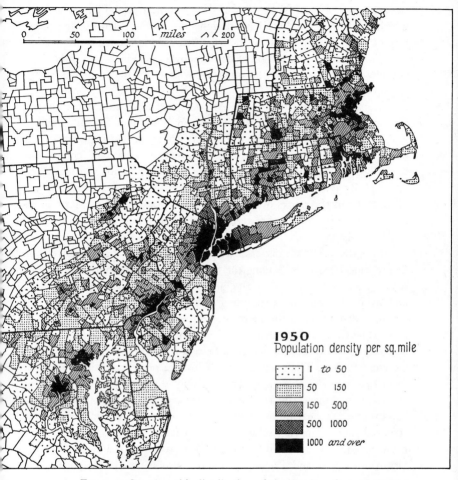

1950
Population density per sq. mile

1 to 50
50   150
150   500
500   1000
1000 and over

FIG. 122. Compare this distribution of the density of population by minor civil divisions in 1950 with the same for 1940 on Fig. 121 and for 1960 on Fig. 1 (p. 6).

subdivisions, and the people are counted where they live, not where they work. The statistics may therefore give a misleading picture as to the nature of the landscape. Within a New England township an area thoroughly built up with industrial plants may appear to be not much more populated than wooded suburban areas peppered with scattered residences, such as, for instance, the area south of Lowell, Massachusetts, (the land use of which is shown for 1950 on Fig. 67, p. 233).

What population changes were occurring throughout Megalopolis between 1930 and 1950 is demonstrated on another map (Fig. 73, p. 248), which emphasizes interurban and peripheral growth of density, and therefore of urban land uses, along the axial belt joining the main historic nuclei. The resulting distribution of densities by 1950 (Fig. 122) testified to a considerable expansion of the territory with more than 150 inhabitants per square mile. Along the axial belt, a ribbon of this density had become practically continuous from Cape Ann to Alexandria, except for narrow interruptions in the northeastern corner of Maryland. For all practical purposes the suburbs of Baltimore and Washington had grown together enough to be counted after 1950 as one great urban system, comparable to the Boston-Providence complex or the Delaware complex around Philadelphia. By means of a narrow neck of high density following the axis of U. S. I and the tracks of the Pennsylvania Railroad, the latter had almost joined with the northeastern part of New Jersey that gravitates towards Manhattan.

During the 1950's the dispersal went on with greater speed and freedom than during the 1940's. Among the factors that led the sprawl to develop were better highways, more cars, and more families with small children looking for homes with a suburban setting. The detailed map of density for 1960 demonstrates the increasing dispersal of residences (see Fig. 1, p. 6). The Census taken in 1960 showed for New York City and several neighboring counties in New York State a migration to the periphery in clear-cut fashion. The great city itself lost 1.4 per cent of its population from 1950 to 1960; of its five boroughs only the more peripheral Queens and Richmond grew (by 16.7 and 15.9 per cent respectively), while Manhattan was the heaviest loser (−13.4 per cent). Great increases were achieved by the outlying suburbs on Long Island (where Nassau County grew by 93.3 per cent and Suffolk by 141.5 per cent), and north of the city Westchester and Rockland counties also counted substantial gains (29.3 and 53.2 per cent).[2]

The growth of the population of New Jersey by counties from 1950 to 1960 (see Fig. 9, p. 41) showed a sharp increase for the whole state. Few places added less than 20 per cent to their 1950 population, most of these being in the vicinity of large urban centers or in more dispersed areas that were already densely built up before 1950. Through most of Megalopolis, however, the areas where the more massive increases have taken place on

[2] U. S. Bureau of the Census, *1960 Census of Population, Advance Reports*, PC(A2)–34, Washington, D. C., March 1961.

Opposite FIG. 123. Percentage change in population of continental United States by counties, 1940–50. *Courtesy of the U. S. Bureau of the Census*

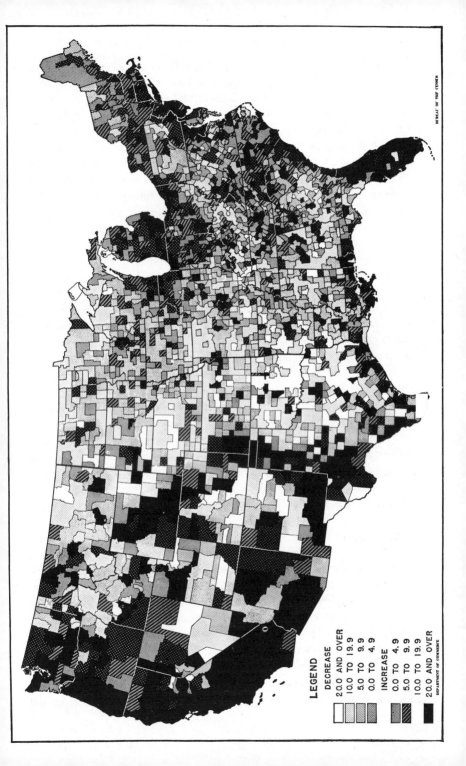

LEGEND

DECREASE

20.0 AND OVER
10.0 TO 19.9
5.0 TO 9.9
0.0 TO 4.9

INCREASE

0.0 TO 4.9
5.0 TO 9.9
10.0 TO 19.9
20.0 AND OVER

DEPARTMENT OF COMMERCE

BUREAU OF THE CENSUS

substantial acreages seem to be located largely on the suburban periphery of the main nuclei or along the main axial belt. It was on the outer reaches of New York's suburbia in Long Island that Levittown, New York, arose, and it was along the main axis between Trenton and Philadelphia that Levittown, Pennsylvania, and Fairless Hills were built, both linked to the large steel plants on the banks of the Delaware River below its falls. Similar trends can be observed along the main roads linking Baltimore and Washington, or in the outer ring of Washington's suburbs. Farther away from the old nuclei and from the axial belt, the filling in of more or less rural territory proceeded during the 1950's by scattered growth along the roads and around the ponds and creeks, rather than by massive advances of an urbanized front.

The scattering of buildings for various purposes along the roads has taken on such magnitude and frequency throughout most of Megalopolis that one seldom loses sight of buildings except on the landscaped parkways and turnpikes or inside public parks and forests. This was true by 1960 not only of the densely settled parts of Massachusetts and Connecticut (Figs. 67, 68, and 69, pp. 233, 235, 238) but also in the relatively rural parts of southern Megalopolis (see the 1960 densities on Fig. 124).

Residences, obviously, did not scatter alone. The Megalopolitan sprawl came partly because residences followed industrial or commercial establishments out of old urban territory, and partly because retail and wholesale trade establishments followed their customers toward new residential areas. However, as the location of either residences or industries required well-organized means of *access*, the dispersal remained dependent on the network of highways. In this era of the automobile it has been much easier to decentralize and scatter people as well as trade and light industry than it was previously, when the attraction of the rail lines or major waterways was stronger.

The maps of distribution of urban uses of the land in Megalopolis have thus been taking on an increasingly *nebulous* character. This has been fostered by the desire of many people to have their residences in rural landscapes; by the vogue of the suburban way of life among certain categories of urbanites; and by the advantages of "decentralized" locations for new industrial or even bureaucratic establishments. The functions of the neatly delimited "downtowns" and "uptowns" of the past have now begun to mingle in disconcerting fashion with farming, woodlands, or just highly populated suburbs.

The whole process, one might observe, has not been for the past fifteen years a monopoly or even a specialty of Megalopolis. Such urban and

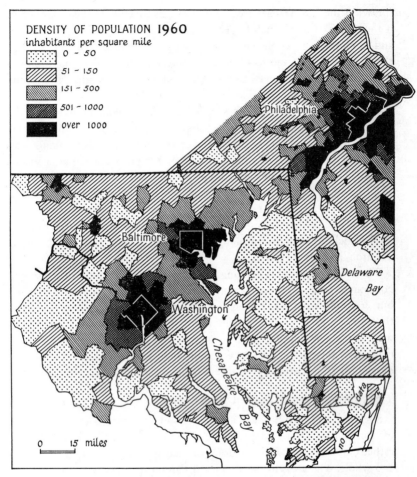

FIG. 124. Density of population in 1960 by minor civil divisions in the southern part of Megalopolis. Compare with the situation in 1950 on Figs. 14 and 15 (pp. 60, 62).

suburban sprawl, leading to many a new metropolis with nebulous structure, can be found in various parts of the United States from the San
Francisco Bay area to Florida's Gold Coast. In fact, many people believe
that the most spectacular case has developed around Los Angeles, and so
it might seem on casual inspection. The arid, barren lands in southern California make every group of buildings stand out boldly in the landscape,
while much of the Megalopolitan suburban sprawl is shielded from sight
by the wooded nature of the area. But those who are so impressed by the

sprawl of the Los Angeles area might perhaps tone down their enthusiasm if they realized how much larger the Megalopolitan sprawl is in territory and in number of people, and how much more complicated and costly is the organization of means of access to the hub of Manhattan, to downtown Philadelphia, or even to the center of Washington than it is in the case of Los Angeles.[3]

This phenomenon, sometimes called the "metropolitanization" of the United States, has developed in Megalopolis on a scale that is unique so far in the nation and in the world, and over vast areas there is an almost *colloidal* interpenetration of urban and rural that gives the region a special quality. Despite this interpenetration, Megalopolis has also continued to build up its several enormous nuclei of densely occupied, congested central cities. Skylines have been changing more rapidly than ever, not only on the island of Manhattan but also in the old downtown business districts of Philadelphia and Boston and in the much smaller cities of Newark, Trenton, and New Haven.

The suburban sprawl, fanning out horizontally, at times in dense and continuous formations and at times as a sparse dispersal, has not prevented but, it would seem, has merely accompanied and perhaps complemented the vertical rise in the central districts of the old urban cores. These various trends, while displacing many people and organizations and fostering many new fortunes in the real estate business, have also caused the pattern of each metropolis to acquire a new form, a rather *nebulous structure*.

The Morphology of These Urban Growths

Such a many-sided process of urbanization has assumed a wide diversity of forms throughout Megalopolis. The general trends have followed rather closely the general evolution of metropolitan growth in the nation as a whole. The areas in the vicinity of large urban centers and along the historical axial belt from Boston to Washington have been increasing in population and activities more rapidly, at least since 1900, than the outlying areas of Megalopolis, just as metropolitan areas in general have grown at a faster pace than the rest of the United States. And the suburban rings have been growing in all respects more rapidly than the old

[3] In 1950 the average population density of Los Angeles County was 1,020 inhabitants per square mile, while that of neighboring and smaller Orange County was 277. The average for the metropolitan area stood at 900. In the New York–Northeastern New Jersey Standard Metropolitan Area the average density was 3,278; in the Philadelphia area, 1,034; in the Boston area, 3,078; in the Providence area, 1,492; and the central cores were more crowded in each of these and in other metropolitan areas of Megalopolis than was the core of Los Angeles.

urban cores. Here again Megalopolis follows the national trend as described by Donald J. Bogue:

> Since 1900, a remarkable reversal in the pattern of growth within S.M.A.'s [standard metropolitan areas] has taken place. In 1900–10, the central cities had higher growth rates than the metropolitan rings, but in 1940–50 the rings were growing at a much more rapid rate than central cities. This change appears to have taken place about 1920 . . . The advent at that time of the use of automobiles for commuting marks the beginning of the more extended pattern of settlement around metropolitan centers which has now become an outstanding characteristic of population distribution. About 11 percent of the total population of principal S.M.A.'s was living in the metropolitan ring outside central cities in 1900. By 1950, this proportion had risen to 24 percent.[4]

The older metropolitan areas in the country, that is, those of Megalopolis, led the way, and their suburban rings began growing more rapidly than the central cities before this tendency developed in smaller and newer metropolitan units (see Table 17). The early beginning of this evolution in Megalopolis reflects the greater congestion of the central cores there. Of the many factors that have contributed to this congestion some are perhaps regrettable, such as the high population density and the greater age and therefore obsolescence of housing, but others testify to the resilience of the old cores. For example, there must be economic opportunity and growth in a core city to attract more people to work or to live in it, and there must be good organization of access to the central city from the outside. Many people who have moved their residences out to the suburbs have continued to work in town; others who do not work in the city still take advantage of its nearness to profit by the commercial, entertainment, and social facilities it offers.

To be successful a city must have a well-organized network of transportation and communication facilities, making it easily accessible from various directions. How could it otherwise preserve any "centrality," remain a "central city," even if only on a modest regional scale? This organization of good relations with its environs is what makes a city grow in terms of the activities located within it, but at the same time it may cause the city's nighttime population to decline or remain stabilized while the suburbs around it and even its satellite communities increase much more rapidly in population as recorded by the Censuses.

While a good deal of the explosive quality of suburban sprawl after 1920 can be attributed to the growing use of automobiles, in Megalopolis connections between central city and suburbs or satellite towns had been

[4] Donald J. Bogue, *Population Growth in Standard Metropolitan Areas 1900–1950*, Housing and Home Finance Agency, Washington, D. C., December 1953, p. 18.

Table 17
Rates of Growth of Standard Metropolitan Areas in Megalopolis, 1900–1950

Standard Metropolitan Area	Population 1950	Percentage Increase or Decrease					
		'40–'50	'30–'40	'20–'30	'10–'20	'00–'10	1900–1950
Manchester, N. H.	156,987	8.4	3.4	3.4	7.5	11.9	39.4
Central city	82,732	6.5	1.1	-2.0	11.9	22.9	45.2
Suburbs	74,255	10.5	6.1	10.9	2.0	0.6	33.4
Boston, Mass.	2,875,876	8.3	1.7	12.8	14.3	20.1	70.6
Central cities (Boston, Lawrence, Lowell)	979,229	2.4	-1.0	1.2	10.7	20.1	36.3
Suburbs	1,896,647	11.6	3.3	21.0	17.0	20.2	96.1
Brockton, Mass.	189,468	12.2	4.0	3.4	8.8	26.6	66.2
Central city	62,860	0.8	-2.3	-3.7	16.5	42.0	56.9
Suburbs	126,608	18.9	8.1	8.6	3.7	18.3	71.3
Worcester, Mass.	546,401	8.3	2.7	7.9	13.9	15.2	57.5
Central city	203,486	5.1	-0.8	8.7	23.1	23.3	71.8
Suburbs	342,915	10.3	5.0	7.5	8.6	11.0	50.0
Fall River, Mass.	381,569	4.6	0	1.6	12.7	26.4	51.4
Central cities (Fall River, New Bedford)	221,152	-2.0	-0.9	-5.7	11.9	29.1	32.2
Suburbs	160,417	15.5	1.6	16.6	14.3	58.6	12.1
Pittsfield, Mass.	132,966	8.7	1.3	6.8	7.4	10.0	39.0
Central city	53,348	7.4	0	18.9	30.0	47.6	145.1
Suburbs	79,618	9.7	2.2	-0.3	-2.6	-1.0	7.7
Springfield, Mass.	455,565	12.6	-0.9	10.4	25.5	25.7	94.3
Central cities (Springfield, Holyoke)	217,060	6.8	-1.5	8.8	29.4	36.1	101.4
Suburbs	238,505	18.5	-0.3	12.1	21.6	16.9	88.3
Hartford, Conn.	539,661	19.9	6.9	25.3	34.3	28.0	176.1
Central cities (Hartford, New Britain, Bristol)	287,084	8.3	1.7	19.6	43.1	35.9	156.1
Suburbs	252,577	36.5	15.3	35.9	20.7	17.3	203.0

New Haven, Conn.	545,784	12.7	4.5	11.6	23.1	25.3	102.8
Central cities (New Haven, Waterbury)	268,920	3.5	−1.0	3.3	23.0	34.4	74.8
Suburbs	276,864	23.4	11.7	24.8	23.3	13.2	140.2
Bridgeport, Conn.	504,342	20.5	8.2	20.5	30.8	33.2	173.8
Central cities (Bridgeport, Stamford, Norwalk)	282,462	20.2	2.5	11.0	53.9	44.1	203.3
Suburbs	221,880	20.9	16.4	37.6	3.0	22.1	143.6
Providence, R. I.	681,815	7.5	2.9	14.9	12.2	28.7	83.4
Central city	248,674	−1.9	0.2	6.5	5.9	27.8	41.6
Suburbs	433,141	13.8	4.7	21.6	17.7	29.5	120.8
Albany, N. Y.	514,490	10.5	1.9	11.8	6.4	15.0	54.0
Central cities (Albany, Troy)	299,091	3.7	−2.5	8.0	9.7	34.0	60.4
Suburbs	215,399	21.5	10.1	19.6	0.2	−9.0	45.9
New York–Northeastern N. J.	12,911,994	10.7	7.4	27.9	20.5	39.6	155.7
Central cities (N.Y.C., Jersey City, Newark)	8,629,750	5.4	6.5	21.4	17.7	38.4	121.9
Suburbs	4,282,244	23.2	9.6	46.9	29.5	43.8	269.5
Trenton, N. J.	229,781	16.5	5.4	17.1	27.2	31.8	140.9
Central city	128,009	2.7	1.1	3.4	23.2	32.1	74.6
Suburbs	101,772	40.1	13.8	57.1	40.7	30.8	361.4
Atlantic City, N. J.	132,399	6.7	−0.6	48.8	16.7	54.9	185.3
Central city	61,657	−3.8	−3.2	30.6	9.9	65.8	121.5
Suburbs	70,742	18.0	2.3	76.5	29.0	38.7	281.1
Wilmington, Del.	268,387	21.0	12.1	7.1	23.1	11.1	98.5
Central city	110,356	−1.9	5.5	−3.2	26.0	14.3	44.2
Suburbs	158,031	44.5	19.8	22.3	18.9	6.9	169.1
Reading, Pa.	255,740	5.7	4.4	15.4	9.6	14.8	60.2
Central city	109,320	−1.1	−0.5	3.1	12.2	21.7	38.4
Suburbs	146,420	11.5	8.9	29.5	6.8	8.1	81.5
Scranton, Pa.	257,396	−14.6	−2.9	8.4	10.3	33.9	32.8
Central city	125,536	−10.6	−2.1	4.1	6.1	27.3	23.0
Suburbs	131,860	−18.0	−3.7	12.4	14.5	41.3	43.6

Table 17 (continued)

Standard Metropolitan Area	Population 1950	Percentage Increase or Decrease					
		'40–'50	'30–'40	'20–'30	'10–'20	'00–'10	1900–1950
Wilkes-Barre, Pa.	392,241	−11.2	−0.8	13.8	13.9	33.5	52.6
Central cities (Wilkes-Barre, Hazelton)	112,317	−9.6	0.7	16.3	14.6	40.3	70.3
Suburbs	279,924	−11.8	−1.4	12.9	13.7	31.1	46.4
Harrisburg, Pa.	292,241	15.9	8.0	10.3	11.0	15.7	77.3
Central city	89,544	6.7	4.4	5.8	18.3	27.9	78.5
Suburbs	202,697	20.4	9.9	12.8	7.4	10.3	76.8
Allentown, Pa.	437,824	10.4	1.3	12.9	19.7	25.2	89.2
Central cities (Allentown, Bethlehem, Easton)	208,728	10.4	2.2	17.3	69.0	37.3	207.2
Suburbs	229,096	10.3	0.5	9.3	−3.8	20.2	40.2
Philadelphia, Pa.	3,671,048	14.7	2.0	15.6	19.7	19.9	94.0
Central city	2,071,605	7.3	−1.0	7.0	17.7	19.7	60.1
Suburbs	1,599,443	26.1	6.9	33.2	23.8	20.2	167.3
Lancaster, Pa.	234,717	10.5	7.9	13.3	4.1	4.9	47.4
Central city	63,774	4.0	2.3	12.8	12.5	13.9	53.8
Suburbs	170,943	13.1	10.4	13.5	0.7	1.7	45.1
York, Pa.	202,737	13.9	6.5	15.6	5.9	17.2	74.2
Central city	59,953	5.7	2.6	16.3	6.2	32.8	77.9
Suburbs	142,784	17.7	17.7	15.3	5.8	10.8	72.6
Baltimore, Md.	1,337,373	23.5	10.0	15.6	18.3	12.7	109.2
Central city	949,708	10.5	6.7	9.7	31.4[a]	9.7	86.6
Suburbs	387,665	72.9	24.7	52.0	−27.0[a]	24.2	197.3
Washington, D. C.	1,464,089	51.3	44.0	17.5	28.4	17.6	286.7
Central city	802,178	21.0	36.2	11.3	32.2	18.8	187.8
Suburbs	661,911	117.1	64.5	38.0	17.5	14.5	562.7

Source: Donald J. Bogue, *Population Growth in Standard Metropolitan Areas 1900–1950*, Housing and Home Finance Agency, Washington, D. C., December 1953, pp. 61–71.

[a] The unusually large percentage of increase for Baltimore in the decade 1910–20 and the accompanying decrease in population in its suburbs reflect the city's annexation of extensive suburban areas on June 1, 1918.

started much earlier, even before the railroad era. Around 1800 it was already common, when comparing the populations and the metropolitan role of New York City and Philadelphia, to count with the latter its suburbs, the small towns that were later linked with the central city by the "main line" of the Pennsylvania Railroad. To Philadelphia the "main-line families" meant something similar to what the society of Long Island or Westchester estates meant to New York.

A distinguished European, visiting the United States in 1912–13, was deeply impressed by the marked sprawling of American cities:

In America the city has spread out with heretofore unknown proportions . . . The American city has a transportation apparatus that makes it possible to specialize its various wards, to separate the "town" of business from the "town" of the *home*, to place between them vast parks, to keep the countryside within itself. "The locomotive," Anthony Trollope wrote half a century ago, "is here a domestic animal." What would he say nowadays? Swarming all around, indefinitely expanding its suburban districts, the city is the most perfect expression of Americanism.[5]

We may ask in the same vein: what would this author have said today, after another half century has elapsed? His prognosis certainly appears even more correct in 1960 than it must have seemed in 1912. It reminds us who live in the automobile age that Megalopolis knew metropolitan sprawl before the automobile's advent.[6] As seen in Table 17, in the New York–Northeastern New Jersey Standard Metropolitan Area the three central cities increased by 38.4 per cent from 1900 to 1910 and by 17.7 per cent in 1910–20, while the suburban ring grew by 43.8 and 29.5 per cent in these two intercensal periods; the disparity of the rate widened, of course, in the 1920's (21.4 and 46.9), was reduced through the depressed 1930's, but increased in the 1940's and, as far as we can tell, to an even greater degree in the 1950's. In the Philadelphia, Boston, and Providence metropolitan areas the rate of increase of the suburban ring was only slightly above that of the central city in the 1900's, while in Fall River, Scranton, and Baltimore it was quite marked. In other cities this more rapid growth of the suburbs did not begin until a later decade, but it is now characteristic of most of the standard metropolitan areas in Megalopolis, and indeed in the country as a whole.

[5] Paul Vidal de la Blache, *Principes de Géographie Humaine*, Librairie Armand Colin, Paris, 1921. This is a posthumous work, the author having died in 1917. The quotation, in our own translation from the French, is from the unfinished fragments annexed to the book, p. 295.

[6] In fact, Vidal de la Blache mentions Chicago and St. Louis, as well as New York, Philadelphia, and Boston, on the page from which the above quotation was taken.

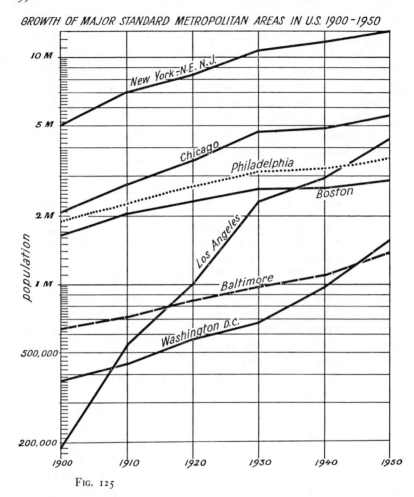

GROWTH OF MAJOR STANDARD METROPOLITAN AREAS IN U.S. 1900-1950

FIG. 125

The growth of the suburban rings has continued at an increased pace through the 1950's. Even before the publication and analysis of detailed data gathered by the 1960 Census, many records, observations, and even counts have demonstrated this. An approximate evaluation made by the Bureau of the Census in 1956 estimated that 85 per cent of the increase that took place in the civilian population of the United States between 1950 and 1956 went to the standard metropolitan areas (in their limits as defined in 1950). While this meant a *rate of increase* of 14.8 per cent for the country's metropolitan population, that rate had been only 4.7 per cent for the central cities but 29.3 per cent for the suburban rings; and within those rings the urban areas (as defined in 1950) had increased by

17 per cent and the "rural" areas by 55.8 per cent. There can be no doubt that the suburban sprawl rolled on through the 1950's.[7]

The more rapid growth of the suburbs did not result only from the shift of former central-city residents to new homes in greener pastures. In fact, had such a migration been the essence of the whole process of metropolitan growth, the central cities would have been emptied at a much quicker pace than has been the case. The speed of population growth in the suburbs indicates, in Megalopolis as well as in the rest of the country, that *most of the newcomers to the suburbs have come from outside the metropolitan area*. Exactly how many of them there have been and from how far away they have come we do not know. However, we can gather some indications about their origins from statistical data available on interstate migration,[8] and we may deduce a little more from the characteristics of each metropolis. It can thus be logically inferred that the Washington metropolitan area, because of its role as the national capital, will draw from the entire United States to a greater degree than will any other sector of Megalopolis. The New York metropolitan area may be expected to rank second in this respect, because of its size and its role as the major financial and commercial hub of the continent. In other metropolitan areas the mixture may not have been as diversified, but there is no doubt that natural increase within a large metropolitan area could not be responsible alone for the population growth.[9]

The days of the frontier may have passed, but metropolitan sprawl has

---

[7] See U. S. Bureau of the Census, *Current Population Reports, Population Characteristics*, Series P-20, No. 71, Washington, D. C., Dec. 7, 1956; see also the comments in Donald J. Bogue, *The Population of the United States*, The Free Press, Glencoe, Ill., 1959, pp. 42–52. Projections for the future on the basis of the 1900–1956 data are offered in Jerome P. Pickard, *Metropolitization of the United States*, Research Monograph 2, Urban Land Institute, Washington, D. C., 1959.

[8] See the graphs of Figs. 54a to c and 125, pp. 192–193 and 398, and the comments about them in Chapter 4, for some general indications.

[9] The City Planning Commission of New York City estimated in 1951 (as reported in *The New York Times*, Aug. 6, 1951) that during the 1940–50 intercensal period the city's net gain in population from excess of births over deaths would have amounted to 580,000. In actual fact its gain was only 445,000, for a massive out-migration of 750,000 and an in-migration of only 615,000 left a negative balance of 135,000 from migration movements into and out of the city. Probably most of the out-migration was to the suburbs, but some of it may have gone farther – to the Washington metropolitan area, which grew so rapidly in the 1940's, to the army, and elsewhere. According to calculations of the Regional Plan Association (see its *Bulletin*, No. 78, June, 1957) the entire metropolitan region of New York (which by the Regional Plan's definition includes twenty-two counties in three states) had a natural increase in 1940–50 of a little more than 2 million and a net in-migration increase of about 800,000. Comparison of these figures with those for New York City indicates clearly that a good deal of the population growth in the suburbs must have come from other sources than migration out of the central city.

become in several respects the modern version of the frontier, and the American people still show great mobility. It has been estimated recently that one out of every five Americans moves during a year — a high mobility rate. From this it would appear that there must be a good deal of moving from one metropolitan area to another, in addition to the migrations from the central cities to the suburbs and from nonmetropolitan territory into metropolitan areas.

The importance of suburban sprawl may be measured not only by population figures but also by the distribution of increase in retail trade sales. On a map showing the rate of this increase from 1948 to 1958 for the counties in and immediately around Megalopolis the peripheral growth of the main metropolitan conglomerations is clearly shown (Fig. 157, p. 508). The growth of retail trade has been made visible in the landscape by the rise of large shopping centers, many of which include branches of department stores from the central cities. These establishments take space, all the more so as they need generous parking areas, and they provide employment.

For what the Census of Business calls the "selected service trades," the distribution of receipts in 1954 (Fig. 160, p. 513) showed a definite emphasis on the more metropolitanized counties, and also, of course, on the major central cities, which still hold the greatest concentrations of people and of business. Between residences and establishments of retailing and special servicing a mutual attraction develops in obvious sequence: trade and services follow the migrations of residences and then, by creating more employment in the residential areas or in their vicinity, they cause more people to settle in that general area. Until recently manufacturing and such commercial activities as wholesale trade and transportation were held to be the essential job providers in urban areas. This is still true of the central cities and their more industrial satellites, especially if office work is added to the categories of employment mentioned above. However, the fields of employment more directly in touch with the consumer cannot be disregarded nowadays. In a suburban but still industrialized section such as Nassau County, on Long Island, manufacturing occupied some 69,000 persons in 1954, the selected service trades 17,000, and retail trade 52,600, the two latter together thus employing almost exactly as many as manufacturing. In heavily industrialized and urbanized Union County, New Jersey, retail trade employed 24,700 people in 1954, the selected service trades 11,000, and manufacturing 81,000. Situated in the axial belt, on the main line from New York to Philadelphia, Union is much more heavily industrialized than the more outlying Nassau County, and yet even there dealing with the consumer involves a substantial part of the labor force.

Manufacturing has thus been a prime factor in determining suburban densities. In a country and a period of generalized motorization and well-organized routes of access, industry did not need to go to the very heart of the labor market and yet when selecting a new plant site it could not afford to move out of easy commuting range of prospective workers. Management had to take various other criteria into consideration when choosing locations, such as accessibility to and from markets and sources of supply, taxation, availability of large enough tracts of land that are not too expensive, labor relations, and, for certain kinds of manufacturing, specially skilled personnel. Most of these criteria usually work together to favor some location not far from at least one large city, and preferably close to and therefore between two or more larger urban nuclei. Thus the extraordinary industrial concentration of the axial belt of Megalopolis has grown. The more division of labor a manufacturing process involves, favoring a contractual structure, with an involved pyramid of subcontracting factories or firms, the more the factors of transportation facilities and sometimes of proximity weigh heavily in the choice of location.[10]

Employment in manufacturing is still heavily concentrated in the region's main central belt, because it has been better equipped for such purposes for a longer time. It is concentrated in especially large numbers in the major cities (with the exception of Washington, D. C.) and in their immediate vicinities, except in New England, particularly in eastern Massachusetts (Fig. 137, p. 457), where for historical reasons it is more widespread. In the years 1939–54, however, the trend of evolution has been rather to get away from the older agglomerations, at least in terms of increase percentagewise (Fig. 138, p. 459). This trend has meant consolidation and widening of the axial belt, some shifting of manufacturing southward within Megalopolis, and some shifting northward from the already heavily crowded Philadelphia–New York City axial belt.

On the whole, outside the more fully urbanized areas high residential densities often coincide in Megalopolis with a higher proportion of manufacturing workers in the labor force (Fig. 126). This is to be expected. As we look at the pattern of these relationships on the map we are still re-

[10] The factors of industrial location come into this study at several stages of the analysis and must be considered from various angles. The brief remarks in this chapter are therefore complemented in other passages, especially in Chapter 5 above and Chapter 10 below. See also National Resources Planning Board, *Industrial Location and National Resources*, Washington, D. C., December 1942; and for a recent case study, James B. Kenyon, *Industrial Localization and Metropolitan Growth: The Paterson-Passaic District*, University of Chicago (Department of Geography Research Paper No. 67), Chicago, 1960.

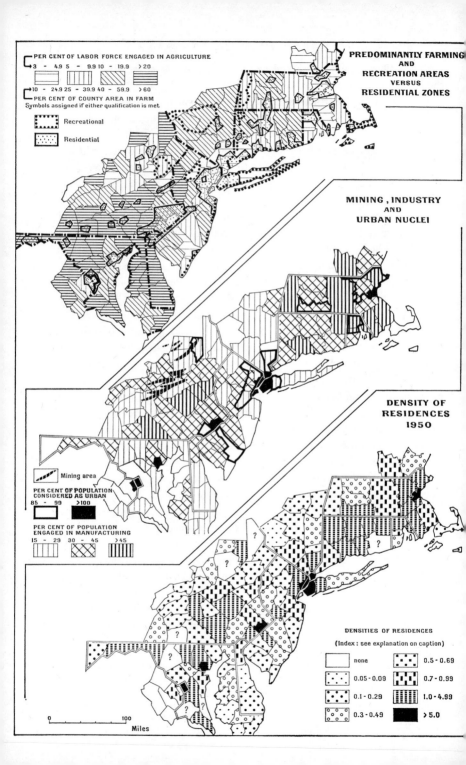

PER CENT OF LABOR FORCE ENGAGED IN AGRICULTURE

3 - 4.9   5 - 9.9   10 - 19.9   >20

10 - 24.9   25 - 39.9   40 - 59.9   >60

PER CENT OF COUNTY AREA IN FARM
Symbols assigned if either qualification is met

Recreational

Residential

PREDOMINANTLY FARMING
AND
RECREATION AREAS
VERSUS
RESIDENTIAL ZONES

MINING , INDUSTRY
AND
URBAN NUCLEI

DENSITY OF
RESIDENCES
1950

Mining area

PER CENT OF POPULATION
CONSIDERED AS URBAN

85 - 99   >100

PER CENT OF POPULATION
ENGAGED IN MANUFACTURING

15 - 29   30 - 45   >45

DENSITIES OF RESIDENCES

(Index : see explanation on caption)

none   0.5 - 0.69

0.05 - 0.09   0.7 - 0.99

0.1 - 0.29   1.0 - 4.99

0.3 - 0.49   >5.0

0   100
Miles

minded that the great numbers of manufacturing workers are in the highly urbanized counties, where they do not, nevertheless, account for a majority in the labor force. Modern urbanization and suburbanization in Megalopolis do not entirely depend on nor develop from manufacturing activities. Although these industries are very important both to the prosperity of Megalopolis and to the distribution of people within it, there are various other activities that share, with increasing responsibility, in determining the direction and characteristics of the metropolitan sprawl.

Thus the seaboard metropolis explodes in a great many ways. From the overcrowded central city some population spills over, scattering over a radius widened by the ease of circulation through the area. This same ease of movement induces newcomers, who have come from distant points to work in the central city, to settle in the outer suburban ring. Other factors bring more industrial and commercial establishments to the suburban districts. Thus broad dispersal goes on, appropriating more and more land for urban or special uses and thickening the urban character of the region. In describing the various aspects of the dispersal we have already mentioned and sometimes analyzed the forces at play, for in such a complex process one can hardly describe the "hows" without touching upon some of the "whys." Once it is realized that land is in relatively scarce supply, particularly as it is desirable to keep a good part of it green, either in farms or in forests, the question arises as to *why so many people and factories move out of the more crowded section.* Is there really no space left for them there, or are they moving away from undesirable obsolescence in the areas that were first urbanized?

The Process of Obsolescence

Obsolescence in buildings, whether homes, factories, or offices, is a very complex and largely subjective notion. Whether a given building is obsolescent now for its current use depends on the investment capability of its owner, on the taste of the occupant, and on the existing possibilities for replacing the present building with a new one that is

Opposite FIG. 126. Specialization of various areas within Megalopolis. The data were taken from U. S. Bureau of the Census, *County and City Data Book: 1952, A Supplement to the Statistical Abstract of the United States,* and used as indicated in the legends on the maps. The index of density of residence (lower map) was calculated as follows:

$$\text{Index} = \frac{\text{occupied dwelling units} - \text{commercial farm units}}{\text{land area of county} - (\text{area in farms} + \text{woodland area})}$$

more profitable or more fashionable. In an affluent society, obsolescence of buildings becomes a matter of fashion as much as of cost of maintenance. Thus a building may be considered less desirable either because the material necessities of maintaining it have grown too cumbersome or because it has gone out of fashion — in terms of its outside appearance, its internal layout, the personnel it requires, or its neighborhood.

So many factors are thus at work in a rapidly changing and prosperous community to cause the obsolescence of buildings that the very physical condition of the structure itself and of its basic equipment is seldom a primary criterion of obsolescence. A much-deteriorated building may be worth full repair and refitting for new use if its internal layout meets the requirements developing in its neighborhood at the time. Such restorations in previously blighted sections of large cities have occurred in Sutton Place and Washington Mews in Manhattan, and in Georgetown in the District of Columbia; and in similar fashion some old farms have been converted to fashionable suburban residences or summer homes.

On the other hand the social obsolescence of a neighborhood may often cause the physical deterioration of its buildings to progress at a faster rate than would otherwise be expected, because maintenance costs are cut and less care is given to upkeep. Urban territory in Megalopolis has been expanding very rapidly for the past century, and during the last half century suburban sprawl has progressed with increased impetus. Since this has been also a time of great technological progress and rather general prosperity, except for the 1930's, the social and economic factors determining desirability of various locations for either residential or commercial uses have been undergoing rapid change, causing many and frequent shifts in the patterns of land use.

Studies of obsolescence in urban buildings have usually been devoted to dwellings and have concerned themselves with the grave social problems of slums, the essential element of blight on the urban landscape and community. A great deal of very useful literature has been published in America on these problems of slums and urban blight. They are basic problems and should be given first priority whenever urban renewal is undertaken. *The whole question of obsolescence of buildings, however, cannot be reduced to the problem of slums, for slums are the result, not the cause, of obsolescence,* a process that may accelerate and generalize blight in some places but spur on renewal or displacement in others. The process of obsolescence is not simply ended by the redevelopment or the renewal of slum areas and the relocation of the residents in better quarters. The matter reaches much more deeply into the region's social and economic structure.[11]

To understand the recent and present trends in urban uses of the land it seems worthwhile to consider briefly the roots of this process of obsolescence of buildings and neighborhoods. These two factors are constantly reacting on one another: the more obsolescent the buildings in a district, the less desirable is this district as a location, unless the whole neighborhood undergoes rejuvenation. Such renewal or redevelopment usually modifies the kind of residents or the type of activity characteristic of the area. Whether it spurs on blight or renewal, obsolescence accelerates displacement of people, activities, entire neighborhoods. In areas of increasing population and employment, it must mean the occupation of *more land* by urban uses. Thus, accelerating the process of obsolescence in a developing urban area will accelerate the sprawl of buildings, as has happened recently over large sectors of Megalopolis.

Before we come to define the process of obsolescence itself, we must examine the general status of housing in Megalopolis around 1950. Was it actually good or bad? The question is in fact a difficult one, for the quality of a building, especially as a dwelling, is a most debatable question. The yardsticks of good and bad can be defined in many different ways, and only a few qualitative features of housing seem quantitatively measurable.

The Census has a category of relatively good dwellings, defined as not dilapidated and equipped with hot running water and private toilet and bath. In 1950, the Census of Housing recorded that 63 per cent of all the

[11] In the early 1940's the Twentieth Century Fund made a careful study of housing in the United States, and the problem of slums was well summed up in the introduction of the report by Miles L. Colean:

"Housing is confused with the slum problem because slums are made up of houses, and because the deteriorated condition of slum housing, and in many ways the character of its original planning, aggravate the slum situation. Many factors, however, contribute to the existence of slums, among which are the problems of poverty and of the demoralization that comes from poverty. Almost equally pertinent are the problems arising from the structures of cities and the methods of city growth, from the techniques of land valuation, assessment and taxation, from the hopes of property owners for increases in value, and from the complicated nature of laws affecting the reassembly of scattered ownerships.

"All these things make for the creation and preservation of slums. All of them are probably more directly responsible than the dwellings of which the slums are composed. The remedy for slum conditions can never come from attempts to improve housing conditions unless the whole problem of urban organization is attacked at the same time." (Miles L. Colean, *American Housing: Problems and Prospects*, Twentieth Century Fund, 1944, p. 4.)

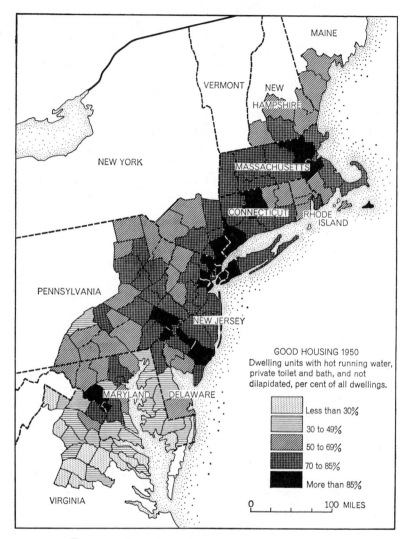

GOOD HOUSING 1950
Dwelling units with hot running water,
private toilet and bath, and not
dilapidated, per cent of all dwellings.

Less than 30%
30 to 49%
50 to 69%
70 to 85%
More than 85%

0   100 MILES

FIG. 127

dwelling units in the United States belonged in that category. Among the main regions in the country, the Northeastern seaboard ranked quite high, with an average of 79.2 per cent of all dwelling units classed as relatively good in the Middle Atlantic states and 73.9 per cent in New England; only California had a higher ratio of good housing, with 86 per cent. The distribution of this ratio over Megalopolis, on a county basis, is quite interesting (Fig. 127). There was a predominance, especially along the axial belt of the region, of percentages greater than 70, and in and around the main cities (except Philadelphia and Baltimore) they were greater than 85. Within Megalopolis the less well-housed sections were toward the south and away from the main cities. Beyond the fringe of Megalopolis, too, in northern New England, in the Appalachian Mountains, or even more in Virginia, the average quality of housing declined.

The good showing of the more crowded and more urbanized districts may shatter the old association in the minds of many between urban areas and slums. Although many people do live in blighted housing in the large cities, they make up, in this midcentury, only a minority of urban and suburban population. In fact, while 63.1 per cent of *all* dwellings in the entire country were classified in this better category in 1950, that ratio rose to 69.5 per cent for the nonfarm dwellings and 77.8 for urban dwellings. Only 6.5 per cent of the urban dwelling units were classed as dilapidated, 2 per cent were not dilapidated but lacked running water, and 10.5 per cent had no private toilet or bath.[12] These proportions were higher for rural nonfarm dwellings and much higher for rural farm. For the country as a whole, therefore, people were better housed in urban territory than in rural areas, and this was true even in Megalopolis, as the map of housing shows, for although its cities are older, many of the buildings are relatively new or in good general condition.

To conform to current standards of good housing, then, a dwelling must have running hot and cold water and private toilet and bath, and must be, of course, in a good state of repair. Proper equipment and maintenance are more important than age, but obviously they are more difficult and costly in an older building than in a newer one. In 1950 the proportion of old dwellings (more than thirty years old) was much higher in the rural farm category than in the urban, but urban dwellings were on the whole older than rural nonfarm dwellings, because of the recent expansion of outer suburbia. The urban houses, however, seemed better maintained.[13] Perhaps the relatively high rents in the cities warrant more repairs.

This Census definition of good housing is concerned mainly with

---

[12] U. S. Bureau of the Census, *U. S. Census of Housing: 1950, Vol. I: General Characteristics, Part 1: U. S. Summary*, U. S. Government Printing Office, Washington, D. C., 1953, p. 4.

[13] *Ibid.*, pp. 1–3.

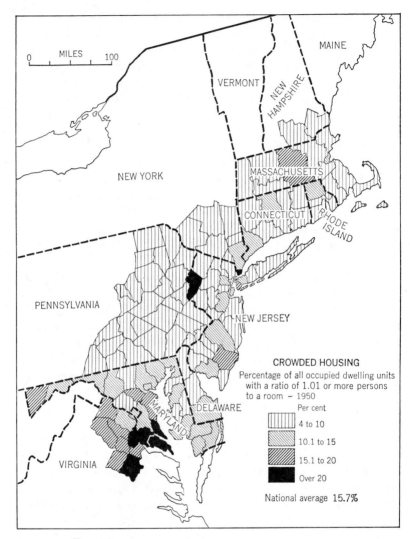

CROWDED HOUSING

Percentage of all occupied dwelling units with a ratio of 1.01 or more persons to a room – 1950

Per cent

4 to 10

10.1 to 15

15.1 to 20

Over 20

National average 15.7%

FIG. 128

sanitary conditions, which are important considerations but not the only important ones. A dwelling adequately equipped and repaired will not provide actually good living conditions if it is crowded with too many people in every room. Moreover, overcrowding will also make good maintenance more difficult and may well accelerate the rate of obsolescence. We must, therefore, consider the "persons per room" or "P.P.R.

ratio" [14] as an index of crowding. This can be expressed for an area by giving either the average number of persons per room or the percentages of all dwelling units having a low or a high density of occupants. Crowding in a household really begins when there is more than one person per room, which gives a P.P.R. ratio greater than 1, and a map of the relative degree of crowding in housing may be obtained by showing the percentage of all dwellings in which the ratio is greater than 1 (Fig. 128). In this respect Megalopolis does relatively well, and the larger cities do not appear especially blighted in terms of crowding. In fact, it is remarkable that in the United States higher *regional density* of population does not make for more crowded *housing*. The P.P.R. ratio in 1950 was relatively low — 0.66 — in the densely populated Northeast, while it was 0.78 in the South and 0.70 in the West (all ratios for nonfarm households).[15]

Neither the physical condition and equipment of the structures nor the density of occupance per room can serve, of course, as entirely satisfactory measures of housing obsolescence, but they provide valuable indications. Related to income, household size, racial distribution, value, and rent, as has been done by Louis Winnick, the P.P.R. ratio proves a significant index. From such studies it is evident that housing is more adequate for white families than for nonwhites. In many areas the crowding per room is usually greater in Negro neighborhoods than in white districts, and the higher ratios in this respect in the South reflect the higher proportion of Negroes in that section's population. This crowding stems, of course, from the unwillingness of white people to let Negroes settle where they would like to. However, the minorities whose areas of residence are thus crowded because of such restrictions usually have a relatively lower income level, which also decreases their capacity to secure better housing.

As a result of urban studies carried on by American sociologists since the beginning of the century it has become almost commonplace to stress how the history of an old house in a large city tells the story of successive waves of settlement and migration through a given area — how, as the structure has aged, it has sheltered households of newcomers and of people with relatively decreasing incomes. This succession used to be true of many (though not all) districts in the larger urban nuclei of Megalopolis, especially as long as immigrants from abroad kept pouring

[14] For a very good analysis of this ratio and a discussion of the various measurements of housing, see Louis Winnick, *American Housing and Its Use* (Census Monograph Series for the Social Science Research Council in cooperation with the U. S. Department of Commerce), John Wiley and Sons, New York, 1957.

[15] Winnick, *op. cit.*, pp. 61–65.

in, and the most recent layer among them usually corresponded to the lowest income level. Then, as the influx of immigration slackened, the in-migration of Negroes from the South took on increasing importance in Northeastern cities, and still more recently the Puerto Ricans have come, especially to New York City.[16] Such successive use of older structures by group after group of poorer people accelerates the rate of obsolescence. Often the new occupants would be willing to contribute to better maintenance, but they seldom own the buildings; and in a socially declining neighborhood a landlord is less interested in keeping up his property than in making as much profit from it as possible before the building becomes completely obsolescent, leaving merchantable value in the land only.

In the process of obsolescence age is therefore a very important factor for other reasons than the fatigue of materials used in the structure. It must be remembered that in the United States by 1950 some 55 per cent of all nonfarm dwelling units were more than thirty years old, and only 21 per cent were less than ten years old.[17] The Internal Revenue Service uses thirty-three and one third years as the standard of the useful life of a one-family frame dwelling.[18]

The U. S. Treasury's valuation of the useful life of a dwelling house does not correspond with the usual assumption by banks and mortgage loan companies that it will last fifty to one hundred years. The former estimate is based on the depreciation of rented housing, which undoubtedly is more rapid than for owner-occupied dwellings, and it allows for a reasonable profit on the capital investment. The latter estimate is oriented more toward the owner-occupied house. Whatever the point of view of an evaluation, age becomes an essential component of a house's value. It is therefore interesting to consider the distribution in Megalopolis of recently built houses (Fig. 129). By 1950 in most of the counties of Megalopolis the percentage of dwelling units in structures built after 1940 was below 20, i.e., below the national average; it was more than 30 per cent only in the parts of Maryland and Virginia where the suburbs of Baltimore and Washington had been sprawling, and in Nassau County on Long Island. Despite the relatively good condition and little

[16] Oscar Handlin, *The Newcomers*, New York Metropolitan Region Study, Harvard University Press, Cambridge, Mass., 1959.

[17] *U. S. Census of Housing: 1950, Vol. 1, Part 1*, pp. 1–3.

[18] We are indebted for a good deal of research on housing to Dr. John Rickert, a research assistant with the Study of Megalopolis in 1957–58. The tables and graphs of his report on the obsolescence of housing have been used in the preparation of the following pages.

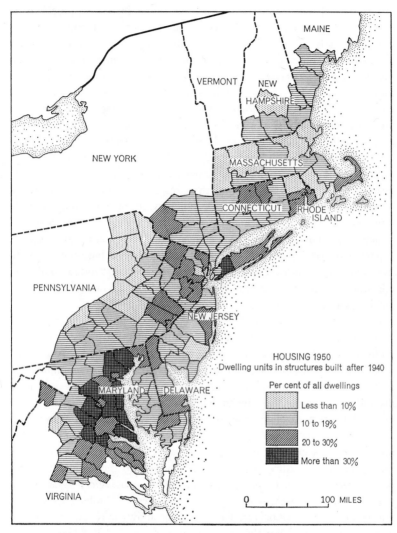

FIG. 129

overcrowding of housing in Megalopolis, the age of the great majority of the buildings could cause some concern for the not-too-distant future.

True, because of the heavy urban concentrations in the old cities a higher proportion of the population lives in large structures built of heavy masonry. The physical wear and tear on a building is, of course, influenced by the materials of which it is made, and upkeep is in many respects easier and less costly for masonry than for wood, especially in terms of exterior maintenance. As to the interior, wear and tear again depend greatly on the quality of the materials originally used in the construction, and at a later stage on the kind of maintenance and repair provided. "Adequately modern" contemporary residences, whether one-family detached structures or multi-storied apartment houses, require a constantly increasing internal equipment of growing complexity. As mechanization spreads, a home uses more and more electrical apparatus, and periodic or continuous overloading of the electrical wiring causes the wires to overheat and burn out the insulation, creating a fire hazard. A number of machines or gadgets that used to be luxuries, occasionally installed by residents according to their respective whims and means, are increasingly becoming indispensable components of a dwelling unit. In America hot running water and private baths are no longer criteria of luxury but essentials of decent dwellings. New houses and apartments are expected to have a mechanical refrigerator and even built-in air conditioning quite as naturally as they are expected to have windows and electric outlets (see the maps of dwellings with refrigerators and central heating, Fig. 130).

Real estate salesmen often hold that "gadgets sell houses." Such gadgets, to name a few found in the better suburbs, included in the late 1950's built-in stoves and ovens, vacuum cleaners and dishwashers, garbage disposals and air conditioners, and in many cases radio intercommunication systems and radio-controlled garage doors. It is easy for many people to do without many of these technological improvements, but social standing and relative dwelling comfort increasingly depend on many such features in a home. The rapid pace of technological refinement in mechanizing homes requires a building to be adaptable to all these changes. Unadaptable houses may be considered obsolete to the extent the occupants desire this sort of progress. Thus new *technological obsolescence* must be reckoned with, which quickens the pace of obsolescence in general as long as the rising standard of living allows it to go on and on. This trend also increases the significance of the age of buildings.

Both technology and taste have recently modified the whole design and plan of houses and apartments. Space is now distributed within the structures differently from what was usually the case before 1940. On the whole, space for living has been shrinking (perhaps with the exception of the living room proper), while space for "gadgets" has increased. Homes of smaller cubic footage have been accompanied by much larger garages, which must hold one and preferably two bigger cars per family.

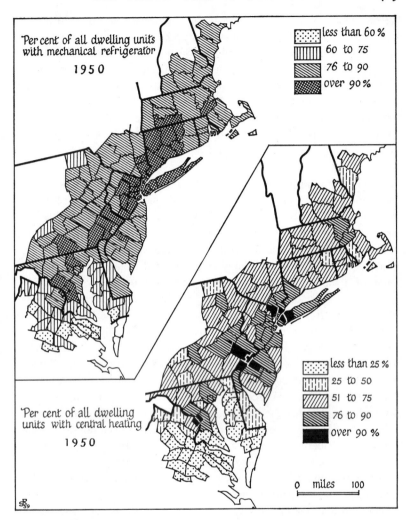

Per cent of all dwelling units
with mechanical refrigerator
1950

less than 60%
60 to 75
76 to 90
over 90%

Per cent of all dwelling
units with central heating
1950

less than 25%
25 to 50
51 to 75
76 to 90
over 90%

0   miles   100

FIG. 130

The one-level or split-level plan is in many cases preferred to the older multi-storied homes. These fashions in design, which, of course, are not unrelated to considerations of comfort (elimination of stair climbing, for example), have added to the general trend of an accelerated rate of obsolescence.

Obsolescence means depreciation for the great majority of structures, though there has always been a market for unusual homes and historic relics, which may be compared to the demand for antique furniture.

Certain kinds of old structures have been especially glorified by history or literature; and though they may be especially costly in terms of upkeep and equipment with modern gadgets, the wealthier members of a community may well accept the expense in exchange for the aesthetic feeling and the prestige value derived from such surroundings. This is why Sutton Place and Georgetown have been rejuvenated and made fashionable, and why many manorial farms have been restored and kept up in areas of estate farming from northern Virginia to Rhode Island, and why former fishermen's houses on Cape Cod or Nantucket have taken on new value.

The relationship between age and the adequacy of a house as a dwelling could certainly not be formulated in simple and constant terms, but it could generally be agreed that *the older a house is, the higher is its propensity toward obsolescence*, though measures can be taken to offset the trend if the owner is able and willing to go to such expense. In 1937 a study of one-family dwellings in the United States showed that the value of a building went down to 93 per cent of the original amount three years after construction, to 60 per cent after thirteen years, to 37 per cent after twenty-three years, to 12 per cent after forty-three years, and to 4 per cent after sixty-three years.[19] Happily for the owners, the value of the land usually goes up as the building itself depreciates. The predominance of U-shaped graphs showing the changing values of houses and the land they stand on, in the Megalopolitan cities of Providence, Rhode Island, Worcester, Massachusetts, and Trenton, New Jersey, indicate also that the land becomes more valuable than the house on it forty-two to fifty-five years after construction; in the non-Megalopolitan city of Richmond, Virginia, this occurs after about a 60-year period (Fig. 131). These trends suggest that, but for a few exceptional cases or locations, some fifty years after it was built a residence becomes obsolete and is worth essentially only what its land is worth.

The obsolescence of housing is affected not only by age and technological, economic, and social changes, but also, and to a substantial degree, by existing legislation on such matters as zoning, taxation, and credit. Many authors have pointed out that zoning, at least in the way it has been used, does not help much to control obsolescence. It rather "petrifies urban improvement";[20] and, as Arthur B. Gallion has shown, taxation

[19] Data used in this paragraph and in the construction of Figure 131 are from U. S. Department of Commerce, Bureau of Foreign and Domestic Commerce, *Financial Survey of Domestic Housing*, Washington, D. C., 1937.

[20] Arthur B. Gallion and Simon Eisner, *The Urban Pattern: City Planning and Design*, Van Nostrand Company, Princeton, N. J., 1950, p. 367.

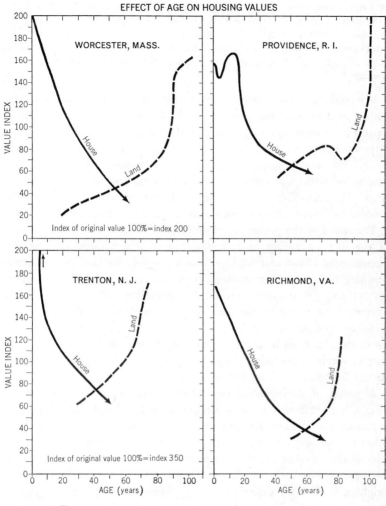

EFFECT OF AGE ON HOUSING VALUES

WORCESTER, MASS.

PROVIDENCE, R. I.

Index of original value 100% = index 200

TRENTON, N. J.

RICHMOND, VA.

Index of original value 100% = index 350

Fig. 131

works in reverse of what it might have been expected to do for the conservation of built-up lands:

Physical and social self-maintenance is the urgent need — a form of pre-
ventive treatment that will build resistance to decay and render major operations less necessary. . . . Buildings are built to provide space in which to live
or conduct business. Taxes are collected to support the public services that
make these building ventures possible and profitable. Today taxes are measured

by the assessed value of land and buildings. The value of land may increase. The value of physical improvements, on the other hand, depreciates with age and use. At the same time the cost of public services increases as physical deterioration continues. Yet the present assessment of taxation actually works in reverse of this: *tax revenue goes down as the cost of urban maintenance goes up*.[21]

It would seem that a great many factors of different kinds work together to accelerate the process of obsolescence of buildings. This is especially true of housing, which is the category including the great majority of the nation's buildings. The process and the trends are nationwide. They acquire a special urgency in Megalopolis because the higher density of settlement creates more pressure on the land, increases distances between places of residence and of work, and therefore raises problems of transportation and access to the hubs of crowding.

The speed of the process of obsolescence and the number and variety of the forces favoring its accelerated development point to a massive phenomenon of considerable significance not only for land use and urban planning but also for the national economy as a whole. The real estate market and the construction and transportation industries are deeply affected by the trends that speed up the obsolescence of housing; for speeding up obsolescence, in a society that likes comfort, wishes to be up to date, and has both the means and the will to drive toward these targets, means accelerating urban redevelopment and renewal, suburban sprawl, highway building, and so forth.

A group of distinguished city planners and architects, gathered to discuss with this writer the obsolescence of housing,[22] overwhelmingly expressed the opinion that gadgets, materials used in construction, and other technological changes were not essential in determining the rapid pace of obsolescence. Basic to the process was the *mobility of the American people*, their social fluidity that constantly modifies the character of neighborhoods, their desire for change, improvements, and new experimentation. It seems likely indeed that none of the factors of obsolescence could have developed to the extent now observed had the users of the buildings opposed all this change, so enormous in amount and so rapid that it seems almost incredible by the standards of any other nation.

Had Americans really cared for staying where they lived, they would have found means of maintaining their houses well enough, of rejuvenat-

[21] *Ibid.*, p. 368.

[22] This meeting, kindly organized at our request by the School of Architecture of Princeton University, took place on December 1, 1958, at Princeton under the guidance of Professor Robert McLaughlin, Director of the School.

ing and equipping them, of maintaining the social standing of their neighborhoods, in order to avoid undesirable obsolescence and the ensuing mobility. But to most of them, moving was a good and easy solution. Their acceptance of mobility made for more slums and blight in the central cities, but also for more newly built suburbs, and in the final analysis, for more renewal in the old urban cores. It helped the construction industry to expand, real estate speculation to develop, and more space beyond the old city limits to be occupied by urban uses. These trends have for long been familiar to urbanites in Megalopolis, many of whom move to a new home every time the old one needs a new coat of paint.

Redevelopment, Renewal, and Relocation in Urban Areas

The constant migrations within, around, and between the old urban cores of Megalopolis have caused much change and much new building throughout the region, especially in its axial belt. For a long time urban growth in Megalopolis could proceed through expansion in space. On the one hand the "downtown" districts expanded because of the development of commercial, industrial, and, in a few cities, governmental activities; and the additional ground needed was usually acquired partly at the expense of the neighboring residential sectors and partly at the periphery, on suburban land. On the other hand, the "uptown" districts expanded because of the sustained rise in the number of residents, and most of the necessary ground was obtained on the periphery or even at some distance from the old core at the expense of farms, woods, or sparsely settled suburban areas.

In the past this process went on smoothly without greatly disturbing the standing buildings of the urban core, except for the erection of new office or industrial structures in certain locations, and on the whole these occupied relatively little acreage. A good part of the process consisted in a change of residents in the older houses. Those who had lived in them moved out to the newly built sections of the city or to suburbs, and their places were taken by newcomers with lower incomes: immigrants from abroad or in-migrants who belonged to the poorer strata of the population, especially Negroes. A few residential sections located close to the business districts usually succeeded, especially in the larger cities, in preserving the quality of the neighborhood and of the housing at a high cost, and kept undesirable newcomers out just by pricing themselves far above their reach. Thus we find the Fifth Avenue–Park Avenue section between 60th and 96th streets in Manhattan, or the section of "Embassy Row" centered on Massachusetts Avenue above 16th

Street N. W. in Washington, and smaller but no less restricted districts in Philadelphia, Boston, and Baltimore. Elsewhere the process of obsolescence went on until more and more of the residential sections in the older parts of the cities, close to downtown, became actual slums.

In the larger cities there were, however, enough wealthy residents and enough attraction to the business activities of downtown to cause certain sectors to be well defended, as has already been indicated, and others were rehabilitated or even rebuilt in order to attract the kind of residents who were willing to pay adequate rents and live in high-rise apartment buildings, and who valued locations with convenient access to their places of work and to the social and recreational resources of the central cores of the great cities. Such resources are obviously much more limited in the medium-sized central cities and in small industrial cities, and the power of attraction for the higher-income residents of urban nuclei outside the five great cities in Megalopolis is very small. As a result obsolescence and relative decline of housing in the cores have been more rapid and have caused more obvious changes in the smaller cities than in the five larger ones.

A city, it has often been observed, is a dynamic organization — always changing, always in transition. In Megalopolis we could add that it is always growing. In the past the growing population made good use of relatively obsolete structures; but newcomers in search of work and economic opportunity opened the door to the spread of blight and slums in the hearts of the central cities. Although the statistics and maps analyzed earlier in this chapter seemed to point to a relatively favorable condition of housing on the *average* in Megalopolis, and though in the 1950's overcrowded and blighted buildings were occupied by only a minority of the population, it must still be realized that a "small minority" out of more than 37 million people meant *several million persons living in substandard and sometimes slum conditions* of housing within the region.

As long as the recently arrived immigrants were rapidly improving their lot and moving up, at least with every generation, in social and economic standing, the dynamics of housing and land use remained in a certain traditional framework, full of promise and progress within the city. In recent years the process has been somewhat modified, for the inflow of immigrants from abroad has been reduced to a trickle, and increasingly these aliens are not poor but are highly skilled professionals assured of making an adequate income within a short time. Some of the in-migrants from other parts of the country are of this type too, lured to Megalopolis by higher profits, wages, and prestige. The great majority of the newcomers, however, are Negroes and Puerto Ricans, who still belong definitely in the lower-income brackets. They find it doubly difficult to secure good housing, not only because of the cost but also because they are restricted in space by racial discrimination.

A new problem, the result of social opposition and too-sharp economic contrasts, has arisen in the larger cities. Middle-income families, especially those with small children, have found themselves caught between two advancing fronts: more expensive new housing on the one hand, and on the other the rapidly worsening housing in the areas toward which Negro or Puerto Rican settlement is moving. Most of these medium-income families have chosen to move out toward the suburbs and even farther away. The sharpening contrast in Manhattan between Harlem and the richer Upper East Side and similar situations in Washington, Boston, and Baltimore cause local and national concern.[23] At the same time the smaller cities of Megalopolis have decayed more rapidly, and the average income of their residents has declined in both absolute and relative terms, in contrast to a general rise throughout the region and the nation. In 1958, at a forum conducted by the National Health Council in Philadelphia, a distinguished expert in urban problems could ask the question: "Will the central city be left with a population consisting of the lame, the halt and the blind, the poor, the aged and the minority group?"[24]

This was a threatening but a deliberately pessimistic way to formulate

[23] A few statistics showing the distribution of lower and higher incomes in and around the major cities reveal these trends convincingly. *The County and City Data Book: 1952* (U. S. Bureau of the Census, U. S. Government Printing Office, Washington, D. C., 1953) reports Bureau of the Census figures for the 1949 incomes of all families living in specified areas in 1950, and these show that in central cities of Megalopolis the wealthier group (incomes of $5,000 or more) and the poorer group (incomes of less than $2,000) were relatively large and more or less equal in size, while in the suburbs the wealthier category was much larger and the poorer category smaller. For the New York City area, the two groups made up the following percentages: Manhattan, 24.7 and 27.1; the Bronx, 27.6 and 17.4; Brooklyn, 25.7 and 19.7; Queens, 36.0 and 12.5; Westchester County, New York, 42.2 and 13.2; Nassau County, New York 43.8 and 10.5; Bergen County, New Jersey, 39.2 and 10.9. Note that the outer boroughs of New York City represent a condition transitional between the core city and the adjacent suburbs. In the District of Columbia the percentages were 34.6 and 17.6, while in Fairfax County, Virginia, they were 39.0 and 14.9 and in Montgomery County, Maryland, they were 53.3 and 10.3. In Baltimore City the percentages were 23.1 and 22.7, but in Baltimore County they were 27.1 and 14.3. Philadelphia had 22.9 and 21.6 per cent for the two groups, and adjacent Camden County, New Jersey, had 25.9 and 17.5. Boston (Suffolk County, Massachusetts) had 20.9 and 21.0 per cent, and adjacent Middlesex County had 26.7 and 16.5.

[24] William C. Wheaton, "How Far Will Our Central Cities Slide?," in *Urban Sprawl and Health* (Report of the National Health Forum) National Health Council, New York, January 1959, p. 175.

the problem. The outcry has been general, however, among experts concerned with recent trends, in an effort to warn of the need for action to obtain better redevelopment and renewal than have yet been achieved if the old urban cores are to be saved. The process of free migration and relocation accentuates the traditional American propensity to mobility, and at the same time it has driven the suburban sprawl to devouring more land and rendering metropolitan transportation increasingly difficult and costly. Regulation by public authorities appeared necessary. But such regulation would only worsen the situation unless it could provide efficient help for the central city and endow it with new attraction for residents other than underprivileged.[25]

In fact, public authorities have been concerned with urban housing for quite some time. National legislation had been adopted many years ago to help solve the riddle, and Federal funds had been brought on the scene. As early as 1892 Congress decided to make an investigation of slums in cities of 200,000 inhabitants or more. During World War I, Congress authorized several government agencies to provide housing for war workers, and an executive order of the President established a United States Housing Corporation to handle wartime housing and rent grievances. However, it took the depression of the 1930's to bring on large-scale Federal action on housing. In 1933 the Home Owner's Loan Corporation was established, and it functioned successfully until 1951. In its first four years it helped many homeowners threatened with foreclosure by accepting poor-risk mortgages held by private financial institutions and converting them to new longer-term mortgages at a lower interest rate, to bring the refinancing within the reach of the impoverished owners. In 1934 Congress made an essential step forward by passing the National Housing Act providing government insurance for residential long-term mortgages.[26] To carry out the objectives of the Act, the Federal Housing Administration was established June 27, 1934, as an emergency agency to help revive the home-building industry. Twenty-five years later, the F.H.A. had become "a major arm of the Federal Government. It is solvent and self-sustaining, having repaid in 1954 the last

[25] Miles L. Colean, *Renewing Our Cities*, Twentieth Century Fund, 1953; Coleman Woodbury (ed.) *The Future of Cities and Urban Redevelopment*, University of Chicago Press, Chicago, 1953; Nathan Straus, *Two-Thirds of a Nation: A Housing Program*, Alfred A. Knopf, New York, 1952; Raymond Vernon, *The Changing Economic Function of the Central City*, Committee for Economic Development, New York, 1959.

[26] *Your Congress and American Housing: The Actions of Congress on Housing from 1892 to 1951*, H. Doc. No. 532, 82d Cong., 2d sess., Washington, D. C., 1952.

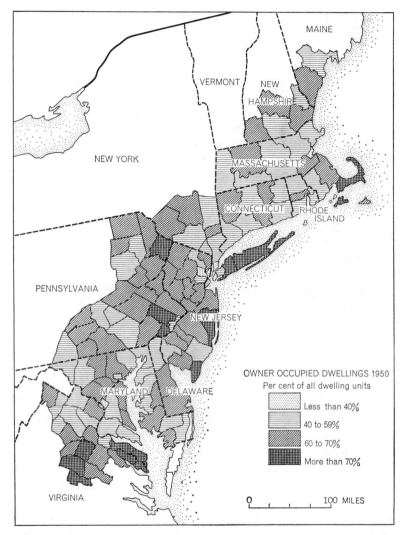

OWNER OCCUPIED DWELLINGS 1950
Per cent of all dwelling units

Less than 40%

40 to 59%

60 to 70%

More than 70%

0   100 MILES

Fig. 132

dollar owed the Treasury. . . . The agency has helped 5,000,000 families to buy their own homes and has helped provide 800,000 others with housing in rental or cooperative developments." [27] There is no doubt, even among the critics of the F.H.A., that it has helped greatly to provide better housing throughout the United States, while at the same time it

[27] *The New York Times*, June 28, 1959.

has helped the construction industries and has contributed toward the achievement of sound design and better planning. Since 1934 the National Housing Act has been amended several times, extending the life of the F.H.A.

In 1944 the "G. I. Bill of Rights" authorized the Veterans' Administration to help veterans buy housing by guaranteeing up to 60 per cent of a loan made for such purpose by a lending institution. There have been other Federal agencies (the Home Loan Bank Board, the Federal National Mortgage Association, and others) entering the field of public help to housing. After various reorganizations the general coordination of these government programs was entrusted (1947) to the Housing and Home Finance Agency.

Until 1947 Federal aid to housing could be described as resulting from various national emergencies: the two World Wars, the depression of the 1930's, and the return of veterans after 1945. The restoration of relatively normal economic conditions after these very special periods did not make the public authorities abandon their interest in this field, for the new problems arising from urban and metropolitan growth were too great. The general welfare of the American nation was at stake, and it required more governmental assistance, as set forth in the National Housing Act of 1949. As early as 1937 Congress had created an authority, later renamed the Public Housing Administration, to aid local public-housing agencies for low-rent housing and slum-clearance projects. This brought about government cooperation on the Federal, state, and local levels in supplying low-rent housing with the help of public funds, while the F.H.A.'s insurance of mortgages, because of the standards required, had been of help mainly to medium-income families.

The Housing Act of 1949 introduced innovations by widening the provisions in favor of public housing and by starting *urban redevelopment and renewal*. Federal funds were authorized to help build new low-rent housing. At the same time slums were recognized as a national problem, and Federal aid was suggested for clearance and reconstruction or rehabilitation areas in cities. In 1954 the housing legislation was further amended, providing for more Federal participation in slum clearance, urban renewal, and planned redevelopment. Title I of the National Housing Act, dealing with housing renovation and modernization, was substantially expanded in 1949 and even more in 1954, helping many cities to obtain Federal aid in rebuilding many blighted sectors of the old urban cores.[28]

---

[28] For a good discussion of the Federal government's participation in the housing field see Glenn H. Beyer, *Housing: A Factual Analysis*, The Macmillan Company,

Megalopolis has benefited greatly by this Federal participation in the fight against urban decay.

The original F.H.A. program, insuring mortgages of relatively good new homes, was of benefit chiefly, as most experts acknowledged, to people in the middle-income brackets, and it contributed to the sprawl of detached one-family dwellings in the inner and outer rings of suburbs. Federal policy should not be accused of having caused this sprawl, which was an inevitable result of the accelerated rate of housing obsolescence (to which many other factors contributed) and the continuing growth of metropolitan populations (though the pattern of in-migration had changed in Megalopolis). This policy made the whole process less painful, almost easy. It contributed to rapid urbanization and to improvement in the average quality of housing. It did not cost the taxpayers much, for F.H.A. repaid all the money advanced to it by the U. S. Treasury and it guaranteed and insured loans rather than contributing funds directly. However, this policy worked against the old urban cores, where it could only accelerate obsolescence.

At the same time, the old cores benefited from Federal aid to public housing and urban renewal. The relevant provisions in the national legislation made it possible to relocate at least some of the less fortunate people displaced by slum clearance in new, well-planned, low-rent dwellings. In many cases Federal and local governments cooperated effectively in such programs. The groups of high-rise apartment buildings, often called "villages," thus erected with the help of public funds in Harlem and other parts of New York City considerably improved the physical conditions of housing and the health conditions in the rebuilt neighborhoods. The new provisions in the National Housing Act called for urban renewal plans drawn for an entire neighborhood. Federal aid became more readily available in old urban cores for projects involving the renewal of an entire area rather than of just a building or two. Since 1949, Title I has authorized the use of land obtained by slum clearance not only for new dwellings but also for parks, shopping centers, and even parking lots.

During the 1950's Megalopolis has used these means of development more extensively than any other section of the country. Baltimore redeveloped, predominantly for residential use, two former slum areas (with

New York, 1958, especially Chapter 10. Also various pamphlets put out by the Housing and Home Finance Agency, Washington, D. C., and a good critical appraisal by Catherine Bauer, "Redevelopment: A Misfit in the Fifties," in Woodbury, *The Future of Cities and Urban Redevelopment, op. cit.*, pp. 7–25.

a total of about sixty acres), known as the Waverly and Broadway projects, and has planned others. Philadelphia quickly completed several smaller projects, chiefly for housing Negroes (Spring Garden Homes, Penn Towne, Harrison Plaza, and Cambridge Plaza Homes). Providence rebuilt the Willard Street Commercial Area, a project providing a shopping center and a city school, and has plans for a large residential project in the Mount Hope area, some 200 acres in size. Somerville, Massachusetts, made interesting plans, and New Haven began the redevelopment of major parts of its old downtown section. With Federal help, New York City built impressive groups of high-rise apartment towers (Delano Village in Harlem, Kingsview Homes in Brooklyn, Grant Houses on the Upper West Side, and the I.L.G.W.U. Cooperative Village at Corlears Hook on the Lower East Side), and undertook the spectacular, multi-faceted Coliseum project on Columbus Circle. More and more of such redevelopment projects are being started,[29] but not as many as was expected when the legislation was passed, for from 1949 to 1958 only one tenth of the credits appropriated by Congress had been disbursed. Renovation of the old urban cores proceeded at a much slower pace and with much more caution than did the suburban residential sprawl.

Much more spectacular indeed has been the rise, in the central sections, of large and medium-sized "cities" of *office towers and expensive luxury-type apartment buildings,* put up by private funds. Manhattan pioneered once more in this respect. Building of its magnificent Rockefeller Center was started as early as the late 1920's and continued through the 1930's. The great depression kept this development from exercising over the midtown area all the stimulating influence that might have been expected. After World War II, however, the trends it suggested became dominant between 42nd and 60th streets, giving this district a new look. New office towers of glass, set in various metals, began to rise along Park, Madison, and Fifth avenues, replacing expensive apartment buildings, millionaires' mansions, or older and smaller office buildings already classified as obsolescent in choice locations. In 1947 the establishment of the United Nations headquarters on the East River between 42nd and 47th streets added to the momentum of the renewal of Manhattan's East Side, both north and south of 42nd Street, and the removal of the Third Avenue "El" (a part of the city transit system on elevated tracks) in the mid-1950's provided

[29] Housing and Home Finance Agency, *Approaches to Urban Renewal in Several Cities,* Urban Renewal Bulletin No. 1, U. S. Government Printing Office, Washington, D. C., 1954; and "Redevelopment Today" in *Architectural Forum* (New York), April 1958, pp. 108–113.

new stimulus for the construction of luxury apartment houses. During this same period there has been much renovation activity also on Manhattan's Upper West Side, as evidenced by the Lincoln Center for the Performing Arts and the Morningside Gardens housing development undertaken by Columbia University and other institutions in the area; and in between these two centers many new high-rise residential buildings have been built or are being planned by both public and private agencies. Even *The New York Times* has decided to move from its celebrated location near Times Square to the bank of the Hudson River near 70th Street. And Rockefeller Center expanded westward near 50th Street. During the 1950's, too, vast programs of renovation, including many new and impressive skyscrapers, were started or announced in the old downtown section of Lower Manhattan, where even the Wall Street financial district had seemed for a while threatened by the midtown development along Park and Fifth avenues.

The obvious success of the daring experiments conducted in Manhattan from 1947 on set an example that many other American cities have decided to follow, although on a more modest scale. The essential lesson of New York's hub development has been that investment in renewal of the central business district can pay handsomely in terms of real estate values and long-term profits. Pittsburgh was probably the first large city outside Megalopolis to undertake a comparable program, apparently with success. Since World War II great new office towers have arisen around Mellon Square, and the "Golden Triangle" has been redeveloped, with a large new civic center added back of the business district. Many other cities have followed suit — Philadelphia with its Penn Center in the very heart of town, Washington with the rebuilding of its southeastern section, and Boston, Baltimore, Newark, New Haven, and Trenton with ambitious renewal programs in their old downtown areas. By 1959 more than 200 municipalities in the United States were engaged in some sort of urban renewal.

Altogether the modifications thus introduced in the central hubs of the old urban nuclei have affected as yet only a minor acreage, a very small fraction in terms of space and numbers of buildings of the total urban core areas. Manhattan, where the churning has more drive and power, is the only actual exception to that rule — a very notable exception, to be sure, due apparently to the unique concentration of needs for office space, hotels, and luxury apartments in New York City. Thus the question arises: how exceptional are the Manhattan trends? No other American city has shown any signs of success in attracting anything comparable to the massive centralization of the nation's financial, managerial, and mass-media functions in New York City, and singularly in the hub of Manhattan. No other city could get another "United Nations" with a whole diplomatic corps of its own, almost duplicating the role of Washington in foreign and international relations. But, on a more modest scale, could other cities apply some of the same economic principles that have succeeded in New York, and put to better use their respective facilities and assets as regards industrial and regional management, financial operations, political role, and cultural endeavors? In other words, is Manhattan's evolution *unique*, because of the *nature* of its national and international role? Or is it merely unusual in terms of *degree* and *size*, demonstrating in powerful manner what could be achieved also on a smaller scale by many other smaller but still dynamic metropolises?

The answer to this query could reach deep into our whole knowledge of urban economics and growth. It involves the definition of the basic functions of the city today, and of the changes presently occurring in these functions. Experiments that have been under way for only a few years and on relatively small fractions of the old cities can hardly provide as yet more than a few preliminary and somewhat vague indications. Nevertheless, these are noteworthy. It might seem expected for great regional centers outside Megalopolis, such as Pittsburgh, Detroit, Chicago, or San Francisco, to succeed in rejuvenation and renewal of their business districts, for they are less dependent on New York by virtue of distance. But when this occurs even in Megalopolitan cities like Philadelphia, Baltimore, Newark, and Trenton, lying between the two great concentrations of offices in Manhattan and Washington, D. C., it suggests that Manhattan's development is not unique. Very little has been attempted, however, in smaller towns outside the axial belt, such as Reading, or Scranton, Pennsylvania, or even Worcester, Massachusetts. These do not seem to offer hopeful prospects.

It must be realized that *renewal and rebuilding provoke displacement and relocation* of people and business, a process bringing new profits to the real estate trade, the construction industry, and various other local interests, and new worries and expenses to the local government. An abundant literature has dealt with the problems arising out of the relocation of the residents of blighted areas being cleared. Since slums degrade the people who live in them as much as, and often more than, they make the buildings decay, the cost of clearing them and providing their residents with better housing must be considered as a long-range investment, the profits from which cannot be reaped immediately or assessed in dollars and cents. The local society as a whole shares in these benefits in the long run, for the environment of daily life ought to be improved by the removal of slums not only for those who once lived in them but also for those who lived or worked in adjacent districts. Insofar as slums often breed crime, the community on an even larger scale should be directly interested in their eradication.

When the redevelopment or renewal of an urban area displaces people the new buildings erected on the site do not correspond in most cases to the same use and are not fitted, even when dwellings succeed dwellings, for the same users. In the case of low-rent public housing some of the former occupants of the place may be rehoused in the new buildings on the site, but most of the former residents will move elsewhere, generally farther away from the city's center. The number of people officially relocated by local urban renewal agencies by December 31, 1958, was not very high: 17,882 in New York City, as a result of the demolition of 2,210 buildings; 1,458 in Boston, where 580 buildings were demolished; 12,600 in Washington, D. C., where 1,949 buildings were demolished; 4,000 in Newark, New Jersey; 121 in Cambridge, Massachusetts; 123 in Elizabeth, New Jersey; 250 in Hartford, Connecticut; 2,545 in Providence, Rhode Island; 500 in Passaic, New Jersey.[30] These numbers varied greatly from city to city, and not in proportion to the extent of actual rebuilding carried out within the central core or the periphery but rather to the economic level of the population. Thus in Norfolk, Virginia, where most of the people involved were Negroes, more people were relocated (almost 20,000 before 1959) than in New York City.

Obviously most of the actual renewal and displacement of people in Megalopolis, which has affected a few million people in the last twenty years, has taken place without intervention of public authorities. However, it has been helped and to some extent fostered by legislation making it financially easier, especially through F.H.A., to acquire new individual homes for those who could afford them, and they have been many. In addition to helping chiefly people who had at least a minimum of credit, this legislation and the various provisions in tax legislation favoring real-property owners with incomes in the higher brackets have fostered the building of new homes in the form of one-family detached structures. Families with small children and many other American households have certainly liked this solution, but it has contributed to the great suburban sprawl of recent years, devouring space, materials, and services,

[30] Data from *The Municipal Year Book: 1959*, published by the International City Managers' Association, Chicago, 1959, especially Table XV, pp. 332–339.

while it has also accelerated housing obsolescence in the cores of central cities.[31]

The Balance of Recent Trends

Since 1930 new construction of dwellings has developed mainly outside the old urban nuclei, but more in the axial belt of Megalopolis or on its immediate fringes than on the periphery of the region as a whole. This trend is well demonstrated on the maps of population density for 1960 and 1950 (Figs. 1 and 122, pp. 6 and 387) and of population change, 1930–50 (Fig. 73, p. 248). It results largely from the fact that the axial belt, born out of the fusion of early elements in the economic hinge, offers locations between old nuclei with the advantage of easy access to two or more central cities.

This observation for Megalopolis agrees with general trends noted in the United States.

Where [metropolitan] areas are located in close proximity to one another the advantages of accessibility to two or more centers rather than to one only may be manifested in a more pronounced tendency to deconcentration than occurs where areas are widely spaced. The presence of two or more metropolitan areas within short distances of one another suggests, too, that the extent of metropolitan development in that locality may have advanced further than where areas are located far apart.[32]

In the whole United States, Megalopolis is the section most likely to exploit fully the consequences of a chain of adjacent metropolitan areas, the central cities of which are very close to one another. A speedier urbanization of the interurban areas has resulted. The general remarks of Amos Hawley apply to this region:

Until 1920 the differences between relative growth rates of satellite areas were negligible. Following 1920 the highest ratios developed in areas the central cities of which were within 50 miles of other central cities. The more isolated areas had the lowest ratios of satellite growth. The outlying zones of [metropolitan] areas 50 to 100 miles from other areas, however, had higher ratios than did similar zones in areas within 50 miles of other areas, in both 1910–20 and 1940–50. The less the distance between central cities the smaller was the

[31] The statistical data gathered in the *U. S. Census of Housing: 1950* has been well analyzed with respect to these trends by Richard U. Ratcliff, Daniel B. Rathbun, and Junia H. Honnold, *Residential Finance, 1950* (Census Monograph Series for Social Science Research Council in Cooperation with the U. S. Department of Commerce), John Wiley and Sons, New York, 1957, and in Winnick, *American Housing and Its Use, op. cit.*

[32] Amos H. Hawley, *The Changing Shape of Metropolitan America: Deconcentration since 1920,* The Free Press, Glencoe, Ill. 1956, p. 75.

proportion of all increase gained by central cities and the larger was the share received by satellite area. . . . When the rates are standardized for size of central city, deconcentration is found to have been inversely related to distance between central cities.[33]

Most of the studies of metropolitanization in the United States try to establish general or average trends developing all over the country. There are always exceptions to such rules. The coal-mining region of eastern Pennsylvania is in many respects such an exception within Megalopolis, for it has been declining more than any other part of the area. Even there, however, new construction of housing and retail-trade establishments has been occurring mostly outside the main cities; and the decline of that area would certainly have been much worse had it not been for its relative proximity to the prosperous axial belt of Megalopolis.

Some measure of the distribution of new residential building in the 1950's is provided by computing the total of new dwelling units authorized in the eight years 1950–57 in various places around Megalopolis.[34] Thus in these eight years the small township (including the borough) of Princeton, New Jersey, with about 25,000 inhabitants in 1957, gained 938 new dwelling units, while the neighboring central city of Trenton (with a population greater than 150,000) added only 558. Washington, D. C., added 27,728 dwelling units, but its suburban counties in Virginia added more (14,838 in Arlington alone, and 34,403 in Fairfax County), and the Maryland suburbs of Washington expanded even more rapidly (40,846 new dwelling units in Montgomery County). In Connecticut there was a great deal of new residential building. Stamford (74,000 people in 1950), having grown in population 37.6 per cent in 1940–50, authorized 7,234 new dwelling units in 1950–57, while New Canaan township (population 8,000 in 1950) authorized 1,304, but the city of Hartford (177,000 in 1950) added only 3,727. Both Stamford and New Canaan definitely had a more suburban or satellite function and location with reference to New York City than did the state capital of Hartford. Similar examples could be given in Massachusetts and Rhode Island: 11,641 new dwelling units for Boston and 4,395 for Framingham, which belongs to Boston's outer suburbia; 3,353 for Providence and 6,190 for the satellite township of Warwick. In Pennsylvania a similar picture can be obtained in the Philadelphia metropolitan area. That central city had been relatively active, adding 49,695 new dwelling units, but the small suburb of Upper Darby built 2,161 and the indus-

[33] *Ibid.*, p. 163.

[34] U. S. Department of Labor, Bureau of Labor Statistics, *New Dwelling Units Authorized by Local Building Permits*, Annual Summaries, 1950–53, 1954–55, 1955–56, 1956–57, U. S. Government Printing Office, Washington, D. C., 1954, 1956, 1957, 1958.

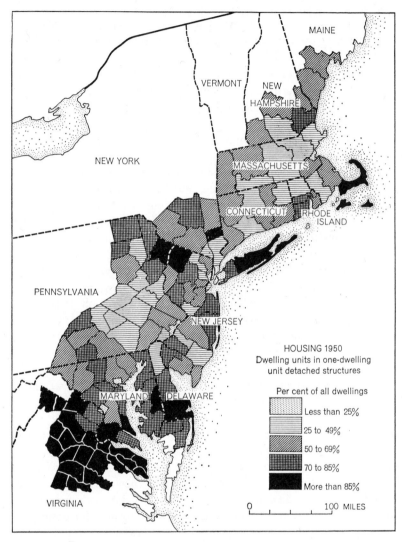

FIG. 133

trial satellite of Bristol, on the main Delaware Valley axis, 9,242. During the same period Wilkes-Barre in the coal-mining area (76,800 inhabitants in 1950) built only 222 new dwelling units! In New York City, Queens was by far the most rapidly developing borough, adding 85,000 new dwelling units, more than in Manhattan and the Bronx put together. Manhattan alone authorized 41,425 new units, but the township of Babylon on Long Island recorded 14,743, and the smaller Massapequa Park 4,075.

Since 1957 the construction rate has continued to increase in Megalopolis, but its acceleration has "taken a breather" in the outer suburbs. This has been especially clear in the tri-state New York Metropolitan Region, as observed by the Regional Plan Association;[35] however, while the one-family detached structures remain predominant in the outer suburban rings, a definite trend has developed, especially since 1959, toward multi-family units in the inner suburban ring, as has long been true in the central core. This is true of the larger cities and their suburbs, while the trend is less obvious in smaller places. The main reason for this development is, of course, the higher average cost of one-family units. Construction costs rose in the 1950's, land values increased considerably in the major cities and their immediate vicinity, and the tight money policy prevailing in the late 1950's raised interest rates for loans and mortgages.

The average valuation of a dwelling unit authorized in 1954 in the New York–Northeastern New Jersey metropolitan area was estimated at $10,811 for a one-family house and $8,209 in two-or-more family structures. That same year 63,172 new dwelling units were added in one-family houses and 31,952 in apartment buildings. By 1956 the average valuations stood at $12,893 for one-family houses, of which 51,732 were built, and at $7,958 for apartment units, of which 25,918 were built. The percentage of the latter in the total of new dwelling units was edging up slightly. In the Philadelphia area the trend was different. There 26,410 one-family houses were authorized in 1954 (at an average value of $10,043) and 22,215 in 1956 (average value $11,357), while the number of new apartment units fell from 4,134 in 1954 (average value $5,140) to 1,723 in 1956 (average value $7,713). Thus the Philadelphia area was still adding a higher percentage of individual houses, more than 80 per cent of them in the suburbs, for it is on the whole less crowded than the New York area. The demand for new apartments in the city is mainly for the more expensive kinds and is a much less sustained demand than in the New York area.[36]

The trends in the middle 1950's in the other large metropolitan areas in Megalopolis can be seen in Table 18. It thus seems that only in the New York area did the average valuation of new apartments authorized go down in 1954–56. Elsewhere the cost of new apartment units rose sharply, but these remained everywhere much less costly on the average than one-family houses, the latter being everywhere predominant in numbers,

[35] See the Regional Plan Association's series of Bulletins, *New Homes in the New Jersey–New York–Connecticut Metropolitan Region*, especially No. 5, "First Six Months 1959," RPA Bulletin 93, New York, February 1960.

[36] U. S. Department of Labor, Bureau of Labor Statistics, *Trends in Building Permit Activity*, Bulletin No. 1243, U. S. Government Printing Office, Washington, D. C., 1959, pp. 107–110.

Table 18

NEW DWELLING UNITS IN SOME MEGALOPOLITAN CITIES, MID-1950's

	Boston		Baltimore		Washington, D. C.	
	1954	1956	1954	1956	1954	1956
New one-family houses						
Number	10,204	9,490	14,275	11,205	17,758	12,102
Average valuation	$10,286	11,467	9,618	10,913	9,941	12,998
New apartment units						
Number	541	446	1,189	333	6,151	3,809
Average valuation	$6,919	8,101	7,211	8,610	5,443	7,484

Source: U. S. Department of Labor, Bureau of Labor Statistics, *Trends in Building Permit Activity,* Bulletin No. 1243, U. S. Government Printing Office, Washington, D. C., 1959, pp. 107–110.

though less so in the New York area than in the other four major metropolitan areas.

In the New York Metropolitan Region (a larger territory than the standard metropolitan area of the Census) new apartments rose percentagewise in the total number of new homes authorized through 1959. In the first six months of 1957 they accounted for 30 per cent of all new homes authorized in the whole region, in the first six months of 1958 for 47 per cent, and in the first half of 1959 for 50 per cent. These same percentages stood at 86, 91, and 94 in New York City and at 20, 36, and 41 in the seven inner-ring suburban counties.[37] The great city of New York still experiences a demand for apartments in its old core and in its surburbs that can be explained in part by the higher degree of crowding and in part by the enormous concentration of higher- and lower-income people around its hub and its industrial and commercial establishments.

As such an enormous metropolitan system grows on and on in population and in territory, the problem of choosing between "spacious living" and "easy access" becomes acute. A careful analyst of this problem has observed:

The balancing of access convenience against the desire for space and other amenities works out differently for individuals who have different tastes and housing needs — and different levels of income to satisfy them.[38]

The lower-income category cannot afford to commute from afar because of the cost. The upper-income category can very well afford long-distance commuting, but they can also afford the more expensive apartments of the residential towers that increasingly characterize Manhattan's

[37] Regional Plan Association, *Bulletin 93, op. cit.*
[38] Edgar M. Hoover and Raymond Vernon, *Anatomy of a Metropolis*, New York Metropolitan Region Study, Harvard University Press, Cambridge, Mass., 1959, p. 152.

expanding hub. Such expensive apartment buildings close to business districts are also rising in the old cores of other major cities in Megalopolis and on the West Coast. They are usually associated with important concentrations of the office industry, the higher-salaried officers and employees of which like such residences. Among those in the higher-income range, suites in luxury hotels are also popular.

The towers, either for residential or office occupancy, do not devour space as the one-family houses do. But their inhabitants live in a world of stone, brick, glass, and cement with little greenery in it. Growing bushes and other plants on terraces is undertaken by some, especially in Manhattan, to make up for the lack of natural greenery around the homes. The residents of expensive apartments with such terraces also can often afford a country house that is relatively far away, though still situated within Megalopolis. This is another way in which a great deal of space is used per family.

For many inhabitants of Megalopolis access to their place of work means long commuting. Data are not yet available to tell in precise figures the numbers of commuters whose daily trip to work by train, bus, or private car is greater than ten miles, greater than thirty miles, or even greater than fifty miles. In fact, mere distance is hardly a proper measurement within the larger cities, especially in New York City or in Philadelphia. A distance of more than ten miles from home to work does not necessarily make one a commuter, for it is not infrequent within the city limits; but it certainly means commuting in Connecticut or New Jersey. Whether the commuting trip by car on a rural New Jersey road is more disturbing in any way than a subway trip of the same distance from Queens to lower Manhattan may be long debated. Although the answers to all these questions may be very important to specialists on metropolitan transportation, to local politicians, and last but not least to the commuter or subway user himself, they do not matter decisively for the pattern of land use.

If the commuter makes his daily trips despite the distance and other odds, it is in the great majority of cases because he chose to do so. The possibility of choice can be said in recent times to be denied by existing circumstances only to a few minorities, especially to the Negroes and Puerto Ricans. The choice to commute may have been dictated by many various considerations — financial factors, emotional factors (such as special attachment to a certain location, neighborhood, or even building), or preference of a certain mode of life for reasons of taste, career, social contacts, children's education, and so forth. These various considerations may become so entangled that although people often know why they move to a new house, they have great difficulty finding out why they do not move but remain in a spot even after its position has changed with relation to the considerations that originally led to its choice.

Study of changes in land use within the urbanized districts of Megalopolis reveals a complex network of motivations contributing to such changes. The push of the residential expansion toward the periphery is a logical and centuries-old trend in large urban centers, observed in many cities around the world. Where topography permitted, the city in old times grew by more or less regular concentric rings, initiating the custom that is still followed of speaking of the "center" of the city and an "inner ring" and "outer ring," as if city growth always proceeded along a circular pattern. Beyond the limits of the city proper, strongly emphasized by walls in early days, suburbs usually developed at the gates or farther out along one of the main lines of traffic radiating from the city's crossroads. Thus, beyond the well-constructed outer ring of a given period, the beginnings of the next period's outer ring are found. Sir Patrick Geddes of Edinburgh, one of the leading initiators of modern urban studies, compared London's growth to that of a coral reef and suggested the name of "man-reef" for such developments.[39] He was also conscious of the decisive role of the major lines of traffic in orienting the spread of urbanization. Half a century ago he foresaw the shaping of Megalopolis:

> Greater New York, now linked up, on both sides, by colossal systems of communications above and below its dividing waters, is also rapidly increasing its links with Philadelphia — itself no mean city — and with minor ones without number in every direction possible. For many years past it has paid to have tramway lines continuously along the roads all the way from New York to Boston, so that, taking these growths altogether, the expectation is not absurd that the not very distant future will see practically one vast city-line along the Atlantic Coast for five hundred miles, and stretching back at many points; with a total of, it may be, as many millions of population.[40]

Megalopolis has come of age probably more rapidly than Patrick Geddes expected and, at least in this century, with a much more modest num-

---

[39] In his often-quoted *Cities in Evolution*, London, 1915, Patrick Geddes wrote: "This octopus of London, polypus rather, is something curious exceedingly, a vast irregular growth without previous parallel in the world of life — perhaps likest to the spreadings of a great coral reef. Like this, it has a stony skeleton, and living polypes — call it, then, a 'man-reef' if you will." (p. 9 of the new and abridged edition published by Williams & Norgate, Ltd., London, 1949). Despite Geddes' warning against too-easy biological comparisons, cities are too often likened to growing "organisms," for instance by Eliel Saarinen, in *The City*, Reinhold, New York, 1943, pp. 8–26.

[40] Geddes, *op. cit.*, pp. 23–24.

ber of inhabitants than he envisioned. Perhaps even a man of his breadth and daring of vision could not imagine in 1915 the rate at which the Megalopolitan people could devour space and produce wealth, to plow it back as rapidly into the land. For here the suburban symbiosis of urban and rural has developed on an especially lavish scale, with one-family detached houses, lawns and backyard gardens, parks, shooting grounds, country summer homes, and other such uses of the land. This represents such an intensity of transportation movement and a source of profits for so many industries and trades that the rapid consumption of land is coupled here with a remarkably high rate of capital accumulation and redistribution.

The metropolitan explosion, which has here conquered so many acres and subordinated to its daily use or comfort so many more acres (chiefly wooded areas apparently left empty), has generated a great deal of wealth by providing work for so many people and consuming so many materials and services. It is perhaps difficult to estimate in millions of dollars all the business these trends in land use have brought to the realtors and shopping centers, to the construction and transportation industries, to the basic manufacturing of cement, steel, lumber, glass, machinery, furniture, etc., and to others because of the daily use of motor cars, rubber tires, gasoline, and do-it-yourself tools, to mention only a few of the beneficiaries. To every individual of the families involved, suburban sprawl may mean increased expenditure, but they can generally afford it, although this way of life, as compared with others, may leave less money for other possible expenditures or for savings. Again, this is a matter of choice by the individual, and since many millions chose such metropolitan living, an enormous amount of capital is turned over again and again, and much wealth is generated within the region. Whether such growth of wealth can be expanded indefinitely remains a problem for theoretical economists, perhaps not an easy one to solve.

For the purposes of this study, the consideration of such processes reminds us of the fact that it costs a great deal of money to devour space as residential sprawl has done in Megalopolis during the past twenty years.[41] The cost is not paid up when the essential plant is in place. Maintenance is necessary for houses and highways, and the latter must be widened or otherwise improved as traffic swells. Schools must be expanded, and more parking facilities and more parks must be provided. More wir-

[41] An interesting outline of the complexity of the process involved in building cities can be found in *Building, U.S.A.*, by the editors of *Architectural Forum*, McGraw-Hill Book Co., New York, 1957.

ing, sewage, and piping of all kinds must be laid and maintained through the areas where homes scatter or agglomerate. This means upward revision of rates of servicing and in the long run more taxation. The circuits breeding more wealth may well reach saturation, and individual budgets may tighten up. Then the momentum of the rising tide of urban expansion may slacken, and the problems of increasing population may be solved in less expensive ways.

Many of the studies of the metropolitan "explosion" and of its consequences in terms of land use have assumed that the means of financing what the people wanted would always be found. Such discussions have too often been restricted to defining the people's desires, generally established on the basis of the trends in previous years, even though those trends may have been started by another generation than the one whose wishes ought to be decisive in the forthcoming years.[42] If the availability of credit for expansion and maintenance were to decrease, people might look for less expensive solutions that would still take them out of the slums or prevent the obsolescence of their present homes. The answer might lie partly in high-rise apartment buildings, built far enough apart to leave enough air, light, and, if possible, recreational space for the dense population of the towers. We have already noticed, in the figures on building permits, a trend in the late 1950's toward these types of multi-storied houses. This trend could well develop more strongly in the 1960's. In this case the threat, instead of being to devour too much space, would become to gather too high a density of population over vast areas built-up uninterruptedly. While development of some of the recent suburbs may look wasteful, similar and worse waste of human resources could result from overcrowding.

Another partial solution to metropolitan growth with less sprawl could be achieved through more rehabilitation of obsolescent or aging buildings. Recently thought and discussion have been turned increasingly in that direction. By American standards it may seem too conservative, and in the long run almost wasteful, to attempt to control obsolescence and fight blight by rehabilitation short of full redevelopment, but it is not impossible for these standards to be revised and for techniques of rehabilitation to be worked out and applied that would greatly improve buildings with-

[42] This kind of discussion, trying to find out what is happening by estimating what has been and will be the free and unobstructed choice of the people, is often encountered in the land-use studies in such books as, for instance, *The Exploding Metropolis*, by the Editors of *Fortune*, Doubleday, Garden City, New York, 1958, or William H. Whyte, Jr., *The Organization Man*, Simon and Schuster, New York, 1956.

out actually rebuilding them. The remarkable organization known as The American Council to Improve Our Neighborhoods (ACTION) has already achieved substantial results in this direction and has contributed to educating the public as well as the national leadership in such matters. Recently Miles Colean, the distinguished housing expert, reminded the specialists of the enormous resources available in the "standing stock" of buildings housing the nation:

> The value of the residential structures in our urban communities, exclusive of land, has been estimated (as of 1955) to be $320 billion, or nearly one-quarter of all national wealth.
>
> From its magnitude alone, this vast investment merits attention and concern. From its bearing on the general welfare, in terms of the health, safety, comfort, and happiness of the people, its meaning is not surpassed by any of our other assets. In terms of the business generated through real estate and financing transactions and property repair and improvement, its importance is hardly less. It provides a large source of local revenue. . . .
>
> If we find that the tasks of maintaining and improving the existing housing supply and of adapting it to altered environmental conditions can make for good business and satisfactory investment, then we may point the way both to an important economic opportunity and to a means for reducing governmental burdens. Or, if we find that the business opportunities are unexploited, then we may seek the reasons and undertake to suggest remedies.[43]

These statements prefaced a careful survey of the opportunity existing for residential rehabilitation. Starting with so-called "prestige rehabilitation," of which Foggy Bottom in Washington is the prime instance, the survey dealt also with middle-income and low-rent housing rehabilitation, with the problem of financing, possible aid from public funds, and the general need to expand the volume of rehabilitation. It concluded:

> What are the alternatives to using rehabilitation more extensively in local housing programs? To place complete reliance on new, private construction may accelerate the outward expansion of urban population, producing entirely new city forms replacing existing urban centers. To rely primarily on publicly aided construction in existing urban centers requires an extremely high level of public and private expenditures. Rehabilitation at standards as closely approximating the abilities of local users to pay, without sacrificing a realistic standard of human decency, deserves a larger role in the housing programs of every community.[44]

[43] Miles L. Colean in "Preface" to William W. Nash, *Residential Rehabilitation: Private Profits and Public Purposes* (directed by Miles L. Colean) (ACTION Series in Housing and Community Development), McGraw-Hill, New York, 1959, pp. xix and xx.

[44] Nash, *op. cit.,* pp. 196–197.

It is noteworthy that almost all examples of successful rehabilitation quoted in this survey are in large cities, most of them in the five major cities of Megalopolis. This ought to have been expected, for because of the chronology of American settlement and urban growth the main cities on the Northeastern seaboard have more aged housing, higher urban residential densities, and a great turnover of population in more diverse income brackets.[45] The need for some stabilization and rehabilitation is greatest there, and some of the more successful experiments have already taken place there. It is unfortunate, however, that the most impressive successes have been on the side of "prestige rehabilitation," in the service of the wealthier residents or newcomers.

More emphasis on rehabilitation should decrease the mobility of residents within the large metropolitan areas and cause less obsolescence, as well as less new scattering eating up more suburban space. However, more buildings will have to be added anyway, to accommodate the increase in population. It is probable that more new buildings will be in multi-storied buildings for all levels of income. Many families with small children may prefer detached structures in outlying locations, while parents of already grown-up children may prefer apartments in central locations. As both these categories of families will grow in number, more dwellings of both kinds will be needed. The mobility of Megalopolitan residents will still be marked, though perhaps slightly less so.

This mobility, which has contributed much to residential obsolescence, was never caused by the physical deterioration of buildings alone. As a matter of fact, if the various forces at play in this intra-regional mobility could be assessed with some precision, it would probably be found that several other factors have been more effective in spurring it on. First, the desire for a homogeneous neighborhood of a certain sort has often caused large groups to move to another district in the community once they thought their territory had been "infiltrated" by newcomers of an "undesirable" race, creed, or social status. Panics have occasionally developed along entire streets, many houses being sold in a hurry at relatively low prices. Second, residences are attracted by employment, and migration of industrial plants has caused sudden local sprawls, and at times entire townships, to be built up. Third, the spread of residences is greatly influ-

---

[45] Harland Bartholomew, in *Land Uses in American Cities* (Harvard University Press, Cambridge, Mass., 1955), studied many middle-aged cities, only one of which, Newark, New Jersey, is in Megalopolis. He found Newark deviating from the "norm" especially as only 8.44 per cent of its developed area was in single-family homes by 1957 (his footnote, p. 32). Megalopolitan cities are on the average built higher than other American cities.

enced by transportation facilities, and new highways, bridges, or subways (there has been little recent extension of them) may determine the
development of new places and increased scattering in some areas. Thus,
even though residential rehabilitation may be favored and extended, bringing more stability to some communities, the traditional mobility of people
in Megalopolis will continue to be influenced by transport, by location of
industrial and commercial employment, and by social and racial prejudice.

We have been dealing almost exclusively with residential land use in this
chapter on urban uses of the land. Residents come to or stay in a place
sometimes because of its attractiveness but more commonly because of the
economic opportunities it offers. Land use in an urbanized region can
hardly be separated either from the economic activities by which its population makes a living or from the social structure which determines the
character of neighborhoods, and the social structure in turn is bound to
reflect the occupational characteristics of the region.

Form and Function

The urban economy has always differed from agriculture in the proportion of space allocated to *residential occupance* on the one hand and
economically productive functions on the other. In farming regions dwellings occupy an almost negligible fraction of the space given to agricultural production, and this is still true of most of the farms in Megalopolis.
In urban territory, on the contrary, residential needs take up most of the
land area, only a fraction of which is indeed occupied by the factories,
stores, warehouses, offices, and transportation facilities that make up the
"productive" part of a city's physical plant. This fraction, minor in area,
is, however, the very essential condition of a city's existence. It produces
the profits out of which the residents are paid the wages, salaries, fees,
and other revenue on which they subsist.

Thus in the past the traditional distinction grew up between *downtown*
and *uptown* in American cities, *downtown* being where people worked
and transacted business and *uptown* being where they lived. The two sections of the city were quite distinct, having different functions and different looks. Not all industrial and commercial functions could be kept in
the old downtown district, and many industrial plants and warehouses
moved toward the periphery or were built in adequate suburban locations.
Little by little the urbanized districts of large metropolitan areas became
complicated puzzles, made up of an irregular pattern of many districts
with different specializations. From study of this puzzle for the New York
or Philadelphia metropolitan area three main generalizations can be

drawn: (1) residential occupance still covers much more acreage than all other uses combined and is found in all parts of a city except in a few heavily industrialized waterfront sectors; (2) main lines of transportation attract industrial establishments and warehouses, as is obvious along the water channels of the great seaside ports, along major rail lines, and along certain highways such as Route 128 around Boston (sometimes surnamed "Electronics Boulevard"); (3) business offices and entertainment establishments are usually concentrated in or near the old "downtown."

To what extent factories, warehouses, or offices move in or out of the various parts of Megalopolis is a rather complex question, better studied for each category in terms of the economics of its function. As a *use* of the land, industrial and commercial occupation is less well known to us than housing, for it has never been as carefully surveyed on a national or regional scale in the United States as has been done for housing in the Censuses of housing. Censuses of business and manufacturing provide a good deal of data about employment, payrolls, value added by the manufacture, sales, or receipts, but do not inform us about the extent of the physical plants, the frequency of displacement, or the kind, age, and condition of the buildings.[46]

We know, however, that certain manufacturing specialties concentrate in certain areas; that space for expansion is important to any industrial enterprise that is not folding up; that the recent trend in architecture of industrial buildings has been toward more space on the ground floor and buildings with fewer stories. This has meant greater acreage consumed and more cases of moves "out of town," for such acreage can be secured more easily and more cheaply in less crowded districts. Since to an industry accessibility is expressed in terms of transportation costs, which represent an increasing share of all costs, the axial belt of Megalopolis between important city markets has remained a favored location, although an improved highway system has helped to widen many parts of the traditional axial ribbon of territory along the Fall Line.

Meanwhile, architectural trends for many categories of establishments employing white-collar personnel have gone in the opposite direction. Manufacturing plants and even specialized warehouses have indicated a tendency to relative dispersal and to sprawling on the ground in single-story structures, but corporation offices, banks, department stores, hotels, and even hospitals have shown a definite preference for high-rise towers

---

[46] See John Rannells, *The Core of the City*, Columbia University Press, New York, 1956. This is a pilot study, especially concerned with the central district of Philadelphia.

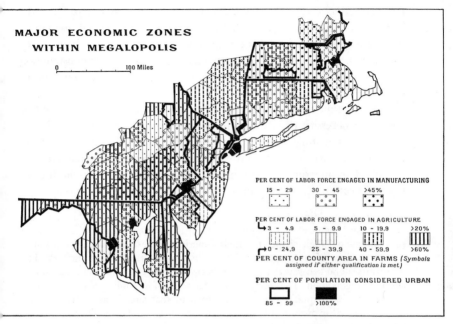

Fig. 134. The economic zones on this map result from superimposing the various characteristics shown separately on the three maps of Fig. 126. The data are from the Censuses of 1950.

and for congregating in or near central business districts. At the same time more separation in space has developed between the production and the nonproduction facilities of the same firm or industry and, within their nonproduction activities, between warehousing, research laboratories, and administrative offices. The latter two categories of activities, however, seem to prefer locations not too distant from one another. Manhattan has attracted in increasing number the offices of industrial corporations, which meet their ever-expanding need for more floor area by rising toward the sky rather than by spreading over more ground acreage. At the same time, research laboratories of the same corporations are beginning to crowd in obvious fashion within relatively easy reach of New York City, especially in New Jersey and Connecticut. In such locations the laboratories find themselves, of course, within easy reach also of much else that they often need besides advice or instructions from their administrative offices.

All these trends occur to diversify the built-up landscapes in Megalopolis and each of the major metropolitan units of the region. *A sort of increasing division of labor for the metropolitan space works itself out as form and function tend to link themselves more obviously in the patterns of land use.* These patterns result from an increasingly refined division of labor among the activities that must cooperate in complex modern society to bring about the finished products of manufacturing, the consumption of business transactions, and the final profits at which the economic process aims.

For some time architects and urbanists have been talking and preaching about the necessity of adapting form to function in buildings and city plans. In this century the teachings of Frank Lloyd Wright and Le Corbusier especially have insisted on what is often called the "organic requirements" of architecture and planning. More than a century ago, in discussing architecture, the American sculptor Horatio Greenough wrote:

To plant a building firmly on the ground; to give it the light that may, the air that must, be needed; to apportion the spaces for convenience, decide their size, and model their shapes for their functions – these acts organize a building. No college of architecture is a quorum to judge this part of the task. The occupants alone can say if they have been well served; time alone can stamp any building as solid. The monumental character of a building has reference to its site – to its adaptation in size and form to that site. It has reference also to the external expression of the inward functions of the building – to adaptation of its features and their graduation to its dignity and importance; and it relates, moreover, to that distinction which taste always requires between external breadth and interior detail.[47]

This statement, remarkably advanced for 1852 (when its author died), could apply today as general instruction for the planning of a whole development or new town, as well as for buildings.

Since the 1920's Le Corbusier has championed an urban architecture favoring high-rise large apartment buildings, generously spaced, with a good deal of greenery around them, and within easy reach of large parks.[48] As often happens to theoreticians, he has been more successful in inspiring the work of others, architects or town planners, than in designing such structures himself. Although other schools of architecture have prevailed in Megalopolis, nowhere else have so many buildings been erected of the general sort he foresaw. The rules of the real estate market seldom have allowed for the actual "vertical green city" Le Corbusier preached.

---

[47] Horatio Greenough, *Form and Function: Remarks on Art, Design and Architecture*, University of California Press, Berkeley, 1957, pp. 20-21, being a reprinting (in paper-bound edition) of *Memorial of Horatio Greenough*, edited by Henry T. Tuckerman, Putnam, New York, 1853.

[48] See especially his summary of general views on urban development: Le Corbusier, *Propos d'Urbanisme*, Bourrelier, Paris, 1946.

However, he was less Utopian, perhaps, than Ebenezer Howard, the prophet of the garden city.

The emphasis on the garden, the green, the open space in twentieth-century urbanism is quite significant. As the density and mass of the various cities neighboring on one another in Megalopolis have increased, *the need for recreation has grown also, especially in terms of the space devoted to it.* A new function has thus appeared in the expanding gamut of urban uses of the land — recreational space for urban crowds.

In the past, such use of land was a great luxury. Only the wealthier or more powerful people could afford to set aside pieces of land just for their own enjoyment, like the vast gardens and parks designed after the Renaissance for Florentine princely merchants, French kings and counts, or English barons. For such wealthy persons, even the greatest artists, such as Leonardo da Vinci, were called upon to design parks, and gardening became a great and respected art. The principles then laid down for parks and gardens seem to have influenced city planning to this day.[49] But it was only in the nineteenth century that the need for the recreation of large urban crowds made imperative the establishment of parks in the cities and around them. In the capitals of Europe grounds set aside in previous centuries for the pleasure of the reigning families were often thrown open to the public and became city parks (thus the Luxembourg Gardens in Paris, Kensington Gardens in London, and the suburban Forêt de Soignes next to Brussels or the Forêt de St. Germain near Paris).

In the cities of Megalopolis, however, other kinds of land had to be found for parks. At a very early time (in the 1850's) New York City set aside land for the impressive expanse of Central Park. Land for Prospect Park (in Brooklyn) and Bronx Park was obtained by the purchase of large private estates in 1859 and 1884 respectively. The Bronx and Brooklyn had to emphasize the educational value of botanical gardens in order to set up more large parks. The District of Columbia took advantage of a valley too steep for buildings and established Rock Creek Park. The size and mobility of the Megalopolitan crowds, early motorized, have made it unnecessary to keep the major recreational grounds immediately adjacent to the major residential concentrations. Parks have been scattered at some distance, maintained by state or local authorities, but within easy driving reach from the great nuclei of crowding. The average urbanite wants also

[49] Pierre Lavedan, *Histoire de l'Urbanisme*, Vols. 2 and 3, Henri Laurens, Paris, 1947 and 1952; and Jean Gottmann, "Plans de villes des deux côtés de l'Atlantique," in *Cahiers de Géographie de Québec*, Vol. III, No. 6, April-September 1959, pp. 237–242.

to have hunting grounds preserved for him conveniently near his residence (a privilege reserved for feudal lords in the Old World until a few generations ago),[50] and he often goes boating or fishing and indulges also in winter sports.

More leisure and more means for recreation, now available to the common people in this area, create an enormous problem in terms of the space to be allocated for these functions. The spaces that seem empty along the Northeastern seaboard and in the hilly ranges bordering on Megalopolis may help to meet this need (some sections have already been put into public parks, state forests, or reservations), which the green space available within urbanized districts could not satisfy. To some extent it might be claimed that the spread of detached one-family houses in suburban areas, with patches of green around them, and all the recent trends toward a symbiosis of urban and rural land uses [51] meet this need of open space for the recreation of every family, especially if it has small children. For most of the suburbanites, however, these small gardens or lawns around their homes, while improving the conditions and landscape of daily relaxation, do not fully satisfy the urge for recreational activities that require more space.

Thus in some parts of this vast area the uses of the land create sharply differentiated and specialized districts while in others they interpenetrate and mingle so much that they cannot help causing adverse reactions, such as the fencing off of various areas in an effort to reserve them for their proper occupants, the owners or tenants, and to defend their privacy and property against intrusion that may also threaten the land values. Thus the farmer posts his land against hunters, and the urban community resorts to zoning and other legal devices such as the incorporation of villages, the establishment of country clubs, and the like.

Such a partitioning, aiming at stabilization and conservation, is in many respects necessary. Zoning legislation in the urbanized areas is an indispensable foundation for organizing the community and its land space from within, preventing anarchy through various *limitations on the use* of the land. It has been traced back in American legislation to the ordinances of colonial days that banished powder mills and stores from the vicinity of dwellings in Boston (1706) or set up limitations on buildings to secure bet-

---

[50] See Chapter 7 above, pp. 341–383. For the past history of city parks see Paul Zucker, *Town and Square: From the Agora to the Village Green*, Columbia University Press, New York, 1959.

[51] See Chapter 5 above, pp. 217–257.

ter fire protection (Boston, 1692).[52] The first comprehensive zoning regulation in the United States was enacted in 1916 by New York City. In
1920 Congress passed a zoning law for the District of Columbia, and by
the 1950's zoning laws regulated almost all the densely settled districts in
the country.

Zoning, however, cannot and should not be thought of only as a tool for
conservation and stabilization. It has been recognized by many courts
throughout the United States as aiming at protecting the future as well as
the present.[53] The future of land use in a region such as Megalopolis, and
in each of its growing and changing cities, is obviously endowed with
great fluidity. Zoning has the great advantage of providing for such fluidity if needed, and for being administered on the local, usually the municipal, level. Land use here again appears as one of the essential resources of
a community by which it may provide for its well-being and "well-grow-
ing." Zoning should thus express the community's intent, its wisdom, and
its resourcefulness.

It becomes obvious at this stage that the land-use patterns, which have
been and still are changing rapidly in Megalopolis, cannot be determined
or administered according to simple formulas dealing with location, density of occupation, or immediate profits to be earned. Many forces and
principles are at play that cannot be quantified. We have to describe land
use in broad terms and major categories. The inner details and the orientation of their evolution must be considered in the light of a full understanding of the region's activities and modes of life, of the economic and
social structure of its component communities.

The recent revolution that has occurred in land use in Megalopolis stems
from deep changes in the ways and means of the local society, and some
of these have been applied to the use of the land, vast but not unlimited,
with that Promethean impulse characteristic of Megalopolitan tradition
and momentum. The space available to the people has been devoured in
some sections vertically, in others horizontally, and in still others by being
emptied and abandoned to undesirable kinds of flora and fauna. But Megalopolis has reshaped its environment more than once and will not stop
at this stage. Among the recent trends of change the renewal of the cen-

[52] James Metzenbaum, *The Law of Zoning*, 2nd ed., Baker, Voorhis & Co., New
York, 1955, 3 vols., especially Vol. I, Chapters 1 and 2.

[53] See on this score Gallion and Eisner, *The Urban Pattern, op. cit.*, Chapter 11;
Metzenbaum, *op. cit.*; and Richard L. Nelson and Frederick T. Ashman, *Real Estate
and City Planning*, Prentice-Hall, Englewood Cliffs, New Jersey, 1957, especially
Chapters 18 to 22.

tral districts in the larger cities is a significant symptom. It points to new functions presently congregating in the hub of the modern metropolis.

The old "mix" of activities, inherited from the nineteenth century, and consisting mainly of manufacturing, retail and wholesale trade plus some government offices, is replaced by a different congregation of businesses. The new "mix" consists of activities pertaining to finances, industrial management, research, education, government, and entertainment. The first and last of the fields mentioned have been associated for ages. The mutual attraction of research and education on the one hand, and financial and industrial management on the other, appears as a newer feature and a promising one. The new "mix" of functions for a great metropolitan "downtown" requires novel centers, stadiums, laboratory and school buildings. The imperative necessity of satisfying this trend will grow more obvious as we turn to a study of the economic functions of Megalopolis.[54]

[54] Not every city in Megalopolis can easily develop in its central district the new mix of activities on a substantial scale. As trade and manufacturing stop growing or, sometimes, move out, a number of medium-size cities lose much of their activity, and begin to question their *raison d'être*. In as dynamic a region as Megalopolis has been, with a constant remaking of the economic system that sustains the population, local soft spots are bound to appear. Not every part of Megalopolis is necessarily growing and progressing even though the region as a whole is doing so. There have been in recent years several "depressed areas" within Megalopolis, in places where adaptation to the economic changes was more difficult to achieve. The coal-mining towns of eastern Pennsylvania and some of the textile towns of Massachusetts and New Jersey have been clear examples, for reasons rooted in the evolution of the industry on which the local economy was founded. It is difficult in this volume, concerned mainly with the region as a whole, to account for each particular component of it. (See National Planning Association, *Depressed Industrial Areas — A National Problem* (Planning Pamphlet No. 98), Washington, D. C., January 1957.

PART THREE

EARNING A LIVING

INTENSELY

The preceding chapters of this study have been concerned mainly with the historical processes by which Megalopolis has become such a huge concentration of people, economic power, and activities, and then with the present uses of the land over its vast area. In other words, we have tried to describe the genesis and present structure of Megalopolis. The sketching of the dynamics of past growth gave little opportunity to deal with the economic foundations on which the present prosperity of this region rests, although the formula of the "economic hinge" helps to make clear the general principles of the regional economy and its great emphasis on large-scale commercial business. Now comes an analysis of the ways, industrial and commercial, by which the Megalopolitan people make their living.

The modes of life described in connection with the uses of land suggest a rather intensified economy, yielding high profits widely redistributed through the region and probably beyond it. Our study of the use of farmland and woodland [1] indicated that these nonurban and traditional activities, although earning financial profits for a few people, do not represent on the whole a basic element in the money-making system that allows Megalopolis to live as it does. In fact, the very organization of Megalopolitan agriculture and forestry suggests an entire dependence on special kinds of benefits stemming from the suburban character of the locale, from the immediate proximity to the densely urbanized districts with all their needs and resources.

Megalopolis earns its living on small patches of territory, the total ground acreage of which represents only a small fraction (possibly by 1960 one twentieth) of the region's total area, which itself extends over only 1.8 per cent of the land area of the continental United States. *Thus the places of work that earn the living of a little more than one fifth of the American nation,* and that the richest fifth, *occupy less than one thousandth of the country's area.* This means a dense concentration indeed of industrial, commercial, and administrative activities, for this space was the locus in 1950 of 22.8 per cent of the nation's labor force and 21.2 per cent of the population. In 1954 it accounted for 28 per cent of the nation's wholesale-trade payroll; 32.6 per cent of the merchant wholesalers' sales; 31.2 per cent of the selected-services-trades payroll and 32.8 per cent of their receipts; 26.4 per cent of the total value added by manufacturers in the United States; and 24.2 per cent of the retail-trade payroll. In 1956 its banks held 37 per cent of the deposits in all American banks, and its financial institutions handled well over half of all financial transactions in the country. This impressive concentration means that the intensity of all activities in the region is greater than the national average. Even by American standards, and certainly in terms of international averages, we are justified in speaking here of *intense living and working* on a very small acreage.

The size of the spaces devoted to these business or manufacturing activities is such as to make it difficult to examine them as one of the components in the pattern of land use. As a matter of fact, some of the important white-collar activities in this system are carried out in space officially defined by zoning as in residential use. The money-making activities, insofar as they provide the means of living, spending, and saving for the population, affect much more than land use alone. We must study them now for themselves, their size, their diversity, and their trends, not only

[1] See above, Chapters 6 and 7.

in location but in general evolution as well. We may thus better understand what is now happening and what the prospects are for the future.

Historically, the commercial activities of the great seaports in this region laid down the true foundations of local prosperity and urban growth, and, in more general fashion, of the region's role in the world. Today commercial and financial establishments again employ more people than do manufacturing establishments, and personnel of the latter is in good part occupied in administrative, financial, trading, and research functions, so that employment in manufactures directly engaged in production represents only a minority (probably close to one fourth) of all the jobs in Megalopolis. Nevertheless, manufacturing has played such an essential role in the building up of this region's wealth and in its urbanization [2] that we may well examine it first when reviewing the economic activities.

For at least 150 years, as a result of the Industrial Revolution, urban densities resulted essentially from the gathering in cities of factory workers and their families. Never would Megalopolis have grown and consolidated as it did through the first half of the twentieth century had it not attracted and developed so many manufactures. The recent tendency for industrial plants to move out to other, less crowded sections and the relative drop in Megalopolis' share in American manufacturing have caused a great deal of concern in the region as to its future. We shall therefore devote the next chapter to the present condition and distribution of manufactures in Megalopolis.

Future growth in employment, so necessary to maintain the whole area's momentum, would seem, however, to depend less and less on manufacturing. All the modern economic evolution, spurred on by recent technological advances, points to the decisive and increasing role of commerce and of the white-collar occupations. These two categories of activities will be examined after the survey of manufactures.

Both manufacturing and commerce in Megalopolis are greatly dependent on the region's retaining its role as the nation's economic hinge. This poses the problem of transportation, both in terms of the networks linking the region to the outside and in terms of the facilities for transportation and communication within the region. A hinge between sea lanes on the one hand and inland waterways, railroads, and highways on the other is built around an exceptionally intricate network of railroads and roads. Can Megalopolis retain its role as an essential hub in an era of planes and pipelines, of telephone, radio, and television, when the lines separating land, sea, and air seem to lose their ancient significance? We shall exam-

[2] For the historical development see Chapters 3 and 4 above.

ine this entanglement of problems in the following chapters, but without letting it obscure the more immediate and possibly greater threat offered by the worsening metropolitan traffic within the region.

In the contemporary economic evolution of the metropolis in general, and in Megalopolis especially, the growing emphasis placed on commercial and administrative functions and on white-collar occupations is bringing about a redevelopment of the "downtown." However, the capacity of the old areas of business concentration to manage and accommodate the rising tide of the expanding "office industry" is being questioned, chiefly because of the hardships faced by traffic to and through the business districts. Other problems, however, are the costs of servicing such a concentration, and the increasingly unpleasant consequences of such crowding in terms of pollution of the natural environment and worsening of the social environment. This last threat may become the greatest of all if it is allowed to develop and to deepen, and unpleasant conditions for working and living may hasten the trend toward decentralization or deconcentration already evident for many stages of industrial production. If such decentralization should increase in the white-collar occupations, as seems technologically feasible already, although not yet managerially desirable, all the modern metropolitan structures would be deeply shattered, and the suburbs might suffer as well as the central cores. Urban life is founded on the advantages of living and working together in a society that is highly diversified but can function as one well-organized community. The survival of the multi-million society of Megalopolis as a going concern could be threatened if to waste of space and materials, which on the whole is profitable, were added waste of human resources.

CHAPTER 9

Manufacturing in Megalopolis

It has often been stated that the Northeastern seaboard of the United States has been losing manufacturing establishments to other areas so that it no longer represents as important a part of the nation's manufactures as it used to. In relative terms this is certainly true, reflecting a general trend toward a wider distribution of industries within the country. Megalopolis accounted for about one half of all wage earners in manufacturing in the United States in 1904 but for only 28 per cent in 1954. However, such has been the growth of American industries on the one hand and of Megalopolis itself on the other that in *absolute* terms, either in numbers of employees or in value added by manufacturing, these industries are greater than ever in Megalopolis as a whole. Many locational shifts have taken place, of course, and the specializations characteristic of the manufactures still concentrated in the area have been slowly evolving.

In 1954 the concentration of manufacturing in Megalopolis still made up a little more than one fourth of the total manufacturing activities in the United States.[1] The aggregate size of these industries in Megalopolis kept it ranking among the leading manufacturing areas of the world. Its factories employed more people than all those of Italy and Sweden put together, or a number equal to three fifths of all manufacturing employment in the United Kingdom. In terms of value added by manufacturing the Megalopolitan production surpassed that of all these three European countries combined.[2] Only the industrial Middle West, in the triangle broadly defined by Chicago, Pittsburgh, and Buffalo, could boast a comparable concentration, perhaps even a greater one, but so differently oriented in its major specializations as to make detailed comparison difficult.

Such has been the integration of the huge American economic system that the Northeastern seaboard has been a part of the whole and has never felt any need for self-sufficiency in its manufactures. A rather free competitive system has determined what is to be produced here rather than to the west or south. Because of the enormous consumption of the regional market, new production establishments are constantly attracted to Megalopolis. The magnificent system of transportation facilities, both by land and by sea, worked out by the economic *hinge* has also helped to attract new manufactures and to stabilize old ones. Manufacturing in Megalopolis is thus based on the commercial system the region has built up for itself. What has been happening to industrial activities here will be better understood once present distribution and recent trends within the region have been examined.

Employment in Manufacturing

In 1954 the total manufacturing employment in Megalopolis reached the highest figure recorded by any Census. This increase in personnel was all the more remarkable because between 1947 and 1954 a good deal of automation had considerably increased the productivity of the average employee in many sectors. Thus the rise in number of jobs testified, better than many other statistics could, to an expansion of the industrial production in this region. During 1954 the average total manufacturing employment amounted to 4,363,000 people, about one third of the whole non-

[1] In more precise terms, according to data computed from the *U. S. Census of Manufactures: 1954*, the region held 27.9 per cent of the annual average number of employees, 27.3 per cent of that year's payroll, 28.1 per cent of the wages paid to production workers, and 26.4 per cent of the value added by manufacturing.

[2] Based on data in the United Nations' *Statistical Yearbook 1958*, New York, 1958, Table No. 66. Such broad comparisons between countries with different modes of life and different wage scales do not necessarily mean much, but still they may provide a general indication as to size of industrial production.

agricultural labor force in the region.[3] While manufacturing is therefore responsible for the subsistence and prosperity of only a minority (though a substantial one) of the Megalopolitan population, it is still the most important of all major categories of employment in Megalopolis.

How manufacturing was distributed through the region in 1950 can be ascertained from the map showing the percentage of the whole labor force employed in manufacturing (Fig. 135). The higher percentages (especially those above 40 per cent, clearly above the average for the whole area) are found in southern New England, but away from Boston; in eastern Pennsylvania, but at some distance from Philadelphia; and in a few counties of New Jersey, but there again at some distance from both New York City and Philadelphia. Among cities, the larger percentages of employment in manufacturing were found in the medium-sized and smaller central cities — in such places as Fall River, New Bedford, and Worcester, Massachusetts; Bridgeport and Waterbury, Connecticut; Trenton, Camden, and Paterson, New Jersey; and Allentown, Pennsylvania (see graphs in Fig. 60, p. 212). The list would be longer, of course, if cities with less than 100,000 inhabitants were included. Many of these smaller central cities have such a high proportion of their people employed in manufactures not so much because manufactures are outstandingly successful in them as because they are unable to attract many other kinds of economic activity. In cities of comparable size where other types of business have developed to a notable degree, such as Newark, New Haven, Hartford, or Wilmington, the proportion of employment in manufacturing drops below 40 per cent of the total.

There is thus a marked trend for manufacturing to play a greater role in the economic life of the parts of Megalopolis *not* in the immediate vicinity of the larger cities. In the great cities and their suburbs the proportion of the labor force employed in manufacturing is generally as low as 25 to 40 per cent, for these areas provide other means of livelihood on a larger scale than can smaller cities or less densely urbanized areas. In absolute figures, however, these great cities remain the major concentrations of manufacturing employment, as is shown on the map of the *numbers* of manufacturing employees by counties in 1954 (Fig. 137). Despite their small area the counties of the old urban cores each counted more than 100,000 employees, and so did two New Jersey counties close to Manhat-

---

[3] Precise figures for the labor force by counties are not available for 1954 but only for 1950. The approximate proportion of "one third" was therefore estimated in broad fashion, projecting the 1950 Census figures for the labor force on the basis of official estimates of the 1950–54 growth of employment by states.

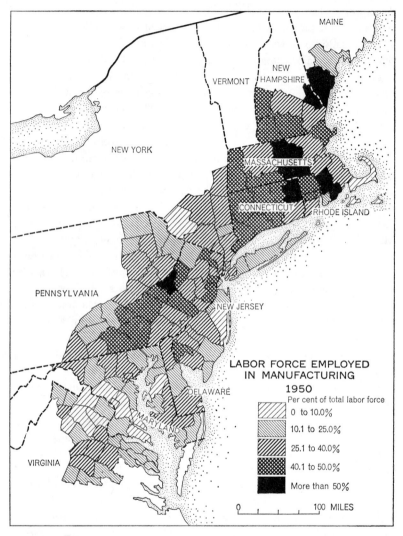

LABOR FORCE EMPLOYED
IN MANUFACTURING
1950
Per cent of total labor force
0 to 10.0%
10.1 to 25.0%
25.1 to 40.0%
40.1 to 50.0%
More than 50%

0   100 MILES

FIG. 135

tan (Hudson and Essex) and one of Boston's suburban counties (Middlesex). These areas have most of the industrial workers but are not as highly
specialized in manufacturing as are some outlying districts. For such purposes as trade, finance, and recreation the smaller cities that are more dependent on local manufacture become satellites in the orbits of the larger
metropolises with a more diversified economy.

Modern urban growth thus appears to be less rooted in manufacturing activities than is usually believed and than used to be the case. Nevertheless, manufacturing remains, as we have already noted, *the most important supplier of jobs* of all the principal occupational categories throughout the whole area, and the total employment figures are still growing. This growth, however, is unequally distributed over the Northeastern region (see Fig. 136). During the period 1904–1954 manufacturing employment showed an especially rapid rate of growth south of Delaware Bay (that is, in Delaware, Maryland, Virginia, and the District of Columbia), and in this southern part of Megalopolis it continued to rise rapidly during the early 1950's. A similar trend may be observed in New Jersey, which benefits from its location between New York City and Philadelphia, receiving some of the overflow from both larger metropolitan regions. Connecticut showed some progress too, though at a slower pace, but Massachusetts, Rhode Island, and New Hampshire seem to be levelling off or even slightly declining. In these last three New England states the maximum reached in 1919, at the end of the spectacular industrial development caused by World War I, remained above the figures of 1947 and 1954, whereas from Connecticut southward the level of 1919 was surpassed in both 1947 and 1954.

The number of employees does not necessarily reflect the volume or value of the production. Mechanization and, more recently, automation have considerably increased the individual worker's productivity in many industries, but in proportions that vary greatly from one type of manufacturing to another. Nor would the value added by manufacturing be a much more significant index than the number of employees. However, a general impression emerges, from examination of the maps and graphs showing manufacturing employment in Megalopolis, that manufacturing has been pushing southward and has developed west of the Hudson more rapidly (especially since 1920) than in New England. To a large extent this has been a move out of the more congested section of Megalopolis, out of the states that were the first to industrialize on a large scale and that may therefore have suffered more from obsolescence. This trend was probably accelerated by the general economic growth of the South, particularly after 1930, and by the search for locations better linked to the rapidly developing markets in other parts of the country. Many factors have been at play here.

This general observation seems to be confirmed by the changes that occurred in manufacturing employment from 1939 to 1954 (Fig. 138). The 1947 figures were still much under the spell of the growth of "war-baby

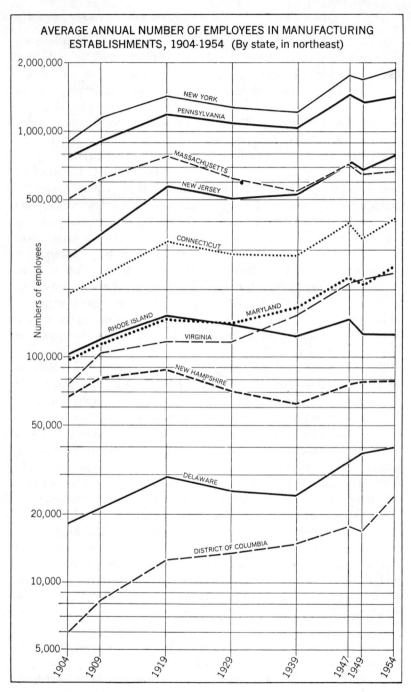

FIG. 136

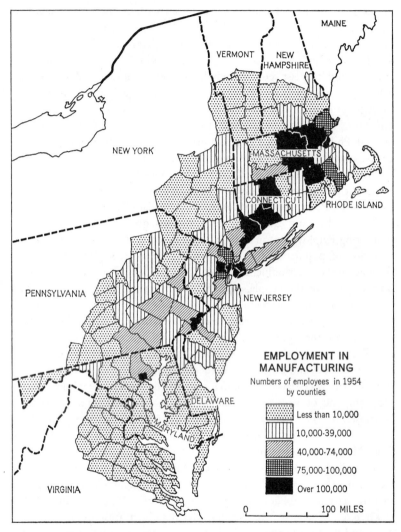

EMPLOYMENT IN
MANUFACTURING
Numbers of employees in 1954
by counties

- Less than 10,000
- 10,000-39,000
- 40,000-74,000
- 75,000-100,000
- Over 100,000

0   100 MILES

FIG. 137

industries" and of the overexcited demand of the first postwar years, reflecting the endeavor to make up for restrictions imposed on consumption
by wartime conditions (see the distribution of 1947 manufacturing employment on the lower map, Fig. 139). By 1954, however, Megalopolitan
manufacturers had become adapted to conditions of the postwar era. The
period 1939–54 saw the whole employment in manufacturing in the United

States grow by 63 per cent. Thus counties with an increase of less than 51 per cent (see Fig. 138) were notably behind the national trend. They are relatively numerous in southern New Hampshire, in Massachusetts and Rhode Island, in eastern Pennsylvania, and even in central New Jersey, although this last state as a whole experienced a remarkable expansion at that time. Growth was especially impressive, much above the national average, in most of the New York–Northeastern New Jersey Metropolitan Area, around Baltimore, and, to a lesser extent, in Connecticut and around Philadelphia. In a few counties manufacturing employment declined, especially around Washington, D. C., and in Suffolk County, Massachusetts (i.e., in Boston itself). The main industrial growth in Megalopolis in that period took place south of Hartford, Connecticut, and west of the Hudson River, mostly in the traditional axial belt but with some widening of it. In many essential features the changes in distribution of manufacturing employment in 1939–54 tend to coincide with changes in distribution of population for 1930–50 (Fig. 73, p. 248). This comparison testified to the great influence the distribution of manufactures still exerts on the spread of the people, especially outside the greater cities — at least on the scale of our observations.

In many ways manufacturing remains the backbone of the Megalopolitan economy throughout the whole area, with the exception of the metropolitan region of Washington, D. C. It is understandable, therefore, that local authorities and experts concerned with the section's economic future insist on the necessity of retaining most of the already established manufacturing and of attracting as much more as possible. Some worry may be caused by the often-remarked shrinkage of the relative role of Megalopolitan manufacturing in the national total. In 1904 the seaboard states, from Massachusetts to the District of Columbia inclusively, held 51.6 per cent of all the manufacturing wage earners in the United States. Every Census has shown a regular decrease in this percentage: 50.1 in 1909, 47.2 in 1919, 42.1 in 1929, 40.8 in 1939, 38.1 in 1947, 35.8 in 1954. Included in this region, of course, are the non-Megalopolitan areas of upstate New York and western Pennsylvania, but the general trend seems valid on the whole for Megalopolis. It had 28 per cent of the nation's manufacturing employment in 1954, or 4,363,000 employees, more but not much more than the almost four million thus employed in the same area in the peak year of 1919. A growth of only about 10 per cent in the number of jobs, during a period when the national increase in such jobs came close to 60 per cent, may justify concern.[4] That the population and wealth of Mega-

[4] See Murray D. Dessel, *Long Term Regional Trends in Manufacturing Growth: 1899–1955, Area Trend Series*, No. 2, Office of Area Development, U. S. Department

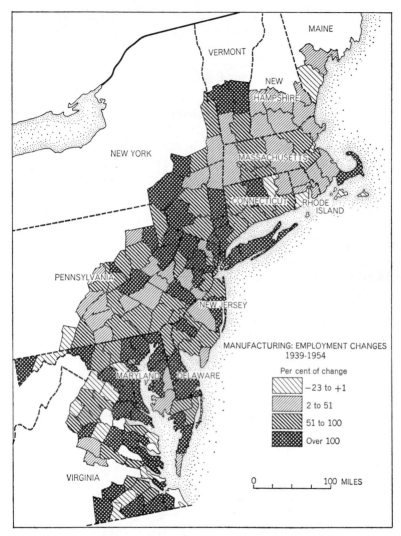

FIG. 138

lopolis increased during this same time by much more than one tenth, although not necessarily at the same rate as for the whole nation, means, of course, a decreasing local dependence on manufacturing. This dependence remains large enough, however, to warrant a closer look at the basic advantages of Megalopolis for manufactures, at the specializations and migrations of manufactures that have developed within the region, and at the trends of migration to other areas.

Which Industries Are Located Where?

The various kinds of manufactures do not all follow the same lines of development and do not all obey the same forces. Factors causing the prosperity or decline of one category, out of the great numbers gathered in Megalopolis, may have a quite different effect or no effect at all on other types of manufacturing found there. Before we consider the intricate dynamics governing industrial location, we must first review the great variety of manufactures now located in the region and see which groups or types of establishments are situated where. We may then begin to understand the reasons for this distribution and the factors that may or may not modify it.

The variety of manufacturing carried on in Megalopolis is such as to discourage any attempt at presenting a full tableau. Of the New York metropolitan region alone it was recently said:

> The industries . . . run almost the whole range of the industrial lexicon, from airplanes to zippers. In fact, of the approximately 450 industries listed by the federal Bureau of the Census in its detailed breakdowns of the nation's manufacturing economy, some 420 appear in the New York Metropolitan Region.[5]

And almost every category that does not appear in this central part of Megalopolis can be found elsewhere in the region. For example, although there are no large steel mills around New York City, they can be found in eastern Pennsylvania or the suburbs of Baltimore. Such variety is not surprising, for one fourth of American manufacturing, located within a relatively small area that also contains one fifth of the nation, is bound to endeavor to satisfy the enormous demand of the local market. Moreover, since this is a seaboard region well equipped with seaports and means of transportation inland, many of the industries located here may be attracted by the access to faraway markets or sources of materials, domestic or foreign. Thus some of the manufacturing is for export and some of it processes imported unfinished materials.

A few maps based on the numbers of manufacturing establishments by main categories of goods in each county give us a general picture of the

---

[5] Edgar M. Hoover and Raymond Vernon, *Anatomy of a Metropolis*, New York Metropolitan Region Study, Harvard University Press, Cambridge, Mass., 1959, p. 25.

situation in the middle 1950's.[6] The map showing the distribution in 1954 of establishments manufacturing textiles, apparel, and related products (Fig. 140A) clearly indicates a concentration of textile mills in New England (especially eastern Massachusetts and Rhode Island) and in Pennsylvania north of Philadelphia (especially Bucks, Berks, Montgomery, and Lehigh counties). In contrast, apparel factories are scattered throughout the whole region, with a definite concentration in and around New York City and Philadelphia.

Establishments manufacturing machinery of all kinds (including electrical), transportation equipment, fabricated metal products, instruments, etc., are also scattered throughout Megalopolis but are rather impressively concentrated in the axial belt from Boston to Baltimore (via Worcester, Hartford, New Haven, Greater New York, Trenton, Philadelphia, Lancaster, and York). Clustering is quite evident in and immediately around the central cities, especially in the older centers of industrialization (Fig. 141B). Primary metals manufacturing (Fig. 141A) shows somewhat less dispersion. South of the Mason and Dixon line it is found mainly in Baltimore, while north of that line it is concentrated toward the seaside, which includes the great tidal rivers, especially the Delaware. It is also attracted toward the larger cities and ports and is found in relatively impressive numbers, and often with at least a few large establishments, in the coal-mining area in Pennsylvania and on its fringe (especially in Bethlehem and Reading).

The chemical and petroleum industries are distributed in a fashion rather similar to that of the primary metals: there are not many establishments outside the axial belt, and there are strong concentrations in or around the larger cities. The huge consumption of petroleum products in Megalopolis and the large quantities of crude oil brought in by sea (either

[6] Statistical data about "establishments" are more readily available by counties than are detailed statistics about number of employees or value added by manufacture for each category of manufactures. The number of establishments does not necessarily provide a full or accurate indication of the size of the industry in a small area. Thus, according to the Census Bulletin MC-203, *Size of Establishments*, the *1954 Census of Manufactures* recorded in the United States a total of 287,000 manufacturing establishments of all sizes, among which 2,008 had 1,000 or more employees each and accounted for one third of all manufacturing employment and 37 per cent of value added by manufacture, while 107,000 small establishments, with less than five employees each, accounted for only 2 per cent of employment and value added. However, the concentration in a county of a large number of establishments, even if they are small, means something in terms of local specialization. The maps (Figs. 140 to 143), based on the *1954 Census of Manufactures*, thus indicate general trends in distribution rather than actual size of either production or employment.

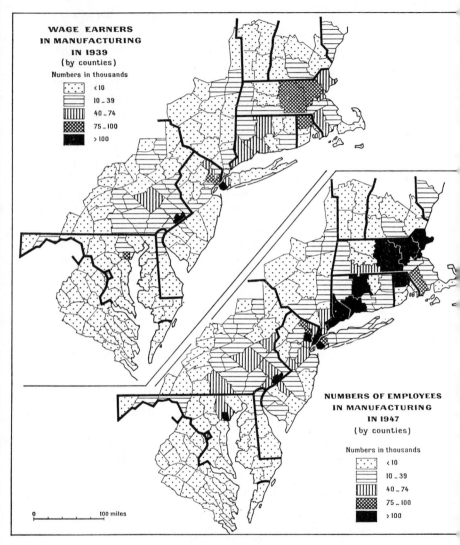

FIG. 139

from the Gulf, California, or foreign countries like Venezuela or Kuwait) have fostered on this seaboard one of the more impressive concentrations of oil-refining and oil-processing plants in the world. Along the lower Delaware River are to be found the most massive groupings of oil refineries, but there are others in Baltimore, around New York, Boston,

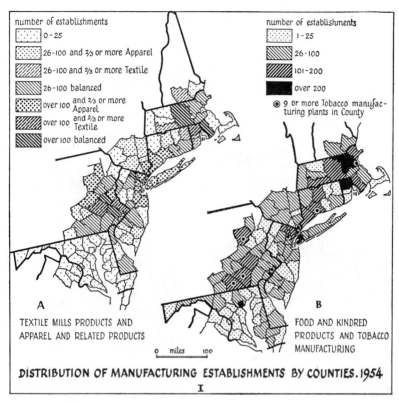

number of establishments
- 0-25
- 26-100 and ⅔ or more Apparel
- 26-100 and ⅔ or more Textile
- 26-100 balanced
- over 100 and ⅔ or more Apparel
- over 100 and ⅔ or more Textile
- over 100 balanced

number of establishments
- 1-25
- 26-100
- 101-200
- over 200
- ⊚ 9 or more Tobacco manufacturing plants in County

A
TEXTILE MILLS PRODUCTS AND APPAREL AND RELATED PRODUCTS

B
FOOD AND KINDRED PRODUCTS AND TOBACCO MANUFACTURING

0   miles   100

DISTRIBUTION OF MANUFACTURING ESTABLISHMENTS BY COUNTIES.1954
I

Fig. 140

and elsewhere (Fig. 143). Although oil refineries and steel mills are much larger plants and process bulky and crude materials, in Megalopolis they are just as much attracted by the mass of local consumption as are the industries traditionally classified as producing consumer goods and foods.

The maps of establishments manufacturing lumber and wood products, pulp and paper, furniture and fixtures on the one hand (Fig. 142A), and tobacco, food, and kindred products on the other (Fig. 140B) give us again a picture similar in many respects to that of the previously considered categories of manufactures, with concentration in the axial belt, especially in the vicinity of the greater cities. However, for these industries that are somewhat "lighter" than primary metals, chemicals and petroleum, numbers of establishments are higher in New England than in areas southwest of the New York metropolitan region. This also holds for printing and publishing plants (Fig. 142B), which usually belong in the

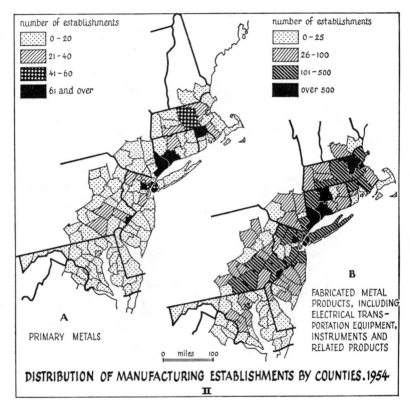

Fig. 141

lighter-industries category. However, more than any of the other industries represented by this series of maps, printing and publishing are heavily concentrated in the old and large urban cores, particularly in Manhattan (where 3,765 establishments were counted in 1954).

One aspect of local specialization revealed by these maps showing the density of establishments is that "light" industries, more immediately linked with the consumer, are more important in Megalopolis east of the Hudson River, while the "heavier" types of industries are more concentrated west of the Hudson. This is a *relative* concentration again, and some samples of both types are found throughout most of the region's axial belt, at least from Boston to Baltimore. This very generalized kind of specialization may well be increasing in some respects. Although New England has often wished for its own heavy steel and other metals plants, and for oil refineries and the like, the larger plants of these categories built

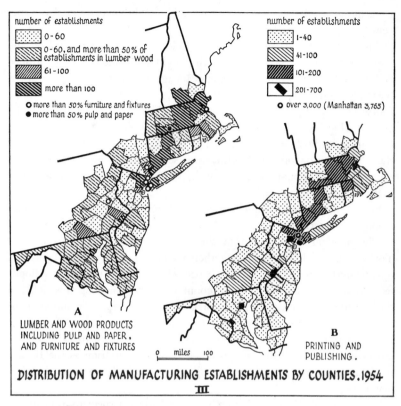

FIG. 142

recently on the Northeastern seaboard have chosen locations between Manhattan and Baltimore rather than New England.[7]

A brief survey comparing the distribution of large manufacturing establishments (employing 1,000 or more) in 1947 and 1954 shows their number shrinking (from 235 to 186) in New England as a whole, with Massachusetts, Rhode Island, Connecticut, and Maine each experiencing some decrease. This was also the trend in New Jersey and Pennsylvania, but the number of large establishments increased somewhat in New York State and in Maryland. In fact, among all the sections in the country, Megalopolis lost the greatest number of manufacturing establishments and showed in this respect the steepest ratio of decline during the 1947–54 pe-

---

[7] Witness, for instance, United States Steel's Fairless Steel Works and the large Tidewater oil refinery, both on the west bank of the Delaware River.

riod, although the national total of such establishments rose by 4 per cent.[8]

The emphasis in Megalopolis as a whole, and in its New England and New York parts in particular, on the "lighter" products, more finished and ready for mass consumption, appears again on the maps of the distribution of some specialized industries: drugs and medicines (Fig. 144), footwear (Fig. 145), household furniture (Fig. 146), and electrical machinery (Fig. 147). For all four of these Megalopolis had the greatest concentration in the United States in 1956, and in at least three of the four the concentration on the Northeastern seaboard outlines rather exactly the region of Megalopolis except in its southernmost district, the Washington metropolitan area.

For the manufacture of electrical machinery Chicago was the leader among all American cities in the first quarter of 1956, with 12.5 per cent of the national employment in this industry. However, Boston, New York City, and Philadelphia together accounted for 15.9 per cent, and northeastern New Jersey alone for 8 per cent, and the whole of Megalopolis held about 36 per cent of the country's employment in this field. In the manufacture of electrical industrial apparatus, too, Megalopolis contained a little over 30 per cent of the national employment (Fig. 148). For this latter category of manufactures the southern half of Megalopolis, especially in Pennsylvania, has as much of a concentration as the Boston to Bridgeport area, producing chiefly the "heavier" types of electrical machines.[9]

In Megalopolis there is definitely a trend toward specialization in the finishing stages of manufacturing and in the making of more complicated and delicate types of products. This trend started in New England, as have many other economic tendencies that later spread through the whole region, and it partly explains the decrease in the number of large establishments at the same time that growth has continued in terms of total employment and value added by manufacturing. It does not explain why some categories of manufactures have remained in the region and others have moved out, for it might seem that they all should have reacted in

[8] "Employment Size of Manufacturing Plants," *Area Development Bulletin,* Vol. III, No. 6, December 1957–January 1958, Office of Area Development, U. S. Department of Commerce, Washington, D. C.

[9] Data for these maps, Figs. 144 to 148, and the statistics above are from *County Business Patterns, First Quarter 1956,* a cooperative report of the U. S. Bureau of the Census and the U. S. Bureau of Old-Age and Survivors Insurance, U. S. Government Printing Office, Washington, D. C., 1958.

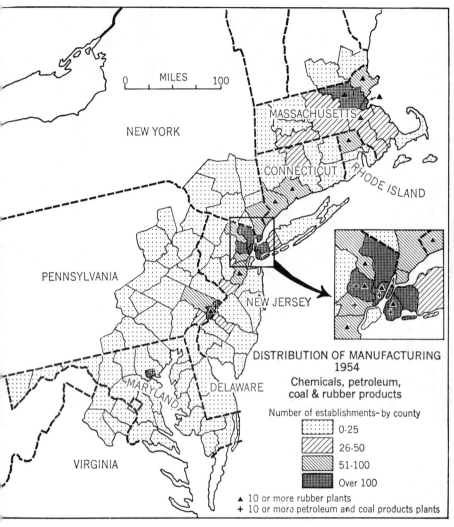

DISTRIBUTION OF MANUFACTURING
1954
Chemicals, petroleum,
coal & rubber products

Number of establishments- by county

0-25
26-50
51-100
Over 100

▲ 10 or more rubber plants
+ 10 or more petroleum and coal products plants

Fig. 143

rather similar manner to the impact of crowding, the proximity of the consumer market, and the other basic factors according to classical theory.

Table 19 provides data broken down by states and principal categories of manufactures about the recent evolution of specialties in Megalopolis, compared to the national trends for the same industries. On the whole, in

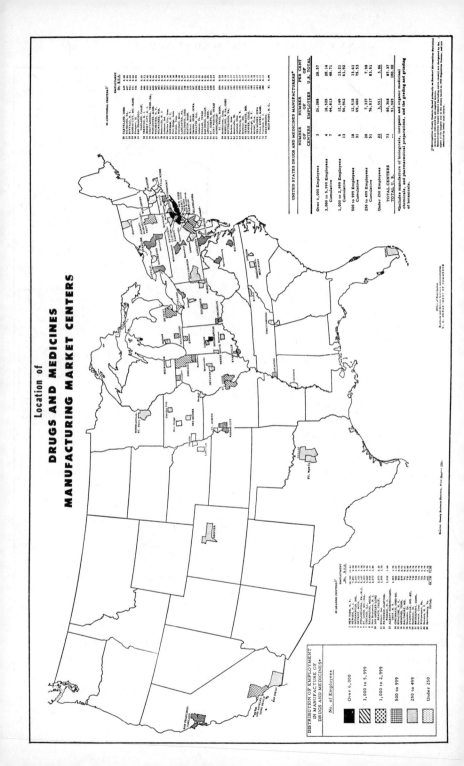

Location of
DRUGS AND MEDICINES
MANUFACTURING MARKET CENTERS

INDUSTRIAL MARKETS FOR SUPPLIERS TO SHOE MANUFACTURERS

LOCATION BY COUNTIES
Footwear Industry

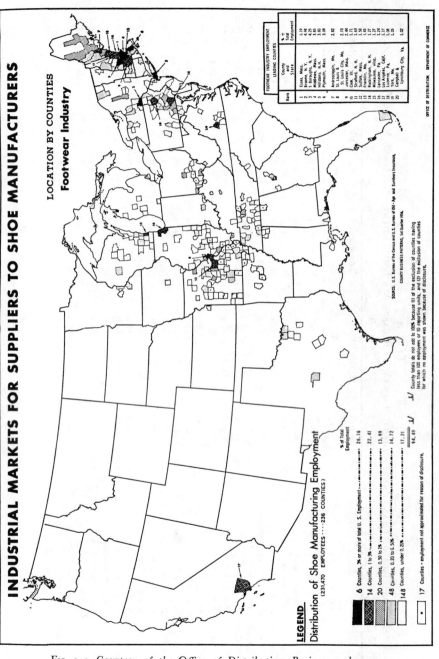

LEGEND

Distribution of Shoe Manufacturing Employment
(231,470 EMPLOYEES····236 COUNTIES)

		% of Total Employment
6	Counties, 3% or more of total U. S. Employment	26.16
14	Counties, 1 to 3%	22.41
20	Counties, 0.50 to 1%	13.99
48	Counties, 0.20 to 0.50%	14.72
148	Counties, under 0.20%	17.21
		94.49 ¹⁄

17 Counties - employment not appraised for reason of disclosure.

¹⁄ County totals do not add to 100% because (1) of the exclusion of counties having less than 100 employees or 10 reporting units, and (2) the exclusion of counties for which no employment was shown because of disclosure.

SOURCE: U. S. Bureau of the Census and U. S. Bureau of Old - Age and Survivors Insurance,
COUNTY BUSINESS PATTERNS, 1st Quarter 1954.

Rank	County and State	% of Total Employment
	FOOTWEAR INDUSTRY EMPLOYMENT LEADING COUNTIES	
1	Essex, Mass.	5.19
2	Broome, N.Y.	4.98
3	S. Broughs, N.Y.	4.25
4	Middlesex, Mass.	3.86
5	Hillboro, N.H.	3.85
6	Plymouth, Mass.	3.09
7	Androscoggin, Me.	2.82
8	St. Louis, Mo.	2.70
9	St. Louis City, Mo.	2.44
10	Worcester, Mass.	1.71
11	Cook, Ill.	1.63
12	Strafford, N. H.	1.58
13	Suffolk, Mass.	1.43
14	Franklin, Mass.	1.27
15	Rockingham, N.H.	1.27
16	Milwaukee, Wisc.	1.24
17	Lancaster, Pa.	1.17
18	Los Angeles, Calif.	1.08
19	Luzerne, Pa.	1.05
20	York, Me. Campbell & Lynchburg City, Va.	1.02

OFFICE OF DISTRIBUTION   DEPARTMENT OF COMMERCE

FIG. 145. *Courtesy of the Office of Distribution, Business and Defense Services Administration, U. S. Department of Commerce*

Opposite FIG. 144. See caption to FIG. 145.

Table 19

CHANGES IN MEGALOPOLITAN MANUFACTURING, 1947–54, AS REGARDS ALL EMPLOYMENT (A.E.) AND VALUE ADDED (V.A.)
(Percentages)

Industry	Massachusetts A.E.	V.A.	Rhode Island A.E.	V.A.	Connecticut A.E.	V.A.	New York A.E.	V.A.	New Jersey A.E.	V.A.
All industries	-5.7	29.8	-15.9	5.8	3.3	51.7	6.9	46.4	6.6	51.2
Food & kindred products	-9.4	12.9	-8.5	46.6	5.8	32.7	-.3	25.3	14.7	69.7
Tobacco manufactures	-7.1	54.9	Dᵃ	D	D	D	-27.4	1.4	-27.7	10.6
Textile mill products	-45.0	-34.3	-42.3	-35.3	-31.7	-21.1	-26.6	-1.2	-26.6	-17.4
Woolen & worsted manufactures	-63.2	D	-76.1	-60.9	-53.2	-41.1	-47.4	-30.3	-53.3	-52.5
Broad woven fabrics	-40.9	-47.6	—	—	-36.5	-38.1	-74.8	-61.0	-36.3	-31.8
Cotton	-44.9	-52.2	—	—	-50.8	D	-91.1	-80.2	-28.6	-21.9
Synthetics	-32.5	-39.2	-60.4	-46.0	D	D	-57.3	-47.1	-41.8	-38.5
Apparel & related products	24.0	41.5	33.0	67.3	8.1	22.6	-.2	0.7	10.3	24.3
Lumber & wood products	-20.2	1.4	-6.0	8.1	8.6	54.9	0.0	25.8	10.1	21.8
Furniture & fixtures	16.0	41.2	-22.0	27.6	9.6	71.4	2.1	34.5	13.9	57.6
Pulp & paper products	-1.6	24.3	-9.7	11.0	14.0	47.5	.5	29.0	18.7	32.5
Printing & publishing	5.2	38.5	12.4	54.4	23.8	37.4	1.2	39.7	22.3	61.6
Chemicals & products	-13.4	29.0	-3.9	-0.1	23.7	140.0	.6	49.1	-5.4	50.9
Petroleum & coal products	-10.8	-12.4	D	D	57.0	D	-24.2	-18.1	6.5	-29.4
Rubber products	-6.7	39.9	-20.2	18.9	23.4	67.5	12.9	46.2	-16.7	17.6
Leather & leather goods	-7.5	-9.1	67.0	99.8	59.8	51.9	-11.1	-5.5	10.7	10.7
Stone, clay, & glass products	-.7	34.8	90.5	221.6	-15.5	14.8	-0.1	51.4	10.5	55.2
Primary metal industries	-7.1	54.8	24.7	85.2	21.2	32.8	-4.0	64.5	-6.7	33.4
Fabricated metal products	-11.6	29.4	-6.3	7.5	-21.2	15.8	11.2	51.6	19.4	93.9
Machinery, except electrical	-12.1	38.9	29.4	13.8	-6.2	47.7	3.3	70.1	4.3	58.1
Electrical machinery	34.5	115.2	-24.3	12.5	-.4	49.3	23.6	105.7	9.9	96.7
Transportation equipment	29.2	170.3	D	D	115.8	260.1	57.2	190.9	22.4	116.8
Instruments & related products	11.8	71.9	31.7	57.8	-15.3	26.0	-8.4	64.4	45.9	139.9
Miscellaneous manufactures	3.9	42.7	21.3	31.4	D	D	53.1	113.2	-3.2	25.1

Table 19 (continued)

Industry	Pennsylvania A.E.	Pennsylvania V.A.	Delaware A.E.	Delaware V.A.	Maryland A.E.	Maryland V.A.	National A.E.	National V.A.
All industries	-1.4	43.4	13.5	92.9	10.7	65.8	9.5	57.4
Food & kindred products	-8.2	17.7	7.2	54.4	3.1	18.2	1.1	32.2
Tobacco manufactures	-15.6	15.1	D	D	D	D	-15.2	54.0
Textile mill products	-27.7	-20.4	3.9	31.8	-33.0	-24.3	-15.8	-10.8
Woolen & worsted manufactures	-59.1	-58.7	—	—	—	—	-49.1	-42.4
Broad woven fabrics	-30.3	-30.5	—	—	14.7	34.8	-9.3	-20.0
Cotton	-43.0	-45.8	—	—	—	—	-10.3	-22.2
Synthetics	-27.9	-26.9	—	—	—	—	-7.8	-13.4
Apparel & related products	10.7	25.5	31.8	95.7	1.8	10.9	10.0	15.9
Lumber & wood products	-12.6	15.6	-32.7	D	12.7	58.9	-11.1	11.0
Furniture & fixtures	28.8	77.5	D	D	62.2	129.9	-7.7	46.1
Pulp & paper products	7.8	47.7	1.7	2.3	38.1	111.5	16.7	57.2
Printing & publishing	13.0	50.4	51.0	121.0	8.2	36.8	12.5	47.4
Chemicals & products	3.5	64.3	-14.7	69.9	-29.8	2.9	18.0	77.6
Petroleum & coal products	-11.0	21.2	-12.0	D	41.0	88.8	4.0	29.7
Rubber products	-13.9	49.5	D	D	9.8	59.4	-4.5	47.0
Leather & leather goods	-1.8	-3.7	-35.3	-24.4	-20.5	-2.5	-7.0	6.8
Stone, clay, & glass products	-9.7	48.6	102.0	217.9	4.0	74.2	6.7	66.3
Primary metal industries	-9.0	45.0	45.0	234.8	2.4	113.8	-3.5	63.5
Fabricated metal products	-8.4	42.1	-58.8	-8.2	-1.9	70.0	4.8	54.4
Machinery, except electrical	-5.2	51.6	1.3	21.3	9.7	71.9	-0.7	57.5
Electrical machinery	12.2	87.4	D	D	42.9	189.9	20.4	91.8
Transportation equipment	5.8	64.8	D	D	26.5	114.9	45.1	138.4
Instruments & related products	23.3	96.1	D	D	63.0	170.5	11.3	86.5
Miscellaneous manufactures	45.9	103.7	D	D	D	D	50.2	116.5

Source: U. S. Bureau of the Census, *U. S. Census of Manufactures: 1954*, Vol. III, *Area Statistics*, U. S. Government Printing Office, Washington, D. C., 1957.
a D means information was withheld to avoid disclosing figures for individual companies; a dash indicates no industry of that type in state.

471

1947–54 the percentage of change was substantial both in number of workers and in value added by manufacturing, but the change was often in different directions for these two factors. The value added by manufacture increased for most industries and in most states, as well as in the country as a whole, because of increases in the dollar cost of manufacturing as well as because of the larger volume produced. The numbers employed decreased rather widely, even when the value added by manufacture showed a marked rise.

There were, however, significant variations from these predominant trends. In textiles, for example, there was a rather general decrease, nationally as well as locally, both in value added and in employment. This decrease was greatest in New England, but it was felt in Pennsylvania and Maryland too. In certain textile specialties the decline came close to liquidation in parts of Megalopolis; thus the value added by manufacturing cotton broad woven fabrics declined by 22 per cent in the whole of the United States but by 52 per cent in Massachusetts, 80 per cent in New York State, and 45.8 per cent in Pennsylvania. In 1947 American industries had been supplying a post-war world market then hungry for cotton goods, while in 1954 this extraordinary demand had been largely satisfied and new manufactures had developed, especially in Japan and Hong Kong, competing with American mills even on the domestic market. In the country as a whole the situation for woollen and worsted goods seemed to be better than for cotton and synthetic fabrics, but states in Megalopolis lost one third to one half of their production and employment in this industry; this trend went on from 1954 to 1958.

Food and kindred manufactures showed better progress in New Jersey and Delaware than in the nation as a whole. Increases in apparel and related products were greater than the national average in New Jersey, Pennsylvania, Delaware, and most of New England, while the industry was essentially stationary in New York, where it has so long been concentrated. For many other categories of industries Delaware and Maryland showed an expansion that corresponds with the general southward movement of manufactures. In most parts of Megalopolis there was an impressive growth, in terms of both production and employment, in instruments and related products, transportation equipment, and electrical machinery (especially in Massachusetts, New York, and Maryland). While pulp and paper industries grew less rapidly in Megalopolis than in the rest of the country (except in Maryland), printing and publishing activities expanded more rapidly than the average, especially in Rhode Island, New Jersey, and Delaware.

There are some curious anomalies in the figures relating to petroleum and coal products. On the whole these industries declined, except in Maryland, but employment in them rose in New Jersey and Connecticut at the same time that value added by manufacturing declined! Such apparent contradiction can perhaps be reconciled by the development, in both these states adjoining New York City, of research installations of large petroleum concerns, these laboratories often using plants formerly engaged in commercial production. Thus the employment of the petroleum industries in these areas could grow while the value added by manufacturing was curtailed.

Such variations in certain categories of manufactures, as indicated by the ratios of change set forth in Table 19, seem to confirm at least two deductions made earlier on the basis of previously examined data: the moving of manufactures southward within Megalopolis itself; and the gradual shifting of Megalopolitan specializations toward the more complicated and "upper stages" of production or of the manufacturing process, as exemplified by rapid growth in the fields of printing and publishing, instruments, electrical machinery, and petroleum research.

This last conclusion may seem to be contradicted by the faster-than-average growth, in Rhode Island, Delaware, and Maryland, of the primary metal industries and of the manufacture of stone, clay, and glass products. The latter was obviously linked to construction activity and needs no additional explanation after what has already been said about suburban sprawl, highway development, and urban renewal in the region. The former responds also to the market provided by the construction industries, which consume large quantities of such materials as fabricated steel, aluminum, and copper, but other factors are involved too. The primary metals industries, having started some 200 years ago on the seaboard, grew chiefly west of the Appalachian Mountains, and few producers were left in Megalopolis. Since World War II, however, a new trend has brought more of these plants into the region, reflecting the attraction of the huge local market and other factors.

First, in the 1940's and 1950's the United States became a net importer of iron ore, copper, and bauxite, and imports are supplying an increasingly large share of the national consumption of these metals. In the case of iron ore, for example, the gradual exhaustion of higher-grade ores accessible by open-pit mining and close to the Great Lakes led American industry to look abroad. Abundant sources of highly concentrated iron ores were found in several countries of the Western Hemisphere and on the west coast of Africa. Net imports of iron ore increased from 1.3 million

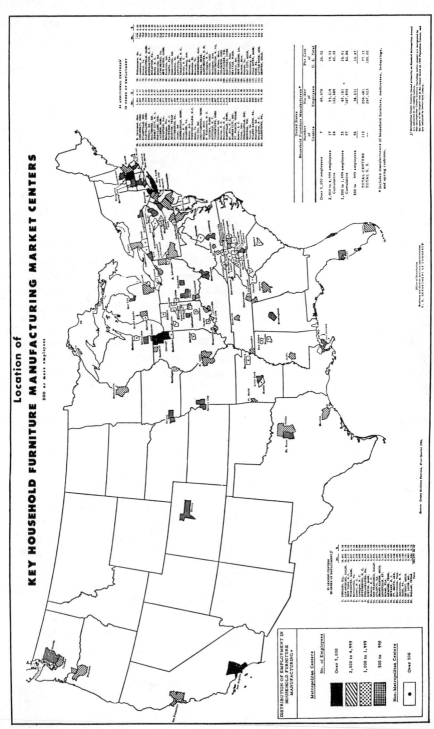

FIG. 146. *Courtesy of the Office of Distribution, U. S. Department of Commerce*

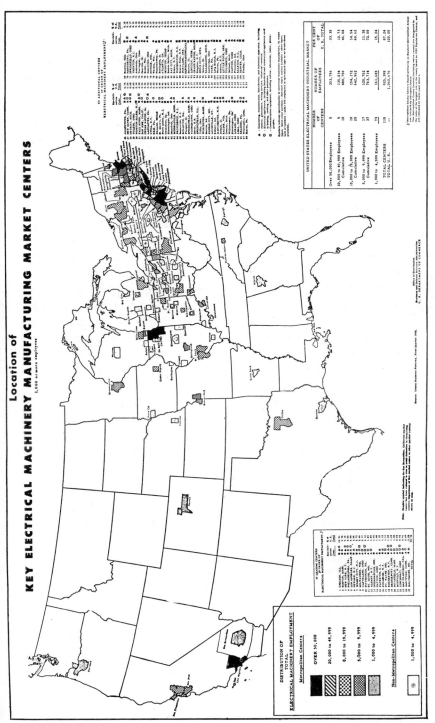

Fig. 147. *Courtesy of the Office of Distribution, U. S. Department of Commerce*

tons in 1937 to 2.7 million in 1947 and 32.1 million in 1957, the latter figure being 21.5 per cent of the national consumption that year.[10] Despite the possibility of bringing these ores into the Great Lakes by way of the St. Lawrence Seaway, it was a logical move to build more steel plants on the shores of Megalopolis, open all year to sea navigation and in the heart of a large steel-consuming and scrap-generating market.

Second, the increased costs of mining and transportation have made it profitable to reuse the metallic scrap accumulated by an economy that uses and discards metal objects liberally. Such recovery pays when the quantities of scrap are large enough and the supply is regular enough, and these requirements are met better in Megalopolis, with its high density of population and large cities, than in any other section of the country.[11] Metallic scrap is generated not only by individual consumers but also, in large amounts, by the industries working in metals. What is called "prompt industrial scrap generation," provided principally by the fabricating operations of manufacturing or construction industries, plays an important part in the supply of raw materials for the iron and steel industry. In 1954, out of a total of 8.5 million tons thus generated in the country, the seaboard states from New Hampshire to Maryland provided 1.8 million, being second only to the Michigan-Ohio region of the great automotive and mechanical industries (which supplied 4.2 million). The scrap generation ratio, a measure of the rapidity of turnover of iron and steel in the industry, was highest in Connecticut (31.8 per cent), Michigan (30.9), Massachusetts (26.7), and New York State (25.1). For copper industrial scrap the Northeastern seaboard states (Maryland was the leader) ran ahead of any other similar section of the country in 1954, with 141 million pounds out of a national total of 341 million. Large copper smelting and refining plants are located in Baltimore, and in Perth Amboy and Carteret, New

[10] U. S. Department of the Interior, Bureau of Mines, *Minerals Yearbook, 1957,* Vol. I, *Metals and Minerals,* U. S. Government Printing Office, Washington, D. C., 1959, and American Iron and Steel Institute, *Statement of American Iron and Steel Institute on Iron Ore,* New York, December 31, 1958.

[11] Steel consumption by metal fabricators is highest in the Chicago-Detroit-Cleveland-Pittsburgh area, which is also the leading steel-producing belt. However, consumption is also quite high in Megalopolis. In 1954, in the metropolitan areas of Philadelphia, New York, Newark, and Baltimore it amounted to 4,288,000 tons, or 11 per cent of the national total. Each of the three Middle Atlantic states normally consumes more than a million tons annually, while Massachusetts, Connecticut, and Maryland use between 300,000 and 1,000,000 tons. But generation of purchased scrap from sources other than metal-fabricating industries is especially important in Megalopolis, with its density of automobiles and other metallic goods, which are used and discarded in large numbers every year. Michigan leads in making cars, but Megalopolis leads in destroying them.

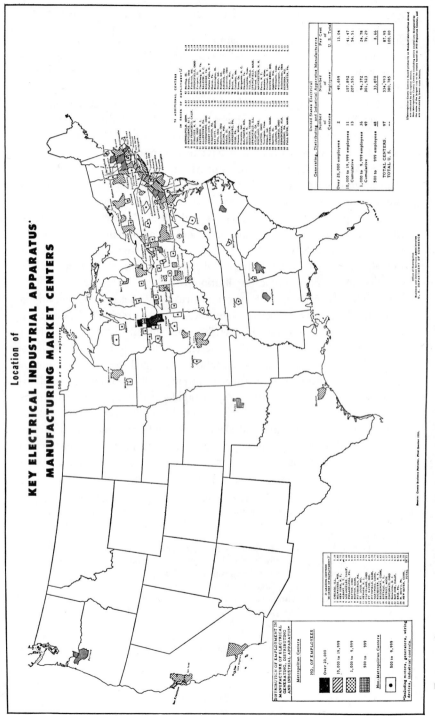

Fig. 148. *Courtesy of the Office of Distribution, U. S. Department of Commerce*

Jersey. For aluminum the Megalopolitan states generated about 23 per cent of the national total of industrial scrap.[12] These relationships illustrate how industry may attract industry. The metal fabricators are consumers of metal produced by the primary industries. In turn they furnish the latter with scrap, both directly from their own processing and indirectly by way of the consumers they supply. This cycle within the region becomes quite important in times of crisis or shortages, as World War II and even the Korean War have demonstrated.

This sketch of the manufactures of Megalopolis shows that underlying their location in the region there is a *transportation equation*, for costs of supply and delivery play a great part in the final accounting of a manufacturer's profits. Over the years technological advances have modified the meaning of this factor somewhat, and labor organizations have entered the picture. Nevertheless, the fundamental factor of accessibility has influenced both the early industrial developments in the region and the more recent changes in their distribution pattern.[13]

Consider, for example, the matter of proximity to a massive consuming market. The great size, density, and wealth of the region's population is one of its important assets, one that has contributed to the magnitude of the industrial development and to the emphasis on lighter goods and finished products ready for use. It has also discouraged the migration out of the region of many manufactures supplying consumer goods: food industries, some of whose products spoil rapidly and need proximity to the consumers; apparel, which is sensitive to fashions affected by the market's moods; electrical apparatus and electronics products, which need careful handling if they are shipped long distances and which are also sensitive to fashions; printing houses, to whom proximity to the customer means a great deal unless they work on long-range contracts and for distribution

[12] U. S. Department of Commerce, Business and Defense Services Administration, *Industrial Scrap Generation: Iron and Steel, Copper, Aluminum*, U. S. Government Printing Office, Washington, D. C., 1957; also *Minerals Yearbook, 1957, op. cit.*, see especially Vol. I.

[13] The pre-World War II factors affecting decisions about location were well presented in the report of the National Resources Planning Board, *Industrial Location and National Resources*, Washington, D. C., December 1942, and in the report of the National Resources Committee, *The Structure of the American Economy*, Washington, D. C., June 1939 (2 vols.). More contemporary conditions and the relative weight of various factors were thoughtfully analyzed by Coleman Woodbury in *The Future of Cities and Urban Redevelopment*, University of Chicago Press, Chicago, 1953 (see Part II, pp. 103–288). Similar problems in the New York metropolitan region have been discussed by Hoover and Vernon in *Anatomy of a Metropolis, op. cit.*, Chapters 2 and 3, in a way that is valid for much more than the New York region.

over an area much vaster than Megalopolis itself; and, of course, construction industries. These are some of the obvious industrial specializations that to a large extent remain in Megalopolis in order to be "on the spot." Even these may be subject to shifts in location because of technological evolution and changes in the labor market.

For many factories it is the region's well-organized links to many varied and often distant sources of raw-material supply that has favored their location in Megalopolis. In this respect Megalapolis differs somewhat from many other industrial areas. As a result of the Industrial Revolution in the nineteenth century it was long accepted that industries prospered best on coalfields or in their immediate vicinity. Coal was originally the major source of industrial power, and the early coal-driven steam engines used large amounts of it because of their relatively low energy productivity. For many industries coal is also an essential raw material. Location of a given plant on a coalfield therefore helped reduce the cost of transportation of this bulkiest of the raw materials indispensable to most stages of the manufacturing processes. And the clustering of plants near the coalfield reduced the cost of transportation to and from factories that were customers or suppliers of the given plant. Observing in 1915 that each of the British conurbations except Greater London was located on a coalfield and that in many other countries similar coincidence existed, Patrick Geddes associated the future of urbanization with the distribution of collieries and added: "Our population map of the United Kingdom may thus be a forecast of the future of the coalfield areas of the United States." Megalopolis, however, has only the eastern Pennsylvania coalfields, and although they played a notable role during the nineteenth century in assuring the energy supply of the Northeastern seaboard and in spurring on some substantial industrial development, particularly in Pennsylvania, they were neither the original nor the decisive factor in Megalopolitan urbanization. Both from its own vicinity and from distant sources Megalopolis has managed to secure an adequate supply of power, that is, a supply both abundant enough and cheap enough. Fuel wood and charcoal from the woodlands, waterfalls on local streams, and local coalfields were first put to use. Then, as each of these local supplies soon proved insufficient, more energy was brought in from afar. Petroleum now comes to this seaboard from many parts of the world; natural gas comes from Texas, Louisiana, and elsewhere; hydroelectric power is fed in from the regions to the north and west; and soon electricity from nuclear reactors will be available. While urbanization has progressed in the coal-mining areas of the United States, as Geddes forecast, in Megalopolis much more has developed at a distance from them. This reflects the predominantly light character of the industries of the region, as well as a changing technology that has made available an abundant supply of other sources of energy. Manufactures have therefore proved less and less dependent on proximity to energy supplies. This is true of other raw materials too. For example, iron and copper, obtained from local ores in the early days, have been increasingly brought in from the West or from overseas.

The concentration of industries on a coalfield reflects not only the attraction of the coal but also, as has been noted above, the attraction of other industries that serve as suppliers or customers of each other. That is, "industry attracts industry." In Megalopolis this rule applies also, for to the supply of materials is added the vast local labor market. The very diversity of the industries that have been attracted has favored further industrial growth and further clustering, especially since with more specialization each industry needs more access to many other industries.

Because technological advances have now made transportation easier and faster, there has been a decrease in the significance of local accessibility in determining industrial location. Many parts of the country that formerly seemed out of the way of the major arteries of traffic have equipped themselves to attract manufactures, a notable example being the Southeast, to which textiles have been migrating since the beginning of the twentieth century. This is not so much a move closer to the cotton-producing areas, for at the same time cotton cultivation has been shifting westward, to Arkansas, Oklahoma, Texas, Arizona, and California. Much more important have been the influences of abundant labor, cheap and little organized, of relatively inexpensive real estate, and of tax advantages. These same considerations have attracted synthetic textile fibers to the Southeast also, some apparel industries, and recently a variety of others.[14]

Many of these new establishments represent additions resulting from growth rather than simple displacement of previously existing factories. An industrial plant, even of modest size, always represents a substantial investment, and its operation rests on a carefully elaborated system of multiple relations with suppliers, customers, labor, banks, and local authorities. Because moving such a plant is a much more expensive and involved enterprise than moving a home, *there is a tendency toward greater stability of manufactures than of residences.* Nevertheless, despite all the power of

---

[14] Calvin B. Hoover and B. U. Ratchford, *Economic Resources and Policies of the South,* The Macmillan Company, New York, 1951. See especially Chapters 2, 4, 6, 7, 15, and 16. See also Jean Gottmann's *Virginia at Mid-Century,* Henry Holt & Company, New York, 1955, Chapter 7.

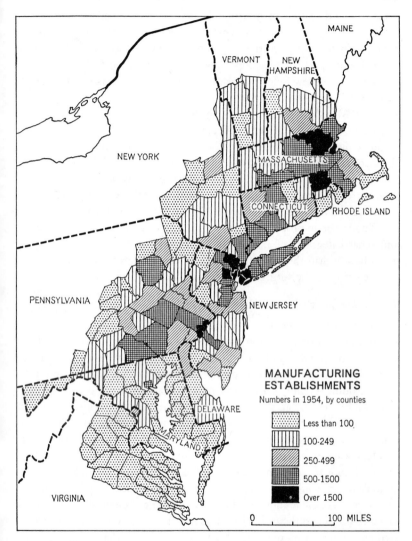

MANUFACTURING
ESTABLISHMENTS
Numbers in 1954, by counties

Less than 100

100-249

250-499

500-1500

Over 1500

0   100 MILES

Fig. 149

inertia, moves of existing manufacturing plants are not too infrequent in
Megalopolis, especially in the older urban cores, because of the pressures
of overcrowding. Once a certain density of industries is reached in an
area, it appears that industry ceases to attract industry. That is, saturation
can be achieved.

The earliest and densest crowding of manufactures developed in the

New England section of Megalopolis and on the immediate outskirts of New York City, and it is from these areas that most of the outgoing moves have originated. Many of the moves, but not all of them, have been made toward other parts of Megalopolis west of the Hudson Valley. As to the springing up of new industrial plants all over the country, one may safely venture the hypothesis that many more of them would have elected to locate in Megalopolis had the region been less crowded and less tightly organized, especially in terms of labor and taxation. The Northeastern seaboard has both profited and lost because of its historical heritage as the manufacturing pioneer of North America.

Thus we have seen which industries are growing in Megalopolis and which are moving out of the region, and how the various parts of the region have been affected recently. We must still examine in closer detail how much the metropolitan structure has been modified by these trends and what categories of manufactures present the brighter prospects for growth. We shall thus understand better how manufactures may keep on congregating in the future in highly crowded regions.

The Suburbanization of Manufactures

Manufacturing used to be a major urban occupation and land use. Plants were at first located in the core of a city, and only when the latter became too crowded and more space was needed for industrial activities would a peripheral location be preferred. True, in New England and parts of the Middle Atlantic states early industrialization developed many scattered "mill towns," at a distance from already existing cities. Each mill needed near-by residential facilities for its personnel, for transportation was slow and difficult in those days. As transportation, even on the individual scale, was made easy by the automobile, a plant became able to draw its labor force from a greater radius, twenty to fifty miles, and new establishments could be located at a distance from any large city if their sites were accessible enough. However, large new establishments seldom failed to attract to their vicinity some new housing. This process accelerated the filling in of the space between the older urban nuclei and the consolidation of the axial belt of Megalopolis.

Most industries preferred sites between two large markets, serviced as well as possible by a dense transportation network, and these conditions were usually found along the axial belt. Some plants, however, could locate outside this belt, along one of the spokes of traffic radiating in several directions from each metropolis. On the whole, suburbanization of manufactures proceeded apace in various directions around old central cities and between them, often turning "exurbia" into more ordinary "suburbia" and constantly expanding the more densely occupied and trafficked districts of Megalopolis.

Since the beginning of this century, and especially since the expansion of manufacturing after World War I, the trend for industries to shift to the suburbs or to interurban "satellite places" has been noticeable in Megalopolis and in the whole country. Analysis of Census data to reveal this trend is made difficult because some cities have annexed pieces of previously suburban territory and because many people living in one metropolitan area go to work in another adjacent one. Such complications existed before 1950,[15] but they have grown much more involved since then.

In a detailed survey of this suburbanization trend Kitagawa and Bogue [16] stress the differences in evolutionary pattern in the various metropolitan areas throughout the United States, and for the purposes of their study they divide the country into thirteen regions. The first of these, called the Atlantic Metropolitan Belt Province, differs little in extent from Megalopolis as defined in this study.[17] About this region they write:

> Metropolitan manufacturing in this region is more suburbanized than in most of the other economic regions . . . Even though the S.M.A. population suburbanized very rapidly, the rates of manufacturing growth for central cities and rings were almost equal and, hence, led to no appreciable change in the pattern of industrial location.[18]

This observation was based on comparison of data from the *U. S. Census of Manufactures* for 1939 and that for 1947. Between 1947 and 1954 the suburbanization of manufacturing was accelerated, as is apparent on the map showing changes in employment from 1939 to 1954 (Fig. 138). However, that map gives the distribution by counties and does not account for the differences between central city and metropolitan ring within small S.M.A.'s, such as those of Lancaster or York, Pennsylvania, or New Haven and Hartford, Connecticut. While we know that decentralization progressed rapidly in the 1950's in the rings around the greater cities (including Boston, Baltimore, and even Providence), this was not necessarily or

[15] See Evelyn M. Kitagawa and Donald J. Bogue, *Suburbanization of Manufacturing Activity Within Standard Metropolitan Areas*, Scripps Foundation Studies in Population Distribution No. 9, Scripps Foundation, Miami University, Oxford, Ohio, 1955. These difficulties are discussed in Chapter 7, "Reports from Local Analysts."

[16] *Op. cit.* For other careful studies of this trend see also Amos H. Hawley, *The Changing Shape of Metropolitan America: Deconcentration Since 1920*, The Free Press, Glencoe, Ill., 1956, and, for a more up-to-date discussion, the already quoted volumes of the New York Metropolitan Region Study directed by Raymond Vernon.

[17] Our region of Megalopolis includes a smaller part of Virginia.

[18] Kitagawa and Bogue, *op. cit.*, pp. 29 and 31.

generally as much the rule for smaller and less congested cities, such as Lancaster or Scranton.

On the whole, it seems certain that in most parts of Megalopolis suburbanization of workers' residences has developed more rapidly, since 1920, than has suburbanization of manufacturing plants, although the two are closely related.

The dispersion of metropolitan population is closely associated with industrial deconcentration, though it is not entirely dependent on the outward movement of manufacturing industry. Actually, dispersion moved more rapidly, at least after 1920, in areas with high proportions of their populations engaged in manufacturing industry . . . than in areas of deconcentration . . . There are factors associated with large proportion of manufacturing employment that encourage the centrifugal movement of population over and above that produced by industrial deconcentration itself.[19]

One of the factors referred to by Amos Hawley in the above quotation is the congestion, often accompanied by blight, in central cities of highly industrialized metropolitan areas. The population can afford to move out more easily than can industry, and homes have become obsolescent more rapidly than have factories.

However, some of the "obsolescent characteristics" of central cities that were heavily and early industrialized may also drive some manufactures out to the metropolitan ring, and the labor force is not always willing or able to follow. Thus, in relatively rural parts of New York City's or Philadelphia's outer rings some large plants have been welcomed by local authorities with the understanding that the labor force is not to come en masse and settle around the plant. First, such a community often resents the very threat of such invasion by newcomers, especially if there has been a restrictive tendency, favoring the admission only of people of a certain sort and income level. Second, while a community welcomes a substantial addition to its taxable base, it is not always willing to assume the cost of all the services that would be needed for an additional population of not-too-high income; for even in Megalopolis wage earners in manufacturing are on the whole in the lower-income brackets.

Moreover, new and large plants have sometimes been built on sites in the immediate proximity of which there is no prospect of housing for most of the employees. These had then to commute from adjacent towns, often from the central city. Developers usually spot such situations quickly, however, and help solve the problem by building not too far away a brand new town, and thus the dispersal of residences has gone on.

<hr />

[19] Hawley, *op. cit.*, p. 145. This conclusion, based on 1900–1950 data for the whole country, seemed rather correct for Megalopolis in the 1950's.

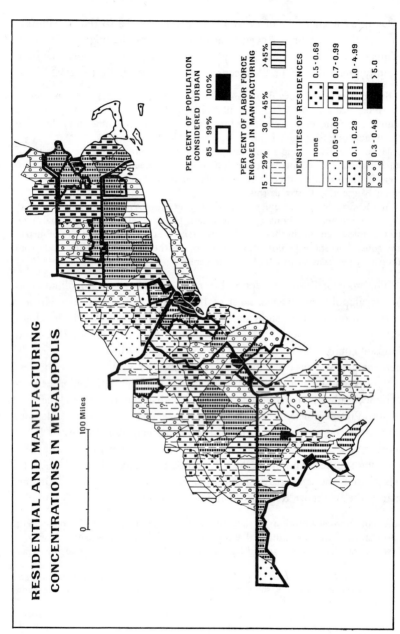

RESIDENTIAL AND MANUFACTURING
CONCENTRATIONS IN MEGALOPOLIS

PER CENT OF POPULATION
CONSIDERED URBAN

85 - 99%   100%

PER CENT OF LABOR FORCE
ENGAGED IN MANUFACTURING

15 - 29%   30 - 45%   >45%

DENSITIES OF RESIDENCES

none   0.5 - 0.69

0.05 - 0.09   0.7 - 0.99

0.1 - 0.29   1.0 - 4.99

0.3 - 0.49   >5.0

0   100 Miles

Fig. 150. Data are for 1950 and by county. Compare with Figs. 126 and 134. See caption of Fig. 126 (p. 402) for explanation of the index used for the density of residences.

Despite the endeavor of many municipal authorities to retain manufactures in their territory or even to attract new ones, the migration of such plants out of the central cities, especially out of the larger ones, has been steadily going on and on. A recent report on Greater Boston stated:

Between 1947 and 1957 downtown Boston alone lost some 9,000 manufacturing jobs, that is, almost half of all such employment lost to the City as a whole. . . . The new techniques usually require a large one-story building for which sufficient land is no longer available downtown.

More recently, changes in transportation technology and the growth of superhighways have made it possible for much manufacturing to move to areas in the suburbs other than those served by rail. The industrial expansion along Route 128 illustrates this trend. . . .

In the decade under review manufacturing employment beyond corporate Boston increased by about 35,000 jobs and by 1957, about 70 per cent of all such employment in the Boston Metropolitan Area was located in the suburban environs. The share in downtown Boston, on the other hand, declined from almost 13 per cent to just under 9 per cent.[20]

The story of Boston is repeated in most other large metropolitan areas in Megalopolis and even in most of the United States. We have already noticed it on the maps showing the recent growth of employment (Figs. 136 and 138). In New Jersey the two older industrial giants, Essex and Hudson counties, close to New York City, showed a loss in 1954, not only percentagewise but even in absolute number of jobs, whereas the less congested and outlying counties of Bergen, Middlesex, and Union had experienced substantial growth, at a faster rate than the state as a whole.[21]

Both Philadelphia and New York City have, of course, shown a definite outward trend of manufacturing. Even in the metropolitan area of Baltimore, a city comparable to Boston in size and located at the more rapidly growing southern end of the heavily industrialized axial belt of Megalopolis, there is the same growing suburbanization of manufacturing. On this matter the Baltimore Regional Planning Council has written as follows:

A common assumption is that the central city is principally dependent upon small firms for industrial employment. With an ample supply of low cost central floor space vacated by larger plants, and with a dependable array

[20] Greater Boston Economic Study Committee, *A Report on Downtown Boston*, Policy Statement, Part 2, Associates of the Committee for Economic Development, Boston, May 1959.

[21] Horace J. De Podwin and Morton M. Binenstock, "Manufacturing Industries," in *The Economy of New Jersey*, a report prepared under the direction of Salomon J. Flink, Rutgers University Press, New Brunswick, 1958, pp. 191–260. See also John I. Griffin, *Industrial Location in the New York Area*, New York Area Research Council, Monograph 1, The City College Press, New York, 1956.

of services, the central city is a natural incubator of the small firm. While Baltimore has these advantages to offer, only 10% of its manufacturing employment in 1956 was in firms employing less than forty employees.

. . . firms with 1,000 employees or more constitute 36.5% of Baltimore City's manufacturing employment. Adding to this the 10.7% in firms employing 500 to 999 employees and the 14.5% represented by firms employing 250 to 499, it is soon evident that the economy of Baltimore City is now dependent upon large firms . . . Such plants have substantial floor space and land area requirements.

The middle group, firms employing 40 to 249 workers, constitute 28.2% of the total manufacturing employment in the City. . . . These are the size firms most apt to expand, and therefore are likely to relocate in the suburbs if the City does not plan for their expansion.[22]

Although local variations are obviously considerable in an industrial system as vast and complicated as that in Megalopolis, the trend toward suburbanization of manufacturing is general. It affects almost all kinds of production, and especially establishments that need or plan expansion rather than smaller or well-stabilized firms. Expansion, however, has been a steady feature and need of most healthy manufactures in a growing economy. Additional outward migration of plants is to be expected within the metropolitan areas in Megalopolis, from central cities toward outer rings and from one metropolitan area to another that is less congested though well serviced. In the working of such centrifugal forces one cannot help recognizing a general tendency similar to that which, on a larger geographical scale, takes manufactures out of Megalopolis to other parts of the United States and even beyond. In spite of this the whole of employment and value added by manufacturing continues to grow within Megalopolis, because of the need of certain industries to cluster there.

The Centripetal Forces in the Distribution of Manufactures

Recent technological and social evolution has definitely worked for the dispersion of manufactures throughout the United States. At the same time some forces, developed on the whole within the same economic process, have helped certain kinds of production to cluster, and especially to gather around the old nuclei of the Northeastern seaboard. By approaching the matter from several angles and by analyzing the available statistical data some of these factors favoring concentration can be clearly recognized — for example, the attraction of the consuming market; the attraction of the extremely well-organized transportation network; the attraction of other

[22] Baltimore Regional Planning Council, *Industrial Land Development*, Technical Report No. 2, Maryland State Planning Commission, Baltimore, May 1959, p. 34.

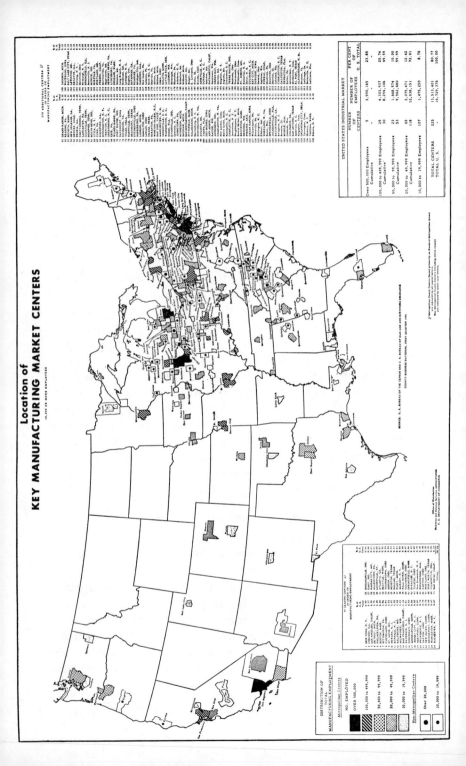

Location of
KEY MANUFACTURING MARKET CENTERS
10,000 OR MORE EMPLOYEES

industries that serve as suppliers or consumers of the one considered; the abundance of qualified labor. In brief, one could say that in one way or another it is the *mass* of Megalopolis that attracts or retains production — mass of people, money, consumption, transportation, labor, even the mass of junk, as is illustrated by the importance of scrap generation for metal-producing industries.[23]

The ease of suburbanization, that is, the ease of finding adequate land and servicing in other but still Megalopolitan parts of the seaboard, is another centripetal force in the large regional scale, though it may look centrifugal on the local scale of the internal structure of each metropolitan area. Obviously, if plants not satisfied with locations in downtown Boston can still multiply in its suburbs or in the next county, this facility increases the chances of their locating within the general area rather than choosing a place in another section of the country. If a manufacturer that wants to leave Connecticut can find convenient conditions in New Jersey or eastern Pennsylvania he may well prefer this shorter displacement, which keeps him close to familiar grounds, to moving to Texas. And throughout almost all of Megalopolis one can still find not-too-congested sites for many manufactures.

The "massive organization" of the region brings to most parts of it many advantages in terms of services, but *at a cost*, for Megalopolis is in several respects an expensive region for manufacturing. Wages are relatively high — won by labor, together with other benefits, by means of a good deal of unionization. Not only are unions powerfully organized, but their locals in this region are usually rich and influential, in terms of more qualified, and sometimes more aggressive, officers, better legal counsel, occasionally more influence in local political life. These circumstances may complicate the task of management, especially for medium-sized or small firms that cannot depend on nationwide contracts for their labor-management relations. Some other costs, too, are increased by the very quality of the space organization — local taxes, for example, the value of real estate, and in some places water supply.

Despite it all, in 1954 Megalopolis held a little more than one quarter of the nation's manufactures, and some categories of production were growing within its limits more rapidly than in the rest of the country. While locational inertia, a powerful consideration with many a manufacturer, could be the basic reason why much of the older manufacturing has remained in the area, it could not account for the growth in certain specialties. A penetrating analysis of manufacturing trends in the very heart of

[23] See above, p. 476.

Opposite Fig. 151. *Courtesy of the Office of Distribution, U. S. Department of Commerce*

Megalopolis has been made recently by the New York Metropolitan Region Study, and its conclusions deserve our close consideration.[24]

On the one hand this study emphasizes in various ways the centrifugal forces that foster dispersal of manufacturing and will continue to do so: the search for more not-too-expensive space; the preference for cheaper, less organized, and abundant labor; the flight from local and state taxes. Each of these three great factors is indeed quite complex and too often "steeped in pure emotion and impure data." [25] At first, summing up all that could be said *against* locating manufactures in Megalopolis, and especially in its axial belt, close to the main old nuclei, one may wonder whether any force other than inertia could be responsible for keeping so many of them there. However, consideration of the recent trends in detail (Table 19, and the maps illustrating this chapter) shows at once that these industries are not inert at all, but very lively. After all, locational decisions are made firm by firm, plant by plant. General theory must take into consideration not only the massive phenomenon of the exodus of certain types of production (textiles and apparel especially) from the region, but also the no less massive fact that many other specialties stubbornly cling to this region. The latter specialties run a diversified gamut, from great steel mills to small electronic or printing plants. All of them could be said to have been kept or attracted here by "marketing considerations," but *market* has very different meanings for each of the various components of the gamut. To some it means the mass of consumption, as already noted, to others, a certain special kind of organization.

The manufactures directly attracted by the size of the regional market and its favorable transportation facilities are often large plants, many of which have recently undergone modernization, and through automation they may have reduced the figures of employment without reducing productive capacity. Steel mills, oil refineries, and some of the manufactures of foods belong in this category. These industries will go on growing to some extent with the region's needs, but they may also renounce any endeavor to supply most of that market in favor of supplies brought from the outside. This suggestion is made not merely in terms of local consideration. Large plants, manufacturing in great quantities, usually belong to

[24] What follows is based on Hoover and Vernon, *Anatomy of a Metropolis, op. cit.*; Max Hall (ed.), Roy B. Helfgott, W. Eric Gustafson, and James M. Hund, *Made in New York*, Harvard University Press, Cambridge, Mass., 1959; and Martin Segal, *Wages in the Metropolis*, Harvard University Press, Cambridge, Massachusetts, 1960 (all volumes in the series of reports of the New York Metropolitan Region Study). See also our remarks above, p. 401.

[25] Hoover and Vernon, *op. cit.*, p. 55.

great corporations, the decisions of which are influenced by national policies rather than local conditions. Such plants also represent large investments, which adds to the stability of their locations.

The second category of manufactures recently attracted to Megalopolis consists of a great variety of smaller establishments. They have been defined as "the communications-oriented industries," that is, industries for which "face-to-face contact" is most important.

On the average, plants in these industries are generally half the size of the average plant in the Region, measured by the number of employees per plant. Geographically, the employment in these "communication-oriented" industries is highly concentrated. More than three-quarters of the employees work in New York City. And an added 5 per cent are found in Hudson County just across the river. . . . A clue to the reason for the heavy clustering of these industries is to be found in the interrelations of speed, small size, and uncertainty of outlook. . . . The firms are not offering, as their stock-in-trade, the products themselves but the products-by-a-time-certain.[26]

The last two sentences of this quotation are not contradictory: working to produce for a given date, most of these industries work on contract with the buyer, but at the same time they feel a constant uncertainty about future contracts and also about the future desirability of the precise product they are making at a given moment. Tastes and fashions change rapidly in these communications-oriented industries, and to keep abreast of the market in terms of forthcoming fashions and contracts the manufacturer must be constantly on the alert and in touch with current developments. These imperatives require clustering, in an area close to the main sources of both contracts and fashions.

The printing and publishing business is, of course, in several of its stages precisely this kind of communications-oriented industry, for which it is used as a model in the New York Metropolitan Region Study.[27] The steady growth of printing and publishing in Megalopolis, confirmed again by the 1958 *Census of Manufactures*, must obviously be related to the concentration in the region of the mass-media market for the whole nation and, in some respects, for the world.[28] The concentration in New York is well known and easily understandable; but it is also observed, though on a somewhat smaller scale, in each of the major nuclei of Megalopolis. In the Washington, D. C., metropolitan area, printing and publishing is by far the leading industry, providing about half of the jobs in manufacturing. In Boston, Philadelphia, and even Baltimore it is important

[26] *Ibid.*, p. 63.
[27] *Ibid.*, and Hall, *Made in New York, op. cit.*, pp. 135–239.
[28] See below, Chapter 11, pp. 597–615, and Fig. 142B, p. 465 above.

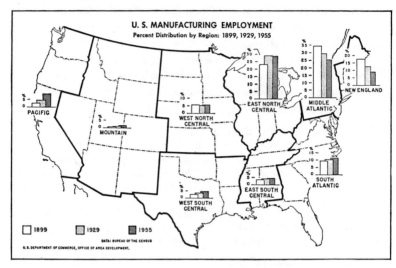

Fig. 152. *Courtesy of the Office of Area Development, U. S. Department of Commerce*

and growing, although more in the metropolitan ring than in the central core, and it is beginning to leave the downtown districts where it used to be concentrated (especially in Boston, and to some extent also in New York City).

Besides printing and publishing, two other communications-oriented industries play an essential part in the New York metropolitan region: women's and children's apparel and electronic products. The common traits between these two apparently very different industries — those traits that foster clustering — have been well pointed out in the recent New York Metropolitan Region Study.[29]

Of all subdivisions of manufacturing, women's outerwear and related trimmings have always been most obviously linked to and commanded by fashion, and New York City remains the undisputed center of fashion in America. This is emphasized by its dominance of the mass-media market, its function as the main hub of overseas relations and travel, and its concentration of wealth because of its financial and managerial supremacy. In the past the garment industry located in Manhattan, partly for these and partly for very different reasons, and, although it has recently been grow-

[29] Hall, *Made in New York, op. cit.*, especially the chapters by R. B. Helfgott and J. M. Hund.

ing more rapidly elsewhere in the United States, women's fashionable outerwear will be the last sector of the industry to cling stubbornly to the city that is the national capital of fashion.

The electronics industry would seem at first to belong in another world, and indeed it does; but it is a young industry, the field of which is expanding rapidly and the products of which are constantly being reshaped, diversified, and applied to new uses. There are at least three recognized categories of electronic industries. Consumer electronic manufactures produce rather standardized consumer goods (radios, television sets, etc.) for a large market, and their fashions change slowly following technological innovations. This category of electronics has already been decentralized from Megalopolis and is the least communications-oriented. Component electronic industries produce parts, tubes, transistors, and other items to be used by the manufacturers of the finished apparatus. Military and industrial electronic products encompass all those that do not fall into either of the two other categories, and this is the most shifting field, the most manifold, the most affected by "fashions" and by contractual arrangements. Because it is evolving and expanding so rapidly, this industry depends greatly on research and experimentation, which is pursued either in the industry's laboratories (largely under government contract) or in independent research institutes, many of which are located in Megalopolis and connected with this region's academic institutions.

When research for an improved electronic instrument requires a certain type of transistor, not yet widely used, the engineer or scientist in charge may have to shop around quite a bit, almost like a woman looking for a dress, before he finds the precise thing that would best fit his purposes. Thus the research laboratories benefit by being located close to many producers of industrial electronic products and components, and this is the case throughout Megalopolis, for many electronics factories are near the leading centers of research in such cities as Boston, New Haven, New York, Princeton, Philadelphia, and Washington. Most of the new gadgets, which are adopted at a given moment and needed in large quantities, are produced by small firms working on contracts for larger organizations. Such a firm must always face the possibility, which arises quite often, that a contract may require quantities it could not, with its own means, deliver in the time required, and subcontracting is the solution for such dilemmas. The cluster of electronics plants becomes a sort of market place for shoppers looking for either special products or special orders. The garment industry in Manhattan used to work along similar lines, and women's outerwear is still made there according to a business strategy not very different from that of industrial electronics.[30]

Following a pattern that has characterized many other industries, the electronics industry is already providing an ever-increasing number of articles in large amounts, to supply a steady demand from all over the country; but new shapes and functions are constantly being invented, and these yet unstandardized articles will for some time remain a specialty of Route 128 around Boston or of Greater New York City. Similar factors keep drug industries clustering there.

With the stabilization of demand and with the standardization of the product and the methods of manufacture, firms in a maturing industry find it possible to pursue opportunities for cost reduction via large scale production. At the same time their market horizon has broadened to encompass the whole nation. Being less dependent on the "incubator" advantages of the metropolitan area, they are left free to seek out locations which are attractive either in terms of geographic position with respect to a national market or in terms of the favorable cost structure they afford for critical factors of production.[31]

The above remarks, made for the New York metropolitan region and with respect to the electronics industry, are true for the general trends in manufacturing distribution and for the whole of Megalopolis. *The Northeastern seaboard has indeed served as an incubator for most of the various categories of manufactures now scattered through the United States.* As an industry "comes of age," deconcentration of its production is a normal process; however, as the uses of its products increase and diversify, the volume of them consumed in Megalopolis reaches a level that often justifies the building of more plants in the region, despite its congestion and other liabilities, to be close to the large local market and perhaps also to ports. Such an evolution has taken place in the production of steel and some other metals. It may also develop in the electronics industry some day, although it produces a rather light kind of merchandise, not expensive to transport. But when the daily life of the average person requires enough electronic gadgets, which will be built into homes and will become indispensable to the usual work in stores and offices, then the mass of the Megalopolitan consumption may well bring more plants to the region, making quite standardized apparatus.

A last centripetal force must be recorded here, although it is somewhat difficult to demonstrate by precise statistics or examples how it works. This force is the availability in Megalopolis of a vast pool of labor pos-

---

[30] Hoover and Vernon, *Anatomy of a Metropolis, op. cit.*, Chapter 3.
[31] Hall, *Made in New York, op. cit.*, p. 313.

sessing a great variety of skills and offering a great diversity of wage levels.

While it is an area renowned for its expensive labor, Megalopolis, particularly in the old cores of its main cities, still offers a good supply of relatively cheap, though not very skilled, personnel. These cities still attract such labor: Puerto Ricans, Negroes from the South, and some immigrants from abroad. This sort of labor supply is not as abundant as it used to be in the time of massive immigration from Europe, but it is nevertheless a feature in the structure of the labor force; it still furnishes a good part of the production workers in various industries such as foodstuffs and apparel.

At the same time the metropolitan areas of the Northeast still produce and attract in large numbers a whole spectrum of skilled and competent workers. This feature of the Megalopolitan labor force is more important to the white-collar professions than to manufacturing personnel; but manufacturing, too, needs skills on various levels, and needs them increasingly in the nonproduction sectors of its employment, such as management and research. In this region a good many manufacturing firms have industrial laboratories and research plants. Such aspects of manufacturing activities do not show in the figures of value added by manufacturing and have only moderate effect yet on the statistics of employment; but they help to swell the local payroll and attract more communications-oriented plants to their vicinity.

The Shifting Role of Manufactures in Megalopolis

Since the beginning of the century there have been a great many shifts in Megalopolitan manufacturing, and a great deal of churning is still going on. This constant evolution is a factor of growth and a proof of vitality. Speaking of the New York metropolitan region, Martin Segal has described a mechanism that brings vitality to Megalopolis as a whole and continues the age-old process of the division of labor.

The stability of the Region's share in manufacturing employment is explained chiefly in terms of the industrial composition, or *mix*, of its manufacturing sector. The Region has continuously had a high concentration of industries whose employment in the nation as a whole has been growing relatively fast. . . . the Region has not been merely a passive beneficiary of the changes which mitigate the tendency toward standardization. The Region's economic environment — the combination of external economies and relatively high wages — has itself provided a stimulus toward development of differentiated and variable products. As firms producing more standardized types of apparel or toys begin to feel the impact of outside competition, they are under pressure to modify their product in order to protect themselves, temporarily at least, from the competitive pressures based on lower labor costs elsewhere. . . . the Region's nursery benefits have enabled it to attract other new and fast-growing activities to take the places of the ones that have left.[32]

A center of "fashion" for much more than garments, an "incubator" and "nursery" for new types of industries, the region of New York and, to a somewhat smaller extent, the whole of Megalopolis have been playing a very essential role in the enormous and intricate structure that is the manufacturing system of the nation. It is not only the *kind of articles* manufactured in the region that has been rapidly shifting but also the *kind of workers* the manufacturing firms employ. Like other regions, but perhaps at a somewhat faster rate, Megalopolis has steadily shifted its manufacturing employment toward the nonproduction functions. The map of the proportion of production workers in total manufacturing employment in 1954 [33] (Fig. 153) shows a striking pattern of distribution: the percentage of production workers was higher than the national average of 79 per cent in the outlying parts of Megalopolis and still higher beyond the region's limits; but *in most of the counties of the axial belt, where most of the manufacturing employment is concentrated, this percentage is below the national average* — much below, of course, in the District of Columbia and its Maryland suburban counties. This feature of the axial belt, emphasizing the nonproduction aspects of manufacturing, would probably appear in an even sharper way on a similar map for 1960.

This trend does not mean that production is going out of the axial belt. While some categories of it may be, a good many others are staying or growing there. The map just mentioned must be compared with the map (Fig. 154) giving the density of value added by manufacturing, calculated per square mile of nonfarm land area in each county. This density of the value of manufacturing production shows a higher concentration precisely in those same parts where the proportion of production workers in total employment was low: most of the counties with value above a million dollars per square mile were in the category having only 70 to 79 per cent of the workers in production. These maps demonstrate the specialization of Megalopolis in the "upper" and "final" stages of manufacturing as well as in the "incubator" or "nursery" stages, which depend

---

[32] Segal, *Wages in the Metropolis, op. cit.*, pp. 157–160.

[33] The figures for 1954 are used here rather than those of the Census of Manufactures for 1958, as the latter was a year of depressed industrial activity.

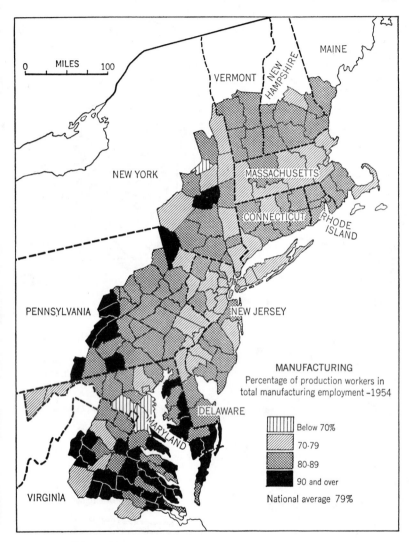

FIG. 153

so heavily on research and organization. All these trends in specialization seem destined to remain and even to increase in the future.

The ordinary function of modern manufacturing — the mass production of standardized goods — still goes on, of course, in Megalopolis, but it plays a declining role in the region. Neither the recent and expected growth of the regional economy nor its present prosperity could be ex-

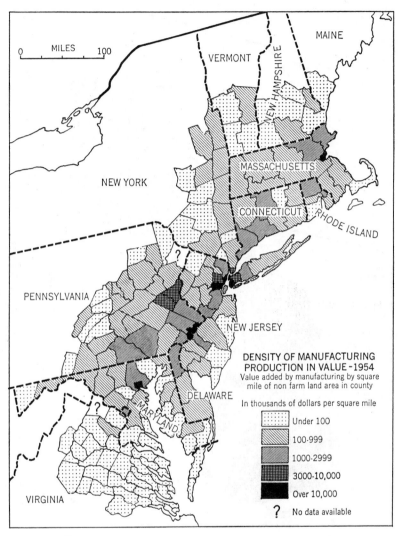

DENSITY OF MANUFACTURING
PRODUCTION IN VALUE - 1954
Value added by manufacturing by square
mile of non farm land area in county

In thousands of dollars per square mile

- Under 100
- 100-999
- 1000-2999
- 3000-10,000
- Over 10,000
- ? No data available

FIG. 154

plained by that normal, usual kind of manufactures. The fact that manufacturing remains one of the essential foundations of the region's employment is the result of an extraordinary versatility and a quite exceptional ability to reshape itself continuously. In a way this is a comforting characteristic, for it means that this region retains a very great concentration of manufactures of the kinds in which it is especially difficult to replace hu-

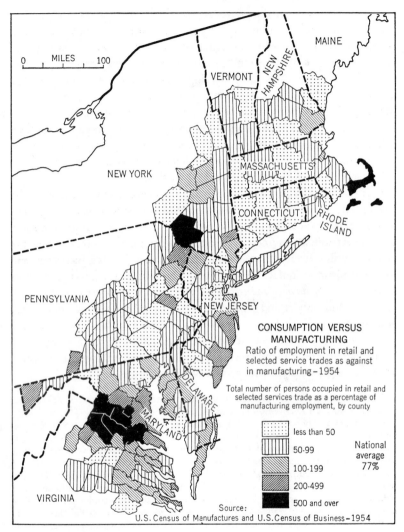

CONSUMPTION VERSUS
MANUFACTURING
Ratio of employment in retail and
selected service trades as against
in manufacturing – 1954

Total number of persons occupied in retail and
selected services trade as a percentage of
manufacturing employment, by county

less than 50		
50-99		National
100-199		average
200-499		77%
500 and over		

Source:
U.S. Census of Manufactures and U.S. Census of Business – 1954

FIG. 155

man labor by machinery. But the kind of labor needed has been changing
and will keep on changing, and what used to be a "blue-collar" job may
soon require a degree in engineering.

Thus the relative role of manufacturing as an employer is decreasing in
Megalopolis. It is interesting to compare the 1954 employment in manufacturing on the one hand and in retail trade and selected service trades

on the other. The latter represent daily consumption of goods and services as against the production of goods by manufacturing. As could have been expected from the distribution within Megalopolis of manufacturing and residences (Fig. 150), a map of "consumption versus manufacturing" (Fig. 155) shows a ratio of consumer-serving trades above the national average in and around the major cities; but in 1954 in most of the counties of Megalopolis, even in the axial belt, these *consumption-serving trades employed fewer people than did manufacturing*,[34] in many counties less than half as many. Manufacturing therefore remains an essential element of the region's prosperity, although it may no longer spearhead its growth.[35]

For some time to come the future growth of manufactures in Megalopolis will remain linked to the unique commercial organization of the region — its internal commercial organization that serves such a huge and demanding market and its external commercial network that gives it some great assets difficult to find elsewhere. This commercial system makes the area especially attractive to the communications-oriented industries and to the kinds of manufactures that need incubating and nursing, in short to *the more speculative industries*, which often turn out to be the more profitable but only if and when they are adopted by a large commercial system. Perhaps Megalopolis could not have been such an *incubator* for new industries without the exceptionally favorable environment provided by its vast and bold commercial organization, the development of which preceded and supported the growth of manufactures.

[34] Wholesale trade was omitted from these figures, since it is often linked with production or with distribution beyond the regional market.

[35] Between the two Censuses of Manufactures taken in 1954 and 1958, the manufacturing employment in the United States decreased by 1 per cent. The year 1958 was marked by a recession of business activity, felt particularly by manufacturing and, much more than on the national average, by Megalopolis. The figures indicate a decrease in manufacturing employment of 2 per cent in Massachusetts and New Jersey, 6 per cent in Connecticut and New York State, and 7 per cent in Rhode Island, although Delaware showed an increase of 13 per cent and Maryland 3 per cent. Thus in spite of some local increases Megalopolis on the whole was hit harder than the rest of the nation, with only the Midwestern industrial belt suffering more severe loss of employment (18 per cent decrease in Michigan, 8 per cent in Ohio, etc.). Although 1959 and 1960 showed some recovery, not everything was regained. The southern tier of states, from Florida to California, meanwhile continued to attract manufacturing. See "Shifts in Manufacturing Employment: 1954–1958," *Area Development Bulletin*, Vol. V, No. 6, December 1959–January 1960, published by the Office of Area Development, U. S. Department of Commerce, Washington, D. C.

CHAPTER 10

The Commercial Organization

The history of the continent's economic hinge [1] has shown the fundamental role of the commercial relations of Megalopolis, domestic and foreign, in developing the economic structure of this vast urban region. This commercial organization is still the basic support of the region's present economy. In 1954 it employed 4,056,000 people directly, in wholesale and retail trade and selected services, including the proprietor-merchants of unincorporated businesses. This was close to 30 per cent of Megalopolis' total labor force, and about 27.4 per cent of the nation's employment in these categories.

In terms of number of people employed in Megalopolis in 1954, trade and services together were somewhat below manufacturing, but they about equalled manufacturing in terms of proportion of the national em-

[1] See Chapter 3 above.

ployment in their fields.[2] Considered as entire categories, these two sectors of economic activity cannot be thought of as opposed one to another. Even though they may occasionally and on a local scale compete for some piece of land or a certain kind of labor, they are and have been for a long time complementary. Trade distributes the products of the manufactures within the region and beyond it and supplies the plants and the people working in them with the whole variety of goods they need. The service industries, too, meet needs of the workers in manufacturing. In the early years the vast commercial organization of Megalopolis supported local manufacturing by opening up markets for its products, first all over this continent as settlement proceeded, and more recently overseas. As has already been noted, since 1920 many plants have been moving out of the area, particularly out of the section between Boston and Philadelphia. However, the convenience of distribution provided by this commercial organization has kept many manufacturers in the region, has attracted some new ones, and has maintained this region's role as the "incubator" of novel industries in America.

Actually the commercial organization of Megalopolis includes much more than merely wholesale and retail trade. It involves also a series of services that take care of all the operations of *transfer* — transportation and communication, corporate and business legal counsel, accounting, advertising, real estate, banking, brokerage, insurance, and other financial transactions. As the products and markets of Megalopolitan commerce grow more diversified, the terms and operations of transfer become more involved, and a greater variety of specialized professional services is needed. The local payrolls based on each of these services in the region vary considerably, ranging from relatively small amounts for legal counsel to substantial figures for transportation and communications. In this chapter we shall not consider all these services in full detail, but several distinct aspects of commerce must be reviewed separately.

The retail and selected services trades, serving the mass of the population within Megalopolis, are consumer-oriented. Wholesale trade, much oriented toward the supply of local and regional retailing, has broader horizons too, reflecting the "hinge" function of this seaboard. The maritime commerce of Megalopolis must also be considered, for it was from skillful use of their advantages in this field that the seaports of the Northeast developed such a vast network of connections and accumulated such wealth. Last but not least, the services extended by the financial communities in the region must be reviewed. Such a survey will make more

[2] Compare the above figures with those on page 452.

meaningful the significance of these four categories of commercial activities to the regional economy as a whole, in terms of land use, employment, present prosperity, and prospects.

The Scattering Retail Trade and Selected Services

Since retailing and "selected services" (i.e., business and personal services) exist to serve the crowds of individual customers, they are found where the most customers are located. The customer prefers to have them at his doorstep. In the past, however, when consumers were rather thinly spread across the vast expanse of the United States, even retailing was relatively concentrated in the areas of higher population density, most of which were in Megalopolis. Since these were also areas of higher income, the total sales of the retail trade were rather heavily concentrated in the Northeastern seaboard and especially in its major cities.

Such was still the situation in 1939 (Fig. 156). In the national volume of retailing there was a quite impressive predominance of the entire Northeast, defined by a Boston-Washington-Chicago triangle, and especially of the axial belt of Megalopolis within that triangle. In other words, there was still a concentration of sales where people were the most crowded and where there were enough wealthy customers living within short distances to warrant many large stores, offering a wide choice of diversified merchandise. These conditions existed in the main urban centers, and more particularly in New York City, by far the leading retailing center in the country despite the substantial volume of sales in not-too-distant places such as Boston, Philadelphia, Newark, New Haven, and others. This was, of course, a concentration of sales of the more expensive and durable goods, for, as has often been observed: "Food retailing is usually restricted to a market of exceptionally short radius, whereas retail markets for furniture or expensive style goods may cover wide areas, especially where a major center offers strong attractions." [3]

Since 1939 these Northeastern areas have lost a good deal of their previous relative supremacy. Retailing tends to follow the consumer, and the great prosperity of the 1950's increased the consuming capacity of almost every section of the nation. It lifted the average American standard of living to a level that made the consumption of food rather uniform throughout the country, except for the more expensive specialties and for certain foods favored by some localized groups in the population. The

[3] Wilbert G. Fritz "Markets and Marketing," Chapter 10 in the National Resources Planning Board's, *Industrial Location and National Resources, December 1942,* U. S. Government Printing Office, Washington, D. C., 1943, p. 206.

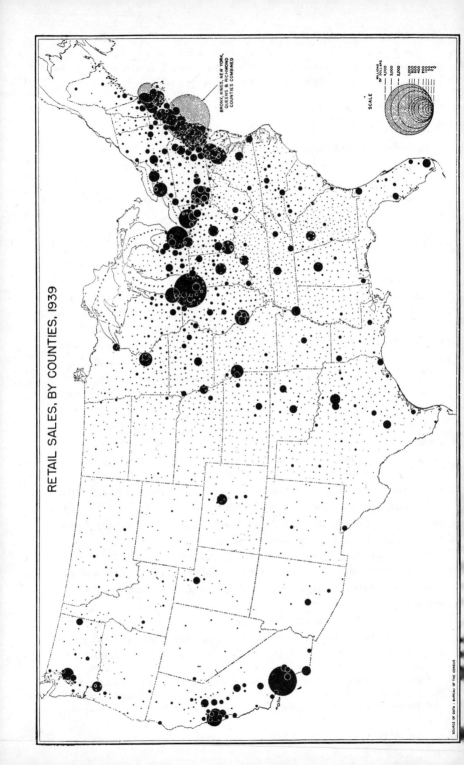

RETAIL SALES, BY COUNTIES, 1939

BRONX, KINGS, NEW YORK,
QUEENS & RICHMOND
COUNTIES COMBINED

SCALE

MILLIONS
OF DOLLARS
4,000
3,000
2,000
1,000
800
600
400
200
100

SOURCE OF DATA: BUREAU OF THE CENSUS

average American family acquired its own home and came to use a rapidly increasing number of mechanical gadgets. To meet all these needs shopping areas developed in nearly every town, carrying a larger listing of merchandise and a greater choice than ever before. True, there was an increase also in number of people who could afford more expensive, fashionable furniture, clothing, and so forth, and these wealthier customers still needed the wider choice that could be found only in the great stores in places where wealth had been concentrated for some time, especially in New York City, Boston, Chicago, or San Francisco. But, in spite of the general prosperity of the nation, such a clientele could represent only a small fraction of the retail business. On the whole the main cities' share of sales in the national total was bound to decrease, and this tendency was accelerated by the stores' own endeavors to pursue the consumer by establishing branches.

Formerly the main shopping area of a town or city was rather localized in the central business district, near the places where other major commercial operations were transacted. This concentration downtown was rooted in the old tradition and organization of the *market place*, and main roads or means of mass transit converged toward that hub of trade. As the volume and variety of business transactions expanded, so did the area in which these activities thrived. These developments in New York City have been described as follows:

As the years went on, the consumer facilities of Manhattan crawled northward like almost everything else. By 1850, "the" shopping district stood at about Canal Street and Broadway, just south of the then finest residential section of the City. It continued to travel in the wake of better residences and was centered at 14th Street in 1880. . . . Twenty-third Street became the center for a while, only to yield to 34th Street, which became the heart of the department store area just after the turn of the century. Once more the decisions on the location of the Grand Central Station and the Pennsylvania Station were important in determining the rate of northward crawl. . . .

Today, the main retail "nucleus" of Manhattan is more diffused than ever before, being strung along miles of streets and avenues in the midtown area.[4]

New York's central shopping area was defined by the New York Metropolitan Region Study as bounded by Third and Tenth avenues and by Canal and 59th streets, being in the center of the "hub" of Manhattan but much smaller than the whole central business district.[5] In 1960 New York

[4] Edgar M. Hoover and Raymond Vernon, *Anatomy of a Metropolis: The Changing Distribution of People and Jobs within the New York Metropolitan Region*, New York Metropolitan Region Study, Harvard University Press, Cambridge, Mass., 1959, p. 115.

[5] *Ibid.*; see footnote on p. 13.

City's hub was still by any standard the main retailing center in the nation, in terms of volume as well as of the extraordinary variety of its business. However, it owes its role and size to a national and even an international function as much as to the local clientele on the metropolitan level.

Pioneering in this respect, New York City's department stores began to decentralize rather early. Not only did they establish branches in various other cities far away from New York (such as Miami Beach, for instance), but they invaded the suburbs in the wake of the residents' exodus to the metropolitan ring. Their first suburban branches were opened in the late 1920's. By 1951 there were eighty of these throughout the metropolitan region (that is, in twenty-two counties), twenty-one of them being in northern New Jersey and about half of the total having been opened between 1946 and 1951. From 1929 to 1948 the increase in retail sales was 57 per cent in Manhattan, but it was 503 per cent in Garden City on Long Island, 165 per cent in White Plains, 180 per cent in Bridgeport, 341 per cent in Millburn, New Jersey, and 248 per cent in Hackensack. Not only Manhattan but also the two other main central shopping areas in the region, those in Brooklyn and in Newark, had an increase much inferior to that of the suburbs.[6] Similar trends developed in other central cities throughout Megalopolis, and they were accelerated after 1950.

These suburban developments have taken place in spite of the fact that the larger stores would seem to be more strongly rooted in their downtown or midtown locations than smaller stores would be. To offer all the diversity of merchandise a large department store in a major city carries on its shelves, it must count on fairly large crowds of customers, and the numbers shopping in a suburban town, even one serving a whole county or two, could not be expected to equal those normally shopping in the central business district of a larger metropolis. The suburban branches therefore often carry only part of all the variety of goods offered in the main store. Moreover, the various stores have tended to space their suburban branches so as to avoid easy competition between any two, even though the mother establishments may very well be competing next door to each other in the center of Manhattan, Washington, or Boston. However, the suburban branches do usually find themselves competing in many kinds of merchandise with small specialized stores that cluster around them. More and more frequently the larger building of one such branch store rises above the general one-story level of a sprawling suburban or exurban shopping center.

[6] Regional Plan Association, *Suburban Branch Stores in the New York Metropolitan Region*, RPA Bulletin No. 78, New York, December 1951.

The *shopping centers* scattering all over the inner and outer rings of metropolitan areas, large or small, have created new market places or small "downtowns" within the apparently unorganized, nebulous structure of Megalopolis and of many other metropolitanized parts of the country. By 1960 there remained only a few small towns in the United States that did not have at least one shopping center, usually established on the periphery, even at some distance from the built-up area, but close to some major highway. Accessibility from both the near-by town and the countryside at large is the very *raison d'être* of the shopping center.[7] Several shopping centers begin to congregate around a few major suburban crossroads: new business districts thus may be born.

The success of what has become, in the last twenty years, a fundamental institution of suburban America recalls a similar process of urban growth in past centuries throughout Europe and Asia. Beginning in the Middle Ages, markets or "fairs" were established near the gates of towns situated at important crossroads. Merchants gathering there preferred the location outside the city walls to avoid the crowding of the town's center, the local tolls and taxes, the competition of the town's stores; and yet they could benefit from easy access to and from both the city and the surrounding country, and from the protection of the guards at the city gates. For the latter advantage, merchants who used the place for their transactions paid a tax to the feudal lord or authority who commanded the walls towering above the field. Such cooperation profited everybody concerned, including the townsmen residing within the walls. It always attracted more permanent activities and residences to the vicinity of this "suburban market," which served as an incubator for a suburb that ultimately developed around it. Such commercial activities *extra muros* made cities grow and expand. In many cases the modern shopping center has had a similar influence. It attracts more buildings, commercial or residential, to its neighborhood. It gives its customers the advantages of easy access by not-too-crowded roads, of abundant parking space (a *must* for a shopping center), and of a compact gathering of a variety of retail stores and often of various service establishments.

The structure of the shopping center illustrates how retail trade is ultimately coupled with a variety of services in its pursuit of the consumer. In the urban business districts the shopping areas tend to be next to the

---

[7] Alan M. Voorhees, Gordon B. Sharpe, and J. T. Stegmaier, *Shopping Habits and Travel Patterns*, Technical Bulletin No. 24, Urban Land Institute, 1955; also Saul B. Cohen and William Applebaum, "Evaluating Store Sites and Determining Store Rents," *Economic Geography*, Vol. 36, 1960, pp. 1–35.

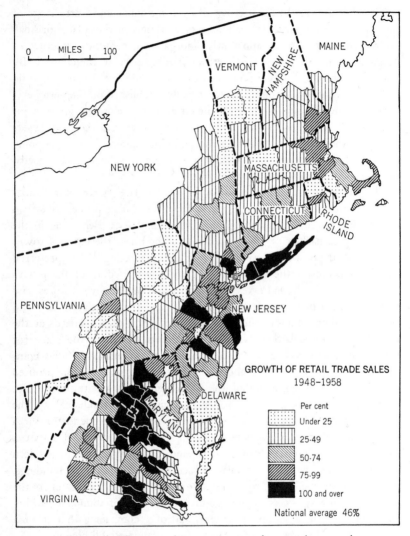

FIG. 157. The map shows percentage increase by counties.

districts where entertainment establishments, hotels, and restaurants congregate. Similarly, the shopping centers offer not only the logical array of retail stores but also services such as restaurants, banks, service stations, occasionally a post office branch, barber shops and beauty salons, sometimes a movie theater. In addition to serving shoppers, they gradually attract social life and become community centers in more than a commercial sense. Since World War II shopping centers have had such phenomenal success that they have already put their imprint on the American way of life and can be rated one of the major conveniences of suburban dispersal in the automobile age.

An abundant technical literature has dealt with the various aspects of location, development, and management of shopping centers.[8] Some of these have brought forth an almost scholarly analysis of the policies and principles regulating the "shopping center market." [9] In the mid-1950's the multiplication of these centers began arousing some concern as to whether their development may have been too fast, causing an undesirable overfractionation of the suburban consumer market. Moreover, there is the question of their effect on the central cities. There can be little doubt that the shopping centers take a great deal of business away from the downtown shopping areas of the old urban cores. The effect has been more adverse on the smaller cities, but even the major cities have lost a good deal of their potential growth as a result. In some cases, however, this competition may have forced improvements on the old downtown.

The advent of a shopping center tends to pull merchants in an older district together to meet the common threat. This cooperation results in the rehabilitation and renovation of Main Street, the provision of better parking facilities, and more cooperative merchandising; which all in turn stimulate trade.[10]

Inevitably the massive displacement of Megalopolitan population into the outlying areas has been accompanied by a good deal of displacement of consumer-oriented trade and services. What these shifts have been can be assessed by an examination of the growth pattern of retail sales from 1948 to 1958, a decade of great suburban sprawl (Fig. 157). During that period retail sales in the whole nation grew by 56 per cent;[11] the in-

[8] See, for instance, Saul B. Cohen, *Selected Annotated Bibliography on Shopping Centers*, The Kroger Company, Cincinnati, Ohio, 1957.

[9] J. Ross McKeever, *Shopping Centers Re-studied*, Urban Land Institute, Technical Bulletin No. 30, 2 parts, 1957; and Homer Hoyt, *A Re-examination of the Shopping Center Market*, Urban Land Institute, Technical Bulletin No. 33, 1958. See also "Shopping Centers: 6th Annual Special Report," a special issue of *Chain Store Age*, New York, Vol. 34, No. 5, May 1958.

[10] McKeever, *Shopping Centers Re-Studied, op. cit.*, Part 1, p. 17. New Brunswick, New Jersey, is cited as a case in point.

[11] The map, Figure 157, is based on the county data of the *U. S. Census of Business* for the years 1948 and 1958, which are not entirely comparable. However, as the map aims at a generalized picture of the growth ratio it is not much affected by the differences in the detailed computing of sales statistics. We have had to use the preliminary data for 1958 but do not think that corrections on the final edition of this Census would modify in any appreciable way the picture presented on this map.

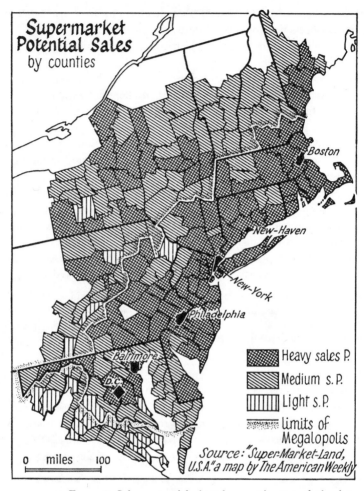

Fig. 158. Sales potentials based on estimates of the late 1950's

creases were definitely higher than this, however, in most counties of the axial belt of Megalopolis, especially around New York City and Philadelphia, and to an even greater degree around Baltimore and Washington. They were below average in the larger cities themselves (Boston, New York City, Philadelphia, and Baltimore) and in the highly urbanized counties of New Jersey such as Hudson, Essex, and Mercer. As was to be expected, growth was greater southwest of New York City than in New England, where population had increased to a lesser degree. Finally, the more outlying counties in Megalopolis and those adjacent to but outside the region showed a low ratio of increase.

This map of shifting retail trade seems to reflect rather closely the pattern of population growth in the two preceding intercensal periods (compare Fig. 73, p. 248), which increased the density and continuity of the axial belt, especially toward the south. Another map (Fig. 158), prepared from 1958–59 data on potential sales of supermarkets by counties, demonstrates that the nation's most massive concentration of counties with "heavy sales potential" is to be found on the Northeastern seaboard, and that the boundaries assigned to Megalopolis in this study approximate rather closely the outline of this concentration. It reflects both the density and the high income level of the population.

Diffusion of consumer-oriented trade and services following population dispersion proceeds with speeds that vary according to the types of trade or service. The "supermarket" trade usually moves most rapidly in the wake of the customers, with personal and repair services following closely (Fig. 159). The selected service trades scatter (Fig. 160), too, but much less rapidly than does retailing proper,[12] for some of these services remain a function of the urban core. It provides the very substantial market needed for such services as entertainment, hotels, and even catering. Moreover, the large seaboard cities, because of their old hinge function, serve and entertain many visitors from beyond their metropolitan areas, and this group of customers for expensive and fashionable goods and services is found only at the great national and international crossroads.

Thus, while downtown districts of suburban or satellite places and new shopping centers can take some of the trade away from the main cities, they must leave to them certain functions always localized at hubs of great size. In the suburbs the people are too thinly spread to justify duplicating all the services of the central city with the frequency of the shopping centers. And to the suburban population, used to commuting, the better variety and quality of the services available in the central cities justify a trip to them. It must be remembered, too, that the Megalopoli-

[12] Figures 159 and 160, based on 1948 data on personal and repair services and 1954 data on selected service trades (see the *U. S. Census of Business* for these two years) are not strictly comparable because of some differences in the definitions of the two Censuses. Moreover, by showing number of establishments on the 1948 map and receipts on the 1954 map, we have deliberately avoided straight confrontation of data. Nevertheless, the maps are complementary. In general fashion they show that these services are closely related to the density and mass of the population; and they show a striking concentration of the receipts, that is, of the volume of business, in the larger cities and their immediate surroundings. It is significant that even in 1954 these old nuclei agglomerated more of such business than did the countryside.

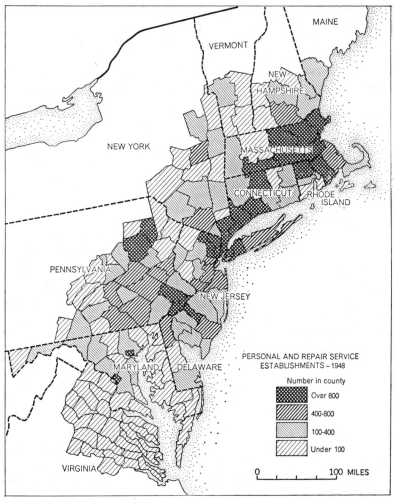

FIG. 159

tan population is rather demanding and is not ready to accept poorer services, especially of types not required daily, as a result of moving out to the suburbs. A good many residents of the wealthier suburban places continue to patronize specialty shops, barbers and beauty salons, dentists and opticians in Boston, New York City, or Philadelphia. The sorts of trade establishments they patronize could not survive in a smaller town.

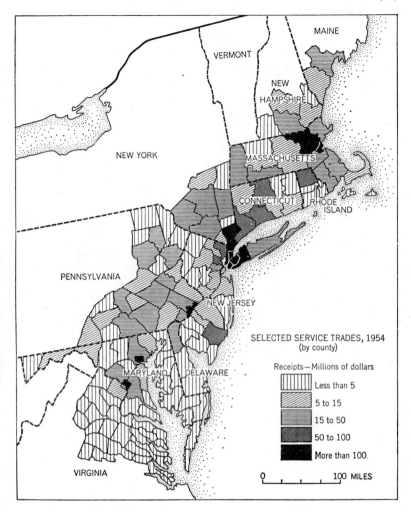

FIG. 160

The Wholesale Trade

Although wholesale trade employs fewer people than either retailing or the selected service trades, it consists of larger establishments with a wider system of commercial relationships. The activity of the wholesale market is what actually determines the commercial significance of a crossroads. It generates in its vicinity more transportation, more white-collar

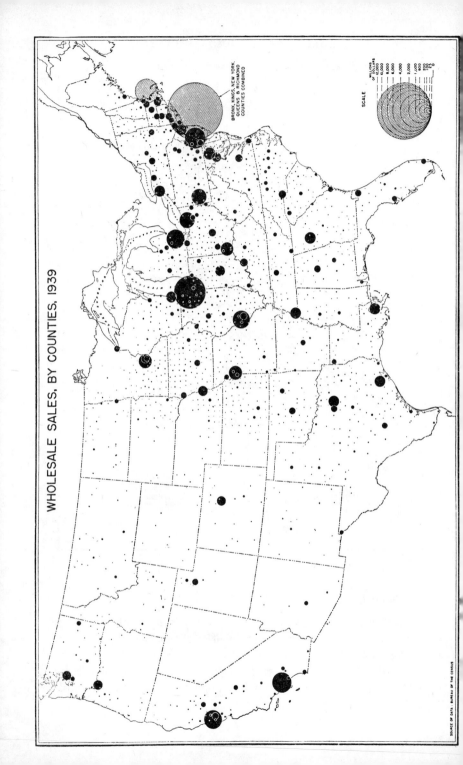

WHOLESALE SALES, BY COUNTIES, 1939

BRONX, NEW YORK, KINGS, QUEENS & RICHMOND COUNTIES COMBINED

SCALE

MILLIONS OF DOLLARS
12,000
10,000
8,000
6,000
4,000
2,000
1,000
500
200
100
0

SOURCE OF DATA: BUREAU OF THE CENSUS

jobs, more credit management, and sometimes it attracts banking and manufacturing also.

Since the end of the seventeenth century the seaports of Megalopolis have been the great wholesale markets of America. The seaboard location and the early development of the "economic hinge" function set up and maintained there the largest organization of wholesalers in the country. In the eighteenth century Boston and Philadelphia vied for first rank, but New York City took the lead at the close of the War of 1812, when the British chose to dump in that port the big bulk of the exports they had gathered to send to the United States as soon as normal relations were resumed. The quantities of merchandise thus suddenly accumulated on her wharves presented New York City with a real challenge, and its merchants rose to the occasion, rapidly establishing the city as the largest wholesale market in the nation, the main hub of its foreign trade.[13] It was New York's role as the great American *emporium* that attracted to it a great concentration of transactions in securities, insurance, entertainment, and advertising, which the city has not yet relinquished.

By 1939 New York City's leadership as a wholesale market, as evidenced by the volume of sales, was even more marked than its leadership in retailing; and from Boston to Washington the axis of Megalopolis appeared on the map of the United States as a continuous chain of substantial centers of wholesale trade (Fig. 161). Nowhere else in the country was there then any comparable grouping, not even in the Chicago area. In 1956 the situation was very similar, despite the consolidation of various regional centers in other parts of the country, an unavoidable consequence of the diffusion of retail trade and manufacturing. The map for 1956 (Fig. 162) still shows a rather long and solid chain of counties, each with more than 2,000 employees in wholesale establishments, that follows exactly the Megalopolitan axial belt. Nowhere else is there such a massive and continuous concentration, for wholesale trade is of course the first foundation and characteristic of the "hinge" function. In 1956 Megalopolis held about one fourth of the employees occupied in wholesale trade in the whole country. According to the *U. S. Census of Business: 1954*, the exact figures for the region were: 23.5 per cent of the country's active proprietor-merchant wholesalers, 26.8 per cent of the paid employees, 28 per cent of the annual payroll, and 32.6 per cent of the sales. In other words, the employees in this region are paid a little better than average, and the business transactions are larger in terms of dollars.

These proportions result both from the size of the region's wholesale

[13] Hoover and Vernon, *Anatomy of a Metropolis, op. cit.*, pp. 79 ff.

markets and their diversity. Some very specialized markets, commanding the country's entire trade in their specialties, have elected to locate in Megalopolis. Among these are the fur and diamond wholesale markets of Manhattan, in which relatively few people handle small quantities of goods with considerable value. Fur and diamond wholesalers have traditionally had their main markets in Manhattan for more than a century, as have apparel wholesalers. And there are even some such concentrations in food specialties, forming a much smaller but still appreciable part of the total wholesale trade of Megalopolis. Many special exotic foods, especially imported delicacies, such as caviar, French champagne, and pistachio, are distributed throughout the United States from one or two major wholesale markets, set up in the leading importing seaports such as New York and perhaps San Francisco. The total quantities consumed in the nation do not warrant many specialized warehouses, and the high value of the products can easily absorb the costs of more transportation, handling, and intermediaries.

In contrast, wholesalers of ordinary foods, handling larger quantities and serving a much wider public, will of course locate as centrally as possible in terms of accessibility to the broadest possible market area. The more densely an area is settled, the more closely spaced will such wholesale markets be, and each major metropolitan area will have its own large produce markets serving the central city and its suburbs.

The very great size and variety of wholesale markets neighboring on one another in a great city help each of the specialized markets to retain its attraction for both sellers and buyers, for they make possible the concentration in the city, and in the vicinity of the business district, of various services that benefit both wholesale and retail merchants. These services, ranging from legal advice to various forms of entertainment, attract the customer from afar and help the local merchant when he needs counsel, wants to entertain well, and so forth. New York's advantage as regards organization of local amenities is largely a result of the efforts of its merchants to attract a large clientele to their developing entrepôt. It was partly owing to its reputation for entertaining the customer lavishly that in the first half of the nineteenth century the New York wholesale market rapidly surpassed those of Boston and Philadelphia, where merchants showed more reserve in this respect.[14] This concentration of entertainment services is important, but so also is the concentration of a variety of other specialized services, such as advertising, legal counsel, various technical consultation agencies, shipping, and insurance. All the preparatory

[14] *Ibid.*, p. 80, quoting the historical testimony of Jacob Knickerbocker (pseud.), *Then and Now*, B. Humphries, Inc., Boston, 1939.

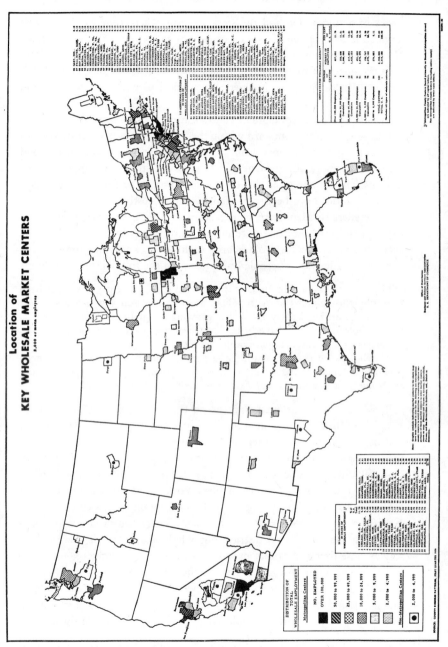

Fig. 162. *Courtesy of the Office of Distribution, U. S. Department of Commerce*

stages of a transaction and the steps resulting therefrom would be well serviced in a large center as well organized as are the major cities of the Northeastern seaboard. For the past century New York City has definitely been the queen of the specialized wholesale markets, but Boston, Philadelphia, and Baltimore have retained a good deal of wholesale trade in and around their central cores (see Fig. 162).

In spite of these advantages of centralization, there is some tendency for wholesaling to spread outward within the main metropolitan areas. Wholesale handling of bulky merchandise requires large warehouses with good accessibility, especially for trucks. The crowded streets of congested business districts do not offer this easy access, nor space for parking, unless special facilities have been provided, which is costly on expensive land. For travellers to Manhattan or Brooklyn additional expenses result from the tolls collected on bridges, tunnels, and turnpikes built to improve the accessibility. In the New York area such an outward migration of the wholesale trade was noticeable by 1930, when the following was written:

> The Market has not the solidity it once had and in recent years it has been scattering throughout the metropolitan area. One reason was the heavy cost of trucking, arising largely from that growing congestion of the streets . . . Some wholesale grocers have had to pay nearly 4 per cent of their net sales for expenses of transportation within the city.
> Warehouses necessarily play a large part in wholesale markets of all nonperishable goods. . . . the newer ones find Manhattan too expensive and are being built in almost every case in Brooklyn or New Jersey.[15]

This trend has continued right up to the present time. From 1929 to 1954 New York's metropolitan region, encompassing twenty-two counties and half of the people in Megalopolis, showed an increase in the number of wholesale employees from 269,000 to 381,000. However, Manhattan's share fell during this period from 76.4 to 58.8 per cent of the region's total, while the other four boroughs of New York City pushed their share up from 11.7 to 16.5 per cent, and the share of Hudson and Essex counties in New Jersey went up from 6 to 9 per cent. There had been decentralization from the old central district, but wholesale trade still preferred to stay as close to it as possible, and in 1954 the counties of the region's central cities accounted for 84 per cent of the total employment in wholesale trade. In 1956 Manhattan still held 94 per cent of the wholesale trade in dry goods and apparel and 75 per cent in furniture and home furnishings, but only 41.8 per cent in edible farm products, 37.6 in hardware and

---

[15] R. L. Duffus, *Mastering a Metropolis*, New York, Harper and Brothers, 1930, p. 57.

plumbing, and 26.6 per cent in scrap and waste materials. Obviously the markets requiring more space for cheaper materials were the first to decentralize.[16] One of the most recent examples of such decentralization is the decision, made in 1959, to move the fruit and produce market of the Washington Street district, on Manhattan's lower West Side, out of the island to a new site in the Bronx. A short time later, early in 1960, the Governor of New Jersey approved the choice of a large area in the Jersey Meadows for another new and large produce market, obviously intended to serve at least part of New York City as well as part of northern New Jersey.

Similar changes have taken place in other Megalopolitan cities. In Boston the downtown district lost 5,000 jobs in wholesaling between 1947 and 1957, and in the latter year it retained only 28 per cent of the metropolitan area's activity in this trade. During the same period the rest of the area gained 11,000 wholesale jobs. Physical decay, obsolete goods-handling facilities, and traffic congestion worked together to make it uneconomical for the large warehouses to remain downtown.[17] Baltimore and Philadelphia have experienced similar trends, although their business districts were not quite as crowded as those of Manhattan and Boston.[18] In Philadelphia the city has moved most of its food wholesaling to a new, less central, but more spacious and accessible location, which by 1960 was serving a large area in southern and central New Jersey besides a good part of eastern Pennsylvania. Philadelphia's success in this relocation has been studied carefully by the other major centers in Megalopolis.

The wholesale establishments located or relocated outside the central core of a metropolis still feel the pull of its commercial organization and prefer to remain close to it. Even in New Jersey, so advantageously situated, the area linking the two great metropolitan regions of New York and Philadelphia did not attract as many wholesalers as one might have expected. In 1954, the whole of New Jersey had only 5,697 merchant wholesalers as compared with 23,045 in New York City and 5,009 in

[16] Hoover and Vernon, *Anatomy of a Metropolis, op. cit.*, pp. 83–88.

[17] Greater Boston Economic Study Committee, *A Report on Downtown Boston*, Policy Statement, Part 2, Associates of the Committee for Economic Development, Boston, Mass., May 1959, and, in the same series, *Recent Changes in the Employment Structure of Greater Boston*, Economic Base Report No. 3, Boston, 1959.

[18] Alderson and Sessions (prepared for the Philadelphia City Planning Commission), *Philadelphia Central District Study*, Philadelphia City Planning Commission, 1951 (see Fig. 15, p. 38); Baltimore Regional Planning Council, *Industrial Land Development*, Technical Report No. 2, Maryland State Planning Commission, Baltimore, May 1959; and John Rannells, *The Core of the City*, Columbia University Press, New York, 1956.

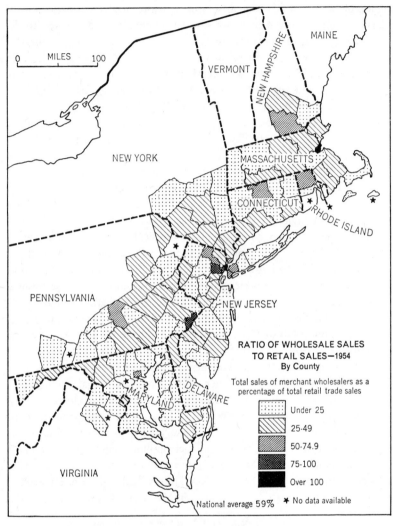

FIG. 163

Philadelphia. And most of the wholesaling went on in the counties of Essex, Hudson, and Union, most directly suburbanized by New York. It is noteworthy that in 1956, when wholesale trade accounted for 5.1 per cent of the total employment in the United States, it provided only 4.5 per cent of New Jersey's employment.[19]

[19] Salomon J. Flink, *The Economy of New Jersey*, Rutgers University Press, New Brunswick, N. J., 1958.

Moreover, it must be noted that these decentralization trends do not involve all phases of the wholesale trade. A certain division of functions has developed within it. It is the wholesale handling of goods requiring large warehousing facilities that moves to the periphery of metropolis, while the business offices often remain downtown. In Philadelphia, for example, a study made in 1951 showed that "wholesaling without stocks" had been occupying increasing amounts of floor space in the central district of the city, while the downtown space used by "wholesaling with stocks," which involves warehousing, had been shrinking.[20] This trend seems to be developing in most large cities of Megalopolis. "Perhaps in time almost no goods will be brought into the center of the city that are not to be consumed or processed there. But this will not prevent the city from performing the very important function of price-fixing, for that can be done by samples whenever a business is sufficiently well organized and standardized."[21] As the old metropolitan cores become more crowded and the operation of warehouses therein grows more costly, the future for warehousing wholesale establishments will be most promising in suburban and outer-ring areas. However, *the markets, in the sense of the places where transactions are negotiated, will remain fairly concentrated*, particularly those dealing in the more valuable kinds of merchandise.[22]

In its handling of large quantities of often bulky materials wholesale trade is linked to good means of transportation and, especially in Megalopolis, to the seaboard, that is, to areas accessible to seagoing ships. In its handling of large commercial transactions, often involving considerable amounts of money, wholesale trade is dependent on close links with financial institutions that may provide credit, and, as has already been noted, with the various services that may be needed by both resident and visiting merchants. These two sets of relationships integrate the wholesale trade into the region's powerful commercial organization, of which overseas trading and the financial community are two other essential elements.

[20] Alderson and Sessions, *Philadelphia Central District Study, op. cit.*, Chapter 4.
[21] Duffus, *Mastering a Metropolis, op. cit.*, p. 57.
[22] This can be well demonstrated by the wholesale-retail ratios. In New York City, for every $100 in sales by retail establishments in 1958, sales of all wholesalers amounted to $468 and of merchant wholesalers alone to $210. In the four suburban counties nearest to the city in New York State the ratio of merchant wholesalers' sales to retailers' sales stood at $31 to $100, which was even lower than the upstate ratio of $45 to every $100 of retail sales. See "Wholesale Trade, 1958," *New York State Commerce Review*, Vol. 14, No. 4, April 1960. For the ratio in 1954 see Figure 163.

The Maritime Commerce

The maritime commerce of Megalopolis is concentrated in four main port areas, corresponding to the region's major urban nuclei, all of them old. From north to south there are Boston, the Port of New York, the Delaware River ports, and Baltimore. It was the great overseas trade of these ports that built up the whole area as the nation's economic hinge and, in so many respects, as the nation's *Main Street*. As the United States evolved, by the end of the nineteenth century, toward a higher degree of economic self-sufficiency, the role of oceanic traffic in the national economy declined. The twentieth century has turned the tide once more and has given increased importance to the seaports in general and especially to those of the Northeastern seaboard. Four factors have concurred in this further expansion of Megalopolis' sea trade: the growing part assumed by oil fields of Texas and Louisiana in supplying petroleum to the Northeast; the opening in 1914 of the Panama Canal, which fostered easier sea connections with the West Coast and the Pacific realm in general; the increased stress put on exports of American manufactures and raw materials during and after the two World Wars; and finally, the growth of American imports, mainly from countries bordering on the Atlantic Ocean.

According to a long-standing international usage, seaports are ranked according to the volume of their trade with foreign countries. This was a wise tradition for the time when and the nations where domestic coastwise traffic involved only bulky materials moved short distances, mainly the construction materials that still make up the big bulk of the *local* trade in such ports as New York and those on the Delaware. However, the domestic coastwise traffic of the United States consists largely of important shipments from the Gulf and West Coast ports to those of Megalopolis, involving large ships, a variety of goods, and a long oceanic voyage. Such domestic trade should not be disregarded in assessing the role and problems of the maritime traffic of Megalopolis.

Foreign trade still ranks first, however, among all the components of the ports' activities. This is essentially commerce that could not be carried otherwise than by sea (unless some day air freight is able to handle such enormous volumes). In terms of ship movements and of merchandise handled, *the ports of Megalopolis lead the nation in every respect except for outbound shipments*. In 1958, out of a grand total of 48,455 vessels entering all United States ports, with an aggregate net registered tonnage of 149 million tons, the ports in Megalopolis accounted for 23.4 per cent of the number of vessels and 44 per cent of their tonnage, with the port of New York alone accounting for half the Megalopolitan total.[23] These figures show that the large Megalopolitan harbors attract more of the larger vessels and, especially in the case of New York, many liners that carry the great majority of passengers coming from or going to foreign lands by sea.

In terms of cargo handled, in 1957 [24] the ports in Megalopolis unloaded 105 million tons of imported cargo, or 60 per cent of the total United States seaborne imports, and shipped 27.4 million tons, or 19 per cent of the United States exports. The imbalance is striking both in the volume of cargo and in the proportion of the national total. Megalopolis imports much more than it exports. Since it is a huge consuming market itself and a redistributing center mainly for expensive goods, this quantitative imbalance should not cause surprise. In value the region's foreign trade deficit almost disappears (in New York and Baltimore exports actually exceed imports in value), for the great harbors export mainly costly manufactured goods, while the imports consist largely of raw materials. The massive importation of crude petroleum and iron and manganese ores boosts the incoming trade, particularly on the Delaware River and in Baltimore.

In tonnage of raw-material imports the Delaware ports have outstripped New York, the recognized queen of American seaports for a century and a half (see Table 20). Actually, the complex of ports on the Delaware is much more diversified and less unified than is the port of New York, even including all its components, such as Port Newark in New Jersey. If the figures of the ports of Philadelphia and Camden were considered separately they would show smaller imports than the port of New York, for they would not include the petroleum brought to Marcus Hook or to the Tidewater Oil Company's refinery downstream, or the iron ore unloaded at the Fairless Works of the United States Steel Corporation upstream. Nevertheless, it is significant that in a year of high industrial activity, such as was 1957, the Delaware River ports combined surpassed, in volume of imports, the powerful grouping of port facilities

[23] Data from U. S. Bureau of the Census, *United States Foreign Trade: Vessel Entrances and Clearances, Calendar Year 1958*, Summary Report FT 975, May 27, 1959.

[24] A year more typical than 1958 for the recent period's foreign commerce. Data from U. S. Bureau of the Census, *Statistical Abstract of the United States: 1959*, U. S. Government Printing Office, Washington, D. C., p. 591.

Table 20

COMMERCE OF SELECTED UNITED STATES SEAPORTS, 1957

(Seaborne Traffic Only, in Thousands of Short Tons of Cargo)

Selected Ports	Foreign Trade		Coastwise Trade	
	Imports	Exports	Receipts	Shipments
In Megalopolis				
Boston	4,976	1,423	11,531	1,148
Providence	1,271	102	5,773	504
New Haven Harbor	873	2	5,244	1,163
New York Harbor	32,012	9,991	41,510	10,982
Delaware River Harbors	41,344	6,225	28,929	8,230
Baltimore Harbor	22,567	9,477	6,461	1,744
Outside Megalopolis				
Hampton Roads { Norfolk	2,907	30,076	4,956	4,846
Hampton Roads { Newport News	3,200	23,677	67	3,560
New Orleans	4,588	10,220	908	9,506
Houston, Galveston, and Texas City	2,319	13,642	1,406	32,606
Los Angeles and Long Beach Harbors	5,402	5,170	6,333	8,252
San Francisco Bay	5,833	2,897	10,218	9,927
Total United States	176,236	146,890	196,307	196,370

Source: U. S. Bureau of the Census, *Statistical Abstract of the United States: 1959,* Table No. 776, p. 591.

on and around the lower Hudson River. In that same year Hampton Roads, Virginia,[25] surpassed even the Delaware River total in foreign trade, owing to massive exports of coal; with a total of 60 million tons of cargo handled, Hampton Roads ranked first that year among all United States ports in volume of foreign trade, ahead of the Delaware River group (47.6 million) and the port of New York (42 million). Hampton Roads' lead was especially striking in exports (about 54 million tons), and in this function it was followed by the Houston-Galveston-Texas City group, then by New Orleans, and only then by New York and Baltimore.

In contrast to the raw-materials-exporting ports of the South, the Megalopolitan ports definitely receive more than they ship out, although their exports are large. This characteristic is even more marked if coastwise

[25] During the World Wars and in the years immediately following them, when there was great need for port facilities, the great ports on both sides of Hampton Roads, just outside of Megalopolis, rose to importance. Their functions are very different from those of the crowded Megalopolitan ports they complement, for their chief activity is the export of bulky materials, such as coal, tobacco, and grains, from the West or South, and their outbound traffic is many times the inbound in volume. Moreover, even in peacetime the Navy's activities make up a very important part of the maritime life of Hampton Roads. See Jean Gottmann, *Virginia at Mid-Century,* Henry Holt & Company, New York, 1955, pp. 491–503.

trade is taken into account. Then the port of New York definitely regains first rank, for in 1957 its total tonnage of cargo, both foreign and domestic coastwise, was 94.5 million short tons, or 13 per cent of the national total. The Delaware River ports were second, with 85 million tons, followed by Hampton Roads (73 million), the Houston-Galveston group (50 million), and Baltimore (40 million). Thus three (including the two greatest) of the five leading, enormous, commercial seaports of America are in Megalopolis. All the ports in Megalopolis, among which Boston, Providence, and even New Haven are still of respectable size in terms of their traffic, aggregate close to 40 per cent of the national total in foreign and coastwise trade by sea. These figures do not include the purely local traffic, which boosts to much higher values the total tonnages handled in the major ports, where construction materials are carried by water.

The domestic long-distance traffic consists chiefly of petroleum and petroleum products carried in tankers from the Gulf ports (and occasionally from California via the Panama Canal) to the ports of Megalopolis. This category of merchandise is largely responsible for the massive shipments of the Gulf ports, and for the large coastwise receipts of ports in Megalopolis. This also explains the scattered deliveries along the Megalopolitan coast, with New Haven and Providence receiving some five million tons, Bridgeport over a million and a half, Norwalk and Stamford smaller but still substantial amounts, and so forth. The comparison of tanker and dry-cargo traffic in domestic sea transportation is significant in this respect (see Figs. 164 and 165). This special role played by petroleum in sea transportation has been developing in recent years all around the world. In the dry-cargo category coal used to play a dominant role, and although this has been on the decrease it is still notable. Ores, especially iron ore and bauxite, are now becoming more important in international trade by sea, and their increasing significance is clearly apparent in the imports of Megalopolitan ports.[26]

[26] A recent trend in port traffic studies has been the differentiation between "tanker" (that is, petroleum and petroleum products) cargoes and "dry" cargoes. In certain quarters it has been suggested that ports be classified and ranked according to their dry-cargo trade only, for the tanker cargoes flow through pipes and cisterns, from the land to the tanker and back to the land, without actually requiring much in the way of port facilities or much port labor other than the fastening of one pipe to another for the loading or unloading operations. However, petroleum is an essential fuel and industrial raw material, the abundant supply of which is of paramount importance to the motorized economy of any region. One must remember, of course, that its transit through a port provides less local business than do most dry cargoes, and yet the volume of this specialized traffic is of great importance to a port and its environs. It should not be deducted when ports are being ranked in terms of the amount of cargo they handle.

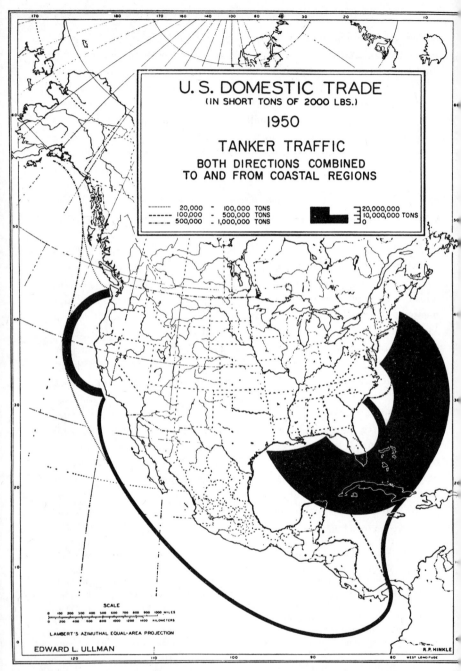

FIG. 164. *Reproduced by permission from Edward L. Ullman,* American Commodity Flow, *University of Washington Press, Seattle, 1957, p. 176*

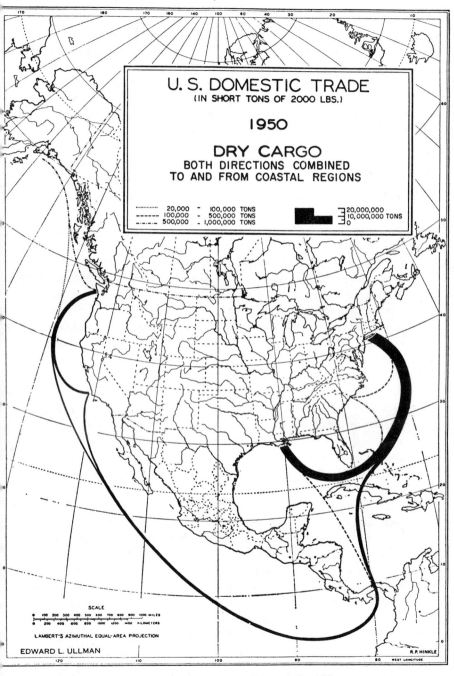

FIG. 165. *Reproduced by permission from Edward L. Ullman,*
American Commodity Flow (*see caption of Fig. 164*), *p. 175*

In addition to receiving more than they ship, the major ports in Megalopolis have a more diversified commerce than does any other group of
American ports, in terms both of variety of goods handled and number of
ports with which regular relations are maintained. Routes plied at regular
intervals by ships under American or foreign flags from the Megalopolitan ports form a network neatly enveloping the globe. This regular contact with many places has helped the seaports of the region to specialize
in shipping and receiving small cargoes, not bulky enough to fill up a vessel, but for which speed of delivery is important. Such shipments, which
need more speedy, careful handling, converge on the major Northeastern
ports, especially New York, both from within the country and from
abroad. Goods coming from the interior of the country will find here a
ship going their way with a minimum delay, and goods enter here from
many overseas sources because many ships sail frequently and regularly
from ports all over the world for New York, Philadelphia, or Baltimore.
This function of "maritime express" is always centered in ports with the
greatest number of regularly scheduled entries and departures, giving contact with many other places. The frequency and regularity of movements
to and from the port of New York are unequalled, for in addition to its
extensive network of foreign commercial relations, in which London and
Rotterdam are also outstanding, New York is the greatest port in the
world for liners and transoceanic passenger traffic. The liners can also
carry cargo, if it is not too bulky, in their spacious holds. For occasional
shipments to Europe of some machinery or expensive manufactured goods
for which quick delivery is desirable, a manufacturer usually finds it
advantageous to ship via New York, Philadelphia, or Baltimore, even
if his product originates at a plant located in some smaller seaport. The
liners sail regularly and according to schedules announced months in
advance.

The international trade in machinery, electrical apparatus, and the like
is steadily developing and will probably keep on growing as more underdeveloped countries improve their equipment. Such shipments will benefit by the organization of what we have called the "maritime express," a
function slowly but solidly built up by the great commercial seaside hubs
of Megalopolis. While the bulk trade can and even must be "decentralized" to avoid too much congestion in the greater ports, a diversified,
selected trade based on the versatility of the local traditional commerce
will remain very much centralized. This function of the great ports is one
of the factors favoring the concentration of national wholesale markets

for the more expensive kinds of merchandise in these same cities, and particularly in New York.[27]

A more detailed analysis of the traffic of the main ports in Megalopolis is provided by the graphs of Figure 166, showing for each main port from Portland to Hampton Roads the inbound and outbound shipments according to the kind of trade (foreign, coastwise, or local) and according to the kinds of goods handled. The preponderance in Megalopolitan maritime traffic of manufactured goods in the outbound trade and of foodstuffs and raw materials in the inbound shipments was to be expected, given the region's manufacturing function and its enormous appetite for materials to feed its people and its machines. The graphs are based on averages for the years 1953–56 and include local traffic. In Boston manufactured products are predominant in both the incoming and the much smaller outgoing cargoes, with petroleum products leading in both cases. That is, Boston redistributes a large part of the petroleum products it receives. New York, too, is a redistributor of petroleum products, but there dry-cargo manufactured goods play a greater role than in any other of these ports, making up about one fourth of the total loaded cargo. They include a variety of goods outside the main categories listed, representing the whole gamut of merchandise attracted by the frequency and diversity of sailings at New York. Philadelphia still dominates the Delaware group. Local traffic, "internal" to one harbor area, is particularly important in New York, partly because the city spreads over several islands and partly because of the excellence of the waterways provided by the Hudson River, the East River, Long Island Sound, and other channels.[28]

The physical operation of waterfront facilities could hardly be listed among the principal sources of employment in Megalopolis. It takes relatively few hands to perform each of the operations in the life of a port, but there are many of them, and in a large port many sailings. To pilot

[27] See U. S. Department of Commerce, *Essential United States Foreign Trade Routes*, U. S. Government Printing Office, Washington, D. C., May 1957; Edward L. Ullman, *American Commodity Flow*, University of Washington Press, Seattle, 1957; F. W. Morgan and James Bird, *Ports and Harbors*, Hutchinson University Library, London, 1958; and Benjamin Chinitz, *Freight and the Metropolis*, New York Metropolitan Region Study, Harvard University Press, Cambridge, 1960.

[28] The figures on which the graphs of Fig. 166 were based were calculated from statistical data in U. S. Department of the Army, Corps of Engineers, *Waterborne Commerce of the United States* (Annual), 1953–1956, Part I: Waterways and Harbors, Atlantic Coast. See also John I. Griffin, *The Port of New York*, Monograph No. 3, Institute of New York Area Studies, The City College of New York, Arco Publishing Co. (for the City College Press), New York, 1959.

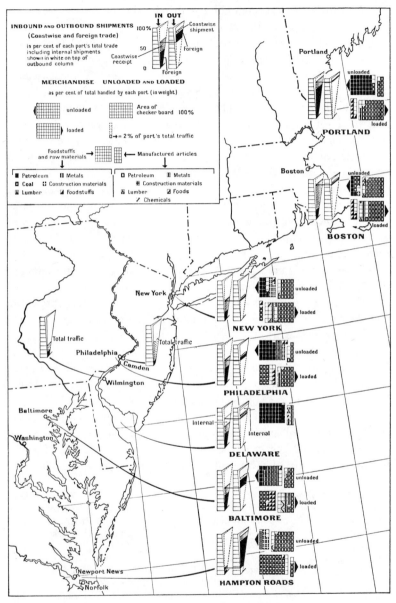

FIG. 166. The graphs, designed by Jean Barbier, are based on averages for the years 1953–56. See also Table 20 for the year 1957.

and berth the vessels, load and unload goods and passengers, dredge the channels, furnish the various services and supplies the vessels need, all require skilled labor. These activities taken altogether make a major port a large-scale industry and a substantial source of revenue, and still more business is provided by the commercial organization on which the management of oceanic transportation depends. In addition the flow in and out of the metropolitan area of cargoes, passengers, and crews generates, at a distance from the waterfront, various profitable activities: more transportation by truck, rail, or inland waterways, for example; more trade in the local wholesale and retail establishments; more office work for traffic management, freight forwarding, freight brokerage, marine insurance, travel services. All told, a whole world of diverse specialists lives in the port and as a result of the port, in addition to the people who handle the cargoes directly. To receive and ship over 200 million tons of goods annually is a huge enterprise. Moreover, a well-organized and well-serviced port attracts manufacturing, at least to process some of the goods handled at this breaking point of their transportation. It also attracts industries that service the ships, build and repair them, supply them, and keep the harbor adequately equipped for the traffic.[29]

At least as much as "industry attracts industry," commerce attracts commerce. The growth of New York through the nineteenth century exemplified this influence, for the volume of business to be transacted by the port forced upon the city a commercial organization of constantly growing size and diversity, and this organization in turn attracted more trade and more shipping. To serve its clients better, New York initiated *liner* service as early as 1816, when it inaugurated the "Black Ball Line," sailing on schedule at regular intervals on the transatlantic run to Europe. Since then the port has attracted some 160 scheduled lines plying sea lanes all around the world, the greatest concentration to be found in any port, and this concentration in turn has brought more traffic both in passengers and in cargo. At a time when all overseas connections were by ship, the con-

[29] As an illustration of the economic significance of these port-related activities, see the Port of New York Authority's *The Port and the Community*, New York, 1956. At that time the Port Authority estimated that in the Port District over which it functions (an area radiating outward about twenty-five miles from the Statue of Liberty) there were 430,000 jobs directly related to port activities, bringing in yearly wages of $2.1 billion. Estimating further that each of these dollars "generates or creates two dollars of additional income within the area," the Port Authority concluded that the port-generated income in the Port District was $6.3 billion yearly, or more than a quarter of the total yearly income ($23 billion) earned in the area. In a pamphlet on *The Economic Impact of the Delaware River Ports*, the Delaware River Port Authority estimated that 96,300 jobs, generating an income of $516 million, depended in the area on the ports.

vergence of liners, tramps, and other trading vessels on the port of New York was a major factor in locating in that city the major commodity and securities exchanges. The importance of the money market and of the financial community in New York, as well as in Boston, cannot be understood apart from the pre-existent organization of overseas relations.[30]

The growing concentration could not help crowding the harbors with ships, wharves, and other equipment, and the waterfront with various industrial establishments. Looking for more seaside land to develop and for greater accessibility to the shore's installations, the sea traffic moved, though unwillingly, away from the main hubs, either to the periphery of a metropolitan port or to another port in the vicinity. Thus some facilities or functions of these ports have migrated or, more often, expanded outside the old core harbors. For instance, from New York City proper some business has moved to the opposite shores of New Jersey and to the docks of Port Newark, administered by the Port of New York Authority. In addition there has been steady expansion southward, toward the Delaware River ports and toward Baltimore on Chesapeake Bay. This trend corresponds to the generally more rapid increase of population density and manufacturing activities in the southwestern parts of Megalopolis. To the northeast, in New England, the pace of maritime activity has been slackening somewhat, and there have been complaints that the port of Boston is "drying up," partly as a result of the competition of New York and the other Atlantic and Gulf ports to the south.

Each of the great Northeastern seaports must beware of two different kinds of competition. On the one hand there is *competition between the ports in Megalopolis,* which are situated close to one another and the four largest of which (Boston, New York, the Delaware River ports, and Baltimore) have enough in common to be to some extent interchangeable for shipments that only transit there. On the other hand, there is *competition*

---

[30] For the past relationships see Chapter 3 above; Robert G. Albion, *The Rise of New York Port: 1815–1860,* Scribners, New York, 1939, and Samuel Eliot Morison, *The Maritime History of Massachusetts: 1783–1860,* Houghton Mifflin Company, Boston, 1921 and 1941. For recent years the best description of the trade and facilities of each of the ports in Megalopolis can be found in the reports of the *Port Series* published and frequently revised by the Corps of Engineers of the U. S. Army and the Maritime Administration, U. S. Department of Commerce. For this study we consulted the following volumes in the Port Series: *The Port of Boston, Mass.* (No. 3, Revised 1956), 1957; *The Ports of Southern New England* (No. 4, Revised 1952), 1954; *The Port of New York, N. Y. and N. J.* (No. 5, Revised 1953), 3 vols., 1955; *The Port of Philadelphia, Pa., and Camden and Gloucester City, N. J.* (No. 7, Revised 1955), 1956; *The Port of Wilmington, Del., and Ports on the Delaware River Below and Above Philadelphia, Pa.* (No. 8, Revised 1955), 1956; *The Port of Baltimore, Maryland* (No. 10, Revised 1955), 1956. Finally, it is useful to consult the reports of the Port Authorities of Boston, New York, and the Delaware River.

between the other main groups of ports on the Atlantic and Gulf coasts, from the St. Lawrence River to the Rio Grande, *and the Megalopolitan group.* The major ports in Megalopolis do not display much solidarity in resisting the competition of these rivals outside the region. For a long while they seemed united in a stubborn opposition to the completion of the St. Lawrence Seaway project; then, after World War II, even in this respect the common front crumbled. The Seaway was opened in 1959, bringing the Great Lakes ports into the ring and thus increasing the competition in the hunt for cargoes. Since the success of its port means much more, to a city and to its metropolitan area, than just merchandise in transit, the competition has been stiff at times.

Within the regional framework of Megalopolis the following recent trends are noticeable: the relative "drying up" of the port of Boston, especially in terms of decrease of liner calls and general-cargo traffic; the consolidation of New York as the main Atlantic "gate" of the United States for passengers and general cargo; the growth of the Delaware River ports, largely owing to increased shipments of petroleum and ores; the steady progress of the port of Baltimore, less rapid in the 1950's than earlier. All these ports seek to serve the continent's maritime transportation needs to as great a degree as possible. Ideally each one would like to count the whole of the United States, and in the winter a good chunk of Canada, in its "hinterland." Careful study of oceanic transportation and port economy shows that often the concept of hinterland is too much oversimplified. With the present ease and speed of transportation over almost the whole North American continent, four great seaports situated within distances of 100 to 200 miles of each other cannot expect each to have a commercial realm of its own, well-partitioned from the others.[31] Such concepts are inherited from an outdated past, when distance, natural barriers, and political or administrative boundaries governed the costs and modes of transfer. In the United States this has never been the case since the Revolution. In fact, had it been the case, the four great Megalopolitan ports, tucked in a small corner of the country, would not have been allowed to develop and maintain for so long their role as the whole continent's economic hinge, and to dominate the foreign maritime trade, especially in general cargo, for two centuries.

The mechanisms that fostered the existing concentration on this short section of the Atlantic seaboard functioned under conditions of great economic freedom, which allowed these more experienced, better equipped

---

[31] See the attempt made in Donald J. Patton, "General Cargo Hinterlands of New York, Philadelphia, Baltimore, and New Orleans," *Annals, Association of American Geographers,* New York, 1955, Vol. 48, No. 4, pp. 436–455.

and organized, more wealthy hubs of commerce to attract customers and currents of trade through a competitive rivalry of which American history can be proud. Each port had its own *clientele* in the interior of the continent and overseas, but the geographical distribution of this clientele has shifted from year to year and from season to season, varying according to merchandise and sometimes according to destination or with respect to delays involved in shipping.

Many factors were instrumental in a client's choice to ship via one port or another. Freight rates, steamer schedules, and costs of handling at the port of loading or at the port of unloading were among the more obvious components of the individual equations. When, as was often the case, there was little difference in costs or timing between one port and another, the decision could then be made on the grounds of personal or business relations established between the sender and one of the carriers or another intermediary, such as the freight broker or insurance agent. Thus the merchants and agents in each port have had to work hard to win clients for their port, and successful efforts of this kind earn worthwhile rewards.

The ports of New England, led by Boston, have fought a long battle to retain currents of trade that are shifting southward. New England is located in a corner of the United States, clearly to the north of the main transcontinental routes that have developed in the last hundred years; it is also away from the southward movement of industrialization resulting from the economic revival of the Southeast since the 1930's. Among the various reasons given to explain the slower-than-average growth of New England and the decline of its maritime commerce are: the freight rate differentials by rail and truck (higher than to Philadelphia and ports farther south); the obsolescence of much of the equipment, which was among the first of its kind to be installed in America; and the barrier to westward transportation formed by the Hudson River, crossed by only a few bridges.[32]

---

[32] Three stages of the examination of New England's problems including its freight and maritime difficulties will be found in John K. Wright (ed.), *New England's Prospect: 1933* (Special Publication No. 16), American Geographical Society, New York, 1933 (especially pp. 344-403); Council of Economic Advisers and Committee on the New England Economy, *The New England Economy: A Report to the President*, U. S. Government Printing Office, Washington, D. C., 1951 (especially Chapters 11 and 12); Arthur A. Bright, Jr., and George H. Ellis, *The Economic State of New England*, Report of the Committee on New England of the National Planning Association (published by arrangement with the New England Council), Yale University Press, New Haven, Conn., 1954 (especially Chapters 12 and 13). See also the reports of the Port of Boston Commission and the Massachusetts Port Authority.

The slow "drying up" of the port of Boston since at least 1900 has been a result both of the supremacy of New York and of the gradual southward displacement of the center of gravity of the national economy. Since 1814 New York has organized its inland commercial relations more effectively than has Boston. New York has tried, and rather successfully, everything it could to attract traffic, from lavish entertainment, scheduled liners, and the early completion of the Erie Canal to the dominance of the Eastern railroads, which had chosen it as the major terminus in the Northeast by the end of the nineteenth century. Boston could neither acquire good trunkline connections to the interior nor even gain control of the major railroads serving New England.

The rail connections inland, especially toward the Great Lakes and Middle West, are still, in this era of highways, of considerable importance to the port of Boston. During the 1950's Boston received increased quantities of western grain for export. Whether this favorable trend can be maintained and developed seems to depend largely on the quantities of grain that will be shipped by the St. Lawrence Seaway, opened in 1959. Since the Seaway is closed by ice for four to five months every winter, the question arose for Boston whether the rail facilities could be depended upon to move out to its port during the winter months at last some of the bulky materials stockpiled in the West. Competition for such trade is not, of course, competition between Megalopolitan ports only. The St. Lawrence ports and even New Orleans come into the arena to vie for Midwest grain and other exports. The commercial organization of the major ports of this seaboard is too vast and reaches too far to lend itself to an analysis contained in the regional frame.

Still, of the Megalopolitan "big four" ports, Boston has today the most modest plans and ambitions. New York, Baltimore, and the Delaware River ports reach farther into the continent, in almost all directions. The competition between them is sharper and clearer. In this game a port's facilities play a great part, for as ships grow larger, more specialized, and more costly to operate, the time spent in a port for unloading and loading becomes a significant element in the cost of a journey. Thus more traffic has been and will increasingly be attracted to the ports providing quicker turnaround for the larger vessels. In this respect the port of New York is indeed without rivals on the Atlantic seaboard, but it may become so crowded as to slow down the movements of ships inside the harbor. Such crowding is already felt in terms of the difficulty of adding well-situated new facilities; and the obsolescence of many of the wharves calls for improvements on this score too. Obviously, one would not consider erecting new large oil refineries or steel mills on the main harbor of New York (although the New Jersey Meadows near Newark could still provide such space, after necessary improvement of the ground); a location on the lower Delaware or even on Chesapeake Bay would seem more reasonable, and such has been the decision in some recent selections of new sites for such plants. The Delaware River traffic grew in the 1950's partly owing to the more "central position" of the area and partly to its lesser degree of crowding.

Proportionately it would thus seem that Baltimore and the Delaware River ports ought to grow more rapidly, in terms of the volume of cargo handled, than New York and Boston. The Delaware River ports specialize in bulky materials carried in specialized vessels, such as tankers and ore ships. Some division of labor was worked out between these rivals, which are too close neighbors not to divide between themselves the main functions of the maritime façade. New York continues to attract a greater amount of general cargo and more steamship liners than any other port on American shores. In 1959, a year of relatively average economic activity, the port of New York's total tonnage in foreign-trade general cargo increased 1.1 per cent as against 1957, but the port's share of the United States total in this trade declined from 24.9 per cent in 1957 to 21.4 in 1959. Among bulky imports, New York received more bauxite, lead, and copper than the other ports in Megalopolis, but most of the iron, manganese, and chrome ores go to the Delaware and Baltimore.[33]

While specialization was shaping, stressing some complementarity between the huge ports of Megalopolis, more cooperation resulted from the very proximity of each of them to the others. It is not always easy for a ship to fill up its holds with merchandise to be unloaded in one port, in which she could also load a full outbound cargo for a destination agreeable to her operator. But it is easier to be loaded to a large extent both ways if the ship can call at two or three of the Megalopolitan ports. As can be seen from the three-day sample listing of sailings into and out of the port of New York (see Table 21), the freighters calling here often come from or sail for Boston, Baltimore, or Philadelphia. Such co-operation between Baltimore and the ports on the Delaware has been enhanced, despite the competitive spirit prevalent in these two port districts, by the Chesapeake and Delaware Canal, which greatly shortens the voyage by sea between them and eliminates the need to round the Delmarva Peninsula. Of course the same canal also shortens the distance from Balti-

[33] See Port of New York Authority, *Oceanborne Foreign Trade at the Port of New York, 1960*, New York, 1960. This Annual Report gives figures through 1959.

more to New York and even to Boston. The distance between the great city of Massachusetts and the other ports of Megalopolis has also been somewhat reduced by the Cape Cod Canal. Such cooperation between the leading ports helps each of them in some way. The ease with which a freighter gathers a full cargo is a major consideration for shipping-traffic management. Steamship companies whose freighters come regularly to New York will find it worthwhile to have agents in Philadelphia and Baltimore also, and perhaps in Boston. While vessels flying the pennants of about 160 steamship lines come to New York, about 110 (mostly the same companies) are listed as sailing regularly from Philadelphia, about 90 are registered in Baltimore, and close to 40 in Boston.[34]

Thus the modern functioning of the *hinge* becomes more obvious. The four great ports in Megalopolis share the same general hinterland (that is, most of the developed area on the North American continent), through which is spread their clientele. They share the same vast ocean and many of the opportunities offered overseas. They also share the indispensable function of servicing the seaborne transportation needs of the people and industries of Megalopolis, no mean task in itself. This seaside region remains as a whole the major gate and hinge of the continent's relations with the outside and especially with the transatlantic world. In the relative specialization that has been slowly worked out, largely as a result of the national economy's evolution and of too much congestion in New York, the port of Boston may feel it has been the loser; but it may still in the future regain more activity because of the need to redistribute the huge total burden somewhat more evenly. Today Boston seems resigned to fourth place on the Megalopolitan team; it is hoping to improve its position if it is granted, at least for certain goods, equality of inland freight rates with Baltimore. On the major North Atlantic runs, sea-freight rates have for some years been equalized for the ports of the Northeastern seaboard, giving them a better chance both for free competition and for cooperative division of labor.

In one specialty, however, the port of New York has acquired almost a monopoly: the traffic of passengers arriving from or departing for foreign countries by sea. In 1956, of all the passengers arriving by sea in the United States, 81 per cent landed in New York; in 1957 this percentage stood at 74; in 1958, at 75. For departures by sea New York scored in the

---

[34] Calculated from the individual *Port Series* reports quoted above (see footnote 30, p. 532). On the usual practices of traffic management for ships, see Carl E. McDowell and Helen M. Gibbs, *Ocean Transportation*, McGraw-Hill Book Co., New York, 1954.

Table 21

Movement of Ships into and out of New York Harbor

(On three ordinary days in May 1960)

Arrivals		Departures	
May 11		*May 11*	
Passenger and mail ships	*From*	*Passenger and mail ships*	*Destination*
INDEPENDENCE (Amer. Export)	Naples	AFRICAN GLADE (Farrell)	Dakar, Freetown, Monrovia, Abidjan, Accra, Takoradi, Lagos, and Pointe Noire
C. COLOMBO (Italian)	Genoa		
STATENDAM (Holland-America)	Rotterdam	BERGENSFJORD (Norwegian-America)	Kristiansand, Copenhagen, and Oslo
		BREMEN (North German Lloyd)	Cherbourg, Southampton, Bremerhaven
Freighters	*From*	EXFORD (American Export)	Genoa and Rijeka
SEAFAIR	Cristobal	GEN. W. O. DARBY (Military Transport)	Bremerhaven
PLATIDIA	Curação	LIBERTÉ (French)	Plymouth, Havre
ESSO CHILE	Amuay Bay	QUEEN ELIZABETH (Cunard)	Cherbourg and Southampton
ANGELO PETRI	Los Angeles	FAIRLAND (Pan Atlantic)	San Juan
ARCHANDROS	Bridgeport	HIBUERAS (United Fruit)	Santiago and Kingston
KERKEDYK	Antwerp		
MASTER NICKY	Falmouth	*Freighters*	*Destination*
SOMMELSDYK	Norfolk	OCEANIA MARU	Osaka
OLEANDER	Bermuda	MORMACWAVE	Philadelphia
AMER. LEADER	Philadelphia	HINDSIA	Las Piedras
BISCHOFSTEIN	Philadelphia	KAMOHARU MARU	Kobe
FINNSAILOR	Hamburg	HOOSIER STATE	Bremerhaven
LEISE MAERSK	Freetown	CORN'S MAERSK	Norfolk
MILL SPRING	Houston	SVENSKUND	Boston
INGWI	London	STANREALM	Djeddah
NEW JERSEY SUN	Oilport	WHITE ROSE	Copenhagen
TROPICANA	Pt. Canaveral	GULF TIGER	Freeport
EURYMEDON	Yokohama	MORMACOAK	Reykjavik
EXPRESS	Boston	BARBARA BROVIG	Ft. de France
FLYING EAGLE	Mayaguez	AFR. LIGHTNING	Capetown
TURANDOT	Baltimore	EVGENIA	San Pedro
MAIPO	Baltimore	CD. DE BARQ'TO'	La Guayra
GEZINA BROVIG	Philadelphia	ELIN HORN	Genoa
SUNOAK	Trinidad		

Freighters

Ship	From
PERIKLES	Charleston
RAPHAEL SEMMES	Jacksonville
RONDA	Baltimore
SADO MARU	Norfolk
BANGGAI	Philadelphia
FINNBOARD	Newport News
URUGUAY	Boston
R. L. RUSS	Baltimore
VIRGINIA TRADER	Houston
SANTA CATALINA	Cristobal
LAGO VIKING	Baltimore
FREDENHAGEN	Baltimore
WANGARATTA	Norfolk
RAGUNDA	Norfolk
SEATRAIN N. J.	Texas City
MEIJOY MARU	Charleston
RAVENSBURG	Hopewell
ASSYRIA	Norfolk
SAN JOSE	Barrios
CORVIGLIA	Hamburg
HVIDEFLINT	San Juan
SPENSER	Trinidad
HELLENIC STAR	Philadelphia
ATLAS	Atreco

Passenger and mail ships
May 12

Ship	From
ARGENTINA (Moore-McCormack)	Buenos Aires
SANTA PAULA (Grace)	Kingston

Freighters

Ship	From
AMER. ARCHER	Boston
BEAUREGARD	Houston
CITY OF MADRAS	Boston
DEGEMA	Freetown
HEREDIA	Armuelles
KEYTRADER	Norco
MATTAWUNGA	Boston
MORMACSEA	Baltimore

Freighters

Ship	Destination
NEW YORK CITY	Bristol
JARAMA	Newport News
HOEGH DRAKE	Philadelphia
STERNENFELS	Beirut
AULICA	Curaçao
FAROVI	Havana
PRES. TYLER	Baltimore
BLACK FALCON	Boston
CITY OF BIRK'H'D	Boston
LOIDE MEXICO	Philadelphia
PALLIUM	Oilport
NEW YORK	Oilport
BAHIA DE NIPE	Havana

Passenger and mail ships

May 12

Ship	Destination
ACORES (East Coast Overseas)	Angra, Ponta Delgada and Funchal
CRISTOFORO COLOMBO (Italian)	Gibraltar, Naples, Cannes, and Genoa
EXERMONT (American Export)	Lisbon, Casablanca, Tel Aviv, Haifa, and Larnaca
RANENFJORD (Norwegian Amer.)	Oslo
UNITED STATES (U. S. Lines)	Havre and Southampton
ALCOA POLARIS (Alcoa)	San Juan and St. Croix
BEATRICE (Bull)	San Juan
REINHART L. RUSS (Alcoa)	Trinidad, Georgetown, and Paramaribo
RIO TUNUYAN (Argentine State)	Rio de Janeiro, Santos, Montevideo, and Buenos Aires

Freighters

Ship	Destination
FLY INDEPEND'T	Southampton
ORIENT M'CHANT	Beirut
HAVMOY	Rotterdam
L. ECUADOR	Santos
LAGO VIKING	La Guayra
TRANSBORINQUEN	San Juan
TURANDOT	Manila
THOMAS SCHULTE	Puerto Barrios
PIONEER MIST	Manila
PERIKLES	La Ceiba

(Continued on following page)

Table 21 (continued)

Arrivals

May 12

Freighters (contd.)

	From
MUNESHIMA MARU	Cristobal
NAT O. WARREN	Houston
SANTA OLIVIA	Philadelphia
SEATRAIN N. Y.	Savannah
THORUNN	Caripito
NORDERHOLM	Jacksonville
H. W. LARSEN	Pto. la Cruz
ESSO HUNT'GTON	Baton Rouge
TILLAMOOK	New Haven
MAR DOW CHEM	Paulsboro
SANTA OLIVIA	Philadelphia
MARILU	Philadelphia
ANTONINA	Baltimore
TRANSCARIBBEAN	Norfolk
DEGEMA	Freetown
AMPENAN	Philadelphia
GEN. BEM	Baltimore
HAVANA MARU	Newport News
BAHIA DE MAT'ZAS	Richmond
HILDA KNUTSEN	Maracaibo
FOUR LAKES	Oilport
CITIES SVC. N'F'LK	Oilport

May 13

Passenger and mail ships

	From
ZION (Zim-Israel)	Haifa
NASSAU (Incres)	Nassau

Departures

May 13

Passenger and mail ships

	Destination
AMERICAN ARCHER (U. S. Lines)	Havre
AMERICAN HARVESTER (U. S. Lines)	Rotterdam and Antwerp
AMERICAN LEADER (U. S. Lines)	London
AMERICAN SCIENTIST (U. S. Lines)	Liverpool
AMERICAN SCOUT (U. S. Lines)	Bremerhaven, Bremen, and Hamburg
EXETER (American Export)	Cadiz, Gibraltar, Barcelona, Marseilles, Naples, Alexandria, Beirut, and Piraeus
FINNBOARD (Boise-Griffin)	Helsinki
INDEPENDENCE (American Export)	Algeciras, Cannes, Genoa, and Naples
RAGUNDA (Thor Eckert)	Tunis
STATENDAM (Holland-America)	Southampton, Havre, and Rotterdam
ANCON (Panama)	Port au Prince and Cristobal
ANGELITA (Dominican)	Trujillo City
COSTA RICA (Mamenic)	Corinto
ELIZABETH (Bull)	San Juan
GLOMEGGEN (Amerind)	Havana
JOHAN (Grancolombiana)	Port Limon
NASSAU (Incres)	Nassau
SAN JOSE (United Fruit)	Puerto Cortez and Puerto Barrios
SANTA LUISA (Grace)	Cristobal, Buenaventura, Salaverry, and Callao
SANTA OLIVIA (Grace)	Barranquilla, Cartagena, Guayaquil, Arica, Antofagasta, Chanaral, and Valparaiso
SANTA PAULA (Grace)	Curaçao, La Guayra, Aruba, Kingston
PARTHENON	Ecuador
CONCORDIA STAR	Naples

Freighters	From	Freighters	Destination
QUEEN OF BERMUDA (Furness)	Bermuda	HELLENIC STAR	Basra
OCEAN MONARCH (Furness)	Bermuda	L. M. D'IBERVILLE	Havre
SANTA CLARA (Grace)	Cartagena	RONDA	Antwerp
ALBERT E. WATTS	Houston	ASSYRIA	London
AMAZONAS	West Indies	GEN. BEM	Bremen
AMER. ARCHER	Boston	BLACK TERN	Antwerp
AMER. TRAPPER	Baltimore	BISCHOFSTEIN	Rotterdam
ANDREW JACKSON	Rotterdam	CD. DE BAR'Q'LLA	Callao
CARMELA FASSIO	Leghorn	OBERON	La Guayra
EXHIBITOR	Boston	VALERIA	Aruba
GATEWAY CITY	San Juan	MAIPO	Arica
JYTTE SKOU	Havana	NORDERHOLM	Cartagena
KALINGA	Pta. Cardon	RIO DE JANEIRO	Santos
K. LEONHARDT	Med. Ports	SPENSER	Recife
LA PLATA MARU	Cristobal	RAVENSBERG	Santos
LOSMAR	Baltimore	ANTONINA	Santos
PARTHENON	Guayaquil	MORMACTIDE	Buenos Aires
VALERIA	Philadelphia	HEREDIA	Cristobal
ALABAMA	Port Arthur	GEZINA BROVIG	Tampico
CITY OF MADRAS	Boston	MAJORKA	Havana
NORTH DAKOTA	Portland	OLEANDER	Bermuda
MAJORKA	Philadelphia	FREDENHAGEN	Pt. au Prince
EXPORTER	Norfolk	DONA ALICIA	Manila
ELENI D	Philadelphia	HAVANA MARU	Kobe
ROBIN LOCKSLEY	Philadelphia	SADO MARU	Kobe
GYPSUM QUEEN	Hanstport	TANA	Freetown
HESS DIESEL	Sabine	B. DE MATANZAS	Havana
CONSTABLE	Dublin	BAIE COMEAU	Baie Comeau
TOMASHIMA MARU	Capetown		

Source: Adapted from the daily listing in *The New York Times*, May 11–15, 1960.

same years 78, 81, and 81 per cent. While almost every day several passenger and mail ships sail through New York's Narrows (see the sample listings in Table 21), they have become an infrequent sight in Boston and even more so in Philadelphia and Baltimore. These great cities occasionally see cruise ships call, and a few passengers sail on some of the freighters; but none has any crowds of passengers comparable to those at New York, where nearly a million people board ships or land. One can easily imagine what an annual movement of about a million steamship passengers means to the retail and selected service trades of the city.[35]

New York's dominance of the transatlantic passenger traffic has been carried over from the seaport to the airports. The great metropolis' airports serve as terminal points for the majority of flights from and to Latin America, Europe, and the lands beyond. Air traffic does not know the imperious reasons seaborne traffic has for recognizing the seaboard as a breaking point. It is not New York's site or physical environment that have made of it the greatest hub of air traffic in the world.[36] Instead, the size and function of New York have made it the breaking point for the great majority of flights linking the United States with Europe, Africa, and the Middle East. So much national and international business is transacted here that the airports of New York have become the obvious location for the hinge articulating the domestic and overseas networks of air traffic.

This is a rapidly growing function, for air travel and air freight are expanding rapidly, within the continent and abroad. In 1950 the total number of passengers arriving in or departing from the United States by air was 1.1 million, just 26,000 more than the passengers travelling by sea; in 1959 the air passengers numbered 4.1 million, while 1.4 million travelled by sea. Air freight will hardly surpass the volume of seaborne freight in the foreseeable future, but its progress ought to be spectacular with the coming of age of the larger jet planes. It may be expected, however, that with the growth of air traffic and more congestion on the airlines and airfields around the main hubs of traffic, more decentralization will occur there as well. The other main central cities of Megalopolis will then have a good chance of developing their airports: Washington, D. C., owing to

[35] Statistical data from the Port of New York Authority, *Oceanborne Foreign Trade at the Port of New York, 1959*, New York, 1959, and *Statistical Abstract of the United States: 1959, op. cit.*, Table 122.

[36] The major airports of New York (Idlewild International Airport, La Guardia, and Newark) are administered as one integrated system by the Port of New York Authority. The traffic, domestic and international, has been expanding so rapidly as to make a fourth airfield necessary, which in this congested area may have to be put at some distance from Manhattan, in central New Jersey or in Orange County, New York.

its government role; Boston and Philadelphia because of the size of their metropolitan areas, their interests in faraway places, and the suitability of much of their products, of small size but high value, for travel by air freight.

At present New York remains the main hub of air transportation, but its passenger traffic (see Fig. 204, p. 646) shows that Boston and Washington are two major destinations of the scheduled airlines traffic it originates. The axial belt of Megalopolis is also one of the greatest arteries of air traffic of our time. This is due to the great density of activities, to the intensity of movement generally observed in the area, much of it being obviously inherited from the maritime trade of its seaports.[37]

The relative importance of the maritime trade of Megalopolis may gradually decline, of course, as the needs and resources of the other sections of the nation grow, justifying the convergence of more ships and currents of traffic on the ports serving these other later-developed areas. Since 1959, however, a question mark has arisen over the future of the Megalopolitan maritime trade even in absolute quantities. The St. Lawrence Seaway is threatening a very important component of the hinge mechanism, that is, the function of Megalopolis as the maritime façade of the great industrial system developed south of the Great Lakes. Once Buffalo, Cleveland, Detroit, Chicago, and Duluth become seaports, once the technical difficulties experienced in the early stages of the Seaway's operation are overcome, how much trade may be lost by the ports of the Northeastern seaboard, until now a natural intermediary between the realm of the Great Lakes and the world overseas?

Many experts tried to figure out the answer while the Seaway was being built and during the first season of its operation in 1959.[38] By early 1961 it seemed clear that more outbound grain, from both the United

[37] Statistics of the traffic using the New York airports are regularly published and analyzed by the Port of New York Authority. In 1958 they handled 13,610,000 passengers, 2,029,400 of them arriving or departing by international flights, and 168,000 tons of air cargo plus 59,000 tons of air mail and parcel post. In 1959 these figures rose to 15.6 million passengers (2.48 million international) and 200,000 tons of cargo. Forty-one scheduled airlines serve New York, whose share in the United States international air passenger traffic in 1959 was 62 per cent.

[38] We are especially indebted to Professor Pierre Camu of Laval University, Quebec, to Mr. Frank Herring, Deputy Director of the Port of New York Authority, and to Mr. Frank L. Orfanello, Director of the Port of Boston, for a great deal of data concerning the Seaway's probable influence on the Megalopolitan ports. Professor Camu prepared a detailed report on this matter for our use. We also had the privilege of debating the matter with Professor Harold M. Mayer of the University of Chicago (see his volume, *The Port of Chicago and the St. Lawrence Seaway*, University of Chicago Press, Chicago, 1957) and Raymond Vernon, Director of the New York Metropolitan Region Study. See also Chinitz, *Freight and the Metropolis, op. cit.*, and The St. Lawrence Seaway Authority, *Annual Report 1960*, Ottawa, 1961.

States and Canada, was taking the Seaway, being transferred to seagoing ships either in Montreal or in Quebec. Several new steamship lines now ply regularly between Great Lakes ports (mainly Chicago) and western European ports. For the winter season, when ice closes the Seaway, some of these lines are considering keeping a sailing schedule but terminating at an American ice-free port, and Boston hopes to become the winter terminus of several of them, thus increasing the frequency of sailings from its port in that season. The Port of New York estimated that in 1959 it lost less than 2 per cent of its general-cargo business to the Seaway. In the first and second seasons the traffic did not come up to expectations; in 1960 it totalled only 20.3 million tons of cargo (11 per cent of which was general cargo). When the Seaway reaches its full capacity, estimated at 50 million tons by 1968, it may well divert from the Megalopolitan ports a substantial proportion of the grain exports and, in the case of New York, about 10 per cent of the general cargo.[39] Baltimore and the Delaware River ports are worried too. The railroads and pipeline operators throughout the Northeastern United States may view such diversion of trade with concern. The future performance of the Seaway hinges, however, on a series of variables, the forthcoming behavior of which is difficult to forecast at this time; these variables include the Seaway's tolls, the freight rates in the Northeast, the financing of improvements of navigation channels presently planned between the Lakes, the traffic capacity of the Welland Canal, and the general trends of international trade.

If the volume of goods handled by the maritime trade continues to grow, the Seaway could have its full share of it without causing actual harm to the already rather crowded Megalopolitan harbors. For the Great Lakes region this new channel of transportation raises high hopes that it will at last be able to develop a commercial organization that can rival and perhaps some day dwarf the commerce of Megalopolis. When ocean-going ships can carry bulkier or heavier merchandise directly to and from the ports of Chicago or Detroit, and air freight can take care of the lighter cargoes, the advantages of an advanced seaboard position may be lost to Megalopolis.

At present such a threat still appears quite remote. Much work remains to be done on the Seaway to bring its carrying capacity to a hundred million tons or so of dry cargo, and in the meanwhile the trade of the Megalopolitan ports may go on increasing. The Seaway will probably improve the position of the Great Lakes region, especially for the location

---

[39] *The New York Times,* Sunday, May 8, 1960, p. 14–S. See also Chinitz, *Freight and the Metropolis, op. cit.,* pp. 63–78, and the Seaway Authority's annual reports.

of heavy manufacturing dependent on bulky shipments, and by doing so it may prevent some such new plants from being built in Megalopolis. On the other hand, the Megalopolitan market has grown to a mass that exerts its own gravitational pull on transportation currents and the moving of large plants. The traffic of goods that only transit through the great Northeastern ports, without being processed or consumed in the region, is not basic to local prosperity. Because of its importance to the railroads, the shipping interests, and the wholesalers, it cannot be disregarded, but it can hardly be classified today as a major factor in the metropolitan economy of the four bigger seaports. Much more important is the traffic serving Megalopolis itself, carrying the products it turns out in such large amounts and supplying its huge demand for goods and services, a demand that will exist as long as the people can pay the bill. This traffic to meet the needs of local producers and consumers is a much more permanent foundation for the maritime trade of the region, not easily affected by the growth of the traffic in other ports.

Another permanent foundation is the region's business organization, in the categories of transactions that used to be called the "invisible" ones in international trade. Although these transactions of the money market do not lead to much visible loading or unloading of merchandise, they can hardly be called "invisible" in Megalopolis, for they contribute in a spectacular fashion to the landscape of the great cities.

The Money Market and Related Activities

By the middle of the twentieth century Megalopolis had become the greatest money market in the world. The expression "money market" should not be taken in a too-restricted sense, for the exchange of national currencies and the free estimation of their rates of exchange into dollars, which were formerly the major types of transaction on a money market, are nowadays only a minor part of an extremely diversified business. Much more is involved than the recording of moneys shifted from account to account or promised for such transfers within an indicated time. Modern finance has attained such a degree of variety and complexity, and such penetration of the whole economic process, that the expression "money market" has often been replaced by that of "financial community," which suggests more effectively the diversity of interdependent professions and the substantial number of jobs resulting from the activities related to the handling of money and credit.

However, the rather vague and broad term "financial community" may be misleading if it is interpreted to mean a group of people concerned with financial matters only, a distinct "community" set aside from the people engaged in the management of other industries. In a restricted sense, of course, the financial community of New York may be defined as the holders of some 130,000 jobs in offices clustered in lower Manhattan, below Chambers Street. A more comprehensive definition would include many people who work in the skyscrapers now mushrooming along Park, Madison, and Fifth avenues and on the side streets for a few blocks east and west of these thoroughfares in Manhattan's midtown, for they are vitally concerned, in a professional fashion, with the market of money, credit, insurance, and securities. In other words, the financial community includes not only bankers, brokers, and insurance agents but also corporation lawyers and their staffs, the financial divisions of many great corporations, chamber-of-commerce officers, foundation officials, professors and journalists who specialize in economics and finance. It has intimate connections also with manufacturers, government officials (including foreign consular officers), and advertisers. It is not a merely local group, rooted only in the interests of the city and its metropolitan area, but is the central knot of a vast international network, including not only residents of the area but also others living and working in other parts of the country and abroad. Moreover, the financial operations carried out in New York City probably cause more movement of travellers into and out of the city than does any other category of activities, except perhaps that other complex professional clustering, the mass-media market, which may be more closely associated with the financial community than one might expect from the sound of the words.

In the financial activities of the American nation and more recently of the free world the city of New York has achieved a rather extraordinary supremacy. It has by far the biggest concentration of such activities in the Western Hemisphere. Since 1800 it has attracted many of the functions and transactions that had previously been located in the other cities of the Northeastern seaboard, or that might have developed in them if there had been no larger rival. However, some important financial institutions have risen in some of these cities because of their proximity to New York. Like all the other concentrations of specialized industries in one place, the financial transactions of Manhattan have in the twentieth century begun to move outward, as new specializations and subdivisions of professions have arisen and as the Federal government's increased financial role has given rise to another substantial "financial community" in Washington, D. C. Almost every large city in Megalopolis and a few of the medium-sized cities have acquired and developed some "markets" of a financial nature. New York is the classical great American money market, much described and analyzed, but it is actually the region of Megalopolis as a whole, in the entangled working together of markets scattered along its axial belt from Boston to Washington, that today plays the decisive managerial role too often ascribed to Manhattan alone.

Originally this whole growth stemmed from the lively commerce developed early by the seaports of the region. For New York, now the most successful hub in the trade, the historical role of the waterfront in fostering the clustering of financial operations has been well defined as follows:

> At the outset of the nineteenth century, the banking, insurance and securities-trading functions . . . were barely separable from the general wholesaling and shipping activities of the Port of New York. The chief financing problem was the financing of the movement of goods, and the major insurable risks were the risks of the sea — of piracy, barratry, mutiny, and shipwreck. Besides, the Port was a gateway for news of war and politics, a fact of some consequence to traders in securities. Accordingly, the Region's financial community to the extent that it existed, was closely anchored to the Port area.[40]

The same factors were at work in other Megalopolitan cities, mainly in Philadelphia (which had the first bank, the Bank of North America, and was in 1800 a greater financial center than New York) and in Boston. From the very start, however, the port activities were not the only factors spurring on the growth of the financial community. Handling of money has been needed by more local activities such as the real estate business, which was from an early period a field of active speculation in and around the fast-growing cities; and various services that had to be rendered in the cities on a large scale involved financial activities leading into banking. The first bank in Manhattan, the Bank of New York, began its operations in 1784 having been organized by a group of merchants who agreed with Alexander Hamilton, one of its first directors, that stock should be paid up "in specie only"; they would not take land as security for their capital, although the list of early shareholders included many of the leading landowners in New York. The second bank chartered in New York grew out of the Manhattan Company, formed in 1799 officially to provide the city with an adequate water supply.[41]

Similarly, the insurance industry grew out of concerns rooted either in local problems, such as the threat of fire in the cities, or in long-range trading, such as the risks of transportation by sea. What is called "prop-

[40] Hoover and Vernon, *Anatomy of a Metropolis, op. cit.,* p. 91.
[41] Allan Nevins, *History of the Bank of New York and Trust Company: 1784 to 1934,* privately printed, New York, 1934.

erty insurance," or "fire and casualty insurance," started in Philadelphia in 1721. John Copson opened an office there where underwriters would assemble to discuss insurance contracts on vessels and merchandise. In 1752 another group, of which Benjamin Franklin was a partner, founded the "Philadelphia Contributorship for the Insurance of Houses from Loss by Fire," a company that was still in business in 1960. Other Philadelphians established the Mutual Assurance Company in 1781 and the Insurance Company of North America in 1794. The great city on the Delaware seemed to have taken a decisive lead, but this did not last. The importance of maritime activities and the growth of city real estate values fostered the creation of other companies in the main seaports of the Northeast. Thus by 1800 marine underwriting companies had been organized in New York, Boston, New Haven, and Baltimore also; and a New York fire insurance company was founded in 1787, the Baltimore Equitable Society in 1794, and the Mutual Assurance of the City of Norwich in 1795.[42]

Connecticut entered the picture early, but it was not until the nineteenth century that Hartford became interested in insurance. In that small city a few business leaders started some of the larger insurance concerns in the country — the Hartford Fire Insurance Co. in 1810 and the Aetna Insurance Company in 1819. Its location between Boston and New York, with good relations maintained with the financial communities of the two great seaports, proved beneficial; and the Hartford companies set up a network of agents scattered throughout the country, a policy later adopted by other insurance companies.

While they started by specializing in either fire or marine insurance, the major companies soon underwrote both kinds of contracts and provided coverage also for other possible property or casualty risks. From the 1830's on, life insurance began to interest business, and large companies were established for that special purpose, beginning of course in Megalopolis, where the density and wealth of the population offered a substantial market. By 1850 there were 48 companies with assets estimated at $10 million. Today life-insurance companies are among the larger business concerns in the American economy, and, as a group, through their investments and loans, one of the regulating factors of the flow of capital in the nation. New York, Newark, Philadelphia, and Boston are the homes of many of the largest of these concerns, which usually specialize in life insurance only. However, some of the leading Hartford companies have added this type of insurance to their other, older activities.

---

[42] See Sidney M. Robbins and Nestor E. Terleckyj (with the collaboration of Ira O. Scott, Jr.), *Money Metropolis*, New York Metropolitan Region Study, Harvard University Press, Cambridge, Mass., 1960, Chapters 6 and 7.

Of the fifty largest life-insurance companies of the United States and Canada, each of them with more than $1.8 billion of total insurance in force at the beginning of 1959, eighteen had their national headquarters in Megalopolis. New York City housed five of them (including the Metropolitan Life, the Equitable, and the New York Life — these three adding up to $138.3 billion of total insurance in force, or one fourth of all the life insurance in force in North America); Hartford was home to five others (among which Travelers, Aetna, and Connecticut General ranked high); Newark, Boston, and Philadelphia had two each (among them the Prudential in Newark and the John Hancock in Boston), Springfield and Worcester, Massachusetts, one each. It thus appeared that the Newark-Boston section of Megalopolis held an extraordinary concentration of national insurance centers, for it was home to all seven of the life-insurance companies that held more than $20 billion of insurance each.[43]

If the ranking were based on admitted assets on December 31, 1958, the concentration in Megalopolis would appear even more striking, with twenty-one out of the fifty leading companies, and with fourteen out of seventeen reporting more than $1 billion of assets each.[44] Among the fire casualty companies, classified according to the net premiums in 1957, a similar concentration is noted, with a greater focus on Hartford, which is the home of three of the four biggest; out of the twenty largest groups in this field, fifteen are in Megalopolis, including the five leading ones.[45]

On the whole the insurance industry is still rather concentrated in the Megalopolitan region that started it and has pushed its development for more than two centuries. This leadership is not necessarily permanent, for younger companies are developing elsewhere, and their rate of growth has been greater in recent years than that of the older and much bigger companies in Megalopolis. Life and health insurance especially, the major sector of the whole insurance business, is almost as easy to decentralize as is retail trade. With a greater spread of the population from coast to

[43] Data from *The National Underwriter*, Vol. 63, No. 17, April 25, 1959, p. 6, which published a list of the ranking 766 main companies in the order of the total insurance in force held by each. We are also indebted to Mr. Morton Miller, Vice President of the Equitable Life Assurance Company, for having discussed with us the location of and the factors influencing clustering in the industry.

[44] The smallest of these had assets of more than $1.3 billion. See the statistics in *Life Insurance Courant*, Vol. 64, No. 4, April 1959, pp. 68–70.

[45] In the number of life insurance companies Texas leads all the states in the Union. However, any classification by this standard gives an aberrant view of the matter; for Texas legislation allows for the chartering of small, almost family-size partnerships as "life-insurance companies." The actual importance of these establishments and their geographical distribution are better understood with the help of criteria such as insurance in force, premiums written, or assets reported by the companies.

coast and a more even distribution of income it becomes easy to do insurance business from almost any part of the country. Pursuing the customer, the insurance companies are sending more agents into the field and establishing more scattered local offices, and even impressive regional offices to which more authority can be delegated. The home office does not have to centralize all the huge amount of business, files, and personnel required by the operations of the larger companies. Neither the amount of insurance in force nor the amount of the assets determines how much employment the leading companies will have in Megalopolis. A large part of their personnel is distributed in the regional offices, and their agents are scattered throughout the country. With the present ease and speed of communications, even the home office could be set up in almost any large city in the country; and such headquarters of important insurance companies are already found in Milwaukee, Fort Wayne, Los Angeles, Chicago, Nashville, Cincinnati, Galveston, Des Moines, St. Louis, Omaha, Dallas, Minneapolis, Sacramento, San Francisco, and even Skokie, Illinois.

Although there is some need for close contact at the top to determine the terms of insurance and underwriting and the investment policies, this central-market function occupies rather few people and would not represent any large fraction of a company's total personnel. Still the policy-making and general managerial activities may well profit by being carried on in the proximity of the main national money market and of the mass-media market. Home offices are therefore attracted by the size and competence of the financial community as a whole, and this may well be another reason, in addition to inheritance from the past, for the clustering of national headquarters of so many leading companies in New York, Newark, and Hartford. Megalopolis has thus attracted the more communications-oriented kinds of activities in finance as well as in manufacturing. Because of the growing complexity of business problems and increasing specialization, the management of any large-scale modern business requires more and more advice and consultation.

The insurance industry thus offers a good illustration of the play of forces that have brought about the rise of the financial community in Megalopolis and maintained its national supremacy, and these same forces are deterring the much-talked-about trends of central-office decentralization from Manhattan or from the downtowns of Boston and Philadelphia. A recent study of New York's money market has well indicated this:

It was New York's experience that whenever a major money-market segment became established, its existence contributed to the development of other segments at the same location. Two main factors . . . lay behind this

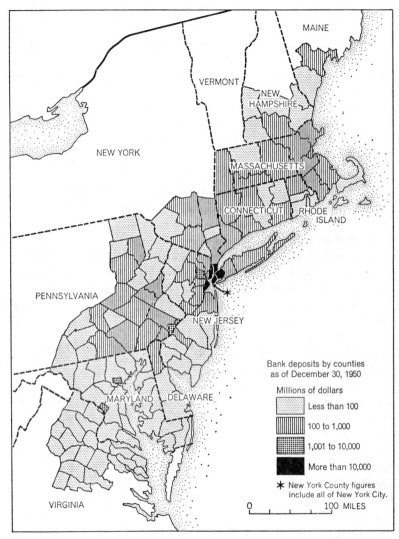

FIG. 167

phenomenon. Briefly, one of these was the urgent need for quick and effective communication among the decision-makers of the money market. The other was the hoary principle that the size of the market determined the degree of specialization — the growth of money-market segments brought the proliferation of specialists offering services which provided "external economies" to the money market as a whole. Because of the need for communications and the common use of specialists, the various segments of the money market became closely interwoven and the entire complex became a formidable entrenched entity.[46]

A third factor may perhaps still need stressing in the snowballing process of a large money market. The size of the whole, in terms of the sums involved in the operations, provides security for each of the individual participants. We have already noted how in the past the great seaboard cities and especially New York, attracted more deposits from smaller cities to their banks, because a business that dominated the economy of its mill town would feel its money was safer if deposited in a bank that carried many other accounts of similar size; and the borrowing possibilities would be better for the depositor at such a bank.[47]

The volume of money handled on the markets of Megalopolis is enormous, but it is difficult to assess it with any degree of precision, even though the various operations transacted on the money market and in related activities are each and all defined in dollars and cents in at least some of their aspects. However, accurate statistics are regularly published by the Federal Reserve Board giving the amounts on deposit in the various banks, and the value of the banks' assets. If we want to use the bank deposits as a measurement, we learn that on June 30, 1956, for instance, all the deposits in Megalopolitan banks amounted to $81.3 billion, or 37.7 per cent of the total figure for the United States,[48] greater than the region's share (then 21 per cent) of the nation's population. Within Megalopolis the distribution of these deposits was quite uneven, as is evidenced by the maps of bank deposits by counties in 1950 and 1956 (see Figs. 167 and 168). Comparison of these maps shows some changes had taken place during the early 1950's. A good number of suburban counties around New York City, Boston, Baltimore, and Washington, D. C., had moved up by 1956 into a higher category, as the deposits in their banks rose above the $100 million or the $1 billion mark. During these six years New York City's bank deposits climbed from $29.7 billion to $43.2 billion, an increase of 45 per cent; but in the same period bank deposits in the whole United States rose by almost 48 per cent. Until 1960 the laws of New York State forbade the banks in the city to branch out beyond the city's limits; as they are now authorized to establish branches in the suburban counties, the increase in deposits there may become more rapid, but this would not affect the total amount of Megalopolitan banking.

---

[46] Robbins and Terleckyj, *Money Metropolis, op. cit.*, p. 24.

[47] See above, Chapter 3, pp. 147, 148.

[48] U. S. Bureau of the Census, *County and City Data Book, 1956: A Statistical Abstract Supplement,* U. S. Government Printing Office, Washington, D. C., 1957.

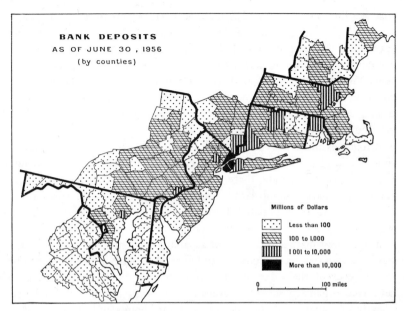

BANK DEPOSITS
AS OF JUNE 30, 1956
(by counties)

Millions of Dollars

- Less than 100
- 100 to 1,000
- 1 001 to 10,000
- More than 10,000

0   100 miles

FIG. 168. The figures for New York City are given as a total without breakdown by counties; that is why the black extends over all of them.

Figures of deposits alone do not measure adequately the amounts of money handled. For some time the Federal Reserve Bank of New York has calculated an index of "velocity of demand deposits," a measure of the speed with which the money represented by the demand deposits on the banks' accounts revolved. Taking the average velocity of the years 1947–49 as a base index of 100, the index in New York City reached 174.8 in December 1956, and 198.9 in December 1957; in the country at large (defined as "337 centers," which did not include New York City or the other leading cities of Megalopolis), the velocity of demand deposits reached an index of only 138.1 and 148.1 on these same dates.[49] Thus a dollar deposited in a Manhattan bank revolved more rapidly, was used more times within a year, than a dollar deposited in one of the banks of the 337 smaller centers. Some difference in the velocity of demand deposits in Manhattan on the one hand and in the rest of the country on the other certainly existed well before 1949; but the indices quoted imply

[49] According to the table of selected economic indicators in the *Monthly Review of Credit and Business Conditions,* published by the Federal Reserve Bank of New York, Vol. 40, No. 2, February 1958, p. 32. At the time of writing, this was the most recent issue of this Monthly Review to give these economic indicators.

that the difference increased from 1949 to 1956 and to an even greater degree during 1957. Thus, since the deposits in New York City were spent over and over again with a greater frequency than was the case in the country as a whole, perhaps we would be justified in suggesting that New York City had a larger share in the flow of money throughout the nation in 1956 than in 1949 or 1950, even though in terms of bank deposits calculated at the close of business on one given day New York City's relative position had declined slightly.

Banking is more a dynamic than a static process, and it is especially dynamic in places such as the major cities of Megalopolis. Little money is allowed to remain idle there. However, many of the transactions on the money market involve the cash transfer of only small fractions of the values actually negotiated. Credit and accounting can endow figures with great elasticity for those who know the art of handling them.

The money market today is not separable from the market of securities. The two securities exchanges in lower Manhattan account for almost 90 per cent of the value of all operations transacted on the country's seventeen organized securities exchanges. In 1949 it was estimated that "nearly 90 per cent of the sales of corporate bonds and 39 per cent of the sales of corporate stocks . . . were consummated over the telephone and teletype wires which collectively make up the nation's over-the-counter system. But even so, the 'inside' market for these securities is believed to be largely in the hands of New York dealer firms, which include practically all the biggest ones in the country." [50]

The firms dealing in securities hold for their clients large amounts of securities and cash, which also revolve rapidly. The clients themselves may be scattered over the whole country and abroad, but the transactions remain concentrated on the market. Once the activity of the much smaller markets in Boston and Philadelphia is added to that of New York City, Megalopolis appears to take care indeed of more than 90 per cent of the money and related market transactions in the United States, although no one of the various indices formulated in dollar value comes up to that proportion.[51]

[50] Robbins and Terleckyj, *Money Metropolis, op. cit.*, pp. 11–12. See also Margaret G. Myers, *The New York Money Market, Vol. I: Origins and Development*, Columbia University Press, New York, 1931.

[51] For instance, if the figures of bankers' acceptances outstanding are considered, by city of accepting bank, New York accounted, in 1954, for 66.3 per cent of the national total, Boston for 5.6 per cent, and Philadelphia for 1.7 per cent; the total for Megalopolis can be estimated at 74 per cent of the national total. (See *Federal Reserve Bulletin*, Washington, D. C., Vol. 41, No. 5, May 1955.)

Banks, trust companies, securities dealers, and investment and mutual funds are not the only important members of the financial community. We have already mentioned the insurance industry, which is a very important lender and investor. The real estate business must also be included, for it is active and large in the busily expanding metropolitan areas. However, it presents a problem, not one that affects the statistics significantly but one that points to a more general difficulty in neatly delimiting the financial community. Many real estate firms, besides acting as brokers and dealers in real estate, engage also in building, in developing, and even in the management of the buildings they erect on their own or someone else's land. That is, an interpenetration often develops between real estate and the construction industry, perhaps even with the hotel industry, and others. Since in this case the number of jobs penetrating the partitions between the various industries and professions involved is quite small, we have no reason to elaborate upon the situation; but a similar and more complex interrelationship exists between the management of large manufacturing firms and the financial community.

At the present time a large corporation manufacturing a certain specialized line of goods needs within its management a whole staff engaged in financial matters. The large sums of money involved in the operation, in the expansion, and in the profits of such a corporation require its budgetary matters to be administered by people in close touch with the money market. The financial management of the corporation decides about borrowing, issuing bonds or recalling them or other securities, keeping a larger share of the profits in the corporation's hands to avoid seeking more funds outside it, or investing some of the profits in securities or other enterprises to diversify the interests of the company.

In all these ways the larger corporations, handling hundreds of millions of dollars each, exert an important influence on the nation's money market, on the securities exchanges, and on the general management of the country's wealth and its redistribution. As mergers and growth proceed, the number of such large corporations increases, each having almost a small or medium-sized banking establishment within its headquarters. This "financial division" of a corporation, the business of which may be manufacturing, retail trade, utilities, or transportation, needs the same services as a bank or insurance company in terms of "external economies," and it needs also close contact with the purely financial professions of bankers, securities dealers, insurance brokers, and so forth. All this causes the financial staff responsible for the money management of such large concerns to prefer locating in a central city, where such a concentration already exists. In this way the number of offices busy with financial matters increases in the few cities that provide such conveniences. The clustering goes on, especially in New York City, and in San Francisco,[52] in Chicago, and even in Boston. However, such is the attraction of New York City for this type of activity that Boston and Philadelphia have some difficulty continuing to grow.

The most remarkable feature in the snowballing of the financial decision-making function of Megalopolis is perhaps the steady growth of the concentration in New York City, despite the growing role assumed in financial matters by the Federal authorities located in Washington, D. C. When Washington was planned and built just below the falls of the Potomac, it was expected to develop into a great seaport and commercial center. Instead, it remained specialized in its Federal-government role as the national capital and, as the nation grew, as an international center. Gradually the needs of national defense, centered there, developed on a large scale, and since the 1930's the Federal authorities have had to intervene increasingly in various sectors of the national economy. Such interventions arose on the one hand from the need to regulate certain economic activities and on the other from the sheer size of governmental expenditure.

The regulatory agencies have to deal with and supervise transactions or plans that would be detrimental to the interests of the people if they were allowed to be carried out without regulation. Many such transactions involve substantial financial interests. Moreover, the very functioning of the securities exchanges and of banking is being regulated by the Securities and Exchange Commission and the Federal Reserve Board. Interstate commerce and communications, the distribution of power and fuel, transportation rates, and other interests are within the jurisdiction of Federal regulatory agencies, and the specialists in the management of large-scale private finances have to keep in touch with one or more such agencies. The Federal government deals also with import tariffs and export regulations, and to some extent it finances some foreign trade transactions, either through the Export-Import Bank or because they involve government-held or subsidized stockpiles of strategic materials or agricultural surpluses. In this way, and also through its policies of supporting

[52] San Francisco is really the most remarkable financial community in the United States outside Megalopolis. It serves as financial headquarters for many Western mining or manufacturing corporations. It is the only American city besides New York to have agencies of leading foreign banks, and it is the home town of the Bank of America, at present the largest bank in the United States and in the world, outstripping the biggest Wall Street institutions.

the prices of farm products, Federal decisions and regulations influence the markets, national and international, of various commodities.

As the greatest disbursing agency in the country, and in the free world, the government greatly influences the money market and the variations of the nation's industrial activity. The gross debt of the Federal government on June 30, 1958, amounted to $276 billion, almost ten times what it was in the early 1930's. No wonder that trading in United States government securities now makes up an essential sector of the activities of the money market. Since 1952 Federal expenditures have oscillated between $65 billion and $75 billion annually; in 1945, the peak year, they reached $98.4 billion.[53] There is little need to stress the impact of these sums on the nation's money market and general economic activities. Nor is it any wonder that the number of government officials concerned with the administration of these expenditures has been growing, and that an increasing number of corporations have felt it necessary to maintain permanent offices in Washington. Since World War II Washington has been concerned also with international financial problems, symbolized by the location in that city of the World Bank for Reconstruction and Development and of the International Monetary Fund. Today New York is perhaps more worried about the growing role of Washington in money management and economic policy-making than about the gradual decline of New York's share in the total deposits or assets of all American banks.

The decentralizing trends that have been decreasing Manhattan's supremacy in financial matters have been at work largely within Megalopolis rather than all over the nation. That so many younger centers of banking, insurance, and other financial activities are growing in other cities does not necessarily signify the decline of the money and associated markets of New York. Even if Manhattan is not the only location in the country where certain transactions can take place, where loans of a certain size can be secured, it is still a very great center of business. The growth of the American economy and its increasing involvement with the international scene are expanding the volume of financial and related business to such a degree that concentration of it all in one city seems neither desirable nor feasible. The number of workers employed in banking alone rose from 330,000 in 1946 to 540,000 in 1957, a 63 per cent increase.[54] The total financial employment in the nation is estimated to have risen from 1,312,000 in 1947 to 1,941,000 in 1956, or from 2.3 per cent

---

[53] *Statistical Abstract of the United States: 1959, op. cit.*, p. 364.

[54] See "Banking's Fast-Growing Family," in the *Business Review*, Federal Reserve Bank of Philadelphia, February 1959, pp. 7–11.

to 3 per cent of the total national employment; and it is expected to go on growing and to make up about 3.9 per cent of the total national employment by 1985.[55] It would be unreasonable to expect this rapidly developing profession to concentrate in one spot.

However, large regional centers of banking may be expected to look toward one national center that is *the market,* indeed the central clearing house of the various types of transactions, the central exchange determining rates and policies. New York City has a fairly good chance of keeping this role for some time to come. The recent New York Metropolitan Region Study gave a good deal of attention to this function of the great metropolis,[56] concerning itself mainly with forecasts of the number of jobs the financial activities will provide in the region and with the probable future location of firms. Such projections into the future are based on available statistics, and little attention was given to what might happen if the forces acting in the region were to be drastically modified. Indeed, there are no impending changes that justify a detailed examination of such improbable developments. However, the early nineteenth-century evolution that brought about New York's supremacy on the seaboard, strictly restricting the role of Philadelphia and Boston, and even more of Baltimore and Washington, may have seemed just as improbable to observers in the 1790's. It may therefore be worthwhile to glance briefly at the very foundations of the financial community of New York and of the whole of Megalopolis.

Basically, the role of the central market is dependent not only upon the whole commercial organization of the regional community but also upon the economic structure and orientation of the nation. The latter may be modified either because of legislative reforms or because of a reorganization of the system of transportation.

Some changes in legislation have brought about new controls exercised from Washington and the growth of what may be called the financial community of the national capital. This may somewhat restrict the freedom of operations on the other markets in the country and especially in New York. As long as the American economic system remains founded on the principles of free enterprise and on the free functioning of the money, securities, and commodities markets according to the interaction of demand and supply, the powerful commercial organization of New

[55] Robbins and Terleckyj, *Money Metropolis, op. cit.,* p. 179, Table 33.

[56] See Hoover and Vernon, *Anatomy of a Metropolis, op. cit.,* pp. 88–97; Robbins and Terleckyj, *Money Metropolis, op. cit.;* also Martin Segal, *Wages in the Metropolis,* New York Metropolitan Region Study, Harvard University Press, Cambridge, Mass., 1960, pp. 8–26 and 127–28.

York will be able to carry on its present role, propped up by all the locally available services of the "external economies" that complement the financial community proper. If more governmental controls and government participation should develop in American economic life, the resulting bureaucracy might substantially decrease the role of New York and of Boston, Hartford, Newark, and Philadelphia. If the government bureaucracy were to take over from the New York markets more of the role of arbiter of business transactions within the nation and of intermediary between the national economy and financial operations overseas, the role of Washington would grow, and regional operations would probably be delegated to field offices scattered throughout the country. Insofar as the American business community appears prepared to carry on its present share of responsibility and decision-making with a minimum of help or interference from government, the present financial role of New York is bound to go on developing, although the types of transactions that will form the specialties of this "money metropolis" will gradually shift.

Such shifts will result from the process of growth and of constant readaptation of the methods of business to changing conditions. They have been going on constantly in the past, modifying the types of negotiations and work carried on in the financial offices in the Megalopolitan cities and elsewhere. For a time they caused more concentration of all kinds of financial activities in the lower Manhattan district, often referred to as "Wall Street." More recently they have caused some decentralization in several directions: growth of deposits in suburban banks, rise of Washington's influence over all financial activities, and expansion of the office space needed by financial and related business. This expansion has pushed out of the downtown sections of the major cities toward the uptown areas, creating "midtown" business districts.[57]

The maps of bank deposits help reveal some of these trends within Megalopolis. A map showing the payrolls of the financial community in the strict sense — that is, including only finance, insurance, and real estate firms — may add to this picture (see Fig. 169). The very impressive concentration in the larger cities is almost according to city size. Hartford and Newark are notable nuclei, chiefly because of the size of their insurance companies. Some expansion of the business districts outside the large cities will undoubtedly go on.

---

[57] This has been especially true in Manhattan but it has also occurred to some extent in Boston and in Washington, and there have even been some suburban expansions, such as the new headquarters of the Connecticut General Insurance Company outside Hartford.

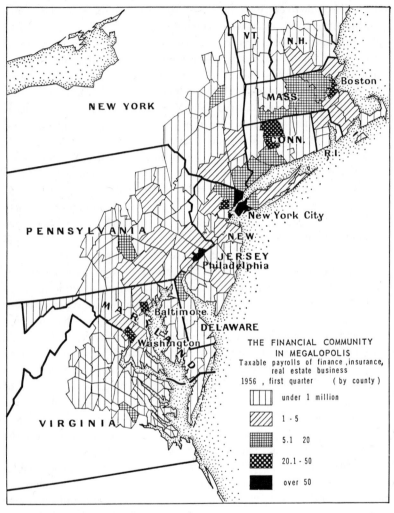

THE FINANCIAL COMMUNITY
IN MEGALOPOLIS
Taxable payrolls of finance ,insurance,
real estate business
1956 , first quarter   (by county)

▥	under 1 million
▨	1 - 5
▦	5.1 20
▩	20.1 - 50
■	over 50

Fig. 169

In Manhattan the early 1960's may witness a spectacular struggle between two already obvious trends. One is the concentration of more
financial business in the midtown area, symbolized by the huge building
of the First National City Bank on Park Avenue and by the move of the
Hanover Bank to the same area; the other, the effort to maintain the old
Wall Street center, is symbolized by the erection there of the new Chase
Manhattan Bank building and the plans, announced early in 1960, to

rebuild another section of that area, creating more facilities and institutions for international financial business.[58] Both districts may very well continue to grow at the same time if the recent growth rates of the national and the international economies are maintained. Mushrooming skylines in Boston, Philadelphia, and even Baltimore may go on expanding the old notion of "downtown" to midtown locations. The success of such plans, however, hinges on the ability of the communities involved to provide adequate access to the districts of the rising skylines, as well as on the ability of business leaders to maintain the vast and complex network of relations, both within Megalopolis and outside it, that has always constituted the essence of the commercial organization.

Some migration of offices associated with the financial markets to suburban locations must of course be expected, as well as continued outward spread of the residences of financial workers.[59] This is the result partly of the whole process of metropolitan growth, to which the financial community is not immune, and partly of the growing together of several great metropolitan areas in the axial belt of Megalopolis. Such tendencies testify to the momentous rate of growth of financial activities and employment in the region as a whole, and especially in its Philadelphia-Boston sector.

The financial community of Manhattan must now be considered, as was done by the New York Metropolitan Region Study, within the framework of a large metropolitan system in which are included even such nuclei as Newark. Indeed, the larger concerns whose home offices are located in Newark would have had some difficulty in operating as smoothly as they do had they been far removed from all the services

[58] These are to include an international stock exchange, a hotel, a heliport, and so forth. See *The New York Times*, January 28, 1960. On February 11, 1960, the Port of New York Authority agreed to study the planning, financing, and activation of this "World Trade Center."

[59] It is interesting to see a survey of *The Economy of New Jersey* (Flink, *op. cit.*) include a whole chapter on the financial community (by Eugene E. Agger, pp. 424–444). It points out on p. 440 that "the problems and issues that confront New Jersey banking and finance may be regarded primarily as growing pains," and it stresses the advantages and disadvantages of New Jersey's position between the two large banking centers of New York and Philadelphia. Some concerns serving a variety of banks have recently moved or considered moving to New Jersey from downtown Manhattan. Thus Kennedy Sinclaire, Inc., specializing in advertising and sales training for banks, and serving some 450 banks in this way, moved from Manhattan to Montclair, New Jersey, in 1958 (*The New York Times*, July 13, 1958). Other firms serving the banking industry are making similar moves to intermediate locations in New Jersey or Connecticut, even though the banks themselves keep their main offices in central cities. See Robbins and Terleckyj, *Money Metropolis, op. cit.*

available in the New York–Northeastern New Jersey metropolitan area to serve the great cluster of institutions in Manhattan. Even Hartford might not have developed as it did in the insurance field had it been much more remote from New York City. The interpenetration of interests between large-scale firms of neighboring sections in Megalopolis is rather obvious in every commercial field. The basic strength of the region's financial activities, including those in Manhattan, rests on the whole commercial organization built up in the last 300 years by the seaboard communities. It is a diversified and shifting organization, and the future of the region's financial role depends on its ability to adapt to changes in the future as well as it has done in the past.

The Changing Ways and Means of Commerce

The commercial organization of Megalopolis is certainly one of the most remarkable achievements of man's art of trade. The history of America's economic *hinge* tells an exciting story of the skill with which the traders in the seaboard cities adapted to changes taking place rapidly on the developing continent of North America as well as in turbulent overseas areas. In the seventeenth and eighteenth centuries these traders developed both maritime activities and inland penetration, harvesting the fruits of the era of great maritime discoveries. From the later eighteenth century on, the successive stages of the Industrial Revolution were used to their full advantage; transportation and manufacturing were developed in order to maintain or expand the network of trade currents focusing on the business districts in this region. In the twentieth century more changes have occurred, and the Megalopolitan traders have taken enough advantage of them, even initiating some of them, so that by midcentury they have risen to a rather commanding position in world commerce.

The greatly increased consumption of an ever-rising variety of goods by the common man has been one of the major "inventions" and factors of growth of the American economy. Nowhere else is this more obvious than in the major metropolitan areas of Megalopolis, despite the elements of obsolescence remaining in the local picture, resulting from a relatively long history. Retail trade has adapted to the recent trends, pursuing the consumer to the outer suburban ring with shopping centers at the same time that it has modernized the stores within densely built-up districts, and developing both chains of self-service stores and facilities for home deliveries.

Wholesale trade has had a more complicated evolution. The map of the wholesale-retail ratio in 1954 (see Fig. 163, p. 520) may cause some surprise, for only the two greatest wholesale hubs, New York City and Boston, show a value of the ratio above 100, and only in New York is it very much above this (388). Even in such great redistributing centers as Philadelphia and Baltimore, wholesale trade did not net as much as retail trade in the city alone. But wholesaling is here measured by the sales of merchant wholesalers, while a large and increasing part of the supply of goods to retailers no longer transits through such merchants. If wholesaling were taken to mean all the distribution supplying the retail trade, it would include also "manufacturer-owned sales outlets, petroleum bulk stations, agents, merchandise brokers, assemblers of farm products, and distributors of industrial goods."[60]

In 1954, for the whole country the sales of merchant wholesalers represented only 59 per cent of retail sales, and in fact sales by wholesalers to retailers for resale constitute normally only about 40 per cent of all the proceeds of wholesale trade if the latter is taken in its larger meaning. In that case "wholesale establishments" come to be defined as "separate places of business primarily engaged in selling or acting as an agent in selling merchandise to (or buying it for) business concerns regardless of whether the latter purchased for resale or for business use. The place of business may be a warehouse from which sales are made at wholesale, a sales or brokerage office, or part of an office that may be shared with others."[61]

Today for many products retail stores are serviced by a system of distribution organized and controlled by the manufacturer, short-circuiting the "wholesaler" of old times as an independent intermediary. In some special cases the manufacturer goes directly to the consumer, establishing his own retail outlets. In such marketing methods, increasingly preferred by the larger, more integrated firms, the "merchant wholesaler" is left out, and the system of distribution is managed by agents who are employers, concessionaires, or contractors of the producer. More decentralization is then bound to occur from the hub of trade, from the priv-

[60] Such was the definition of wholesale trade used in the *U. S. Census of Business: 1948* (see U. S. Bureau of the Census, *County and City Data Book, 1952*, U. S. Government Printing Office, Washington, D. C., 1953, p. xxi). The *U. S. Census of Business: 1954* gave separately the figures for "merchant wholesalers," whose activities correspond better with the old concept of "wholesale" as a profession and as a form of business independent of manufacturing.

[61] U. S. Bureau of the Census, *County and City Data Book, 1952: A Statistical Abstract Supplement*, U. S. Government Printing Office, Washington, D. C., 1953.

ileged geographical locations where special facilities and services used to be provided.[62]

If the various kinds of trade follow the evolution of manufacturing and scatter all over the consuming market, which itself tends toward uniformity, what advantages do the large cities offer to the commercial organization besides the crowding of consumers within small areas? The answer lies in the basic novelty of the ways and means of commerce in our time. *While the flow of materials from production to consumption becomes more and more independent of the business districts of the central cities* (except for certain goods of high value and small volume), *the management of the swelling flow of materials requires increasing employment and activity in the hubs of commerce.*

There is more *office work* involved than ever in the management of modern distribution. Today commerce as well as manufacturing requires more negotiations, more contracting and subcontracting, more information about a constantly diversifying gamut of facts and trends. That is why the commercial organization is becoming more subdivided into specializations, why it is more than ever communications-oriented and needs more legal and technical advice, why it uses more paper, more telephone service, and finally more people, particularly great numbers of better-educated and specially trained people.

The expansion of employment in the "white-collar" professions and the increase in the use of a diversity of services are the two factors that have in recent years forced more concentration of economic activities, of the commercial or managerial categories, in the expanding downtowns and the rising lines of skyscrapers in Megalopolis. This region has been once again a pioneer in these trends. Indeed, in the 1950's it became the leading laboratory for an experiment that may perhaps be called the "white-collar revolution," succeeding the "industrial revolution" that began 200 years ago.

[62] ". . . the rise of the department store, the specialty outlet, and the chain store checked the growth of wholesaling. Large scale retailing — and above all specialty retailing — is an urban affair, so we may say that urbanization restricted the scope for wholesaling." Harold Barger, *Distribution's Place in the American Economy since 1869* (A Study by the National Bureau of Economic Research, New York), Princeton University Press, Princeton, N. J., 1955, p. 71.

C H A P T E R 1 1

The White-Collar Revolution

A recent report on the economy of New England [1] recalls, in outlining the past evolution of the area, that Sir William Petty wrote, as long ago as 1682: "There is much more to be gained by *Manufacture* than by *Husbandry;* and by *Merchandise* than *Manufacture* . . ." [2] The report then goes on to show how the region's recent economic development illustrates this concept, following the general pattern described by the Australian economist, Colin Clark. [3] The proportion of workers employed in agriculture has decreased, while the proportion of those employed in services (transportation, finance, communications, and personal services) has increased and is now actually greater than the proportion of those employed

---

[1] George H. Ellis, "Transition in New England," in *The Economic State of New England*, Report of the Committee of New England of the National Planning Association, Yale University Press, New Haven, 1954.

[2] Sir William Petty, *Political Arithmetick*, London, 1691. The manuscript had been completed in 1682 but was not published until after the author's death.

[3] Colin Clark, *Conditions of Economic Progress*, The Macmillan Company, London, 1940.

in manufacturing. While this has been the trend of the labor force of the United States as a whole, it has been particularly characteristic of New England, which may claim to have spearheaded this evolution.

This growing category of "service" or "tertiary" industries [4] does not quite correspond to the notion of the "white-collar" occupations, for the service industries include such fields as transportation and the utilities, which employ more "blue-collar" than "white-collar" workers. In addition, however, the tertiary category encompasses all employment classified as clerical, commercial, financial, educational, and medical, as well as government work and the special professions, such as law, architecture, and designing. These are essentially white-collar occupations.

The increased importance of the service industries reflects the steady rise of the general standard of living, for these tertiary services are usually associated with the higher levels of personal income per capita. They are also essentially urban. Sir William Petty recognized this as early as the seventeenth century, when he studied the expansion of Greater London far beyond the limits of the city, and he suggested that some day such metropolitan development would cover almost the whole of England.[5]

As it turned out, this prediction proved to be more applicable to New England and the American seaboard immediately to the south of it, for by mid-twentieth century these areas appear to be leading in the evolution toward predominance of the tertiary activities. This evolution is a worldwide phenomenon, certainly well advanced all over the United States and in several European countries, but Megalopolis is outstanding because of the unusually rapid rise there of the *white-collar* occupations. To most educated people in various parts of the world, this Northeastern seaboard of the United States still means one of the biggest manufacturing concentrations on the globe, associated with a great deal of overseas trade converging on the major seaports of the region. This picture remains to a large extent true; but the most spectacular and most unique characteristic of the Megalopolitan economy and growth today is the expansion of the white-collar labor force, of which the towering skyline is the rising symbol.

[4] The term "tertiary industries," originated by A. G. B. Fisher of New Zealand (in the *Clash of Progress and Security*, 1935), was used by Colin Clark in the first edition of his book, *Conditions of Economic Progress* (1940, *op. cit.*). In his third edition (1957), however, he preferred to use the term "service industries," in which he included building and construction, which in our opinion are better classified as secondary industries. See footnote by Clark, *ibid.*, 3rd ed., p. 491.

[5] Petty, *Political Arithmetick, op. cit.*

White-collar employment appears at present to be the most difficult type to decentralize and scatter over the countryside, and when such dispersal can be obtained it brings about the rapid urbanization or at least metropolitanization of the land area involved. In many of their consequences these trends can be described as a "revolution," the long-range results of which may well be compared to those of the Industrial Revolution.

Numerical Growth of Jobs in Tertiary Occupations

The 1960 Census will show a majority of "white-collar" workers in the total nonagricultural employment in the United States.[6] This has never before occurred in a detailed population count, and for this reason if for no other the Eighteenth Census of the United States will rank as a great landmark in history. In a nation of 180 million people the numerical dominance of "white-collar" workers in the whole labor force introduces deep changes in the national way of life, and once one of the larger countries in the world has achieved such new structural characteristics many other nations are bound to evolve in the same direction. In Megalopolis better than anywhere else one can observe the process and the consequences of this rapid growth of employment in the tertiary occupations and in white-collar jobs.

Though in some ways the present situation may look strikingly new, it is, of course, the result of a steady evolution. The statistics available for the last hundred years are not fully comparable, for the classification

[6] The first results of the 1960 Census, in terms of occupational groups, have broken down nonagricultural employment into three main categories: blue-collar, white-collar, and service workers. This third category comprises private household workers as well as general service workers, such as policemen, barbers, and elevator operators. "Service workers" are often difficult to classify in either the white-collar or the blue-collar groups. Most of them however are nonmanual workers, and, providing services, they ·belong in the tertiary industries. Why barbers and policemen should be classified in another great occupational group than sales clerks in a retail store or butchers is a complicated matter and beyond the scope of our study. It is significant for our purpose here to note that in 1960 the white-collar workers, in their restricted definition, still made up 46.6 per cent of the nonfarm employment (as against 42.8 in 1950). The service workers represented 13.6 per cent (instead of 12.5 per cent in 1950). The white-collar workers plus one half of the service workers would have made up a majority of the nonagricultural labor force in 1960 and the "tertiary" occupations altogether employed much more than one half of the total labor force by any count. In 1960 employed white-collar workers numbered 28.5 million people, an increase of over six million jobs since 1950. See Carol A. Barry, "White-Collar Employment: I. Trends and Structure; II. Characteristics," *Monthly Labor Review*, U. S. Department of Labor, Bureau of Labor Statistics, Washington, D. C., Vol. 84, No. 1, January 1961, pp. 11–18, and No. 2, February 1961, pp. 139–147.

and definitions of the major occupational groups have not been consistent. Nevertheless, the available data concur in making one general trend quite clear: the steady increase, in absolute number of jobs and in their proportion to total employment, in *those occupations that do not produce or process goods but service either production and processing industries or the consumer in all his diversified needs*, from the transportation and distribution of goods to the education of the people and the government of communities. The progress of that evolution from 1870 to 1930 is shown in Figure 170 left. Manufacturing and agriculture together made up about 75 per cent of the total employment in 1870. By 1930 they made up barely 50 per cent of the total, but these two combined with mining still kept the tertiary activities from attaining dominance. The clerical, professional, and public-service occupations accounted for less than 5 per cent of the employment in 1870 but for some 16 per cent in 1930. These trends continued at a quicker pace after 1930 (see Fig. 170 right),[7] and the Bureau of Labor Statistics has estimated that by 1953 nonindustrial jobs clearly dominated in nonagricultural employment and that they have continued to increase their lead.[8]

Agriculture has been the section of employment most clearly declining in numbers, and this trend will probably continue, at least through the 1960's, for the nation as a whole. It shows definitely on all graphs and tables, despite increases in the output of many agricultural products. Employment in mining seems to be declining too. Manufacturing employment is still rising and will probably continue to increase in absolute figures, but it seems destined to decrease in proportion to total employment. The case of manufacturing is complicated by the sharp increase in the personnel of manufacturing firms of *nonproduction* workers.[9] As such firms go on developing their own staffs busy with sales, research, transportation, maintenance, and administrative matters, the category of "manufacturing employment" is bound to include more white-collar jobs, more blue-collar servicing jobs, and a lesser proportion of craftsmen, foremen, operatives, and kindred workers. This accounts for the greater need to differentiate such categories as white-collar, service, and blue-

[7] The two graphs on Figure 170 are not quite comparable though both are based on U. S. Census data, for the Census method of classifying occupations was somewhat modified in 1940. However, the general trends are clear enough for the purposes of this inquiry.

[8] See "Recovery in Labor Market," in *Federal Reserve Bulletin*, May 1959, pp. 471–476; and for an earlier discussion of this development see p. 52 above. Nonindustrial employment includes trade, service, finance, and government, essentially white-collar work.

[9] See above, Chapter 9, especially pp. 495–500, and Fig. 153, p. 497.

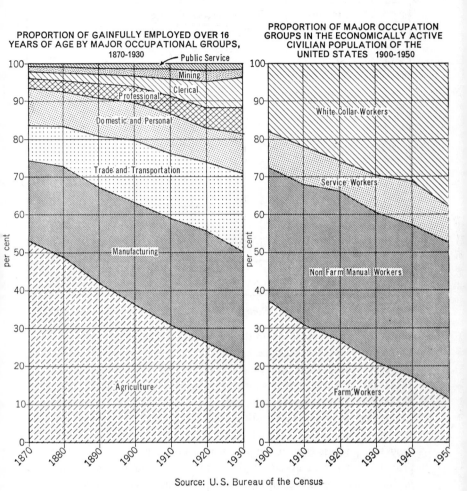

Source: U.S. Bureau of the Census

FIG. 170. Major occupational groups in the labor force, according to two different classifications, 1870–1950

collar workers in nonfarm employment, instead of the pre-1940 categories of "manufacturing," "trade and transportation," etc. We have depicted both Census classifications (see Figs. 170 and 171) and have found them following the same trend.

That trend involves first towards a rapid numerical growth of jobs in the *tertiary* economic activities, and second an expansion of the white-collar occupations any way one figures it out. The forecasts for the

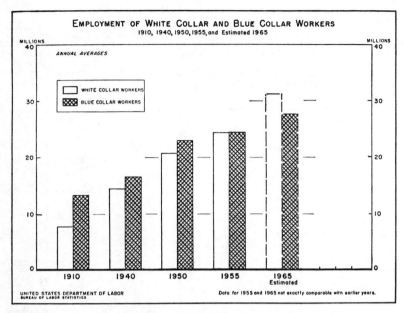

FIG. 171. *Courtesy of the U. S. Bureau of Labor Statistics*

evolution of the labor force in the 1960's reflect the same trend. The U. S.
Bureau of Labor Statistics has estimated that white-collar and blue-collar
workers came to share about equally in the national employment around
1955, and has forecast that white-collar growth will be much faster than
blue-collar growth up to 1965 (see Fig. 171). By 1960 Ewan Clague,
Commissioner of Labor Statistics, could confirm the trend once more.[10]
It is noteworthy that he singled out the financial community as promising the quickest ratio of employment increase in the 1960's, while he
placed construction ahead of the industries employing large numbers
of blue-collar workers, on the assumption that more building will be
needed to house more people and more offices, especially in cities.

In similar fashion the New York Metropolitan Region Study, dealing
only with the area at the heart of Megalopolis, has forecast that by 1985
there will be a considerable increase of the tertiary sector and of white-
collar jobs in both absolute and relative terms.[11] In this region they already

[10] See above, Chapter I, pp. 50–54, and Ewan Clague's address on May 25, 1960,
to the Conference on Occupational Outlook. (*The New York Times*, Sunday, May
29, 1960). Also Barry, "White Collar Employment: I. Trends and Structures," *op. cit.*

[11] See Edgar M. Hoover and Raymond Vernon, *Anatomy of a Metropolis*, 1959,
especially Chapter 4; Martin Segal, *Wages in the Metropolis*, 1960, and Raymond
Vernon, *Metropolis: 1985*, 1960, all part of the New York Metropolitan Region Study,
Harvard University Press, Cambridge, Mass.

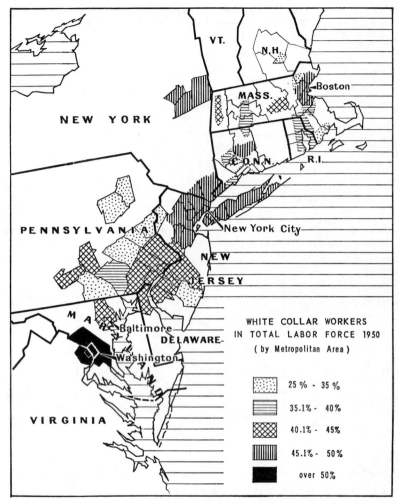

FIG. 172

represent a very substantial part of the labor force, of course. In 1950 white-collar workers accounted for more than 25 per cent of the total employment in every standard metropolitan area of Megalopolis; for more than 50 per cent in the Washington, D. C., area; and for 45–50 per cent in the New York–Northeastern New Jersey, Boston, and Hartford areas (see Fig. 172).

The increase in the numbers and proportions of jobs led, of course, also to a similar trend for personal income provided by the service industries in the total revenue of the nation and especially of Megalopolis.

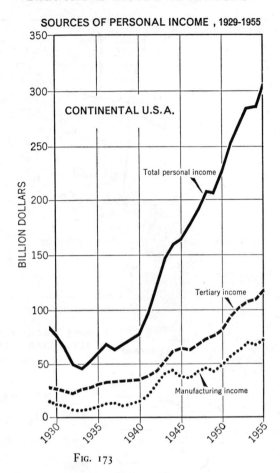

FIG. 173

How important the *tertiary* activities have become as sources of personal income can be seen from the graphs in Figures 173 to 175, which show for the whole nation and for the major states in Megalopolis the changes in total personal income, in wages and salaries from manufacturing, and in wages and salaries from the tertiary occupations, between 1929 and 1955.[12]

[12] See the publication of the U. S. Department of Commerce, Office of Business Economics, by Charles F. Schwartz and Robert E. Graham, Jr., *Personal Income by States Since 1929, A Supplement to the Survey of Current Business,* U. S. Government Printing Office, 1956. Lines 10, 11, 14, 18, 21, and 27 of their Tables 4-62 (in Part V) have been combined to derive the income from tertiary occupations as shown in the graphs in Figs. 173 to 175. It includes salaries from: wholesale and retail trade; finance, insurance, and real estate; transportation, communications, and public utilities; services; and government.

Payroll disbursements of manufacturing and tertiary industries do not, of course, account for all personal income, but they form a good part of it. In all the Northeastern seaboard states the tertiary payroll has been rising significantly since the early 1930's. The most impressive feature of this rise appears to be its *continuity*, for while the tertiary payroll does not always exceed the manufacturing payroll, it demonstrates almost everywhere *more stability* than the less regular income from manufacturing. This continuous and regular rise of the tertiary activities must have been due largely to the growth of the white-collar occupations, which have been more stable than the blue-collar fields, such as transportation, and Federal military payrolls.

An exception to the common features of the trends demonstrated on these graphs can be found in the case of Virginia, where manufacturing, which played a very minor role before 1935, has been growing more steadily than on the seaboard north of the Potomac. Since 1933 the economy of Virginia has been very dependent on Federal government expenditures, especially in the vicinity of the national capital and also around Hampton Roads, the main naval base of the Atlantic fleet. But most of Virginia does not belong in Megalopolis, and the special behavior of its income graphs reflects its peculiar position and evolution in the past thirty years. In the Old Dominion, Megalopolis and the old South border on one another and almost interpenetrate.

For Megalopolis itself, the general conclusion remains well demonstrated that the tertiary activities, the various services, have been in the recent past *a more stable and more regularly growing source of income* than manufacturing. For the country as a whole this appears to be true also, not only in terms of manufacturing but also of agriculture. The greater stability of the tertiary income reflects both the fact that it is the "growth sector" of the modern economy and the fact the bulk of the people have reached a high level of living and expenditure. Mass consumption and mass culture generate intimately interwoven economic processes, some of which produce the contemporary trend of employment and of disbursements toward the nonagricultural and nonindustrial activities. In the United States these processes are rather advanced; one has at present little doubt that most of the other nations will follow on this path.

The fact that Megalopolis has shown the way, at least in America, is chiefly owing to this region's focus on commercial organization. Behind the present spread of offices, so characteristic of the business districts of Megalopolitan cities, is a long tradition of traders thirsty for information

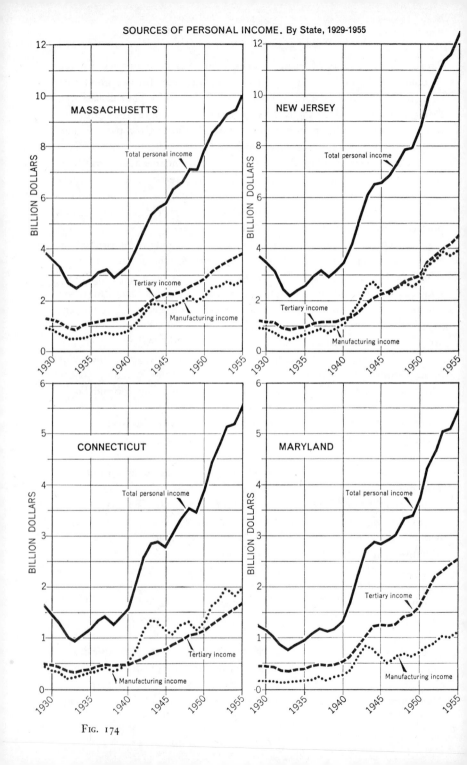

SOURCES OF PERSONAL INCOME. By State, 1929-1955

MASSACHUSETTS

Total personal income

Tertiary income

Manufacturing income

NEW JERSEY

Total personal income

Tertiary income

Manufacturing income

CONNECTICUT

Total personal income

Tertiary income

Manufacturing income

MARYLAND

Total personal income

Tertiary income

Manufacturing income

BILLION DOLLARS

FIG. 174

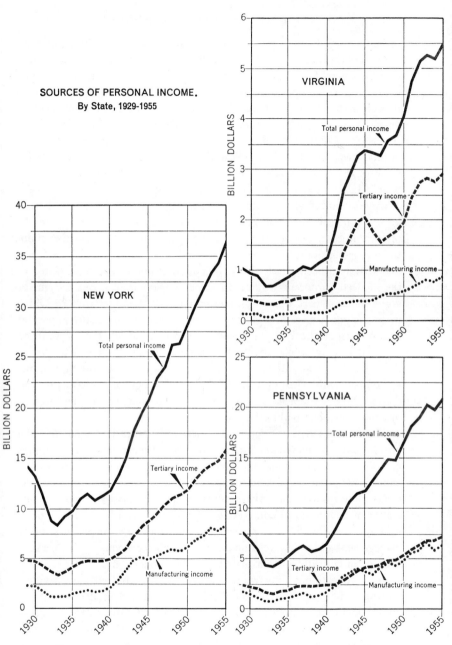

SOURCES OF PERSONAL INCOME.
By State, 1929-1955

VIRGINIA

Total personal income

Tertiary income

Manufacturing income

NEW YORK

Total personal income

Tertiary income

Manufacturing income

PENNSYLVANIA

Total personal income

Tertiary income

Manufacturing income

Fig. 175

to better the conduct of their commercial operations. Information is indeed the very life blood of commerce anywhere, unless the distribution of goods merely conforms to a traditional, set pattern of moving certain goods from certain places of production to certain consumers. Conducted in such static fashion, trade renounces actual commerce to become almost purely a matter of transportation and accounting. The cities of the American wilderness would never have become great commercial centers in their own right had they followed the conservative path of established trade relations. To develop a continent's yet barely known resources, to benefit by the opportunities of merchandising on the open seas, a very dynamic concept of commerce was needed, and it was early and stubbornly pursued by New York and Yankee traders. To recognize the opportunities that came their way, these traders needed information about the ways and means of commerce and industry.

It has often been asserted that the counting house was the ancestor of the modern corporation office. In some respects it was. But the inn or coffee house where news was exchanged and the waterfront to which news and goods were brought from overseas have been equally important forerunners of the modern spacious offices, in which they have been replaced by conference rooms, telephones, and ticker tape. The "over-the-counter" markets of a nation have come to be diffused through countless offices, with wires or waves linking them together, just as the residences of the workers have scattered over metropolitan outer rings instead of being contained within the walls of a mill's dormitory.

The growing mass of goods and of data to be taken into account in the operation of business aimed at markets of Megalopolitan size requires much space and more and more personnel. Servicing modern production and consumption requires handling the goods on the one hand and the transactions on the other. Managing the transactions is no longer a simple matter of counting and contracting, or arithmetic and legal forms; today it involves information and research on the technology of products or of management and public relations, as well as on the events in the markets, local or distant information that cannot be obtained and used efficiently without education, competence, and special skills. Indeed, one wonders whether a new distinction should not be introduced in all the mass of nonproduction employment: a differentiation between *tertiary* services — transportation, trade in the simpler sense of direct sales, maintenance, and personal services — and a new and distinct *quaternary* family of economic activities — services that involve transactions, analysis, research, or decision-making, and also education and government. Such quaternary types require more intellectual training and responsibility. The numerical increase in the tertiary and white-collar jobs appears to be related to an accompanying rise in the number of the professions and specializations classified under these older labels.

A Self-Refining Division of Labor

As the factors bringing about the clustering together of large offices in the "downtowns" of large cities are analyzed, many centripetal forces are exposed. Among them are always mentioned the need for *good and reliable information*, since office work is so often communications-oriented, and the need for *a pool of skilled labor*. A good part of office or white-collar work consists in gathering, analyzing, classifying, filing, and distributing information, a great diversity of it — from data about the taxation rules of places where certain raw materials can be obtained to publicity about the virtues of a product to be sold. In between these two ends of the long line of information needed either by manufacturers or importers, a great many intermediate links are found, each of them corresponding to another kind of information.

The larger the organization concerned and the wider the gamut of goods it puts on the market, the longer and the more variegated will be the chain of kinds of data that organization will on the one hand require for its own use and on the other hand distribute to the outside. Every category of data in this long chain will be best handled by a "specialist," or even by a profession, if the demand for that particular link is widespread enough. As has already been pointed out several times, for trade and services large cities offer the advantage of an agglomeration of all the various "external" specialists needed by the various industries. Such an agglomeration can be expected to arise and last in any place only if at that place there is a large enough clientele of firms all interested in using the services of these various external specialists.

Once such a cluster is achieved, be it for electronics manufacturers, for contract builders, or for banks, it will tend to attract more external specialties and more industries to be serviced. In this process of growth the specialties will be refined, spawning new subspecialties and constantly adding self-perfecting and self-subdividing specializations. In a city of a million people one may count on finding, for instance, a variety of catering firms. In New York City or Philadelphia there will be a whole range of caterers, suitable for various possible occasions, for large or small gatherings, and for different tastes. Newark or Trenton, in contrast, will obviously not equal Manhattan or Philadelphia in the choice, quality, and capability of their catering firms, because the market of these smaller cities, with less entertaining to perform, is so much smaller. As a result, the largest occasions in these New Jersey cities may well be catered by firms from either Manhattan or Philadelphia; and this extension of the market of the larger cities will induce more competition and specialization, with perhaps subcontracting by the firms in the two bigger metropolises.

What is true of caterers, a special service trade, applies to truckers or movers as well, to take an example from the truly tertiary activities. It applies even more to the more complicated quaternary specializations, in which competence requires more training and yields higher fees — for example, the law, the brokerage business, engineering, and education. The pooling of skills expands and subdivides itself, according to a mechanism of the division of labor well described long ago by Adam Smith.

In the progress of society, philosophy or speculation becomes, like every other employment, the principal or sole trade and occupation of a particular class of citizens. Like every other employment too, it is subdivided into a great number of different branches, each of which affords occupation to a peculiar tribe or class of philosophers; and this subdivision of employment in philosophy, as in every other business, improves dexterity, and saves time. Each individual becomes more expert in his own peculiar branch, more work is done upon the whole, and the quantity of science is considerably increased by it.

It is the great multiplication of the production of all the different arts, in consequence of the division of labor, which occasions, in a well-governed society, that universal opulence which extends itself to the lowest ranks of the people.[13]

While extolling the benefits derived from the division of labor, Adam Smith pointed out that it was "the necessary, though very slow and gradual, consequence of a certain propensity in human nature . . .; the propensity to truck, barter, and exchange one thing for another. To this he added:

As it is the power of exchanging that gives occasion to the division of labor, so the extent of this division must always be limited by the extent of that power, or, in other words, by the extent of the market. . . .

There are some sorts of industry, even of the lowest kind, which can be carried on nowhere but in a great town. A porter, for example, can find employment and subsistence in no other place.[14]

[13] Adam Smith, *An Inquiry Into the Nature and Causes of the Wealth of Nations*, first published in 1776. The above quotation is from Book 1, Chapter 1, of the fifth edition, 1789, reprinted by the Modern Library of Random House, New York, 1937, pp. 11 and 12.

[14] *Ibid.*, Chapters 2 and 3; quote, p. 17.

Thus this process, which has been going on in the more urbanized and industrialized cities for centuries, has an obvious relation to the size of the market and more specifically to the crowding of consumers. This is what the commercial organization of Megalopolis has been developing constantly since the *Wealth of Nations* was published. In this constant refining of the division of labor in services and white-collar professions there have been two associated developments. On the one hand, new firms have been undertaking to provide the very specialized services needed by a goodly number of older firms, and these new establishments have attracted people qualifying for the new professions. On the other hand, some already existing establishments, if they are large enough, have felt they needed a competent specialist of the new profession servicing them on their own staff. By this double process the numerical growth of new professions has been accelerated.

Such narrowing down of specialties may encourage research and progress within each one, and this may expand the knowledge or skill in a given point that induces a new subdivision. This self-refining of the division of labor is well known in the professional fields of science, technology, law, and medicine. In such "quarternary" activities it seems preferable to speak of a division of labor rather than a specialization, for to improve his performance of the particular kind of work in which he specializes *the professional worker has to be trained and competent in a much broader area than the narrow one* in which he applies his knowledge professionally.

Let us consider dentistry as an example. A century or two ago teeth were pulled by barbers. Now dentistry is completely distinct from barbering and belongs instead in the medical community. The dentist must know a good deal about general medicine, though he does not practice it. In the not-too-distant past a dentist himself did almost any work his clients' teeth required. Now there are specialized categories in the profession, and there are springing up entire industries supplying dentists with various kinds of machines, gadgets, chemical materials, artificial teeth, and other supplies they may need. To use properly this ever-expanding arsenal of tools, drugs, and other materials, the dentist, even narrowly specialized, must learn about the physics, chemistry, and mechanics of his equipment and supplies. The more he has to know, the more he will tend to specialize in the practical work, to avoid blunders and risks in a too-wide field. No longer can every variety of dental work be done in a small isolated community, whose market would not normally support a large enough number of specialists.

It must be remembered, therefore, that *the specialist is not a member of the profession who knows less than the general practitioner.* Actually he must know more, for while his specialization reflects only a sub-division of labor within his profession it usually requires more science, more training, than does more general work. This is true of every pro-fession in what we have called the *quaternary occupations*, those supply-ing services that require research, analysis, judgment — in brief, brainwork and responsibility. This becomes a process in the "division of labor" rather than in "specialization" in a restricted sense. Actual narrowing down of specialization is possible in the practice of primary, secondary, and even tertiary economic activities, but it should not occur in the activi-ties that require broader knowledge.

In the field of education the implications of this trend are considerable. Anyone familiar with academic life since the beginning of this century knows that on every campus the number of different courses and of chairs and departments has been steadily increasing in ways rather inde-pendent of the numerical growth of the student body. The latter has been the result of population growth as well as of the greater demand, in a rapidly advancing culture, for more and better education and more specialized people to man the white-collar jobs. The expansion of quater-nary occupations was the result of an economic and social evolution that did not wait for the universities to turn out graduates in large enough numbers. However, continuance of this evolution is dependent on the expanding and improving of university activities, to supply the needed regular flow of adequately trained people able to assume the tasks and responsibilities of the newly opening fields of employment.

In the first place college faculties have seen new subdivisions estab-lished within the long recognized disciplines. To teach just "chemistry" or "physics" or "geography" or "civil engineering" has become increas-ingly difficult and, at a certain level, impossible. Each of these fields has been subdivided in a whole series of specialties, which are being gradually partitioned further. In addition, new disciplines, respectable and even necessary, have been developed, spanning the traditional partitions be-tween formerly distinct fields such as physics, chemistry, mathematics, and biology. As a result there are now such specializations in science, and in professorships, as mathematical physics, physical chemistry, and even physico-chemical biology, which spawned the whole new field of genetics. Similar trends are observable in the social sciences. While the all-encompassing term "natural history" is today seldom used, so out-dated is its rather encyclopedic quality, the varied specialties constituting the staff of a Museum of Natural History (such as the New York institution bearing that name) include social studies in the social anthropology field; and at least one university in Megalopolis has established a separate department of history of mathematics.[15]

What is taught to the students is soon reflected in the professional line-up of the quaternary activities. The demand for these professions, new and old, has been expanding rapidly in all the research establishments financed by either government funds or private industry. As the Federal government has become increasingly concerned with technology, for both civil and military purposes, the Civil Service Commission has had often to revise, and every time to refine, its listing and definitions of white-collar occupations. For example, by 1957 thirty-nine different occupations were listed under the general title of "engineering," including not only the rather traditional and comprehensive types, such as "civil engineering" and "electrical engineering," but also many new kinds of engineering. For highways alone, an important field of modern government expenditure, at least four specializations were listed: highway engineering, highway research engineering, highway design engineering, highway construction and maintenance engineering. Bridge engineering forms still another profession.[16] Federal employment in the engineering field is still increasing steadily — for instance, by about 8 per cent between 1954 and 1957. In the same period the number of jobs in the Federal civil service concerned with accounting and budget increased by about 12 per cent, and the number of physicians increased by 26 per cent.[17] These professional categories were continuing to grow in 1961.

Similar trends are observable for white-collar jobs in manufacturing[18] and in other occupational groups. Automation may to some extent reduce employment in some of the purely tertiary occupations, but it will hardly affect the quaternary group much, for it will produce new professions to tame the complicated machinery. As the numbers of white-collar jobs grow, so the numbers of the occupations in which they belong increase too. This process may go on for quite some time to come, for it follows Adam Smith's principle that the size of the market governs the further

[15] Brown University, in Providence, Rhode Island.

[16] U. S. Civil Service Commission, Employment Statistics Office, *Occupations of Federal White Collar Workers*, February 28, 1957 (Pamphlet 56–1), U. S. Government Printing Office, Washington, D. C., June 1958, Table A, p. 30.

[17] *Ibid.*, pp. 7–13.

[18] Herman Travis, "White Collar Jobs in Manufacturing," *The Occupational Outlook*, October 1957 (a report of the U. S. Bureau of Labor Statistics); and David M. Blank and George J. Stigler, *The Demand and Supply of Scientific Personnel*, No. 62, General Series, National Bureau of Economic Research, New York, 1957.

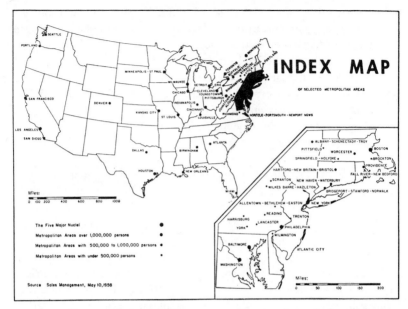

FIG. 176. Index to Figs. 177 to 186, showing telephone messages between selected cities. *Courtesy of Neil C. Gustafson of Minneapolis, Minn.* (See footnote 26, p. 588.)

partitioning of the division of labor.[19] However, size was not the only important influence of the labor market on the division of labor, even in Smith's time. He pointed out that many professions can exist only in large towns, for the market must not only be large and expanding but also it must be *dense* enough to spur on the self-refining division of labor. This is obvious in Smith's examples of porters and philosophers.[20] Thus crowding was an influence to be reckoned with even in the eighteenth century, and it certainly is at least as significant in our time.

The urbanization and metropolitanization of as vast a region as Megalopolis was bound to produce an especially advanced state of the division of labor in services and in white-collar work. However, this process of division of labor is not only accelerated by the concentration of service industries and offices in the axial belt of Megalopolis but has certainly, in recent years, been itself a factor causing concentration.

[19] Recently this principle has again attracted the attention of economists, as is pointed out in *The Study of Economic Growth: Thirty-ninth Annual Report; a Record for 1958 and Plans for 1959*, National Bureau of Economic Research, New York, May 1959, p. 7. See also George J. Stigler, *Trends in Employment in the Service Industries*, National Bureau of Economic Research, General Series, No. 59, Princeton University Press, Princeton, N. J., 1956, especially Chapter 8.

[20] See quotations from *The Wealth of Nations*, p. 578 above.

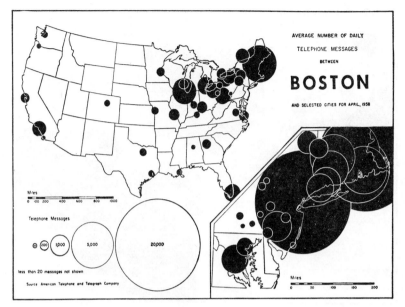

FIG. 177. *Courtesy of Neil C. Gustafson*

The Need for the Concentration of Skills and Offices

The office worker is characteristic of, and was formerly seldom found outside of, the business districts of central cities, where business is transacted by and professional services are available to a large clientele drawn from the whole city, its suburbs, and beyond. Many out-of-towners come to the "downtown" of a city to transact business, and while they are there these visitors may take advantage of the retail trade and personal and professional services available in the vicinity, which they could hardly find in a smaller place or in a purely residential district.

All this pool of skills has clustered in the business district more to service the people who come to work there regularly than because of the frequency of out-of-town callers, but the latter should not be disregarded, of course. They are part of the consumer market on which those who offer their services in the area count; but they are only a complementary component of a market the big bulk of which consists of the daytime population at work in the offices. The labor force in a busy downtown area during weekdays and office hours is the densest agglomeration of people to be found regularly in any category of place throughout the country. It is particularly so in Megalopolis, because the region's cities have put the skyscraper to good use to achieve daytime densities of tens of thousands per square mile and in some blocks of several thousands per acre. Such densi-

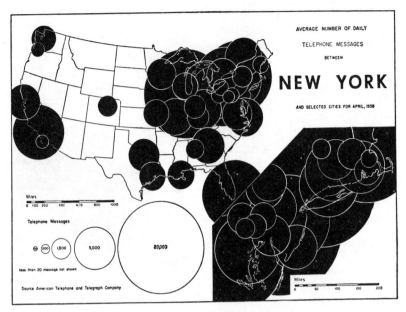

Fig. 178. *Courtesy of Neil C. Gustafson*

ties supply an enormous clientele for all the trade and services in the area. The mass and density of these concentrations afford commercial interlocking opportunities that cannot be disregarded and that must attract more shops and offices to the district.

Manhattan's midtown between 34th and 60th streets offers the most striking concentration of this kind. Lower Manhattan, with the financial district and the government institutions clustering around City Hall, forms another smaller one, not as well serviced as the midtown business district in terms of retail trade and personal or professional services, especially in the medical field. The midtown part of Manhattan's hub has the advantage of adjoining on the one hand the Broadway theater and entertainment district and on the other hand the most expensive residential districts of New York City, and thus this midtown area has attracted the main concentration of hotels, restaurants, department stores, specialty shops, and medical and dental offices, all located close to both the office-worker crowds and the residents of near-by fashionable apartments. These two categories of potential customers belong in the higher income brackets and therefore in the group that can and does spend more than average.

The crowding of all these services in the vicinity of the office towers

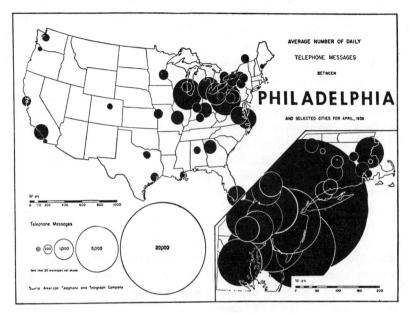

Fig. 179. *Courtesy of Neil C. Gustafson*

makes it desirable to be employed in such well-located offices or to pay them a visit for business purposes. In the hub of Manhattan, especially its "midtown" part, there is a good deal of attraction for the kind of personnel the offices are looking for, particularly for the young women who form a very important component of the office labor force.[21] The same factors favor the central business districts in the other main cities of Megalopolis, such as Boston, Philadelphia, Baltimore, Washington, and even Newark, Wilmington, and Providence. Therefore, when an important insurance company moved its headquarters office out of Hartford to a suburban location, only a few miles from the city limits but in a not yet too vast or too crowded metropolitan area, it was felt wise, in order to avoid difficulties in personnel recruitment, to have available next to the new headquarters at least some special services, such as beauty shops. Similarly, Federal government agencies have begun scattering around the District of Columbia, and some of them have at times experienced difficulties in finding precisely the kind of competent workers they need, difficulties that do not seem to occur when the location of such work is in Washington itself, in or near the center of the city where most of the

[21] This has been well described and analyzed by Hoover and Vernon, *Anatomy of a Metropolis, op. cit.*, pp. 98–112.

government offices are gathered. Young people particularly place high value on a central location for their jobs.

The problem of finding adequate personnel for office work has been one of the centripetal forces concentrating offices in central cities. This problem has many facets, the two principal among them being: first, the need to recruit enough competent workers for all the great variety of tasks to be performed in the offices; second, easy access to all the services, needed in connection with the office work by the management and also by the rank-and-file workers, but available only from sources outside the office. Among the many different services needed, some are available *within the office* (they may vary from typing to general administration), while others are *external but complementary to the office* (these range from beauty shops to financial and scientific advice).

Easy access to this whole variety of skilled employees, when one needs to hire them, and of competent and reliable servicing or advice, when one wishes to call on them, cannot be expected just anywhere. In fact, there are only a few places in the United States and not many elsewhere where these needs of the headquarters of a large modern industrial concern can be easily satisfied. For such businesses Megalopolis is the choice location, and that is why so many of them have congregated there.

Among the 500 largest industrial firms in America, listed in 1958 in *Fortune's Directory*,[22] 202 had their national headquarters in Megalopolis, and 156 of them were in the New York metropolitan region. A breakdown by industry shows that out of the "50 largest in the United States" Megalopolis holds seventeen banks, eighteen transportation firms, twenty-two merchandise establishments, twenty-two life-insurance companies, and twenty utilities.[23] Most of the large concerns whose home towns are outside Megalopolis have a financial division in New York City. Such concentration, already pointed out with regard to the commercial organization of Megalopolis, the very foundation of this region's economic success and growth,[24] has some good reasons behind it.

Today the most compelling reason is easy access and proximity to all the desirable external services and to an adequate labor market for the "inner" personnel. But these considerations exert imperative pressures to bring about concentration as a result of the present "self-refining subdivision of labor" in the tertiary and the quarternary occupations. The ever-expanding chain of useful specialists, needed either permanently on the

[22] "Directory of the 500 Largest Industrial Corporations" *Fortune*, Vol. 58, No. 1, July 1958, pp. 131 ff.
[23] "Fortune Directory: Part II," in *Fortune*, Vol. 58, No. 2, August 1958, pp. 115 ff.
[24] See above, Chapter 10.

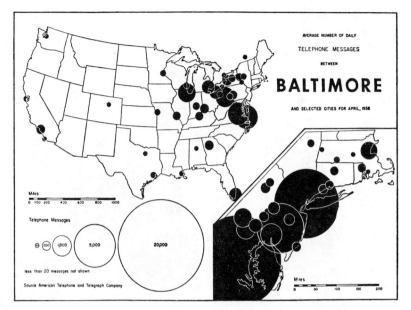

Fig. 180. *Courtesy of Neil C. Gustafson*

staff or occasionally for consultation, will congregate at a place where
they can be assured of satisfactory employment. For most white-collar
professions Megalopolis offers by far the best possible market for jobs,
whether on a full-time, part-time, free-lance, or consultative basis. In such
diverse fields as accounting, publishing, or scientific research, the talented
young man or woman today seldom has to "go West" from Megalopolis,
unless some special or personal conditions are involved.

However, personnel and external services are not the only reasons calling today for concentration in white-collar work. There are many other
aspects of communications that are instrumental in this process. The quaternary occupations are *all* communications-oriented. We have already
seen how in manufacturing and in commerce the activities so oriented
have tended to cluster together and to be found in great numbers in this
largest cluster of metropolitan areas. Office work also needs and produces
large amounts of documents on paper. The volume of papers necessary to
the financial operations transacted in Manhattan seems to be one of the
reasons keeping close one to another the diverse establishments between
which flows this great stream of documents.[25] The huge volumes of mail
that flow through Megalopolis are quite astonishing compared to the size

[25] Sidney M. Robbins and Nestor E. Terleckyj, *Money Metropolis*, New York
Metropolitan Region Study, Harvard University Press, Cambridge, Mass., 1960.

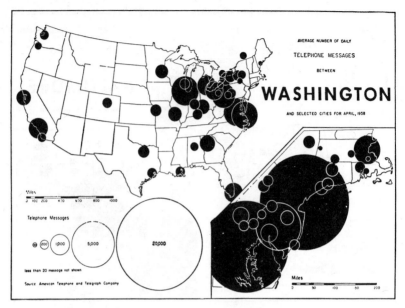

FIG. 181. *Courtesy of Neil C. Gustafson*

of the mail carried over similar distances in any other part of the world. New York City originated 18 million pieces daily in 1959.

However, communication by mail is often too slow for Megalopolitan white-collar workers, and therefore the telephone rings in this region with greater intensity than anywhere else, be this intensity measured by the absolute number of calls or their density, per acre or per inhabitant. The series of maps (Figs. 176 to 186) showing the flow of telephone calls from the main cities in Megalopolis to other major centers in the country testifies strikingly to the greater density of telephone communications in this region than in other parts of the country.[26] Whether one considers the total number of calls or their number per capita, the flow between the great Megalopolitan cities is much more intense than is the flow between them and other cities in the United States.

In order to ascertain what went on in the medium-sized cities of Megalopolis we mapped the flow of telephone calls made during a sample pe-

[26] We are indebted for these maps to Mr. Neil C. Gustafson of Minneapolis, who prepared them as part of his study of "Metropolitan Linkages of the Eastern Seaboard," in the Department of Geography, University of Minnesota. Mr. Gustafson has kindly authorized us to reproduce these maps, prepared on the basis of data supplied to him by the Long Lines Department of the American Telephone and Telegraph Company.

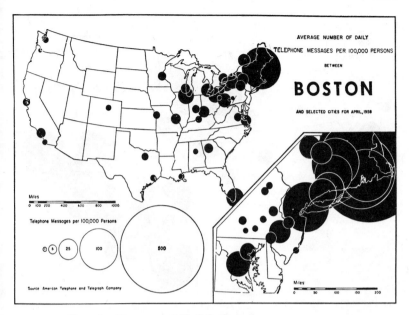

FIG. 182. *Courtesy of Neil C. Gustafson*

riod in 1959 from the three main centers in Connecticut — Hartford, New Haven, and Bridgeport.[27] The result (Fig. 187) corroborates the study of the flow of calls from the large cities. If only out-of-the-state calls are counted, the function of the main Connecticut cities as links in the chain of Megalopolis' axial belt appears clearly, for the two centers that receive many more calls than any others are New York City and Boston. These two great cities are not necessarily the terminal points of all these thousands of calls per day; they redistribute some of them to other communities in their vicinity. In this fashion Newark's rank in third place must be explained, for its central switchboard redistributes calls to some of its suburbs (especially person-to-person calls). However, the community of interests existing between the great insurance companies having their central headquarters located in Newark and in Hartford must explain part of the volume of this flow. During the ten-day period only New York, Bos-

[27] We are indebted for the figures from which this map, Fig. 187, was prepared, to the Southern New England Telephone Company's head office in New Haven. The detailed data kindly supplied to this study were generalized in order to be fitted into a not-too-complicated map. It is based on a ten-day run of long distance calls, March 9–20, 1959, excluding the week end. It was assessed that multiplication of this sample figure by 31.133 would provide a good annual figure for 1959, according to the Company's statement.

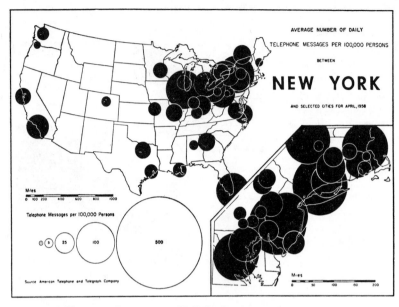

FIG. 183. *Courtesy of Neil C. Gustafson*

ton, and Newark received more than 10,000 calls each from the main Connecticut centers. In the group that received 5,000–10,000 calls we find Springfield, Worcester, Providence, and Philadelphia. The latter city is another major hub in Megalopolis, but the other three probably owe the intensity of the telephone flow between them and the Connecticut cities to proximity, to many interconnected interests, and even to the fact that residents of one occasionally work in the other. This map underlines the integration of the various sections of Megalopolis with the neighboring sections, consolidating the concept of the region. In like manner the series of maps showing the flow of calls between the major cities stresses how much more involved each of them is with its neighbors in Megalopolis than with other sections of the country.

The density of the flow of telephone calls is a fairly good measure of the relationships binding together the economic interests of the region. Telephone calls represent not only economic and governmental relationships but also social and family links. The main use of these communications belongs to the sphere of the "white-collar occupations" and may be adopted as an indication of the usefulness of close contacts between all the offices strewn along the Megalopolitan axis.

On January 1, 1959, the United States had 66,645,000 installed tele-

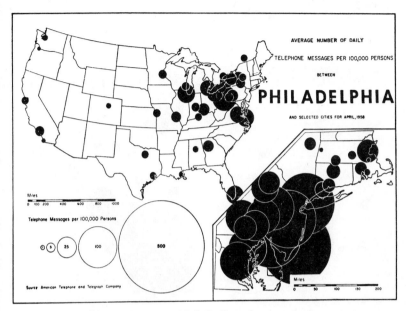

FIG. 184. *Courtesy of Neil C. Gustafson*

phones, about 53.4 per cent of the world total. This number amounted to 38 telephones per 100 people in continental United States, while the world average stood at 4.3 per 100. The only countries to have telephone densities approaching the American record were Sweden (34 per 100 people), Canada (29.6), Switzerland (28.3), and New Zealand (27.5).[28]

These higher national averages can be compared with the figures for the principal cities, which, of course, have a greater telephone density. Outside the United States, the highest figures are found in Stockholm (59 per 100 people), Toronto (49), other Swedish and Canadian cities, then Wellington (44), Milan (40), London (37), Copenhagen and Oslo (36), Paris (33), etc. In the United States almost every city has more than 30 telephones per 100 inhabitants. Among cities of more than 50,000 inhabitants Washington, D. C., has the highest figure, 71.4 and it is followed by White Plains, New York (68), Atlantic City, New Jersey (64.4), Skokie, Illinois (62.5).[29] Residential suburbs and resort places show a particularly

[28] These figures and the statistics in the next paragraph are from *The World's Telephones*, 1959 issue, published by American Telephone and Telegraph Company, New York, December 1959.

[29] Practically every city in Megalopolis has a density per inhabitant above the national average. However, dormitory cities such as White Plains and hubs of office

FIG. 185. *Courtesy of Neil C. Gustafson*

high average of installed telephones in proportion to population. However, the primacy of Washington among all large cities in the world is significant and appears to be linked to the great concentration of offices in and around the Federal agencies. Office work and administration, being communications-oriented, need the telephone and use it intensively.

A last indicator of the relations between the concentration of offices and the telephone may be found in the ratio of business telephones to residential telephones as figured for the counties of Megalopolis for 1955 (Fig. 188). Manhattan seems to be the only area in Megalopolis where the number of business telephones installed was then much above the number of the residential. Nowhere else is there such a concentration of large offices and such an impressive skyline. The ratio was also quite high in Washington and Boston. These three cities are indeed the three major concentrations of offices and of white-collar workers on a huge scale, not only in Megalopolis but also in the whole eastern part of the United States.

There seem to be many good reasons for concentrating office work, and the current white-collar revolution has been a factor contributing to the growth and crowding in the central business districts of central cities.

work (New York City, 55; Hartford, 56; Harrisburg, 56) have higher ratios than do purely manufacturing cities (Lowell, 36; Manchester, 34; Jersey City, 37).

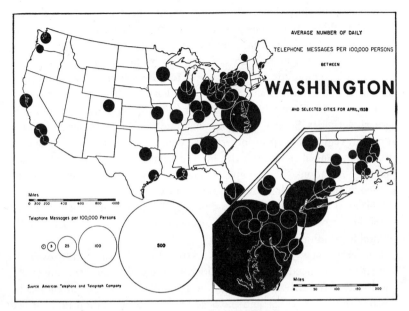

FIG. 186. *Courtesy of Neil C. Gustafson*

For some years, however, one has heard constant talk of decentralizing these economic activities. The scattering of white-collar workers from Megalopolis through the country and from the central cities through their metropolitan rings has, of course, been going on to some extent for some time. This reflects the general evolution, in every local economy, toward having more services supplied locally, and toward having a greater percentage of white-collar employment in almost every industry.

These migratory trends of white-collar employment and of the office industry have been carefully analyzed by the recent New York Metropolitan Region Study in several of its volumes,[30] and in surveys of other large metropolitan areas. The tertiary and quaternary occupations are expanding both in the central business districts of Megalopolitan cities and in the country at large. The same trends noticed earlier for employment in manufacturing, trade, and services are being repeated in the office industry. As a greater percentage of all employment shifts to these occupations, the proportion of the national total achieved by the older centers for these activities must decrease. This relative decline is not necessarily

[30] See especially Hoover and Vernon, *Anatomy of a Metropolis, op. cit.*; Robbins and Terleckyj, *Money Metropolis, op. cit.*; Raymond Vernon, *Metropolis: 1985, op. cit.*; and an unpublished survey of the office industry in the region, prepared for the New York Metropolitan Region Study by Professor Herman E. Krooss, of New York University.

a decline in absolute figures. Peacetime employment in the Federal agencies in Washington and in the office industry of New York City and of Boston has in fact been rising, despite a systematic policy of decentralization applied by the Federal government and by many large corporations.

Figures of employment alone cannot tell the whole story involved in the spreading of offices and white-collar workers all over the urbanized areas. These trends involve a manifold redistribution of tertiary and quaternary activities. Some offices may well move to the periphery of a metropolitan region if they do not require constant contact with the special profession concentrated in the business districts and if they do not require "prestige locations." For some white-collar professions, especially the academic and research personnel, some outlying suburbs or a small town in the axial belt may serve as a "prestige" location at which a special gathering of selected scientific and academic activities creates particularly favorable conditions for work.

Princeton, New Jersey, is such a prestige location for high-brow intellectual and advanced scientific activities. By the early 1940's the university, the Institute for Advanced Study, the research laboratories of the Radio Corporation of America, and the headquarters of the Gallup Poll formed there a small but very selected concentration of such quaternary activities. Since 1945 this town of about 25,000 people has attracted many other research laboratories of large and small firms, many services, and offices of certain sorts (even the headquarters of a publishing house, which moved from New York). In addition it has been chosen as the place of residence of many professors, foundation executives, and distinguished intellectuals who may work in other cities, including New York and Philadelphia (approximately equidistant from Princeton), and even as the official residence of the Governor of New Jersey. Although many of these residents may commute to Manhattan or Philadelphia, where their places of work are located, they find in Princeton a community where their problems can be debated after office hours and on week ends. Like any other "town with a personality," and there are many in Megalopolis, Princeton is unique in many respects; it may well be the prototype of a new category of "brains town." However, some other towns are similar in some ways, having concentrations of intellectuals, corporation executives, or professional people of some other category. In some ways Cambridge, Massachusetts, and New Haven, Connecticut, have such communities, but each of these is surrounded by the much larger community of a substantial industrial center, which Princeton has as yet avoided.

As part of the white-collar revolution white-collar workers are occupy-

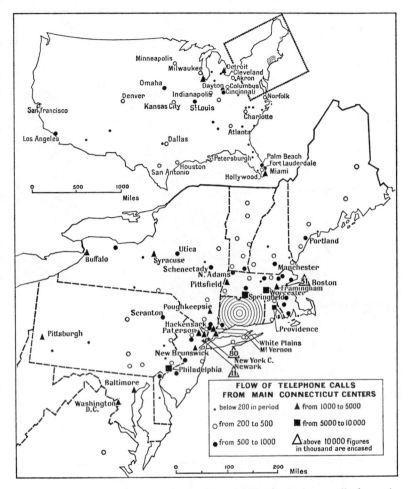

FIG. 187. The map shows the number of telephone calls from the main cities in Connecticut (Hartford, New Haven, and Bridgeport) during a sample period in March 1959, according to data supplied by the Southern New England Telephone Company. See explanation on p. 589 and in footnote 27 on that page.

ing more space, and such expansion has been of several types. Some former "downtown" activities have crawled in an "uptown" direction, leading to the development of "midtown" business districts, already well formed in Manhattan, Boston, and Washington. The "boom in skyscrapers," which pile offices up to great heights, has been especially spectacular in New York but has begun to take shape in the other major cities also

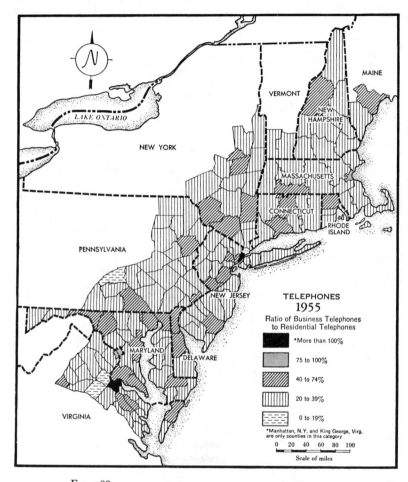

Fig. 188

(for example, Penn Center in Philadelphia, a group of insurance buildings and hotels in Boston, Charles Center in Baltimore). Finally, smaller concentrations have grown up in some specially selected towns of the Megalopolitan axial belt, such as Hartford, New Haven, and Princeton, or in certain favored suburban locations, such as Cambridge, Massachusetts (suburban with respect to Boston) or the Swarthmore-Haverford area in Philadelphia's suburbs.

Ultimately most of Megalopolis' axial belt will be urbanized more densely than it is now, and the white-collar occupations will predominate in the labor force living and working there. The increasing ease of transportation and communications ties this vast and elongated area together better every year. The managerial and policy-making activities that still congregate there do not seem to be as easy to decentralize as production has become. The higher brackets of the communications-oriented activities seem to require three conditions that can be achieved only in a place where there is enough crowding of tertiary and quaternary occupation, these three conditions being: a large enough pool of diversified but competent labor, a large pool of various external services and skills; and easy access for personal contact. The latter condition means that a meeting could be arranged and take place within a day, possibly within half a day. With modern automobile and air transportation and telephone such meetings can easily take place between people residing or working in Washington, New York, Boston, and intermediate places. In a way, Manhattan may be favored by its position at about the midpoint on the Boston-Washington axis.

Megalopolis is just about large enough for the economic, cultural, and political function it is now assuming. If it were to grow more in length, the distances might become bothersome for a smooth functioning of the system. Moreover, its position could deteriorate rapidly if any one of the three above-mentioned conditions should cease to be operative there, particularly in the main hubs of the office industry. Difficulties of physical access to the hubs could precipitate out-migration of functions vital to the region's prosperity. Loss of variety in the labor force and deterioration of the special services, or even of the ever-increasing gamut of these, would seriously jeopardize the whole structure.

The Concentrated Mass-Media Market

Since the office industry is communications-oriented, its essential raw material is *information*. Just as the small counting houses of former times have grown to be huge banks, stock exchanges, and insurance companies, so the exchange of news and the launching of rumors by chatting in the coffee houses and on the strand and the wharves have been replaced by great newspapers, publishing or broadcasting corporations, and advertising companies. Around Times Square and Madison Avenue on the island of Manhattan there is concentrated a *mass-media market* whose impact on American life is quite comparable to that of the money market clustered around Wall Street and Rockefeller Center. Megalopolis considered as a whole appears to enjoy a strongly established dominance over the field of information and over the mass media in the United States, a dominance that does not seem to be seriously threatened despite what some employment figures may be.[31]

In many ways Megalopolis is a center of cultural diffusion in the United States, and with the nation's growing influence in this era the diffusion reaches far beyond the national boundaries. First, this region is the center of the financing and production of "cultural goods": books, magazines, newspapers, radio, television, etc. Second, it is a place in which taste is set and developed for the entire country. Although Megalopolis is sensitive to the development of tastes outside of itself, in order to tap whatever market there may be for its products and directions, it is, nevertheless, a prime mover in the elaboration of such tastes. It draws in all elements, and then these elements are diffused through and from Megalopolis. This process is possible because the region has a high concentration of both the producers and the main consumers of culture in this country.

As a new medium of mass communication comes into the ring to participate in the diffusion of information and culture, the new medium must draw its personnel from the previous media and the professions related to them; that is how the subdivision of labor operates in the white-collar fields. Thus in their early stages radio and television personnel came in large part from other forms of entertainment already centered in Megalopolitan cities. These cities had been the first in America to concentrate in those media that do not reproduce cultural products mechanically but participate directly in the creation of taste and fashion, media such as museums and art galleries, live concerts and the theater, libraries and learned societies. Owing to its early start in these fields, Megalopolis has had for some time an elite with the education and the wealth to appreciate and afford such primary cultural activities. The elite of Boston, New York, Philadelphia, and the smaller places of Connecticut, Rhode Island, Delaware, New Jersey, and Maryland were in the past looked upon as almost alien by the rest of the country. This is not yet forgotten. The success of Turner's theory of the frontier as the mainspring of the real American tradition perhaps owed much to this popular attitude. When modern technology provided new media for the massive diffusion of information and culture, in periods of prosperity the average consumer was usually delighted to acquire the fashions and tastes previously reserved for that same

[31] We are greatly indebted for the following analysis of the mass-media market in Megalopolis to Professor Morroe Berger, of the Department of Sociology, Princeton University, who prepared a substantial unpublished report, supplemented by detailed inquiries on certain aspects of the matter, especially for this study. His main points and conclusions are summarized in the following pages.

elite he had branded strange. The concentration in Megalopolis of these very select consumers in rather large numbers became a major factor in locating the national mass-media market there.

This market encompasses a variety of enterprises adding up to a respectable and fast-growing slice of the national economy, as may be seen from a few examples. In 1946 some 236 magazines in the United States had a total circulation of about 95 million copies; in 1955 there were 268 magazines circulating 166 million copies. In the same decade, 1946–55, the number of daily newspapers in the country dropped from 1,800 to about 1,600, but their total circulation went up from 51 to 56 million copies. By 1955 radio was in virtually every home, "in three-fourths of the 38 million passenger cars on the road and in 10 million public places." Television was in three out of four American homes and within reception range of all but three per cent of all homes.[32] The increase of expenditures in the average American's budget for what may be called "cultural products" has been steady and is likely to continue (Table 22). In good part it has been responsible for the growth and prosperity enjoyed recently by industries such as electronics (which include radio, television, and phonographs) and printing and publishing.[33] For example, it has been estimated that at least $2 billion were spent by Americans in 1950 for reading materials, libraries, and museums.[34] As will be shown in the following pages, Megalopolis is to a marked degree a central market for the rather elusive stuff fed to these media of mass communication, much of which becomes mass culture, although little of it deserves to last.

The book is the oldest and most durable medium for the diffusion of information and culture. In 1957, there were 544 book publishers of all kinds in the United States, and 381 of them had their main offices located in Megalopolis (306 in the New York metropolitan area). The only other area of importance in this respect in the United States is in and around Chicago (58 book publishers in 1957). American agents of foreign publishers, representing 160 of them, are all located in Megalopolis (mainly in New York, with a small number in Philadelphia).[35] In 1954 the Megalopolitan publishers sold about 60 per cent of all the books made and sold in the United States, not counting the sale or distribution of books produced by the Government Printing Office in Washington, D. C., probably the

[32] Figures and quote from Leo Bogart, *The Age of Television*, Frederick Ungar, New York, 1956, pp. 7–8.

[33] See above, Chapter 9, especially p. 491 and Fig. 142B, p. 465.

[34] J. Frederic Dewhurst and associates, *America's Needs and Resources: A New Survey*, Twentieth Century Fund, 1955, pp. 359 and 396.

[35] *Literary Market Place, 1957–1958*, R. R. Bowker, New York, 1957, pp. 77–93.

Table 22

EXPENDITURES FOR SELECTED CULTURAL MEDIA, 1929–50

Cultural Media	Expenditures (Millions)			Increase, 1929–50	
	1929	1941	1950	Amount (Millions)	Per Cent
Book rental and repairs	$ 2	$ 4	$ 9	$ 7	350
Books	307	247	611	304	99
Magazines, newspapers, sheet music	538	619	1,338	800	149
Radios, TV sets, musical instruments (not repairs)	1,012	636	2,848	1,836	181
Movie theaters	720	756	1,247	527	73
Legitimate theater and opera	91	40	90	(−1)	(−1)
Total	$2,670	$2,302	$6,143	$3,473	130

Source: Selected and adapted from J. Frederic Dewhurst and associates, *America's Needs and Resources: A New Survey,* Twentieth Century Fund, 1955, Table 162, p. 368.

largest of all book-publishing institutions in the country.[36] Also, the *Literary Market Place* lists twenty-nine national trade associations in the publishing and allied fields — twenty-five located in New York City, one in Philadelphia, and three outside of Megalopolis.[37] To recruit their personnel the Megalopolitan publishers have been combing the country for talent. Although many new firms have started out in various other regions, "the editors and better salesmen watch these local firms, and the authors and books of real quality that start under their auspices gravitate to New York." [38]

In book selling, too, Megalopolis dominates. New York is the home of the two largest book wholesalers, and the five largest cities in Megalopolis held a majority of all the substantial bookstores in the country, according to a 1947 survey. The retail outlets are so numerous because the Megalopolitan fifth of the nation spends more on book purchasing per capita than

[36] U. S. Bureau of the Census, *U. S. Census of Manufactures: 1954,* Industry Bulletin MC-27A. *Newspapers, Periodicals, Books, and Miscellaneous Publishing,* U. S. Government Printing Office, Washington, D. C., 1957, Table 6G, p. 19.

[37] *Literary Market Place, 1957–1958, op. cit.,* see pp. 77–93 and 113–136. It is also noteworthy that Megalopolis dominates in more spectacular fashion the field of trade books (65 publishers in this region out of 71 in the country) and also that of inexpensive editions. The Boston Society for the Diffusion of Knowledge, founded in 1829, sponsored two years later the American Library of Useful Knowledge, the first series of low-priced informational books in America, and from this early start to the pocket books and the recent paper-back series Megalopolitan publishers have led in the field.

[38] Alfred Harcourt, *Publishing Since 1900,* Second of the R. R. Bowker Memorial Lectures, The New York Public Library, New York, 1937, pp. 11–12.

the national average, despite an excellent local network of public libraries. Book clubs have now become very important distributing channels, and in 1957, out of ninety-eight adult and juvenile book clubs listed by *Literary Market Place*, eighty-six had their headquarters in New York, two in Philadelphia, and ten elsewhere.

Because there is a centralized market for the sale of books in Megalopolis, and mainly in New York, there is also to be found there a concentration of all the major transactions in the sale of, or contracting for, manuscripts. It is, of course, an "over the counter" market, but the transactions take place where the major concentrations of publishers' offices are located. *Literary Market Place* lists some 130 agents of writers for magazines, books, television plays, and radio, 110 of them in New York and four in other Megalopolitan cities. Out of sixteen literary and writers' associations, twelve have headquarters in New York and one is in Washington, D. C. Although the writers themselves may be scattered all over the world, the transactions leading to the publication and distribution of their works are concentrated in this region.[39]

The book "market" has been increasingly concentrated in the New York metropolitan area, though a few important firms have moved out of Manhattan toward the suburbs. Around 1900, it was Boston publishers that "set the standards of taste in literature and publishing practice for the whole country," [40] including New York. Today New York has definitely eclipsed Boston in all these respects and has, in both quantity and quality, a larger share of the field than any one city used to have in the past, a supremacy that Harcourt attributes to typography and design as well as content:

New York became a great Jewish city, a great Italian and German city, and it was inevitable that the cultural heritage and emotional life of these races should find expression. While Boston publishers were bringing out sets of Longfellow and Emerson in new bindings, new publishers sprang up in New York . . . who began to publish translations of contemporary foreign authors and books by young American authors who had broken away from the Victorian point of view. These books found an audience at once all over the country in cultivated groups with foreign backgrounds and among Americans of

[39] Data compiled from Fred B. Millett, *Contemporary American Authors*, Harcourt, Brace & Company, New York, 1940, indicate that, out of 195 American-born authors surveyed, 136 lived at that time in Megalopolis, and 55 of these had been born in the region, which suggests a rather heavy concentration of literary talent born and resident in a small section of the country; even more than were born there had come to live in the region, probably because of its cultural and economic functions.

[40] Harcourt, *Publishing Since 1900*, *op. cit.*, p. 4.

international training. The older New York houses were quick to recognize the new trend, and New York publishing became international and cosmopolitan . . . The new New York publishers brought something colorful and unhackneyed to the jackets, title pages, and typography of their books, and American bookmaking has been greatly improved by their influence.[41]

The publishing of periodicals and newspapers is much less centralized than that of books. Newspapers are the most localized of mass media in publication and in influence, as well as in advertising and content. However, the number of daily newspapers has been decreasing (from 2,042 in 1920 to 1,563 in 1955) in the country as a whole since radio and television came into the field; but the circulation of the daily press as a whole has kept rising, suggesting more concentration than formerly. Megalopolis itself has a good many dailies, but its main cities have papers of general regional influence (Fig. 189), and a few of its newspapers and associated institutions have considerable influence over the whole United States and beyond.

The great *news-gathering agencies* located in New York City supply much of their materials to every daily and to most magazines in America. The Associated Press is the leading one of these agencies; from Manhattan, it serves more than 100 of its own regional bureaus located in various cities and it also serves its members (i.e., newspapers, magazines, broadcasting stations, and foreign news agencies that subscribe to the service) directly in their news rooms. The Associated Press, begun as a monopoly in 1848, was set up by the morning newspapers in New York City as a means of sharing the cost of telegraphing news from European papers brought to North Atlantic ports by ship. These papers also pooled their news coverage from Washington and other eastern cities, and the A.P. sold all this news to newspapers outside New York, a clientele that developed rapidly as the telegraph lines were extended. By 1900 outside pressure forced the A.P. to reorganize itself as a cooperative group. It had an enormous influence on the whole American press. Not only did the A.P. central office edit the news, but most newspapers, tempted by the way of least effort, adopted the style, presentation, and opinions of the A.P. "The result was a standardization of content going beyond the beneficial and needed cooperative coverage of significant non-local news." [42] Now the A.P. has some competition from another huge news association, the United Press, the main offices of which are in New York and Washington.

[41] *Ibid.*, pp. 5–6.
[42] Edwin Emery and Henry Ladd Smith, *The Press and America*, Prentice-Hall, New York, 1954, p. 542. See also Oswald Garrison Villard, *The Disappearing Daily*, Alfred A. Knopf, New York, 1944.

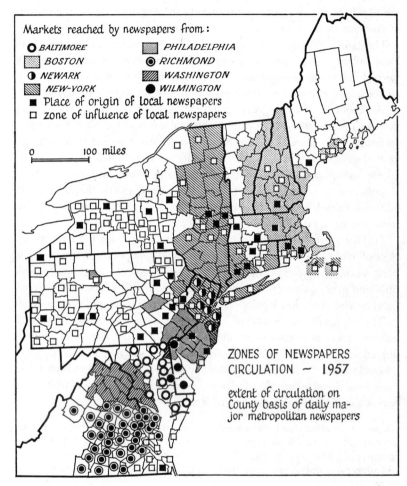

Markets reached by newspapers from:

○ BALTIMORE   ▨ PHILADELPHIA
▦ BOSTON   ◉ RICHMOND
◑ NEWARK   ▨ WASHINGTON
▧ NEW-YORK   ● WILMINGTON
■ Place of origin of local newspapers
□ zone of influence of local newspapers

0 ——— 100 miles

ZONES OF NEWSPAPERS
CIRCULATION – 1957

extent of circulation on
County basis of daily ma-
jor metropolitan newspapers

FIG. 189

A somewhat more diversified but still standardizing and centralizing influence is exerted by the newspaper feature syndicates. *Ayer's Directory* [43]
lists 151 newspaper features, pictures, and news sources, 104 of them in
Megalopolis (78 in New York City). These syndicates enable local and
even rural newspapers to compete to a reasonable degree with the large-
city press but on the condition of diffusing the material the large-city
agencies, and mainly the Megalopolitan agencies, are feeding them. While

[43] *N. W. Ayer and Son's Directory of Newspapers and Periodicals: 1957* (annual),
Philadelphia.

the numbers of newspapers seem to indicate decentralization, the sources of their information remain very centralized.

The main newspapers of Megalopolis are also widely read by editors of local dailies. A poll, specially conducted by this study in 1957 among editors of newspapers in medium-sized cities in thirty-six states outside Megalopolis, brought answers from eighty-six editors, eighty of whom (i.e., 93 per cent) said they regularly follow at least one newspaper from a city in Megalopolis. Only *one* of these eighty did *not* read the New York press, and nineteen followed *only* the New York papers. Some of those who answered gave several reasons for following the Megalopolitan press: its intrinsic importance because of the political and economic power of Megalopolis itself; its wide coverage of national and international news; its editorials on public affairs. It is clear that the daily press in Megalopolis has some influence beyond its own readership.

This daily press certainly influences also the magazines, the *editorial offices* of which are heavily concentrated in Megalopolis and especially in New York. In 1957 *Ayer's Directory* [44] listed some 283 magazines of cultural and general interest. Of these 177 had editorial offices in New York City, 35 elsewhere in Megalopolis, and only 71 (i.e., 26 per cent) outside it. The degree of domination of New York City would be even greater if only the more important magazines, in terms of circulation or of cultural influence, were considered. The main reasons for locating all these editorial offices in New York seem to be the abundance of editorial and art talent there and the presence of the large advertising agencies, for advertising revenue is the key to magazine finance.

Costs, competition and the necessity of speedy distribution directly and indirectly influenced the dispersal of operations in magazine publishing. They encouraged publishers to select New York as headquarters for their editorial and advertising operations, some outlying city as their printing and distribution point.
. . . even magazine publishers who began elsewhere, like the Fawcetts of Minneapolis, David A. Smart of Chicago, and Gardner Cowles, Jr., of Des Moines, moved their editorial and advertising offices to New York. . . .
. . . In September, 1925, Hadden and Luce moved the offices of Time, Inc. from New York . . . to Cleveland, Ohio, where rent and clerical help were cheaper. But they returned to New York in August, 1927, for two reasons. First, they missed the supply of adventuresome young intellectuals whom they could hire for comparatively small salaries in New York. Second they missed up-to-date copies of the *New York Times*, indispensable to their coverage of the news. [45]

[44] *Ibid.*
[45] Theodore Peterson, *Magazines in the Twentieth Century*, University of Illinois Press, Urbana, Ill., 1956, pp. 99 and 223.

In fact, throughout the whole history of the United States, Boston and Philadelphia are the only cities besides New York that have had lasting roles as important centers for magazine publication. In recent years Chicago has been pressing hard for third place; but the general predominance of Megalopolis seems unchallenged today.[46]

The type of audience that has for some time been characteristic of this region, and that has helped develop and retain here the central mass-media market, may in a way be evaluated by examining the circulation of magazines. Table 23 shows the circulation of ten leading magazines, of different types of interest, in seven states entirely or partly within Megalopolis and in the District of Columbia, and compares them with the national circulation. The total circulation of the ten magazines in 1956 amounted to 33,286,000 copies, of which 27 per cent was in the area enumerated, a proportion virtually equal to these states' proportion in the country's total population. Individually, however, the magazines have varying proportions of their total circulation in the Northeastern urbanized seaboard. Some of them are bought in disproportionately greater numbers in Megalopolitan states: this is the case for *Esquire, Holiday, Life, The New Yorker,* and *Time,* all magazines obviously catering to more metropolitan and cosmopolitan tastes. Some other magazines are bought in disproportionately lesser numbers in Megalopolis: for example, *Grit* and *True Story,* which appeal to rural areas and to less educated groups. Finally, some magazines are bought in seven states and the District in roughly the same proportion as the distribution of population would suggest. This is the case for *Better Homes and Gardens, Reader's Digest,* and *Saturday Evening Post,* apparently the category of magazines reaching a large proportion of all types of groups all over the country. It seems significant that, among the ten magazines considered, the one with the highest concentration of circulation in the Northeastern seaboard (44 per cent) is *The New Yorker,* which addresses itself to a metropolitan public. Its prospectus stated:

The *New Yorker* will be a reflection in word and picture of metropolitan life. . . . the *New Yorker* will be the magazine which is not edited for the old lady in Dubuque. It will not be concerned in what she is thinking about. This is not meant in disrespect, but the *New Yorker* is a magazine avowedly published for a metropolitan audience and thereby will escape an influence which hampers most national publications. It expects a considerable national circulation, but this will come from persons who have a metropolitan interest.[47]

[46] For an excellent history of the magazine field, see Frank Luther Mott, *A History of American Magazines,* Vol. I, D. Appleton & Century, New York, 1930, Vols. II to IV, Harvard University Press, Cambridge, Mass., 1938–1957. The four volumes available cover the period 1741 to 1905.

[47] Quoted in Peterson, *Magazines in the Twentieth Century, op. cit.,* p. 236.

Table 23

CIRCULATION OF TEN "CONSUMER" MAGAZINES IN SOME MEGALOPOLITAN STATES, DECEMBER 31, 1956[a]

(In Thousands)

Magazine	National Total	New York	New Jersey	Massa- chusetts	Connec- ticut	Pennsyl- vania	Dela- ware	Rhode Island	District of Columbia	Regional Total	Regional Per Cent of National Total
Better Homes	4,300	382	161	119	76	280	13	18	26	1,065	25
Esquire	790	96	31	20	11	52	3	4	6	233	28
Grit	816	24	2	3	2	140	0.5	0.5	0.1	172	21
Holiday	870	90	31	35	16	53	3	5	9	242	28
Life	5,700	736	255	237	122	387	20	35	54	1,846	32
New Yorker	410	100	16	20	13	21	1	2	9	182	44
Reader's Digest	10,700	1,048	361	363	163	622	26	49	71	2,703	25
Sat. Ev. Post	5,000	439	169	190	88	311	19	29	28	1,273	25
Time	2,000	234	70	88	45	130	8	12	26	611	31
True Story	2,700	205	84	66	32	189	8	10	10	604	22

Source: Selected from Standard Rate and Data Service, *Consumer Magazine and Farm Publication Rates and Data,* Vol. 39, No. 6, June 27, 1957, pp. 24–31.

[a] Certified by Audit Bureau of Circulation.

This expectation has proved correct as metropolitanization has gained through the United States. In 1960 it was announced that the New Yorker had consolidated into one both its New York and its out-of-town editions. This example supports the trend, already observed many times, for new fashions to be started in Megalopolis and then to be adopted rather nationally in due time.

Wholesale distribution of magazines to newsstands and other retailers has also been directed from Megalopolis. In 1952 the American News Company (founded in New York for such wholesaling in 1864) and its affiliate, Union News, were charged with monopoly in this activity. The Department of Justice's action led to reorganization in 1955–57. There are today five other big distributors, all centered in Megalopolis.

Although there are some very large companies in magazine publishing, most of the existing magazines are relatively small businesses. A publisher can get articles from free-lance writers, advertisements are prepared by the advertising agencies, wholesalers can distribute copies to the newsstands, and printing can be done in a regular printing establishment. With enough contracts securing all such adequate servicing, the publisher does not need a large staff, just as a Megalopolitan farmer does not need much land any more. As a result, magazine publication has been endowed in recent years with great fluidity, but it is all the more important to be located at a place where all the necessary services are readily available, especially insofar as information and advertising are concerned. As Peterson put it: "Advertising converted the magazine publisher from a dealer in reading matter into a dealer in consumer groups as well." [48] The publishers understood quite some time ago that a magazine could sell for much less than its cost of production and bring profits if its circulation could attract a large enough volume of advertising. When they compete for a wider audience, the magazines (and the newspapers as well, in most cases) are fighting in fact for more advertising revenue. And the latter is concentrated in the accounts of a few magazines. "In 1955 the gross revenues of just three publishers — Crowell-Collier, Curtis, and Time, Inc. – amounted to almost half of the total sum spent on national advertising in consumer magazines." [49] The volume of money involved may be gauged from the fact that in 1956 the ten important magazines whose circulation was analyzed in Table 23 collected a total of $342 million in advertising revenue. [50]

Advertising, handling such huge sums of money, binds together the financial community and the mass-media market. In certain respects it be-

[48] Ibid., p. 64.
[49] Ibid., p. 79.
[50] Advertising Age, Vol. 28, No. 3, January 24, 1957, p. 54.

longs to both, but it is more closely related to the field of mass media, without which there could hardly be any large-scale publicity. In the economics of radio and television, and even of music and art, advertising's influence is as great as, and perhaps greater than, it is in the economics of the press. It has also its own ways of diffusion, independent from any other medium, such as billboards along the highways, posters on walls, in subways, buses, and railroad cars, and direct mail.

In 1956 advertising distributed through the various mass media brought a total of $8,026 million, about 2 per cent of the gross national product. The agencies directing this flow of capital are heavily concentrated in Megalopolis. To list the names of advertising agencies in 1957 the *Standard Advertising Register* [51] required 99 columns, of which 25.5 columns gave only agencies in New York City (it alone had 18 columns), Boston, Philadelphia, and Washington, D. C. The only other large clusters of advertising agencies are in Chicago, Detroit, and Los Angeles–Hollywood. Of the ten agencies with the highest amount of domestic billing in 1956, seven were located in New York City, two in Chicago, and one in Philadelphia. Of thirty-four agencies having billings of $25 million or more that year, nineteen had headquarters in New York City, five in Detroit, four in Chicago, one each in Philadelphia, Cleveland, St. Louis, and Minneapolis. The New York metropolitan region has accounted for more than 40 per cent of all receipts and employment by advertising agencies in recent years. The firms concentrated in Manhattan have been setting the general tone and style of the whole advertising industry, which is commonly referred to as "Madison Avenue" (some of the most important agencies are not on that avenue, but they are not far away from its midtown section).

How strongly advertising, either in general or in its Megalopolitan concentration in particular, influences national taste and "creates fashions" is an involved and debatable question. There is little doubt, however, that it has some influence on consumers as well as distributors, and that it has a considerable role in spreading fashions whether it originates them or not. If such had not been the demonstrated case, advertising would not have been given its present share in the American economy. Whether the achievements and the role of advertising have been a good or bad influence on the nation, and especially on its mass media, is another matter of considerable moral portent but beyond the immediate purposes of this rapid review of the mass-media market. The center of advertising was quite naturally located in the heart of that market and within the commercial or-

[51] In its *Agency List*, No. 121, New York, May 1957.

ganization of the hinge. This industry specializes in an old endeavor of traders, described in Montesquieu's aphorism: "It is in the nature of commerce to make the superfluous useful, and the useful necessary."

Publicity and public relations are important to movie stars and to new automobile models in similar fashion. The former are celebrated because they are displayed as celebrities; the latter become known to and attract the interest of the potential customer once they are displayed and celebrated enough for him to wonder whether he should get one. Advertising (and public relations, which in the self-refining division of labor becomes a new occupational group or industry) must therefore procure more sales and profits for the artist and for the manufacturer. Mass media are used for this end, and according to reasonable estimates advertising revenue supplies the following percentages of their total receipts: about 70 for newspapers, 60 for magazines, and 90 for television stations. These figures alone indicate a considerable influence on the mass media.

Radio and *television* thus appear especially dependent on their advertising contracts. They are also dependent on a good supply of information and of "talent." It is in Megalopolis and especially in New York City, the major "markets" for these items, that the radio and TV networks may expect the greatest concentration of them to be found. The extent of the radio and television industry in the United States and its impact on the American way of life hardly need to be elaborated upon. The domination of Megalopolis in this field is certain, but it cannot be measured by a few simple figures. For example, the number of stations means little, even less than does the number of daily newspapers, because a whole series of technological and legal factors requires stations to be scattered widely through the territory they serve. In the middle 1950's Megalopolitan cities had only 131 AM, FM, and TV stations, a very small proportion of the 4,352 authorized by the Federal Communications Commission in the entire country. *Megalopolitan influence in radio and television is exercised in other ways: through the networks, the advertising business, and the concentration in the development and promotion of radio and TV talent.*

For the scattered radio and television stations, cooperation and centralization are provided by the "networks," [52] which constitute the essential

[52] Giraud Chester and Garnet R. Garrison, *Television and Radio*, 2nd ed., Appleton-Century-Crofts, New York, 1956; also U. S. House of Representatives Committee on the Judiciary, 85th Cong., 1st sess., *The Television Broadcasting Industry, Report of the Antitrust Subcommittee*, March 13, 1957, and U. S. Senate, Committee on Interstate and Foreign Commerce, 85th Cong., 1st sess., Staff report, Committee Print No. 2, *The Television Inquiry: Television Network Practices*, June 27, 1957, Washington, D. C., 1957.

working framework of the industry, with advertising supplying most of its revenue. The main function of the networks is to make possible the broadcasting of programs to all parts of the country at the same time. Whether these programs be live or recorded and filmed, they are of a quality and variety that an individual station could not obtain with its own resources only. Moreover, the scattering of many stations in various parts of the country, each serving its own localized audience, in its turn improves the programs, for the wider the audience, the easier it is to secure a better advertising contract to sponsor a program. Congressional investigations have demonstrated that a network affiliation is virtually indispensable to the success of a television station. By 1957, all but 38 of the nation's 455 commercial television stations had some kind of network affiliation, and the average station devoted about half of its time on the air to network programs.[53]

In the late 1950's three such national television networks were in operation: The Columbia Broadcasting System (CBS), the National Broadcasting System (NBC), and the American Broadcasting Company–Paramount Theaters, Inc. (ABC). Each of these has about 200 affiliated television stations and a similar number of radio stations. The control the networks may wield *de facto* over the radio and television industry is much greater than any influence that advertisers or news agencies can exert on the other mass media. For all three networks the headquarters are in Megalopolis, and although their functioning is regulated by Federal agencies in Washington, D. C., it is largely directed from Manhattan.

As one adds together the influences of Megalopolitan networks and advertising on radio and television, this region's domination of the field appears irresistible. In addition, the National Association of Radio and Television Broadcasters, the main channel of self-regulation of the broadcasting industry, is located in Washington, D. C., and of the "rating services," which determine by audience research the degree of popularity enjoyed by the various programs, four are in New York City and one is in Washington. (The only other one is in Chicago.)

Finally, Megalopolis influences broadcasting through its impact on the development and exploitation of entertaining talent. The "market of talent" in the performing arts and in literature must, of course, be closely linked to the mass-media market, nowadays the essential customer of such talent. Here again one medium has borrowed from another that had developed previously. "By and large, both television and radio in the past have depended on the legitimate theater, the music hall, and the night clubs to provide them with performers and program material." [54] More recently, however, television has found it has its own requirements and has begun developing its own performers and writers. Recently some television hits have been transferred to the legitimate theater, adding to the interconnections between these industries, and there are instances in which NBC and CBS have participated in theatrical ventures on Broadway. The possibility of monopolistic practices in the broadcasting industry has been hinted at in Congressional hearings, which have also noticed the networks' heavy influence in the creation of talent used in broadcasting. The only center in the country seriously competing with New York in the production of talent and of TV programs is Hollywood. However, the products of Hollywood need to be adopted by New York audiences to gain national success, while New York productions do not need Hollywood's approval. In fact, the only important mass medium not centered in New York is the motion picture industry, and its financing is directed from New York. [55]

The concentration of talent in Megalopolis results partly from the past history of the region, which had the first clustering of cities, with their universities, theaters, and other cultural centers, and which had an educated and wealthy elite that could afford and use all of these facilities. However, while other more impersonal businesses have been slowly decentralized as they have pursued the customer, in the case of the performing arts the major "market," the audiences that pass the decisive judgments, has remained in this region. People still come from all over the country to see the plays on Broadway and attend the other major performances of the season, mainly in Manhattan. Broadway attracts talent from outside and then radiates it back to the outside. If the number of theatrical productions in New York has somewhat declined, as well as attendance at the city's theaters, this has been largely the result of more out-of-town travelling by shows that have appeared in New York or that are being tried out before being brought to Broadway. In part, of course, the decrease in New York theater business reflects the competition of the movies and television, and the rising costs of producing shows in Megalopolis.

American music and ballet, too, had their early development in Megalopolis, and are still largely dominated by it. Boston was the birthplace of symphonic music in the United States, for it organized a Philharmonic Society in 1810. Ten years later the Music Fund Society of Philadelphia gave the first performance in America of a Beethoven symphony. The Moravians had brought an even older musical tradition to Bethlehem, Pennsyl-

[54] Chester and Garrison, *Television and Radio, op. cit.,* p. 13.
[55] "Movies: End of an Era," *Fortune,* Vol. 39, April 1949, pp. 101–146.

vania. Hundreds of foreign musicians came to America in the wake of the 1848 revolutions in Europe, many of them settling in Boston and New York. Thus for more than a century the Megalopolitan cities have been major centers of musical performance and education. Such schools as the Julliard School of Music in New York, the Curtis Institute in Philadelphia, and conservatories in Baltimore and Boston enjoy worldwide reputations. Carnegie Hall in New York has become a consecrated shrine of symphonic music.

Today Megalopolis influences the musical scene through various other means also, such as publishers and licensers (i.e., the owners of copyrights), broadcasters and record companies, musical clubs, and the concentration of composers, performers, and their various agents. Many non-Megalopolitan influences have, of course, gone into the making of such popular American music as cowboy music, hillbilly music, Dixieland jazz, and so forth, but as Theodore Dreiser commented in 1898:

In New York the work of booming the song is followed with the most careful attention, for it is well known among music publishers that if a song can be made popular around New York City, it is sure to be popular throughout the country.[56]

The hearings conducted in 1956 by the Anti-trust Subcommittee of the House Committee on the Judiciary gave new examples of the lasting truth of this overriding influence of New York in the manipulation of taste and in the selection of the music to be played over broadcasting facilities. Such manipulation does not occur with "popular music" only, but with serious music as well. The choice of music offered on the market throughout the nation is largely determined by the broadcasting networks, which are closely associated with the leading record companies.

Since World War II there has been an extraordinary increase in the number of record companies, and by 1950 a musical guide listed 699, of which 315 (including the more important ones) were in Megalopolis.[57] The organization of distributors of music is, perhaps, a less centralized force than is the labor union of performers. The American Federation of Musicians, presided over by James Petrillo and with headquarters in New York City, is one of the most powerful agencies in the entire field of music, exerting influence over all purveyors of music in the country. In 1957

[56] Theodore Dreiser, in an article in the *Metropolitan Magazine,* November 1898, quoted by Isaac Goldberg, *Tin Pan Alley,* John Day, New York, 1930, p. 200.

[57] Calculated from *The International Who Is Who in Music* (Fifth, Mid-Century Edition), Who's Who in Music, Inc., New York, 1950, pp. 539–547. On "music economics" see also Roger Sessions, *Reflections on the Musical Life in the United States,* Merlin Press, New York, n.d., circa 1953, pp. 12–14 and 54–59.

this union had 700 locals with nearly 260,000 members (though only one third of the membership were estimated to earn more than half of their incomes by playing music). Their main problem has been the widespread use of mechanical recording devices, which reduce the number of opportunities for musicians to play. The American Society of Composers, Authors and Publishers (ASCAP), located in New York, is the main collector of performance fees and controls most of the copyrights on music in the United States. Its chief competitor is Broadcast Music, Inc., organized by the broadcasting networks.

Because of the concentration of the mass-media market in Megalopolis, a sizable profession of agents has developed there who act as personal representatives or publicity agents for artists. These agents deal with managers and booking agents of performers. In 1955, in an anti-trust action, the Federal government charged that two management agencies, both located in New York City, acting as concert bureaus, together accounted for 80 per cent of all bookings of musical artists and had no real competitors. They were charged also with allocating among themselves the various locations throughout the country where they had set up audience associations.[58] The natural desire of audiences outside Megalopolis to hear the successful performers from the great Megalopolitan centers, especially those consecrated by success in New York, is exploited and cultivated by the publicity agents of the performers and by the concert bureaus. Thus success in New York is made compelling both for the artists and for audiences throughout the nation. In fact, the audiences themselves are influenced by subsidiaries of the major booking agencies to a much greater degree than they even suspect. In 1952 the two main audience-group agencies controlled audiences in 1,900 American communities.[59] Thus the talent market, even in music, has its brokerage houses, as well organized as and more concentrated than the brokers on the securities and money markets. It has been observed that "nowadays the American public spends more on professional music than on professional baseball,"[60] and the substantial sums of money handled by the music market should increase rapidly in the 1960's, for there will be more people with more leisure and a higher level of education.

The tableau of the mass-media market in Megalopolis and of its influ-

[58] *The New York Times*, October 21, 1955, p. 29; and December 25, 1955, Sec. 2, p. 9.

[59] Cecil Smith, *Worlds of Music*, Lippincott, Philadelphia, 1952. The two agencies are the Columbia Artists Management and the National Concert and Artists Corporation. In 1957, S. Hurok started a third booking agency.

[60] *Ibid.*, p. 17.

ence on the nation's taste and culture would hardly be complete without some reference to the role the region plays in the American art world. In recent decades the growth in popularity of traditional and modern art has been phenomenal throughout the nation. It may be illustrated by the attendance at two retrospective exhibitions of the work of Van Gogh. The first, organized by the Museum of Modern Art in New York in the mid-1930's, was shown in several American cities to a total of 900,000 people; the second, held twenty years later by the Metropolitan Museum of Art, travelled through the whole country and attracted several million viewers. The number and frequency of such exhibitions has been constantly increasing, the whole movement being directed by the major museums, the private galleries, and occasionally the art dealers. Although the first museum in America was established in Charleston, South Carolina, in 1773, the Megalopolitan cities soon took over leadership in the field and kept it. Because for a long time they have had many millionaires (see above, p. 58), famous collections have been developed in these cities, most of them going to local museums. To serve the collectors and the museums, the art dealers have congregated here too, especially in Manhattan. Museums, private galleries, and art exhibits help to form, modify, and diffuse the fashions of taste. Thus the International Exhibition of Modern Art, held in 1913 at the 69th Regiment Armory in New York, resulted in dividing the republic of taste into two major parties: the "modern" party and the "traditional" party.[61]

Something similar occurred for a new period in art when the Guggenheim Museum opened in 1959 on Fifth Avenue. In 1960, of the sixteen more important art museums in America, twelve are located in Megalopolis (six in New York alone).

Most museum directors are trained at Harvard, Princeton, and New York University. There are sixteen national organizations of practicing artists, all of them with headquarters in New York. In an exhaustive list of various organizations, museums, associations, and clubs dealing with art, New York City occupies about twenty-two pages of names, Washington, D. C., six pages, Philadelphia five, Boston three and a half, Baltimore three, and New Haven two pages. Non-Megalopolitan centers are left far behind, for Chicago takes only three pages, as does Detroit, while San Francisco and Los Angeles occupy two pages each.[62] Of twelve periodicals

[61] Russell Lynes, *The Tastemakers*, Harper and Brothers, New York, 1954.
[62] American Federation of Arts, *American Art Directory*, 1955, Vol. 39, edited by Dorothy B. Gilbert, R. R. Bowker, New York, 1955, pp. 19-33.

dealing especially with art, ten are published in New York, one in Detroit and one in Cleveland.

Much the same picture is obtained as we turn to the commercial dealers in art and to the auctioneers. The domination of Megalopolis and especially of New York City is very strong. There are in New York alone about 180 art galleries, which hold at least 1,500 exhibitions annually. While there are no statistics available about the residences of the artists, it seems certain that most of the better known cluster around Megalopolis, or come to visit there regularly, largely because the market is there, and also because of all the museums, exhibitions, educational institutions, and other attractions, which maintain in the world of art an intense activity that produces inspiration. In this respect New York is probably second only to Paris at the present time.

The mass-media market is a complicated, manifold organization, fairly interdependent, however, for advertising, the press, and even industrial design constantly use artists or draw some inspiration from the success of certain styles or formulas that originated in painting, in literature, or in the political and social news. The mass media have become part of both national culture and industrial organization. As they develop, the ranks of white-collar employment swell. And this field may be one of those least open to decentralization because of the entangled interdependence of its various organizations, and because it needs so special a pool of skills that it could not expect to find everywhere.

Education, Research, and the Labor Force

While the mass-media market has created within itself a "talent development" division, the very functioning of its various branches and of the industries linked with it require numerous competent personnel. The financial community and the large corporations' headquarters face the same problem. Their personnel can be gathered from all over the country and beyond. In the routine of daily recruitment, however, all the various offices in Megalopolis looking for competent white-collar workers cannot be scouting the whole continent. Instead, they expect to find on the spot a good number of adequate applicants among whom to choose for the jobs they may offer. Undoubtedly this matter of personnel has been a decisive factor in the mushrooming office industry in Megalopolis, and in New York City especially.

All we have said about the process by which tertiary and quaternary employment has been growing recently indicates an increasing need for specialized, well-trained labor of diverse kinds and at various levels of pay and responsibility. The trend points to an increasing need for more education and more research, to produce a competent enough labor force and to make the daily decisions with an adequate knowledge of a fast-changing world and technology. Megalopolis has been for some time better equipped than any other region in the United States to meet this challenge.

Because of its early start the Northeastern seaboard has more colleges, more institutions of advanced learning, more libraries, general and specialized, and more laboratories than any other region, at least insofar as density of these establishments goes. It is hardly necessary to remind the reader of the considerable influence exerted on American education by the older universities of the Northeast, especially Harvard, Yale, and Princeton, and by at least two younger universities, Johns Hopkins and the Massachusetts Institute of Technology. The number of colleges and graduate schools and their enrollments have, of course, expanded with population in all parts of the country, but many Megalopolitan educational institutions still play a great national role because of their selective recruitment of a student body drawn from all parts of the country; because of the standing, quality, and diversity of their faculty; and because of the attention paid to their policies and curricula by educators all over America.

Around the better universities and colleges entire centers of learning and research have grown, constellations of establishments that are officially independent of the university but that in practice are attached by the local environment to a major campus. Such has been the case not only in Princeton, which we have already singled out, but also in Cambridge, in New Haven, and even in New York and Philadelphia. Although in these enormous cities the academic activities may appear to be only a small detail, they do in fact play an essential part in the industrial and commercial life of even the larger metropolis, a part that cannot be measured quantitatively but that is of enormous help and significance to many policy makers, data seekers, and personnel divisions at work in the downtown or midtown skyscrapers. Many times an executive from these offices in Manhattan needs the advice of some specialist whose office is located on the campus of Columbia or Rutgers, Fordham or Yale, Princeton or M.I.T.

All the education in Megalopolis and the research carried on would be impossible without resources of well-supplied and numerous libraries, and by any standard Megalopolis has the largest concentration of libraries in the world.

In terms of the total number of volumes in all the libraries of a city, Washington, D. C., leads all American cities, with 25.4 million volumes in

1955. It is followed by New York City and the Boston-Cambridge area (with 24.7 and 18.3 million volumes respectively in 1955). Of the twenty leading library centers in America, each with more than 3.5 million volumes in its libraries in 1955, Megalopolis contained ten.[63]

Megalopolis has also the largest individual libraries. In 1956 the Library of Congress, in Washington, D. C., the New York Public Library, the Harvard University Library, and the Yale University Library were the only four in America to hold over four million volumes each, and only two libraries in Europe belonged in the same "size" (the Bibliothèque Nationale in Paris and the British Museum in London). All Megalopolitan libraries together now have more than 100 million volumes, which is about one third of the holdings of all libraries in the United States. No other region of the world of comparable area or population has as many books (see above, p. 65). Especially important is the fact that the largest *special libraries* in a great variety of fields are concentrated in Megalopolis, particularly in New York City and Washington, D. C., but also in several much smaller cities in the region. Special libraries are valuable chiefly for research and specialized reference. They are rapidly becoming an indispensable tool for the kind of work large modern industrial and financial concerns pursue.[64]

Libraries are a basic resource for education and research at any level. However, they cannot replace the laboratory. It is almost impossible to collect any simple quantitative data about laboratories that would be meaningful, for the term includes too many diverse establishments. Universities have laboratories for both teaching and original research on their campuses. Industrial corporations have laboratories to test the materials they use and to conduct the research needed to improve and modify the prod-

[63] The seven besides the enumerated three largest were Philadelphia (7.8 million volumes), Newark, New Jersey (6 million), New Haven (5.3 million), Baltimore (4.9 million), Princeton (4 million), the Providence–Fall River–New Bedford area (3.6 million), and Hartford (3.6 million). Data from Robert R. Downs, "Distribution of American Library Resources," in *College and Research Libraries*, May 1957, pp. 183–189 and 235–237.

[64] Thus, according to the *New York State Commerce Review*, Vol. 13, No. 3, March 1959, pp. 9–10, the New York metropolitan area had more than 600 special libraries in 1956, most of them in Manhattan. Among these, the Federal Reserve Bank of New York had 50,000 volumes and pamphlets and 248 file drawers; near by the First National City Bank had 40,000 volumes and classified pamphlets and 108 vertical file drawers; and the Chase Manhattan Bank had a collection of 27,000 volumes and 240 vertical file drawers of data. The Metropolitan Life Insurance Company had 109,000 volumes and pamphlets. The library of the Engineering Societies had 170,000 volumes and received 1,400 engineering periodicals. The library of the American Geographical Society held 145,000 volumes and a collection of 275,000 maps.

ucts, services, and patents they supply to their customers. Hospitals have laboratories too, as do drug stores. Megalopolis has a great many laboratories of all kinds and sizes, from great scientific institutions like the Bell Telephone Laboratories and the R.C.A. research center in New Jersey to a great many small private testing shops scattered in every city of more than 50,000 people.

A significant fact for the role of Megalopolis in directing education and research throughout the country is the concentration there, and once more in New York City, of many foundations. In 1955, of a total of 4,164 foundations in the United States with total assets of $4.5 billion, New York City alone was the location of 27 per cent of all foundations, holding 56 per cent of all foundation assets. At that time seven foundations reported assets of $100 million or more, five of them being in New York City, one in Philadelphia, and one outside of Megalopolis, in Battle Creek, Michigan.[65] One of the larger, the Ford Foundation, after trying to operate out of California, gave up the attempt and came to Manhattan. To the world of private foundations one should add the larger expenditures for research decided upon in Washington, D. C., by the Office of Naval Research, some other offices in the U. S. Department of Defense, and in other Federal agencies (such as the Department of Agriculture and the Bureau of Mines). Not all the money paid out for research and education by Megalopolitan bureaus, public or private, is put to work in Megalopolis — in fact, it may be spent all over the country and around the globe — but the sources of these means and the central clearing houses of the ideas and projects supported by them are concentrated in this region.

Education in America has long been influenced by such Megalopolitan establishments as Columbia University's Teachers College (in New York) and the National Education Association, first organized in 1857 in Philadelphia and now having its headquarters in Washington, D. C. The N.E.A. has had considerable influence in this country upon teachers' attitudes and especially upon school administrators, who themselves exercise considerable power in the school system. Finally, the market of textbooks is also largely dominated by publishers located in Megalopolis.

Many decisions of importance to the whole nation are made in the offices of such establishments, and the people who staff them, living and working in Megalopolis, cannot fail to influence the education provided in their communities. Many of the office workers and an even higher proportion of the "executives" have come to Megalopolis (chiefly to New York

[65] Wilmer Shields Rich, *American Foundations and Their Fields,* 7th ed., American Foundations Information Service, New York, 1955.

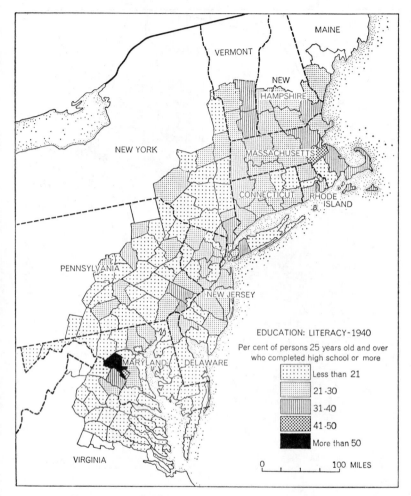

FIG. 190

and Washington) after their education was completed, but they help to raise the average level of education of the population. Four maps (Figs. 190 to 193), based on the Censuses of 1940 and 1950, show on a county basis the educational status of the adult population. In 1940 only a few counties, mainly suburban, had, among their population twenty-five years old and over, more than 30 per cent who had completed high school or more (Fig. 190). The more striking concentrations of better trained persons were in and around Washington, D. C., and also, though to a lesser degree, around Boston. By 1950 a spectacular change had taken place

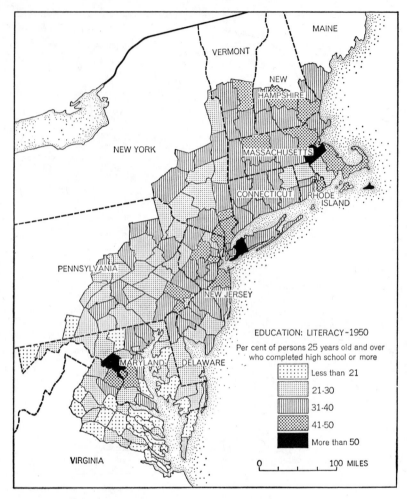

EDUCATION: LITERACY-1950

Per cent of persons 25 years old and over
who completed high school or more

- Less than 21
- 21-30
- 31-40
- 41-50
- More than 50

0   100 MILES

FIG. 191

(Fig. 191). The metropolitan areas of Washington and Boston still led, but New York's suburbia had progressed greatly, as had the suburban counties around Philadelphia and Baltimore also. In most of Megalopolis' axial belt more than 30 per cent, and in the suburban rings of the major cities more than 40 per cent, of the adults had completed high school or more, which is essentially the literacy requirement for modern employment. At the same time the great cities and some of their suburbs showed also the highest proportions (more than 12 per cent) of adults having completed fewer than five grades (Fig. 192). This latter map, which may be called one of "illiteracy" in 1950, in contrast to the map of "literacy," demonstrates how Megalopolitan cities attract both extremes in American society, and how certain suburban counties have attracted only the "upper brackets" and have avoided the less educated strata, which often correspond to the recently arrived "newcomers," mainly Negroes and Puerto Ricans. The contrast between most of Megalopolis and Virginia, beyond Washington's suburbs, appears striking on these maps and helps convince us that Megalopolis should not as yet be extended farther south.

Despite the existence of these contrasts in the levels of education in the major metropolitan areas, the map of the median number of school years for persons twenty-five years of age and older (Fig. 193) sums up the situation in 1950 by showing that the metropolitan areas were better educated, but chiefly owing to residents of the outer ring, many of whom commuted to the central city's business district to work.

All these trends were accentuated in the 1950's. The Census for 1960 will show a still better educated population, at least insofar as years of schooling are concerned. Better education has usually come with higher income (compare Fig. 191 with Fig. 220, p. 717), or vice versa; the two have been closely related, whether one or the other came first, and the mass of the people knows it well. Thus the prosperity of the 1950's should have helped the trend. More important, however, has been the growing realization that *more education helps to get better-paid jobs,* and that there is now and will be in the future a brighter employment prospect for those with more education and training. The white-collar revolution calls for a very literate labor force.

To provide the younger generation with adequate educational opportunity becomes an imperative necessity for the nation. Mechanization and automation have already demonstrated that they can replace a good deal of manpower in the processes of production, either agricultural or manufacturing. In the service industries, however, they have not saved much in terms of payrolls. The first reason for this is that *the machines themselves have to be serviced.* The more "intelligent" the machines are, the more servicing they need. Even a rather simple machine, by modern standards, such as a refrigerator or a typewriter, needs servicing to keep it running smoothly, and this must be provided by specialists who know the whole mechanism and its various parts. In fact, to service and repair a machine usually requires more knowledge than does operating one, where simple "know-how" is usually adequate, for repair involves diagnosis. This means that automation of services will require better trained "blue-collar" workers. The more involved machinery that is rapidly invading the larger

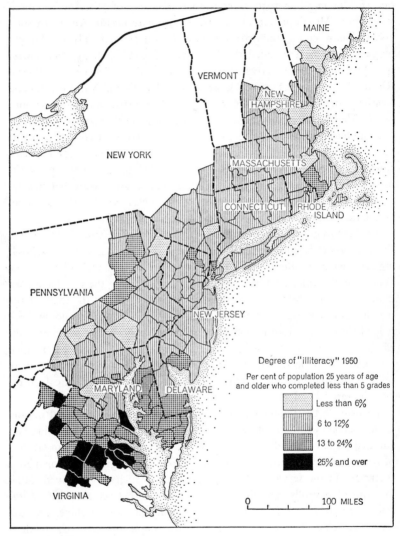

Degree of "illiteracy" 1950

Per cent of population 25 years of age
and older who completed less than 5 grades

Less than 6%

6 to 12%

13 to 24%

25% and over

0   100 MILES

FIG. 192

offices requires not only regular servicing by maintenance and repair crews but also servicing by operating crews consisting of highly specialized workers.

The use of electronic computers, for instance,

. . . has created a number of new office occupations and has changed the functions performed in others. Some of the new jobs, especially in programming . . . require considerable related experience or education at the college level. Many of the other jobs related to operation of computing systems also require other types of clerical work. In general high school graduation is the minimum educational requirement.[66]

Among the important groups of "quaternary" activities, the financial community is one that is being rapidly mechanized nowadays with *diverse* electronic devices, including elaborate computing systems. Nevertheless, it is still cited by labor specialists as a category of employment expected to expand more rapidly than most other industries through the 1960's (see above, p. 558). From 1946 to 1959, commercial bank employment in the country increased 65 per cent compared with 20 per cent for total non-agricultural employment. Bankers are afraid of what may happen to their staffs if this rate of growth continues. A recent joke maintains that if this should happen, by the year 2100 everybody then in the labor force would be working in a bank. In fact, mechanization is expected to lower the operating costs of banking and, by "taming the paper tiger," make it easier for banks to expand their business. A survey conducted by the Federal Reserve Bank of Philadelphia observed:

The installation of machinery tends to upgrade some workers in both prestige and pay. Banks tend to draw on their existing staff for personnel to operate new equipment and this applies even to electronic computers. Thus many workers are rescued from routine, boring jobs and given something that makes better use of their true skills . . . Why not let the machines take over the dull, stultifying jobs and save people for the things they do best — thinking? [67]

To be able to think well, however, most people need a good deal of education and information. Provision of these to meet the expanding need will require more personnel competent to teach, train, gather and process information, file, catalogue, and so forth. Even manufacturing, while increasingly mechanizing its production, needs more research and laboratory personnel, more managers and public relations people, and, for all of these, more secretarial and general clerical help. Indeed, education at all levels must expand rapidly in all directions, and it will remain a field hard to saturate or even to satisfy fully, because of the rapidly changing world in which we live. Today technical training and scientific knowledge grow

[66] U. S. Department of Labor, Bureau of Labor Statistics, *Automation and Employment Opportunities for Office Workers,* Occupational Outlook Series Bulletin No. 1241, U. S. Department of Labor, Washington, D. C., October 1958, p. 4. See also 84th Cong., 1st sess., *Automation and Technological Change,* Hearings before the Subcommittee on Economic Stabilization of the Joint Committee on the Economic Report, October 1955, U. S. Government Printing Office, Washington, D. C., 1955.

[67] "How Banking Tames Its Paper Tiger," *The Business Review,* Federal Reserve Bank of Philadelphia, May 1960, p. 5.

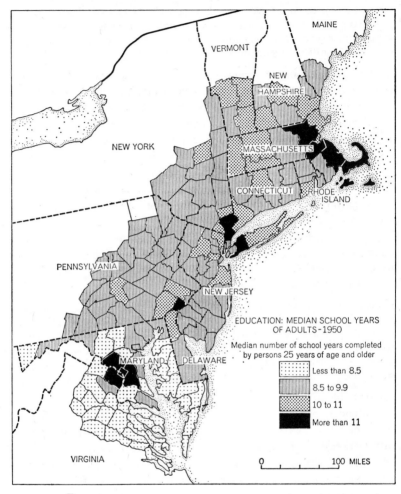

FIG. 193

obsolete rapidly unless they are brought up to date constantly or periodi-
cally.

The preparation of the younger generation for these sorts of work
should start as early as possible. In a recent timely report, Dr. James B. Conant stressed the great variety of high schools encountered throughout
the United States.[68] He advocated a "comprehensive high school" whose

[68] James B. Conant, *The American High School Today*, McGraw-Hill, New York,
1959, pp. 77–95.

programs would correspond to "the educational needs of *all* the youth in the community." His survey showed that an adequate degree of comprehensiveness is difficult to attain outside the large city. "The enrollment of many American high schools is too small to allow a diversified curriculum except at exorbitant expense." However, "in many of the eastern cities of considerable size and in a few of the medium-sized cities, one finds specialized high schools for the academically talented youth and for those with other talents."

Thus even in this field Megalopolis seems to be favored. However, as this region is the seat of such a considerable concentration of offices, research laboratories, and those activities that are rapidly expanding their "quaternary" employment, it obviously has also a greater than average need for more and better educational institutions, for it could not constantly rely on the rest of the country for its personnel. Its whole system of present prosperity depends much on the region's specific ability to supply in large numbers the specialized labor force desired; and this asset is largely a matter of the schooling of the population.

One of the remarkable features of the "white-collar" labor force is *its high proportion of women*. True, "womanpower" has gained a large share of the employment in various sectors of the modern economy, including the production workers of certain manufacturing, the so-called "light" industries (such as textiles, apparel, tobacco and cigarettes, and food processing). In the white-collar jobs, however, the differences between men and women employees tend to decrease except for the upper "executive" strata, where men remain clearly dominant. By 1960 women were more numerous than men among the service workers and in several white-collar occupations.

The proportion of women in the whole labor force was already rather high in 1950 throughout the axial belt of Megalopolis and especially in the large cities (Fig. 194), amounting to more than 30 per cent in most of the counties and to more than 33 per cent in many cases. This percentage dropped sharply as one entered Virginia, where in few counties did women make up more than 25 per cent of the labor force, whereas the national average stood at 29. The average for the whole of Megalopolis was somewhat above the national average, and the average for the axial belt was still higher. In early 1959 it was estimated that female workers, having increased about 20 per cent since 1950, supplied 31 per cent of the total labor force. Of the country's female population 14 years of age and older, the proportion in the labor force rose from 31.4 per cent in 1950 to

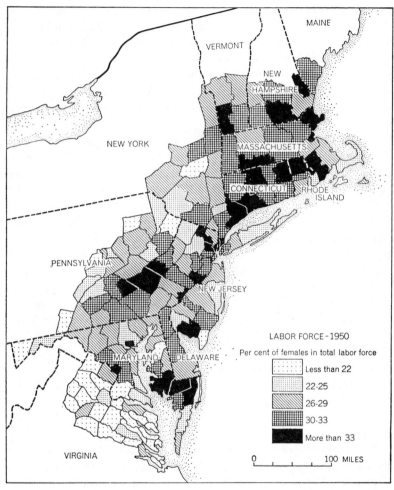

Fig. 194. "Womanpower" in Megalopolis, by counties, 1950

35 per cent in 1958, and this proportion rose especially rapidly among married women.[69] Thus women now play a larger role in the nation's labor force, and office or factory work plays a greater part in the life of women. In this evolution, which seems destined to proceed and expand, the white-collar revolution and the increasing employment in the service industries have been powerful factors.

[69] Statistical data from the U. S. Bureau of the Census, *Statistical Abstract of the United States: 1959*, U. S. Government Printing Office, Washington, D. C., 1959.

In 1950, women made up 52 per cent of the clerical and sales workers in the country and 42 per cent of the professional workers. In 1960 these percentages came to 63 and 38 respectively. The women lost on the professional level mainly for lack of adequate education. In 1957, the National Manpower Council stated:

> The demand for women office and clerical workers has been influenced by the increasing scale of industrial and commercial activity, by growth in the size and complexity of business enterprises, and by greater specialization in managerial functions. It has also been directly stimulated by innovations in systems of communications and record-keeping. . . .
>
> While the growth of urban centers creates new demands for women workers, urban life also tends to make more women, particularly more married women, available for paid employment by encouraging higher standards of living and by making housekeeping easier and less time-consuming. . . .
>
> . . . The predominance of women in office, clerical, and other white-collar work has been made possible by the great number of girls graduating from high-school. The importance of women in the professions rests upon the large proportion of young women among college graduates.[70]

The white-collar revolution has been reaching deep into many essential characteristics of American society and its way of life. It was a revolution largely started by the Megalopolitan ways and means of doing business and is still more advanced in Megalopolis than in the rest of the country because it is a product of urbanization, of better education of the people as a whole, of the concentration in this region of so much office industry and other activities that require mainly white-collar labor.

The Consequences for Land Use and Living Conditions in Megalopolis

The consequences of the predominance of white-collar workers in the labor force are just beginning to be felt even in Megalopolis, which in 1960 had about eight million of them. The people in these occupations have a way of life somewhat different from that of a manufacturing production worker. Their main work consists in relations with other people in the office or outside it, rather than in the operation of machines or the handling of materials. Therefore their general interests will tend to be different, more oriented toward social and, at a certain level, intellectual questions. The work they have to perform has so much to do with information that it will lead to more reading and often to much more travelling.

[70] National Manpower Council, *Womanpower*, Columbia University Press, New York, 1957, pp. 13–14. See also Barry, "White-Collar Employment," *op. cit.*, for detailed characteristics of the female white-collar labor force.

It is a well-known fact that professional and sales workers "rush around" much more than do foremen or operators in a manufacturing plant. They do so partly because their work requires it, or so they believe, and partly because they have more financial means for it and more curiosity.

Not only do these trends modify this composite and somewhat abstract concept, the "way of life," but they also have immediate consequences for the living conditions of individuals and for their behavior as consumers. Because of the greater demand for travelling, more passenger transportation facilities are needed, and the transportation industry in this region must thus look for more space, more equipment, and more employees. The expanding desire for information calls for more publications and mass media of various sorts. More leisure entails a whole variety of new activities, and more spending in fields that used to be much more restricted. We have seen, as an instance, the requirements resulting in Megalopolis from the taste developed by city dwellers for hunting and fishing (see above, pp. 368–378). It is estimated that in 1958 Americans spent more than $2 billion for boating,[71] while $2.6 billion were spent on fishing and another billion on hunting; the cost of golfing was estimated at $750 million. The Federal Reserve Bank of Philadelphia's *Business Review* observed: ". . . it's likely that total outlays for participation sports now top $10 billion a year. By comparison, this sum is more than half of all expenditures for education." [72] Resort business has been booming too, and within Megalopolis itself summer and week-end homes or resort facilities on the seaside or in the hills occupy a substantial amount of land on both sides of the axial belt.

The living conditions of the white-collar labor force are still greatly affected by the fact that these workers belong in occupations chiefly employed in communications-oriented industries. These cluster in business districts, most of which, in Megalopolis, are becoming very congested. As "the boom in skyscrapers" goes on in almost every large city, access to the congested hubs becomes more difficult or at least uncomfortable. Those who can afford it take up residences in the immediate vicinity of the hub and speak of walking to their offices or getting there by a relatively short bus or taxi ride. As the residential sections close to the business hubs are rebuilt in the process of urban renewal, the cost of living in the areas within easy reach of the business districts rises rapidly and gets out of reach of the average office worker. The white-collar workers have

[71] "Much Ado About Doing," *Business Review*, Federal Reserve Bank of Philadelphia, July 1959, pp. 7–13.
[72] *Ibid.*, p. 8.

made up the big bulk of the migration to the outer rings of metropolitan areas, to the kind of suburbia that is greener and less tightly built up.[73]

Whether they live on the periphery of the central city in still very urban surroundings or in greener suburban locations, the white-collar workers will have a journey to work that may become increasingly unpleasant if present trends in commuter and city transit transportation are maintained and no new solutions are brought about to solve the riddle. In Manhattan's hub more skyscrapers are rising or being planned that will hold on a few acres of ground tens of thousands of people during working hours; and the access to the entrance of the buildings is still planned on only one level (the ground floor from the street), except when there is an underground level connecting directly with a subway, as in Rockefeller Center. Crowding threatens to make immediate access difficult and any activity on the street unpleasant. The longer range of access, by subway, bus, or car from other parts of the city and by train, bus, or car from suburbia, is another question that may affect the future land use in the metropolis considerably within the coming decade or two.

Office space has been expanding rapidly in the main city hubs. In Manhattan it increased from 120 million square feet in 1947 to about 138 million in 1956, and in that year the whole city of New York estimated its total office space at 144 million square feet.[74] In Philadelphia the total available floor space in commercial office buildings remained between 10 and 11 million square feet from 1935 to 1955, and a good deal of it remained vacant until 1944. By early 1960 office space reached the all-time high for the city of 11.8 million square feet. About 75 per cent of the space added since 1956 has been in four brand-new office buildings in the very heart of the business district. These have been renting well, but at the expense of older office buildings.[75] It seems that within a city the trend

[73] This is the migration described in Auguste C. Spectorsky, *The Exurbanites*, Lippincott, Philadelphia, 1955; or William H. Whyte, *The Organization Man*, Simon and Schuster, New York, 1956. There are interesting observations about the role of the white-collar workers and their move to the suburbs in Daniel Seligman, "The New Masses," Chapter 6 of *Markets of the Sixties*, by the Editors of *Fortune*, Harper and Brothers, New York, 1960, pp. 103–118. Edgar M. Hoover and Raymond Vernon, in *Anatomy of a Metropolis*, New York Metropolitan Region Study, Harvard University Press, Cambridge, Mass., 1959, have provided a thoughtful analysis of the white-collar corps' desiderata and of the "spacious living versus easy access" problem in the New York metropolitan region.

[74] See Hoover and Vernon, *op. cit.*, pp. 110–112, and "Commercial and Industrial Floor Space Inventory," *Bulletin of the Department of City Planning*, City of New York, December 1957.

[75] "Philadelphia Office Buildings in 1960," *Business Review*, Federal Reserve Bank of Philadelphia, March 1960, pp. 14–17.

is toward consolidating the clustering of large new office buildings; this is true of Baltimore, Boston, and Newark as well as of New York. But the central city is beginning to get some competition from the suburban ring. The space in suburban office buildings around Philadelphia, for instance, is already estimated at one million square feet at least. Decentralization for the office industry is a hard thing to accept. There are objections to it rooted in the difficulties of finding adequate personnel in outlying locations, especially for the larger firms, and in the difficulties of quick and satisfactory communications with many other offices.

To what extent communications by telephone, television, teletype, and other means may be able to offset the present need for clustering is a question to be pondered. For, if conditions of access get worse in the main hubs, if transportation does not alleviate the threat of crowding on the ground and undue delays of access, then the technological progress of communications may bring about the scattering of the office industry in a way that will force much building in many places and ruin the present land use, land values, and trade in the central cities.

Whatever solution may be brought about in the forthcoming decade or two, the needs and whims of the white-collar labor force will be a decisive factor; and much of the present programming ought to concern itself with the living and working conditions of this occupational group.[76] The revolution in the labor force presently taking place will probably use Megalopolis as its main laboratory. This experiment cannot afford to fail, for too much is at stake.

[76] See International Labor Office, *Effects of Mechanization and Automation in Offices,* a report reprinted from the *International Labour Review,* Geneva, Vol. 81, Nos. 2, 3, and 4, February, March, and April 1960; see also Ida Russakoff Hoos, "The Impact of Office Automation on Workers," *International Labour Review,* Vol. 82, No. 4, October 1960, pp. 363–388. Many observations in this article, though based mainly on a survey conducted in the San Francisco Bay area, have a general value and apply to Megalopolis.

C H A P T E R   1 2

Transportation and Traffic

The future course of Megalopolitan development appears to depend to a large extent upon the quality of the transportation services the region will be able to offer its inhabitants and visitors. During the 1950's the problems raised locally and regionally by traffic jams and transportation inadequacy perhaps caused more debate, meetings, and publications than any one of the other questions stemming from the urbanized character of the region and the concentration of economic activities within it.

Megalopolis has a density of population, a "mix" of economic activities, and an average level of personal income that require an extraordinary density of traffic within its cities and between them. The flow of traffic on the ground and in the air above it is just as impressive as the intense flow of telephone communications that ties together the cities of Megalopolis (see above, pp. 582–596). All means of transportation are used. Along a given route there is some competition between the various carriers, and while this competition often increases the traffic it does not usually work for better service, for each of the carriers complains about its poor finances and asks for more facilities. It seems a curious paradox that the various transportation industries in this region constantly point out their lack of financial means, their insufficient profits, while in terms of markets for its services transportation has here the most massive concentration mankind has ever known. Perhaps in our time transportation has inherited what used to be the farmer's well-known habit of complaining.

Type of transportation may be ruled essentially by technology, size of available facilities, and costs of operating carriers. Traffic, however, is influenced at least as much by the occupational pattern of the community, the level of personal income, the amount of time and money available for leisure, the family structure, the geographical distribution of places of residence and of work, the seasons and the weather, even the rate of interest on the money market.

Thus the recent suburban sprawl has intensified and expanded the tidal currents of commuting. Tidal currents of lesser frequency but quite comparable volume of traffic carry crowds out of the residential areas to the seaside, the hills, the woods, and back to their homes, and because of the rise in the average family's income and the increase in leisure time these movements are more frequent and affect more people than formerly. As all these factors influencing traffic have evolved rapidly in recent years and are still shifting today, traffic and the uses of the various carriers have been continually modified. One may even be surprised that in a region and an era that are both so dynamic the major flows of traffic have been allowed to develop with relatively little hindrance on the whole, though at a cost to the region's people of considerable money and of increasing nervous strain and physical discomfort. At some points and at some times traffic nears saturation. More facilities to move more people can, of course, be added, for engineering or technological solutions can be found to all flow problems; but such solutions might be at the cost of so many dollars to the community and of so much aggravation to the public transported that the wisdom of a purely technical and statistical approach can be doubted.

In a region such as Megalopolis, where increased crowding has become the indispensable alternative to decay, and where the concentration of communications-oriented activities is the very condition of progress, the improvement of transportation for a growing traffic becomes a matter of necessity, almost of survival. No wonder so much has been written and said about these questions. We shall deal with them as briefly as possible, without losing sight of their significance to the whole concept of Megalopolis and to the region's role in the nation and the modern world.[1]

[1] For a good part of the research that provided data for this chapter we are indebted to Dr. Aloys A. Michel of the Geography Department, Yale University.

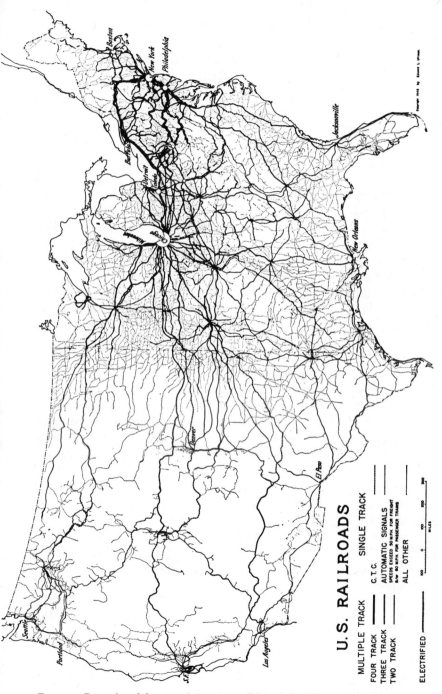

FIG. 195. *Reproduced by permission from Edward L. Ullman,* American Commodity Flow, *University of Washington Press, Seattle, 1957, p. 3*

The Density of Movement within the Region

On this seaboard, coastwise navigation was long the main means of transportation linking its different parts. It still has its importance, and maritime commerce remains one of the pillars of the regional economy (see above, pp. 522–545), but today water transport is used chiefly for bulky freight. Movement of people within the region now depends on railroads or highways on the ground and on airlines above it.

The traffic in and out of the major metropolitan "hubs" requires considerable and diversified facilities. In the case of New York's hub (that is, Manhattan south of 61st Street),[2] the number of persons entering it on a typical business day rose from 2.3 million in 1924 to 3.7 million in 1948 but decreased to 3.3 million by 1956. The recent decrease may be explained by a combination of several trends, such as the moving down into the hub of residences previously situated outside it; the moving to uptown locations (and beyond) of certain places of work previously located in the hub; the rapid growth of manufacturing and retailing on the periphery of the city; and even the increasing inconveniences caused by increased congestion in the hub and along its approaches.

While the number of persons entering (and therefore leaving) New York's hub daily has declined slightly in the 1950's, the number of motor vehicles entering the hub on business days has not stopped rising: from 200,000 in 1924 to 382,000 in 1948 and 519,000 in 1956.[3] The proportion of persons entering by automobile or taxi has risen also, of course, from 10.6 per cent of the total in 1924 to 22.2 per cent in 1956, while the proportion of those travelling by railroad declined in the years 1924–56, despite the migration to the suburbs and to exurbia, from 9.3 to 7 per cent, and among those moving about within the city the proportion using rapid transit and public surface facilities decreased from 72.2 to 59.5 per cent. The number of trucks moving in and out of the hub increased during those years too, reaching about 75,000 on a typical business day in 1956. Thus there is little wonder that congestion of the hub's streets has increased, although a somewhat smaller daytime population is being serviced.

Because of this increased dependence on cars and trucks, railroads, which for about a century have played an essential part in moving Mega-

[2] The territory of the hub is expanding northward and may soon reach 72nd Street, or perhaps 80th Street, especially east of Central Park.

[3] Statistical data in this and following paragraphs are from *Hub-Bound Travel in the Tri-State Metropolitan Region*, Regional Plan Association Bulletin No. 91, New York, April 1959.

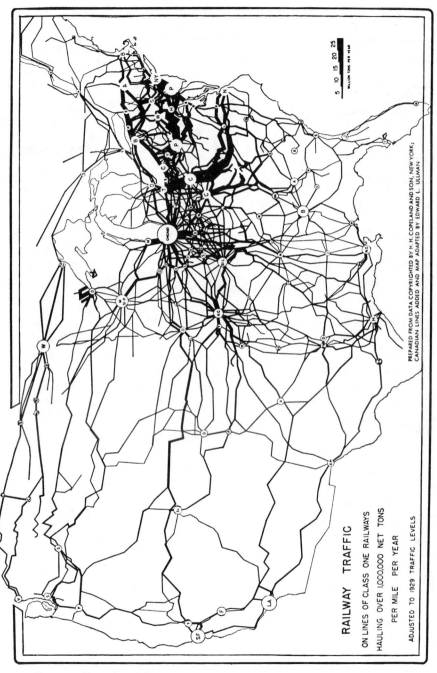

RAILWAY TRAFFIC

ON LINES OF CLASS ONE RAILWAYS

HAULING OVER 1,000,000 NET TONS

PER MILE PER YEAR

ADJUSTED TO 1929 TRAFFIC LEVELS

PREPARED FROM DATA COPYRIGHTED BY H. H. COPELAND AND SON, NEW YORK; CANADIAN LINES ADDED AND MAP ADAPTED BY EDWARD L. ULLMAN

5 10 15 20 25
MILLION TONS PER YEAR

FIG. 196. *Reproduced by permission from Edward L. Ullman,* American Commodity Flow, *University of Washington Press, Seattle, 1957, p. 5*

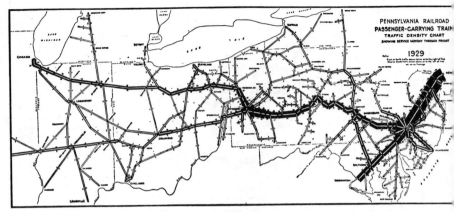

FIG. 197. *Reproduced from Exhibit 45-2 in* Transportation Plan for the National Capital Region: Hearings before the Joint Committee on Washington Metropolitan Problems, *86th Congress of the United States, November 1959, Washington, D. C., 1960, p. 401*

lopolitan people around,[4] are now considered somewhat "outdated" as carriers for passengers. The 1920's seem to have marked the apogee of their role in American transportation. How thoroughly their net covered the country in 1929, and how intense was the flow of freight traffic on the railroads of the Northeastern seaboard, may be seen in Figures 195 and 196. Since that time the traffic, especially the passenger part of it, has declined. The number of passengers carried by the Pennsylvania Railroad in 1929 was much higher in both intercity and commuter traffic than in 1959 (see Figs. 197 to 200). In the latter year, however, it was still quite substantial, and the hubs of the major cities remained dependent on the railroads for their daily transportation requirements. The greater the city and its business district, the more it needs mass transportation, which, outside the city limits, has traditionally been supplied by trains, though scheduled bus lines are taking a growing part of it.

The daily movement of more than three million persons into and out of Manhattan's hub represents a great intensity of traffic, all the more so since the tide reaches its crest in the morning and evening rush hours.

[4] How important the railroads were to the region before the era of superhighways is indicated by the fact that the Pennsylvania and New Haven lines, running along the axial belt of Megalopolis, have four tracks (electrified) most of the way from New Haven to Washington, D. C. When they were built these installations evidently were profitable. See Edward L. Ullman, "The Railroad Pattern of the United States," *Geographical Review*, Vol. 39, No. 2, 1949, pp. 242–256.

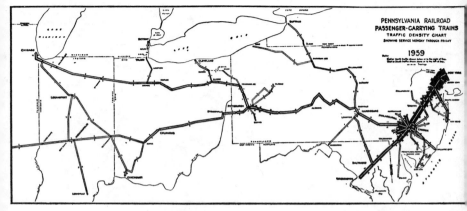

FIG. 198. *Reproduced from Exhibit 45–3 in* Transportation Plan for the National Capital Region (*see caption of Fig. 197*), *p. 402*

On a 1956 business day, 1,551,000 persons or 46.8 per cent of the day's total inbound traffic entered during the morning rush hour, 7–10 A.M. About as many moved out of the hub between 4 and 7 P.M.[5] The transportation must be adequate to handle a flow of traffic that can reach close to a million people within one hour, twice a day. Obviously, servicing this traffic requires readiness for the average flow of the peak hour.

Manhattan is the greatest and most congested of all metropolitan hubs in America and is likely to maintain this position. However, the intensity of travelling into and out of the central hub in proportion to the total population of the metropolitan area is not highest in the New York area. In 1955 in the Washington, D. C., metropolitan area, with a population of 1,870,000, about 1.6 million people entered and left the hub on an average weekday.[6] The Washington suburbs have many fewer centers of employment than have New York's periphery and outer ring, and the central city, a more purely white-collar city, generates more daily traffic per capita of Census population. This observation may be worth remembering, for office and white-collar occupations, Washington's predominant economic activity, may be expected to become increasingly important in most central cities, especially in Megalopolis.

In Philadelphia, the total number of commuters entering the central business district daily appears rather stabilized just above the 600,000 level;

---

[5] *Hub-Bound Travel . . . , op. cit.*

[6] Joint Committee on Washington Metropolitan Problems, *Washington Metropolitan Area Transportation Problems*, Hearings, 85th Cong., 2d sess., May 22, 23 and June 10, 1958, U. S. Government Printing Office, Washington, D. C., pp. 88–110.

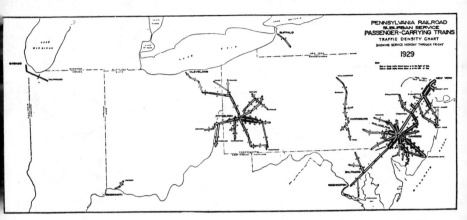

FIG. 199. *Reproduced from Exhibit 45-4 in* Transportation Plan for the National Capital Region (*see caption of Fig. 197*), *p. 403*

even projections for 1980 do not expect it to rise much above 637,000.[7] In 1955 the movement into Philadelphia's hub was thus considerably less than half what it was into Washington's hub, despite the much larger size of the metropolis on the Delaware. The lesser importance of white-collar employment in Philadelphia and the greater development of manufacturing on the periphery are probably the essential reasons for this. In Philadelphia, as in New York and Washington, the proportion of persons travelling by automobile and taxi was increasing, and the proportion using public transportation was decreasing, trends that have in each case resulted in greater congestion of the city streets and the access routes.

Similar observations may be made in the Boston and Baltimore metropolitan regions. As in New York, the number of persons entering downtown Boston decreased, from a daily average of nearly 600,000 in 1950 to about 560,000 in 1956; railroad and mass-transport facilities have suffered an even greater loss, while the number of persons commuting by automobiles has increased slightly. Since 1956 the latter trend has been accelerated.[8] Even by 1956, some 57 per cent of all persons travelling to downtown Boston went by automobile. Of the total number for a day almost one half arrived in the peak hours, between 7:30 and 9:30 A.M.

It is interesting to observe once more that Boston's hub attracts a daily flow of people almost equal to that entering Philadelphia but only about

[7] City of Philadelphia, Urban Traffic and Transportation Board, *Plan and Program 1955*, Philadelphia, April 1956, pp. 20–33.

[8] See Boston College, Seminar Research Bureau, College of Business Administration, *Transportation Facts and Public Policy for Downtown Boston*, Boston, 1958.

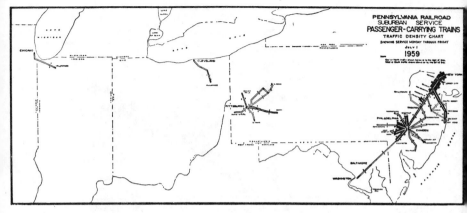

Fig. 200. *Reproduced from Exhibit 45-5 in* Transportation Plan for the National Capital Region (*see caption of Fig. 197*), *p. 404*

half the volume entering Washington's hub, while in terms of population it is close to Washington's size and much below Philadelphia's. As a component of the city's economy, white-collar occupations play a *relatively* greater part in Boston than in Philadelphia, but definitely a smaller part than in Washington. The relative importance of white-collar workers in the daytime labor force seems to be a factor affecting the flow of commuters in and out of metropolitan hubs. It is by no means the only such factor, but it is a significant one in Megalopolis. The office industry has proved to be one particularly resistant to decentralization from the main hubs; moreover, it employs people who like to enjoy life, who appreciate residence in quieter and greener surroundings, and who can often afford the expense of commuting. As offices expand and white-collar jobs multiply, one may expect the intensity of traffic to and from the major cities to keep on rising.

A great deal of the traffic in Megalopolis does not converge on the business hubs, although these currents are, during the peak hours, the most intense. A considerable amount of automobile traffic flows between homes and places of work outside the hub; more flows to and from shopping centers and business districts of small towns, or even between residential sections. For example, the importance of home-to-work currents crisscrossing heavily industrialized northeastern New Jersey in almost all directions may be ascertained on the map of this traffic in Middlesex County (Fig. 201).

The total amount of intercity motor traffic on Megalopolitan highways is certainly the most dense one could find in any region of similar size in

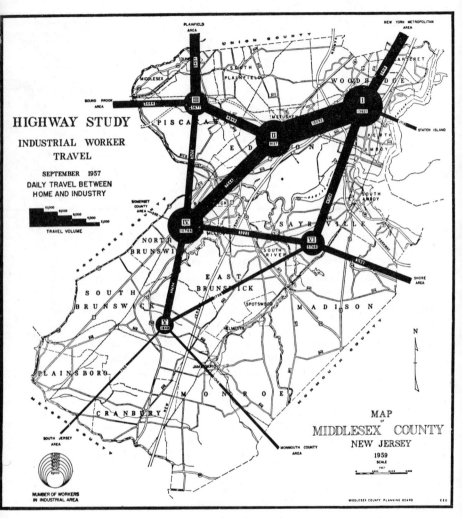

FIG. 201. *Reproduced by permission of the Middlesex County Planning Board*

the world. A comparison with the rest of the country is offered by the map (see Fig. 202a) of highway traffic flow in the United States prepared by the U. S. Bureau of Public Roads for 1952, which shows that nowhere is there any comparable volume of flow involving distances of several hundreds of miles. The traffic around Detroit, Cleveland, San Francisco, and Los Angeles is very impressive too, but for much shorter distances.

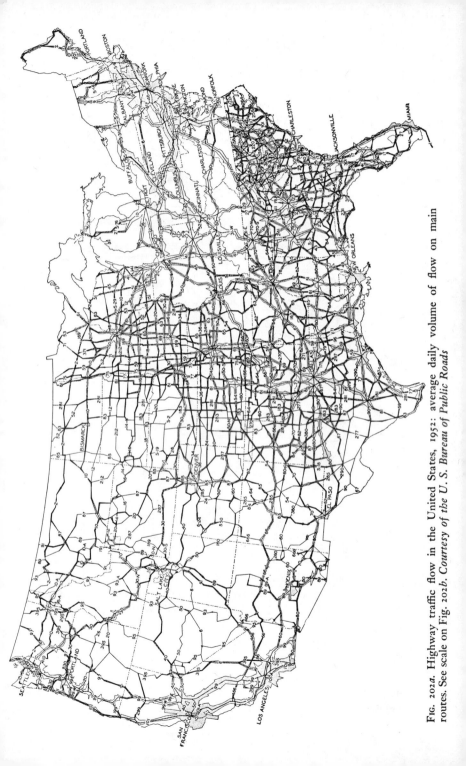

FIG. 202a. Highway traffic flow in the United States, 1952: average daily volume of flow on main routes. See scale on Fig. 202b. *Courtesy of the U. S. Bureau of Public Roads*

FIG. 202*b*. Highway traffic flow in Megalopolis, 1952: average daily volume of flow on main routes. *Courtesy of the U. S. Bureau of Public Roads*

Although California led all the states in the nation in 1960 in the number of driving-license holders, the traffic on longer intercity routes, such as from the Bay area to the Los Angeles–San Diego area, does not yet approach in intensity that developed between Boston and Washington.

The northeastern section of this same map, shown on a larger scale (Figs. 202*b* and 202*c*), demonstrates in spectacular fashion the massive flow through the whole region we have defined as Megalopolis. So close one to another are the heavily trafficked roads that it was difficult to distinguish them on a map for the whole country on such a scale. However,

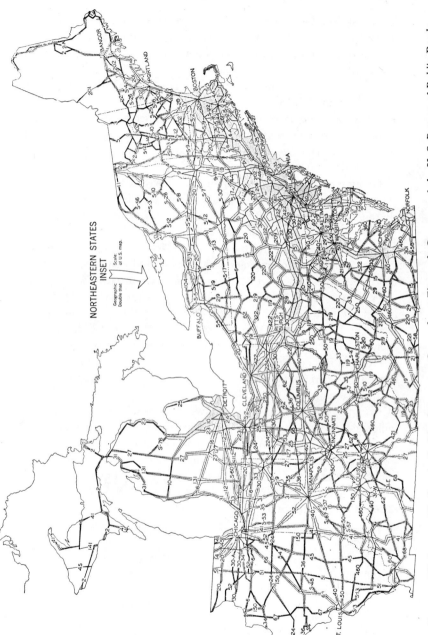

NORTHEASTERN STATES
INSET

Geographic
Double that | Scale
of U.S. map.

Fig. 202c. Highway traffic flow in the Northeast, 1952. See scale on Fig. 202b. *Courtesy of the U. S. Bureau of Public Roads*

it seemed desirable to analyze into its various components this huge flow of traffic within the region. We have attempted to do this by classifying all the routes shown on each state's highway map into seven categories, according to the number of vehicles per average day in 1957–58 (see Fig. 203). The map thus obtained does not show all the traffic in full detail, for routes that are city streets do not appear on state highway maps and they make too dense a network to be represented at such a scale. We were therefore able to show here mainly intercity traffic on essential routes. This map provides a fair analysis of the highway traffic flow through Megalopolis.

Traffic is clearly concentrated along the axial belt and radiates out in all directions from each of the main hubs, especially New York City, Boston, and Philadelphia. The convergence of so many heavily trafficked routes on New York and on Philadelphia is noteworthy, as is the rather extraordinary density in northeastern New Jersey of highways each carrying more than 20,000 vehicles daily. One is hardly surprised after looking at this map to learn that the gasoline tax collected from motorists plays a large role in New Jersey's state finances (see Table 25). It is also interesting to observe the density of major highways in southeastern Pennsylvania and eastern Massachusetts. In the District of Columbia, however, the movement of vehicles is much less impressive than around Philadelphia and Boston, even though the flow of people is considerable. Two main differences between Washington and the great metropolises to the north are responsible for this. First, practically all the traffic that comes to Washington goes toward its downtown section, where the Federal office buildings stand, while in Philadelphia and Boston the industrial and manufacturing peripheries attract even more traffic, throughout the whole day, than do the central business districts in more concentrated fashion. Second, either for commuting or other purposes, there is a great deal of intercity flow in eastern Massachusetts, northeastern New Jersey, and southeastern Pennsylvania, while the traffic around Washington consists mainly of relatively short-range trips between the metropolitan ring and the central city.

It was in this Northeastern region that the network of "parkways" and "turnpikes," meaning new superhighways, first developed, and although they are now found in other areas too [9] — Florida and West Virginia, for example, and Kansas and Oklahoma — their main concentration centers on

[9] See the maps in the Annual Reports of the Bureau of Public Roads for a record of the spread of toll roads through the country after 1950.

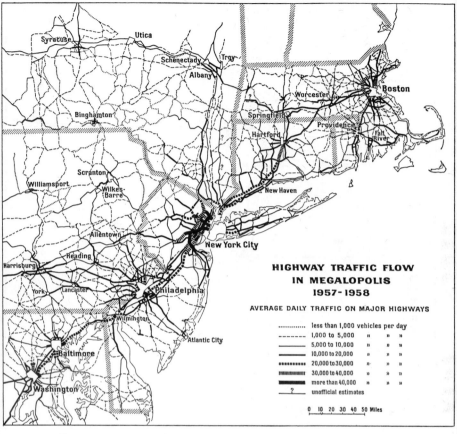

HIGHWAY TRAFFIC FLOW
IN MEGALOPOLIS
1957-1958

AVERAGE DAILY TRAFFIC ON MAJOR HIGHWAYS

.... less than 1,000 vehicles per day
– – – – – 1,000 to 5,000   »   »   »
————— 5,000 to 10,000   »   »   »
————— 10,000 to 20,000   »   »   »
■■■■■■■■ 20,000 to 30,000   »·   »   »
|||||||||||||| 30,000 to 40,000   »   »   »
————— more than 40,000   »   »   »
___?___ unofficial estimates

0   10   20   30   40   50 Miles

Fig. 203

New York City and branches out of Megalopolis westward and north-ward, improving the access of this region to automobile traffic.

The detailed map of traffic flow by major highways leaves the justified impression that the metropolitan regions of Megalopolis are on the one hand well integrated, each within itself, and on the other well interconnected one with another, particularly along the region's axial belt. It is difficult here to differentiate fully between "commuting" and "intercity" traffic, for the two interpenetrate intimately, their interpenetration taking somewhat different forms in winter and in summer. In the latter season a good deal of "week-end commuting" develops for fathers who have sent their families to a vacation spot within weekly commuting distance. Some

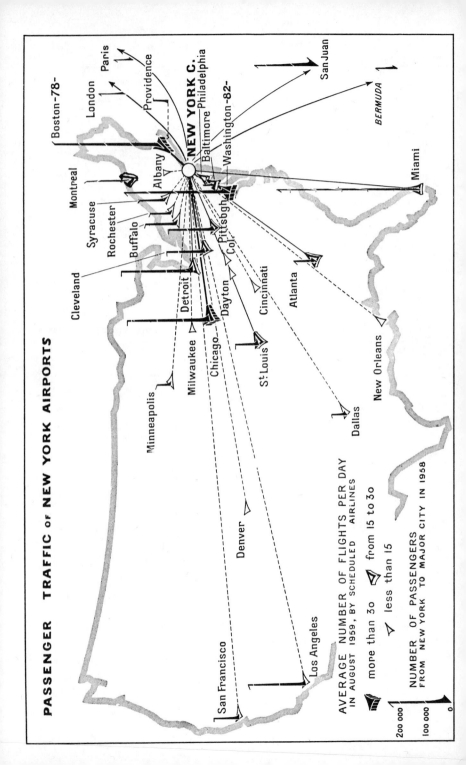

PASSENGER TRAFFIC OF NEW YORK AIRPORTS

NEW YORK C.

Boston-78-
London
Paris
Providence
Albany
Philadelphia
Baltimore
Washington-82-
San Juan
BERMUDA
Miami
Montreal
Syracuse
Rochester
Buffalo
Cleveland
Detroit
Pittsbgh.
Col.
Cincinnati
Atlanta
New Orleans
Dallas
Minneapolis
Milwaukee
Chicago
Dayton
St. Louis
Denver
San Francisco
Los Angeles

AVERAGE NUMBER OF FLIGHTS PER DAY
IN AUGUST 1959, BY SCHEDULED AIRLINES
more than 30   from 15 to 30   less than 15

NUMBER OF PASSENGERS
FROM NEW YORK TO MAJOR CITY IN 1958

200 000
100 000
0

of this latter kind of commuting takes place by plane (for instance, between Washington or even New York and resort areas of New England).

The distribution of the passenger traffic of the New York airports for the whole year 1958 shows that though Miami was the destination that attracted the greatest number, Boston and Washington came immediately after it despite the relatively short distance involved. But the average number of flights per day scheduled through the month of August 1959 (see Fig. 204), indicated only three destinations with more than 30 flights daily: Washington with 82 flights, Boston with 78, and Chicago with 43.[10] The extraordinary frequency of the flights on the New York–Washington and New York–Boston runs suggests in some respects the most intense scheduled airlines connections one could find at present between three cities within 500 miles of one another as the crow flies. This means congestion of two sorts. In 1956 there were 123 planes in the air at one time (10:30 A.M. on July 14) within a fifty-mile radius of New York City, and it is anticipated that by 1975 there will be 350.[11] The dangers inherent in this situation were illustrated by the December, 1960, collision of two planes over New York City, with a loss of 132 lives.[12] Associated with these congested airways, and contributing to the danger of collision, is what might be called a congestion on the ground as regards airports. It has been suggested that from the point of view of safety the major airports in the New York area are too close together — there is a distance of only eight miles by air between La Guardia and New York International airports and about twice that between either of these and Newark Airport.[13] In the spring of 1961, Eastern Air Lines started an "air shuttle" between New York, Boston, and Washington, with planes leaving every two hours on the hour; tickets could be bought on board.

Thus by car, bus, train, or plane the traffic along the axial belt of Megalopolis is the most intense in the modern world. This is not simply because of the area's density of population. There are, as we know, some other regions on our planet as thickly settled or more so. In these other regions,

[10] Figures from *Combined Timetables All Scheduled Airlines*, August 1959, and data from Port of New York Authority.

[11] Seymour Deitchman and Alfred Blumstein, "Air-Traffic Control," *Scientific American*, December 1960, pp. 47–63.

[12] *The New York Times*, December 17, 1960.

[13] *The New York Times*, December 25, 1960. See also Chapter 14 below for a discussion of the lack of space for additional airports close to the city.

Opposite FIG. 204. Data on the number of passengers in 1958 were kindly supplied by the Port of New York Authority. The average daily number of flights from the New York airports to the various destinations was calculated (counting departing flights only) from the *Combined Timetables of All Scheduled Airlines* for August 1959.

even in the relatively prosperous triangle Amsterdam–Paris–Bonn, or in central England, there may be some comparable crowds moving from home to work and back, commuting at rush hours to London or to Paris; but this is purely internal to one metropolitan region and seldom involves movements of more than fifteen miles per person. In Megalopolis the scale is quite different, both in terms of daily and yearly averages and in terms of the much longer distances involved.

Megalopolis is largely integrated as a region and stands out as a regional system on every map of the nation, largely owing to its remarkable system of transportation, complicated but powerfully developed and continually growing, using all the various means available. This has been achieved because the people wanted all these links and relationships (had they not been this kind of people they would probably not have been so successful with communications-oriented industries) and because the economy and technology developed here both require them and have made them possible.

The Competing Means of Transportation

The existing means of carrying freight and passengers have not been equally well developed and have not grown at the same rate. Railroad traffic has in fact been declining, while the importance of motor vehicles and airplanes has been increasing in recent years. These three categories of carriers are not the only ones competing in the Megalopolitan arena, or in the United States as a whole. There are nowadays at least six major types of transportation on the domestic scene: merchant marine for coastwise navigation, inland waterways, railroads, motor vehicles, oil and gas pipelines, and airplanes. All six are at work moving freight and passengers to and through Megalopolis. Historically, however, their relative shares in the task have been constantly changing. This past evolution must be considered first on the national scale.

Coastwise navigation was originally the major means of transportation between the first American cities and colonies along the seaboard. Today the merchant marine still is an important carrier of freight in domestic coastwise trade, but mainly for petroleum products, for the flow of dry cargo has been very much reduced (see above, Chapter 10, and especially Figs. 164 and 165, pp. 526, 527). While the merchant marine's role remains essential in foreign trade, it is declining in domestic transportation. Inland waterways, however, have recently regained some of their past importance. In Megalopolis their use is largely limited to the carrying of building materials for the great amount of construction going on in the cities

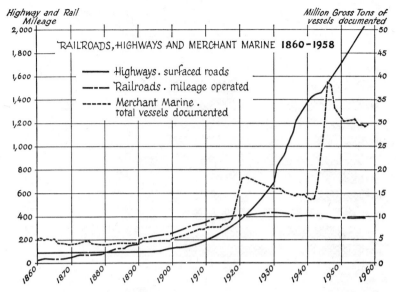

FIG. 205. Trends of major surface carriers in the United States

and their suburbs, and to the regional redistribution of cargoes imported by sea from distant shores. In contrast, the great rivers of the Middle West, the Great Lakes, and the new St. Lawrence Seaway have regained a more diversified role. These trends are external to Megalopolis, and some of them have been viewed with concern by the Northeastern seaports as deflecting currents of trade from them.

The modern competition among means of transportation has been keener between the various carriers on land than between them and the carriers on water. The major means of transportation on the ground have been railroads, highways, and pipelines. Railroads developed and increased their operated mileage rather rapidly from the 1860's to the 1910's, and then slowly through the 1920's, when they seem to have reached their maximum expansion. In the meantime highways were slowly extended, until by 1910 the total network of surfaced roads reached about 200,000 miles in length. Then progress became very rapid, and in the early 1920's, as expansion of the rail network slackened, the surfaced roads surpassed the rail tracks in mileage, exceeding one million miles in 1934 and two million miles in 1956 (see Fig. 205).[14]

[14] Based on material from two U. S. Bureau of the Census publications: *Historical Statistics of the United States, 1789–1945*, 1949, and *Statistical Abstract of the United States: 1959*, 1959, both U. S. Government Printing Office, Washington, D. C.

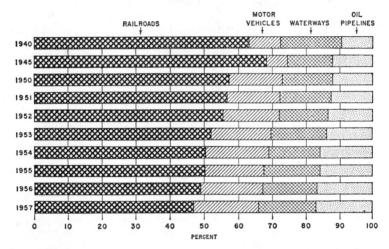

PERCENT DISTRIBUTION OF DOMESTIC INTERCITY FREIGHT
TRAFFIC, BY TYPE OF TRANSPORTATION: 1940 TO 1957
Airways not shown separately—less than one-tenth of 1 percent.

Source: Chart prepared by Department of Commerce, Bureau of the Census. Data are from Interstate Commerce Commission.

FIG. 206. *Courtesy of the U. S. Bureau of the Census*

In the movement of domestic intercity freight for the nation as a whole, railroads declined rapidly in significance after 1945 (see Fig. 206), their total loads dropping from more than 60 per cent of all intercity freight to 50 per cent in 1955 and about 47 per cent in 1957. This decline could not be ascribed to competition from the waterways, which carried about the same share — 14–17 per cent — of a rising total volume of freight throughout the 1950's, nor from the airways, which carried less than 0.05 per cent of the nation's freight in 1957. Instead it reflects the greater use of trucks and pipelines, which carried respectively about 19 per cent and about 17 per cent of the country's total freight in the late 1950's.[15]

Many factors have contributed to this decline in railroad freight traffic, one of the chief ones being the increased dependence on petroleum products for heat and energy. National consumption of anthracite and bituminous coal actually declined from 523 million short tons in 1930 to 494 million in 1950 and 434 million in 1957,[16] and this decreased the shipments of what had long been a major freight item for the railroads. The petroleum products and natural gas used in place of and in addition to coal — for transportation, heating, and power development — are carried to a very

[15] Data in this paragraph are from the *Statistical Abstract of the United States: 1959, op. cit.,* p. 565.
[16] *Ibid.,* p. 727.

small degree by the railroads in the East. Gas moves by pipelines, of course, and oil and its refined products are carried chiefly by pipeline, tanker, and tank truck. Moreover, much other freight has shifted from the railroads to trucks (which are among the users of petroleum products) because of their greater flexibility.

In passenger traffic the railroads have lost even more heavily, to both planes and motor vehicles, both powered by petroleum products. The total passenger-miles travelled on American railroads dropped from 47,370 million in 1920 to 23,816 million in 1940, rose to 31,790 million in 1950, and decreased again to 23,295 million in 1958. Since the number of passengers carried dropped in even more spectacular fashion, from 1,270 million in 1920 to 382 million in 1958, the average trip by train is evidently much longer now than it used to be.[17] Passenger trains are still doing relatively well in the West, but the service has been cut in all respects in the East, even in Megalopolis, despite its greater density of passenger traffic. Because of the constant cutting down of the passenger services offered by the Eastern railroads (more passenger trains were dropped from the railroad schedules in 1959 than in any previous year), it has even been forecast that all intercity passenger movement by rail might be eliminated in the United States by 1970 or thereabout. By 1958 it was estimated that about 90 per cent of all passenger-miles travelled in the country were made in passenger automobiles,[18] of which there were then some 57 million. Trains, buses, and planes vie for the remaining 10 per cent.

In such competition, trains are at a disadvantage for intercity transport, for they are much slower than planes and not much faster than express buses on express highways or turnpikes. Moreover, they can move only on their own tracks, providing only station-to-station service, whereas buses can follow varying routes and make frequent stops, and automobiles can go from door to door, on routes that suit the driver. Thus motor transportation saves a good deal of walking and luggage or package carrying and gives more freedom of action. At the same time an automobile requires the constant attention of the driver instead of allowing him to relax as he can on a common carrier. This responsibility may be very taxing if traffic congestion is heavy, as it typically is in the main hubs of the larger Megalopolitan cities at rush hours and on the approaches to the cities during the weekly rush hours at the beginning and end of summer week ends.

The density of the rush-hour traffic in the main hubs would seem to

---

[17] Ibid., p. 567; also Statistical Abstract of the United States: 1960, op. cit., p. 569.
[18] Automobile Manufacturers Association, Automobile Facts and Figures: 1959–60 Edition, Detroit, p. 40.

call for mass transportation rather than for individual passenger cars. For example, the hub of Manhattan obviously could not service the daily movement of people into and out of it without trains, subways, and buses. The American Transit Association has demonstrated this very strikingly by the following estimates of the carrying capacity of a single lane for different forms of transportation, in passengers per hour: [19]

Passengers in autos on surface streets	1,575
Passengers in autos on elevated highways	2,625
Passengers in buses on surface streets	9,000
Passengers in streetcars on surface streets	13,500
Passengers in streetcars in subways	20,000
Passengers in local subway trains	40,000
Passengers in express subway trains	60,000

These are approximate figures, which in practice have been actually exceeded and could certainly be increased. However, it is the relative volume of the carrying capacity that is most significant, not the absolute numbers. The flow of automobiles can be improved on controlled-access highways with safety devices, higher speed limits, and the use of smaller cars, and there are also ways to speed up the flow in the subways. Subway trains can carry ten to twenty times as many passengers as automobile traffic can in urban surroundings. Even the relationship between buses and street cars on surface streets and automobiles on elevated highways requires some thought, for the former types of transportation are obviously more economical in cost and in time. Nevertheless, the automobile's share in daily transportation has been gaining in recent decades and in recent years, not only in the country as a whole but even in the most crowded hubs of Megalopolis — that is, in Manhattan, Philadelphia, and Boston.

In Megalopolis the competition of the automobile with urban buses, subways, and suburban trains creates many practical problems, and it also suggests a few questions as to the future of transportation in crowded urbanized areas. Is traffic on rubber tires going to eliminate most of the passenger transportation on steel rails? Among those most worried by such a prospect are urban authorities, who visualize the traffic and parking problems that would develop in their congested business districts if all those who used to come in from out of town by train were to come instead in their own cars. Logically rail service would seem to answer a

[19] From the Joint Committee on Washington Metropolitan Problems, *Washington Metropolitan Area Transportation Problems, Hearings* . . . , May-June 1958, *op. cit.,* p. 160. It was mentioned that even before 1940, trains in one of the New York subways have transported on a local track 61,800 passengers per hour, and on an express track 123,000.

growing need of metropolitan areas, especially in Megalopolis. But the railroads said passenger traffic did not pay.

With the development of suburban sprawl and the increasing number of commuters, one would expect an increasing need for and use of mass transportation. Actually, fewer people are coming into the busiest hubs daily, and they are carried by many more automobiles. As the number of train passengers declines, the network of highways expands and highway traffic swells. A general impression grows with the public, and seems accepted by the regulating authorities, that in the competitive struggle for the passengers the railways are losing while in both commuting and inter-city traffic the highways and the automobile are winning.

Why are the railroads losing a function in which they would seem at first glance to be more "economical" than motor vehicles? The official answer of the railroad management is that passenger traffic brings them only deficit while, as private corporations, they must make profits so as to pay dividends to their shareholders and interest to their bondholders. Staying in the business of passenger transportation, it is said, would make them lose too much money.

While the railroads were cutting down their passenger services, the automobile demonstrated its many advantages over any collective form of transportation. Production in series and in great numbers quickly made it an indispensable piece of equipment in the American way of life, especially outside the larger cities. The number of passenger cars and taxis registered in the United States rose from 8,000 in 1900 to 8 million by 1920, 27.4 million by 1940, 59 million in 1959 (one passenger car for every four inhabitants in 1940 and for every three in 1960). In 1957 about 75 per cent of the 51.2 million families in the nation owned at least one car, and as there were then about 55 million privately owned automobiles, one may forecast that soon there will be more American households with two cars than with no car. Until 1957 the percentage of families that owned a car had been steadily increasing. In 1958 this steady growth showed hesitation, for only 74 per cent of all families seemed to own a car that year. Some kind of saturation of the market had been achieved, at least temporarily.[20]

Thus almost everybody owned a car in America, and this had been a fairly generalized situation even in some large cities, especially Detroit,

[20] The above figures are from *Statistical Abstract of the United States: 1959, op. cit.*, pp. 556–562. The annual publication of the Automobile Manufacturers Association, *Automobile Facts and Figures*, in its 1959–60 edition, p. 33, gave the following percentages for families owning automobiles: 75 in 1957, 73 in 1958, 74 in 1959. This was the first setback in this ratio's advance since World War II.

Los Angeles, San Diego, and Houston. Among the large cities, only the main Megalopolitan nuclei (New York City, Philadelphia, Washington, and Boston), and also San Francisco and New Orleans, showed a ratio of more than 1.1 household per passenger car in 1959.[21] This higher ratio obviously corresponds to dense agglomerations of urban population, to more crowded cities, and somewhat better means of public transportation. The density of traffic on the city streets is not actually measured by the number of cars registered in a city, or even in the county to which that city belongs, for commuters, shoppers, and other visitors often come from the outside in their cars, crowding the streets.

Whatever the detailed indications of the car-per-household ratio, almost every family has been motorized in the United States. And as one owned and drove a car, one preferred using it for travelling whenever practicable, rather than taking the train or the bus. As highway traffic rose, more and better highways were built in Megalopolis and across the nation. A diversified and prosperous trade developed servicing cars and motorists along the highways. The automobile industry, highway construction, the service station trade became huge organizations and essential pillars of the national economy. These industries consumed or distributed large quantities of steel (more than 20 per cent of national consumption in 1958), rubber, petroleum products, glass, nonferrous metals, cement, and various machinery (for instance 30 per cent of the radio sets produced in 1958 in America were for automobiles);[22] as this demand rose the whole economy grew. The leaders of the motor-car industry began to consider themselves the prime movers of American prosperity, a state of mind expressed in the mid-1950's by the famous statement: "What is good for General Motors is good for the country."

This growth of motor transportation took a great deal away from the railroads. The trains lost most of their passenger traffic; they also lost some freight traffic in proportion to the nation's total (Fig. 206). The decline of the railroads was a gradual and complicated evolution. Many factors were at play, concurring in the present painful results; some of these factors were indeed permanent, while others may be termed temporary, as they were a result of the need for (and lack of) adaptation of the railways to new conditions of competition in the transportation field. A good deal of the traffic on short distances was taken over by cars and trucks, and a good deal of the longer distance traffic by the airplane. Whether the railroads had to lose as much as they did is a much-debated question.

---

[21] *Automobile Facts and Figures, 1959–60, op. cit.*, pp. 22–23.   [22] *Ibid.*

In a special issue entitled "Who Shot the Passenger Train?" the magazine *Trains* has presented a thoughtful analysis of that question as seen by the railroads.[23] Passenger traffic has become too expensive, causing a deficit that the railroads cannot carry any more. The railroads also have not been subsidized recently as the airlines were; they had to build their own tracks, and they pay taxes on every parcel of land they occupy, while trucks and motorists ride on highways built with public funds and on which no taxes are levied. The railroads blame the special expenses incurred for commuting traffic, the excessive demands of the labor unions, the mail and express traffic, which in the railroads' opinion should not use passenger trains and stations but be considered as freight (though paying much more than other kinds of freight), and so forth. However, the conclusion is that passenger trains should be saved and the service on them improved:

On the face of it, a passenger instrument which can propel 200 to 300 people at 80 miles per hour with only 1500 horsepower and a crew of three or four men is not bound for the museum for the same reason that the stagecoach landed there. Man has yet to invent an overland passenger mode of transport with the train's unique combination of speed, safety, comfort, dependability and economy . . . its native profitability has been frustrated by archaic regulation, obsolete labor contracts, unequal taxation, and publicly sponsored competition. Moreover an essentially wholesale and industrial breed of management has been unable to afford the passenger train the retail-minded direction which it requires.[24]

This statement implicitly admits that railroad management has not been capable of managing passenger traffic as it should have and has concentrated its preferences and care on industrial freight. While discussing the fact that railroads have been doing better in the West than in the East and that some of the Western railroads have found passenger traffic profitable, it is argued that such figures can be achieved through tricks in accounting,[25] and that Western railroads are gradually coming to accept the Eastern method of accounting, which stresses the passenger deficit as the right result. This is an argument that may be reversed as well. Accounting is a subtle art, and in as involved a matter as separating the costs of passenger traffic and freight traffic using the same railroads, a great deal becomes interpretation and could be debated for long.

There are many entanglements in the accounting and financing of the railroads. They have certainly not been much interested in passenger

[23] *Trains*, Milwaukee, Wis., April 1959, Vol. 19, No. 6.

[24] *Ibid.*, p. 51.

[25] *Ibid.*, p. 19: "many roads have felt they could write their passenger deficits off as advertising or public relations."

trains recently, and to continue the service in the East they call for government subsidy and other help, and they would like to see the management of passenger service established as a separate entity accorded separate responsibility and authority over revenues and costs, and committed
therefore to separate (that is, additional) profits. Such demands were
made in western Europe earlier in this century and they have led to the
nationalization of most of the European rail networks (in France, Germany, the Netherlands, Italy, Switzerland, Britain, for example). Such a
solution is certainly not what the present railroad management wants, and
it would be contrary to American economic tradition. And yet, to insure
proper transportation, public authorities have been put in charge of the
construction and operation of highways, bridges, and tunnels needed by
motor traffic, of airports, city subways, and even of some of the major
seaports. To meet the present railroad crisis, especially that of passenger
traffic, would seem to call for a re-examination of policy.

Any prospect of nationalization still appears far-removed, but some
subsidies or help from public funds may well be forthcoming. Such a
trend could hardly avoid increasing the influence of government in the
regulation and management of rail transportation. The last forty years
have seen a rapid decline of the position of railroad management in the
American economy. From the 1880's to about 1920 the railroads were,
with banking, the more select sector of business; the securities of the
railroads were considered an excellent investment — "blue chips" and
"growth stocks." Since the 1920's much of railroading has seemed to rest
on its laurels. It has been replaced by other industries as "growth sectors"
of the American economy, among these fast-growing industries being the
automobile manufactures and the large petroleum concerns. These became
"blue chips" and were favored until recently by investors, including the
specialists of investments, the men of "power without property" whose
great influence on contemporary business has been analyzed by Adolf A.
Berle, Jr.[26]

As the investors, led by their experts, turned away from the railroads,
and as motor transportation took a leading role on the national scene, it
became more difficult for the railroads to obtain more money and better
managers. Their competitors were being boosted by all the complex of
forces that follow prestige, success, and belief in future growth.

The need for remedying the railroad situation has been increasingly felt
since 1958. Concluding his report on a study conducted under the auspices
of the Brookings Institution, James C. Nelson wrote:

[26] Adolf A. Berle, Jr., *Power Without Property: A New Development in American Political Economy*, Harcourt, Brace and Company, New York, 1959.

It is noteworthy that the current difficulties of the railroads developed in times of prosperity rather than of depression. Important contributing factors have been declining passenger traffic and rising passenger deficits, the failure of expansion in railroad freight traffic to keep pace with the growing economy, and heavy losses of the most profitable types of traffic to the trucks. Government provision of facilities for competing agencies and limited rail rate and service adjustments to inflation and to competition have also been significant. Finally, the failure of railroad management to make greater progress in increasing labor productivity, in improving or discontinuing service, and in dealing with rate and service competition must not be overlooked . . . the troublesome railroad situation is primarily the result of long term factors, including, to an indeterminate but obviously important extent, technological substitution.[27]

It is rather normal that technological substitution progresses more rapidly in times of expansion than in times of economic stagnation. America has known little stagnation in this century. If rail transportation had been completely outdated, however, it would have been relegated to the museum as the stagecoach has been. On the contrary the feeling is gaining that such should not, could not, be the case, that the railroads still have a useful and even necessary function in present conditions. Passenger service is obviously an important part of that function, especially in the more densely populated and integrated metropolitan areas. It is in Megalopolis, curiously enough, that the plight of the railroads has appeared worst, and it is here that public authority has undertaken to help some suburban and metropolitan rail traffic to survive. A recent report of the U. S. Department of Commerce recommended that the Federal government

should encourage local authorities to do more long range land-use planning, in which transportation has a critical part . . . Encourage urban long-range community planning, including total transportation planning to make full use of highway, transit, rail commutation, and all other capacity to minimize total transportation cost and congestion, in full coordination with activities under the Housing Act of 1949 as amended . . . With local communities and the same coordination, investigate basic approaches to such plans and their financing. Methods might include amendment of existing highway legislation to allow charges on city highway gateways to help divert auto commuter travel to mass transport means, higher community parking fees to help similarly, diversion of such funds to pay for other transport facilities, etc. . . . Urban transportation planning should in the long run help the railroad commuter deficit problem.[28]

[27] James C. Nelson, *Railroad Transportation and Public Policy*, The Brookings Institution, Washington, D. C., 1959, p. 413.

[28] U. S. Department of Commerce, *Federal Transportation Policy and Program*, U. S. Government Printing Office, Washington, D. C., March 1960, quote from Sections 6, p. 25, and 9, p. 29.

In its statement of long-range objectives the same report observed: "There is general and growing realization that less improvement has been made in distribution than in production of goods and that much of the remaining potential improvement of the Nation's economic efficiency lies in the area of distribution. Transportation is the largest single element within that area." [29] It is significant that in its recommendations this report, transmitted by the President to the Congress for consideration, found it necessary to emphasize the crisis of the railroads and the need to solve it rapidly; urban transportation with its commuter problem; and the need for coordinated planning of all available means of transportation in order to "divert auto commuter travel to mass transport means." This would appear as a new trend in government thinking at a high level in the United States. The shift of emphasis from the individual car to public transportation indicates a change of mind that probably has not yet been achieved or even desired all over this vast country, but increasing numbers of responsible people are realizing its urgency in the more urbanized regions: in the area around San Francisco Bay, in metropolitan Chicago, and in Megalopolis.[30]

Commuting and Urban Traffic in Megalopolis

In every section of Megalopolis conditions have become severe enough, in terms of congested traffic and difficult access to city hubs for business and to places of relaxation for week ends, to stir local and state authorities to action. In most cases this has meant making increased provisions for cars, in the form of highways, bridges, tunnels, garages, and parking facilities. For example, more has been done to keep automobile traffic flowing in and around Manhattan than in any other spot on our globe. For the last forty years this has been traditional thinking and acting.[31] It has given Megalopolis an unrivalled intensity of automobile traffic flow, but it has also given the region its celebrated traffic jams and delays. Because

[29] *Ibid.*, p. 1.

[30] Many experts still feel that it is too late to save public transportation in America, that it may "survive" in as congested a place as New York City and perhaps develop around San Francisco Bay but that elsewhere the car and the plane will keep the future to themselves. Such seems to be the forecast by Gilbert Burck and Sanford S. Parker (see the Editors of Fortune, *Markets of the Sixties*, Harper and Brothers, New York, 1960, pp. 165–189).

[31] The past story of transportation policies can be followed in a series of important publications of the Brookings Institution of Washington, D. C.: Charles L. Dearing, *American Highway Policy*, 1941; Charles L. Dearing and Wilfred Owen, *National Transportation Policy*, 1949; Wilfred Owen, *The Metropolitan Transportation Problem*, 1956; James C. Nelson, *Railroad Transportation and Public Policy*, 1959.

of them increasing attention is being given also to public rapid transit systems and to railroad service for commuters.

In the fight to reduce automobile traffic congestion Boston has been a leader. Perhaps this is because Boston and Massachusetts remember how hard-hit they have been by their geographic location, eccentric to the interior of the continent as it was settled and developed; and how the disadvantages of that location were increased as the major railroads chose New York and coastal points south of it as their Atlantic terminals. Perhaps the Port of Boston would not have "dried up" as it has if the access to it from the west had been improved by a few more railroad bridges over the Hudson River. With all these memories in mind, Boston has been striving to maintain as good means of access to its downtown area as possible, and it has been waging a rather dramatic battle.

The first problem in this mushrooming metropolitan region, already densely occupied and centered on an old city with rather narrow downtown streets, was to keep too many cars *that did not need to* from coming into the hub. Of the traffic approaching a city, the central business district is the destination for only 17–33 per cent, depending on the city's size (Fig. 207). And yet a study of travel patterns in many cities throughout the United States, conducted by the Bureau of Public Roads in the years 1946–54, showed that there was more passing through the central parts of cities than was necessary,[32] because of the lack of good peripheral routes. Recognition of this situation led to the idea of a circumferential route to skirt the densely built-up hub of Boston, so that those whose destination was not in that central sector would not need to cross parts of it. Accordingly, in the early 1950's the Massachusetts Department of Public Works built Route 128, the outer belt highway proposed by the master highway plan of 1948 for the Boston metropolitan area. Route 128 has been a huge success, attracting a great deal of traffic and many industries, especially in the electronics field, and by 1960 it already seemed to need enlarging, for it was becoming crowded.

The great success of Boston's Route 128 has led to planning for similar circumferential routes in other cities, particularly Philadelphia, Baltimore, and Washington, where peripheral belt expressways are being built. Such by-passes have often been provided around the downtown center of smaller cities, and in a way some of the major turnpikes in Megalopolis allow long-distance traffic to by-pass large cities in the axial belt. This is

[32] See Frank B. Curran and J. T. Stegmaier, *Travel Patterns in 50 Cities*, Division of Highway Transport Research, U. S. Bureau of Public Roads, circa 1956 (mimeographed).

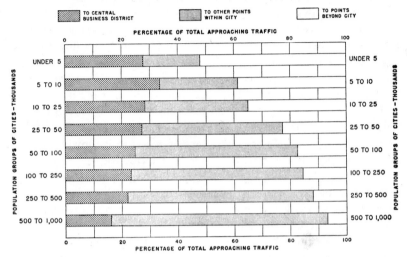

FIG. 207. *Courtesy of the U. S. Bureau of Public Roads*

true in part in the New York area, where a number of by-pass routes already exist while others are still in the planning or construction stage.

There are fewer such by-pass facilities for avoiding crowded city streets while driving from point to point within one city. In Europe and Asia the steady growth of older cities resulted in the abandonment of city walls, on the sites of which circular boulevards were built. In American cities, however, there were no walls the removal of which could provide such circular routes. In most cases the central city was laid out on a "checkerboard" plan,[33] but growth out from this center has been irregular, extending radially along the main routes to and from the city. Movement within the city area often requires following one radial route into the hub of the city and another out from it to one's destination. In recent years the planning and building of inner-belt routes to by-pass city hubs has begun, for these are typically badly congested, especially at daily rush hours.[34] Washington has planned such a route. Manhattan as a whole has one, in the Henry Hudson Parkway–West Side Highway, the Franklin D.

[33] See Jean Gottmann, "Plans de villes des deux côtés de l'Atlantique," in *Mélanges Géographiques Canadiens Offerts à Raoul Blanchard*, Presses Universitaires Laval, Quebec, 1959, pp. 237–242; also Chapters 3 and 4 above, pp. 176–178.

[34] In contrast, intercity traffic is little troubled by rush-hour peaks on a daily basis, unless two cities are linked by a very active flow of commuters.

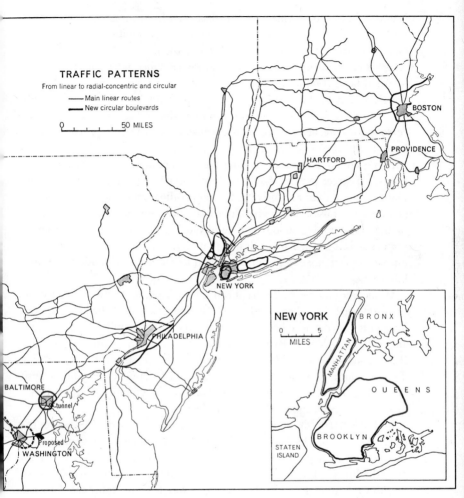

FIG. 208

Roosevelt Drive, and the Harlem River Drive (Fig. 208, inset). In lower Manhattan plans have been drawn up for a more localized inner loop, to be provided by widening existing streets, and part of the work has been completed.[35] Boston's 1948 plan included a recommendation for an inner-belt expressway around the most crowded heart of downtown Boston, as well as an expressway system with spokes radiating from the inner belt toward the periphery. Building of these radial expressways has made good progress, and they have been extremely helpful, but the inner belt has

[35] *The New York Times,* October 16, 1958.

been delayed, and at times the plan has even been threatened with abandonment, for it has aroused much speculation and political struggle in the city. However, it remains a major need of the metropolitan highway system.[36] The same need is recognized in Philadelphia, where part of such a loop has been completed.

In addition to the problem of diverting through-traffic from the hubs of cities there is the problem of handling the traffic that has legitimate reasons for entering these crowded central areas. Many approaches have been tried: one-way traffic to permit more continuous flow; metered parking; elimination of all parking from congested areas during business hours; off-street parking facilities, both public and private; off-street facilities, both public and private, for the loading and unloading of trucks and intercity buses. Everywhere this is an increasing problem, but in most of the cities of Megalopolis it is aggravated by the narrow and often irregular streets in their older downtown sections, inherited from the earliest days of settlement and quite unsuited to the needs of modern automobile traffic.

While automobile traffic has been multiplying, and efforts to meet its growing needs have been made in the various ways described above, public transit systems have been plagued by decreasing numbers of passengers and increasing deficits. Paraphrasing the famous Latin motto, the Regional Plan Association of New York entitled one of its newsletters, "Sick Transit Gloria Manhattan," [37] and this could be applied to public transit generally, in Megalopolis as in other parts of the country. Various forms of aid have been suggested or undertaken.

In Boston, for example, by act of the Massachusetts legislature the transit system of the bankrupt Boston Elevated Railway Company was turned over in 1947 to the Metropolitan Transit Authority (M.T.A.). In 1949 the Boston Transit Department was abolished, and the ownership of its subways, tunnels, and other facilities was likewise transferred to the M.T.A. This Authority, composed of Boston and thirteen other towns and cities in the inner metropolitan area, now owns and operates a rapid transit system and surface facilities (buses, trackless trolleys, and streetcars). Under this system of public ownership, and under the control of

---

[36] The desirability of the inner belt in Boston has been stressed again recently by several studies, among them the valuable report of Boston College's Seminar Research Bureau, College of Business Administration, *Transportation Facts and Public Policy for Downtown Boston, op. cit.* See also Coverdale and Colpitts, *Traffic Studies for the Boston Metropolitan Area,* Boston, July, 1957.

[37] Regional Plan Association of New York, *Newsletter,* November 1953.

the state legislature, Boston's transit has been maintained and in some respects improved. Nevertheless, the M.T.A. faces a substantial annual deficit (which is paid off by the fourteen cities and towns on a proportionate basis) and a steadily though slowly declining patronage. Although there were 205 million revenue passengers in 1958, this still was 3.2 per cent less than the number carried in 1957.[38] Faced also with growing needs of metropolitan transportation, the M.T.A. had the courage in 1959 to extend its rapid transit service to Newton over the abandoned right-of-way of the Boston and Albany Railroad's Newton Highlands Branch. Although the M.T.A.'s managers have not been too happy about this step, they felt they had to provide the service, which extends about twelve miles from the center of the system, farther than any other rapid transit line.[39] Large parking facilities at the new stations were planned to attract "park-and-ride" passengers, as had already been done near the outermost stations on other lines. Such a reconversion of an abandoned railroad line to rapid transit under public ownership was a significant step.[40] Studies based on a questionnaire issued to passengers indicate that this line has attracted enough former automobile users to reduce traffic congestion in downtown Boston by about 7 per cent.[41]

The case of Boston, a central city already endowed with a relatively efficient rapid transit system, well illustrates the position and urgency of the traffic crisis in the larger cities of Megalopolis. Boston realized that it could not afford to let transit slowly decline and to rely only on the automobile, more highways, and more parking spaces. Balanced cooperation and coordination between rapid transit and automobile traffic have become a necessity for Greater Boston.

This same necessity has been recognized for some time in metropolitan

[38] Metropolitan Transit Authority, *Twelfth Annual Report: Year Ended December 31, 1958*, Boston, 1959. See also the League of Women Voters of Massachusetts, *Massachusetts State Government: A Citizen's Handbook*, Harvard University Press, Cambridge, 1956, pp. 239–245.

[39] In 1947 the Metropolitan Transit Recess Commission, known as the Coolidge Commission, recommended extension of the M.T.A. lines along twelve routes. (See Commonwealth of Massachusetts, Metropolitan Transit Recess Commission, *Report of the Legislative Commission on Rapid Transit 1947*, April 1, 1947.) Such extensions are still being urged. (See Greater Boston Economic Study Committee, *Commuting: A Policy Statement*, Boston, June 1958.)

[40] In similar fashion, New York City's rapid transit facilities were extended, in 1956, to the Rockaways using tracks of a branch of the Long Island Rail Road, which discontinued service in 1950 after fire destroyed a trestle.

[41] Greater Boston Economic Study Committee, *A Survey of Commuters on the Highland Branch*, Boston, August 1960.

New York, which is often cited, even by the champions of highway traffic, as the outstanding example of a city where rapid mass transit must be allowed to survive. In the hub of Manhattan the concentration of urban activities is so great as to convince everybody of the necessity of some public transit.

In New York, as in Boston, the debt-ridden rapid transit system has been reorganized. In 1953 all rapid transit and surface lines owned by the city and operated by its Board of Transportation were turned over, under a ten-year lease agreement, to the New York City Transit Authority. This public benefit corporation (established by the New York State legislature in 1953 and revised in 1955) maintains and operates the lines, using the income from the fares, but capital costs are paid by the city, which thus subsidizes the system.[42] The recent capital improvement program has included such items as modernization of the signal system, improvements of stations, new lighting in stations, new subway cars and buses. While the number of passengers has increased slightly in the last year or two (after about a decade of steady decline) there is still an operating deficit, though it has decreased.[43]

In addition to its subsidization of the publicly owned rapid transit system the City of New York has provided tax relief for the privately owned Staten Island Rapid Transit Railway, by the device of leasing it from the company and then leasing it back again with abatement of all taxes.[44]

It has often been suggested that more efficient operation of the transit system would be possible if the load were spread over a greater part of the day by staggering the working hours in the city. At the present time more than half of the total load is carried during the morning and evening rush hours, about two and three hours long respectively.[45] While a stagger plan might require a greater number of subway cars it would permit present transit lines to carry a larger total load, thus reducing the need for additional lines; and it would increase passenger comfort, thus perhaps inducing more people to use the public transit facilities. A number of studies have been made of the feasibility of such a program. Already individual stagger systems have been adopted by some city departments

[42] New York City Transit Authority, *First Annual Report, July 1, 1953 to June 30, 1954*, New York, 1954.

[43] New York City Transit Authority, *Annual Report for the Year July 1, 1958 to June 30, 1959*, New York, 1959. Fare increases contributed to this drop in passengers, but another factor was the decrease in number of people entering the city's hub. See above, p. 634.

[44] *The New York Times*, October 7, 1957.

[45] New York City Transit Authority, *Annual Report for the Year July 1, 1958 to June 30, 1959, op. cit.*

and by many large private offices, and this has had some beneficial effect on the transportation conditions at rush hours.[46]

Numerous other proposals have been made for the improvement of the rapid-transit facilities of the New York area. In 1957 the Metropolitan Rapid Transit Commission recommended a bi-state rapid-transit loop linking Manhattan's subways with the New Jersey rail lines.[47] This plan was doomed, however, by opposition from many sides, including both New York City and various New Jersey municipalities. Another proposal is the extension of the Hudson and Manhattan Railroad Company (the so-called Hudson Tubes, which runs from New York to Jersey City and Newark) out to Morristown, Montclair, and other suburban areas, using railroad tracks already in existence. It has also been proposed that operation of this line, now in bankruptcy, be put in the hands of the Port of New York Authority, which, after long study of the problem, offered early in 1961 to buy it.[48] This, of course, would require legislation by both New York State and New Jersey. In New York the proposed Second Avenue subway line, promised to Manhattan's East Side after the dismantling of the Third Avenue Elevated Line, seems to have been forgotten. Several proposals to put the Port of New York Authority in charge of rail commuting, subway, or other large-scale transit operations have met with opposition from the Authority itself, because of the fear that such deficit-endowed operations would wreck its finances. It has been concentrating on facilities for motor-vehicle traffic (bridges, tunnels, bus and truck terminals), airports, and waterfront installations.[49]

---

[46] See, for example, *The New York Times* for July 27, 1959, and January 22, 1960.

[47] Metropolitan Rapid Transit Commission, *Metropolitan Rapid Transit Survey: Report of the Project Director*, New York, May, 1957; *idem, Report on Rapid Transit for the New York–New Jersey Metropolitan Area*, New York, January 1958.

This commission was established in 1954 by the states of New York and New Jersey to make recommendations concerning rapid transit in the New York metropolitan area. Its study was financed by appropriations from the individual states and from the Port of New York Authority. In addition to the plan mentioned above the Commission recommended also that the two states set up a Metropolitan Rapid Transit District to work for improvements in transit facilities. Neither plan was adopted, and the Commission went out of existence in 1959.

[48] *The New York Times,* January 28, 1961.

[49] It is widely claimed that by providing so many facilities for motor vehicles the Port Authority has actually aggravated the whole transportation situation, for each new facility brings additional cars into the city, increasing its traffic congestion and reducing the use of public transportation systems. For this reason, and because of its endeavor to remain specialized in the more profitable sectors of metropolitan transport, the Port Authority is meeting with increased criticism, in the press and in the U. S. Congress. See Edward T. Chase, "How to Rescue New York from Its Port Authority," *Harper's Magazine,* June 1960, pp. 67–74.

Baltimore and Washington are still without rapid transit, but as a result of recent surveys of their transport needs experts are beginning to talk about it, especially in Washington.[50] And in 1960 Congress considered a bill, backed by the mayors of many cities, to establish a fund from which cities could borrow for the purpose of improving their urban transportation facilities.

Philadelphia is one of the cities that hopes to obtain some sort of Federal aid in support of its most interesting transportation plan.[51] Under contract with the city the two railroads involved, the Pennsylvania and the Reading, provide frequent service from outlying parts of the city to its center at a new reduced fare of thirty cents. During the trial period, beginning in the fall of 1958, the system was operated on two routes, with the city paying the railroads a subsidy ($340,000 a year on one route, $105,000 on the other) to cover the cost of the extra service and the low fares. The plan's marked success — there was a significant increase in passengers — proved that lower fares and better service attract more riders, many of whom had previously been rush-hour automobile drivers from peripheral parts of the city or from the suburbs. The city has estimated that the cheaper fares mean a saving to the passenger over automobile operation and an annual saving of perhaps $1 million in the cost of maintaining existing roads and policing them, not to mention the avoidance of new road construction. Early in 1960 the plan was extended to other routes, and its operation was placed in the hands of the nonprofit Passenger Service Improvement Corporation, whose directors represent the two railroads and the railroad labor unions as well as the city.[52] The railroads are guaranteed fixed payments, and if the fares do not cover these the city will make up the difference. The Philadelphia Transportation Company, privately owned, has cooperated by providing feeder buses to the railroad stations on these routes, and transfers to and from the local subway and bus lines are available at a reduced rate. Plans for the future, for which Philadelphia will seek Federal aid, include electrification of all the lines, building of more parking facilities, purchase of new air-conditioned cars, integration of the new system with the city's other transit facilities, and expansion of the subway system. While it is hoped that ad-

[50] Eighty-sixth Congress, First Session, Joint Committee on Washington Metropolitan Problems, *Hearings on Report of the Washington Mass Transportation Survey*, 1959; *idem, Final Report* (No. 38), 1959.

[51] See City of Philadelphia, Urban Traffic and Transportation Board, *Plan and Program, 1955*, Philadelphia, April 1956; *Hearings on Report of the Washington Mass Transportation Survey, op. cit.*, pp. 429–434; Fred J. Cook, "Railroads Versus the Commuter," *The Nation*, December 20, 1958, pp. 67–71.

[52] *The New York Times*, January 21, 1960.

jacent suburban counties may join the system, it is at present limited to the city of Philadelphia. However, commuters can and do benefit from it by driving to the city limits, where they park and board the train, paying the reduced fare into the heart of the city. Thus they avoid the higher fares that are still charged from suburban stations, and their cars are kept out of the city. Simultaneously, therefore, Philadelphia's Transit Improvement Program provides additional rapid transit within the city, decreases the number of automobiles entering the hub area, and increases the income of the commuter railroads.

Other efforts, too, have been made to help the commuter railroads, which face many of the same problems as do rapid transit companies. Morning and evening rush hours, four to five hours each business day, require crews and equipment that are little used the rest of the time. Property taxes must be paid on railroad holdings, while automobiles, buses, and trucks use public highways, built and maintained at public expense. Because of this competition, railroad passenger and freight traffic has been continually declining, and the resulting loss of income, together with rising costs, means poorer service and further loss of patronage. This vicious circle involves, of course, larger and larger deficits and darker prospects for the future. And yet the need for commuter rail service is widely recognized.[53] In general, what seems to be expected from trains in Megalopolis is not that they should reduce the number of automobiles or their use but that they should keep their numbers from soaring to a point at which the growth of the city's economy could be strangled by congestion in the hub and on its approaches.

In Boston, for example, every business day more than half a million people move into and out of the downtown area of the city. In 1956 about 57 per cent travelled by private automobile, 34 per cent by M.T.A. facilities and private buses, and only 9 per cent by the commuter trains of the New Haven, Boston and Albany, and Boston and Maine railroads. The seriousness of the problem has been well stated by the Greater Boston Economic Study Committee.

> Every year as more commuters take to the highways, downtown traffic conditions deteriorate and parking troubles multiply. These conditions weaken the competitive position of downtown Boston in retail trade and many other activities. They lower real estate values and are, in part, responsible for the City of Boston's chronic fiscal embarrassment.[54]

[53] For a general discussion of the railroad commuter problem, see *Hearings on Report of the Washington Mass Transportation Survey, op. cit.*, pp. 389–434.

[54] Greater Boston Economic Study Committee, *Commuters: A Policy Statement,* Boston, 1958, p. 8.

At the same time the increased use of automobiles means decreasing business and therefore deficits for the M.T.A. and the railroads. While the publicly owned M.T.A. has tried to expand its network in spite of its deficit, the railroads have continued to cut down their commuter service, decreasing the number of suburban trains and even abandoning individual lines.[55] The abandoned Highland Branch of the Boston and Albany Railroad has been taken over by the M.T.A. as described above. When the New Haven Railroad threatened to end commuting service on the Old Colony line, which served the South Shore suburbs, the Massachusetts legislature, in 1958, voted the railroad a special subsidy to keep these trains running for one year more. In 1959 renewal of the subsidy was refused, and the trains were discontinued. The Greater Boston Economic Study Committee statement [56] considered an extension of the M.T.A. over the tracks of the Old Colony, perhaps as far as Brockton. The same report noted that replacing the commuter trains by a bus service from the South Shore would bring some 140 additional buses into downtown Boston at rush hours, which did not seem practicable. Letting all the commuters who took trains in 1957–58 ride in their own cars would mean some 75,000 additional automobiles in the city every day, mainly in its business district, which would require more than doubling the parking facilities.[57] The conclusion of the Greater Boston Committee seemed wise. The M.T.A. should be extended and improved and its deficit dealt with in more imaginative fashion; commuter trains should be maintained and the service improved; and finally, a metropolitan planning commission should be given authority to coordinate all plans affecting the movement of people within the metropolitan area.

While the continued prosperity of the New York metropolitan economy is partly dependent on rapid transit, this huge tri-state region is dependent also on rail commuter service. But here, as elsewhere, the number of railroad passengers has been decreasing,[58] while more and more travel

[55] In the summer of 1960 the Boston and Maine Railroad inaugurated an experimental program offering more frequent service at lower fares, with new air-conditioned equipment. See the *Boston Daily Globe*, April 14, 1960.

[56] *Op. cit.*

[57] According to estimates of the Greater Boston Economic Study Committee (*op. cit.*, p. 14), "these additional spaces in six-story garages would require land equivalent to 40% of all the land now devoted to commercial and industrial uses in the central business district. And still more valuable land would be required for widening streets, building access ramps and the like to handle the additional downtown traffic."

[58] The maximum number of railroad commuters, more than 350,000, entered New York City in the late 1920's. This number decreased to a low of about 230,000 in 1941,

by automobile and bus. Because of this loss of patronage and rising costs the commuter railroads serving the New York area operate their passenger service at a loss, and by 1957 all of them were asking for government aid. As *The New York Times* put it: "Metropolitan commuters and railroads are trapped in ruinous fiscal squeeze." [59] Because of the severity of the problem, the states in the area have begun to search for ways of helping the commuter railroads.[60]

New York State's earliest efforts were exerted in behalf of the Long Island Rail Road, which went bankrupt in 1949 and spent the next five years in the hands of a series of trustees. In 1954 the state legislature discharged the railroad from bankruptcy and placed it under the management of the Long Island Transit Authority. For twelve years it is to be relieved of half of its state, county, and local taxes and of the interest on a debt owed to the Pennsylvania Railroad. At the same time it is to undertake a $60 million modernization program. Several sizable fare increases contributed to a marked decrease in passengers, from the 1949 peak of 87,500 daily to a low of 74,000 in 1955. Since that time there has been a slight increase, but again in 1960 there were setbacks because of a long strike and several heavy storms, and in early 1961 the Long Island was again calling for help to avert a financial crisis.[61]

During a 26-day strike that halted all traffic on the Long Island Rail Road in July 1960, New York City took several measures to check the

rose during the war years to about 325,000 in 1944, and has declined steadily since then to about 208,000 in the late 1950's. See *The New York Times*, March 23, 1954 and February 22, 1959. See also the comparison of New York's case with that of London and Paris by David Neft, "Some Aspects of Rail Commuting: New York, London, and Paris," *Geographical Review*, Vol. 49, No. 2, April 1959, pp. 151–163.

[59] *The New York Times*, October 7, 1957, pp. 1 and 20. See also "Time for Decisions on Commuting," *Business Week*, September 6, 1958, p. 164; "The Long Island Rail Road Works Its Way Back," *Business Week*, March 21, 1959, pp. 106–114; Fred J. Cook, "Railroads Versus the Commuter," *op. cit.*; Charles E. Stonier, *Long Island's Transportation: Resources and Needs*, Hofstra College Bureau of Business and Community Research, Hempstead, New York, December 1957. We are also indebted for our analysis of the commuting problems in Megalopolis to Dr. Herbert Askwith, who gave us the benefit of his advice and several reports.

[60] Until 1960, however, relieving the railroads of some of their financial difficulties did not induce them to improve their services; and the more passenger trains they have cut, the more their deficits have increased. This is true everywhere. *Newsweek*, in an article entitled "Who Pays for the Ride?" (August 11, 1958, pp. 71–73), observed that from 1950 to 1957, while eliminating more than 981 trains, the railroads throughout the nation claimed that the deficit in their passenger operations rose from $509 million to more than $700 million. Reducing operations does not seem to put the railroads on the way to prosperity.

[61] See *The New York Times*, March 2, 1959, and January 4, 1961.

threatened increase in automobile flow into Manhattan. Subway service from Queens and Brooklyn to Manhattan was intensified, two cars being added to most trains, especially at rush hours; special bus service was established outside the areas served by the subway lines; and parking regulations in Queens were relaxed, allowing motorists to drive to the subway, park in the vicinity of the stations, and then ride into Manhattan.[61a] As the strike started after July 4th, when the summer vacation period had already somewhat reduced the daily traffic, the compensation worked out rather well without causing the worsening of traffic that had been expected in Manhattan and on the bridges. However, the measures that had to be taken point out that reduction or complete halting of railroad commuter service can hardly be dealt with, especially in seasons of fuller activity, without an expansion and ultimate extension of subway or similar service, assumed by a public authority.

By 1959 New York State's aid to railroads became more general.[61b] The state legislature voted partial exemption from local taxes on railroad property, with the state reimbursing communities for half of the lost tax revenue. It is estimated that the saving to the railroads will rise from about $5 million in 1960 to $15 million in 1962–63. In addition, local taxes are to be eliminated on future improvements to railroad property. The legislature also initiated a State Commuter Car Program, under which the state has loaned $20 million to the Port of New York Authority, which is to act as agent to buy 400 new air-conditioned commuter cars and lease them to the New York Central, the New York, New Haven, and Hartford, and the Long Island Railroads. The first fifty of these cars were purchased for the New York Central in December 1960.[62] In addition, Governor Nelson Rockefeller recommended revision of the laws specifying size of train crew.

Several states and a Federal agency have joined forces to help the New York, New Haven, and Hartford Railroad. In October 1960, it declared it was on the verge of bankruptcy, and an interstate committee was appointed by the governors of New York State, Connecticut, Rhode Island, and Massachusetts to consider a program of tax relief. To tide the road over until such relief can be put into effect the Interstate Commerce

---

[61a] See *The New York Times*, July 12, 1960.

[61b] See "1959 Legislation Affecting Business," *New York State Commerce Review*, Vol. 13, No. 5, May 1959.

[62] *The New York Times*, December 16, 1960. The Port Authority was authorized also to borrow an additional $80 million for this purpose, with the state guaranteeing to make good any loss incurred. The New Jersey legislature accepted these proposals.

Commission guaranteed two loans (for $4.5 million and $3.5 million).[63] Nevertheless the railroad went bankrupt in July 1961.

New Jersey, too, has begun to look for solutions to its rail commuting problem. Located between and partly within the two great metropolitan regions of New York and Philadelphia, New Jersey is especially interested in attracting and keeping as many commuters as possible. The state has built a beautiful network of highways, which carry the densest flow of traffic in the world (see Fig. 203), but maintaining a good rail commuting service remains essential. In 1959 Governor Robert B. Meyner proposed a scheme by which the surplus profits from the New Jersey Turnpike's tolls would be used to subsidize rail commuting, but in November of that year the voters refused to approve this scheme.[64] However, in June 1960 the state legislature approved a railroad subsidy plan based on contracts. A state appropriation of $6 million yearly will be shared, on the basis of passenger-miles, by commuter railroads serving New Jersey, in return for their contracting, for a one-year period, to maintain essential commuter service with no fare increase, and to consolidate passenger facilities. Eight lines have signed such contracts.[65]

The subsidy thus granted to the railroads is the largest any state has yet authorized, except for the generous tax relief granted by New York State to its railroads. However, New York's program did not at first stipulate two essential conditions attached to New Jersey's subsidy: the maintenance of existing commuter services at a standard satisfactory to the state, and no increase in existing fares. Despite the substantial tax relief granted to it in March, 1959, by New York State, the New Haven line enacted three successive fare increases in the following fifteen months, the latest in the summer of 1960, and by the end of the year the New York Central, too, was asking for higher fares.[66]

For the future, Governor Meyner has set in motion another more controversial plan, for imposing an income tax on all who commute between New York and New Jersey, the funds to be used to help the commuter railroads. Already about 150,000 New Jersey residents who work in New York pay a New York State income tax, the total reaching $35–$40 million a year. New Jersey decided in 1961 to impose a similar tax on them and on the 70,000 New Yorkers who commute to New Jersey. Un-

[63] *The New York Times*, October 28, 1960, and December 31, 1960.
[64] *The New York Times*, June 6, 1959, and November 4, 1959.
[65] *The New York Times*, June 7, 1960, and August 22, 1960.
[66] *The New York Times*, December 28, 1960.

der the reciprocity clause in the New York tax law, and a similar clause that would be included in the New Jersey law, a New Jersey resident working in New York could claim a credit on the New York tax to pay his New Jersey tax, and vice versa. Transfers of funds between the states would be mandatory under the reciprocity clauses.[67]

Thus by the summer of 1960 a change had become obvious in the opinion of the state and local authorities responsible for metropolitan transportation in Megalopolis. To their endeavors in favor of highways and the automobile, and some help for rapid transit, they were now eager to add measures helping rail traffic, especially for commuters.[68] So far, however, little progress has been made in coordinating the planning for all these modes of transportation, and this is necessary for final solution of the problem. The following statement about the needs of the Boston area is applicable equally well to the other great urban centers of Megalopolis:

Development of a master transportation plan which expresses the general objectives of the community is essential. It will be achieved only when the many agencies engaged in highway and street construction and those engaged in mass transportation begin to develop plans that complement rather than compete with one another.[69]

Cost, Waste, and Wealth

Determining the actual cost of any means of transportation is a very complicated matter. Rail transportation appears to require constant subsidies in order to maintain passenger traffic, while in contrast it is generally agreed that automobile transportation "pays for itself," which means it is

[67] *The New York Times*, May 2, 1960, June 7, 1960, and January 11, 1961.

[68] In Megalopolis, helping the rail commuter service amounts to helping the whole passenger coach service. There the distinction between commuting and intercity traffic is only a matter of accounting and, to a lesser extent, of train schedules, which must be adapted to dual needs. Businessmen or other white-collar workers residing and working in Trenton or New Brunswick, for example, often need to make one or two trips a week to Manhattan or Philadelphia or even Newark. Faced with the choice of taking his car or the train for his trip, such a traveller may prefer to take the train if the commuter service is good; thus, although he is not a commuter he uses the commuting facilities. This is true of the Pennsylvania Railroad line from New York to Washington or from Philadelphia to Harrisburg, as it is true of the New Haven line from Boston to New York. The continuous system of commuter-carrying railroads along the axial belt of Megalopolis becomes a sort of enormous "subway." It has attracted Federal attention. See *Commuter Transportation, Report prepared for the Committee on Interstate and Foreign Commerce, U. S. Senate,* 87th Congress, Committee Print, Washington, D. C., January 31, 1961.

[69] Boston College, *Transportation Facts and Public Policy for Downtown Boston, op. cit.,* p. iv.

Table 24

HIGHWAY AND STREET EXPENDITURES AND REVENUES, 1929–59

(*In Millions*)

A. Expenditures

Year	Capital Outlay	Maintenance & Administration	Interest on Highway Debt	Grand Total
1929	$1,272	$ 750	$315	$ 2,337
1934	1,193	614	226	2,033
1939	1,566	728	191	2,485
1945	368	920	131	1,419
1949	2,154	1,625	129	3,908
1950	2,299	1,706	129	4,134
1955	4,350	2,315	270	6,935
1957	5,605	2,681	318	8,604
1958 (prelim.)	6,207	2,855	352	9,414
1959 (est.)	7,138	3,010	356	10,504

B. Revenues

Year	Federal Govt.	States	County & Local Rural Road Agencies	Urban Places	Grand Total
1929	$ 89	$ 833	$525	$ 725	$2,172
1934	705	765	251	337	2,058
1939	925	1,048	284	382	2,639
1945	83	1,188	271	327	1,869
1949	491	2,249	419	560	3,719
1950	471	2,410	460	566	3,907
1955	779	3,936	606	838	6,159
1957	1,426	4,494	651	931	7,502
1958 (prelim.)	2,275	4,532	670	973	8,450
1959 (est.)	2,985	4,742	688	1,019	9,434

Source: Automobile Manufacturers Association, *Automobile Facts and Figures, 1959–60*, Detroit, 1960, p. 51.

paid for by the users. However, the matter is not as simple as it seems, for the accounting of the railroads can be and has been criticized, as has been pointed out above, and any attempt to figure out the costs of motor transportation has its intricacies. The widely held view that highways and automobiles pay for themselves is true in only a limited sense. The total amount of all taxes, tolls, and fees paid by motorists equals and even surpasses the total government expenditures for highway building, but it does not cover all the disbursements, including such items as traffic control and police service, made by all the public agencies concerned with roads and streets. This is true whether we use the calculations of the Automobile Manufacturers Association (see Table 24) or the somewhat higher figures of the Bureau of the Census,[70] both of which are based on data of the U. S. Bureau of Public Roads. Both sources recognize an increasing deficit since 1956, when a new Federal law enlarged the scope of Federal aid to highway construction throughout the country, adding to former commitments a thirteen-year program to cost some $25 billion in additional Federal funds.

Thus the oversimplified idea, current among motorists, that they pay for the highways with the taxes included in the bill for gasoline is obviously an error. Highway traffic is much more subsidized than people usually realize. Of course, however, users *do* pay for all the costs of highways and automobile travel, used by almost every American even though he may not own or drive an automobile. And the people pay also for all other transportation in their country, for who else would? The question is not, therefore, who pays, but whether the payment is well enough distributed, and whether the present scale of the cost is necessary.

The total highway and street disbursements by all public agencies concerned in the continental United States appear to have grown from $4,456 million in 1950 to $9,927 million in 1958, that is, by 123 per cent, while the national income rose by 50 per cent only.[71] Thus during the 1950's the American people have been spending an increasing proportion of their annual income on highways and related facilities. The estimates for 1959 and 1960 seem to show that this trend has continued. Although the American nation is by far the wealthiest in the world, one may wonder whether it can or should afford to assign such a rising share of its income to the support of only one of the various means of transportation at its disposal.

These huge expenditures cannot be equally distributed over the land. Sparsely populated areas still need highway construction and maintenance, the latter often being quite onerous because of the very climatic and topographic conditions that have made the population sparse. Transportation costs in such areas as the Western mountains and deserts must be paid for partly with receipts obtained in richer, more thickly settled regions, where a more intense traffic brings higher revenue.

[70] See *Statistical Abstract of the United States: 1959, op. cit.,* Table No. 714, p. 551. As an indication of the differences between the two sets of figures, note that receipts for 1955, 1957, and 1959 are given in the *Statistical Abstract* as $7,333 million, $8,601 million, and $10,773 million respectively, while the disbursements for the same years are given as $7,356 million, $9,130 million, and $11,060 million. On the whole the *Statistical Abstract* shows a smaller deficit than does Table 24.

[71] That is, from $241.8 billion in 1950 to $360.8 billion in 1958. See the *Statistical Abstract of the United States: 1959, op. cit.,* Tables 714 and 396.

Table 25

HIGHWAY-USER TAXES IN SELECTED STATES, 1958

State	Total Highway-User Taxes (Millions)	State Tax on Motor-Vehicle Fuel (Millions)	Highway-User Taxes as % of Total State Tax Revenue	Per Cent of Motor Taxes Diverted to Non-highway Purposes
Entirely within Megalopolis				
Massachusetts	$ 92	$ 69	22.2	0.3
Rhode Island	16	9.8	23.4	29.3
Connecticut	59.7	43.8	27.3	a
New Jersey	134	70	46.5	18.0
Delaware	12	7.8	22.5	7.6
Maryland	71.6	47.6	28.3	a
Partly within Megalopolis				
New Hampshire	16.7	10.3	47.6	a
New York	273	140	18.2	2.1
Pennsylvania	237	157	26.7	0.1
Virginia	93	70.8	36.3	a
Outside Megalopolis				
Minnesota	91	52	28.5	1.4
Texas	245	170	36.9	17.4
California	419	302	25.0	16.1
Oregon	59.6	34	32.2	1.9

Source: Automobile Manufacturers Association, *Automobile Facts and Figures, 1959–60,* Detroit, 1960.
a Data not available.

The special automobile-user taxes [72] collected by state governments amounted in 1958 to $4,351 million, or 29 per cent of all state tax revenues. This highway-user revenue was essentially allocated to highway expenditures, but some of it could be used also for non-highway purposes in states with an obvious surplus from such taxes. The state tax on motor-vehicle fuel, more directly related to the actual use of the vehicles and the roads, amounted to almost $3 billion in 1958, or 70 per cent of all the state collections of special motor-user taxes. Table 25 gives the distribution of these taxes and their use for the Northeastern seaboard states and a few others and indicates the importance of highway revenues in the finances of most states. However, this table does not take into account the Federal aid received by the various states for the construction of major highways.

[72] These include the state registration fees, gasoline taxes, and tolls on bridges, tunnels, ferries, and roads (most of them collected by public agencies rather than by state government officers). In addition there are Federal excise taxes on fuel, repair parts, etc.

Without that help the financial situation of this sector of the economy would not look as bright as it does.

The expenditures of state and local governments on highways represent a substantial part of all their disbursements. The *per capita* expenditures for highways in 1957 averaged $45.79 in the continental United States. Connecticut led with $106.69 per capita, followed by Wyoming ($92.80), Nevada ($89.14), Kansas ($82.40), Montana, ($79.02), South Dakota ($78.84), and so forth. In New Jersey the highways took only $38.71 per capita; in Maryland, $55.40; in Massachusetts, $61.46; and in Rhode Island, $36.42. Why Connecticut spent so much more per capita, even more than the sparsely populated states of the West, may perhaps be explained by an exceedingly inflated budget of its highway department. In 1957 Connecticut gave 32.9 per cent of all its expenditures, by state and local government, to its highways, a share not equalled in any other state, though it was approached by South Dakota (32.2 per cent) and by Kansas, New Hampshire, and Vermont (about 30 per cent in each). In Massachusetts the highways received only 21 per cent of total expenditures, in Rhode Island 17.4 per cent, in New Jersey 16.3 per cent and in Maryland 23 per cent. It may be noteworthy that expenditures for education were lower than those for highways in Connecticut, while they were somewhat higher in Massachusetts, substantially higher in Maryland, and more than twice as high in New Jersey.[73]

By 1960, however, Connecticut could boast of an excellent system of roads, in which almost every small rural road could serve as a major highway. In the automobile era, such a highway policy in a state without large cities may have served well the purposes of increased urbanization or suburbanization, helping residences and industries to scatter through the state.

The case of Connecticut in 1957 illustrates the danger of generalized assumptions that more intensively travelled and densely settled areas produce highway-user revenue in excess of local needs and thus should subsidize the less wealthy and more sparsely populated regions. Connecticut may have absorbed outside help for some years in a way comparable to what South Dakota or Wyoming must normally receive. On the whole, however, Megalopolis, with its great intensity of highway traffic and its rather higher average level of personal income and expenditures, certainly covers well the cost of its highway and automobile transportation, even though this cost is rather high.

Many times the question has arisen as to where to look for the money needed to build and maintain roads in this area. In a thoughtful study of

[73] Data from *Statistical Abstract of the United States: 1959, op. cit.,* p. 410.

the needs and costs of metropolitan transportation made in 1956, Wilfred Owen reached the following conclusion:

> Present financial policies governing the provision of transportation in urban areas is in need of a thorough overhauling. There is no indication that present practice could support a truly modern system of urban mobility. But clearly the best chance of achieving the transportation needs of metropolitan areas in the future will be through a self-supporting system. The goal will require revision of state-aid policies, a closer relation between transportation costs and charges, a more effective use of the pricing mechanism, and new administrative arrangements in metropolitan areas. Financial success is not likely to be accomplished short of an integration of facilities and services aimed at self-support for the transportation system as a whole.[74]

Self-support involves coordination between various agencies on the local and state levels, as well as contributions of Federal funds. Except in well isolated metropolitan units, such as Denver or St. Louis, it could hardly be planned on the geographical basis of each metropolitan area separately. Especially is this true in Megalopolis, with its integrated chain of metropolitan areas, and cooperation between them, as well as between states, has already proved necessary. The Port of New York Authority, for example, is a bi-state agency. In 1957 the same two states established the unsuccessful bi-state Metropolitan Rapid Transit Commission (see above, p. 665), and they set up the New York–New Jersey Transportation Agency to deal with the commuter problem. Connecticut declined an invitation to participate in this agency. However, in 1957 these three states did set up a joint traffic control system. In 1959 a new Penn-Jersey Transportation Study was started, encompassing nine counties in the two states and including Mercer County, New Jersey, the Trenton metropolitan area, as well as the Philadelphia area. This study might have been even better rounded had it included also New Castle County, Delaware (though that would have made it a tri-state proposition) for in many respects Wilmington gravitates toward Philadelphia's orbit, while some people in Chester and Delaware counties of Pennsylvania gravitate toward Wilmington.

At this time we have to be grateful, of course, for every bit of progress toward the development of an integrated, or at least a better coordinated, handling of transportation. The planning of transportation must, of course, be closely related to the general planning of the area concerned, especially in crowded urban districts. In them many uses compete for land, some of which might be undesirable or even in conflict with what

[74] Owen, *The Metropolitan Transportation Problem, op. cit.*, pp. 189–190.

the traffic program calls for.[75] In a few of the more congested places in Megalopolis serious efforts have been made to improve traffic, either on highways or on railroads and mass transit, and on the whole the results have been encouraging. For the most part, however, this immense problem has been tackled in piecemeal fashion, and the general results of such management are far from satisfactory.

So far the most comprehensive planning has been in the field of intercity highway traffic. It has been very costly, but it has also given the best results and on the whole seems to produce less obvious deficit than the other means of transportation. If it has been easier to finance, this has been largely because it has been better managed. The user and the taxpayer have paid for it, but at least they have received in exchange a remarkable service. However, even this network of highways fails occasionally to provide satisfactory service in the main hubs and on their approaches at times of peak traffic, either daily or weekly, and it is these rush hours that are held responsible also for most of the hardships of the railroads, the subways, and their passengers. In most American cities the patronage of the transit systems decreases greatly during the day, between the rush hours. At the peak, however, there are enough patrons for all modes of transportation, and at times any kind of transportation becomes deficient, because it is not considered financially possible to run a subway or a railroad or to build highways in terms of the needs of the peak hours. These rush periods are short, while the facilities have to be maintained around the clock all the year. Travellers therefore expect some congestion and discomfort when they travel in peak traffic. However, they resent it when it becomes too frequent and lasts too long. The highways and the automobile have been a great help in alleviating for a time the flow of traffic through the crowding of Megalopolis. Now, however, a degree of saturation has been reached that calls for new solutions.

It must be kept in mind that in the 1960's a new generation, born in the 1940's, will come of age, one much more numerous than the preceding generation born in the 1930's. This is pertinent to the problem, for an individual consumes more space and more transportation after he reaches the age of eighteen or twenty than he did earlier. Coming of age nowadays means driving a car, going separately from the elders or from col-

[75] For a useful study and description of the relationships between land development and transportation analysis see Robert B. Mitchell and Chester Rapkin, *Urban Traffic: A Function of Land Use* (Publications of the Institute for Urban Land Use and Housing Studies, Columbia University), Columbia University Press, New York, 1954. This excellent volume is still a standard textbook for the method of analysis of urban traffic.

lective groups to work, to eat, to be entertained, to relax. On each of these trips the car must find space on the roads and streets, and parking space at every destination. The number of Americans reaching the age of eighteen in each calendar year has been rising since 1958, and it will rise more rapidly during the 1960's (see Fig. 226, p. 766). The transportation requirements for all these young people, and the children they will soon have, create a greater demand for ways and means of moving around than the recently proposed solutions seem to be able to provide.

The problem will be worst where congestion is already greatest — that is, in the larger cities in general and in Megalopolis specifically. This region's concern for city transit and rail rehabilitation was long overdue; it has come to the fore almost at the eleventh hour. Most experts have concluded their reports on these matters by urging action but stressing the costs, which are estimated to be high, and the lack of institutional framework to manage the task ahead. Thus both financial and political obstacles lie in the way.

Any reasonable approach to the question of costs should first ponder the *wastefulness* of the solutions so enthusiastically accepted in the recent past. The successful development of the region's highway transportation, the greatest system the world has seen, was obviously accompanied by a great deal of waste, much of it deliberately planned and accepted. The term *waste* is not used here with any pejorative connotation but rather to indicate that the development of highway travel has not been aimed at saving materials or money. In many ways this will be shown to be a *positive* kind of waste.

That travel in congested areas such as Megalopolis costs more by individual automobile than by train or bus seems fairly obvious, although the individual traveller is not always aware of this. Driving his car, he often compares the cost of only fuel and lubricant to the cost of a train ticket for the distance to be covered. He forgets the price paid for the car, its maintenance, and its insurance, for he would have owned a car anyhow, even if commuting by train. (In two-car families, however, one car would often suffice if the daily trips to work were made by another carrier.) But when he comes into the congested urban district the motorist more often than not pays parking fees, which may add up to a sizable amount; and the increasing frequency of tolls reminds him now that paying for gasoline is not his only cost. Once parking fees and tolls for highways, bridges, and tunnels are added to personal expenditures for automobiles, the total amount spent by Americans for motor transportation comes up to a substantial and increasing part of their personal incomes.

Railroads and rapid transit should be less costly than this. Testifying before the Congressional Joint Committee on Washington Problems in 1959, Mr. W. W. Patchell, a vice president of the Pennsylvania Railroad Company, submitted an exhibit comparing construction costs necessary to handle increased peak-hour loads by rail or by automobile from suburbs served by the Pennsylvania Railroad in the Philadelphia and New York metropolitan areas (see Table 26).[76] In both cases the expressways and parking facilities needed to secure adequate automobile flow appeared to cost many times more than the suburban railroad. The ratio was seven to one for Philadelphia and sixteen to one for New York. In both areas together, for the suburbs served by this railroad, the savings offered by the use of the train amounted to more than $7 billion, a sum that would have to come from public funds if the transport problem were solved by the use of automobiles. Curiously enough, in recent years governmental authorities and public opinion have been as generous in spending billions of dollars for the highways as they have been reluctant to spend millions for the railroads. As patronage of the railroads has decreased, the cost of the service to the individual traveller has increased, making this means of transport increasingly onerous to both carrier and patron.

For a quarter of a century the decay of the railroads remained in sharp contrast with the soaring rise of the automobile and of highway construction, although the latter cost more in terms of fuel, power, rubber, and labor (for the maintenance and administration of the roads). This is obvious if we remember that a train "can propel 200 to 300 people at 80 miles per hour with only 1500 horsepower and a crew of three or four men." [77] Two hundred people riding in 150 automobiles use about 15,000 horsepower, ten times as much energy as by train, plus the personal effort of the 150 people who drive and the service of the policemen to patrol the road.

It may be futile to attempt an estimation of how much more steel, glass, copper, aluminum, rubber, chromium, cement, and other materials are used on the highway than on the rails, because the traveller or his household would in most cases own a car anyhow. How much more rapidly the car is worn out because of greater use appears as another irrelevant question, for many American car owners buy new automobiles not because their old ones are worn out and breaking down but because they look too old. The well known "built-in obsolescence" of American cars,

[76] *Hearings on Report of the Washington Mass Transportation Survey*, 1959, *op. cit.*, p. 417.

[77] As quoted above, p. 655. See footnote 24 on that page.

Table 26

A COMPARISON OF CONSTRUCTION COSTS TO HANDLE INCREASED PEAK HOURS
LOADS BY RAIL OR AUTOMOBILE FROM SUBURBS SERVED BY THE
PENNSYLVANIA RAILROAD

Automobile	Cost (Thousands)	Suburban Railroad[a]	Cost (Thousands)	Cost Ratio
		Philadelphia Metropolitan Area (120,000 passengers per hour)		
1. Philadelphia-Paoli Expressway	$720,000	1. Construction of High-Level Platform[e]	$ 11,000	
2. Philadelphia-Media Expressway	300,000	2. Additional Terminal Station Facilities	55,000	
3. Philadelphia–Chestnut Hill Expressway	324,000	3. Additional Storage Tracks	8,000	
4. Philadelphia-Wilmington Expressway	567,000	4. Additional Electrification Facilities	40,000	
5. Philadelphia-Trenton Expressway	780,000	5. Signal Changes	7,000	
6. Center City Parking Facilities[b]	400,000	6. Additional Parking at Suburban Stations	173,000	
		7. Additional Equipment Requirements	170,730	
7. Total, Philadelphia Area	$3,091,000	8. Total, Philadelphia Area	$464,730[g]	7 : 1[g]
		New York Metropolitan Area (80,000 passengers per hour)		
1. Trenton-Newark Expressway	$1,022,000	1. Construction of High-Level Platforms[f]	$ 6,000	
2. Bay Head–Rahway Expressway	1,064,000	2. Additional Terminal Station Facilities	10,000	
3. Newark–New York Expressway[c]	2,400,000	3. Additional Storage Tracks	9,000	
4. Center City Parking Facilities[d]	266,700	4. Additional Electrification Facilities	22,000	
		5. Signal Changes	7,000	
		6. Additional Parking at Suburban Stations	115,000	
		7. Additional Equipment Requirements	114,120	
5. Total, New York Area	$4,752,700	8. Total, New York Area	$283,120	16 : 1
Grand Total Cost (New York and Philadelphia Areas)	$7,843,700	Grand Total Cost (New York and Philadelphia Areas)	$747,850[g]	10 : 1[g]

Source: Joint Committee on Washington Metropolitan Problems, *Hearings on Report of the Washington Mass Transportation Survey*, 86th Cong., 1st sess., 1959.

[a] Utilizing existing facilities, unless otherwise indicated.

[b] Parking space for 160,000 vehicles at $2,500 each.

[c] Including additional tunnels under the Hudson River.

[d] Parking space for 106,667 vehicles at $2,500 each.

[e] At 74 stations.

[f] At 38 stations.

[g] Totals and ratios corrected so that individual items add up exactly. Corrections made with the approval of the Pennsylvania Railroad and Dr. Frederick Gutheim, of the Committee's staff.

so successfully developed in Detroit by the great automobile industry, has applied a deliberate economy of waste in twofold fashion: first, by the tradition of a new model every year; second, by the trends toward bigger and more ornamented cars with each change of model.

The public's saturation with these policies of built-in obsolescence and of constantly growing size has been demonstrated in recent years by the greater vogue of the small foreign cars (models of which change much less frequently) and, beginning in 1960, of the compact American cars. Despite the stubborn hopes of the automobile industry's management, the public has seemed to prefer smaller cars, the appearance of which is not expected to be outmoded rapidly. Concern has been voiced that such preferences may cause some decline in the quantities of gasoline used by motorists; such decline in consumption would not only mean less revenue for all the gasoline producing and distributing industries, but it could also have serious consequences for the program of highway building, for it would decrease the collection of state and Federal taxes on gasoline.[78] The small or compact cars are designed to give *more miles* per gallon of gasoline. Until recently the trend had been toward cars requiring *more gasoline* per mile travelled. That is, surplus consumption was built into the American automobiles together with accelerated obsolescence. These trends have reached their levelling-off point, at least for a time. Devised to cause more industrial growth, they lose much of their meaning once they cease to stimulate more consumption. The vogue for foreign cars has even decreased the status-conferring value of most large American cars.

This apparent waste, closely and increasingly associated with the generalized use of the individual automobile, has not been an evil in the past. On the contrary, it caused a great deal of improvement in the ease of transportation all over the country, and it also entailed much economic growth. To supply and maintain all these enormous fleets of cars, much used, often renewed, many industries had to develop on a larger scale. We have already mentioned the variety of materials that went in greater and greater quantities into automobile manufacturing and servicing, as well as into the construction and maintenance of the roads, bridges, tunnels, garages, and other facilities these cars needed. So great was the impact of all these industries combined on the national economy that it seemed for a time actually true that "what is good for General Motors is good for the country." If waste there was in terms of materials, this "wastefulness" had become for the nation as a whole a factor of wealth and prosperity.

[78] See Robert Metz, "States Worried About Impact of Small Cars on 'Gas' Revenue," *The New York Times*, June 26, 1960.

But alas, such profitable schemes never last very long. Once such a carefully established system of economic forces seems well set up, the balance on which its momentum rests begins to shift.

There had been a time, in the early 1920's, when the railroads felt as the automobile manufacturers did in the middle 1950's. The railroads had done an essential and magnificent job in providing, throughout the country, the transportation needed for the extraordinary industrial expansion of World War I and its immediate aftermath. In 1958 a report to the U. S. Senate could still recollect:

> For generations the railroads have been the bedrock of our Nation's transportation system. It was the railroads that pioneered the development and growth of the East, the West, the North, and the South. Their history is closely linked with the economic progress of our Nation. It was only a few years ago that the railroads were the biggest business of the Nation. They ranked first as a purchaser of goods and services. Steel mills once counted them as their best single customer as did the fuel oil sellers, the lumbermen, the coal-mine operators, and many others.[79]

The automobile, the pipeline, and the airplane took away from the railroads their economic supremacy. For a time it was handed over to the automobile and the truck, but by 1960 it seemed to begin shifting again. It is the healthful role of technological progress to cause such shifts from one industry to another, from one mode of transportation to another. However, it is too early yet to know what mode of transportation may divert much patronage from the automobile. This kind of evolution can take several paths at the same time, depending on local conditions and on the service to be performed. Air transportation has just begun to develop, but already it has assumed an important role in the passenger traffic within Megalopolis on longer hauls between major hubs. The helicopter is still in its babyhood, but in the future, when this type of carrier has been improved enough to give adequate service, it may well assume a good deal of the function of carrying passengers and even lighter freight in as densely occupied and travelled an area as is Megalopolis. Along the lines of heaviest traffic, mass transit on rails seems to be destined to a revival.[80] Finally, progress in telephone and television communications may remove the need for many trips.

[79] *Problems of the Railroads,* Report of the Subcommittee on Surface Transportation of the Committee on Interstate and Foreign Commerce, 85th Cong., 2d sess., 1958, p. 1.

[80] See Wilfred Owen, *Cities in the Motor Age,* The Viking Press, New York, 1959, especially Chapters 5 to 8; *idem,* "Transportation," in *Metropolis in Ferment, The Annals of the American Academy of Political and Social Science,* November 1957, pp. 30–38.

The automobile has become very deeply imbedded in the American way of life; it could not decline to the extent the railroads did in 1945–60 without causing grave catastrophes. The number of automobiles and trucks will continue to rise as the population grows and spreads over the land, and as its activities multiply. But the pace of the motor-traffic increase is expected to be somewhat less steep in the future than it has been in the recent past.

From at least three different points of view the automobile appears, in 1960, to have reached its zenith as the greatest carrier and perhaps already to have begun a gradual descent. In the first place the automobile as an instrument for leisure and relaxation is no longer what it used to be. This is because people have grown more "sophisticated" or just have been looking for a change, and partly because of the greater congestion of the roads. The American public has taken to other modes of transport for leisure, boating being a leading one among these. The automobile is still, of course, necessary in most cases to get to the boat or even to tow the boat and its crew to the waterside. But the American public has made boating nowadays into a multi-billion-dollar industry, taking away something from the former use of the automobile.

In the second place the expenses connected with the automobile have reached a share in the average household budget that seems too high for what the motorist and his family are getting out of it, when they think of other needs or comforts. This problem has come to worry economists preoccupied with the basic goals of the nation's social and economic evolution. The matter of expenditure on the larger automobiles and superhighways looms important in Galbraith's often-quoted book, *The Affluent Society*.[81]

In the third place there is the traffic congestion that has become endemic in the more crowded areas, of which Megalopolis offers the more spectacular examples. This is, of course, a somewhat regional view of the whole problem. However, it is the aspect of the situation most likely to produce action soon, for although it contains a gradually declining rela-

[81] John Kenneth Galbraith, *The Affluent Society*, Houghton Mifflin Company, Boston, 1958. He wrote, pp. 308–309: "To create the demand for new automobiles we must contrive elaborate and functionless changes each year and then subject the consumer to ruthless psychological pressures to persuade him of their importance. Were this process to falter or break down, the consequences would be disturbing. In the meantime, there are large ready-made needs for schools, hospitals, slum clearance and urban redevelopment, sanitation, parks, playgrounds, police, and a thousand other things. Of these needs almost no one must be persuaded. They are unavailable only because as public officials of all kinds and ranks explain each day with practiced skill, the money to provide them is unavailable."

tive share of the nation's people and activities, Megalopolis is still growing, and its continued growth and prosperity remain an urgent concern and need of the whole country. If this region should falter, the disturbance in the national economy would be great, too great for such a prospect to be tolerated.

A certain kind of planned waste is healthful for an economy of abundance in an industrialized society, and as long as it follows and supports the general tide of growth and progress it is a welcome factor of wealth. But if and when it interferes with the evolution of the rest of the way of life and appropriates for special use too large a share of the money, space, and time available to the population, then this waste must be eliminated. It is bound to be corrected in the field of activity it saturated, although similarly planned wastefulness may then develop in other aspects of the nation's economy.

Urban Land Use and Time Use

Automobile traffic on a good network of highways was one of the essential instruments of the suburban sprawl, which could hardly otherwise have developed as nebulous a structure as it has acquired in Megalopolis. However, other essential factors had to concur with it to bring about the kind of land use we have described earlier in this volume. The construction techniques coming out of the wartime emergency, a regime of credit supporting individual home ownership, the degree of crowding of the central cities, the general prosperity of the population, all these circumstances were instrumental in bringing about the "metropolitanization" of the land. But the highway and the automobile had special responsibilities; for, besides providing powerful help for the spread of those who wanted to scatter, they considerably increased the congestion inside the main hubs of business and, in times of peak traffic, on their approaches.

The densities of people attending to their business in the hubs of central districts during working hours on weekdays are quite high. They vary, of course, from city to city and almost from block to block, but even outside Manhattan they often reach more than 1,000 people per acre in at least a few blocks. If most of those people moved by automobile, how much parking space would be needed? Multi-story garages have become an almost common sight in medium-sized cities, some of them having a new architectural style that is not unpleasant. The customer seems to be willing to pay for this, as he does for parking along metered curbs or in municipal or private parking lots, whenever he can do so at a minimum distance from the place that is his goal.

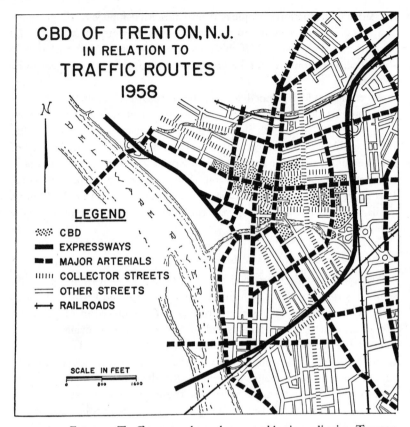

Fig. 209. Traffic routes through a central business district: Trenton, New Jersey. *Courtesy of the Graduate School of Geography, Clark University*

Besides consuming money, parking takes space — all the more so since central municipal parking facilities are provided for anybody who needs to use them, but other large parking facilities are reserved for certain categories of users: for the shoppers at certain stores, for the patrons of a given hotel or restaurant, or for customers who have rented the use of the space, and so forth. In some medium-sized Midwestern cities, zoning regulations require one square foot of off-street parking area for every square foot in commercial use.[82] If such a regulation were to be adopted in the major nuclei of Megalopolis it would mean matching every tower or high-rise building with another of equal square footage for parking, an

[82] See Geoffrey Baker and Bruno Funaro, *Parking*, Reinhold Publishing Co., New York, 1958, pp. 98 ff.

obviously impossible proposition. Less generous requirements may be set up, however, as was done, for example, by the new zoning law adopted by New York City in December 1960. It requires new buildings, except in the hub area, to provide off-street parking to serve a given percentage of their dwelling units or floor spaces, with the percentage being greater in outlying areas than in more built-up sections.[83] Thus it is evident that the local law cannot be as kind to the motorist in larger central cities, especially in their hubs, as it can afford to be in smaller ones. Even the more extreme advocates of the use of the individual automobile agree on the need for some mass transit in the larger cities, especially on the Northeastern seaboard, where densities of both daytime workers and resident population are higher than average.

Disregarding the question of parking, the very movement of traffic is slow in the hubs, and in rush hours it is difficult. More highways take more money and more space; they also consume more time, as congestion grows, for a given mileage. Most systems of freeways in Megalopolitan nuclei improve traffic at first, but they soon become so popular that congestion sets in and more and more lanes are needed. The partisans of highways always stress the fact that mass transit, especially rapid transit, costs a great deal, and that people still prefer riding on the roads. They seldom compare the modest sums usually refused to help transit to the huge sums spent annually on highways, parking facilities, and other automobile requirements.[84]

We have already analyzed the matter of costs, and the assets and liabilities of a certain wastefulness. The congestion of traffic in a central business district has still other implications. It modifies the very function of the district and the type of business transacted. At first manufacturing was gradually driven outside the central hubs toward the peripheries of cities, then toward the peripheries of metropolitan areas, and occasionally beyond them, leaving the central cities to become chiefly commercial. Recently the distributive trades (retail, wholesale, special services, warehousing) have also begun to spread out, pursuing the customers. Even some professions have followed in the wake of this migration. Many central cities have begun to decay with little hope of improvement, and the threat of a "grey zone" hangs heavily over many of them in Megalopolis,

[83] *Report of the City Planning Commission on the Comprehensive Amendment of the Zoning Resolution of the City of New York*, October 18, 1960; and *The New York Times*, December 16, 1960.

[84] Urban Land Institute, *The New Highways: Challenge to the Metropolitan Region*, Technical Bulletin 31, Washington, D. C., November 1957, especially pp. 43–74; also by the same Institute, *Crowded Streets*, Technical Bulletin 26, June 1955.

unless their business districts have developed enough white-collar activities to survive, to continue growing.

Raymond Vernon has carefully analyzed these trends and has pointed out the inherent dangers of the outward movement of people, followed or preceded by an outward movement of jobs.[85] In a few main hubs it may be compensated for by developing "central-office cities" and "communications-oriented" industries. New York City and Washington have such functions on an enormous scale and may well keep on growing. Boston and Philadelphia are valiantly struggling to keep whatever of these functions they have and to attract more. Smaller cities that have the advantage of a large, well-established business or government role (such as Newark, Trenton, Hartford, Wilmington, or Harrisburg) are fighting the same battle. But the white-collar workers often have their residences in the outer ring. The question of easy access to the hub becomes a condition of the successful clustering of white-collar employing industries within it.

While parking, freeways, municipal garages, and heavy costs of roadbed maintenance on streets add to the expenditures of the city government, the space taxable by the city is reduced by the area given to streets, municipal parking facilities, freeways, and so on. A cycle is thus started in which the city is required to perform more services, in more onerous fashion, while its major resource (taxable land) is reduced. The city must then resort to more and higher taxes wherever possible, or ask for subsidies, or do both. Municipal government in central cities thus faces a problem similar to what the railroads face because of shrinking passenger traffic. Most cities face situations in which deficit seems unavoidable.

New York City has resisted these threatening trends better than others. However, as more high office towers rise in its hub, the situation seems likely to be reached soon where congestion will seriously affect movement on the ground. While magnificent elevator systems in the larger office skyscrapers now occupied or in construction boast of their capacity to carry 50,000 to 275,000 riders per day, one wonders what crowding will develop on the ground in neighborhoods where several such giants cluster together. Human bodies are easily compressible, as any rush-hour subway rider well knows, but automobiles are not.[86]

[85] Raymond Vernon, *The Changing Economic Function of the Central City,* Committee for Economic Development, New York, 1959.

[86] Though the New York City Transit Authority has done little indeed to improve the subway or transit system in recent years, trends of decline in patronage appeared reversed in 1959, when the number of revenue passengers rose; it went on slowly increasing through 1960 and the first half of 1961 on both subways and buses.

It may be interesting in this connection to mention also the density of registered

If conditions become bad indeed, what would be the harm of some decentralization, whenever possible, from the main hubs? First, this would mean, of course, a huge increase of transportation needs in those areas to which the people and the business now concentrated in the central districts would move. Second, it would mean more decay, slums, and impoverishment for several million people now dependent on the existing concentration. Third, it would mean shattering the whole present structure of American economic management, decision-making, the central financial and mass-media markets, and much more. However, the rest of the nation could claim that the concentration in Megalopolis is far too great anyhow, that it is undesirable, and that it calls for decentralizing moves. Perhaps they would be right in some respects. Such decentralization can be worked out, however, only when the new techniques of communications permit scattering of the communications-oriented activities. This again might be visualized for a not-so-distant future, assuming due progress in telephone, telegraph, and television transmissions.

It will not come immediately, and if it ever does come it will ruin the last great function left to the central city — and probably also much of the urban economy. Congestion may make us criticize existing concentrations; but we must be aware of the consequences of an evolution, even if gradual and slow, that would spread all the activities evenly over the land, establishing a sort of colloidal solution of land occupance. Urban real estate would lose much in value; the whole capital invested in buildings, services, and the highway system itself would be devalued. The share of all the national wealth now vested in the central cities is so great, though difficult to estimate precisely in dollars and cents, or even in percentages, that one can hardly visualize how the nonurban parts of the national economy could shoulder a serious depression of urban values. Megalopolis would not be alone at stake here, for if New York City and Washington could be decentralized what other cities could still retain any function requiring concentration?

Another more likely possibility is that despite some scattering of various activities, old and new, the central cities, at least the major nuclei, may endure and continue to grow, at least in daytime population. The accom-

motor vehicles per square mile of land area in the Megalopolitan states. In 1959 it reached 278 in Rhode Island, 272 in New Jersey, 196 in Massachusetts, 190 in Connecticut, 96 in Maryland; it was much higher, of course, in the large cities (2,934 in the District of Columbia). To some extent even in Megalopolis, and with the exception of New York City, the density of registered motor vehicles generally follows the pattern of population density. (Figures computed from data in *Automobile Facts and Figures* and the *Statistical Abstract, op. cit.*).

panying traffic congestion would result either in strict regulation, involving increasing discomfort for the mass of the labor force, or in a considerable lengthening of the time a journey would take within the city or the metropolitan area. Perhaps both trends might develop simultaneously unless new bold solutions are found and applied.

Traffic and transportation in Megalopolis, especially in and around the main hubs, affect not only land use but also the use of people's time. The latter is at least as important as the former to the continued performance of this region as a large concentration of free, happy, and intelligent people, assuming responsibilities of leadership in a difficult time. Except for air navigation, which has saved time on many major itineraries, the recent improvement in transportation within Megalopolis has in the long run saved little, if any, time for most travellers. "Time use" cannot avoid influencing the population's leisure and its emotional and intellectual performance. And the time needed to move large crowds would become a factor in survival if the axial belt of Megalopolis, containing thirty or forty million people, should have to be evacuated rapidly because of war conditions or natural disaster. Traffic is a multi-faceted problem and needs urgent and fresh approaches. Megalopolis ought to be able not only to find solutions for its ills but to provide the pattern in this respect for the city of the future.

PART FOUR

NEIGHBORS IN

MEGALOPOLIS

The preceding parts of this book have studied the dynamism of a prosperous society living in relatively crowded conditions on a small but most
important parcel of American land. We have studied this land, the uses
made of it, and the activities of its people in the past and in the present.
We have seen the whole region become urbanized in one way or another,
although much of its landscape does not look the way we have been used
to seeing cities look. We have found the region of Megalopolis closely integrated as one system, but this system remains quite different from what
a city was or is. It is not in any way isolated from the outside by a wall,
a stockade, or any significant administrative boundary; it consists rather
of a chain of crossroads, all intimately connected with other areas or cities
outside the region we have defined. Still, Megalopolis stands out as a well

differentiated and integrated system, which has a "personality" in itself, a set of characteristics not repeated outside it.

The degree of integration of the region has perhaps been best demonstrated on flow maps: actual daily flow of telephone calls (Figs. 177 to 186, pp. 583–593); of highway traffic (Fig. 203, p. 645); of airline passenger traffic (Fig. 204, p. 646); and the longer range, endless flow of population change (Fig. 9, p. 41, and Fig. 73, p. 248). This emphasis on *flow*, especially of people, demonstrates graphically the vast web of variegated and often abstract relationships that unite the different cities and counties of Megalopolis in one regional system. Beyond the limits we have outlined for this region the intensity of all these flows slackens, the density of interconnections weakens.

It is certainly too early to speak at this time of a "Megalopolitan community," and such a thing may never come to be. One can observe within Megalopolis far more competition, rivalry, and diversity than common loyalty or recognition of common interests. In fact, almost every component of Megalopolis is closely linked to and associated with groups, institutions, and interests rooted in other regions of America or even abroad. This may even seem required by the region's historical role as an economic hinge; by its special activities; by the complex maze of contracts, means of transportation, and communication facilities necessary to supply it and to keep its business operating; and last but not least, by the Megalopolitan endeavor to assume leadership in many fields. But even though we do not feel justified in considering this region as one community, much less, of course, as one city, we have found enough integration in the whole and enough interplay between its various parts to indicate strongly that all those thirty-seven million inhabitants counted in Megalopolis by the 1960 Census are close neighbors.

This immense neighborhood is evidenced partly by all the flows within the region, all its tidal currents, and partly by the density of the population, the crowding. The residents of Megalopolis are all neighbors because they have so many problems in common, and most of these problems stem from the crowding due to population density or from the congestion due to the intensity of the various flows. Congestion and crowding have been recorded mainly in the axial belt of Megalopolis, that central ribbon of land that especially deserves the label of the "Main Street of the nation." But the axial belt has been steadily widening, and progress in this sense has been particularly clear between 1950 and 1960 (see Figs. 1 and 9, pp. 6, 41). Even those parts of Megalopolis where the density of population remains thin, or may even be declining, are increasingly used as immediate adjuncts of the more urbanized districts, be it as farmland, parks, hunting grounds, or otherwise.

We have had many opportunities to ascertain how interdependent are the various economic and social facts and trends analyzed earlier in this book. Whether they are conscious of it or not, the people and the institutions in Megalopolis are related one to another by links of neighborhood, both geographically and functionally. They live and work together in a region in which they share many things, both material and immaterial, and the former are very abundant owing to the labor and resourcefulness of its people for three centuries. However, all this sharing must go on in an environment carefully partitioned administratively, politically, emotionally, and in many other ways. The very diversity of Megalopolis, which in some respects makes its strength and wealth, also causes many difficulties and discomforts and calls for constant adjustment and change.

CHAPTER 13

Living and Working Together

Megalopolis is still attracting people, and in the 1950–60 intercensal period its population grew by some five million. For several decades, however, the region's rate of growth has been slower than that of the nation as a whole. This is true not only of population but also of several categories of industries.[1] However, the addition to the Megalopolitan population has been substantial and, during the 1950's, not much below the national average: about 15.3 per cent in the ten years as against 19 per cent for the nation.

Americans have always been mobile people. It has been estimated that one American out of five moves in an average calendar year. Obviously there has been much migration in and out of Megalopolis as well as within the region. The rather special character of the economic activities that continue to cluster and to develop in the region, particularly in its main hubs, has attracted certain kinds of labor from many other parts of the

---

[1] See above, Chapters 9 and 10.

country. Included among the persons drawn to the region are the more highly paid administrators needed for decision-making and managerial positions in private business as well as in government, and those in such professions as education, law, and medicine. And the very presence of these more highly paid groups attracts crowds of poorer immigrants or in-migrants, in recent years chiefly the latter — Negroes from the South and Puerto Ricans.

Thus the highly paid staffs needed by the governmental and managerial functions of the region, by the financial and mass-media markets, live and work together with less-well-paid workers and with large numbers of residents in the lower-income brackets. For the region as a whole, however, the average family income is relatively high (see Fig. 210), and Megalopolis therefore contains the greatest concentration of wealth in the country. While some other counties have as high an average family income, they are in general much more sparsely populated. Nowhere else is there as large a number of households with relatively high average income as in the axial belt of Megalopolis.

This attraction to the central cities of Megalopolis of such sharply contrasted groups of people creates various problems.[2] It affects land use and real estate values; the life of children and teenagers in school and at play; the revenue of local governments and therefore the services they render; the established political patterns.[3] Having served for over 300 years as the main debarkation wharf of crowds of immigrants, Megalopolis is accustomed to such contrasts. The abundant supply of cheap labor was one of the factors that favored industrialization in the past, and it is still a factor of economic growth, for it helps the region to provide, at not too great a cost, the many various services which the people with higher incomes need and can afford. In the past, the leadership of Megalopolis has on the whole successfully handled the tensions and problems rooted in this diversity. In recent times these tensions and problems have taken somewhat new forms, resulting partly from the kinds of people now involved, partly from the new economic specializations that have developed, and partly also from the very fact of greater crowding within the region (where the average density of population rose from 596 per square mile in 1950 to 688 in 1960).

We must outline here the present trends of the Megalopolitan population, especially qualitatively, and the significance of these trends at pres-

[2] See above, Chapter 8, pp. 404–420.

[3] In view of the numbers of people involved, modifications of the political patterns in Megalopolis carry notable consequences for the whole nation.

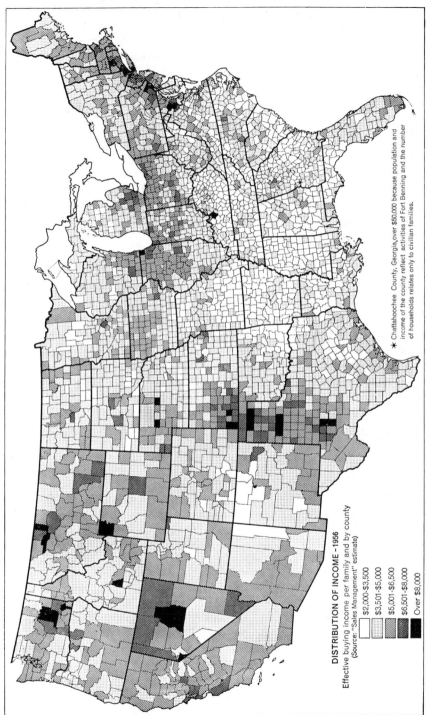

DISTRIBUTION OF INCOME - 1956
Effective buying income per family and by county
(Source: "Sales Management" estimate)

$2,000-$3,500
$3,501-$5,000
$5,001-$6,500
$6,501-$8,000
Over $8,000

* Chattahoochee County, Georgia, over $50,000 because population and income of the county reflect activities of Fort Benning and the number of households relates only to civilian families.

FIG. 210

ent, for the future successful growth of the area hinges largely on the ability of its people to make it a place where all can live and work together pleasantly.

The Diversity of the Population

If a sleeper picked up in a distant country were to awake, at the sudden stroke of a fairy's wand, seated in a public bus in New York City or Baltimore, he would certainly have great difficulty guessing in which part of the world he was. Perhaps the most telling observation he could make, as he looked at the other passengers in the bus, would be the great variety of types, or races, and of social categories assembled in the public vehicle. In most other countries of the world the racial composition would be more uniform; and in those places where it could be as varied, the social "mix" would usually be less contrasted.

Such great diversity seems always to have been a feature of the main cities on the Northeastern seaboard, and it increased with time as successive waves of immigration brought in people from an ever-increasing number of countries. The early waves were British, Dutch, German, or Swiss, with a sprinkling of refugees from varied origins: Portuguese Jews, French Huguenots, and so on. Negro slaves were brought to Maryland and Delaware, and Negroes scattered through the rest of Megalopolis, although their numbers remained low in New England and in the hills of Pennsylvania. In the last hundred years, most of the immigrants have come from Ireland, Italy, and central and eastern Europe, and, in New England, also from French Canada. The ethnic and religious character of the major cities (they attracted the bulk of those immigrants who remained on the seaboard) was thus modified, and in them a mixture of Irish, Italians, and eastern Europeans formed a growing majority. The Irish, who had the advantages of being the first to come in large numbers and of speaking English, rose to political supremacy in New York City and even in Boston. The great cities came to have Roman Catholic majorities, sometimes with a strong Jewish minority (especially in New York City). M. L. Hansen has spoken of "the second colonization of New England," which developed after 1830.[4] Perhaps a third colonization started after 1930, when the Megalopolitan sprawl brought the population "mix," concentrated earlier in the main cities, to the formerly rural townships. There people are beginning to discuss real estate tax assessments with some excitement, for the newcomers to suburbia and interurbia feel they are pay-

[4] Marcus Lee Hansen, *The Immigrant in American History*, Harvard University Press, Cambridge, Mass., 1948, Chapter 7.

ing a disproportionately heavy share of the tax burden, to the benefit of the older residents; and the question of parochial schools is being raised in communities where the proportion of Roman Catholics is steadily rising. The older residents resent the expansion in local government costs necessary to service the newcomers.

New York and New Jersey have experienced a greater number of "colonizations," and their "mix" of population, like that of Maryland, is even more varied than that of New England. Morever, in recent years the section of Megalopolis west of the Connecticut River has received almost all the massive in-migration of Negroes and Puerto Ricans, adding a color problem to the older problems rooted in the ethnic, linguistic, and religious variety of the population (see Fig. 227 inset, p. 767).

The ethnic variety achieved through successive waves of migration shaped an economic and social hierarchy based on national and racial origins. However, a constant broadening of economic opportunity developed in the region from both the westward march of settlement and from the growth of local economic activities on the seaboard; and this process made it possible for many of the newcomers to rise with every generation, first in standard of living and then in social status and educational level. Such social fluidity, of which Megalopolis has many reasons to be proud, was the product of local opportunity, and to rise on the social ladder did not require the immigrants to go West first and then come back East after they had become better equipped with skill and money. In some cases this happened, but the same result was achieved by millions who stayed in Megalopolis, even in the same section of it for several generations. A certain social hierarchy, varying from place to place, is still recognized by custom and public opinion, but it evolves relatively rapidly. As regards race relations, too, most of the leading scholars who have studied the problem agree that the evolution toward greater equality has on the whole progressed most rapidly in the great cities, especially in the great cities of the Northeast.[4a] This seems to have been especially true in the twentieth century, when Megalopolis experienced such an impressive industrial and commercial expansion and the resulting accumula-

[4a] We feel that such a general conclusion can be correctly drawn from the materials on this subject in Gunnar Myrdal, *An American Dilemma*, Harper and Brothers, New York, 1944; Hansen, *The Immigrant in American History, op. cit.*; Oscar Handlin, *The Newcomers: Negroes and Puerto Ricans in a Changing Metropolis*, New York Metropolitan Region Study, Harvard University Press, Cambridge, Mass., 1959; and Oscar Handlin, *Boston's Immigrants, 1790–1880: A Study in Acculturation*, rev. ed., Harvard University Press, Cambridge, Mass., 1959. See also E. P. Hutchinson, *Immigrants and Their Children*, John Wiley and Sons, New York, 1958.

tion of wealth in the region widened the local scope of opportunity for most of its inhabitants. However, this did not mean equal distribution of riches. By increasing the affluence of some, and by attracting larger crowds of underprivileged newcomers, the process of economic growth in the crowded cities could not help sharpening the contrasts offered by their complex associations of palatial life and slums, of virtues and vices, which seem characteristic of any rapidly developing metropolis.

Prosperity and growth were not the only factors that favored the betterment of life for the underprivileged strata of the population in Megalopolis. During the depression of the 1930's the Federal government acquired greatly enlarged powers to regulate economic affairs, and especially to supervise conditions of employment. Many of the obstacles met by newcomers in their search for the kind of work and pay they wanted were simply rooted in accepted practices of discrimination, based on individual or group prejudices,[5] and Federal legislation did a great deal to restrict such discriminatory practices, especially in the Northeastern cities. As the sociologist Morroe Berger has written:

It already seems safe to say that in the "contest" between the implications of political democracy in the United States and the implications of its system of unequal social status based in part on custom and in part on law, the former are prevailing over the latter. The issue is certainly not fully settled. Yet, unless there is a sudden and sharp reversal, all present trends show the "contest" resulting in a clear-cut, if not uniform, victory for the principles of democracy over those of inequality. Such a victory will serve also to demonstrate that legislative and legal techniques can effectively reduce and even eradicate deeply rooted prejudices and habits.[6]

In practice the evolution toward greater equality develops according to different patterns and at different rates in the different sections of the country, and even within Megalopolis there have been substantial variations. In recent years, for example, there has been more resistance to school integration in Delaware and Maryland than north of Mason and Dixon's line, and more discrimination in housing in outer suburbia than in larger cities. On the whole, however, Megalopolis has been one of the regions where recent progress has been relatively obvious and rapid.

This must be attributed in part to the people of Megalopolis. To be

[5] See Ralph H. Turner, "Foci of Discrimination in the Employment of Non-Whites," *American Journal of Sociology*, Vol. 58, No. 3, November 1952, pp. 247–256; also Myrdal, *op. cit.;* and Morroe Berger, *Racial Equality and the Law*, UNESCO, Paris, 1954.

[6] Berger, *Racial Equality and the Law, op. cit.*, p. 10. Gunnar Myrdal has several times expressed concurring opinions to the writer.

sure, both prosperity and depression have worked, in the long run, in favor of greater equality, and legal action has helped to speed the process. But the fact that the process has gone on despite the continuous influx of more newcomers, increasing the variety and the complexity of the population, indicates that the people have accepted the diversity of their region and have favored an evolution that would be in the common interest. They have stood firmly for the principles of equality under the law, of the freedom in pursuit of happiness and other tenets set forth in the Constitution and the Bill of Rights. This could not mean, however, that all individuals or groups passively accept the day-by-day consequences of the region's trends for their particular way of life. Variations in reaction are apparent in the space distribution of the various groups and in the distribution of resources. Ethnic or racial diversity is a basic and constant problem in the region, though not its only one.

Geographical Distribution of the Diversity

The geographical distribution of the various ethnic components in Megalopolis is revealed by the Census data, which provide detailed figures on foreign-born and foreign-stock residents. In 1950 the states of the Northeastern seaboard still presented by far the greatest concentration of foreign-born population in the United States, about 45 per cent of the country's total (Fig. 211). Megalopolis remains the great pole of attraction for immigrants and, apparently, still provides enough suitable jobs to retain many of them.

Always the newcomers to the region have clustered together according to origin and religion. These residence patterns appeared early in all Megalopolitan cities and they have survived partly because of economic forces and partly because of social pressures. Oscar Handlin has well shown how the immigrants established a tradition of hospitality and help for newcomers from their "old country," and how "the immigrants received accommodations of a sort at a price in money within their reach; the cost in health they could not reckon. . . . The process was cumulative; the flight of some [older residents] made more housing available to newcomers, which led to further deterioration and to the flight of more!" [7]

Perhaps the tendency to cluster was reinforced by the fact that in the past most of the immigrants came from small, closed societies, very provincial and often peasant in character. These "uprooted" people could not

[7] Handlin, *The Newcomers, op. cit.*, p. 14. See also his *The Uprooted*, Little, Brown and Company, Boston, 1951, and John Fraser Hart, "The Changing Distribution of the American Negro," *Annals of the Association of American Geographers*, Vol. 50, No. 3, September 1960, pp. 242–266.

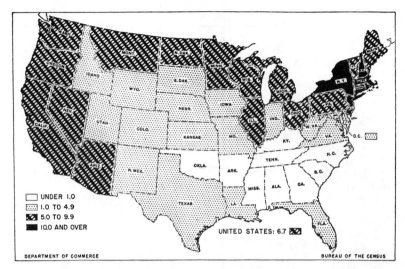

Fig. 211. Percentage of foreign-born whites in the total population by states, 1950. *Courtesy of the U. S. Bureau of the Census*

easily adapt to a cosmopolitan city of the type that would have developed if all the varied components of the population had been thoroughly mixed together from the start. Actually, ethnic influences permeated the map of settlement.

People of every nationality were scattered throughout the city. No ward was purely homogeneous. . . . But those who moved tended to seek out and to settle with people like themselves. Neighborhoods thus acquired a character defined by their churches, shops, and facilities for leisure and entertainment; and individuals with a common background were attracted by common facilities. . . . But the ability of those communities to expand was limited by the entrenchment around them of other groups.[8]

New ground for expansion of the newcomers became available only when some older established groups moved out of deteriorating districts. With the recent tendency toward more children, more automobiles, and more prosperity, suburban sprawl has taken chiefly middle-class groups out of the central cities.

The renewed emphasis on the togetherness of a sound family relationship and the desirability of rearing children in good neighborhoods led directly back to the one-family house on its own plot. . . . The postwar dispersal of residences bore striking similarities to earlier movements of population from the city.[9]

[8] Handlin, *op. cit.*, p. 15.   [9] *Ibid.*, p. 63.

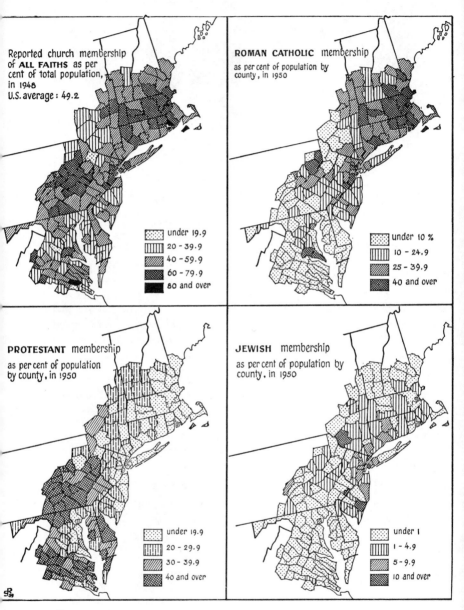

Reported church membership of **ALL FAITHS** as per cent of total population, in 1948
U.S. average: 49.2

under 19.9
20 - 39.9
40 - 59.9
60 - 79.9
80 and over

ROMAN CATHOLIC membership as per cent of population by county, in 1950

under 10 %
10 - 24.9
25 - 39.9
40 and over

PROTESTANT membership as per cent of population by county, in 1950

under 19.9
20 - 29.9
30 - 39.9
40 and over

JEWISH membership as per cent of population by county, in 1950

under 1
1 - 4.9
5 - 9.9
10 and over

Fig. 212

The old clustering tendency of ethnic groups shows up today on the maps of distribution of major religious faiths in Megalopolis (Fig 212). In 1950 Protestant membership was below 20 per cent of the total population in almost all Megalopolitan counties of New England and never as high as 30 per cent. Similar proportions prevailed in the New York–New Jersey metropolitan region. In Pennsylvania and farther south the proportion of Protestants rose above 40 per cent in places, but only at a distance from the major cities.

The distribution of Roman Catholic church membership appears in its general features almost as an inversion of the Protestant pattern. The predominance of Roman Catholics is striking in most of Massachusetts, Rhode Island, and northern New Jersey. It is strong also in Connecticut and in most of the suburban counties of New York City in New York State. The relatively high proportion of Roman Catholics in Orange County reflects in part the suburbanization of the Catskills by New York City, and in part the industrialization of the valley. The Catskills also show a "Jewish area."

The Jewish group is heavily concentrated in the New York metropolitan area, in the other main central cities (Boston, Philadelphia, and Baltimore), and in two outlying counties, both of which have large-scale resort activities servicing New York City — Sullivan County, New York (the Shawangunk Mountains and southern Catskills), and Atlantic County, New Jersey (Atlantic City).

On the whole, the central cities in 1950 were populated less heavily by Protestants than by Roman Catholics and Jews. This reflected the status of the latter groups as relative newcomers, forming a "second colonization" of Megalopolis that is especially noticeable northeast of the Delaware River. However, they are not limited to the cities. With the metropolitanization of the land both Jews and Catholics, many of whom had achieved middle-class status, spread over the suburban counties. During the 1950's this trend became quite obvious through most of Megalopolis for the Roman Catholics, and for the Jews it could be observed all around New York City, Philadelphia, and Baltimore, on a larger scale than previously. The precise extent of the new ethnic "mix" achieved in interurbia through Megalopolis remains difficult to assess with precision, but it appears to be above the national average.

The more recent waves of migration have left the central cities with increasing percentages of Negroes and Puerto Ricans, the result both of continued influx of these groups and of a complementary out-migration of whites. The map of dwelling units occupied by nonwhite households

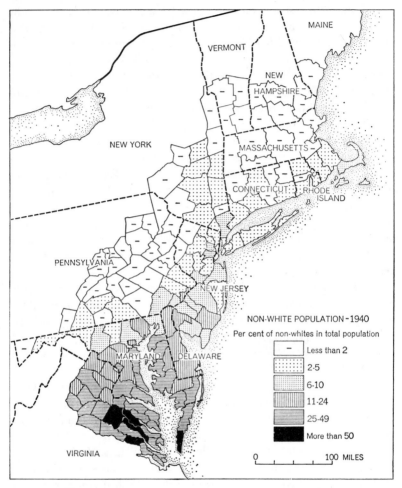

FIG. 213

shows the situation as regards Negroes in 1950 (see Fig. 215 and compare
it with Figs. 213, 214, and 227, showing the proportion of nonwhites in
the total population). The concentration is evident in the major hubs
and in a few areas where domestic servants are in great demand (either
because of the white residents' wealth, as in Westchester County, or because of the needs of summer resorts, as in the Cape Cod–Nantucket
area). Also, of course, the proportion of nonwhite households rises sharply
southward, especially south of Philadelphia. The percentage of nonwhites
in the population of the central cities continued to increase during the

1950's. From 1950 to 1960 it rose in the District of Columbia from 35.4 per cent to more than 50 per cent; in Baltimore from 23.8 per cent to almost 40 per cent; in Manhattan from one fifth to one fourth of the total population. In New York City there was only a small increase in Harlem, most of the growth being in the Bronx, Brooklyn, and Queens. The urban redevelopment in Manhattan has added strength to a migration of Negroes to the outlying boroughs. The newcomers thus are gradually pushing toward the periphery. It still remains difficult for them to find housing in the suburbs, although employment is more readily available there. A counter current at rush hours of Negroes commuting to work in suburbia has developed in the New York area and in several other metropolitan areas. (See Fig. 227, p. 767.)

In New York City the Puerto Ricans have for some time provided a transition between white and nonwhite groups — not because there is much association between them and the American Negroes, with whom they do not wish to be linked, but because of their own racial composition. Seven per cent are classified as Negro, and many more have some Negro blood, but a large proportion of them are white. By virtue of the latter, the Puerto Ricans, white and colored together, gain access to housing in deteriorating tenements that are still closed to American Negroes. Thus the Puerto Ricans have been able to spread much more widely than the Negroes. In 1950 all but twenty-two of Manhattan's 284 Census tracts reported some Puerto Ricans,[10] and by 1959 there were Puerto Ricans living in every one of the city's 352 health districts.[11] In many sections there are few of them, but in some areas these Spanish-speaking people have clustered and increased in numbers rapidly and have come to dominate the neighborhood, sometimes making up more than half of the population in a Census tract. Many of their neighborhoods are contiguous to sections populated by Negroes.

Being the last category of massive migration to come to New York City and other central cities of Megalopolis, Puerto Ricans seem to encounter even more prejudice than do Negroes in many sorts of employment. Their wages appear to be on the average lower than those earned by Negroes in New York. Nevertheless, the attraction of mainland opportunity is still great for the people of the overpopulated Caribbean island, and emigration continues, though the rate has decreased and the in-

[10] For an analysis of the 1950 Census data, see Robert T. Novak, "Distribution of Puerto Ricans on Manhattan Island," *The Geographical Review*, Vol. 46, 1956, pp. 182–186.
[11] *U. S. News and World Report*, December 7, 1959.

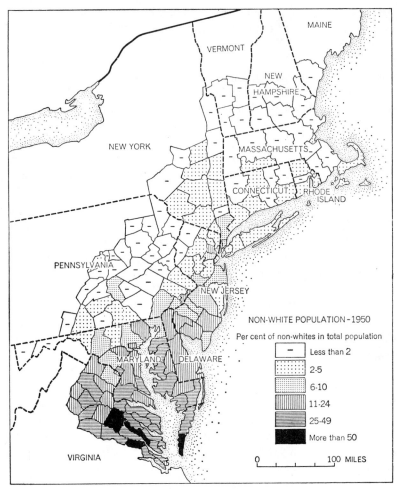

FIG. 214

flux is no longer restricted to the New York area. There is now considerable flow also into Philadelphia, Chicago, and Los Angeles.[12] In 1960 the

[12] According to *A Summary in Facts and Figures*, prepared by the Commonwealth
of Puerto Rico's Migration Division, Department of Labor, April 1957, the increase
of the Puerto Rican-born population from 1940 to 1950 reached 204.9 per cent in New
York City and 355 per cent in the continental United States. Between the 1950 Census
and the end of 1956 the same increase was estimated at 127.3 per cent in New York
City and 212.7 per cent outside it. Still in 1956 New York City held about 577,000
Puerto Ricans, or 78 per cent of all island-born Puerto Ricans on the mainland; New
Jersey had 40,000 of them; Philadelphia, 13,000; Connecticut cities, about 15,000. Meg-

Puerto Rican population in New York City numbered more than 650,000 (750,000 according to some estimates), of whom about one third were mainland born. Although they hold American citizenship they are quite different in language, culture, and many other features from the mass of the Megalopolitan population. Among the new problems they present — these have been carefully studied by sociologists [13] — some of the basic ones are educational, and the city's schools have had a special concern for these newcomers, who already make up about 15 per cent of the total enrollment. That many of them do not speak or even understand much English when they arrive is only part of the problem, and much more than the language must be taught them to help them adapt to the Megalopolitan environment.

The tendency of the older ethnic stocks to move out when the Puerto Rican and Negro neighborhoods have expanded has added to the problems of slums and housing in the central cities. For many, moving out has been the easy solution, but besides devouring space on the metropolitan periphery through the sprawling of suburbia (other factors, of course, have contributed to this too) this flight has also in many ways wasted the value of residential districts in central cities, causing them to decay more rapidly. True, the newcomers were thus able to cluster in the cities, where they pay high but not exorbitant prices for their lodgings. But the lack of provision and foresight, the predominance of day-to-day "easier" solutions, has added to the burdens of local governments in many ways. One of these has been the resulting depreciation of real estate in many sectors of the cities, thereby restricting the taxable values from which cities draw their principal financial revenue. These growing problems have made it less pleasant to live and work in the central cities for many residents, except perhaps those who are affluent enough to keep their neighborhoods well defended and isolated against all odds; and in the long run even such privileged districts will suffer, unless they can find the means to expand and rehabilitate adjacent declining areas (as has been the case in somewhat exceptional fashion for parts of Manhattan and Washington, D. C.).

Such evolution, with the problems and tensions it entails, has come to

alopolis housed certainly more than 90 per cent of the Puerto Rican migrants to the mainland.

[13] For an excellent description of a Puerto Rican neighborhood in Manhattan see Elena Padilla, *Up From Puerto Rico*, Columbia University Press, New York, 1958. Dr. Padilla also prepared a general report on the Puerto Rican migration especially for the study of Megalopolis. See also Handlin, *The Newcomers*, *op. cit.*; and A. J. Jaffe (ed.), *Puerto Rican Population of New York City*, Columbia University, Bureau of Applied Social Research, New York, 1954 (mimeographed).

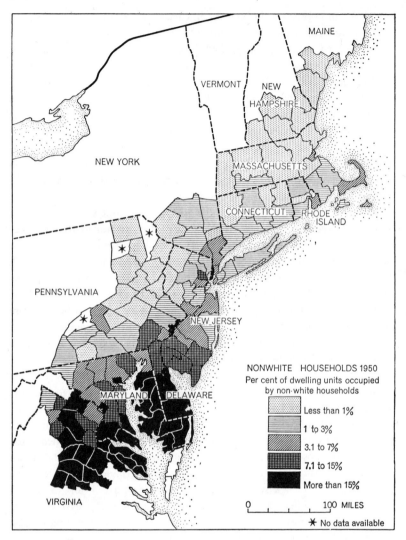

NONWHITE   HOUSEHOLDS 1950
Per cent of dwelling units occupied
by non-white households

Less than 1%

1 to 3%

3.1 to 7%

7.1 to 15%

More than 15%

0   100 MILES

✱ No data available

FIG. 215

many a middle-sized city. An example is provided by the exhaustive and careful survey of its own social trends recently completed by Newark, New Jersey.[14] In 1950 Newark was a city of about half a million night-

[14] *Newark: A City in Transition*, prepared by the Market Planning Corporation for the City of Newark and the Mayor's Commission on Group Relations, Newark, 1959, 3 volumes. See also Louis Winnick, *American Housing and Its Use* (Census Monograph Series, for the Social Science Research Council in Cooperation with the

time residents, with a slightly larger number of incoming daily commuters. This difference between residents and commuters increased in the 1950's, a decade during which the city lost about one tenth of its residents. However, this total figure represents a loss of much more than 10 per cent of the middle-class population and a slightly smaller influx of underprivileged people, largely Negroes. The city's household population [15] was 84 per cent white in 1950 but only 62 per cent white in 1958. As usual there were great variations according to neighborhood. In 1958 the Central Business District was found to be 46 per cent Negro and 33 per cent Puerto Rican, the Central Ward 85 per cent Negro and 2 per cent Puerto Rican, the South Broad Street district 61 per cent Negro and 9 per cent Puerto Rican. The 1950 percentages of Negroes in these same areas were much lower — 33, 63, and 20 respectively (no 1950 data are available on Puerto Ricans). In contrast, the Forest Hill–Silver Lake district showed a decrease in the proportion of Negro households, from 4 per cent to 2 per cent, and there were no Puerto Ricans.

The real estate owners are not necessarily dissatisfied with these trends, for the average monthly rent paid by Negroes is *higher* than that paid by whites in the neighborhoods of greater Negro concentration. But such discriminatory rents do not stop the spread of blight and slums, and the general impoverishment of the city as a community. Race relations become a major concern of government and politics in such a city. If the Negroes should vote as a solid group they could easily swing the balance between the two major parties in most of the large and medium-sized cities of Megalopolis.

Closely associated with these changing patterns of religious and ethnic groups are shifts in the distribution of age and income groups and of educational needs. Changes in these features are modifying the basic features of life and land use in Megalopolis.

Age, Income, and Education

It will cause no surprise to observe that the distribution of age groups is not alike in central cities and suburbia. A great many parents leaving

U. S. Department of Commerce), John Wiley and Sons, New York, 1957; and the series of reports prepared under the auspices of the Commission on Race and Housing and published by the University of California Press, especially Davis McEntire, *Residence and Race*, 1959; Eunice and George Greer, *Privately Developed Interracial Housing*, 1960; Luigi Laurenti, *Property Values and Race*, 1960 (especially Chapter 8 on Philadelphia).

[15] In this study a census was taken only of "the relatively stable and settled portion of Newark's population, those who live in their own households or in rooming houses." (*Newark: A City in Transition, op. cit.*, Vol. I, p. 11.)

city apartments for suburban homes explain that they do it "for the kids"; they accept the troubles of commuting and often somewhat more expensive living in the suburbs in order to provide a better environment for the children — more greenery, cleaner air, better facilities for recreation, better playmates and schools. Seen from this angle, the suburban sprawl was caused partly by the rise in the American birth rate after 1940. The nation's birth rate (adjusted for underregistration) declined from around 30 per 1,000 in 1910–15 to 18.7 in 1935, then rose from 19.4 in 1940 to 20.4 in 1945, 24.1 in 1950, and about 25 in 1952–57. It decreased slightly, to about 24, in 1958–60. The latest trend to a lower rate may be due to a slightly lower marriage rate in 1958–60, which may in turn be explained by the coming of age of the less numerous generation born in the 1930's. This decline should not last long after 1961.

The *median age* of the population in 1950 was not very diversified over Megalopolis, according to a map of its regional variation by counties (Fig. 216). However, on the whole the median age seemed much higher north of Philadelphia than south of it. This distinction between North and South reflects the higher birth rate of the Negro population, especially in Southern rural areas, and also the rather high reproduction rates in the Pennsylvania hills and ridges, which have been a center of white out-migration for some time. New York State outside New York City appeared to have the largest area in which the median age was over 34; but smaller patches of such median age were observed in "out-of-the-way" regions from which the youth have been going away, such as central New Hampshire, the southeastern tip of New Jersey, and the islands of Nantucket and Martha's Vineyard.

The actual features of the geographical distribution of age groups may be analyzed more effectively with the help of the three maps showing, in terms of percentage of the total population in 1950, the relative importance of old people (aged 65 and over), youth (aged 15 to 24), and children (aged 14 and under). These maps (Fig. 217) give a general picture corresponding to the first indications provided by the regional variation of the population's median age. The southern parts of Megalopolis are definitely younger than the region's New England section. Higher proportions of children are found in suburban counties at some distance from the central cities, or in the more rural areas on the fringes of Megalopolis and outside it. A high concentration of youth is often found in the central cities and around them. It is interesting to observe that many counties with a rather high percentage (more than 25) of children showed a relatively low percentage (below 15 and even below 13) of youth, which

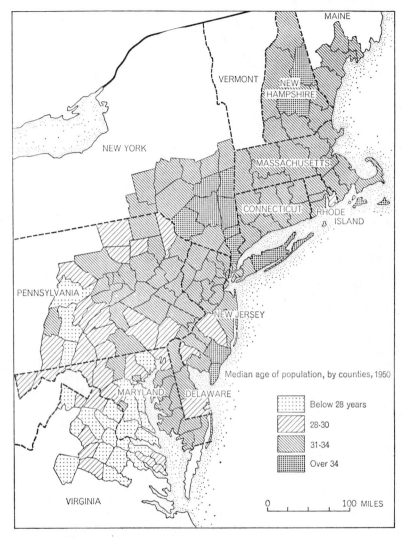

FIG. 216

suggests the strong attraction of the cities for young men and women as soon as they come of age.

Adults aged 25 to 64, who are in the more productive part of their life, are not represented on the three maps of Figure 217. This large age group would, of course, be concentrated in the more densely populated areas, where it forms the mass of the labor force and most of the commuters.

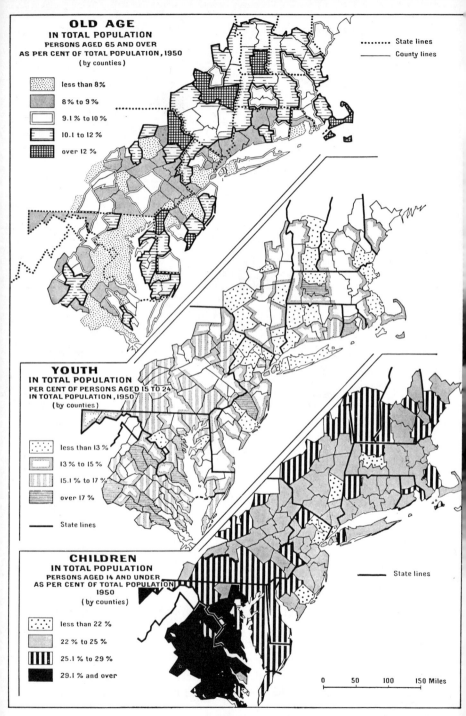

OLD AGE
IN TOTAL POPULATION
PERSONS AGED 65 AND OVER
AS PER CENT OF TOTAL POPULATION, 1950
(by counties)

- less than 8 %
- 8 % to 9 %
- 9.1 % to 10 %
- 10.1 to 12 %
- over 12 %

··········· State lines
———— County lines

YOUTH
IN TOTAL POPULATION
PER CENT OF PERSONS AGED 15 TO 24
IN TOTAL POPULATION, 1950
(by counties)

- less than 13 %
- 13 % to 15 %
- 15.1 % to 17 %
- over 17 %

———— State lines

CHILDREN
IN TOTAL POPULATION
PERSONS AGED 14 AND UNDER
AS PER CENT OF TOTAL POPULATION
1950
(by counties)

- less than 22 %
- 22 % to 25 %
- 25.1 % to 29 %
- 29.1 % and over

———— State lines

0   50   100   150 Miles

FIG. 217. Population distribution according to age groups in Megalopolis, 1950

While these people work chiefly in the hubs or the industrial suburbs of the inner rings, they may settle either in the cities or in the outer ring of the metropolitan areas.

Children make up a larger proportion of the population in areas with a high reproduction rate (for example, the southern parts of Megalopolis), or in areas that serve mainly as suburban dormitories for a great metropolis. Among the latter are such counties as Nassau in New York, Bucks in Pennsylvania, and Plymouth in Massachusetts. The New York City area had a low concentration of children in 1950, ranging in the various counties of the metropolitan region between 17 and 24 per cent of the total population, while the national average stood at 26.9 per cent. The three states of southern New England showed slightly higher figures than did New York City, but the average was still below 26 per cent in most of their counties, and the same was true of suburbanized New Jersey and eastern Pennsylvania. It is quite clear on the maps that suburban districts have a higher ratio of children than do the central urban cores (see, for example, Manhattan, Boston, Providence, Philadelphia, Baltimore, and Washington), and that these same urban cores attract a higher ratio of youth (as is true in Boston, Philadelphia, Baltimore, and New York City as a whole, but not in Manhattan alone). The presence of colleges in these cities and the greater opportunity offered to young job seekers, especially to young women in the white-collar occupations, are probably the main reasons for the attraction of youngsters.

The local variations of the age pyramid indicate that children are being born and reared in the United States largely away from the main urban centers, but increasingly not very far away. The old urban cores have ratios of old and young people below the national average but a higher than average ratio of the adult and mature population. This is true even of nighttime residents, and the ratio of the adults is, of course, much higher for the daytime population, for commuters into the urban hubs are predominantly in those age brackets. Thus, although children today spend most of their time away from the cities, in the sense of crowded, densely occupied, and built-up areas, they will usually spend at least part of their lives in a highly urbanized environment.[16]

The long-range trends in the redistribution of age groups within Megalopolis can be followed on the maps (Fig. 218) showing the changes that

[16] See Eli Ginzberg (ed.), *The Nation's Children*, Columbia University Press, New York, 1960, 3 volumes; among these essays, written for the Golden Anniversary White House Conference on Children and Youth, note especially "The Impact of Urbanization," by Jean Gottmann, Vol. I, pp. 180–208, and "Demographic Trends and Implications," by Eleanor H. Bernert, Vol. I, pp. 24–49. See also Donald J. Bogue, *The Population of the United States*, The Free Press, Glencoe, Ill., 1959.

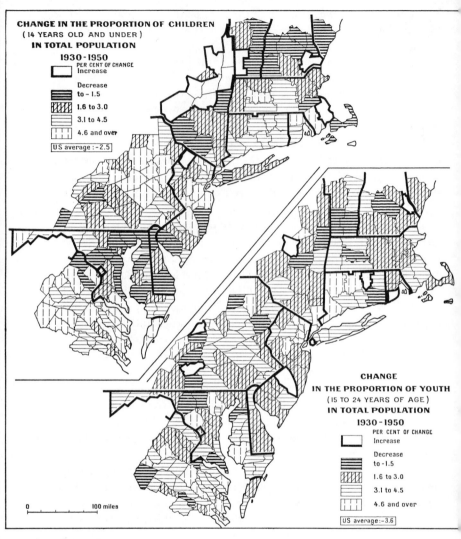

Fɪɢ. 218

occurred in the proportions of children and youth between 1930 and 1950. Despite the rise of the birth rate through the 1940's, its lower level during the 1920's and 1930's had not yet been offset by 1950, and in the whole nation the proportion of children had decreased as against 1930 by 2.5 per cent. In most of the axial belt of Megalopolis, except in Delaware and Maryland, the decrease was greater than average. Few of the more urbanized counties had seen any increase in their population aged 14 and under. For the changes in the proportion of youth the picture was more diversified. Increases, or decreases much below the national average, were found in parts of the axial belt and even in the major cities (particularly in Boston and Brooklyn).

The higher birth rate of the 1950's has again changed the trend and accelerated the urban exodus to the metropolitan rings. The proportion of children has risen even in the axial-belt counties, away from the central cities. When the detailed data from the 1960 Census are fully available, the child population of the suburban areas will be found much increased as against either 1940 or 1950. But the central cities may not have been as much emptied of children as one might have anticipated. The migration of Negroes and Puerto Ricans into the central cities of Megalopolis was first a migration of adults, but families often followed, after some delay, and the rather high birth rate of these newcomers may well have boosted somewhat the reproduction rates of the city population, despite a trend for older persons to come into the cities once their children are grown and have broken away from the parents' home.

The changes developing in the distribution of age groups in Megalopolis do not affect all classes of the population equally. Several times in the course of this study [17] the differences shaping between central cities and their outer rings in terms of income levels have been noted. In 1949 there was a heavy concentration of families with low incomes, especially below $2,000, in the southern parts of Megalopolis (Fig. 219), a situation certainly related to the distribution of Negroes (see Fig. 215, showing the proportion of nonwhite households). Moreover, the concentration of Negroes in Manhattan obviously affects the high proportion of low-income families in this borough of New York City, which, if measured by other yardsticks than the residents' income, would rate as the richest place in the world. Other areas of low-income concentration appear in the Appalachian ridges and valleys, especially in Pennsylvania.

The map of the higher-income brackets (families with incomes of $5,000 or more in 1949) is almost the negative of the previous one. This time the greater concentrations are found in the metropolitan rings around the major central cities (Fig. 220). Especially impressive is the ring of such concentration of "upper-middle-class" residents around New York City and Washington, D. C.

Since 1950 the average incomes have risen rapidly, but the general picture of distribution of the major income groups shows only slight changes.

[17] See above, especially p. 419.

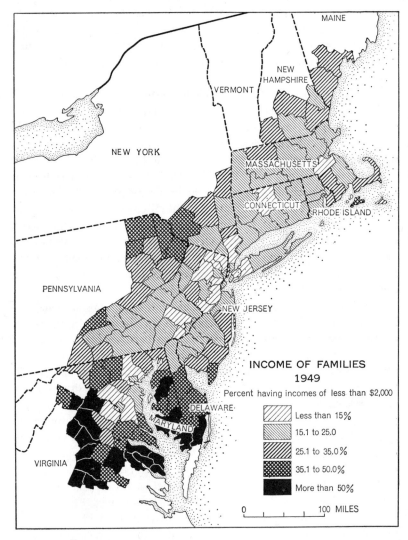

INCOME OF FAMILIES
1949

Percent having incomes of less than $2,000

Less than 15%
15.1 to 25.0
25.1 to 35.0%
35.1 to 50.0%
More than 50%

0   100   MILES

Fɪɢ. 219

However, the rings gathering the upper-middle level around the central cities have broadened and thickened throughout the whole region, for the exodus to the suburbs and particularly to outer suburbia has involved the middle-class population much more than the lower-income level. This is the result both of the partitioning of suburbia into neighborhoods that defend themselves actively against undesired newcomers, by zoning and

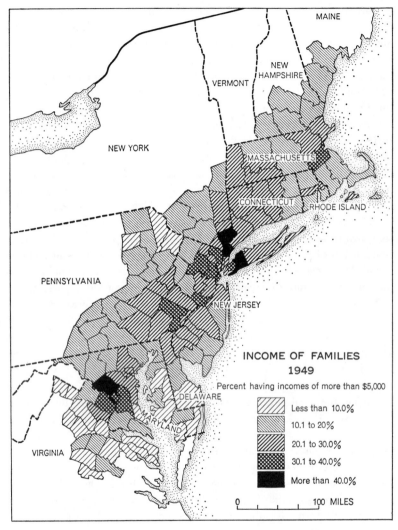

INCOME OF FAMILIES
1949

Percent having incomes of more than $5,000

⫽	Less than 10.0%
░	10.1 to 20%
⫽	20.1 to 30.0%
▦	30.1 to 40.0%
■	More than 40.0%

0   100 MILES

FIG. 220

other means, and of all the economics of Megalopolitan sprawl (in terms of the costs of housing, transportation, and so forth). Another change has been a sharpening of the contrast between the inner and outer districts of the major metropolitan regions, reflecting both economic complementarity (resulting from the division of functions among the different sectors in a metropolitan region) and the residential partitioning noted above.

This partitioning creates different needs in neighboring communities. One common need, however, is adequate schools for the children, whose numbers have risen rapidly since 1945, and this educational need has put a disproportionately increased burden on many communities in Megalopolis (see Figs. 218 and 221). In the suburbs the child population has risen both because of the rise in the birth rate and also because of the influx of families with young children, coming either from the cities or from other parts of the country. Communities serving thus as expanded dormitories saw their school needs shoot up during the 1950's. The central cities should have had less of a burden, because of the migration of parents with children out of the old cores, but the actual trend was not so simple. In part this outflow was offset by the arrival of newcomers with numerous children in greater need of education, for which these newcomers were less able to provide resources. Central cities have had often to lower the standards of teaching in some of their schools to adapt them to the educational needs of the greater numbers of Negro and Puerto Rican children enrolled who came from rural areas or towns with less good schools. Such measures have caused increasing dissatisfaction among white parents.

The costs of school maintenance and expansion have increased rapidly, while the budgetary resources of the municipalities have not increased correspondingly. One of the features that at first made suburban sprawl so attractive to many middle-class families was the relatively low local taxes in small communities. However, as these communities have grown and the demands of their larger population for more services have expanded, the local governments have had to look for more financial resources, which could not be obtained without more taxation. Many suburban communities have been caught in a sort of infernal circle. To expand their resources, by way of their taxable bases, they have encouraged more real estate development and especially have endeavored to attract industries, which would pay higher taxes than mere residents. If such efforts are successful, they result in the gradual urbanization of a community that was formerly suburban or even semi-rural, and at the same time they always cause a rapid increase in the community's demand for public services. Schools are only one among many such services, others being streets with pavement and lighting, adequate highway approaches, expanded sewers and water supply, more policing, more parking space, parks, playgrounds, hospitals, more welfare in general. Such are the expanding burdens befalling local government.

Meanwhile, the central cities have experienced another kind of financial cycle, which has already taken on even more infernal aspects. Insofar as a

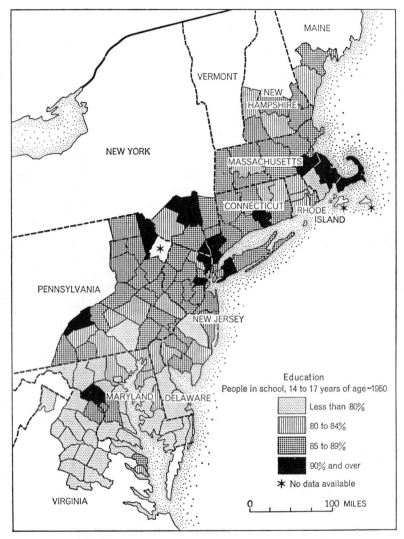

Fig. 221. The map shows the percentage of all residents aged 14–17 going regularly to school in 1950, by counties

city preserves its functions as an active center for trade, industry, entertainment, government, and so forth, the decline of its residential population usually means that those who stay are on the average the less wealthy, who live in more crowded conditions. But during the day the city still must serve all those who work in or visit its commercial or industrial districts. In brief, these new patterns involve more expenditures for the municipality and often less (or less rapidly growing) revenues. If the rate of revenue collection must be increased to avoid chronic deficit, the city may become a less desirable location, and industries or residents who have a choice and can move out may do so, to an even greater degree than they already have.

On the whole, the larger cities still offer the more lucrative jobs, but many of the better-paid people only work in the cities, and their interests thus diverge from those of the less well-paid employees who both live and work there. An opposition of interests grows between those who live and those who only work in the central cities. The business function of the city, of course, depends on both groups. Such trends toward opposition of interests cannot go on indefinitely without deeply disturbing the social and economic cooperation that must somehow be maintained between the various groups in Megalopolis. The Newark survey mentioned above clearly points to many pitfalls that are shaping also in other cities (Trenton and Hartford are two more examples). Many urban renewal projects endeavor to restore the quality of some central city neighborhoods and attract better, middle-class residents to them.[18] However, there is the danger that they may only "protect" against the urban expansion of the newcomers without providing better housing for the latter somewhere else. In that case, while they may locally modify some widely deplored statistical trends, in practice they will only transfer to other areas the more acute and fundamental problems.

The belief in the continued mobility of the American nation and especially of its urban elements (see Fig. 222) is not enough of an answer. Oscar Handlin puts his faith in the belief that the newcomers will gradually rise on the social and economic ladder, as did so many previous waves of immigrants.

The Negroes and Puerto Ricans have followed the general outline of the experience of earlier immigrants. Their latest arrivals diverged from that earlier experience because color prejudice and the social and economic conditions they encountered impeded their freedom of movement, both in space and in social and economic status. That divergence need not be more than temporary, however.[19]

It certainly need not, but Handlin does not argue in detail his assumption that the color discrimination that has been so constant in the past will prove to be only temporary in the long run. He admits that "the Ne-

[18] See above, Chapter 8, pp. 403–439.
[19] Handlin, *The Newcomers, op. cit.*, p. 118.

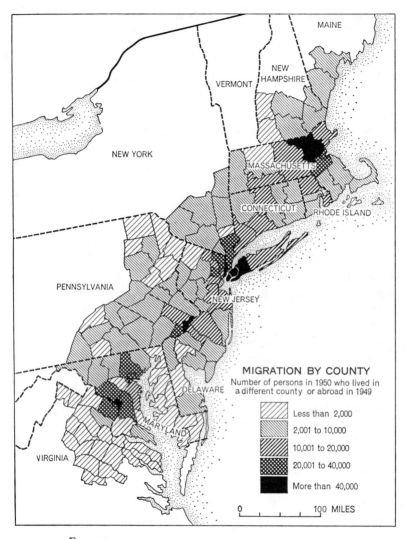

FIG. 222

groes and Puerto Ricans are likely to continue, as they have in the past, to depend more on governmental services for education and welfare than did earlier immigrants." [20] Perhaps this could be merely an outgrowth of the modern evolution toward greater governmental participation in the

[20] *Ibid.*, p. 119. See also U. S. Department of Labor, Bureau of Labor Statistics, *Notes on the Economic Situation of Negroes in the United States* (revised), August 1959, mimeographed.

financial burdens of education and welfare, at all levels and for the whole nation. We know, however, that the answer is not as simple as that. Earlier communities of newcomers were able to organize themselves, despite their "newness" and lack of means, in a way that does not seem possible for the latest influx of migrants. Whether this was a matter of European culture, of basic educational background, or of more affinities with the older ethnic elements than the historian may discern in the shadows of the past is a question to be answered by specialists in social history.

In any case, education is now needed more than ever to enable an individual to take advantage of the economic opportunities of the region. As Megalopolis specializes in the upper stages of manufacturing, requiring more knowledge and skill, and turns increasingly toward the communications-oriented industries and white-collar occupations, will it be possible to overcome the prejudice that stands in the way of closer relations between the different social groups? Will it be possible to open the expanding executive and professional employment widely to Negroes and Puerto Ricans? How rapidly could these groups acquire the proper education and frame of mind for such jobs? The problems remain difficult indeed. Forecasting by sheer projection seems hopeless, but pure optimism may be disappointing.

Besides the new entanglements rooted in the present evolution of the social and economic structure, one must consider the significance of the new opposition that is shaping between those who only work and those who both work and live in the city — between neighbors who seem at the same time linked by close economic interdependence and opposed in their concerns for land use and for the services they desire in their places of work and of residence. This antithesis between the two main functions of the city is a kind of threat to the whole regional system that did not seem to exist in past periods.

The Strength of Local Sentiment

The communities within Megalopolis are many and varied. While they are deeply interdependent in so many respects in their economic and cultural organization, they stand divided sharply differentiated from one another, within each metropolitan area and within each city of some size. The economics of Megalopolis have been founded from the start upon wide open horizons, close relations with distant lands. This cosmopolitan background has come to be highly valued by the American elite; it has been an asset in the leadership Megalopolis has assumed in the economic affairs of the nation and in many facets of international relations. The same process that bestowed this cosmopolitan stamp and these functions of leadership on the main hubs of Megalopolis also attracted to them successive waves of newcomers of various origins.

Some observers, such as Jane Addams, have voiced the hope that the development of urban life, as it has occurred on the Northeastern seaboard, might improve people's understanding of each other and thus work for better international relations. Perhaps some day such hopes may be justified. So far, however, modern society in Megalopolis has reacted to the onrushing and diverse influences of the outside world by partitioning itself into a mosaic of small communities, each of which seems tolerant of the neighboring ones on the condition of being able to keep them out of its own enclosure. Local sentiment is strong and wishes to exclude any intruders, but it can hardly be compared to the provincialism of the European countryside — what the French call their "church-steeple patriotism." [21] Although the Megalopolitan community may be provincial in spirit, it can seldom lead an isolated life, for its interests are too closely woven into the fabric of the daily developments in the vast surrounding area; its sources of revenue are intertwined with the constant flow of people, goods, and events that has made the "hinge" what it is. However, these communities stubbornly seek to divorce the cosmopolitan component of their business from their daily social life. The latter they would like to conduct in a small, homogeneous world of their own.

The causes of this partitioning in the American and especially the Megalopolitan way of life are many, and to conduct a detailed inquiry into them would take us much beyond the proper field of this study. For the purposes of our analysis of the region's problems and evolution, we may be satisfied with recognizing the multiplicity and diversity of the causes. Some of them are obviously rooted deep in the past and reflect the well-established characteristics of early American communities: the New England self-governing township; the self-contained Southern plantation; the settlement by religious sects, each claiming its city, county, or even state; the long-held resentment against neighbors like that developed early between Massachusetts and Rhode Island; the frontiersman's desire to move once his area became "too crowded" with newcomers. Other causes stem from the very pressures that constantly affected the Northeastern seaboard because its fast-growing cities were indeed crowded, and because the immigrants concentrating there came from so many strange places and origins.

[21] "*Patriotisme de clocher*," meaning the local pride and feeling of superiority that exist in every small, isolated village.

In a way it was normal for a well-knit community to strive to preserve itself from being overrun and its unity from being weakened by too-close contacts with all the variety of people who settled near by or with whom business was conducted. The separation of work from home has been an American characteristic. It led Megalopolis to pioneer in the development of office buildings for the transaction of private business. In Europe such distinction has been made, chiefly since the sixteenth century, for government bureaus, but traditionally much private business has been (and still is) conducted in or next to the home. The clear-cut distinction between "downtown" and "uptown" and the daily trip from home to work and back are American contributions to modern life — and they led to the rise of the skyscraper and of commuting on the scale presently observed in Megalopolis. Perhaps the universality in business called for a necessary counterweight in the form of some "provincialism" at home, especially in view of the diversity of people that crowded the hubs of Megalopolis after 1800.

Add to this background the great mobility of the American population and the powerful tradition of community self-government inherited both from England and New England — the individual's urge to keep as close as possible to the administration of his community's affairs. This was a more ambitious and difficult task than it seems, and in large cities there is little or no local government on a neighborhood basis. However, as the population has grown and its density has increased there have been many efforts to keep alive the homogeneous and self-conscious neighborhood because of its social values. If strange influences came to be felt strongly, the neighborhood's people could move out of a given location, in order to preserve a certain homogeneity, scattering some of its members but protecting the family's traditions by avoiding association with neighbors who had different traditions.

Thus suburban sprawl has old and deep roots, many of which may not be felt consciously in the middle of the twentieth century. But mobility to achieve the American "dream" was traditional in this region — and among the components of this "dream," in addition to and probably more powerful than the individual home and the individual automobile, were the desires for church or temple in the *right* kind of community, for the right kind of school and playmates for the children, for the right kind of people to meet at the country club or even on the sidewalk.

Observers of Megalopolitan society have described, some in scholarly and others in more literary fashion, how individuals sought a certain kind of community — looking for more "security," or for "status," or for better identification with an "organization" or a professional category, or often for all those things at the same time. These ends could be achieved by *belonging* to the desired community, a prerequisite being residence at some selected place — a certain suburb or a certain neighborhood.[22]

The American liking for self-government in a not-too-broad community has preserved several strata of community organizations. From the small scale of the neighborhood one rises successively to the local government levels of townships, cities, and counties, then to the level of state government, and finally to the national level. Each of these levels operates by cooperation within the strata and by coordination between the various levels. This interstratified and rather complex structure, the like of which is not found in any other country, could hardly operate as successfully as it has for almost 200 years unless it fitted a complex nation, endowed with extreme diversity when examined from some angles, but with extraordinary homogeneity when looked upon from another perspective. *The homogeneity is more apparent when Americans are at work,* and this is especially striking in the diversified population of Megalopolis.

Perhaps the land use and the whole map of Megalopolis would be quite different from what we have described and analyzed if the way of life had not favored such distinct patterns for the distribution of places of work and of places of residence. Megalopolis works according to one set of rules and lives after work according to another. For some time these two sets of rules coexisted within the same general space without much conflict. New trends and pressures have now developed as the region becomes increasingly integrated into one interwoven system, and as the size and the density of population grow. Three centuries ago those who felt "crowded" in Newtown, Massachusetts, could remove to the Connecticut Valley, causing only a minimum of conflict between their old community and the new. Nowadays places and people are too interdependent for such easy solutions. The needs and resources of central cities and suburbs, of neighboring counties or states do not allow them any more to settle their community problems without concern for outsiders.

[22] There is a great deal of literature on these matters, with more or less emphasis being placed on suburbia or on community belonging. We have had to condense many observations in a few paragraphs for this study's purposes. We may refer the reader to such works as: William H. Whyte, Jr., *The Organization Man,* Simon and Schuster, New York, 1956, and the same author's chapters in *The Exploding Metropolis,* Doubleday and Co., New York, 1958; Robert C. Wood, *Suburbia: Its People and Their Politics,* Houghton Mifflin Company, Boston, 1959 (especially Chapter 4); David Riesman, *The Lonely Crowd,* Yale University Press, New Haven, 1950; Carl J. Friedrich (ed.), *Community,* The Liberal Arts Press, New York, 1959.

Conflicting Needs and Coordination of Resources

Throughout this study many instances have illustrated the bonds that tie together the various parts of Megalopolis, bonds of economic organization and of neighborhood in the sense of proximity.

Cities may compete between themselves or with their suburbs to attract industries, a certain kind of labor, the headquarters of some organization; but until recently there has been enough to vie for, enough growth for every section of Megalopolis. For about twenty-five years, however, despite the economic momentum supplied by World War II and its aftermath, signs of serious and persistent decay have shown in most of the central cities, with the exception of the business districts of some of them (Manhattan and Washington, for example). These cities have been losing resident population and some trade and manufacturing, while the recent growth and progress have gone to the suburbs and to the interurban spaces that until recently could be classified as truly rural. The decline of the cities was quite clear and rather general in Megalopolis in the years 1945–57, although during that time both the country as a whole and Megalopolis were extremely prosperous. This made the case of declining cities look especially hopeless, for if even prosperity did not help them the probability seemed very remote that they might fare better in recession or depression.

Meanwhile, the booming suburban and interurban areas themselves were beset with local problems. Their growth created local needs that these small communities could hardly shoulder without outside help: needs for more facilities of a kind usually paid for out of public funds, such as roads, schools, parks, police, and the like. The state and Federal treasuries have been under constant pressure to bring urgently needed help to *both* the declining central cities and the mushrooming suburbs and small towns. The simple fact that with few exceptions almost no type of community, small or large, can take care of its needs with its own resources witnesses to a general lack of adaptation of the administrative and financial structure to the present situation. To most parts of the region change has come too rapidly, usually overwhelming the local authorities. The lack of adaptation budgetwise affects local services first, and then local politics, threatening to sharpen some of the tensions within many districts.

From analysis of the urban uses of the land, of the symbiosis of urban and rural, and of the main groups of industries employing the people of Megalopolis, we have seen, in many fields and from diverse angles, how complementary are the different parts of Megalopolis and its various economic functions. However, the balance of complementarity is rapidly shifting, with changes occurring in the location of manufacturing plants, trade establishments, currents of traffic, and so forth. In addition, there are elements of conflict and competition.

So many communities, including large cities, have been growing close to one another in Megalopolis that they often run short of space. Since the territory within their boundaries is limited and fairly stable, a community may increase its resources in space either by building in height or, if the local conditions allow for it, by reclaiming for more productive uses any spaces within its territory that may have been lying idle or that have been utilized inefficiently. Thus a group of municipalities in the Hackensack Meadows area of northeastern New Jersey worked out together a plan for fuller reclamation of these marshes and, in 1960, agreed to implement the plan by pooling their resources.[23] In other cases, too, marshes have been drained, and areas previously under water filled in and built upon. New York City, for example, has gained considerable territory in this way. However many communities are running out of space for public purposes. Although New York City has a relatively privileged position in terms of the parks distributed around it,[24] it needs more to satisfy the demands of its very crowded population. In 1960 city authorities complained that the city's residents had not been welcome in the parks of such suburban areas as Westchester County, for instance; and a proposal was made that the city should purchase land beyond its limits to turn into parks, access to which would thus be guaranteed to city residents. Such measures, however, would reflect a sort of deplorable and one-sided segregation of city residents in suburban parks. Indeed, suburban families freely use various facilities maintained by the city (including city parks and zoos) without being discriminated against according to place of residence. It seems that by the city's very nature it is opened to the outsider while the countryside around it claims the privilege of enclosing its own facilities to reserve them to local residents only. The good neighborly relations, so necessary in a crowded area, are here at stake.

For quite some time other forms of competition or coordination have existed between neighboring communities, functioning sometimes through state governments and sometimes through both local and state authorities.

Obvious links exist in the field of transportation, where a good deal of cooperation is necessary despite the competitive position of many of the interests involved. Authorized by Congress, a bi-state compact was estab-

[23] See *The New York Times*, August 11, 1960, p. 29.
[24] See above, pp. 362–366.

lished between New York and New Jersey creating the Port of New York Authority to regulate and coordinate transportation on both sides of the Hudson.

Under the Port Authority's management are the civilian airport facilities of Greater New York. Right after World War II it became obvious that La Guardia Airport, even if coupled and coordinated with Newark Airport under the same Authority, could not satisfy all the new needs of the New York area in the developing air age. Therefore, in the marshy area known as Idlewild, beyond Jamaica Bay on Long Island, there arose the New York International Airport, a bigger and better airfield specializing in long-distance and transatlantic flights.

In 1960, even before the various terminals planned at Idlewild were yet completed, it became necessary to plan for a new, large, fourth airport to serve the New York region in a jet age of intensified relations between Megalopolis and many other parts of the world. The Port Authority selected for the new airfield a site near Morristown, in north central New Jersey, in an area known as the "Great Swamp." Once more, as in many other cases, a major airport was planned in a marshy spot where there was still a large enough area sparsely occupied though close enough to the urban hubs. However, this is an area of estate farms, of wealth and conservative suburbanites who resented and opposed such an intrusion into their area. The suggestion was then made that the new airport should preferably be located in a more central part of New Jersey, possibly halfway between New York City and Philadelphia, to serve both these metropolitan regions. The Port Authority, being born of a New York–New Jersey compact, had no reason to be preoccupied with serving Philadelphia. Moreover, a site in central New Jersey would be farther away from main base. A location in Orange County, New York, has also been proposed.

A major jet airport, opened recently between Washington, D. C., and Baltimore, can serve both these contiguous metropolitan regions. As it seems already unable to carry all the traffic foreseen in the future for the national capital, another location has been selected for a new airfield near Chantilly, Virginia, to the west of the District of Columbia. This may enable Megalopolis to expand further into the Old Dominion but could not be of much use to Baltimore and its suburbs.

Outside the field of transportation, an excellent illustration to demonstrate the competition of the metropolitan areas within Megalopolis for certain supplies may be found in the problems of water allocation and regulation. Water is just as indispensable as space to human activities.

It has come to be almost as disputed, even in Megalopolis, despite the region's rather abundant natural endowment in this respect.[25]

The Case of the Cities' Water Supplies

Rainfall is usually plentiful in Megalopolis all year. From the hills and ranges to its north and west many good-sized streams flow across the area, and well-supplied and rather stable groundwater supplies are found at small depths. Despite all this potential supply, the major cities of Megalopolis have often been threatened with water shortages, because of inadequate facilities of supply or periods of drought or both. To meet present needs and the threat of future shortages, suggested by the rising volume of consumption and its anticipated increase, major metropolitan areas have reached farther and farther into the hinterland. Since this hinterland is common to several cities, each may feel its rights being infringed upon and its own future jeopardized by such enterprises of a too-thirsty neighbor.

Water is needed in Megalopolis for many purposes. In a crowded urban region the vast quantities needed for domestic consumption come first to mind. In the United States every inhabitant uses on the average 200 gallons of water annually just to quench his thirst and 15,000 gallons more for washing, laundry, heating, and waste disposal.[26] In the less densely settled parts of Megalopolis irrigation may consume unexpectedly large quantities of water, especially in summer, to keep in good shape the lawns of many garden-minded residents and to maintain high yields on the intensively cultivated specialized farms.[27] In fact, Megalopolis is the most generous user of supplemental irrigation in the eastern United States. Then the cities need water also for sanitation, and many communities, large and small, need it for recreational purposes. Last but not least, industry consumes huge quantities of water in manufacturing plants and particularly in the steam generation of electric power.

All these various uses of water have been expanding rapidly in the United States during the twentieth century, much more rapidly than the population. Although water requirements per kilowatt-hour have been decreasing, the daily average water use for power generation by steam was estimated at 5 billion gallons in 1900 and 59.8 billion in 1955. In 1900 the public water systems, serving about 30 million people, needed 3 billion

---

[25] See above, Chapter 2, pp. 80–101.

[26] Harry E. Jordan, "Water for Our Cities," *Willing Water* (American Water Works Association), No. 43, December 1956.

[27] See above, Chapter 6.

gallons daily; in 1955, serving some 111 million people, they distributed 17 billion gallons per day. It has been estimated that by 1975 the daily needs of the public water supplies in the continental United States will reach about 30 billion gallons and steam-produced power will consume 115 billion.[28] The per capita average consumption among people served by municipal water systems in the country appears to have increased by about 50 per cent in the first half of the century.

Part of this increase in the national average may be explained by the denser settlement achieved, during this period, in arid western sections of the country. In a dry metropolitan region such as Los Angeles or Salt Lake City the per capita consumption is, of course, higher; but the great Megalopolitan cities, especially New York and Philadelphia, also exhibit high consumption rates, mainly because of greater industrialization. The enormous amounts of electricity now consumed in the great office buildings also require large quantities of water.

The cities of Megalopolis need, therefore, a very abundant water supply, which must be considerably expanded in the years ahead. For the four largest of these cities (New York, Philadelphia, Baltimore, and Boston) the past story of their water-supply systems has been well told by Nelson M. Blake.[29] It is a colorful story, for often hardships were involved, and occasionally the search for water influenced local politics.

New York City is the most thirsty of all great cities, because of its size and its level of economic development. Because local sources are very limited—the city is for the most part located on islands surrounded by tidal channels — the great metropolis has built costly aqueducts to bring water from outlying areas, first from Westchester County, then from the Catskills, and finally from the upper basin of the Delaware River, where the final reservoir, the Cannonsville, is scheduled for completion in 1962. To New Jersey and Pennsylvania, situated downstream along the Delaware River and partly dependent on it, this last development was a threat to their future water supply.[30] Prolonged litigation before the U. S. Supreme

---

[28] American Water Works Association, "Water Use in the United States, 1900–1975," supplement to *Willing Water*, No. 38, February 1956. Similar figures and estimates were given in a report prepared by the U. S. Public Health Service for a Senate Committee and published in *Water Resources Activities in the United States: Future Requirements for Municipal Use*, U. S. Senate, Select Committee on National Water Resources, 86th Cong., 2d sess., Committee Print No. 7, Washington, D. C., 1960.

[29] Nelson Manfred Blake, *Water for the Cities*, Syracuse University Press, Syracuse, N. Y., 1956.

[30] Delaware was concerned also, because its oyster industry in Delaware Bay is influenced by the salinity of the water, which in turn is affected by the amount of river water entering the estuary.

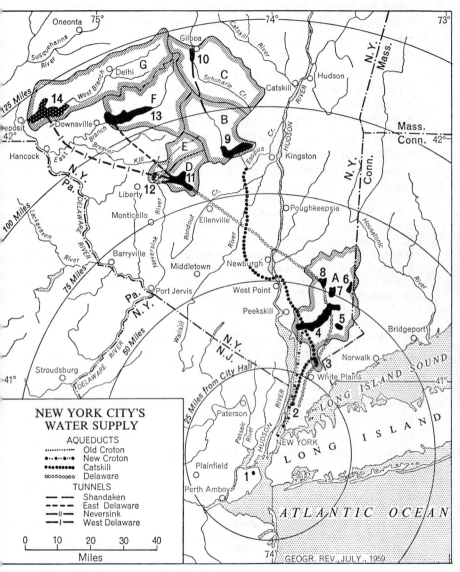

FIG. 223. *Reproduced from the* Geographical Review, *July 1959, p. 371, by permission of Anastasia Van Burkalow and the American Geographical Society*

Court ensued, and limitations were placed (in 1931) on the amount of water New York City could take from the Delaware headwaters, on which the city's construction of Neversink and Pepacton reservoirs was authorized.[31]

For further development of the Delaware River, not only for water supply but also for power development, flood and pollution control, and development of recreation facilities, the four states that share its drainage basin established (1936) the Interstate Commission on the Delaware River, popularly known as Incodel.[32] When New York City's growing water needs led it to seek additional water from the Delaware River, unsuccessful efforts were made to work out a development plan under the auspices of Incodel.

New York, New Jersey, and Delaware accepted the plan, but in 1952 Pennsylvania rejected it. Thereupon New York City reopened the original case before the Supreme Court and asked for an additional 50 mgd from the Neversink and Pepacton Reservoirs and 310 mgd from the proposed Cannonsville Reservoir. This request was granted by a decision in 1954. In both Court decisions the city was directed to release water from its reservoirs in dry periods, to maintain a certain minimum flow in the main valley.[33]

Interstate plans for development of the Delaware River basin, with the cooperation of the U. S. Army Corps of Engineers, are still active, however. Over the next fifty years the water needs of this region are expected to increase fourfold. To meet these needs recommendations have been made for the expenditure of $264 million to build eleven major reservoirs on the Delaware and its tributaries, and to carry out this program a new Interstate-Federal compact has set up a five-member Delaware River Basin Commission, representing the four states of Delaware, New Jersey, New York, and Pennsylvania, and the Federal government.[34]

[31] See Blake, op. cit.; Roscoe C. Martin, Water for New York, Syracuse University Press, Syracuse, 1960; Anastasia Van Burkalow, "The Geography of New York City's Water Supply," Geographical Review, Vol. 49, 1959, pp. 369–386. Our Figure 223 is reproduced from the latter article, by permission of the author and the American Geographical Society, to whom we are grateful.

[32] See Frances A. Pitkin, "Four States Get Together on a River," in Urban Sprawl and Health, Report of the 1958 National Health Forum, National Health Council, op. cit., pp. 198–202. See the thorough study by R. C. Martin, G. S. Birkhead, J. Burkhead, and F. J. Munger, River Basin Administration and the Delaware, Syracuse University Press, Syracuse, N. Y., 1960.

[33] Van Burkalow, "The Geography of New York City's Water Supply," op. cit., p. 374.

[34] See The New York Times, March 25, 1960, April 10, 1960, May 22, 1960, and February 2, 1961. Agencies active in drawing up these plans have been the U. S.

Such cooperation with respect to water-supply problems has been rare in Megalopolis. Figure 224, showing the nature of the water supplies of the major cities in the mid-1950's, illustrates the entanglements of the existing systems and shows that they are most striking in the most densely populated sections, from Boston to Philadelphia. For example, Boston reaches westward beyond Worcester and close to Springfield in its search for water. The watersheds tapped by Springfield and Hartford are close to one another. New York has gone far into the hinterlands of northern New Jersey and even of Trenton and Philadelphia. If the latter wanted to draw more water from the Schuylkill River it would find Reading in its way. In their race for water the great cities of Megalopolis are already outflanking one another, developing more and more competitive situations. Whether they can continue indefinitely their policy of drawing water supplies from costly and ever more distant sources is a serious question. The hinterlands they share are abundantly supplied, to be sure, but future requirements may come to exceed the dependable yield. Moreover, the expenditures already made are enormous, and they increase rapidly with the size and length of the public works undertaken.

Competition is not limited to the larger cities, with their extensive water systems, but is evident even on a more local scale, as is well illustrated in New Jersey. This highly suburbanized state offers a complicated mosaic of water-supply systems, public and private, most of them uncoordinated, and both water and public funds are wasted in large amount by the desire of every area to have its own water supply system.[35] Indeed, outside of the cities and boroughs many people rely on their own individual wells, and groundwater provides an important part of the total supply. In New Jersey some coordination and cooperation were achieved during the emergency of World War II, but little endured after 1946. An exception is the private Hackensack Water Company, "which supplies water to more than 50 communities in northern New Jersey from an integrated

Army Corps of Engineers (Philadelphia District); Incodel; the Delaware River Basin Advisory Committee, composed of the governors of the four states and the mayors of New York City and Philadelphia; the Water Resources Association of the Delaware River Basin, a nonprofit association of more than 250 citizens' groups interested in development of the resources of the area; and the Water Research Foundation, financed by the Ford Foundation to carry out a study of the area, made at the Maxwell School of Citizenship and Public Administration of Syracuse University. The compact, approved on February 1, 1961, must be ratified by Congress and the state legislatures before it becomes effective.

[35] See State of New Jersey, Legislative Commission on Water Supply, *Survey of New Jersey Water Resources Development*, Tippetts-Abbett-McCarthy-Stratton, Engineers, New York, 1955.

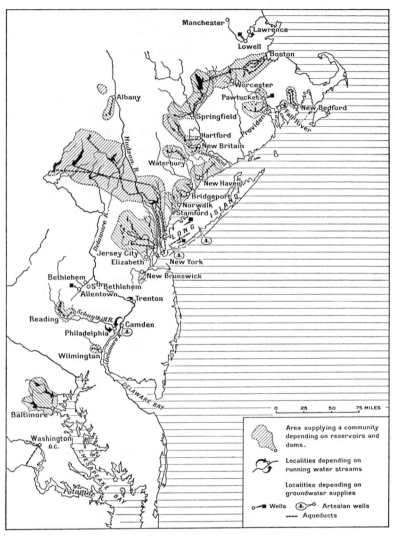

FIG. 224. Water-supply systems of the main cities in Megalopolis.
The map, prepared with the help of Prof. Gordon Wolman of the
Johns Hopkins University, does not attempt to show the details of
the various systems; it only hints at their intricacies with a few
symbols; the shaded areas are *not* watersheds but the general areas
in which a city has established facilities for its water supply; note
the entanglements of the Springfield-Worcester-Boston area in
Massachusetts.

supply and distribution system." [36] Another cooperative undertaking, this time a public one and farther south, is the Washington Suburban Sanitary District, which controls the water supply and sewage disposal for a 300-square-mile area in Maryland.[37]

As the population grows and the per capita consumption of water increases, the time may come when more water-supply regulation and coordination will be necessary in this crowded region. Many factors are involved and interwoven, and what Anastasia Van Burkalow wrote of the greatest city is true also of many smaller communities:

> The story of New York City's water supply is thus one of interactions: between the various elements of the earth environment within the watershed areas; between man and the earth environment both locally and in more distant areas; between the city and individuals in the watershed areas; between the city and other political units or agencies (the United States Supreme Court, New York State and adjoining states, state agencies and departments, counties, townships, villages, school districts); and between man's resource needs and government regulations.[38]

For water supply is a complex, many-faceted problem that affects many interests. Besides competing with other cities for the quantity of water it needs, every city has to decide how much it is willing to spend to obtain this quantity, how much it may regulate use by the consumer in the community to save both water and money, and also what *quality* of water is to be supplied. All this involves such matters as controlling pollution, treating the water supply, and even local politics. The more crowded an area is, the more difficult all such problems of water supply become.

Metropolitan Hierarchy or Nebulous Structures

Water is a good example to illustrate the entanglements and complexities of neighborhood in Megalopolis. It is far from being the only one. We have already spoken about the need for space, about transportation, zoning, and community partitioning. There are many currents flowing through Megalopolis, carrying people, goods, or messages, which do not go always in one direction, as water does, but reverse their directions — some seasonally, others weekly, daily, or even more frequently. Earlier in this study we called them "tidal currents," for they spread people and goods according to an oscillating pattern but irregularly over the space they cover. On a summer Sunday or on an average weekday during office

[36] Jordan, "Water for Our Cities," *op. cit.*

[37] *Ibid.*

[38] Van Burkalow, "The Geography of New York City's Water Supply," *op. cit.*, p. 386.

hours the actual distribution of people in Megalopolis is quite different from that recorded in the last Census. It is still different, though in more fleeting fashion, during the rush hours of a weekday or of a warm week end. And in terms of more permanent shifts, we have seen that while many people and industries leave the central cities for the suburban rings, other people flock to reside in these same cities, and some industries move into some of the hubs.

The central city used to be clearly defined as the "center," the "heart" of a region. If the city was important enough in size and by its impact on the surrounding countryside to rank as a metropolis, then a metropolitan area or region was defined around it. A certain "hierarchy" was established in the web of relationships binding together the city and its suburbs and satellite towns, and distributing the various functions among these communities and among the various neighborhoods and districts of each city or town. There was, for example, a clear distinction between uptowns and downtowns, between rural areas and urbanized districts. The pattern seemed orderly and called for systematization. Some students compared the order to a living organism, others to a solar system; theories and models of "urban hierarchy" blossomed.[39]

Today what we have seen in Megalopolis can hardly be fitted into any of the orderly patterns elaborated by theoreticians. There is too much flow, flux, and constant change within the region. There are too many relationships that link any given community or area of some size to several other areas, cities, and hubs. Perhaps the best comparison of its structure, at a time when astronomical comparisons are in fashion, would be with the structure of a nebula. The expression "nebulous structure" is apt to convey the confusion spreading before us in place of the more neatly organized systems to which we were accustomed in the past. Some central cities are rapidly losing their former "centrality" to become suburbs or satellites or in some way dependencies of communities that do not seem to have either the size or the functions associated with the concept of "central place" and that are multiple instead of one! Downtown functions are moving out of the city's core toward the periphery

[39] For a good summary of these works see Otis Dudley Duncan, W. Richard Scott, Stanley Lieberson, Beverly Duncan, and Hal H. Winsborough, *Metropolis and Region* (Prepared for Resources for the Future), The Johns Hopkins Press, Baltimore, 1960. On the present evolution see also Robert Moore Fisher (ed.), *The Metropolis in Modern Life*, Doubleday, New York, 1955, and the Editors of *Fortune*, *The Exploding Metropolis*, Doubleday, New York, 1958. For the old organization of regions around cities see Robert E. Dickinson, *City, Region and Regionalism*, Routledge and Kegan Paul, London, 1947.

and to other neighborhoods, some of which are based on their proximity to "dormitory" communities, while others grow in the shadow of large industrial establishments set up amidst a rural-looking countryside.

In this study we have given enough examples of the apparent disorder resulting from the recent evolution not to need to elaborate on the "nebulous" and, we are tempted to say, almost "colloidal" pattern of distribution that seems to be shaping in Megalopolis at this time. When we discussed the land-use patterns that evolve in the process, the new forms of the urban uses of the land, the symbiosis of urban and rural outside the old urban cores,[40] we observed some signs leading in those areas to what may become a new order, which would need a new terminology to describe it adequately and which would replace the old categories and specializations of land utilization by new systems founded on *multi-purpose uses* of space. It seems compatible with the Megalopolitan economy and with the needs of as dense a population to have the same geographical area, the same piece of land (if envisioned in "pieces" of a dozen or more square miles at a time), used at the same time for farming, forestry, and recreational purposes; and other such pieces of land used for both farming and residences, or residences and recreation, or industries and forests, and so on.

The "mix" of functions can be left to the resourcefulness of the local people, but such multi-purpose uses are not usual, for people and communities do not yet think in these terms. The distinguished Danish architect S. E. Rasmussen has recently observed that nowadays architecture and town planning are applying a functionalism that has led to the well-separated garden cities for residence and office skyscrapers for downtown work.[41] The actual trends, as evidenced by the recent decades in Megalopolis, are more complex and more numerous than just these, although the two tendencies stressed by Rasmussen were especially strong here in the 1950's.

To adapt to the opportunities of new technological, economic, and social needs and means, the people of Megalopolis must first realize fully the implications of the region's present structure and the assets and liabilities involved in the present tighter neighborhood on a larger scale. As the vast region of Megalopolis grows, regional integration into one interwoven system is bound to progress.

The first evolution must be achieved in the minds of the people, and

[40] See above, Chapters 5 and 8.
[41] See Steen Eiler Rasmussen, *Towns and Buildings*, The University Press, Liverpool, 1956, especially his chapter on "Functionalism."

NEIGHBORS IN MEGALOPOLIS

many signs indicate that it is already occurring. Too often, alas, the inadequacy of institutions is blamed for the difficulties encountered. Governmental institutions, relationships, and regulations now in force have, of course, been established for some time, in accordance with patterns of needs and resources different from those observed today and forecast for the future. Some evolution in the legislation and the governmental structure has already been noticed, and much more is undoubtedly forthcoming. An improved organization and the solution of the major problems will be easier to achieve once the people have fully realized the new features of their life and environment.

CHAPTER 14

Sharing a Partitioned Land

The land of Megalopolis is partitioned in many ways. There is physical partitioning by rivers and bays, ridges and valleys, features that have been serious obstacles to communications in the past and that often to this day remain lines of partition because administrative boundaries follow them.[1] More partitions, purely man-made, were introduced as the region developed. Whether they still carry their original meaning or not, the partitioning of Megalopolis has broken the region into many states. From Manchester, New Hampshire, to Arlington County, Virginia, the

[1] For example, the Hudson River between New York and New Jersey appears to be a barrier much more because it is a political boundary than because of its physical nature. Indeed, it has not been more difficult to overcome the physical obstacle of the Hudson than that of the East River, though it still costs more to cross the former than the latter by car or truck. The cheaper tolls (or their absence) between Manhattan and Long Island point out that it is to the interest of both the City and the State of New York to favor the development of territory under their jurisdiction rather than that in another state.

axis of Megalopolis crosses the boundaries of ten states and the District of Columbia. Thus the administration of Megalopolis involves ten state governments plus the committees of Congress that administer the District of Columbia or are concerned with the National Capital metropolitan region.

On the level of local government the administrative map is much more complicated, for the area includes 117 counties and many cities, and the counties are subdivided into many more townships and boroughs. In New England the townships have most of the governmental functions and authority that are usually vested in the counties west of the Hudson River. The New York metropolitan region as defined for the purposes of the Regional Plan Association of New York, encompasses sections of three states, the totality of 22 counties, and some 1,400 local governments. Besides the state and local governments, a few interstate agencies are beginning to function, and above them all extends the multi-faceted and intricate structure of the Federal government.

The concept of Megalopolis as one integrated system is difficult to realize, for there is so much rivalry between the various components within the region: states, cities, counties, even townships. When New York City resents the possible industrialization of Yonkers or the growth of neighboring counties in New Jersey, how can one ask the Baltimoreans to realize their common interests with the Bostonians or with the suburbs of Providence? The problems of neighborhood have always been ticklish and often unpleasant when examined in minute detail. To get people to behave like good neighbors despite local antagonisms and rivalries requires ethical and moral teaching and the invoking of high principles. Religious and political authorities must cooperate to establish and enforce the law.

Where crowding causes a neighborhood to be more demanding, the law usually must be stiffened, and policing must be stricter. Crowding in Megalopolis is felt in terms of various space needs: housing space, space to move on the streets and roads, space for recreation, and so forth. To most of the inhabitants these shortages of space have brought as yet only temporary discomfort, although this region has known an extraordinary growth, deeply related to a constantly expanding economy and to *expanding abundance*. Its future may well hinge on its ability to maintain growth through abundance, despite the physical limitations of space and the practical partitioning of governmental organization.

Economic Integration and Administrative Divisions

All the preceding chapters of this volume have given examples of the deep interrelations binding together the various parts of Megalopolis. Basically, Megalopolis differs from any other part of the country because it has a denser population, a greater density of activities, and a mixture of industries and trades that altogether endow it with a unique regional economy. This economic development has achieved such intensity and such a high degree of integration largely as a result of the competition between all the large cities and the different states participating in it. From this competition has come a division of economic functions: specializations of the various hubs, division of functions between the districts of a city, between urban cores and suburbia, between adjacent counties, and so on. These specializations are not complete, for similar industries, with some amount of rivalry but also with a great deal of coordination between them, exist in several places within the area. However, no two places are quite alike unless one considers small local details such as two similar shopping centers or two similar dormitory townships.

Competition and coordination together have worked toward economic integration. To some extent the specializations of the various areas have benefited from the administrative partitions between them. Some industries have moved from Connecticut to New Jersey or Pennsylvania, for example, precisely because at a given time the differences resulting from the separate governmental set-ups and backgrounds provide conditions more favorable in one area than the other for the purposes of these industries. Residents with large incomes who work in New York may prefer to live in New Jersey because the latter state's tax structure is advantageous for them. Others who work in the District of Columbia and have children of school age prefer residences in the adjacent counties of Maryland because the public schools there are said to be better than those in Washington. Many other examples could be enumerated. There is little doubt that the frequency with which the main axis of Megalopolis crosses state lines favored the extension of the region along it and the simultaneous growth of many parts of the axial belt. In the seventeenth century the advantages of such partitioning were especially appreciated by the inhabitants for reasons of religion or community politics; in the twentieth century differences in taxation and labor organization have been more important. But, whatever the reason at a given time, it has always been useful to someone to be able to find different administrative regulations by moving just a little distance.

Such advantages reaped from governmental partitioning do not last indefinitely, however. As economic integration has progressed and specialization within the integrated region has proceeded, coordination between neighboring areas has proved increasingly desirable. It has not always been provided, however. Often local antagonisms, traditional local pride, and self-centeredness, rooted in a long past of distrust and resentment among neighbors, have stood in the way of more efficiently coordinated action for the common good. As early as 200 years ago, as Carl Bridenbaugh has noted, some of the present problems of regional neighborhood were very much alive.

A nobleman passing through Connecticut in the early sixties compared it "to a cask of good liquor tapped at both ends, at one of which Boston draws, and New York at the other, till little is left but lees and settlings." This was certainly true, but as the colonial era ended, Manhattan had whittled down Boston's traffic with this province, especially in the Connecticut and Thames valleys . . . by 1770 Yankee annoyance at the hegemony of the Yorkers inspired a "Connecticut Farmer" of New London to dream of the day when "the plumes of that domineering city may yet feather the nests of those whom they have so long plucked." And there were those in New Jersey who agreed with the *New American Magazine's* proposal for an export duty on all Jersey produce shipped from either New York or Philadelphia and a bounty on exports from Perth Amboy and Burlington.[2]

Such feelings are still common today. Although resentment against the big city, and New York especially, has been widespread and frequently expressed in Megalopolis for 200 years, the cities have grown and prospered, as have their suburbs and the interurban spaces. The prosperity of the latter has been less spectacular, since it is not expressed by means of skyscrapers or great monuments, but it is quite real, and today it is increasingly obvious, as is demonstrated by the distribution of income and education, and by many other criteria. At the same time the central cities are losing population and in many cases actually declining. Such downward trends in the cities do not make the outer ring's inhabitants happier, even though for generations the people of Connecticut, Rhode Island, or New Jersey may have wished for the downfall of those mounts of arrogance and conceit, as they have called Boston, New York, or Philadelphia. The recent tendency for a decreased economic role of the large cities is not viewed with favor but instead has even caused concern. Whether they live and work in or out of the cities the inhabitants of Megalopolis know that the well-being of the whole region depends on

[2] Carl Bridenbaugh, *Cities in Revolt: Urban Life in America, 1743–1776,* Alfred A. Knopf, New York, 1955, p. 263.

the successful growth of those activities that are specifically located in the major hubs and that are of a size and nature not found elsewhere in the nation. These hubs make Megalopolis the unique region it is and justify its integration.

Those who govern the hubs are full of complaints about the lack of understanding of their problems on the part of those in Federal, state, or neighboring local governments, who could provide the needed help. There is, of course, a great deal of politics in these complaints and in the "lack of understanding." There is also, however, a new situation of entangled problems, the solutions of which are impeded by the multiplicity of authorities concerned and the lack of coordination between them. The urbanization of the land is an expression of the triumph of the economy fostered by and developed in the central city, but it has been turning against the city that mothered it. If Manhattan and Washington, D. C., still demonstrate vigorous growth in economic activity (not to be measured by the number of inhabitants), it is not indeed because of their regional roles, but because they have concentrated within them national functions that are rapidly expanding at present. Even these two great hubs are seriously worried by the problems of traffic and commuting and by the costs of urban services.

The thoughtful student of metropolitan problems and politics, Robert C. Wood, has remarked:

> Throughout this century, people have debated the question of whether or not the American political system could countenance an unbridled laissez-faire economy — whether it did not have to intervene by selective measures to redress the balance of competition, at times to preserve it, and at times to guide it. But in the modern metropolitan region, the question is reserved. The issue is whether or not a modern economic system, requiring positive stimulation and selective aid and direction by public authority, can tolerate an unbridled laissez-faire profusion of governments which systematically avoid any responsibility for these matters.[3]

Why has this "profusion of governments" become so burdensome today in metropolitan areas, and in Megalopolis especially? The answer is a long and rather complicated one, but fundamentally it is because of the degree of economic integration achieved in a region the many governments of which are more divided than coordinated. This multiplicity of governments, with its accompanying partitioning, has been a deliberate American tradition and a very successful one. It is a necessary feature of

[3] Robert C. Wood, *Metropolis Against Itself*, Committee for Economic Development, New York, March 1959, p. 44.

any federal system. In the United States it has worked especially well owing to a great fluidity of the law as interpreted by the courts and as applied regionally.

The great problem of a decision between *interference* or *laissez faire* has arisen over and over again in every country faced with great economic changes, especially when the distribution of scarce resources is involved. When, at the dawn of history, in the gradually drying up Middle East people gathered around the remaining sources of water, crowding the irrigable land and the approaches to the streams and springs, new laws and new political organizations were elaborated to secure an adequate distribution of water and land for the survival and even the growth (with technological progress) of the population. When, at the end of the medieval feudal period, the cities of Italy and Flanders grew into great hubs of trade, industry, and population, they developed forms of government and political strife that have been studied and analyzed from the time of Machiavelli to our day. In England in the second half of the eighteenth century the Industrial Revolution began the concentration of labor in urban centers and opened new horizons of growth for new industries, At each of these great periods in economic history the question was repeatedly asked: "Laissez faire or interference?" [4]

The present period, with its great momentum of change, has had to ask it again to cope with the remarkable concentration of population and activities in Megalopolis, where cities have been breaking out of old bounds.[5] But the purpose of the present outcry here is not to defend labor against employers, nor to call public authorities to limit the freedom of action of private business. For quite some time governments have been exerting their rights to interfere in these areas. Rather it is a call for reform of the governmental structure, with a view toward securing better coordination and more far-sighted policies in a period of rapid change.

In what ways has the administrative partitioning affected the development of Megalopolis? In the past it seems to have been instrumental in bringing about more local growth and shaping the present general layout of the region. More recently, however, as technological and economic progress has required more regional integration, the multiplicity of governmental divisions and the large degree of autonomy granted to each of

---

[4] See Paul Mantoux, *The Industrial Revolution in England in the Eighteenth Century,* first published in French, Paris, 1906, then in English, Jonathan Cape, London, 1928. See particularly the last chapter (III, 4).

[5] See, for instance, the recent growth on the periphery of Trenton as shown in Figure 225 and compare this map with the land-use maps in Chapter 5, above, Figures 67 to 72.

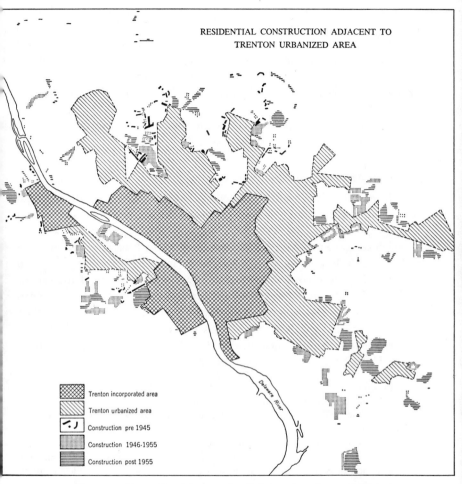

RESIDENTIAL CONSTRUCTION ADJACENT TO
TRENTON URBANIZED AREA

Trenton incorporated area
Trenton urbanized area
Construction pre 1945
Construction 1946-1955
Construction post 1955

FIG. 225. Generalized from a detailed map based on a field survey
by the Graduate School of Geography of Clark University.

them have put obstacles in the way of economic growth and of more
comfortable use of all the region's facilities for anyone who wishes to
use them. Obviously a great economic hub, a continent's hinge, a chain
of international crossroads cannot be satisfied with an organization of
local governments, each of which cares only about its own residents.
These residents make their living from and owe their status to the web of
relations linking each community with the outside. They all participate
in that system, either because of their jobs or at least because of their

location in Megalopolis, but their governments encounter many hardships in trying to give them many of the services they ask for. These difficulties stem from three main problems: lack of money, the problem most frequently raised by public officials responsible for improving the situation; rapid growth of the burdens of local government, which underlines the worsening financial situation; and, last but not least, the lack of understanding and of channels for coordination between neighboring governments, either at the local or the state level. These three areas of tension must be reviewed in succession.

The Financial Difficulties

In the twentieth century throughout the United States state and local governments have become big business, with rapidly growing budgets and employment (see Table 27), and they have accumulated a heavy indebtedness. In recent years the expenditures of local governments have been much above those of the state governments in the continental United States. However, for a long time the actual local revenues of the various types of local governments have not been adequate to cover their disbursements, and cities, counties, and townships have had to turn to their state's treasury for help from funds collected through state taxes. In turn the states have needed financial help from Federal funds. Thus from the U. S. Treasury funds have filtered down even to townships.

In 1932, the States allocated about $800 million to their local governments, and received in turn some $228 million from Washington. In 1956, in the Nation-to-State-to-Local fiscal doubleplay which characterizes the modern Federal system, Washington allocated over $3 billion to the States in grants-in-aid, and the States distributed $6.5 billion to their local governments. Another $309 million came to the localities from the Federal government directly, and the grand total of State and Federal aid was 26 per cent of their revenues from all sources.[6]

This aid from national and state funds usually comes to the localities earmarked for certain purposes, such as highway construction, public schools, hospitals and health services, and so forth. Legislation passed by Congress or the state legislatures thus regulates to a large extent the use of a good fourth of all revenues of local governments. Actually, this limits their freedom of action with regard to much more than one fourth of their budgets, for much of the outside help is allocated to *supplement* disbursements to which the localities have to be committed in order to

[6] Wood, *Metropolis Against Itself, op. cit.,* p. 28.

Table 27

STATE AND LOCAL GOVERNMENT FINANCES

A. Growth of State and Local Government Finances, 1840–1957
(*In Millions*)

Year	Total Revenue	Total Expenditures[a]	Gross Debt[b]
1840	$ 562	$ 560	$ 1,137
1902	968	1,016	1,865
1913	1,602	1,751	3,822
1932	7,416	8,406	17,577
1942	11,396	10,034	17,320
1952	31,013	30,863	30,100
1957	46,033	47,634	52,733

B. State and Local Government Finances, 1957[c]
(*In Millions*)

	Revenue	Expenditures
State governments	$24,656	$24,234
Local governments: Total	29,087	31,014
Counties	5,778	5,905
Townships	1,342	1,320
Cities	11,867	12,751
School districts	9,179	9,924
Special districts	1,396	1,578

Source: U. S. Bureau of the Census, *Historical Statistics of the United States, 1789–1945;* and *Statistical Abstract of the United States: 1959.*

[a] Excluding provision for debt retirement.

[b] Less sinking funds.

[c] For comparison the Federal government's revenue and expenditures in 1957 were $87,926 million and $82,631 million respectively.

acquire the help. A similar relationship exists for the state governments, for uses are specified for the Federal funds they receive. However, the states are much less affected by outside help than are the localities, which do not hesitate to become more dependent on agreements with other, larger, administrative units if this brings them substantial revenue. The relative importance of outside aid varies for the different categories of localities. In most state legislatures, including those of New York, Pennsylvania, and Maryland, rural areas have long held the balance of power. They have therefore received more state aid than would be expected from their share in the state's population.

Given the legislative compassion for rural communities, metropolitan areas do not receive aid in proportion to their population. School districts fare best, receiving on the average 43 per cent of their revenue from outside sources. Counties follow closely with 38 per cent. Townships depend on grants and shared taxes for 25 per cent of their funds, while cities obtain about 14 per cent, and the larger the city, the smaller its share within this average.[7]

Although these ratios were established for the continental United States as a whole, their implications for the region we are concerned with are clear. The large central cities and the metropolitan areas, both of which are numerous in Megalopolis and represent very large parts of its population and business, are not favored in the distribution of Federal and state aid. Both, however, greatly need help: the central cities because, while they are losing resident population, they must provide increasing services for outsiders; the communities in the metropolitan rings because the exodus from the central cities makes their residential population grow locally more rapidly than do industrial activities. The latter are more taxable and bring more revenue, while the residents need more services, in the form of streets and roads, street lights and sewers, schools, playgrounds, and parks. A quick residential growth means that the community must provide more costly services over a wider area, a considerable capital outlay that will not for many years be compensated for by the development of the taxable base.

Despite Federal aid, the states and localities in Megalopolis must levy heavy taxes to meet their present financial needs. However, in this respect the inhabitants are favored by their density and their rather high income. An index measuring the burden of state and local taxes against the personal income per capita in 1957 showed this burden to be lowest among the then forty-eight states in Delaware (index 1.78), Connecticut (2.59), and New Jersey (2.77). Maryland, New York, and Pennsylvania made out relatively well (index between 3.39 and 3.59), remaining below the national average (4.12) and far below the less densely populated and much poorer states, such as Mississippi (index 11.73), North Dakota (8.10), and Arkansas (7.63).[8] Nevertheless, the actual amounts of taxes paid per capita are substantial. While New Jersey could claim in 1959 to have the *second lowest* per capita state taxes ($58.85) of the forty-nine states (Nebraska had the lowest, $55.60), it had also the second highest (New York State was highest) per capita local taxes ($123.99). Delaware had an almost opposite relationship, with high state taxes ($102.05 per

---

[7] *Ibid.* Wood bases his statement on data from The American Assembly, *The Forty-eight States: Their Tasks as Policy-makers and Administrators*, Columbia University Press, New York, 1955, p. 24.

[8] Index from Table III in Henry J. Frank, "Measuring New Jersey's Tax Burden," *New Jersey Municipalities*, Elizabeth, N. J., Vol. 37, No. 4, April 1960, pp. 5–9. The index of tax burden is calculated by taking state and local taxes as a per cent of personal income, divided by per capita personal income.

capita) and low local taxes ($32.09). Delaware's per capita state *and* local taxes together fell below the national average ($169.08), while those of New Jersey were slightly above the average, and New York was far above it ($233.06). However, the New York State figure would have been much lower if New York City's retail sales tax collections had been excluded from the state's computation of local taxes. Obviously many out-of-state residents help to pay this sales tax.[9]

Some friction is caused by the fact that some Megalopolitan states and cities have an income tax, and this is levied not only on the incomes of their own citizens but also on incomes earned within their territory by nonresidents. These situations become significant because of the inter-relationships that exist within a metropolitan area. For example, many residents of New Jersey (which had no income tax) work in New York City or Philadelphia, and on the incomes they earn in those cities they must pay taxes to the state of New York or the city of Philadelphia. Connecticut residents working in New York are in a similar position. New Jersey found it hard to subsidize railroad commuting to neighboring states that brings revenue to the latter's treasuries rather than to the state of residence; a tax on commuters was established in 1961.

To the conflict of interest between neighboring states must be added the conflicts in the sharing of financial revenue developing between central cities and their states. The constant debate between New York City and New York State may serve as a good example. Most of the taxing powers are vested in the state, but the localities have to provide most of the disbursements. The state, of course, comes to the aid of the localities by turning over to them a goodly part of the funds it collects. However, the constitution of New York State assigns a share to New York City in proportion to the Census population, and since that population has been declining in absolute as well as in relative figures, the state aid made available to New York City has been shrinking. The great commercial activities of the hub of New York, the problems involved in urban renewal, in fighting slums and blight, in the expenses for the education and welfare of the less privileged part of the resident population, all these call for more funds.[10]

[9] *Ibid.*

[10] A very good analysis of the state-city relationships in the case of New York is found in the New York State–New York City Fiscal Relations Committee, *A Report to the Governor of the State of New York and the Mayor of the City of New York,* New York, November 1956 (often referred to as the Buttenweiser Report). See also on these questions the U. S. Bureau of the Census, *Compendium of City Government Finances in 1957,* U. S. Government Printing Office, Washington, D. C., 1958.

The very notion of "centrality" expresses a central city's duty to provide for a certain amount of activity involving the people and business of an area larger than its own. The city is merely the *center* for a wider area extending around it, and in serving this wider area, it must incur expenses of which its own residents are not the only beneficiaries. This is somewhat analogous to the situation of a national capital. Because it serves the whole nation the burden of its operations must be shared by the whole nation,[11] and thus the national government often assumes some of the responsibilities reserved to local authorities in other cities. This is the case in London, Paris, and many other capitals. In the United States the Federal capital is located in the District of Columbia, which is still governed by a Committee of Congress.

A central city does not necessarily have national importance, but it often has a regional role that involves extending various services to residents of areas beyond the city's limits. This is the case not only for certain services that must be paid for, but also for such free institutions as parks, zoological and botanical gardens, museums, libraries, hospitals, and so forth, which do not bring revenue but cost a great deal. The great hubs of Megalopolis also have economic functions, which we have summed up by calling them the "continent's hinge," and which serve the nation as a whole. In its managerial and decision-making role, and also as the country's main seaport and airport, New York City serves the nation almost as much as does Washington, D. C. Many other places in Megalopolis, large and small, also perform some national function.

New York City's economic role makes New York the most important state in the nation. Whether that city prospers or declines is a concern not only of its residents and of the state government in Albany. It is also very important to the neighboring states of Connecticut and New Jersey, because so many of their activities are tied to the dynamism of New York City and could shift to other areas if what is now concentrated in Manhattan could be easily decentralized. Similar relationships exist for Boston and Philadelphia, for Baltimore and Wilmington. The weakening of one of the hubs, the chain of which constitutes the framework of Megalopolis, would necessarily affect the others and all the areas between them and around them.

The financial consequences of this metropolitanization and economic integration of Megalopolis call for more help from state and Federal funds for the major cities, unless these cities are to be given new powers to

---

[11] In part also there is the feeling that the policing of the seat of national government ought not to be left in the care of officials of one local government.

develop their own revenue. At present the major revenue sources of American cities are the property tax (which in 1956 supplied about 36.4 per cent of all city revenue and about 75 per cent of all revenue from taxes), the "supplementary revenue" (about 36 per cent of all revenue, and made up of various charges, miscellaneous revenues from nontax sources, and revenue from utilities and insurance trusts), and Federal and state aid (about 14 per cent). Other taxes (such as sales and use) and fees (for licenses and permits, for example) make up 12 to 13 per cent of the total.[12] The role of the property tax has been declining; for revenues from it have not expanded as rapidly as have expenditures. Thus new sources of revenue have had to be developed, and other taxes and fees do not seem yet to have solved the problem. "Supplementary revenue" is a broad category and often a costly one to expand. In absolute amounts aid from other governments has been increasing, but on the whole it supplied a smaller proportion of the cities' revenues in 1952–56 than it did in 1950.

Several bold proposals for new revenue have been offered. One is a revision of the system of property taxes so as to tax heavily the increase in value of the land.[13] A great deal could probably be achieved by revising the policies of real property taxation and especially the assessment policies. However, even such changes would not solve the problem in the larger central cities, for by virtue of their "centrality" they must reserve for special uses, which require tax exemption, a large proportion of their real property.[14] For example, all the real property in the City of New York was assessed in 1958–59 at a total value of $32.33 billion; but 30.6 per cent of this was tax-exempt because it was property of the city itself (used for parks, schools, public buildings and places, public works, sewerage systems, hospitals, harbor piers, airports, and so forth), of the city's Housing Authority or Transit Authority, of the Port of New York Au-

[12] See the Buttenweiser Report, *op. cit.; Compendium of City Government Finances, op. cit.;* and *State and Local Taxes, A Handbook on Problems and Solutions,* published by the American Federation of Labor and Congress of Industrial Organizations (AFL–CIO Publication No. 80), Washington, D. C., December 1958.

[13] Gilbert M. Tucker, *The Self-Supporting City,* rev. ed., Robert Schalkenbach Foundation, New York, 1958. The Buttenweiser Report, *op. cit.,* remarked that in New York City "if expressed in equivalent dollars of constant value, today's real estate tax levy, despite the rise in the rates, is actually lower than it was a quarter century ago." (p. 304)

[14] This is made especially obvious by recent research on Central Business Districts (or CBD's). See Raymond E. Murphy, "Techniques in Central Business District Research," in Perry L. Norton (ed.), *Urban Problems and Techniques,* No. 1, Chandler-David Publishing Co., Trenton, 1959, pp. 101–128; see also R. E. Murphy, J. E. Vance, Jr., and B. J. Epstein, *Central Business District Studies,* Clark University, Worcester, Mass., January 1955.

thority, of the state or Federal government, or of religious and other tax-exempt institutions. In other major cities of Megalopolis also the proportion of the value of real property that is tax-exempt is rather high — 36.2 per cent in Boston, 24.35 in Providence, 22.23 in Philadelphia, 17.9 in Baltimore.[15] The actual value or "full value" of assessed property is higher than that quoted in the assessments, and this is especially true of tax-exempt property, which is generally not reassessed as often and as carefully as is taxable property. In reality, therefore, the percentage of the total value that is exempt is probably higher than the above figures indicate.

The greater are a city's economic and governmental functions, the larger is the proportion of its potential taxable resources that escapes taxation. Note, for example, the relatively high percentages of tax-exempt property in New York and in the state capitals listed (Boston and Providence). At the same time more expenditures are required, much of which must come from the city's budget. Little wonder, then, that a large metropolis, partly deserted by its residents, badly needs financial help from the outside. Whether this could be achieved through more coordination between the finances of the central city and the state is the first question to be asked. Whether an even more urgent need is for greater cooperation between neighboring communities within a metropolitan area and between neighboring states within Megalopolis is the next question.

That cooperation and coordination have not been the major aims of recent trends is indicated by the fact that the number of local governmental units has been steadily increasing in past decades. Their proliferation has been part of the process of metropolitan growth, for as density has increased in suburban and interurban areas, more new incorporated places have been established. Robert Wood has remarked that the New York metropolitan area had 127 governments in 1900; 204 by 1920; and more than 1,000 in 1957.[16] In the continental United States all local governments (except school districts, the number of which has been considerably reduced in recent years) numbered 49,348 in 1952 and 51,833 in 1957. In New Jersey their number rose from 669 in 1952 to 727 in 1957; in Connecticut, in the same period, from 359 to 380; in Delaware from 92 to 116. In Maryland the number remained stabilized, and in Massachusetts it even decreased, from 583 to 568; but in Rhode Island it increased

[15] For New York City see *Annual Report of the Tax Commission and the Tax Department to the Mayor of the City of New York, as of June 30, 1958*, New York, December 1958 (mimeographed). Figures for the other cities are from special communications by letters to this study from the various municipalities.

[16] Wood, *Metropolis Against Itself, op. cit.*, p. 13.

slightly.[17] It is significant that such increases in the numbers of local governmental units can be observed even in as short a period as five years, for governments are not as easy to multiply as are shopping centers or bank branches.

The proliferation means more spending to cover the costs of government in the region, and more partitioning between neighboring communities. Usually it does not help to better coordination and understanding between such communities, which have many more interests in common than they seem prepared to acknowledge. The financial problem runs through the whole gamut of those common interests, but it does not express them all, nor solve all the difficulties local governments experience because of crowding of a partitioned land with people and activities.

The Implications of Neighborhood for Governments

As a specialist of local government, Victor Jones, put it: "Local governments in metropolitan areas are becoming increasingly interdependent in all aspects of community life, except the governmental and the political." [18] This kind of interdependence develops also between local governments in two distinct but adjacent metropolitan areas. The matter involves also state governments where such neighboring metropolitan areas are separated by a state boundary or where (as occurs several times in Megalopolis) a metropolitan area has been recognized as straddling a line between states. The complexities of intergovernmental relations may thus exist at several levels of government simultaneously, and also in the relationships between these levels.

We have already reviewed several of the difficult problems that involve various governments in complex negotiations and debates because they are close neighbors in a dynamic region. Financial entanglements are only the budgetary consequences of the governmental partitioning of a space crowded with people and activities. This density of people would not entail so many problems if the inhabitants spent most of their time within the community in which they live, as is the case in the crowded plains

[17] See *Statistical Abstract of the United States: 1956*, p. 397, and *1959*, p. 400.

[18] Victor Jones, "The Organization of a Metropolitan Region," in *University of Pennsylvania Law Review*, Philadelphia, Vol. 105, No. 4, February 1957, pp. 538–552. One may agree with William T. R. Fox that "the only theory that can describe intergovernmental relations in a metropolitan community is a theory of international politics" (*ibid.*, p. 538). However, even the latter is still far from being in a form that satisfies most students of international affairs. Perhaps the governmental complexities of Megalopolis may in the future justify Jane Addams' hope that the development of the American city may help to evolve better understanding between nations.

and basins of the Far East, where people travel little in a lifetime. In Megalopolis, as we well know, the situation is quite different. There are constant and dense currents of people and goods flowing through the area, and transportation is a major concern of local and state governments in the region and of several bi-state agencies.[19] However, it is not the only system of links binding the region together. Every one of the preceding chapters has given at least one other example of this closer integration produced by the density of activities.

Agriculture in Megalopolis is entirely oriented toward the great market of the urbanized region. The dairy farms, one of the most prosperous of the agricultural industries here, depend largely on the health legislation of the major cities, which have established "milksheds" with a *de facto* monopoly to supply fresh milk to the cities.[20] The uses of the woodlands and other environments of wildlife express the effect of policies determined by the proximity and desires of the large cities. The systems of land use described in Part Two of this study, combining urban and rural features in a sort of symbiosis, would not have been developed except in the vicinity of several large and expanding metropolitan systems.

City growth, transportation facilities, and municipal regulations explain the assets and liabilities of location in the various parts of Megalopolis for manufacturing plants. The suburban sprawl would not have developed in the way it did without the availability near the cities of easily accessible and relatively open, cheap space. Differences in government burdens and taxation were among the factors instrumental in causing the sprawl. The maintenance of easy access remained a responsibility of governmental agencies, and this brings us back to the transportation patterns and the management of traffic.

Neighborhood has not only economic consequences; it also creates concern for public health and safety.[21] Much of the authority and responsibility of the modern municipality has grown out of the threat to health and safety caused by crowding. Water supply came to be a governmental responsibility in the cities largely because of concern for public health.[22] Then came the problem of water pollution in the streams and on the

[19] See above, Chapter 12.

[20] See above, pp. 229-231 and 283-293.

[21] The public-health concerns of the present metropolitan areas were voiced by many experts at the 1958 National Health Forum in Philadelphia, as summarized in its report, *Urban Sprawl and Health*, National Health Council, New York, January 1959.

[22] See above, Chapter 13, pp. 729-735.

beaches, and the recognition that its control could not be achieved by individual governmental units working alone. In the 1930's, for example, the states of New York, New Jersey, and Connecticut therefore set up the Interstate Sanitary Commission to seek pollution abatement in the waters of the New York metropolitan area. In 1958 it was recognized that Washington, D. C., and Baltimore must work together to fight pollution of their water supplies, and a cooperative agreement was reached by the Senate-House Metropolitan Study Committee and the Baltimore Regional Planning Council.[23] Air pollution presents similar problems.[24] Crowding in a limited ground space of so many people, cars, power houses, manufacturing plants, and other sources of smoke, dust, and fumes is bound to fill the air with undesirable polluting elements. Control must be and often is exercised by local governments to achieve abatement. However, air pollution has not yet been effectively controlled in and around the larger cities, for a city's authority does not extend beyond its own limits, while the winds freely blow clouds of smoke or dust across these political partitions. New York City and Philadelphia, for example, can blame much of the pollution of their air on the neighbors in New Jersey across a river. Sometimes the neighbors' guilt or lack of control may be overemphasized in order to excuse nuisances that ought to be taken care of at home. But the lack of coordination as regards air-pollution control and even zoning regulations between communities located close enough together to pollute one another's air remains a hindrance to the best efforts to improve the air Megalopolitans breathe. When so many governments are involved and remain uncoordinated, the people's usual reaction is to look up to Federal authority. "Federal interest in air pollution is mounting not only as an aftermath of the Donora disaster of 1948, but also as a result of the increase in the number of air pollution problems involving interstate and international action." [25] In the same year that this statement was published (1956) the states of New York and New Jersey did undertake joint action by expanding the work of the Interstate Sanitary Commission to deal with air pollution in their parts of the New York metropolitan area.[26]

---

[23] *Washington Star*, January 25, 1958.

[24] See Paul L. Magill, Francis R. Holden, and Charles Ackley (eds.), *Air Pollution Handbook*, McGraw-Hill, New York, 1956, especially sections 1, 2, and 14.

[25] *Air Pollution Handbook, op. cit.*, pp. 2–17. See also the "Bibliography on Urban Climates," largely concerned with air pollution, in American Meteorological Society, *Meteorological Abstracts and Bibliography*, Vol. 3, No. 7, July 1952, pp. 734–773.

[26] Connecticut, a participant in the Commission's work on water pollution, did not join in this new effort, on the grounds that it was not involved in the matter.

Federal authorities have already had to act on another aspect of the control of the air, and in Megalopolis, as elsewhere in the country, all air traffic is under the jurisdiction of the Federal Aviation Agency.

Use of the air for flying requires also some control over uses of the ground, and such problems have sometimes provoked clashes between neighbors in Megalopolis. In 1952, for example, there was a series of tragic accidents involving airplanes that had taken off from Newark Airport, and severe property damage and several deaths resulted in the surrounding residential area, especially in the adjacent city of Elizabeth, New Jersey. The inhabitants of that area, feeling their safety jeopardized, asked that the airport be closed, and for a while this had to be done. A temporary President's Airport Commission was set up to look into the whole problem of airport location and use, and its report, significantly entitled *The Airport and Its Neighbors*, paid a great deal of attention to "community encroachment."

The immediate problem is to find a way to protect present airports and the people residing near them by applying some means of control of ground use in approach zones. Local authorities should prevent further use of land for public and residential buildings near the ends of existing runways. If this is not done, new contingents of home owners will be added to the ranks of those who are now protesting against noise and hazard. In time public pressure may threaten the continued existence of the airport and large investments of public and private funds will be jeopardized.[27]

In 1961 these problems still exist, aggravated by the noise of jet planes and by the continued building up of areas close to the airports, and one of the requirements commonly specified for a new jetport site for the New York metropolitan area is that it must be far from built-up areas, with a "buffer zone" of empty land around it. As has already been pointed out (p. 647, above), distance from the main hubs of already existing air traffic would also reduce the danger of air collisions. Search for a site that will meet all these requirements is a current cause of conflict between urban interests (represented in this case by the Port of New York Authority, which proposes to build the jetport) and suburban interests, such as the residents of Morris County, New Jersey, who immediately resisted the suggestion that the site be located in their Great Swamp area.

Another field of public safety that requires neighborly cooperation is civil defense. To coordinate civil defense in the New York metropolitan area the states of New York, New Jersey, and Connecticut have established a tri-state Civil Defense Committee.

[27] *The Airport and Its Neighbors*, The Report of the President's Airport Commission, U. S. Government Printing Office, Washington, May 16, 1952, p. 7.

The essential fact that causes all the various concerns of local government to interlock in so many fields is that *space densely occupied is not expendable in the long run*. Too many relationships come into interplay within this space, on the ground, in the air above it, in depth below it; and the more such ties of interdependence are established, the more cumbersome, for the daily management of the area as a whole, are the many partitions of authority between local and even state governments. Concluding the National Health Forum in 1958, Dr. Abel Wolman quoted Albert Einstein's remark that "politics is more difficult than physics," reminded the meeting that "growth means problems," and observed:

If we sat down, say in Philadelphia, New York, Baltimore or Washington, and brought out into the light all the services which the old core city now provides — more or less cheaply, more or less smoothly, more or less successfully — we could enumerate at least a hundred separate kinds of services. And we would be led to conclude, at the end of that enumeration, that New York City has no business existing! From a service standpoint, certainly, the old core city could not be made to function. If we listed the hundred multiple services and their competitive nature, our conclusion would be inevitable that it is not a viable community operation.

But the old city was and remains viable to a very large extent. Babies are delivered. Medical care is provided. Milk does arrive at each apartment in the morning. And people do move, even though in bunches and under difficulty. They get to their offices somehow or other, and they do get home. The old core city always had its share of frustrations, and it is gratifying to recall them, because it is an old common heritage of human behavior.[28]

These great cities still concentrate so many activities and people that they continue to be essential nuclei of a regional system. In Megalopolis their relative decline, and even their recent absolute decline, in numbers of residents does not mean that they have been reduced as yet to a minor role. Their economies, though statistically on the decline, remain the major components of the region's prosperity, which could not survive a complete decay of the central cities. Perhaps some of the medium-sized cities are losing many of their functions and will survive only by being absorbed as suburbs (industrial or residential or both) in the orbit of a larger center, new or old. Even this decline is in the long run a discomforting sign for the whole metropolitan system in which such cities belong.

[28] Abel Wolman, "From Urban Sprawl to Healthier Communities," in *Urban Sprawl and Health, op. cit.*, p. 215. The variety of services needed in a city are well illustrated by a look into *The Municipal Yearbook*, edited by O. F. Nolting and D. S. Arnold, published annually by the International City Manager's association in Chicago, especially in Part IV: "Municipal Activities."

Every survey of the conflicts and contrasts between the various parts of a metropolitan region has concluded by stressing the interdependence of the whole. For better economic conditions, to maintain growth and prosperity of the whole, more mutual help and coordination are needed. Local politics, however, do not yet accept these principles as directions for their action. There still is a great deal of pride and some isolationism in large cities, and in the smaller communities there is distrust for the larger neighbor and striving for self-sufficiency and independence.[29] The need for some form of metropolitan governmental coordination is being advocated by most experts in the field, and the idea is gradually gaining strength even in political circles.

The Need for Governmental Coordination

One way or another, Megalopolis has in the past "muddled through" the difficulties of too much partitioning of the land and division of authority. Indeed, the very proliferation of administrative units has not all been for the worse, for some of the more recently established ones do help to offset the partitioning in some ways. "Special districts," for example, can achieve better coordination *in a special field of activity* by performing usually a single function, sometimes several, for an area spanning other types of administrative divisions. In the whole nation the number of special districts increased from 8,299 in 1942 to 14,405 in 1957, and during the five years 1952–57 their number grew by 17 per cent.[30] Most of them fall into the categories of fire protection districts, soil conservation districts, and drainage districts, or they are "authorities" es-

---

[29] This has been well described by Robert C. Wood in *Suburbia: Its People and Their Politics,* Houghton Mifflin Company, Boston, 1959, and a model analysis of the complicated politics of the great city has been offered recently for New York in Wallace S. Sayre and Herbert Kaufman, *Governing New York City: Politics in the Metropolis,* Russell Sage Foundation, New York, 1960. See also Sayre, "Governmental Relations between Cities and the State in New York," in the Buttenweiser Report, *op. cit.,* pp. 281–287.

[30] *The Municipal Yearbook, 1960, op. cit.* These figures do not include school districts, a long-established type of special district that has been decreasing rapidly in the United States, from 108,579 in 1942 to 50,446 in 1957. In some parts of Megalopolis the reduction was even more rapid than the national trend. In Connecticut, for example, the number of school districts fell from fourteen to three in 1942–57. In New Jersey, however, the reduction was by only one unit (from 490 to 489), and in Massachusetts four new school districts were established. The size and authority of the townships in New England make school districts less useful in that part of the country; and the great rise of the child population in suburbanized New Jersey, where communities have been burdened by the growth of educational needs, has not been conducive to a regrouping of the school districts. This trend proceeded very successfully in the less metropolitan parts of New York State.

tablished to undertake the construction and operation of toll roads and bridges, port and airport facilities, and so forth. Authorities have been especially important and helpful in Megalopolis, and they express precisely the inadequacy of other governmental units to take care of the new problems arising from regional integration.[31] Examples are the very helpful Port Authorities of New York, Massachusetts, and the Delaware River.

The needs for certain kinds of coordination or for new governmental frameworks vary greatly from one part of the United States to another and even within the area of Megalopolis. There is, however, a trend toward broadening the geographical scope of the governmental unit, and the need for this is especially felt in Megalopolis. It has taken various forms.

In many cases great cities have sought to solve the difficulties of their relationships with neighboring districts by annexation, as Houston, Texas, did in 1960. In Megalopolis Baltimore annexed large suburban areas in 1918,[32] and some of the early growth of New York was of this type, for it annexed the West Bronx in 1874 and the East Bronx in 1895. Consolidation is another method. As early as 1854 the city and county of Philadelphia were consolidated, and in 1898 the present boundaries of Greater New York, with its five boroughs, were formed by a combination of further annexation and consolidation with the city of Brooklyn. These processes are subject to certain limitations, for they cannot extend a city's area indefinitely, and they can work only within the territory of one state. Moreover, they may bring about a political structure in the greater city that weakens rather than reinforces the practical authority of the city government.[33]

In a few cases the central city has delegated its powers for a certain purpose to a new agency, usually established by the state government, with authority extending also over some of the areas adjacent to the city. In the Boston area the Metropolitan Transit Authority is of this type. In the New York area a somewhat similar example is the Waterfront

---

[31] It must not be thought, however, that every agency named an "authority" involves coordination across political boundaries and was set up because of inadequacies arising from problems of multiple jurisdictions. Sometimes the inadequacy stems from limitations on the borrowing power of *one* jurisdiction. To overcome such a limitation an authority may be established as a public-benefit corporation, with power to borrow money by bond issues to finance certain specified projects. The Triborough Bridge and Tunnel Authority, an example of this type, operates only within the area of New York City.

[32] See above, p. 257, the fight against annexation put up by Fairfax County.

[33] See Sayre and Kaufman, *Governing New York City, op cit.*; and Maxine Kurtz, "The Planning Aspects of Annexation and of Service Areas," in *Urban Problems and Techniques, op. cit.*, pp. 7-30.

Commission of New York Harbor, a bi-state agency set up by New York State and New Jersey in 1953 to control labor conditions on the docks and eliminate racketeering, theft, and related problems. And the bi-state Port of New York Authority operates Newark, La Guardia, and New York International airports for the cities of Newark and New York on fifty-year leases.[34]

Still another possibility is the establishment of a metropolitan type of government, like that developed in Greater Toronto, Canada, and in Dade County, Florida. This is becoming an accepted new category in the vocabulary of political scientists and legal experts. It could not solve all the problems in Megalopolis, for many of them affect areas even greater than one individual metropolitan region. However, within such a region there are many common problems, which a metropolitan government could well tackle. In the New York metropolitan region a start in this direction was made by the establishment, in 1956, of the Metropolitan Regional Council, a voluntary association of the top elected officials of twenty-one counties (in the three states of New York, New Jersey, and Connecticut), twenty major cities, and other minor governmental units of the area, first brought together at the suggestion of New York City's Mayor Robert F. Wagner.[35] Among the topics the Council has discussed, and in some cases acted upon, are transportation and traffic, parks, water supply, water and air pollution, civil defense, and juvenile delinquency. In the fall of 1960 it was announced that in the 1961 sessions of the state legislatures of the three states efforts would be made to pass bills giving the Council governmental status.[36]

The states in Megalopolis have been concerned about metropolitan problems and have studied them attentively. As more interrelationships develop between different governmental units within a state, and as more interstate regional bonds are formed, it will be increasingly the responsibility of the states to deal with the new situations and to help the administrative structure evolve so as to permit easier solutions and greater efficiency in government. The states have recognized their responsibility in the matter and the need for action, more appraisal, and more reform.[37]

---

[34] As regards port facilities the Port of New York Authority is in a somewhat different category, for it supplements or even competes with rather than replaces city agencies.

[35] See The New York Times, June 19, 1956.

[36] See The New York Times, October 19, 1960.

[37] See the very informative Report to the Governor's Conference, directed by J. C. Bollens, The States and the Metropolitan Problem, The Council of State Governments, Chicago, 1956.

Already a number of agencies have been formed, some of which have been described above, and cities have been granted authority to set up various special agencies.

A leading specialist on the matter of legal organizations of metropolitan regions, Victor Jones, has observed:

There is less talk today than before the war about the "integration" of local government into a metropolitan government. The creation of a single local government for a metropolitan area by means of extensive annexations to the central city or of the city-county consolidation has been replaced in post-war discussions by proposals to federate existing units of local government into a limited metropolitan government, or to consolidate particular functions or activities by transferring them to a more territorially extensive unit, by jointly administering them, or by creating special districts or authorities. . . . There must be a community before there can be effective and stable government. . . . local governments are at law, and frequently in fact, creatures of all those political forces we call state governments.[38]

Such considerations are basic, but they are somewhat theoretical. While it is true "that community creates government and that government creates community,"[39] this kind of "creation" is never a simple and direct relationship. The creation takes time, and during that time a whole economic and social evolution takes place, influenced by both community and government, and modifying them both in the process. These relation-ships have been discussed by philosophers and political scientists since Plato and Aristotle at least. In our time and in Megalopolis we are faced with this slow dissolution of past well-structured frameworks evolving toward new, nebulous, perhaps colloidal forms. It appears thus to us at present because things are so much in flux. But we know that the processes of urbanization or metropolitanization, which are going on with great momentum in Megalopolis and, though on a smaller scale, in many other parts of America, Europe, and Asia result from complex technological, economic, and generally cultural features of the societies they affect.

Economic integration is due largely to the status of general prosperity

[38] Victor Jones, "The Organization of a Metropolitan Region," in *University of Pennsylvania Law Review*, February 1957, *op. cit.*, pp. 539 and 552. See also by Jones, *Metropolitan Government*, University of Chicago Press, Chicago, 1942, and his essay, "The Organization of Local Government in Metropolitan Areas," in *The Future of Cities and Urban Redevelopment*, edited by Coleman Woodbury, The University of Chicago Press, Chicago, 1953, pp. 479–606, an excellent summary of the problem at the time.

[39] Inis Claude, Jr., *Swords into Ploughshares: The Problems and Progress of In-ternational Organization*, Random House, New York, 1956. See also Jefferson B. Fordham, *A Larger Concept of Community*, Louisiana State University Press, Baton Rouge, 1956.

and to the techniques of transportation, communication, and financing now available in Megalopolis. All this evolution must be taken into account and constantly borne in mind. New and better governmental concepts cannot be elaborated unless all the patterns of land use, the highways and railroads, the telephone and television, the white-collar occupations and the communications-oriented industries are given a part in the debate about what would be more satisfactory for the present and especially for the future.

Discussing the National Highway Program of 1955–56, Dr. Luther Gulick, president of the Institute of Public Administration, wrote:

> Our new pattern of metropolitanism takes us into a new world of scale, of freedom of movement and association, and of integration. This is, and is intended to be, a turning point in American cultural, economic and social history. As a result of these dramatic changes, many old ideas as to local governmental services are now dead, many ideas . . . are obsolete. Above all we know that there can be no effective attack on the rising problems of the metropolis without a comprehensive and cooperative attack.[40]

New ideas are being taught by experts on metropolitan growth. More new institutions are being established and older ones are being spurred on. Significant developments are the existence in the United States Congress of a Joint Committee on Washington Metropolitan Problems, discussing the "National Capital Region," and the Senate debate on a bill proposing to establish a Commission on Metropolitan Problems.[41] The national capital has been recognized as having expanded beyond the limits of the District of Columbia and to have become a "region." Governmental reorganization may have to follow before a metropolitan "community" can be clearly recognized. Such a community may perhaps be shaped first around Washington because this area is at one of the ends of Megalopolis, adjacent only to the metropolitan area of Baltimore, a city of very different specialization. Nevertheless, the recognition of the "National Capital Region" is rooted in the same entanglements that are found (sometimes even more interwoven) throughout the rest of Megalopolis, and it results

[40] Luther Gulick, "The New Highway Program Requires Metropolitan Cooperation," in *The New Highways: Challenge to the Metropolitan Region*, Urban Land Institute (Technical Bulletin 31), Washington, D. C., November 1957, p. 92.

[41] See "Meeting the Problems of Metropolitan Growth in the National Capital Region," Final Report of the Joint Committee on Washington Metropolitan Problems, 86th Cong., 1st sess., Senate Report No. 38, U. S. Government Printing Office, Washington, D. C., 1959; and "Create a Commission on Metropolitan Problems," Hearings before the Sub-committee on Reorganization and International Organizations, of the Committee on Government Operations, U. S. Senate, 86th Cong., 1st sess., July 24, 1959 (Committee Print), Washington, 1959.

from the same economic and social evolution that forced Megalopolis into its present mold.

Redistribution Is an Urban Function

Each expert analyzes only one aspect of the sweeping processes at work in the region at this time. The expert on government will concern himself essentially with the political and legal aspects of the area's problems, while the economist will study mainly statistics and their distribution, to formulate probable conclusions to the trends he observes. The planner will too often be bent on applying general principles of town and country zoning and planning, principles usually elaborated on the basis of past experiences and not necessarily fitted to the new conditions evolving in a period of changes as revolutionary as those now going on.

Some thirty years ago, Thomas H. Reed wrote that despite metropolitan growth "the old city has not only maintained but actually increased its dominance as a center of trade, banking, amusement and culture." [42] Commenting on this in 1960 Coleman Woodbury remarked that "this indeed must have a comical or even a bitter ring today to many central city merchants suffering from the competition of new outlying shopping centers and suburban retail areas, to redevelopment and other city officials in the older centers trying to combat serious and spreading blight, to church leaders in many central city congregations and parishes, and to many others." [43]

While this remark is certainly true, it does not follow that Reed's statement is no longer true. The detailed examination of the general evolution in Megalopolis shows that one concept need not exclude the other. It may be wise to define such terms as "city" and the cases that serve as yardsticks. Moreover, national averages are interesting but only for the purpose of showing *how much each particular case considered differs from them*. In Megalopolis there are many cities that have followed on the whole the pattern of decline considered to be general, but one could hardly say that New York City is declining at a time when the world influence of Manhattan is greater than it has ever been, and probably greater than the

[42] Thomas H. Reed in the article on "Metropolitan Areas" in the *Encyclopaedia of the Social Sciences*, X, 396 (1933). See also the interesting book by Reed, *Municipal Government in the United States*, rev. ed., D. Appleton-Century Co., New York, 1934, especially his Chapters 2, 3, 22, and 23.

[43] Coleman Woodbury, *A Framework for Urban Studies: An Analysis of Urban-Metropolitan Development and Research Needs*, Highway Research Board, Special Report 52, (National Academy of Sciences, National Research Council, Publication 722), Washington, D. C., October 1959, p. 4.

influence ever had by a city that is not the seat of a national government. New York City may have lost some trade and some residents, but the mass of population, industries, and commerce now contained in the region that lives by and for its proximity to Manhattan is greater than ever and is increasing. Had Philadelphia been declining before it consolidated its city with the county? According to a few statistical yardsticks its central district and adjoining residential areas were even then losing to adjacent municipalities, which had not yet been brought under one roof, administratively speaking, by the old core. The *City* of London was emptied of almost all its nighttime inhabitants and of many industries just about the time when it reached the pinnacle of its economic greatness and power. We could quote many more such examples. The very successful city has always grown beyond its bounds.[44] City limits are determined at a given time for the purposes of the moment, and to strike a relatively stable political balance in the area. The more dynamic is the city's and the area's economic growth, the sooner will this balance be upset and the city limits be rendered obsolete. Megalopolis has been and remains a very dynamic area. Let us not be too impressed, therefore, by local administrative boundaries. Although they command the community's loyalties, they were never meant to weigh in the people's minds as much as national loyalty or devotion to higher moral principles. What happens in Megalopolis must be interpreted as a redistribution of what *used to be* city functions over a wider territory. The economic and social characteristics of the administrative units in this territory and the relationship between them are being modified. The changes must occur in economic and social relationships first; then the legal and governmental framework can be redistributed from time to time to secure as fair as possible a share to all participants. It is when the services normally provided or regulated by governments become unsatisfactory to the users that a redistribution of governmental burdens comes to pass.

Some of the cities in Megalopolis may have declined from any standpoint; but the major cities remain very lively. They may count fewer inhabitants at night, and deposits in their banks may not grow as rapidly as

[44] Sir William Petty wrote as early as the end of the seventeenth century in his *Political Arithmetick*, London, 1691: "There be, Anno 1682, about 670,000 souls in London. . . . By the City of London, we mean the Housing within the Walls of the Old City, with the Liberties thereof, Westminster, the Borough of Southwark, and so much of the built ground in Middlesex and Surrey, whose Houses are contiguous unto, or within Call of those afore mentioned." Petty comprehended 133 parishes in his definition of London in 1682; his expression "within call of" reminds one that the flow of telephone calls is now one of the measures by which metropolitan areas are determined by the U. S. Bureau of the Census.

in neighboring or distant areas, but this does not mean they have lost any kind of "centrality" or "dominance." It means simply that their functions within the region and within the nation have evolved. The role they retain may well remain essential to the metropolitan area, and to a vaster community. There can be no doubt that the relative roles of New York City, and of Washington, D. C., in Megalopolis are essential to the survival of the whole region as a prosperous and essential section of the country. The roles of these two cities in the direction of the economic, political, and cultural life of the American nation have probably grown rather than declined, in the past thirty years, despite what statistical curves may indicate.

Megalopolis as a whole is still growing, and at a faster rate than most other parts of the civilized world. The rate of growth may be slower than the American national average, but this has been a period of exceptionally rapid growth for the United States, both in population and in terms of economic development. In the most recent quarter century, the dispersal of people and their activities was generalized because of the greater mobility provided by the automobile and the highways, the airplane, the telephone, and the ever-expanding mass media. Nevertheless, we have seen how much *denser* are Megalopolitan flows of motor traffic and telephone calls (Figs. 177–186 and 202–203, pp. 583–593 and 641–645) than those found anywhere else; and how centralized the mass-media market is in this area.[45]

The scattering of the growing population of Megalopolis has developed chiefly along the axial belt, in the interurban or suburban areas between the major cities or around them. This has resulted in urbanization of the whole region, as evidenced by the changes in the population during the period 1930–50 (Fig. 73, p. 248). This process continued through the 1950's, with the axial belt widening, as shown by the map of population changes by counties (Fig. 9, p. 41), and with larger old cores continuing to lose residents (see the map of density in 1960, Fig. 1, p. 6). The trends of the 1950's have perhaps accelerated the evolution toward the symbiosis of the *old* "rural" and "urban" modes of life and land use — a symbiosis characteristic of modern urbanization as it is observed in Megalopolis. It spreads people more evenly over the whole region at night, as the densities decrease in the more crowded sectors and increase in sectors that were formerly less crowded. A daily environment that corresponds better to the "garden city" ideal comes to a larger proportion of the region's population and covers a larger part of the region's land area.

The only large section of Megalopolis that continued to show a sub-

45 See above, Chapter 11, pp. 597–615.

Number of 18-Year-Olds

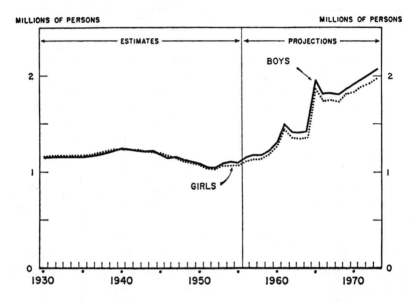

SOURCE: DEPARTMENT OF COMMERCE.

Fig. 226. Number of persons reaching the age of eighteen in the United States, 1930–75. *Reproduced from Chart 34 in* The President's Economic Report to Congress, *U. S. Government Printing Office, Washington, D. C., January 1956*

stantial decline in population during the 1950's was the group of four counties in Pennsylvania, the economy of which was based on anthracite mining. These eastern Pennsylvania coalfields have been declining for quite some time, and their surplus population has been moving out, either toward other sections of Megalopolis or westward. The area still preserved a good deal of active manufacturing. Mining and manufacturing have been moving around much more freely than ever in recent times, having proved to be more easily decentralized than are the "communications-oriented" industries; and coal's share in the American economic system has been steadily declining. It seems quite probable, however, that these coal-mining counties of eastern Pennsylvania would have been emptied much more rapidly of their population, and would have known much worse days, had they been located farther away from the mushrooming metropolitan chain of the Megalopolitan axial belt.

The economy of Megalopolis, despite its crowding and many relative deficiencies, is a very prosperous one. It has been extremely ingenious in

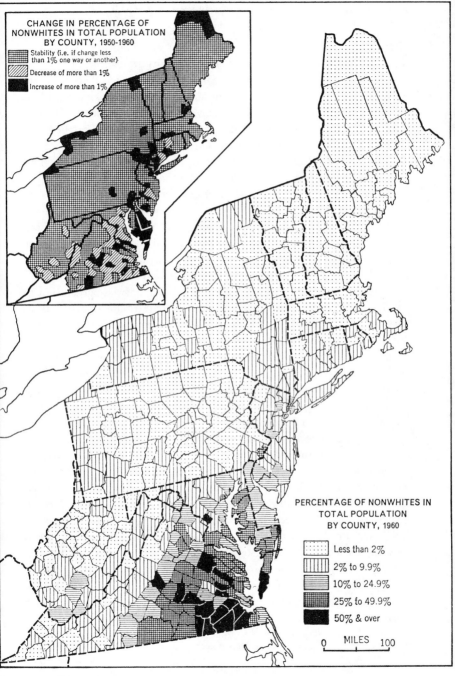

CHANGE IN PERCENTAGE OF
NONWHITES IN TOTAL POPULATION
BY COUNTY, 1950-1960

Stability (i.e. if change less
than 1% one way or another)

Decrease of more than 1%

Increase of more than 1%

PERCENTAGE OF NONWHITES IN
TOTAL POPULATION
BY COUNTY, 1960

Less than 2%

2% to 9.9%

10% to 24.9%

25% to 49.9%

50% & over

MILES
0   100

FIG. 227

finding, throughout its history, new resources at every turn of the winds of trade or production. It has been generally successful in redistributing the surpluses and profits it has had an opportunity to manage. *Any urban economy thrives on the redistribution of surpluses*, whether these are surpluses of food, raw materials, consumer goods, money, services, labor, or even time. What is "surplus" somewhere, within the city itself or in some other location, could perhaps find a customer; and it has been the essential function of the city, with its merchants, its market place, its administrators and brokers, to organize the distribution and the redistribution of all that some people they know might use. Even though the actual transfer of the people, goods, or securities involved does not necessarily take place within the city's territory, the process is managed there. Government, management, trade, finance, and entertainment have been urban functions since the dawn of history. All these functions involve redistributing what cannot be handled otherwise (and what we have called "surplus") to a larger network centered on the city.

The supreme test of resourcefulness for a community is perhaps not to provide more for its members to share, but to redistribute all that is available for redistribution to an ever-expanding circuit of customers. Thus "surpluses" can be used for economic growth, and new "needs" can be created and supplied to the general satisfaction. The latter contentment can never, of course, be attained in absolute fashion, and it should not be; for people who refrain from desiring more have little chance of getting more and achieving progress. The Promethean tradition of Megalopolis is to be both credited with and blamed for the constant notes of dissatisfaction and self-criticism voiced by responsible residents of the region.

This should be so, and it should lead to action, for human progress would soon turn into sheer decay and resentment if men stopped clamoring for "more." In the 1960's Megalopolis will hear much more criticism than in the 1950's because the *adult* population will increase at a much quicker pace than in recent years. The coming of age of the more numerous generation born after 1940 will be the main cause (see the graph showing the numbers of persons reaching the age of 18 from 1930 to 1975, Fig. 226). A further prolongation of the average duration of life, due to recent medical and public health achievements, will be another factor, adding to the numbers of the aged,[46] most of whom will prefer urban residences.

[46] See *Health, Education and Welfare Trends*, 1960 edition, annual published by the Office of the Secretary, U. S. Department of Health, Education, and Welfare, Washington, D. C. See also John J. Corson and John W. McConnell, *Economic Needs of Older People*, Twentieth Century Fund, New York, 1956.

The crowding in Megalopolis is bound to increase. Adults need more space, more money, and more jobs than do children. The distribution of land uses, of residences, of occupations will be shifting once more under new pressures. In this process it may well happen that the share of Megalopolis in the national figures will keep declining in several respects. The crowding could cause more aged people to move to other, more restful parts of America; and it could also accelerate the out-migration of various manufacturing industries or trade establishments. Such relative decrease will not prevent continued growth in absolute figures, especially in the kind of activities for which Megalopolis is at this time best fitted. To provide for all of this, a good deal of foresight is necessary now. More people will be sharing more actively in this increasingly partitioned land. Governments, community leaders, and the general public will all have to cooperate in coordinated action to keep the problems of crowding and the inheritance of the past from interfering with the indispensable process of growth, on which rests the involved structure of the region.[47] The traditions inherited from its history have been a great factor of strength in Megalopolis and they ought to support the forthcoming endeavors to solve the new tide of problems.

[47] The degree of administrative fragmentation now prevalent in Megalopolis may seem to spell increasing anarchy in government for the future. Government, however, reflects the people's ability to cope with existing tensions, pressures, and problems. With the demand for services rapidly rising and the threat of municipal bankruptcy closing in on several of the major nuclei, politics will have to reckon with growing popular concern. See Robert C. Wood, *1400 Governments: the Political Economy of the New York Metropolitan Region* (New York Metropolitan Region Study), Harvard University Press, Cambridge, Mass., 1961.

C H A P T E R 1 5

Conclusion: *Novus Ordo Seclorum*

The growth of Megalopolis is an extremely complex phenomenon. Many factors have combined to bring about its present degree of urbanization and its spectacular concentration of people, industries, and wealth. The geographical location was quite an important asset in the earlier stages of the region's development; and the foundations inherited from the past advantageously support to this day the lofty modern structure that has in recent years dominated the economics and politics of our globe. And yet no combination of material forces alone can be credited with having determined the rise of Megalopolis to its present eminence. The spirit of the people who used the material opportunity within their reach must be recognized as the decisive element in the region's history; such is the lesson of the past, and such is the warning for the future.

The Promethean Momentum

The first towns established on the Northeastern American seaboard from Massachusetts Bay to the Potomac River formed a daring frontier whose people were concerned with solving the problems of human woes at least as much as with developing a continent and controlling an ocean. If these settlements of the seventeenth and early eighteenth centuries are thought of as forming a hinge on the continent's edge, it must be recognized as a "three-dimensional" hinge, the third component being the spiritual aspirations that inspired the various experiments: Puritan Massachusetts, Providence, then Connecticut, Quaker Philadelphia, Mennonite and Amish Lancaster in Pennsylvania, Roman Catholic Maryland, and many others. Each of these groups was led by a faith that burned strong and long and that seemed more capable of achievements in the virgin land of a New World.

New York's origins were somewhat different, and in many ways more materialistic. But New York early became a very tolerant place, open to many faiths, and a great hub of cooperation between people of most diverse origins. All the great seaports, located on this stretch of the continent's façade, were rivals, and therefore they influenced one another. They were all children of the age of the great geographical discoveries, from which they inherited a Promethean disposition soon spurred on by religious fervor and by competition among neighbors.

As one reviews the history of Megalopolis [1] one finds a close association between the spirit of the frontier and the momentum of the great religious experiments. Frederick Jackson Turner's theory of the frontier in American history blends here with Perry Miller's "errand into the wilderness" to produce an endless endeavor toward the betterment of man's destiny through the development of new and unlimited resources.[2] The Promethean ardor flares up brilliantly after independence, as is attested by such writings as Nicholas Collin's statement prominently displayed in the publications of the American Philosophical Society.[3]

Many historians have pointed out that the programs drawn up and the policies followed in this region arose as the daily products of the pressures of the times, which offered opportunity along with obstacles and difficulties. People rose to meet these successive challenges, doing the best they could, without any grand design or conscious planning.

[1] See above, Chapters 1 and 3, especially pp. 67–79.

[2] See especially Frederick Jackson Turner, *The Frontier in American History*, Henry Holt and Company, New York, 1920, Chapter 9, "The West and American Ideals," and Chapter 11, "Social Forces in American History," in which Turner states in fact that the massing of population in the cities, accompanied by urban and industrial growth, is providing the American nation with a new frontier for the twentieth century.

[3] See above, pp. 71–77.

However, there are several ways to face, any particular challenge or to take advantage of a given opportunity. The pre-Columbian Indians did it one way, the New England settlers another way, while the planters in Virginia chose still a third system. The mass of the people in a community are seldom fully conscious of the forces that drive them, and they are usually too busy to spend time investigating them, leaving this to an elite that is more leisurely and intellectual. There can be little doubt that the leadership of the great cities on the Northeastern seaboard paid some attention to the abstract foundations of American strength.

It is significant that the committees that debated and chose the allegoric design of the Great Seal of the United States, shortly after independence, inscribed on one of the seal's faces the Latin phrase, *Novus Ordo Seclorum*, a phrase that appears also on every greenback, printed under the unfinished pyramid the base of which bears the date 1776. The leaders of the young Republic believed that the United States and its way of life ought to be and would be a "New Order of the Ages," a great turning point of history. There were few more striking ways of claiming such a role than by inscribing such a motto on the Great Seal of the federation, and later on its bank notes. An inscription is not worth much in practice unless it expresses a deep feeling alive in the hearts of many people, and such a feeling was characteristic of the leadership of Megalopolitan cities in the latter part of the eighteenth century. Much of this same spirit is still alive in American minds and still inspires American action. The early Boston mariner's policy to "trye all ports" and the more recent formula of the great planners to "make no little plans" represent a Megalopolitan tradition, full of vigor and determination, based on bold experimentation and expressing confidence in the ultimate success of human endeavor.

In terms of ancient Greek mythology such a tradition was indeed titanic; it has proved to be Promethean. An era of great discoveries around the earth and of fervent religious debates lay behind the development of this region, and it achieved its present supremacy at the time when mankind, satisfying an ancient dream, once more opened the gates of discovery and exploration, this time of still newer worlds on other planets. We are constantly reminded today that ideas precede and shape the appearance of new "facts." The ancient philosopher of Alexandria, Philo Judaeus, taught that there is a great *city of ideas* that predetermines and commands the material world in which we live, and this greater city of ideas Philo called *Megalopolis*. It seems, then, especially fitting to apply the same name to this extraordinary region, the present shape and style of which arose from the beliefs and searchings of those who settled there to bring a new order to their brethren on earth.

Unlimited Resourcefulness: A Philosophy of Abundance

What kind of new order was it? Every group certainly visualized it in its own way, but it was to be a *better* order, one of plenty and justice, one in which people would be happy, in which abundance would reign and would be fairly distributed. In their religious fervor the various communities were very much aware of the necessity of material success to demonstrate their truth to the world at large. The Lord's approval of their behavior would be manifested in their general prosperity. To achieve the latter they were all prepared to work hard but intelligently, saving their labor whenever possible, because the people were few and the continent immense, because also the task was enormous, and all devices to advance the community's welfare and its ability to produce would be helpful and would certainly please the Lord.

To these early ideas the nature of the times gave great momentum. The Northeastern seaboard was settled as the era of great discoveries widened horizons in all directions and fired a vast commercial expansion. The early settlements of the seventeenth and eighteenth centuries grew facing the western shores of Europe at a time when the people of the latter were opening in various directions new avenues of scientific and technical progress and were harboring the "enlightenment." The cities of Megalopolis started growing with the Industrial Revolution and with a great upheaval in mass migration and mass consumption.

Megalopolis hungrily absorbed every new device its people learned about, in order to foster its own growth. Commercial development, industrialization, mechanization, motorization, and automation all were put to work on a large scale. The new order to be developed could only be an *urban* order. The old rural economy, which predominated in the "old" countries whence most of the settlers or latter immigrants came, was obviously unfit to support the kind of plenty the Northeastern seaboard had undertaken to secure.

Unlimited resources cannot be found in any small plot of land but must be supplied from a vast radius around it. The Promethean tradition and the urban economy, early based on an active commerce, cooperated to develop the people's resourcefulness as the only possible limitless resource. The continent was settled and developed; but Megalopolis was not satisfied to serve only as the main base for this enormous task. The economic *hinge* was at work both on the continent and overseas. Thirsty for more supplies and more markets, the traders of Megalopolis organized more and more production at home and far away. As surpluses were gathered, they too were marketed and often transformed into necessities through processes several times referred to in this volume. The redistribution of surpluses always has been the function of the market place, and of urban economies.

A certain wastefulness was involved in the accumulation of wealth and in the means of production. Mass consumption was pushed forward by the organization of large-scale advertising, large-scale credit, built-in obsolescence, and by the whole functioning of the mass-media market that remains centered in the main hubs of Megalopolis. It must be realized that such a philosophy of abundance founded on the unlimited resourcefulness of hard-working people with a Promethean drive could lead only to large-scale urban growth and expansion. It led also to a constant and rapidly shifting specialization of a large part of the Megalopolitan labor force into those occupations, those sectors of economic activity, that paid better and were expanding their demand for manpower. From a balanced agricultural-commercial economy Megalopolis shifted as soon as it could to an emphasis on manufacturing plus trade. In the twentieth century the tertiary industries have been taking over the region, and the majority of the labor force has gone into white-collar occupations. By 1960 the major hubs already specialized in what might be called the *quaternary* forms of economic activity: the managerial and artistic functions, government, education, research, and the brokerage of all kinds of goods, services, and securities.

Such activities have always been concentrated in the business districts, the downtowns, the market places that characterized the urban center, the city. For at least a century, and possibly longer, Megalopolis has been at the forefront of the progress and refinement of the urban economy. Its successful expansion suggests that its dynamics have thus rightly followed the basic principles of any urban growth. There is in the mechanics of the city the need for the production of surplus, for a great fluidity in the balance of needs and resources, as well as enough fluidity in the very nature of the revenue-procuring resources.

Abundance of goods and money is also an ancient specialty of the city. The confluence of many currents of supply and traffic is needed to obtain such abundance, which will not be limited to just a few commodities locally produced. However, cities have not always achieved a fair distribution of their abundant supplies. The United States may well claim to be the first large nation to have achieved a high degree of general abundance well distributed among the population, and there can be little doubt that this abundance was due not so much to the extent and fecundity of the land as to the dynamism of the urban economy developed in Megalopolis and founded on the management of redistribution.

The great technological momentum of the period in which Megalopolis grew was a great factor, and the natural riches of the American continent were also instrumental. Still, many nations went through these same years in history without any comparable economic development, although they may have just as rich a natural endowment as the United States. Indeed, vast oilfields, immense ore deposits, and expanses of good land are just being found or surveyed in several continents, even in little old Europe. But the search for and development of all possible resources in the orbit of Megalopolis (which has often coincided, during the most recent 150 years, with part of London's orbit) was not typical of the rest of the world. If one were to ask "why" and dare an answer, the latter ought certainly to be related less to the desire of achieving greater production than to the faith in expanding consumption, even in a wasteful manner if need be, as a constructive factor in economic growth. In a century or two from now the economic historian looking at a detailed accounting of the past may conclude that the natural endowment of the United States, especially east of the Rockies, was nothing exceptional; it might even look then as below average. But the resourcefulness with which its people put it to use, under the direction of the Megalopolitan hubs, may even then appear exceptional.

What the future holds for people is a question to be answered elsewhere. We may, however, wonder how much of a lesson the past and present of Megalopolis may provide for its own people and for the population of other lands.

The New Order: How Exportable?

It would certainly have immensely pleased the Founding Fathers of the cities in Megalopolis to find that the way of life and the economic organization developed there serve as a model to many other parts of the world undergoing the process of urbanization. The actual trends, however, are not quite so simple. The process of urban growth is in our time a worldwide phenomenon and a source of concern for many communities and governments. In every region this growth develops along specific lines, most of which differ from place to place; every community has its own variety of the usual problems, and its own ways and means of tackling them. These local characteristics must be respected. But to be informed of more or less similar problems in other places, and how they have been dealt with, is helpful; and what is learned in this way may be used to help solve one's own problems in one's own way.

Naturally countries faced with the questions of modern urbanization look first at the precedents set and the experiments tried in areas where leadership has been established. In our time Megalopolis is being thus studied and examined, for many of its various problems are or will be repeated, with some variance and on different scales, in most other countries. Whether the action taken concerning any of its urban and suburban problems warrants it or not, Megalopolis should know that it will be examined by many outsiders, some of whom will copy it just because of the prestige the region enjoys today, and some of whom may be inspired to improve on the techniques applied there. Whatever is done, whatever its real worth for the people involved, the example of Megalopolis will be followed more often than not. Observers travelling around the world nowadays report from most varied areas many instances of the obvious influence of American methods of coping with urban problems; and as Megalopolis remains the most impressive and largest urban system, as it is the main façade of the United States toward the outside world, it is mainly Megalopolitan examples that are impressed on so many cities and countries around the globe.

Recently this writer has travelled widely through North America, western Europe and some Mediterranean countries. Everywhere he found cities expanding. The larger metropolitan areas are attracting the larger part of population growth. Cities are expanding one toward the other. The nebulous structure of urbanized regions is becoming frequent and hints at a new redistribution of functions within such regions. Residential land use is gaining in all directions around the congested older nuclei. The more densely agglomerated nuclei no longer specialize in manufacturing and administration as they used to. Production industries often move out to the periphery of the city and beyond into spaces that were until recently considered rural or interurban. The functions that continue to gather in what may be called central districts or hubs of the urban nebulae are offices, laboratories, and all the activities related to the various forms of entertainment. As in Roman times, the arena and the forum, in their modern versions, occupy an increasing share of the hubs. Entertainment and offices are related one to another, thriving on proximity. They create a large market for white-collar labor. All these trends started at an earlier time and they have already developed on a great scale in Megalopolis.

The forces bringing about this evolution are rooted in a deep transformation of modern modes of life and habitat. They are not determined in other areas just by an imitation of Megalopolis, and yet the element of imitation spurs the evolution on.

These trends bestow a heavy responsibility upon the present inhabitants and leadership of Megalopolis. In many ways they may be rightly proud of serving as a model. They must, however, be mindful of the long-range consequences of these trends. People imitate those wealthier, more powerful, more successful than they are, in the hope of achieving through such imitation a better and perhaps an equal status. Mahatma Gandhi told how in his youth he tried to eat beef, despite deep repugnance, in the hope that it would make him intellectually and politically equal to the beef-eating British who then dominated India. He soon understood that that was not the way to solve his problem. Megalopolis may feel some concern at the thought that similarly unreasonable but instinctive imitation may and will develop; but in the field of urban and metropolitan problems one cannot prevent such undesirable imitations. Nevertheless, there remains some responsibility in the very fact of leadership, for the behavior of the followers is under the leader's influence.

The prime responsibility of the people in Megalopolis is, however, to themselves. Once they are satisfied they have done all they could, to the best of their ability, to manage their own region and its problems, then they may face boldly the judgment of the rest of the world, today and tomorrow. If they remain faithful to their traditions, if both community and individuals carry on, with the same enthusiasm and endeavor as in the past, the struggle to build in the wilderness of this hard, complicated, and changing world a better and brighter city, then the future of Megalopolis may well be looked upon with optimism. However, this confidence requires the constant doubts, self-examination, and self-criticism of everyone. If complacency and resignation were to set in, the great Megalopolitan experiment would be jeopardized and the balance of our world might shift.

ACKNOWLEDGMENTS

The subject of this study is so wide and manifold that no one could have gathered alone all the information that went into it or commanded the full competence to interpret all the data. The author has called on the help of a great many people, organizations, and sources. He was fortunate in obtaining throughout his widespread inquiry favorable and helpful reactions in varied quarters. The staff directly employed in the inquiry was kept to a minimum, but a listing of all those to whom the study is indebted in one way or another could easily fill another volume. While the author feels much gratitude for the help so generously given, he must ask forgiveness for any omissions in his acknowledgments.

The use to which the publications or writings of others were put has been stated in the many footnotes on the preceding pages and in the captions to the illustrations. Some contributions deserve, however, special mention. First of all, the author wishes to express his deep appreciation to the consultants who contributed to this study specially prepared reports, summing up the results of original research. Professor Edward Higbee of the University of Delaware spent several months in the field studying Megalopolitan agriculture before writing an extensive report, the summary of which appears as Chapter 6 of this volume. M. Henri Morel of the French National Forest Service, an authority on suburban forestry familiar also with American forests, prepared a report, after three months of field study, which is summarized in Chapter 7. Professor Morroe Berger of Princeton University made an extensive study of the mass-media market in Megalopolis and submitted a report, much of which has been used in Chapter 11, and advised us on various sections of Chapters 13 and 14. Professor Pierre Camu of Laval University (Quebec) wrote a report on the effect the St. Lawrence Seaway may have on Megalopolitan seaports, and shared with us much of his knowledge of the Canadian economy and of North American sea trade. Professor Morton White of Harvard University prepared a report on the American concept of urban life and discussed the matter with us many times; his work is being published independently in several articles and also in book form.

Two young and gifted geographers helped us in the capacity of research assistants during their vacation periods, but both contributed much more than that to the study. Dr. John E. Rickert, research assistant in 1957–58, then at Rutgers University, also devised the "index of suburbanization" (Figs. 7, 63, and 64) and helped with the analysis of urban real estate values. Dr. Aloys A.

Michel of Yale University, research assistant in 1959–60, contributed also to the historical and transportation chapters of this study, prepared the maps showing the main economic areas within Megalopolis (Figs. 126, 134, and 150), and devised the index of the density of residences; in addition he read in full the first draft of this volume, and helped to improve it in a number of respects. Professor Anastasia Van Burkalow of Hunter College edited the manuscript and, besides greatly improving the author's English, made many suggestions for other valuable changes.

This study benefited also from the generous help and cooperation of many institutions. We feel especially indebted among these to the U. S. Bureau of the Census in Washington, D. C., where the Population and Geography Divisions (especially Dr. Clarence E. Batschelet and Dr. Robert Klove) were kind enough to supply us with specially prepared data from the 1950 and 1960 Censuses; and to the Regional Plan Association of New York, the publications of which have always been a major source of information on New York and on metropolitan growth in general. As this study progressed we were fortunate in profiting by constant contacts with the New York Metropolitan Region Study and particularly with its director, Professor Raymond Vernon of Harvard University. Mr. McKim Norton, Executive Vice-President of the Regional Plan Association, was very helpful on many occasions. We are also most grateful for the tireless and manifold helpfulness of the American Geographical Society of New York, the Port of New York Authority, the Greater Boston Economic Study Committee, and the Graduate School of Geography of Clark University. Dr. Elena Padilla of Columbia University kindly supplied us with special material on the Puerto Rican problem in New York City. Dr. Herbert Askwith contributed notes on suburban transportation. Mrs. Rose Zeisel of Bethesda, Maryland, wrote a report on the distribution of Federal civilian employment; and Mrs. Laura Jacobson surveyed various developments in the Washington area.

Many times the staff of the study of Megalopolis received efficient help from the New York Public Library, the Brooklyn Public Library, the Library of Congress, the Firestone Library of Princeton University, and the Library of the Institute for Advanced Study in Princeton, New Jersey. Special thanks are due to Mlle. Myriem Foncin, Conservateur des Cartes et Plans at the Bibliothèque Nationale in Paris, and to Mr. R. A. Skelton, Superintendent of the Map Room at the British Museum in London, who assisted us in the study, choice, and dating of the historical maps of our region. Mr. Neil C. Gustafson of Minneapolis, Minnesota, kindly authorized us to reproduce his series of maps of the flow of telephone messages between the main cities in Megalopolis. Other data and figures were kindly supplied by the U. S. Bureau of Public Roads, the U. S. Forest Service, Northeastern Forest Experiment Station, and by the materials published in the many reports and hearings of the Joint Committee on Washington Metropolitan Problems of the Congress of the United

States. It was fortunate for this study that it could profit by the inquiries into metropolitan problems being conducted in 1957–60 on Greater Boston, Metropolitan New York, and Metropolitan Washington.

Among the persons whose advice was of great help and enlightened us on various matters, we wish to express our special gratitude to Dr. Luther Gulick, President of the Institute of Public Administration; Professor Abel Wolman of the Johns Hopkins University; Professor Raymond Murphy of Clark University; Dr. Leona Baumgartner, Health Commissioner of the City of New York; Professors Gilbert F. White and Harold Mayer of the University of Chicago; Professor Perry Miller of Harvard University; Professor Robert McLaughlin, Director of the School of Architecture, Princeton University; Mr. Henry S. Churchill, the distinguished architect, of Philadelphia; Mr. Norman Williams of the Department of City Planning of the City of New York; Mr. Edward Bacon, Director of Planning of the City of Philadelphia; Mr. Nathaniel Elias, the distinguished chemist, of New York; Professor Peter Elias of the Massachusetts Institute of Technology; Professor Gordon Wolman of the Johns Hopkins University; Dr. Gregory Wolfe, of the Greater Boston Economic Study Committee; Mrs. Shirley A. Siegel, Assistant Attorney General of the State of New York; Professor Harold Cherniss of the Institute for Advanced Study, Princeton, New Jersey; Professor Otto Neugebauer of Brown University; Dr. Uriel Manheim of New York; Professor Sidney Ratner of Rutgers University; Professor Louise Rosenblatt of New York University; Professor Edward L. Ullman of the University of Washington; the late Harvey L. Schwamm of New York; and many, many others.

In 1959, at the suggestion and under the chairmanship of Professor Herbert Frankel, of Oxford University, a meeting was held at Nuffield College, Oxford, to discuss some of the findings of the Megalopolis study and their applicability to other areas in the world which are undergoing urbanization, including the underdeveloped countries. Jean Gottmann, Morroe Berger and Henri Morel of this study attended the meeting. They were grateful for the helpful participation of Professor and Mrs. Gunnar Myrdal, Dr. Chr. Van Paassen of the University of Utrecht, Professor Pierre Gourou of the University of Brussels, Professor G. H. J. Daysh of King's College, University of Durham, Professor D. T. Jack, also of Durham, and several other scholars.

Last but not least, this study owes much indeed to those whose daily work, competent and efficient, kept it progressing and brought it to a successful conclusion, particularly my secretaries, who often worked as research assistants, Mrs. Helen Ginsburg and Mrs. Eleanor Friend. Mrs. Ginsburg is to be especially commended for her skillful handling of historical, statistical, and economic materials through the four and a half years which she spent with this project. During the period when study headquarters were maintained at the Institute for Advanced Study in Princeton we received constant and valuable help from Mrs. Marion G. Hartz and Miss Elizabeth Horton.

The abundant illustration of this volume owes a great deal to various government agencies who authorized the reproduction of some of their maps and charts. Most of our illustrations, however, have been specially drawn, and we are greatly indebted to our principal cartographers, Mr. J. P. Tremblay of New York, Mr. Jean Barbier of Paris, and Mlle Sylvie Rimbert of the University of Strasbourg, for their devoted and skillful cooperation in getting so many maps and charts readied for us on time and in the best shape we could have wished for.

To compare what was happening in Megalopolis with what was happening in other metropolitan areas in North America and Western Europe, the author visited many cities outside his region. Everywhere from the West Coast of the United States to Greece, where the original Megalopolis arose, he was well received and helped in his search. To all those who thus assisted him, in one way or another, he wishes to express his very deep appreciation.

ILLUSTRATIONS

End-papers at front of volume: The Extent of Megalopolis ("1950 metropolitan areas" in the legend is meant in the broader sense of the term: see p. 21); Its Density of Population in 1960, by Counties

FIGURE

End-papers at back of volume: A Map of the Area Where Megalopolis Arose and a View of New York City in 1673

TABLES

INDEX

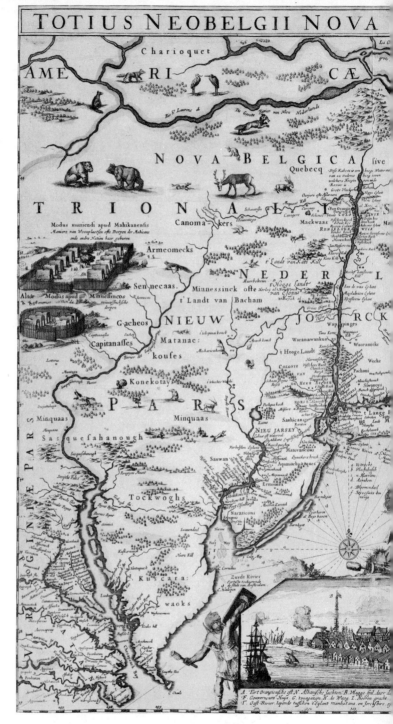

ACCURATISSIMA TABULA

THE M.I.T. PRESS PAPERBACK SERIES